THE FALL AND RISE
OF EUROPE

THE FALL AND RISE OF EUROPE

*A Political, Social, and Cultural History
of the Twentieth Century*

HENRY M. PACHTER

PRAEGER PUBLISHERS

NEW YORK

To Willy Brandt and Jean Monnet
Statesmen of Tomorrow's Europe

Published in the United States of America in 1975
by Praeger Publishers, Inc.
111 Fourth Avenue, New York, N.Y. 10003

Library of Congress Cataloging in Publication Data

Pachter, Henry Maximilian, 1907–
The fall and rise of Europe

1. Europe—Politics—20th Century. 2. Europe—Civilization—20th Century. I. Title

D1058. P32   914'. 03'5   76-189918

ISBN 0-275-3330-4

Printed in the United States of America

Contents

page

LIST OF ILLUSTRATIONS ix

FOREWORD xi

PART I: THE APEX OF EUROPEAN CULTURE AND
       POWER (1900–1914)

1 European Society Before 1914   3
2 The Greatness and Decline of Liberalism   10
3 The New Industrial Revolution   16
4 Imperialism   21
5 The New Right   27
6 Christian Responses   31
7 A View from Below   35
8 Women and Children   38
9 The Labor Movement   41
10 The First Russian Revolution   46
11 Fissures in the Structure   49
12 The Road to War   51

PART II: THE CRISIS OF THE EUROPEAN SPIRIT

1 The Cultural Rebellion   57
2 Mass Culture and Middle-Class Culture   62
3 The Creators of Modern Art   65
4 Literary Perspectives   70
5 The Emancipation of the Senses   73
6 Science and Philosophy at the Crossroads   77
7 Undertakers of Western Civilization   81

v

PART III: WARS AND REVOLUTIONS (1914–23)

page

1	War as Revolution	87
2	The End of the Dynasties	94
3	The Bolshevik Revolution	99
4	European Revolutions	106
5	The New Order of Europe	113

PART IV: THE PERICLEAN AGE OF EUROPE (1924–33) I: POLITICS

1	The Thirty Years' Peace	123
2	The New Social Structure	128
3	Experiments in Democracy	138
4	Weimar and Vienna—Two Splendid Failures	146
5	Experiments in Dictatorship	152
6	Socialism in One Country	158
7	The Great Depression	163

PART V: THE PERICLEAN AGE OF EUROPE (1924–33) II: CULTURE

1	Life and Expression in the 1920's	173
2	The Lively Arts—Popular Culture	180
3	Literature, the Arts, and Society Between the Wars	187
4	Soviet Art and Literature	199
5	Science, Philosophy, and Religion Between the Wars	202

PART VI: THE ECLIPSE OF EUROPE (1933–45)

1	Failure of Nerve	211
2	The Rise of Integral Nationalism	217
3	The Age of Fascism	224
4	The Popular Front and the Spanish Civil War	235
5	The Moscow Trials	241
6	The Collapse of the European System	245
7	The Second World War	251
8	The Powers and the Peoples	259

PART VII: A DIVIDED EUROPE (1945–58)

page

1 Heritage of the War 267
2 The Partition of Europe and the "Cold War" 272
3 The Reconstruction of Western Europe 277
4 The Soviet Empire 282
5 Tito's "Special Way" 286
6 The "Third Force" 289
7 End of Empire 293

PART VIII: EASTERN EUROPE AFTER STALIN

1 The Thaw 301
2 The Khrushchev Era 305
3 The Politics of Coexistence 309
4 Crisis of Empire 311
5 Polycentrism and Revisionism in Eastern Europe 315
6 The Fall of Khrushchev and the New Party Regime 320
7 Spring in Prague, Followed by Winter in the Empire 324
8 Some Notes on Soviet Culture 330

PART IX: POST-WAR SOCIETY IN WESTERN EUROPE

1 The Welfare State 337
2 Technology and Science in the Second Half of the Twentieth Century 349
3 The Third Industrial Revolution and the New Class 354
4 The End of Ideology 361
5 The Youth Culture 366

PART X: CULTURE AND SOCIETY

1 Engaged Literature and Its Disengagement 373
2 Further Developments of the Consumer Culture in the 1950's and 1960's 380
3 Esoteric Art 386
4 Observations on Post-war Movies 393
5 Some Observations on the Stage 397
6 Theology Without God 400
7 The Two Cultures 407

PART XI: THE RESURRECTION OF EUROPE (1958–74)

                                                            page
1 Winds of Change   417
2 The End of the Sterling Club   424
3 Reaction and Reform in Outer Europe   428
4 De Gaulle's Fifth Republic   431
5 May in Paris   436
6 The Northern Countries   443
7 Problems of Nationhood   446
8 Europe, America, and the World   450

A Bibliographical Note   459

Index of Names   473

Index of Subjects   477

Index of Countries, Cities, and Nationalities   481

List of Illustrations

MAPS AND CHART

	page
Map of World War I Europe	90
Map of Europe indicating national borders and nationalities, 1918	120
Chart of lifetimes of the great	196
Map of post-war Europe	347

Artwork by Joel Burton

PHOTOGRAPHS

The following photographs appear between text pages 370 and 371

A slum family in the East End of London (*Radio Times Hulton Picture Library*)
Tea in the garden (*Radio Times Hulton Picture Library*)
Lenin addresses the Second Congress of the Russian SDLP (*Novosti Press Agency*)
Sydney and Beatrice Webb (*Radio Times Hulton Picture Library*)
Picasso's "Man with Violin" (*Philadelphia Museum of Art*)
Rouault's "Les Justiciers" (*Photographie Bulloz*)
Satirical map of Europe (*Imperial War Museum*)
Wounded British soldiers (*Camera Press Ltd.*)
Rudolph Valentino in "The Sheik" (*National Film Archive*)
"The Miracle" (*The Raymond Mander and Joe Mitcheson Theatre Collection*)
George Grosz's "Workers" (*Philadelphia Museum of Art*)
"Dr. Mabuse" (*National Film Archive*)
British Labour Party anti-war poster (*Imperial War Museum*)
Nazi election poster (*Imperial War Museum*)
Hitler and Mussolini (*Süddeutscher Verlag*)
Low cartoon, 1939 (*London Express*)
Polish poster on the 1939 invasion (*Imperial War Museum*)
Albert Einstein (*Radio Times Hulton Picture Library*)
Thomas Mann (*Radio Times Hulton Picture Library*)

Artists in exile (*George Platt Lynes, courtesy of Museum of Modern Art, New York*)

Stalin and Molotov (*Camera Press Ltd.*)

Hungarian refugees, 1956 (*Camera Press Ltd.*)

Coventry Cathedral, built in the 1950's (*Jon Blau, Camera Press*)

Khrushchev and Macmillan (*The Associated Press Ltd.*)

Chancellor Adenauer (*Paul Popper Ltd.*)

General de Gaulle (*Keystone Press Agency Ltd.*)

Pope John XXIII (*Paul Popper Ltd.*)

Monnet and Common Market delegates (*Camera Press Ltd.*)

Zbigniev Cybulski in "Ashes and Diamonds" (*Contemporary Films*)

Fellini's "Juliet of the Spirits" (*Connoisseur Films Inc.*)

Eastern summit conference, 1968 (*Associated Press Ltd.*)

Student protests, Paris 1968 (*Camera Press Ltd.*)

Foreword

*"When all the conditions of an event are
present, it comes to pass."*
—HEGEL

As I reread my manuscript, I notice that it is not about Europe but for Europe—and
in more than one sense. First, it builds a case for a united Europe, not as a recipe for
survival but as a heritage, the result of common experience and a political dream that
has animated both laymen and statesmen. The very quarrels of European statesmen
have often revealed ideas which the hostile nations shared with each other but not
with nations outside Europe. The noblest minds of Europe have at all times looked
for such a synthesis. Almost two hundred years ago Immanuel Kant suggested the
idea that history should be written "with a cosmopolitan intent," and it was Leopold
von Ranke, the father of historism, who entitled his work *History of the Germanic
and Romanic Peoples.* Universal history does not suppress the histories of individual
nations, but tries to understand them as contributions to history in general. Just as one
loses sight of the history of Sardinia after that kingdom had fought for the unity of
Italy, so the histories of Belgium, Holland, and Luxembourg will soon have a merely
provincial interest, and even the histories of greater countries will be submerged in
the history of the development of the Common Market.

But the matter does not end there. The future begets its own past. When an idea
is about to be realized, the historian instinctively looks for its origins and for the
forces that had been striving in its direction. And this brings up the second meaning
of "Europe": the Continent has always been more than a geographical term. It has
had a life that has been determined by certain attitudes, customs, and values that were
shared by no other continent. It has looked on this heritage as something unique,
the culmination of all other history. No nation outside Europe could have produced
thinkers capable of pronouncements such as: "Man is the measure of all things,"
or "History is progress in the consciousness of freedom." It was in this same spirit
that a European philosopher could say, at the time of Hitler's greatest triumphs, "He
is going to perish because he does not belong in our history." For, indeed, as long as
Europeans continued to think in terms of their heritage, their freedom was not lost.

It would be a mistake, however, to look for this idea only among philosophers.
Most intellectual histories deal with writers and artists as though their best works

alone represented the consciousness of their nations. This is not always true; a work of excellence may belong to all ages while mediocre works may reflect the spirit of their contemporaries far more faithfully. Also, often the misunderstandings of vulgarizers and sloganeers may be far more revealing than the true intent of an author. Thus, for instance, the expert may know that Nietzsche would have uttered nothing but contempt for the Nazis, but in a history of popular movements one must note the coinings which were borrowed from Nietzsche. The historian of ideas deals with noble, subtle, and brilliant works, but the archaeologist uses trash as his source. To best study an age, one should not read the esoteric letters of rarely gifted individuals but the low-brow literature, hit songs, and thrillers. One should look at the fashions, furniture, and films of an age, watch its entertainments and vices, and discover its taste in heroes and villains.

Unfortunately, pioneer work in the history of the cartoon, the cabaret, the hit song, the poster, the popular hero, and even the film is still in process, and many of my observations are based on spot checks, memory, and impressions. Nevertheless, my intention will be clear: The trivia of social life should not be recorded as curiosities, as they still are in most histories of manners, but as evidence of changing moods, or as significant expressions of different stages in the development of the human mind. The historian should not defer to the judgment of the critic; social history especially should not substitute the ideas of some for the feelings of many.

Similar considerations apply to political history. I have not dealt with the secret intentions of statesmen but with their overt acts, and I have inserted biographical sketches only in the rare cases where a statesman has embodied the aspirations of his followers or has created a myth of historical significance. In any event, the purpose of European history is better served by the study of broad movements and forces than by character studies, interesting as they may be. For example, Stalin's so-called paranoia adds little to the understanding of the system to which he gave his name; but anybody trying to operate that system would have produced paranoic symptoms. And incidentally, the mediocrity of this individual contrasts so sharply with the greatness of his victories that we must seriously reconsider our notion of the historical individual.

While we know much about what makes heroes tick, I wish I knew more about how organizations work. Though sociology has studied them for fifty years, it is only recently that their impact on history and on the minds of people has become an object of public concern. In this field more archive studies may yield better insight into the make-up of the forces that have shaped the destinies of millions of people. Unorganized goodwill may become historically active but usually falls prey to organized forces. This lesson can be pursued throughout the course of European history in the twentieth century, and it should be heeded by those who have reacted resentfully to the increasing preponderance of big organizations. The answer to arbitrary organizations is not the irrationality of individuals but a more rational organization. This means that for Europe—to come back to my beginning—the question is not simply greater unity, but unity with a rational purpose. Marx and his followers thought that a new society can rise only from the ashes of the old one after a great cataclysm. Experience with apocalypses has been less than convincing, but the steady growth of public control over the Continent's resources in recent years has encouraged the hope that rational alternatives can be formulated and approached in democratic ways of evolution, too.

With these guiding ideas in mind, I shall briefly explain the plan of this history. Part I shows European society at the apex of its development at the beginning of this century; all forces were in full expansion and thereby came to contradict each other. The restlessness which has made Europe so unique also produced dangerous excesses: excesses of refinement and excesses of statecraft, excesses of doubt and excesses of certainty. Awareness of the coming crisis, then, is described in Part II, and its outbreak in Part III, which views the ten years of war and revolution, roughly from 1914–23, as one period of general breakdown and transformation. Parts IV and V, then, deal with the following decade, which included the brief recovery of the middle 1920's and the deep depression of the early 1930's. It was a period of constant crisis and tension, but, perhaps for that very reason, also a period of great creativity and sensitivity. It was also a period of deep contradiction, with the finest flowers of democracy growing in the same social soil that also produced totalitarian vermin. I have called this period the Periclean Age of Europe, reminiscent of the great age when Athens achieved her historic fame amidst unspeakable anxiety.

Part VI, again spanning about ten years, tells of the second collapse of Europe, an age of deep despair and danger when the spirit of Europe itself was in doubt and the totalitarians threatened to take over. Part VII deals with the problems and dilemmas of the immediate post-war period, the partition of Europe, the cold war, the difficult recovery. I cannot agree with those who regard the cold war as the equivalent of a Third World War. There was no crisis but rather recovery and stabilization on both sides of the iron curtain, and the story of this part is actually one of a new start, of gathering forces and forming new conceptions.

The unfortunate result of these years was the partition of Europe, and Part VIII acknowledges this reality by treating the Eastern European countries separately. I do not concede for a moment that Eastern Europe has been cut off for all time or that it has fallen under the sway of an Asian conqueror. On the contrary, I find that Western traditions have not been totally superseded even in the Soviet Union, and while I do not hold with the convergence theorists, I see a growing interaction between the Soviet Union and Europe. Therefore, I have not followed the example of other writers who have excluded the Soviet Union from the history of Europe altogether.

My principal concern, however, is expressed in the three concluding parts, dealing respectively with the social, the cultural, and the political development of Western Europe. I have here collected data indicating that the European crisis is by no means over, but that the forces that are working toward a free and just society are gaining.

For reasons of space, the original manuscript had to be abridged and the lengthy apparatus of scholastic references had to be thrown out. The latter is the more the pity as its inclusion would have shown the enormous labor which my wife has devoted

to this volume. For both of us this has been a labor of love, for in following the
European destiny we have found meaning in the European project. There were times
when it was possible to despair of the future and when we might have prefaced our
present endeavor with the gloomy forebodings that pervade the great work of
Thucydides. But today's Europe is working itself out of the Periclean age and into a
new stage of civilization, less exciting perhaps than the great periods of crisis and
creation but, I hope, more dependable for every man.

The manuscript was completed before the oil crisis of 1973–74 threw Europe into
a panic. Some Western nationalists may have drawn the conclusion that each state
must now fend for itself. I hold on to the belief that now more than ever the nations
of Europe can survive only united. But as the text of my book shows in more than
one place, this unity cannot be conceived as a mere political expedient; Europe must
realize its idea of freedom in a just social order. Zeus, according to Homer, had the
surname *europos*: "calling far and wide."

HENRY M. PACHTER

New York, New York
December, 1974

PART I

The Apex of European
Culture and Power
(1900–1914)

CHAPTER I

European Society Before 1914

THE exuberant nineteenth century—a century of progress and science—left to its successor a legacy of five great institutions: the national state, middle-class culture, industrial capitalism, the technological exploitation of science, and world trade. In combination, these five achievements had made Europe great and her civilization unique. No previous civilization had laid claim to world domination on the strength of its material achievements. No masters before those of modern Europe had asserted that their institutions possessed universal validity and would eventually benefit all races. Western industrial capitalism, Marx had agreed, showed their future to all other continents. Once, Rome had claimed to give one law to her vast empire; the new imperialism proudly proclaimed its intimate connection with progress.

To be alive in 1900 meant to believe that God was good. The generations that matured after World War I do not know what it is to trust that progress is inevitable, to take security for granted, to recognize the established order as beneficial to all. If some classes or peoples still felt excluded from this general bliss for the time being, it was believed that in the long run they too would find their place in the sun.

The great institutions of this order were proof of its harmonious functioning. The national state, creation of conquerors and kings, had developed from a mere tool of power into a subtle organism that welded into purposeful unity peoples speaking different tongues and belonging to different social classes, following different philosophies or educated in different schools. To be sure, the perfect nation-state was an ideal rather than the rule. Many nations had no state, and many states were composed of peoples who later were to declare themselves nations; moreover, as Disraeli had already recognized, each state harbored at least two nations—the rich and the poor. Nevertheless, such heresies were rare, and the nation-state, even if it was a myth, still commanded its citizens' loyalty; its ideology was more powerful than any other since the wars of religion. When a national enterprise proved successful, the minorities and the disinherited also took their modest share of glory and profit instead of questioning the morality of their source. For the national state could not enlist the co-operation of the poor without giving them the hope of social improvement; nor could it obtain the loyalty of minorities without co-opting at least their leaders into the ruling circles. Thus, the "common man," even—in the words of Lloyd George, his great champion—the cottage-born man, was on the rise within the

3

system of each state; old privileges were on the wane, and equal rights were being claimed for all. The very idea of the national state implied a nation of citizens.

The middle class considered itself the pillar of the national state. Its industry supplied the material goods needed for growth; its moralism and its marriage laws, its sense of authority and its respect for learning maintained the nation's spiritual substance; its humility assured the stability of the social order. For all its professional pride, the bourgeoisie in most countries did not aspire to rule but was content to take second place to elites of birth, power, or merit, which assured the security of property and the perpetuation of the class structure. The middle classes looked up to the aristocracy, the military and civil service hierarchy, the financial oligarchy, and the church authorities, but looked down on the laboring classes. All were essential to the social order. So were their values: honor and labor. The middle class itself based its value system on the notion of property: the ability to buy and sell freely, to transform the substance of wealth and thereby to increase it; the power to dispose, to process, to manufacture, to produce, to extract, to change, to exploit, to dominate, to inherit. Untrammeled property rights and achievement made middle-class life meaningful and enjoyable.

The appreciation of material goods is called materialism. So is the philosophy that regards matter alone as real. That the same term is used to define an ethical attitude and a metaphysical assumption may be pure accident, but that both these mental dispositions should have become characteristic of the bourgeois age certainly is not. The economic regime of capitalism was based on the scientific mastery of matter and the systematic exploitation of productive forces.

Middle-class materialism found direct expression in the invention of useful and enjoyable objects, in their fabrication for mass distribution, in the exuberant shapes the new decorative arts gave to dwellings, furnishings, clothing, utensils, and other paraphernalia of daily life. *Art nouveau* still gives us a feeling for our grandfathers' sensuousness, but its unrealistic shapes often seem to deny the materiality of these pleasures.

As if to repudiate the source of its wealth, the bourgeoisie of the young twentieth century surrounded itself with gables and arabesques, pseudo-aristocratic and romantic playthings, or it tried to imitate mannerisms and ideologies of a more chivalrous age. And popular philosophies, we shall see, aimed at the spiritual. These two conflicting tendencies—the submersion in material goods and the quest for pseudo-spiritual pleasures—had marked middle-class culture from its beginnings, but in our century especially, the spiritual leaders were torn between the awareness of being the product of environmental and inherited factors, on the one hand, and the strong assertion of inner freedom on the other.

It has been remarked that persons belonging to the upper bourgeoisie tend toward affirmation of sensuality and materialism, whereas the lower middle class inclines to heroic dreams and must assert its faith in morality. The nation's myth-makers—teachers, writers, artists, politicians, lawyers, clergy—often come from this latter stratum; suspended between the wielders of power and the humble, they responded with mixed and ambiguous reactions to the challenge of modernity. They no longer were sure that science could solve all our problems, and following Nietzsche, a vanguard of free spirits rejected the basic assumptions of nineteenth-century materialism. A cultural pessimism was gnawing at the consciousness of the young elite even while the majority still was basking in its confidence in progress.

For those born before 1870—and they were the makers of history until long after World War I—there could be no conflict between science and freedom. Both were essential to the development of that economic system which had produced the recent acceleration of inventions and conveniences, which had enriched the middle classes and was now spreading wealth abroad, which had girded the earth with a communications network and was involving the entire planet in a great world market, forcing the backward nations to shed their superstitions, tribal customs, and feudal fetters. Industrial capitalism—that is, the technological exploitation of natural and human resources by free enterprise—was still revolutionizing antiquated systems, abolishing obsolete handicraft production, destroying the foundations of despotic government, undermining pagan and even higher religions, and shaking the classical ideals of beauty and truth. Only recently it had produced such marvels as the bridge over the Firth of Forth (1883–90), the dynamo (1875), the horseless carriage (1886); it had created the linotype (1885) and the modern rotary press (*London Times*, 1886), with its promise of instant dissemination of news, and the wireless telegraph (1895), with its promise of instant world-wide communications.

Happily, these benefits did not accrue to the propertied classes alone. After the terrible degradation of the working man that had accompanied nineteenth-century capitalism, industry had begun to provide a decent living for an increasing number of workers. The propertyless proletarians on whose desperation Karl Marx had pinned his revolutionary threat, now bought glass menageries and wore stiff collars on Sundays.

In the dominant view, industrial capitalism had transformed the curses of society into blessings. The masses, no longer vegetating in the brutish ways of the countryside, were being urbanized, educated, accepted as citizens with an equal vote. Culture was being brought to the natives of Africa and Asia. More leisure became available to the metropolitan masses, and—such was the utopianism of that era—this newly won time would be used further to instruct, educate, and refine them. The periodic crises that had attended early capitalism now seemed to become rarer; after a succession of bad years, the nineteenth century had ended in galloping prosperity, and 1900 bid fair to be the "miraculous year," piling up new records.

The rate of progress was astonishing. Life expectancy, which only a generation earlier had averaged 43 years, rose to 53 in 1900. (By 1950 it was to rise to 63 years throughout Europe.) Infant mortality, which had been 25 per cent a hundred years earlier, had dropped to 6 per cent. Real wages increased steadily, so that the masses by the outbreak of World War I could afford coffee, sugar, beer, tobacco, and meat. Although this was progress in absolute terms, relatively speaking the masses still lagged behind. A British worker earning 15 to 20 shillings a week had to spend

8 to 15 shillings on food if he were married and had two children; his master might spend 10 to 20 shillings a week on food for himself alone and pay two servants 10 shillings each. On the average, even in the industrial states, people still had to spend at least half their income on food.

To sell luxury goods, industry at first depended on the rich, but now the century of the common man began to level taste and consumer standards. One such equalizer of great consequence was the bicycle. It competed with the gentleman's vehicle, the horse and carriage, as a means of transportation, and it also afforded opportunities for sports and socializing. No history book of the gilded age is complete without a photo of a mixed bicycle club. The courageous among the well-to-do had a new plaything, the automobile, which sped by at a brisk twelve miles an hour, the legal limit in England, but, before asphalt pavements, also the limit of the endurable. By 1913, as many as 15,000 Englishmen owned one of these contraptions.

Advertisements in fashion journals, impressionist paintings, and the illustrated magazines show us a world in which people took leisurely strolls through lovely parks, rowed on lakes, went to the races, or watched parades. Full-bosomed ladies wore ample skirts and lace-trimmed blouses; dignified men carried canes and wore smart hats, spats, and waistcoats. A beard was not a symbol of rebelliousness but a token of authority, while a mustache characterized the self-confident young man on his way up. On solemn occasions field-marshals and ladies were plumed like African chieftains; the peak of refinement was reached when ladies hid their beauty behind heavy veils. The favorite dances were the sentimental waltz, the gay polka, and the sensual tango; songs from Offenbach, Strauss, Fall, or Lehár operettas gave expression to romantic feelings. Family outings ended in garden restaurants.

The middle classes had grown so grand in their prosperity that they began to challenge the style of living that previously had been reserved for the nobility. Their houses, with balconies and turrets, suggested castles: the interiors seemed designed to combine inutility with expense of upkeep; furniture was imitation Renaissance or baroque; railings and fences swarmed with cast-iron snakes or lions, symbolic guardians of the place, be it mansion or apartment house; curved sofas, ornamented tables, uncomfortable stiff-backed chairs, potted palms, mauve pottery; *art nouveau* china, and gilt trellises. Everywhere decoration took precedence over comfort, and nothing was allowed to reflect its true purpose. Stock exchanges looked like Greek temples, railway stations like cathedrals, factories like army barracks.

Inside, factories were dark, dirty, noisy, and malodorous, cluttered with goods and machines. Workers' tenements were unhealthy. Several families had to share a single toilet, which usually was on a landing outside the apartments. But hygiene was improving, and most city dwellings by the early years of the twentieth century were equipped with water closets and running water. Coal was the household fuel; stored in the cellar, it had to be carried upstairs daily. To take a bath, one had to heat a water tank, and to make that worthwhile, all members of the family had to have their baths one after the other. Poor families, of course, had to use public baths. Well-to-do families were learning about central heating and warm water, and even middle-class families had servants to take care of household chores. The women of the poor were either factory workers or household servants, while well-to-do ladies kept themselves busy shopping in plush department stores and preparing charity balls. Indeed, European society before World War I is unthinkable without an enormous number of servants and without a sharp distinction between rich and poor.

Woman's work was made easier by gas stoves, oilcloth, new cleansers, the treadle sewing machine, and the hand-operated washing machine. When the stores offered ready-made clothing and linens, girls no longer were forced to sew their trousseaus. One could also buy canned food, jam, and fruit preserves, although a really good housewife showed her love of family and her sense of status by putting up her own preserves.

The middle-class home remained patriarchal. Children were obedient, women were playthings and mothers. A strict moral code protected their chastity and ignorance; no similar restrictions applied to men, except the fear of disease. Upper-class women now began to limit the number of children they bore.

The social division of burdens decreed that some must work while others could display, entertain, amuse themselves, talk literature and politics, defend their country, and contemplate eternity. It would be a mistake to view this leisure class as monolithic, however. It was finely shaded, from the top layer of aristocracy to the landed gentry, followed by the *grande bourgeoisie*: doctors, teachers, lawyers, managers, higher civil servants, small manufacturers, engineers. In these circles marriages used to be arranged: the bride had to have a dowry, and an impecunious groom had to have a prefix or a title before his name. Many a gentleman gilded his escutcheon or saved a bankrupt family estate by marrying a banker's daughter. Even in France, which had been a republic for a generation, social climbers still added the *particule* "de" to their names; bourgeois sought distinction by buying old estates or marrying "quality." In the monarchies gentlemen also manned the civil service.

The gentleman with no prefix to his name at least had a title that exactly defined his position on the social ladder. Every member of the hierarchy expected to be addressed by his (or her husband's) rank: *Monsieur l'Inspecteur Général, Madame la Générale, Herr Geheimrat, Frau Oberpostrat, Gospodin Revisor*, Sir John, Your Lordship, *Eccellenza*. (Even today business executives are addressed as "director.") Whoever had business at a court (even the court of a small German prince) was *Herr Hofrat*; should he have the misfortune of having no title, an Austrian businessman could buy the title of *Commercialrat*; his British competitor could be knighted. The public employee or civil servant claimed consideration and respect because wherever he went he was presumed to be a representative of the state. It was not easy to criticize him without questioning all officialdom and in fact the entire hierarchical system. In Eastern countries like Germany and Russia the spirit of functionarism was especially rigid. The *Junkers* (landed gentry who also acted as justices of the peace and district administrators), the military, and the bureaucracy formed a trinity of feudal parasites obstructing the path of liberty and stifling the development of free enterprise. But even critics of the aristocracy did not contemplate the abolition of class society as such: Max Weber and other liberals conceived of the good society as one ruled by men of property and education.

Education was the distinctive mark of "good" society. Although illiteracy was being wiped out in the West and schooling was compulsory for all, differences in education kept the children of the poor in inferior positions and assured a career even to the least talented sons of the rich. In England, communal or church schools contrasted with "public"—that is, elite—schools; in Germany, grade school—"people's school"—until the age of fourteen contrasted with "higher school," where pupils began to study Latin at the age of nine. Only in France did all children go to the same school (either state or church), but a rigorous system of examinations weeded out those who had neither talent nor the means to pay a tutor. In practice, even the most democratic school ever designed, the École Normale Supérieure, which launched some outstanding sons of the lower classes on their careers, still promoted much larger numbers from the upper classes. Although many countries now introduced civil service examinations, none had a true meritocracy. Speech, manners, connections— the old school tie or family contacts—counted more than ability. In all, only a small percentage went on to higher studies. In Germany, 5 per cent of the population finished high school; in England, one in 800 went to university. Germans who had attended high school to their fifteenth year were allowed to serve in the army for only one year instead of three. In every country except Switzerland, speakers of provincial dialects (argot) were virtually excluded from executive positions.

Equal educational opportunity, then, did not mean equality of rich and poor but limited equality of bourgeoisie and aristocracy. The privileges of birth and breeding were being eroded very slowly. Emperor Wilhelm II played cards with Albert Ballin, a Jewish shipowner; King Edward associated with bankers from whom he extracted investment tips.

To join the parade of social climbers was almost an imperative. If liberalism had ever meant yearning for a society of free and equal men, that dream was now being crowded out by the mad scramble for opportunities. To be sure, there were many who failed or were crushed by the increasing intensity of competition or who lost status because of the growth of new, big organizations. Yet those who were ambitious but had found no place in local society had an outlet—the empire, with its fascinating combination of adventure, profit, and personal power. He who had been a misfit at home now found his inferiors abroad: despised minorities, illiterate or decadent neighbor countries, heathen Orientals, naked savages whose backwardness seemed to call for paternalistic domination. The domestic class system was extended into a world system of rule and conquest. The tensions of the hierarchical structure were exported from the metropolitan countries to the frontier areas.

Through her empires and her trade, Europe imposed her own system on all continents. The gold standard ruled commerce, and England ruled the world's gold supply. The international division of labor made Europe the world city whose factories devoured the timber, fibers, and ores shipped from undeveloped areas, whose industrial goods were sold to undeveloped areas, whose bankers provided the capital, whose leisure classes wore the furs and diamonds extracted from foreign countries. Europe's export volume doubled every thirty years; her investments abroad, every twenty.

This was an age of imperialism with scramble for pieces of the world, ardent competition for markets, saber-rattling contests for supremacy among nations, and step-by-step preparations for a world conflagration. Yet, when the Great War broke out, contemporaries were stunned. The more sensitive among them knew that an era of tranquillity had come to an end, an era in which world trade had made the nations more dependent upon one another, an era that had made European culture paramount in a system of world co-operation. The generation that was in its thirties in 1914 had lived in an atmosphere of stability and progress; it had been brought up in the belief that competition was nature's device to achieve God's purposes, that, ultimately, harmony was bound to develop from conflict, that evolution always strives toward higher forms. It could not doubt that the supremacy of Europe meant the betterment of all mankind. It was utterly unprepared for the shock that interrupted this process and precipitated the next generation into an age of revolution.

CHAPTER 2

The Greatness and Decline
of Liberalism

IT is dangerous to read history backward. The chauvinistic and imperialistic trends that led to the catastrophe of 1914 were not predominant features of the preceding decade; one should therefore not speak of the "pre-war period." In its own eyes the age was liberal, not militaristic or imperialistic; its best spokesmen considered militarism and imperialism atavistic outgrowths of a mentality that belonged to a past era and to obsolete classes, like the *Junkers* and Colonel Blimps. Even conservatives adjusted their phraseology to the liberal rhetoric. World trade was expanding; ideas were free; justice followed conscience. When in 1894 a military court in France convicted an innocent Jew—Captain Dreyfus—of espionage and sent him to Devil's Island, world opinion rose to his defense and ultimately (1906) obtained his vindication. It was a great victory of humanity and enlightenment over reactionary militarism, chauvinism, and racism. It was a victory of the republicans over monarchical reaction and its ally, the Catholic hierarchy.

In France, the Radical cabinet of Émile Combes expelled the religious orders in 1902, won the fight for state schools, and carried the *lois laïques* of 1905, which completely separated church and state. The great Radical Party, representative of the vast French middle classes, was slightly left-of-center and anti-clerical, patriotic though anti-militaristic, Jacobin in its rhetoric but devoted to the principles of Adam Smith in its economic policies. In Germany, liberals were divided between the National Liberal Party, which had supported Bismarck and which became increasingly more national and less liberal, and various groups that in 1910 merged in the Progressive Party (*Fortschritt*); it was akin to the French Radicals and famous for the high-caliber professors in its ranks. Even under the domination of the *Junkers*, the authoritarian system began to erode. The officer caste was discredited first by an outrage at Saverne (Alsace), where the entire population had been placed under house arrest after a lieutenant thought he had been insulted; then by a hilarious travesty on militarism when an ex-convict in Köpenick, near Berlin, donning a captain's uniform, commandeered an armed detail to occupy city hall and there issued to himself the passport without which he could not find employment. Public opinion felt the joke was on Germany's ruling class and mores; Carl Zuckmayer later was to immortalize the episode in a play and a film.

Another politically backward country, Spain, was shaken by the humiliation of 1898. When it lost its empire, Spain began to search its soul. A group of brilliant new writers—Angel Ganivet, Joaquín Costa, Miguel Unamuno, Francisco Giner de los Ríos, José Ortega y Gasset among others—turned away from traditionalism. Although by Western standards many of them might be called conservative, their total cultural impact was anti-clerical and liberal; some even were freemasons—the main political rivals of the Roman Catholic Church. A new military disaster, the unending war against the Riff-Kabyles in Morocco, attended by a wave of strikes and protest demonstrations, forced King Alfonso XIII to call on the *Liberales*[1] for support. The new Premier, José Canalejas, permitted non-Catholics to worship in public, taxed church property, outlawed the establishment of new orders (1910), and was assassinated in 1912, after which the *Conservadores* returned to power.

In Portugal, King Carlos, himself a liberal, was assassinated, and, in 1910, the *Liberales* dethroned his son and established a secular republic, which expelled the religious orders and placed education in the hands of the state.

With the advancement of science and the spread of secular knowledge, liberalism everywhere embraced the cause of religious dissent and of the secular state. In England and Ireland, the nonconformists gave electoral victories to the Liberal Party, which fought against the established Church of England. Though the grand old man of liberalism, William Ewart Gladstone, was dead, his legacy, the fight for Irish home rule, was not. In 1900, eighty Irish Nationalists were elected. In coalition with Labour and Liberals, they upset the Conservative government in 1905. The election that followed confirmed the debacle of the military and the imperialists, whose ineffective conduct, cruelty, and rapacious motives during the Boer war had outraged the nation's sensibilities. The Liberal Prime Minister Sir Henry Campbell-Bannerman pledged to expand the franchise, to grant home rule to Ireland, to tax the big landowners and break their power in the House of Lords, to reconcile the Boers, and to dismantle the power of the Church of England in public education. A young Welshman, David Lloyd George, who had attacked jingoism, now became the star of British politics.

Liberal winds also prevailed in other countries. Italy as a secular kingdom provoked the Pope's stubborn opposition, although Italy was not very liberal either in its institutions or in its policies. But the party in power called itself Liberal and its enemies attacked the state as liberal. To be sure, the big estates were safe and the nobles remained powerful; the illiterate Sicilians were miserably exploited, and hundreds of thousands emigrated to America. Prime Minister Giovanni Giolitti ruled by manipulating and maneuvering rather than by democratic principles, yet even his pseudo-liberalism contributed to the general impression that Europe was moving toward freedom. It is true that only France, Portugal, and Switzerland were republics; but most monarchies were tempered by constitutions. With the exception of Russia and Turkey, all major countries had a national legislature with the power to vote the

---

[1] Incidentally, the oldest party of that name in Europe.

budget. However, in key monarchies such as Germany, Spain, and Austria the parliament still could not dismiss the cabinet, and in nearly all legislatures the upper chamber represented the feudal orders. Suffrage had been universal, equal, and direct for men over twenty-five in Switzerland, Spain, France, and Germany (in federal elections, but not in the key state of Prussia) since the 1870's, and in Belgium, Norway, and the Netherlands since before the turn of the century. Finland, Sweden, and Austria (though not Hungary) followed in 1907, Italy in 1912. In Belgium (and to a lesser degree in England) men with educational or property qualifications had more than one vote; in Prussia, the rich, the well-to-do, and the poor constituted three separate constituencies, each of which elected the same number of deputies, and the ballot was not secret. In many countries, workers staged mass strikes for the right to vote, ministerial accountability, or abolition of the upper house. In England and in the Scandinavian countries the government, for all practical purposes, needed the confidence of the parliament, but it took years of battle for that custom to become law. Nowhere, of course, did women vote.

In short, liberalism was on the march, and conservatives often protested that they, too, were democratic and progressive. Especially in the field of education, the liberal philosophy was by and large adopted by all governments. In contrast to U.S. parlance, liberalism, in Europe, meant absolute economic freedom of the individual and rejection of all state regulation of business, all social legislation, and all interference with property. It still means religious, philosophical, and political tolerance, open-mindedness in cultural affairs, and opposition to all traditional powers of the clerical, military, and bureaucratic hierarchies. Everywhere the liberals constituted the party of the bourgeoisie, who tried to curb the power of the landed gentry, and the party of the people, who tried to fend off high tariffs and big military budgets. They were also the party of the educated and sophisticated who fought against obscurantism, clericalism, censorship, and authoritarian education. Their philosophy inclined toward positivism; their relativistic outlook generally permitted them to understand the viewpoint of a foreign government, a suppressed minority, or a disadvantaged class.

In the beginning of the century, liberalism shed its *laissez-faire* image and adopted a program of social legislation. Lloyd George, called to the Exchequer in 1906, repealed the hated Taff Vale Decision of 1902, which had made labor unions liable to damage suits after strikes. A new Trade Disputes Act freed the trade unions from financial liability and allowed them to picket and to contribute to election funds—a fateful step that ultimately made it possible for the Labour Party to defeat the Liberals. The Workman's Compensation Act extended employers' responsibilities; the Children's Act curbed their freedom to exploit minors. The National Insurance Act of 1911 (health and unemployment insurance) and the Old Age Pensions Act of 1908 for the first time gave a measure of security to millions; these acts were expanded into a comprehensive insurance system by an act of 1912, for which Germany provided the model. A slum-clearing and model-housing program completed the turn toward social legislation.

More important, in 1909 Lloyd George submitted a budget featuring steeply progressive income taxes, imposts on large fortunes, heavy death duties, and a tax on undeveloped land and on unearned increments to land value. The almos⁺ punitive attack on landlordism betrayed the hand of Winston Churchill and also the influence of the American, Henry George. When the House of Lords rejected the budget, new elections returned an impressive majority of Liberals, Labourites, and Irish home-rule advocates. The Parliament Act of 1911 abolished the absolute veto of the Lords; they no longer could upset a bill that had passed Commons twice. It also gave £400 a year to members of Parliament. The threat of creating new peers forced the Upper House to accept the law—a double blow for the forces of democracy, since Irish home rule could now be delayed but no longer denied.

The Liberal government laid the foundation for the welfare state, began the re-distribution of wealth through taxes, and preserved free trade against loud pleas from industry, agrarians, and Empire interests; it broke the power of the Lords and land-owners, extended the suffrage, and made the House of Commons sovereign. Moreover, it reconciled South Africa and healed the wounds of the recently fought Boer war. But, as we have seen, it abandoned the strict doctrine of *laissez faire*; economic liberalism became social liberalism. In all these respects English liberals showed more flexibility than their Continental brothers. Social reformers in Germany were usually known not as statesmen but as academic teachers. They were derisively called "lectern socialists."

Another deviation from orthodox liberalism was manifest in Britain's foreign policy. Hitherto liberals had held to the doctrine of "splendid isolation," England's proverbial posture in world affairs. Now the Liberal government committed English forces to the defense of the *status quo* in Europe and strained its resources to stay ahead of Germany in the naval race. As we saw, the German liberals also supported the Kaiser's policy. Trelawney Hobhouse, himself a Liberal, asked in 1904 what had become of Liberal ideals. People no longer seemed to believe in self-government, free trade, peace, disarmament, economical government. "Wherever we look, we see force worshipped, superman adored, saviors expected, humanitarian ideas deprecated, social justice derided," he exclaimed. Lloyd George, who had once been regarded as pro-German, astounded the world with a ringing speech vigorously aligning British democracy with France during the Morocco crisis of 1911. From then on, only small groups denounced imperialism and protested that liberalism could not survive in a world where monopolistic and protectionist interests dictated policy, and empire builders forced the nations to spend their energies in search of glory and power. This was the position of John A. Hobson, the keenest critic of modern capitalism and imperialist policies. Many great writers of the West—among them Anatole France, G. K. Chesterton, Émile Zola, Romain Rolland, and Bertrand Russell—also fought chauvinism and militarism.

Similarly in Germany, the Reverend Friedrich Naumann tried to modernize the Progressive Party. He combined a sturdy liberal's belief in democracy with a social conscience and a cool sense of geopolitical realities. He advocated the creation of a large market area in Central Europe, with dependencies and ramifications in the

Balkans and Eastern Europe. Hundreds of millions were to improve their lot and the German workers would share in the greatness of the Fatherland. However, like all other attempts to bridge the class chasms in Germany, his National Social League (founded in 1896) failed.

German liberalism had always been patriotic, even chauvinistic. It now turned completely imperialistic. The National Liberal Party formed a "Kartell" with the Conservatives to support the Kaiser's naval armament and colonial policies. In the 1906 elections they pinned the label "nigger lovers" on the socialists, who had denounced the suppression of the Hottentots; they also revived Bismarck's *Kulturkampf* against the Catholic Center Party. In a wave of chauvinism the Left was beaten. The protest against militarism was carried on by small groups of pacifists, joined by some prominent writers such as Gerhart Hauptmann, Heinrich Mann, Hermann Hesse, and Friedrich Wilhelm Foerster.

The French Radicals were even less fortunate. Their Jacobin heritage was confined to cultural and military affairs. When their government was forced to deal with economic and social questions, the Radicals proved to be as conservative as the banks. Georges Clemenceau—mayor of Montmartre during the Paris Commune, Dreyfusard, and still at that time a champion of the little man—proposed the eighthour day (since 1905, minors worked eight hours, and the work day of women was limited to ten hours), pensioned retirement at the age of sixty-five, accident insurance, and government control of certain labor contracts, especially in mining. None of these demands passed the Radical legislature; nor did Clemenceau and the ex-socialist Aristide Briand, who succeeded him, hesitate, for all their republican ardor, to call out the troops against striking railroad workers. They also denied teachers, postal workers, and other government employees the right to strike. Joseph Caillaux, who led the government in 1911–12, was unable to push through a tax reform similar to that which Lloyd George had fostered.

Although the army had been defeated in the Dreyfus affair, it was not discouraged. It now proposed to extend the period of service from two to three years on the ground that the Germans could field a much larger and better equipped army. Unable to counter that argument, the Radicals left it up to Jean Jaurès, a socialist professor of history and a great humanitarian, to point out that elite armies and quick victories were things of the past. In *L'Armée Nouvelle* he argued that modern wars required mass armies imbued with the spirit of democratic citizenship, and he expressed the hope that these would refuse to be sent into colonial, dynastic, and commercial wars. However, in 1913 the Chambre adopted three-year conscription, and when World War I broke out, France had an additional class under arms. Thus the word "patriotism" lost its populist overtones, and the Radicals abandoned their antimilitaristic tradition. The only liberal who had a positive program of Franco-German reconciliation and co-operation was Caillaux. When editorials viciously maligned his motives, his wife shot the editor of the Rightist *Le Figaro*. Her trial became a sensation, and Caillaux was forced out of office.

It was in the economic field, however, that liberalism proved to be less than adequate. Business assumed forms unknown to Adam Smith or even to Karl Marx and John Stuart Mill. In underdeveloped countries like Russia, large-scale enterprise was not the climax of a long development, nor was it rare; it was, rather, the typical form of enterprise, usually state-sponsored and financed by foreign loans or operated as a foreign concession. Often these ventures were intimately connected with the government's political plans. The Russian railway system, for example, was designed to move troops, not to transport merchandise; some of the German railways also were strategic. Everywhere the state either had built or was taking over the railways, and it held the monopoly on communications—the postal service, telephone, telegraph, and later radio and television. As a source of revenue, many governments also had reserved for themselves a monopoly on tobacco products and matches. Cities sometimes owned the public utilities and tramways. Government no longer was the "night watchman," as the socialist Lassalle had derisively called the liberal state. As early as 1894, the London *Economist* had warned that "we are advancing toward state socialism."

Governments had to worry about the balance of trade and the balance of payments; defense-minded lobbyists raised a hue and cry over inadequate preparedness and self-sufficiency in case of war. Loans given to insolvent governments had to be safeguarded and new investments directed toward colonies or allied countries. Liberals could deny such pleas only if they completely ignored "world politics." Those who stubbornly held onto their principles condemned themselves to the role of critics, voices of conscience but not serious candidates for office. Walther Rathenau, the German industrialist later turned statesman, said:

> The middle class has won respect on account of the development of the economy, but it has not created any political correlate. To be regenerated, liberalism must free itself from petty-bourgeois superstitions. No great industry grows from the principles of thrift, free trade, and anti-imperialism. Liberalism has always been the party of ideas in Germany, but Leftist liberalism is only the party of criticism.

CHAPTER 3

The New Industrial Revolution

RATHENAU'S father had founded an electro-trust. In 1907, the son expounded its economics:

> Older industries produced articles which consumers needed, merging groups of products and creating new ones, but always leaving their use to the customers' discretion. Manufacturing industries used new techniques, division of labor, mass production, and mechanical power, but essentially continued and improved upon what the old handicrafts had done. With electromechanics, a new *field* of industry is being opened up. It will transform a large part of modern life. Production no longer is ultimately directed to the consumers' needs; rather, these are created or even imposed by the producer. Electricity is not an industry but a complex; it creates new demands, controls new industries, penetrates all spheres of life from lighting to power to traffic and the use of new, centralized machines.

Another revolution occurred in industrial chemistry—paints, drugs, cosmetics, fertilizers, plastics, synthetic fibers, and soon during the war the creation of substitute materials down to synthetic foods. Imperial Chemical in England and I. G. Farben and the potash syndicate in Germany ruled the market. These huge companies differed from traditional firms in everything from production and planning to organizing sales, from their ways of financing to their philosophy of labor relations. Industry was now making materials that did not exist in nature and were not even imitations of natural products. It had succeeded in building up organic substances from amino acids. In 1904, hormones were synthesized. In 1909, the Dutch scientist Leo Hendrik Baekeland invented the first synthetic resin, named bakelite after him. Fritz Haber in Germany and Chaim Weizmann in England produced nitrogen from air, thus liberating Europe from the import of Chilean saltpeter for fertilizer and gun powder. August Wilhelm von Hofmann made synthetic rubber; Wolfgang Ostwald published his *Colloid Chemistry*. Acetate silk or rayon also was developed before World War I; later, filaments were to be invented to meet exacting specifications of tensile strength, heat resistance, resiliency, and so forth.

The word "invention" acquired a fresh meaning. No longer was it the result of a fortuitous discovery or of a lonely researcher's fanatical pursuit of an *idée fixe*; industry itself began to organize research systematically and to put scientists on the payroll. A great deal of money, the teamwork of many experts, and the co-ordination of many inventions were often required to bring a process from the laboratory to the factory. In the production of fertilizer, for example, which enabled Germany to defy the Allied blockade in World War I, the Badische Anilin- und Soda-Companie had to provide for continuous checking of extreme temperature, pressure changes, and gas flow and therefore had to pioneer in related fields affecting its machinery and instruments.

Another example of co-operation among various sciences was the development of aluminum, which is extracted from bauxite by electrolysis. In 1913, the world output of this promising light material had reached 3,000 tons. Man was finally emerging from the Iron Age, and even iron had to accept the new gospel that industrial materials had to be tailored for specific uses: Krupp, Germany's famous arms forge, manufactured a stainless steel containing 8 per cent nickel and 18 per cent chromium. Cynically the Krupps offered to the British Navy an armor plate that would resist any existing shell, and to the German Navy a shell capable of piercing that plate. In construction, reinforced concrete came to be used for buildings of striking beauty.

The new industrial revolution, therefore, was characterized by new industries depending on new industrial processes and new materials; large-scale industrial combinations that no longer followed demand but created and organized their markets; close co-operation among science, government, and industry; and new sources of power—notably electricity, which gave industry a wider choice of location, and the combustion motor, which revolutionized transportation.

The dynamo and the combustion engine had an unexpected consequence, momentarily counteracting the trend toward bigness in industrial production. Unlike the unwieldy steam engine, the versatile motors permitted many craft shops to survive in an age of industrial concentration; they found useful employment on medium-sized farms and averted the fulfillment of Marx's prediction that the middle classes were doomed to be pulverized between big industry and the proletariat. In 1900, about half of the industrial labor force was still working in shops with fewer than twenty employees; only in Russia were nearly 90 per cent of the workers employed in shops with more than fifty workers. In the older countries, two trends are observable: large factories became typical of some industries—the number of steel works was halved while the number of their workers doubled; by contrast, small shops mushroomed in the service industries and occasionally grew to moderate size in the textile and clothing industries.

Technical progress tended to reduce the number of workers as their productivity increased. Industrial capital was increasing at a rate twice as fast as the manufacturing population; the former doubled every fifteen years, the latter only every thirty.

More important, the rapid development of production methods resulted in massive redistribution of the population. The total number of industrial workers increased, both in absolute and in relative figures; the percentage of agricultural population declined. While the countryside was not being deserted, the towns irresistibly attracted the peasants' daughters and younger sons. They found employment in factories, in the homes of wealthy city people, or in the new service trades. Eighty per cent of the British people now lived in towns of over 2,000 population, and

50 per cent of the labor force was employed in manufacturing and mining; in Germany the figures were 60 and 40 per cent, respectively; in France, 44 and 33 per cent.

City life required and created commercial services that once had been provided within the household. Laundries, cafés, restaurants, nursing homes, beauty shops, and similar businesses now catered to the consumer's wishes. The owners of such establishments swelled the ranks of the lower middle class—a stratum that inserted itself between bourgeoisie and working class, smoothing out the social pyramid and mitigating, perhaps even negating, the trend toward a sharp cleavage between capital and labor. A sizable number of independent businesses still studded the cities; commercial and financial establishments were expanding, sales and office forces increasing.

By 1900, German banks were already employing 50,000 office workers. In 1910, Alfred Weber drew attention to the emergence of a "new middle class." The new industries and their organizations required the services of thousands of accountants, planners, and supervisors—a middle layer of management that formerly had hardly existed. In Germany, 8.5 million factory workers had to be directed by 686,000 "bureaucrats," where twenty years earlier 90,000 managers had been sufficient for 5 million workers.

The variety of social roles emerging from these job opportunities helped greatly to refine the crude class divisions of early capitalism, and contributed to the stabilization of the system.

Contemporary observers and critics were thrilled above all by the growth of big enterprise and its combinations: the concentration of related plants under one roof, the merger of several firms, the vertical accretion of supplier and processing plants to a mother firm, the conglomerate, the combinate, the trust, the corporation. To old-fashioned liberals these developments were a dubious blessing. The new giant companies might be able to dominate the market and create a quasi-monopoly; they might enter into combinations to control output, prices, and sales. Cartels, syndicates, quota arrangements, even world-wide understandings threatened to restrict competition. The French Comité des Forges and the German steel, potash, and coal syndicates, several international raw-material conventions (combined in 1926 into the International Raw Materials Cartel), and the grain, sugar, and paper agreements maintained prices high enough to protect inefficient producers; in some countries the government even enforced these agreements. Germany alone had 385 cartels in 1905; other countries had nearly 1,000 conventions, and there were 100 international cartels.

The old family enterprise succumbed to the modern giant corporations, which permit a small group of men to control enormous economic resources and divorce ownership from management. The old-style entrepreneur was a merchant or a production man; the new business leaders are organizers, financiers, lawyers, accountants, or promoters. They may have less substance but, for better or worse, their vision is broader. Often they are bankers; some of the great mergers, syndicates, and foreign ventures were hatched by banking consortiums.

The greatest innovation, however, was the intimate relationship of these new business leaders with all levels of government. Some businessmen took a direct interest in politics, for example, Joseph Chamberlain and Walter Rathenau. Unofficially, business leaders began to act in advisory bodies, helping to shape high policy decisions; formerly their interests and influence had been confined to domestic and especially social policies. Farm leagues, chambers of commerce, and trade associations acted as lobbies; the more strident their demands for protective tariffs, subsidies, or government orders, the more patriotic their gestures to justify their presumptions. Thus monopoly interests also became pressure groups for militaristic and imperialistic forces. Agriculture and heavy industry in almost all countries pleaded for self-sufficiency or, in the name of national power, for "educational tariffs" to protect young industries. Patriotic leagues, generously financed by interested firms or trade associations, were agitating for defense spending; large projects affecting international relations, such as loans to foreign governments, the acquisition of mining rights, or investments in transportation and utilities abroad, were often planned with government aid.

Marxists such as Kautsky and Hilferding feared that eventually a "general cartel" might organize production and distribution in such a way as to avert depressions, but at the cost of putting an end to all liberty. Such gloomy prognostications did not materialize. Monopolistic practices did not curtail competition but were its weapons in the fight for supremacy in world trade. The British and the French defended their markets against the young, aggressive, highly organized German industries, particularly electro-engineering and chemistry.

Even before the turn of the century, Germany had overtaken England in the production of industrial goods, and both were now being overtaken by the United States. The industries arising in these countries (and soon in Russia and Japan) were equipped with the newest machinery and new forms of organization. England's industry, paradoxically, was suffering from the fact that it had been first during most of the nineteenth century; now its equipment was old, and its trading habits tradition-bound. The Germans challenged British supremacy in fields that had been considered British specialties. Thus, an outcry arose from Sheffield when cutlery from Solingen appeared on the English market; a law was passed that all articles must carry a stamp of origin. France, mired in the traditionalism of her family enterprises, also was falling behind; her colonial expansion and her monopolistic practices had to compensate for the backwardness of her capitalistic development.

Monopolistic competition adversely affected the living standard of the masses. If wages rose, so did prices and sales taxes, while the requirements of urban living grew more burdensome. Investments abroad and the capital equipment of industry increased at the expense of the masses, whose low consumption set a limit to the expansion of domestic markets. A depression was threatening in 1905, and by 1907 economists were debating whether another "long down swing" might be in the making. The economy did pick up speed during the following years, but on the eve of World War I another depression seemed imminent. Even during her most prosperous years, Europe was unable to provide employment for her increasing population. In the 100 years before 1914, Europe's population leaped from 180 to 460 million— but another 60 million emigrated. Between 1900 and 1914, 12 million went to the United States and another 4 million to the British colonies. Empire seemed to be the answer to overproduction and overpopulation.

CHAPTER 4

Imperialism

THE world was becoming smaller, not just because steamship and railway shortened distances, the telegraph provided instantaneous communications, and world trade made nations both more dependent on and better known to one another; but also because many frontiers were being closed. Colonial fever, which in the past had seized the European nations from time to time, revived virulently in the last quarter of the nineteenth century, culminating in England's Boer war (1899–1902) and in the joint European expedition to put down the Boxer uprising in China (1900). This was followed by a vigorous arms race and intensive propaganda for "Greater Britain," "Pan-Slavism," "Pan-Germanism," for military values and for the civilizing mission of the European nations—"the white man's burden," as Kipling put it.

Africa was divided up by England, France, and Belgium, with Germany muscling in as a latecomer. In Asia, the powers prepared to dismember two great empires of past glory: China and Turkey. The Sultan still was sovereign over half the Balkan Peninsula and the Levant Arabs. But in repeated Balkan wars the southern Slavs, cautiously supported now by Vienna and then by St. Petersburg, were pushing the Ottoman Empire out of Europe. Italy, having been stopped by the Ethiopian victory of Adua in 1898, was coveting Tripoli (Libya) and some Aegean islands. The Western powers were penetrating into the Near Eastern dependencies, and Russia wanted Constantinople and eyed the areas beyond the Caucasus. Had it not been for the big powers' rivalry, Abdul Hamid's dynasty would hardly have entered the twentieth century.

The same was true in the Far East. Although the major powers divided China into zones of influence and acquired bases, none yet dared to detach any province from the Emperor's sovereignty. Although the China trade was not considerable, governments urged their bankers and railway men to invest capital for the sake of national prestige. Soon the capitalistic sea powers had to contend with the land power of Russia, which thrust the iron fist of railway construction into rich Manchuria, and with the unexpected rise of Japan, "the yellow danger." Japan's appearance as an aspirant for world power at first shocked the racial imperialists: but the practical imperialists of Britain's Foreign Office were free from such prejudices. To stop the Czar in the Far East, they concluded an alliance with Japan in 1902; to protect the route to India, they supported Ethiopia against Italy (1896).

However, colonial rivalries were never strong enough to overshadow European politics. There even was a tendency to sacrifice colonial interests in order to preserve the balance of powers in Europe. French empire-builders, trying to connect East and West Africa, did cross British empire-builders seeking a land bridge from the Cape to Cairo. When Captain Marchand confronted Lord Kitchener at Fashoda, near the Nile sources, in 1898, war seemed imminent. But England was busy in South Africa, and France had a foreign minister whose eyes were unerringly fixed on the Rhine. From 1898 to 1905, under various premiers, Théophile Delcassé labored to encircle Germany. Even earlier, overcoming their ideological scruples, the French republicans had concluded an alliance with the bloody Czar and cemented it with loans. Now Delcassé worked out a deal with England. He conceded to her a free hand in Egypt in return for a British promise to support French claims in Morocco. This understanding was formalized in the *Entente Cordiale* of 1904.

Once England had departed from her "splendid isolation," France could help to reconcile her two partners: Russia and England had points of friction in Persia, in inner Asia, and in China. By the Anglo-Russian Entente of 1907, Russia recognized England's pre-eminence in southern Persia and Afghanistan, while England acknowledged Russia's in northern Persia and Outer Mongolia, and neutral zones were left in central Persia and Tibet. Thus the Anglo-Franco-Russian triangle was joined. These cynical deals demonstrated that colonial conflicts were capable of being compromised.

Germany felt that she was being left out—even "encircled." Eager to be admitted to the club of the world's rulers, Wilhelm II built up a formidable army and started a naval program that forced England into an arms race. Germany wished to be feared—and succeeded resoundingly. Czar Nicholas II, whose meager resources and backward technology did not permit him to keep up with the arms race, invited the major powers to disarm. The first Disarmament Conferences met at The Hague in 1899 and 1907. Two specific agreements, not to use poison gas and not to drop projectiles from the air, were both violated in World War I. All other proposals were rejected by Germany. By so doing, Wilhelm II isolated himself. Hardly had the naval powers parceled out Africa among themselves when he demanded his "place in the sun." Landing at Tangier in 1905, he promised the Sultan of Morocco protection against French designs. A conference was hastily called at Algeciras, where the new Entente stood together and rejected the Germans' claims. But the French cabinet dismissed Delcassé, and there still seemed to be room for accommodation. In a second Morocco crisis, in 1911, Germany received some territory from the French Congo "in compensation" for the establishment of a French protectorate at Fez. At that time the Czar's Foreign Minister, Serghei Sazonov, also agreed that Austria might annex Bosnia and Herzegovina, if, again as compensation, Russia's navy obtained the right to pass through the Dardanelles. But Austria annexed the provinces before the Czar could validate his claim—and pushed Sazonov into the arms of the Pan-Slavists.

Thus the imperialist rivalry was neither capitalistic nor colonial, but followed the traditional conflicts of European powers for preponderance. But this competition now became more arduous and was played out on the economic and on the colonial fronts, too. Upstart Germany was not willing, and moribund Austria was no longer able, to make any "deals," although Britain never tired of offering them. Would Germany, for example, accept a share of the Portuguese colonies in return for a curb on her naval program? Chancellor Bernhard von Bülow indignantly answered: "Germany does not wish to be England's Continental sword." Germans cheered when he thus rejected the chance to stop the encirclement of which he so frequently complained.

Nothing less than supreme power in Europe would have satisfied the German ruling class. They wanted the Ukraine to settle German peasants and the French coal basin of Briey to complement the iron ore of the Saar. They planned to have an army that could beat any coalition of Continental enemies and a navy that could measure up to the British. They also wanted dominion over other races. Under the leadership of Geheimrat Heinrich Class, the Pan-German League (*Alldeutscher Verband*) brought together representatives of big business, the military, and high government officials in its plan to annex millions of non-Germans.

Documents published by the Bolsheviks show similar pre-war agreements among the Entente powers to despoil and dismember their enemies, plans that were partly fulfilled in the Versailles Treaty. The French iron industry, represented by the powerful Comité des Forges, advised the government, which was eager to listen, that to strike down German militarism one must paralyze Germany's arms forge.

The main thrust of Germany's empire drive went in the direction of the Near East, and its main vehicle was a plan to link Berlin, Vienna, and Budapest, via Sofia and Constantinople, by rail with Ankara, Baghdad, and Basra on the Persian Gulf—too close to India for England's comfort. Liberals provided the ideology, a "Central European economic unit." The four big Berlin banks were to finance, and German engineers to build, the link. British diplomacy moved every Moslem contact to dilute or divert the project, and then offered to partition Turkey if the Germans would permit the railway to stop short of Baghdad. But Germany supported the Young Turk revolution (1908) and loaned the new government one of its generals to reorganize the Turkish army. A Prussian commanding in Constantinople was strong cement indeed for the Entente. France, Russia, and England were older imperial powers trying to consolidate their empires; Germany and Italy were new claimants in world politics. Both sides were feverishly rearming. Although by today's standards their armaments were modest—even Germany, the most militaristic nation, spent no more than 4 per cent of her income on defense—contemporaries felt that by 1914 Europe was already bristling with arms. The great munitions-makers—Schneider-Creusot, Skoda, Krupp, Vickers-Armstrong—provided their governments with ever new devices. In the Balkan war of 1912 it was claimed (only half in jest) that the guns of Krupp were defeated by the guns of Schneider-Creusot. In fact, Krupp boasted the biggest gun ever made—Big Bertha, so-called after his wife—a howitzer that in 1914 hurled 42-cm. shells at Paris from a distance of 100 kilometers.

Although guns do not go off by themselves, a would-be conqueror might be tempted

to start war while he was ahead. This consideration certainly weighed in the deliberations of the German general staff when in 1913 France raised the period of service from
two to three years. More inflammatory was the naval race, the "dry war," as it was
called, between England and Germany. Wilhelm's Grand Admiral Alfred von
Tirpitz calculated that, in order to confront England's power, Germany need build
only about half as many battleships as England had. Such a navy, he felt, would make
Germany a desirable ally, and then "we will not be second to the British and the sons
of Jehovah any more." His counterpart, John Fisher, First Lord of the British
Admiralty, thereupon ordered a new class of ships to be built, the dreadnoughts,
which could outrun and outgun any other ship.

Both had miscalculated. By sharing with France the job of defending the sea lanes,
England confronted Germany with superior fire power. But because Fisher's dreadnoughts had made all older warships obsolete, including his own fleet of cruisers, the
Germans needed only to build dreadnoughts to stay close at his heels. In the end,
Germany entered the war with thirteen battleships to England's twenty, and Tirpitz's
surface ships never seriously challenged England's supremacy on the seas. His submarines, however, were a different story. They proved to be a powerful weapon in a
prolonged war of attrition such as no one could have foreseen in 1913. England might
have paid a high price for stopping Germany's naval program. Rebuffed, she
authorized her generals to devise a common defense with France.

In this light, the colonial episodes appear as mere maneuvers in a conflict that was
really focussed in Europe. The great powers, seeking positions of eminence, tried to
outflank each other in the global theater. While this game provided colorful copy for
the press, the leading statesmen were concerned with shifts in the famous "balance
of powers" and with military and naval one-upmanship—what A. J. P. Taylor has
called "the struggle for the mastery of Europe."

No doubt economic interests were the driving force in most earlier colonial
ventures. Queen Elizabeth I shared Walter Raleigh's booty. King Leopold of Belgium,
known for his greed, had made the Congo his personal property, and earned a profit
of 60 million gold francs in the space of thirty years. Cecil Rhodes frankly went in
search of gold and diamonds and engulfed England in an ugly war for the enrichment
of himself and his friends. The Dutch queen owned half of Java's plantations and
trade. The French public had learned from the Panama and Suez scandals what
enormous bribes could be paid out of the shady operations of colonial companies.
The interest of Manchester's cotton mills was clearly served when the British
administrators in India suppressed the village handicrafts.

It was taken for granted that the flag followed the merchandise, that the sword had
to protect business interests. Some economic motive always was invoked, even to
justify obvious power moves. When Wilhelm II tried to stop the erection of a French
protectorate over Morocco, he claimed that he was merely defending the Mannesmann
Pipe Mill Company's access to certain mines. The opposition in every country was
deeply convinced that patriotic appeals were mere covers for the profits of munitions-
makers, shipbuilders, protectionists, and colonial adventurers. Examples of

exorbitant and illegitimate enrichment through the collusion of business and government abound.

Yet, while bankers, traders, and princely despoilers did realize extra profits in colonial and semi-colonial countries, the importance of this surplus—its share in total output and income—was decreasing rather than increasing, and the benefits of colonialism reaped by the metropolis have often been doubted. As early as 1902, John A. Hobson's seminal book, *Imperialism*, showed that monopoly, colonialism, militarism, and imperialism are all unprofitable and even dangerous; far from mitigating the inner conflicts of the capitalistic system, they accentuate them. The extra profits extorted by monopolistic practices are both cause and effect of diminishing home markets; invested abroad, they may mean export of jobs. Monopoly subverts progress and diverts technological advances into the barren venture of the arms race. The mightier a nation may appear to be by virtue of armaments and overseas possessions, the poorer its people and the less competitive its economy. Far from sharing colonial profits with its workers, monopolistic capitalism depresses their standard of living.

During World War I, Lenin expanded Hobson's theories; his pamphlet, *Imperialism, the Highest Stage of Capitalism*, viewed war as the inevitable outcome of intensive monopolistic competition, and the current war as the final stage of capitalism, its death pangs. Many who did not accept Lenin's conclusions nevertheless agreed that the quest for profits had intensified imperialistic rivalries and was the ultimate cause of armament races and war. Yet, while British overseas investments increased from £2.4 billion in 1900 to £4 billion in 1913, only half of that sum had gone into the empire. France's capital overseas was but half that size, and only 7 per cent of it benefited the colonies, while a large amount had been raised under government prompting to equip Russia with strategic railways. Germany, a newcomer, had about a third as much overseas capital outstanding as England, very little of it in her own colonies. Hobson's theory has never explained the colonial expansion of Japan, the United States, Russia, Spain, and Italy—all countries with no capital surplus. Nor did the trade between metropolis and colonies expand faster than trade among the advanced powers. In fact, colonial expansion seems to be more characteristic of a nascent than of a stagnant capitalism, as Marx had seen.

Moreover, instead of revolutionizing the undeveloped societies, the powers were content to subject them to political domination. Instead of enriching both themselves and their possessions, states spent enormous sums to conquer and maintain in subjection colonies that offered neither valuable raw materials nor promising markets and whose climate did not invite European settlers. They entered into a mad scramble over territories that were not desirable in themselves; they added increasing sums to their defense budgets to maintain possession of these white elephants. It almost seemed as though the armies and navies had not been raised to protect these colonies, but that the colonies provided a pretext for maintaining a military establishment. The imperial dreams belonged less to capitalists than to the military and to the colonial administrators, who often conspired with proponents of the imperial idea to force the hand of a reluctant cabinet. The "proconsuls," so branded by Kipling, often acted against the will of their governments, developed a racist, imperial ideology of their own, and used their governorships to embarrass and defeat liberal governments at home.

In much that is called imperialism there is a nervousness, a sense of insecurity, a quality of *nouveau-riche* ostentation, an eagerness to keep up with the neighbors. There also is a note of exasperation and despair. Hobson called militarism and colonialism "organized outdoor sports for the old ruling classes." We may add that imperialism generally attracted people to whom the new bourgeois patterns of value seemed uncongenial: not only adventurers like Eugene O'Neill's Emperor Jones, or would-be pharaohs like Joseph Conrad's Kurtz, or artists like Gauguin and Rousseau, but social misfits who were bored with their existence—men like Jean Rimbaud, Cecil Rhodes, Carl Peters, Jean Baptiste Merchand, Alexandre Bezobrazov—all alienated men who, however, were able to infect the masses with their own delusions of grandeur.

Imperialism thus was the product of an alliance between the old military aristocracy, seeking new outlets for its obsolete values and its parasitic sons; the new bourgeoisie, eager to throw its weight around in the great world; and the lower middle class, compensating for the abandoned dreams of liberalism by the substitute dream of empire. Those who had failed to share in the government at home went in search of a vicarious share in the government of the world. Imperialism was based on an alliance of the mobs with the rejects of the ruling classes.

CHAPTER 5

The New Right

As a new dimension of nationalism, imperialism also had a revolutionizing impact on domestic politics. Liberalism was, as we have seen, poorly suited as an ideology for world politics. Nor could the old-style dynastic conservatives, the army's natural friends, offer the masses a myth of the dynamic future they craved. An answer to their dream was supplied by the Primrose League in England, the Pan-Slav and Pan-German movements in Eastern and Central Europe, the anti-Semitic parties everywhere. The Kaiser's court preacher, Adolf Stöcker, founded the National Social Party, an unsuccessful forerunner of the Nazis. In Vienna, Dr. Karl Lueger led the Christian-Social Party to victory; frequently re-elected, he was one of the best mayors that city ever had, and he maintained his power by violent agitation against Jews, foreigners, the clerical establishment, and liberalism. Both Stöcker and Lueger preached social reform and the style of their agitation offended the taste of traditional conservatives.

Remote from these men geographically but not in spirit, Joseph Chamberlain had started out as a radical reform mayor of Birmingham with a municipal program far ahead of his time, but he suddenly turned imperialist, agitated for empire tariffs, and preached the virtues of Germanic military prowess. In the wake of the Dreyfus affair, French anti-Semites spread their venom against financiers, Freemasons, the republic, and parliament as well. Their propaganda fed on scandals that had beset the parties of the Left. Like the petty-bourgeois they were, they relied heavily on the disclosure of corruption, on revelations about the morals of the mighty, and generally on suspicion of a world conspiracy. The so-called *Protocols of the Elders of Zion* purported to disclose a Jewish conspiracy for world domination. Although proved to be a fake, this famous infamy has been used again and again to support anti-Semitic campaigns. It played a role in Russian pogroms and in the Nazi agitation of the 1920's. Chamberlain too was a ruthless scandalmonger. Guglielmo Marconi's contract with the Liberal government, Persian oil deals, and the sharp practices of Sir Alfred Mond, a liberal Jew who founded England's chemical industry, made good reading in Lord Northcliffe's half-penny sheets.

The spiritual father of modern chauvinism was Maurice Barrès. German nationalist writers borrowed heavily from his programmatic *Un Homme Libre* (published in 1889) and the trilogy *Le Roman de l'Énergie Nationale* (1894). After him Claude Farrère,

Pierre Loti, Louis Bertrand, and other writers took up the banner of chauvinism and imperialism. Charles Maurras, a member of the Académie, joined with Léon Daudet (son of Alphonse) to form the *Action Française*; its youth group, the *Camelots du Roi*, used the monarchist idea as a pretext for beating up people. Neither Maurras's slanderous attacks on political enemies nor his evident paranoia prevented a generation of French writers from looking up to him.

In 1898, Houston Stewart Chamberlain (not related to Joseph) published his two-volume *Foundations of the Nineteenth Century*, a mixture of anthropological and mythological ruminations about the alleged rape of Europe by the Jews, which drew heavily on the philosophy of the author's father-in-law, Richard Wagner. Wagner's music was then enrapturing middle-class listeners all over Europe, but his librettos were understood, at least in Germany, as a plea to bring down the "empire of gold." Wagner's follower Nietzsche enticed immature minds, who probably misunderstood him, with such coinings as Superman, Logic of the Blood, Breeding (*Zucht*), Morality of the Strong, Blond Beast. *Will to Power*, the title of his posthumous major work, sounded like an appeal to the master race to shed the inhibitions of Christian morality and devote itself to the noble art of war. Two other authors widely read by German youth were Paul de Lagarde and Julius Langbehn, who proclaimed the superiority of the German race and inspired their readers with a sense of mission. Pan-Germans felt that German settlers would make much better use of the Ukraine's black earth than Russian peasants.

The idea of war and conquest was exalted in novels and newspapers, in schools and universities. Diaries of the period and the works of such writers as Thomas Mann, Rudyard Kipling, Joseph Conrad, Hermann Hesse, Maurice Barrès, Charles Maurras, and others convey the impression of war as an escape from personal problems or as the only way to serve one's country. Lecturing in 1907 on *The Poet and Our Time*, the suave Hugo von Hofmannsthal called on the Germans to award the accolade "genius" to Frederick the Great; he envied the English language for its ability to "comprise Milton and Nelson in one term."

European authors of the most varied backgrounds denounced liberalism, capitalism, rationalism, cosmopolitanism and, above all, the mechanical, materialistic, and egalitarian philosophy of the Enlightenment. In a general revulsion from eighteenth- and nineteenth-century progressivism, writers now exalted "natural, organic order" tradition, man's need for "roots," instincts, and the aristocratic values of the romanticized Middle Ages as against the philistine world of the middle class. This tendency appeared in the hieratic poetry of Yeats, of Stefan George and Rilke, of the French symbolists and imagists, who hated the masses, democracy, the press, and the very notion of equality. Two Americans, Ezra Pound and T. S. Eliot, were attracted by this anti-bourgeois climate. The Norwegian Knut Hamsun, who had started out with the starkly naturalist novel *Hunger*, achieved fame with *Growth of the Soil* and *The Woman at the Well*, which celebrated the life of the race as against the materialistic forces of capitalism.

Similar ideas are reflected in Joseph Conrad's *Nostromo* and *Secret Agent* and other stories that expose the parasitic emptiness of the financial empire-builders and the hypocrisy of their protestations of faith. Many readers who absorbed the imperialistic spirit of these works may have failed to notice the authors' contempt for the profiteers. On a lower level, American Western fiction, which was gaining popularity in Europe, made the same point. Here were heroes who had escaped civilization and were leading a true life of nature. Two German low-brow writers, Karl May and Friedrich Gerstäcker, exalted the American frontier culture; the frontier novels of James Fenimore Cooper went through numerous editions in many foreign languages.

Just as the anti-rationalists of Western Europe had their roots in Romantic literature, so Pan-Slav ideas reach back to the Slavophiles. In his seminal *Russia and the West* (1871), Nikolai Danilevsky declared that the West was doomed and Russia had to save humanity from going down with it. While the West had lost its soul, Feodor Dostoevsky claimed, Russia still had hers. She would become the "Third Rome," restoring God to the place from which Roman Catholicism had driven Him. Dostoevsky bore violent hatred against Jews, capitalists, the philosophers of the Enlightenment, Anglo-Saxons, and everything else that characterized Western civilization. His charges were taken up by Germans eager to proclaim that they were defending a mystical "soul" against the cold, artificial civilization of France and England. The West was "materialistic" and could produce only "civilization"; the East was mystical and had *Kultur*, as Thomas Mann was to write in his defense of Germany's war against the West. Likewise the Italian, Enrico Corradini, identified the mystical body that harbors the nation's soul. It is to the state that man owes allegiance unto death, and the state must prove itself in war.

It was not difficult to find historical and scientific arguments to bolster this creed. The Russian sociologist Yakov A. Novikov discovered that the law of all organic nature is struggle; hence, nations cannot help fighting each other. The British mathematician Karl Pearson felt that civilization was the product of racial wars; he quoted population statistics to show that the white man was losing the "battle of the cradle." The Swede Rudolf Kjellen founded geopolitics as a science, emphasizing that states needed "space" to realize their identity. His book *States as Life Forms* rejected the liberal axiom that the individual is the ultimate value and exalted the state as a higher form of life. The Frenchman Gustave Le Bon discovered that as part of a "mass" men tend to lose their identity, can be manipulated, and acquire a "mass soul." Lord Northcliffe translated this analysis into advice to the staff of the *Daily Mirror*: Write for the brick-layer; assault the masses with sensational reporting; disregard middle-class pretensions of respectability and education. His technique was imitated by the German press lord, Alfred Hugenberg, later Hitler's ally.

Patriotic Germans were sent abroad not only to earn money for the Fatherland but to gain a cultural and political foothold in foreign countries, to expand the German *Volkstum*, language, and *Kultur*, to create German enclaves, to support German power drives. "With each German battleship that goes out, Goethe and Schiller are also conquering the world," was the technique Hans Grimm cited in *Volk ohne Raum* (1926).

The British were only a trifle more subtle. Cecil Rhodes willed the millions he had made in South Africa to a trust to support the propagation of British culture through scholarship and prestigious studies. The Rhodes Trust had its tentacles in the Colonial Office, in Chatham House with its influential magazine *International Affairs*, in the London *Times*, Lord Lothian's *Round Table*, and even in the United States, in Boston's *Christian Science Monitor*. If France made no similar effort on a comparable scale, the reason was that everybody took the cultural pre-eminence of Paris for granted.

Each nation assumed that it was destined to rule the roost and took offense when others had the same pretension. The tone of public utterances grew provocative and irritated; diplomacy was drowned out by propaganda; writers who had been pacifists and muckrakers before the formation of the Ententes now discovered their nationalistic hearts. The new science of sociology took a special interest in the mechanics of mass domination. The classical books on this subject, written before World War I, mark their authors' turn from an originally democratic to a chauvinistic point of view. Georges Sorel, who had been close to syndicalism, held that the masses were following Marx only because they sensed an apocalyptic religion in his prophecies; he deplored the orthodox and bureaucratized mass organizations, which had lost all virility, and called for a new elite, a war, anything to make people believe in a "myth" once more.

Vilfredo Pareto was a friend of Sorel, and these two are the only masters Mussolini ever acknowledged. Like Nietzsche, they hoped to replace the mercantile, bourgeois elite with a virile, aristocratic one. The son of an exiled follower of Mazzini, Pareto reacted with venom and suspicion to "humanitarian nannies," democrats, and "demagogic plutocrats"; he proposed to "exterminate" the "humanitarian vermin"; he exalted the elites and deprecated ideas. Anti-intellectualism has always been the stock-in-trade of anti-democratic intellectuals.

To summarize a number of disparate movements: This new Right was no longer conservative and quietist; it did not exhort the people to leave government to their betters but called on them to participate, or at least to act as clamorous extras for the big historic pageants. It appealed to the mobs to fight enemies within and without the realm, and it offered them the ideology of an aggressive nationalism which submerged class differences in imperial dreams. True conservatives became rare; their place was taken by the churches and some enlightened scholars.

CHAPTER 6

Christian Responses

TRADITIONALLY, the European churches were allies of the conservatives. In the Protestant states the reigning prince was head of the established church. Dissenters were likely to be liberals, or they voted liberal to get rigid school laws changed. England's Fabian Society attracted Low Church men, and the Labour Party counted a number of leaders whose socialism was based on the Gospel rather than on class war.

But great forces also were at work for a regeneration of the Anglican Church. William Inge tried to renew the faith through an infusion of mysticism. German Protestantism was modernist in theology but conservative in politics. The great theologian Adolf Harnack, whose fame rested on his achievements as a scholar and his liberal interpretation of church history, developed ideas of social reform within the Conservative Party.

Some isolated liberals, like Max Weber, Friedrich Naumann, and Ernst Troeltsch, speculated about a new community of state, church, and society. However, Protestant attempts to cope with twentieth-century realities were deeply intertwined with nationalism. Nowhere except in England did any prominent church official utter a Christian protest when the nations went to war.

It was left to the Catholics, then, to develop attitudes of opposition to both liberalism and conservatism. The Roman Church had always been suspicious of the secular state; its economic doctrines were rooted in rural societies and hostile to financial and big-enterprise capitalism. In some states it represented the minorities. It was, of course, closely allied with the Irish opposition to the Anglican King, with the Polish cause against the Greek Orthodox Czar, with the small particularistic German states against the Protestant Kaiser, with the traditionalist Carlists in Navarra and the Basque provinces against a Catholic monarch who gave power to liberals and Free-masons. It was also opposed to the Italian state, which had taken Rome from the Pope, and to the French Republic, which was ruled (allegedly) by liberals, Jews, and Freemasons. In Germany it relied on the Center Party, which for a long time rallied democratic, anti-Bismarckian, and anti-capitalist forces against the overweening state and the crushing system of free competition. Moreover, it was a truly inter-national institution in an age of increasing chauvinism; north of the Alps its secret agents, the Jesuits, were persecuted as "ultramontane"—that is, subordinate to a foreign sovereign.

Pope Leo XIII had begun to modernize the church with his *Rerum Novarum* (*Of New Things*) encyclical in 1891. Criticizing both capitalism and the liberal state, he declared it nevertheless possible and necessary to live with them. Catholics must believe in authority, but rulers must show responsibility, he said. Social reforms must be restrained by both Christian conscience and the state's benevolent intervention. The Pope encouraged the formation of Catholic trade unions, and he found appropriate instruments in the French Association for Social Work, which tried to develop a Catholic, nonsocialist alternative to capitalism. Its journal *Le Sillon* (*The Furrow*) was founded by Marc Sangnier; a parallel magazine in Germany, *Die Furche*, has recently been revived.

Unfortunately, the Catholic hierarchy of France threw its lot in with cranks, thieves, reactionaries, and anti-Semites. Priests led the anti-Dreyfus mobs and agitated for the monarchy. For another thirty years, Frenchmen remained divided into two great camps, one Catholic, the other laicist. The latter embraced freethinkers as well as anti-clerical Catholics, liberals, Jacobins, socialists, and defenders of the republican form of government. They all adhered to the slogan that no one ought to have enemies to the Left, and many were Freemasons. The victory of the republic therefore entailed the separation of state and church. Since 1905, French Catholics have been able to send their children to their own schools only at their own expense. A quarter of the population has availed itself of this opportunity.

In Austria, too, the Catholic opposition started out with an anti-capitalist slant. But as soon as the Christian Social Party became the second largest in the Reichsrat (parliament), it absorbed conservative ideas, attracted members of the nobility (even the Crown Prince), and became a main support of the monarchy.

Leo XIII died in 1903. His successor took the name of Pius X, indicating that he meant to return to the uncompromising traditionalism of Pius IX. His attempt to obtain an oath of support from all priests nearly split the church. He excommunicated reformers, forbade publication of *Le Sillon*, and ordered the German Catholics to shun interfaith groups. He even repudiated the Christian Social parties and the Catholic trade unions.

A vigorous renascence of Catholic literature supported this new orthodoxy. In France, the novels of Léon Bloy and Paul Claudel; in Austria, Hugo von Hofmannsthal's mystery plays (*The Great World Theater*, *The Castle*, and *Everyman*), his librettos for some of Richard Strauss's neobaroque operas, and the brooding poetry of Rainer Maria Rilke; in England, G. K. Chesterton's Father Brown stories; the Munich magazine *Hochland*, as well as Bruckner's music—all these bore witness to an intellectual trend that ran counter to the liberal and secular mainstream of European culture. Catholic literature and propaganda accompany the shrill symphony of our century like a contrabass, never quite carrying the melody, but at all times discernible or even swelling into a mighty undertone. This was underscored by the conversions of well-known writers such as Henri Bergson, Jacques Maritain, and Julian Green.

Maritain became the leading exponent of Thomism; François Mauriac exposed the Catholic dilemma in harshly thoughtful novels set in the sad landscape of Les Landes, south of Bordeaux.

Some other voices in Catholicism, however, struck new notes. Hilaire Belloc and G. K. Chesterton sympathized with the ideals of patriotic radicalism, attacking "Anglo-Judaic plutocracy," landlordism, the "servile state," the party system, bureaucracy, and liberalism, as well as socialism. Charles Péguy offered a new tune to the young in his *Cahiers de la Quinzaine*. A Dreyfusard and a lifelong democrat, he supported modernism and social reform but remained a Catholic; although sympathetic to syndicalism and pacifism, he fought in the war as a volunteer and was one of its first victims. He became a legend as a literary master, a fighter for free thought, a patriot, and a humanitarian.

These men attempted to make religion palatable in a world that believed in scientific progress and was dedicated to the pursuit of material well-being. But the educated among the believers found it increasingly difficult to reconcile faith with modern science. "Higher criticism," using linguistic analysis, by now had attacked the authenticity of some canonical sources. Julius Wellhausen had shown that Moses could not have written the books attributed to him. The discovery of Hammurabi's code and of a creation story in ancient Babylon further shook the belief that the sacred texts had been received through revelation. The same method applied to the Gospels cast serious doubts on the authenticity of many divine dicta; some even suggested that Jesus of Nazareth may not have existed at all. If Christ was a myth, the scholars concluded, then religion could be saved only by a total divorce from all orthodoxy and theology. It would not really matter what form one's faith took provided that it afforded the believer the religious experience he craved. This was the conclusion of William James, an American who won high praise in Europe.

Such a pragmatic view might legitimize deep new experiences as well as pseudo-religions peddled by mountebanks of many sects, and often it is not easy to tell the crank, the neurotic, and the swindler from the saint. Christian Science and the Rosicrucians tried to reconcile faith with the scientific spirit of the age. The painter Odilon Redon dabbled in the mysteries of the Cabbala; writers Joséfin Peladan and Émile Bernard dealt with the occult sciences. Annie Besant, first a suffragette and then a Fabian socialist, ended as a disciple of theosophist Helena Blavatsky. Rudolf Steiner founded anthroposophy, with the Goetheanum as its spiritual center. Carl Jung and James Joyce immersed themselves in hermetic studies, and W. B. Yeats created a mythology all his own. In the wake of Schopenhauer, Buddhism became a fad for a while; Oriental cults, including the use of hashish, found prophets and adherents in high society.

Above all this bustle, only part of which we can accept as sincere, towered the greatest writer of the age, Leo Tolstoy, a Russian count turned socialist, a warrior turned pacifist, a man who had enjoyed luxuries and who preached the return to nature. There was little that could be called original in his powerful writings on religion and reform; their force springs entirely from his personality, his conscience, and his sincerity. In Tolstoy's view, Christ was a holy man who should be imitated but not prayed to. Tolstoy neither swore nor bore witness in court nor sat as judge over any fellow man; he denied the Trinity, original sin, the sacraments, and the authority of the clergy. The young Gandhi looked up to him. When he died, millions mourned the passing of a modern saint.

CHAPTER 7

A View from Below

UNTIL the end of the nineteenth century, members of the lower classes might appear on the stage as comic characters, in novels or on paintings as picturesque figures, and in social studies as problems for government departments. The "two nations" in each country did not have a common culture and did not even speak the same language. Nowhere did European "society" include the workers, and even their representatives were not recognized by the powers that were. After sitting in the Reichstag for over forty years, August Bebel, the leader of the German Social Democratic Party, complained that no chancellor had ever addressed a private word to him; he always wore sober attire and admonished the younger socialist deputies to do likewise lest they be mistaken for proletarians.

Lack of education and of social graces, indifferent sartorial habits and, above all, uncultivated speech set the working man apart from his betters, prevented him from getting experience in management or administration, and barred him from rising to that status of equality which was the aim of democracy. His schools taught him the three "R's"; in the more advanced countries apprentices also had to attend evening classes in trade school.

The aim of public education was to turn workers' children into good workers and nothing else. Even in England school had become compulsory only in 1870; the lower classes continued to ignore the standard language, did not wear collars on weekdays, and shaved only once a week. They went to their own pubs, took their women to cheap amusements, and brought up their children to fear the landlord, the boss, and the constable no less than God and his vicar.

Living standards had been rising, of course. Compared with his father, a young worker just before World War I was well off: he owned a bicycle and serviceable furniture, ate meat even on weekdays, read a paper, and belonged to a union. On Sundays he donned a white collar and went to a soccer game or bought an excursion ticket on the railroad. When he had a job, he had to save a little against frequent layoffs for seasonal or cyclical depressions. Unemployed workers received a dole, subject to degrading inquiries. A poor man, said Beatrice Webb, the Fabian, was still considered a moral rather than an economic problem. He was not recognized as an equal partner in the production process. The *Times* admitted in 1909 that England's *laissez-faire* system had left "a legacy of multitudes badly born, badly taught, badly

35

fed, and robbed of employment." Factory workers put in ten hours a day, six days a week, and earned £2 to £5 a week.

But the problem was not just poor working conditions and pay. The class system prevented the workers from breaking out of their station, and many of them were afraid to abandon the security of the culture into which they had been born. But the worker still had an artisan's pride in his work. If society kept him in his place, his place also kept him in society; no one else could be a worker, or wanted to be. With luck and effort, his son might become a teacher or a clergyman; talented children of the working class occasionally were given stipends to become functionaries of the ruling class. But such opportunities were rare; the only occasion for the classes to mix was when both descended into vice—a fact attested to by literature and subliterature.

Socialists drew the conclusion that the workers would have to rise as a class; instead of improving their prison, they would have to abolish it. The class-consciousness forced upon them would be the weapon of liberation. They organized their own institutions: a party for the political and a trade union for the social fight, a co-operative to meet the capitalists on their own ground of competition, as well as their own sports clubs. Taking a leaf from the monopolists, the trade unions organized their own labor exchanges to prevent underbidding among wage earners. For many workers the union hall or "people's house" became the center of all activities. In Paris the workers built the "Mutualité"; an inscription above the majestic columns of Berlin's People's Theater proclaimed "Art to the People!"

With memberships in the hundreds of thousands and votes in the millions, labor could think of its organizations as a counter-establishment. August Bebel was some-times called *"Gegenkaiser"* (Anti-Kaiser); German workers were inclined to think of Ferdinand Lassalle as Anti-Christ. Having emerged from Bismarck's anti-socialist laws, the German Social Democratic Party still had memories of its martyrs; its organizers were hounded in the eastern provinces. In Russia, socialists were totally underground. Despite the repeal of Taff Vale, labor unions could not consider their rights secure even in England. Elsewhere, organizing efforts still met with police harassment, especially in the big-estate areas of Eastern Europe. Socialist papers frequently had an editor in jail; some had a "time-serving editor" (*Sitzredakteur*) on their payroll.

But eventually, labor's power had to be recognized. Some of the great naturalistic writers had pictured working people as a class granted its own dignity and its own problems: Gerhart Hauptmann in *The Weavers*, Émile Zola in *Germinal* and *Fertility*, Maxim Gorky in *The Mother* and *Lower Depths*, and Vicente Blasco Ibáñez in *The Cabin* canvassed social problems with workers and poor peasants appearing as people. Käthe Kollwitz's powerful *Rebellion* lithographs (1899) gave a different view of working-class women than Toulouse-Lautrec's grisettes. The historian, Jean Jaurès, spoke eloquently of the historic role of the masses.

To be sure, pamphlets and posters depicted the new proletarian in an idealized and heroic pose—a giant ready to break his fetters, or a grim, indignant witness of scandals in high society. Like the revolutionary middle classes of previous centuries, the class-conscious working men of the nineteenth and twentieth centuries saw themselves as puritans. Having little to spend, they were parsimonious and therefore condemned luxuries. Their work was hard, their day long, their pleasures simple. Their sexual education may have occurred earlier and more spontaneously than that of university students; they may have been more promiscuous before marriage, but workers generally were more faithful to their wives than middle- and upper-class men. Domestic virtue was a symbol of reliability and strength. Class-conscious workers were the true defenders of middle-class morality at a moment when the bourgeoisie was in the process of abandoning it.

Cartoons and subliterary sources are quite eloquent on the view workmen held of upper-class morality. Capitalists wallowed in ill-gotten profits which they spent on women, wine, and caviar. Behind their false dignity, George Grosz was to uncover vileness, depravity, and servility. Zola already had disclosed the perversions of high society, and the pornographic literature of the age without fail attributed monstrous aberrations to capitalists and aristocrats. Rumor mongers knew "for a fact" that Edward VII was ruled by courtesans, that the German Crown Prince liked loose women, that a French president had died naked in the arms of a woman after an overdose of aphrodisiacs, that Alfred Krupp killed himself when his penchant for boys was about to be exposed, that some of the Kaiser's closest friends were homosexuals—all of which was true, too.

This view from below must be juxtaposed to the picture of the late Roman Empire taught in schools and widely disseminated in historical novels: moral dissolution had been the prelude to the successful onslaught of barbarians and Christians, both of immaculate virtue. The doom of capitalist society was not merely an economic necessity, as Karl Marx had assured the skeptics; it was a moral certainty, as the class-conscious knew in their hearts.

CHAPTER 8

Women and Children

As the lower classes were demanding equal rights in society, so the authority of the father was being challenged in the family. Middle-class achievements were under-mining this great institution, the foundation of middle-class society. As early as 1879, Ibsen's *Doll's House* had told European men not to take their wives for granted. The liberal temper also eroded the absolute authority of teachers, beginning at the university; even on the high-school level some reformers were making the bold claim that the learning process ought to awaken the students' interest and develop their critical abilities.

A scandalous play helped to dramatize the plight of youth. In stark, naturalistic tones Frank Wedekind's *Awakening of Spring*, first staged in 1891, showed how Victorian education drove adolescents to their deaths by ignoring their nascent desires. In 1900 a book appeared that was to put its stamp on an entire epoch. In *The Century of the Child*, Ellen Key argued that children should not be treated like miniature adults but should be respected as persons in their own right, living in a world of their own, which was certainly not that of middle-class society and free enterprise. At about the same time, Maria Montessori started her nursery schools, based on the principle that children should not be taught but allowed to discover the world. Soon, being young was seen as a value in itself and as more desirable than being mature. *Art nouveau*, with its sensitive, exuberant lines, was called *Jugendstil* (youth style) in German. Liberal fathers sought to understand rather than restrain their sons; the response, however, was the same as fifty years later—youth wanted not to be understood but to be left alone. The so-called Youth Movement made its first appearance in Germany at the turn of the century as a rebellion against middle-class morality, and even more against middle-class immorality, hypocrisy, and shallowness.

A risqué magazine, *Jugend*, propagated the new liberty and talked of the *Aufbruch der Jugend*, the departure of the young. Their destination was unspecified, but they were resolved to escape from the culture of their parents. In Berlin a group of students started the modern hiking and youth-hostel movement—*Wandervögel* (migratory birds). Their aim was, first, to establish a "youth culture" with expressions of its own: folk songs, folk dancing, a return to nature and, most significant, an honest acceptance of the body and an honest relationship between the sexes. They shunned drinking and smoking, social dancing, dueling, and restrictive clothing, such as girdles and neckties. They advocated health foods and sensible clothes and sang folk songs to the guitar. Gathered in solemn convocation on Mount Hohe Meissner in 1913, they vowed to shape their own lives responsibly. Despite a certain tendency toward cultural elitism and sectarian attitudes toward the uninitiated, the youth movement was democratic in its opposition to caste privileges and its plea for autonomy.

With various time lags, this movement was to reach other countries. It revolutionized traveling, social relations, and education. Full of earnest discourse, still it never got beyond the state of romantic protest. A few members turned to communism after World War I; more went to nationalism.

The youth movement had its greatest impact on education. The tiresome, tyrannical school system was overripe for reform. Cartoons of the period show the archetypal figure of the classroom despot; Heinrich Mann attacked him savagely in his *Small-Town Tyrant* (which later became a world success as the film, *The Blue Angel*).

Meanwhile the "new woman" made her appearance, a woman who could no longer be treated as though she belonged in the home. This was the decade of Eleanora Duse as *La Dame aux Camélias*, of Sarah Bernhardt as *L'Aiglon*, of Emmeline Pankhurst the suffragette, of Lou Andréas-Salomé, the friend of Nietzsche, Rilke, and Freud; the decade of Ellen Key, Marie Curie, Rosa Luxemburg, Beatrice Webb, Colette, Maria Montessori, and many others who were proof that women could excel in fields hitherto reserved for men.

Many kinds of emancipation were beckoning to women: economic, social, legal, political, domestic, sexual. Helene Stöcker fought for birth control and the right to divorce. Career women wanted independence above all; only a few wanted equality and aimed to take the places of men in society. The suffragette went after "woman power," often in an exhibitionist manner; she also fought for the right of women to own property, for equal treatment in court, for equal responsibility in the family, for the right to sue for divorce. The "new woman" did not wear make-up and did not yet smoke in public, but asserted her right to be herself and was not ashamed of being unmarried. She freely associated with men and, although she could not vote, she was active in politics and business. Even fashion relaxed its tyranny. Bustles and whalebone corsets were about to disappear, and women could once again breathe and move freely. The new silhouette was graceful and allowed the new woman to be "natural"— a word that links emancipation with the youth movement. But when women first began to wear riding breeches and gave up the ladylike sidesaddle, the peasants threw rocks at them.

Feminism was a middle-class revolution. Women of the aristocracy either enjoyed or did not care to enjoy the liberties of artists and models. Working-class women were interested in protective laws rather than in political rights. Most Western countries now outlawed female labor on night shifts, in mines, and on construction sites and granted women maternity leave. Still, women did not receive equal pay for similar work—and many women did not want equal pay, for that might mean unemployment.

Working-class women were far behind their well-to-do sisters in the knowledge of birth-control methods. Medical advice was not available to them. Church and society forbade the very inquiry. Cruel laws held them in fear and subjugation. Scientific progress had no remedy as yet for what was called the biological tragedy of woman. Would political representation help?

In 1903, Emmeline Pankhurst, widow of a British socialist barrister, founded the Women's Social and Political Union, which immediately launched into militant action, deliberately provoking incidents, harassing politicians, and heckling speakers. Aided by sensationalist reporting, the suffragettes succeeded in becoming notorious. In 1910, they invaded Parliament and prevented Prime Minister Herbert Asquith from leaving his house. Two years later, under the leadership of Mrs. Pankhurst's daughter Christabel, they resorted to terrorism, smashing windows, setting fires in churches, slashing paintings in museums, and cutting telegraph lines; when jailed, they went on hunger strikes. Just when the terrorist tactics had become self-defeating, war broke out. The public now grew accustomed to seeing women in uniform and doing men's work. Social contacts between the sexes grew more relaxed.

The problem of the sexes was discussed savagely in Strindberg's *Miss Julie* and Wedekind's *Lulu*. August Strindberg, who wrote with brutal frankness of his three unhappy marriages, saw woman as a destructive element to which man is fatally attracted. Wedekind, on the other hand, exalted woman as the "nature" principle, never quite comprehensible to man, whose essence is mere intellect. Woman is elemental; man seeks power. The tragic conflict between them results in the subjugation of woman, who can avenge herself only by becoming a siren. In a similar vein, turning the tragic into the somber, the Viennese Dr. Otto Weininger, a suicide at the age of twenty-three in 1903, divided women into "mother types" and "whore types" in his influential but chaotic *Sex and Character*. He also argued that every person has both male and female components in his mental and physical make-up. Karl Kraus, the eccentric critic of late Viennese civilization, predicted in *Sittlichkeit und Kriminalität* (*Morality and Criminality*) that the white man's culture was doomed unless he recognized the natural rights of women.

CHAPTER 9

The Labor Movement

THE Paris Commune of 1871, exalted by Marx as the first workers' government, had left behind it the memory of both a climax and a cataclysm. Revolution as an armed uprising had now become doubtful. But the attitude of refusal—the exodus to Mount Aventinus as in the Roman legend—remained popular, especially in some areas of France, Spain, and Italy. These workers, raised in the traditions of Proudhon and Bakunin, rejected all contacts with the corrupt state of the bourgeoisie; they did not vote and despised the liberal and democratic politicians. When Filippo Turati founded the Italian Socialist Party in 1892, he pointedly left the word "democratic" out of its name, for these revolutionaries did not wish to be "represented." They relied entirely on "direct action": strikes, sabotage, demonstrations, though not terrorism. As Georges Sorel explained in his epoch-making *Reflections on Violence*, the idea of the general strike was really a "myth," a banner, and a vision that warned workmen never to relax their militancy.

At their Amiens Congress in 1906, the French trade unions and labor exchanges formed the Confédération Générale du Travail (CGT); its "charter" affirmed the labor movement's independence from all doctrines and parties. It also opened the union ranks to those who were neither revolutionary nor socialist; the revolutionary phraseology was compatible with the sober practice of partial strikes, bargaining, and wage contracts. The leaders of the Confederation were Ferdinand Peloutier and Léon Jouhaux, who later on was to go through all phases of syndicalism, reformism, and fellow-traveling with Communists.

In other countries, too, trade unions avoided open identification with the socialist parties, insisting that their goals were purely economic. But ironically, the only great mass strikes in the history of the labor movement, those in Belgium, Sweden, Finland, and Poland, were conducted not for economic goals but for the right to vote or in support of a democratic revolution. As Rosa Luxemburg pointed out, political and economic actions reinforce each other; theory has to learn from practice. Italy's CGL (Confederazione Generale del Lavoro) was consolidated in 1906 under the leadership of "Maximalists," Left-wing socialists who would not hear of minimum demands. But despite its anti-coalition stand, the CGL and its political ally, the Socialist Party, obtained progressive laws through deals with the *Moderati*. The PSI was vigorously supported by the farm co-operatives in the Romagna and Po areas,

41

which engaged in bitter fights with the landlords. In 1908, the farm leader Argentina Altobelli won the eight-hour day for women.

The large, well-disciplined, and well-schooled Social Democratic Party of Germany (SPD) was dominated by the orthodox-Marxist, anti-collaborationist though not revolutionary "center" under Bebel's able leadership. His theoretical spokesman was a Bohemian teacher with encyclopedic interests, Karl Kautsky, whose weekly magazine, *Die Neue Zeit*, was an oracle for Marxists the world over. Among his collaborators were the most brilliant thinkers of the Socialist International: Rudolf Hilferding, Georgy Plekhanov, Otto Bauer, Karl Renner, and the historian Franz Mehring contributed a weekly column. Mehring, Rosa Luxemburg, Klara Zetkin, and Karl Liebknecht (son of the party's co-founder) constituted a Left wing which enjoyed great popularity among young people but was isolated within the party and put its hopes in the "spontaneity" of the workers and the "creativity of the revolutionary day."

The Austrian school of neo-Marxists was close to the German center, but its theoretical output was more original. Hilferding's *Finanzkapital* became one of the sources of Lenin's theory of imperialism. Otto Bauer's work on the nationalities remains a classic, and Renner's ideas on constitutional law and state socialism became the canon of reformist theory in the twenties. Max Adler combined Kant with Marx for a theory of "New Men." These works greatly enlarged the scope of Marxism and responded to modern developments without abandoning basic tenets of socialism. Friedrich Adler assassinated the Austrian Prime Minister Karl von Stürgkh in 1916. Despite this un-Marxist deed, he later on became president of the Socialist International.

For all their intellectual brilliance, however, the Marxist intellectuals were not liked by the practical labor politicians. Their doctrinalism and factionalism were sources of embarrassment, and at the Amsterdam Congress (1904) Jean Jaurès chided them: What has all your orthodoxy achieved? Show me the laws you have got passed. For all your revolutionary doctrines, you still kow-tow to your princes.

Marxism had lost its revolutionary sting. Karl Kautsky and August Bebel in Germany, Jules Guesde in France, and the brilliant Vienna intellectuals were happy with their counter-establishment and reassured each other that capitalism was bound to fall without much pushing. At the founding session of the Second International, in 1889, its secretary, Viktor Adler, expressed that attitude clearly: "When capitalism breaks down—and it will without our help—the proletariat's future will depend on its maturity. . . . We must be ready for that moment," which ostensibly was far off. The revolutionary phraseology won the workers' hearts, but it had nothing to do with the reality of the daily fight for better working conditions, higher wages, shorter hours, housing, progressive taxes, welfare services such as free burial, unemployment insurance, and so on, which all socialist parties now wrote into their programs. The famous "model program" of the German Social Democrats (adopted in 1891 in Erfurt, followed by the Italian program of 1895 and the French program of 1905) dutifully characterized all these demands as "transitorial" or "minimal," a mere rehearsal for the revolution. Elections were interpreted as mere tests of strength, and parliamentary tactics as a means of unmasking the enemy. Much of this was sour grapes, for in Prussia, Austria, Russia, Italy, and elsewhere socialists were considered enemies of the state with no prospect of being invited to sit in its councils. But wherever such chances were offered on the local level, the socialist leaders eagerly campaigned for mayoralties, made deals, and promoted welfare legislation.

In England, socialists had long hesitated to seek political office. But after the Taff Vale Decision, the Trade Union Council recognized that political action was essential. A Labour Representation Committee won 29 seats in 1906. The British Labour Party was formed as a loose coalition of trade unions, co-operatives, Christian socialists, Low Church men, Fabian intellectuals, the Independent Labour Party, and the Parliamentary Labour Party. The latter supported the Liberal government and obtained a statute repealing Taff Vale.

The Fabian Society was a small group of brilliant intellectuals, among them George Bernard Shaw, H. G. Wells, Sidney and Beatrice Webb, Annie Besant, Bertrand Russell, and others. Their famous "essays" advocated the tactics of the Roman dictator, Fabius the Procrastinator, who refused to strike until the time was ripe. Radicals without being revolutionary, socialists without proposing a system or dogma, they tried to change the economic system without upsetting any social conventions. They showed that basic industries should be nationalized, utilities run by the municipalities, and the rest of industry by co-operatives. They were derided as "gas and water socialists." Later, their work was carried on by G. D. H. Cole, a professor of economics and author of a monumental history of socialism, who advocated "guild socialism" based on co-operatives and workers' participation in management, with a Chamber of Economic Deputies replacing the old parliament.

Some of the Fabians, like Shaw and J. Ramsay MacDonald, inclined toward a leadership ideology that was technocratic rather than democratic. The Webbs founded the London School of Economics to train socialist managers. Their main work, *Industrial Democracy* (1897), showed how modern industry had prepared the unions and shop stewards to share in managerial decisions, how collective bargaining increased the workers' share in the product, how this "industrial democracy" helped to overcome the class structure of society. Lenin, who translated this work into Russian, was appalled by its implications. He concluded that the workers, if left to themselves, were capable only of "trade-union consciousness" and that any further impetus toward revolution would have to come from "professional revolutionaries" who submit tô a well trained, well disciplined, philosophically firm party leadership. The Webbs later were to agree with him; when they visited Soviet Russia in the 1930's, they found the technocratic paradise they had dreamed of. So did Cole who then supported the "Left wing" in the Labour Party.

Pointing to the development of parliamentary and industrial democracy in England, Eduard Bernstein told the German socialists that it was time to "revise" (in fact, disown) Marx: Small owners had not been crushed between giant concerns and proletariat; nor had the workers become increasingly pauperized. They were winning the ten-hour day, social insurance, higher wages, freedom to organize, and protective laws. Far from undermining the capitalist economy, these gains were enlarging its consumer basis, mitigating depressions, and diminishing upper-class privileges. The political system, too, was growing more democratic and, as Engels had admitted shortly before his death, socialism might be introduced gradually by parliamentary means, by evolution rather than revolution. In France, at the same time, the warm-hearted and eloquent humanism of Jean Jaurès drew more people to the party than any economic theories could have done. For the best reformists, socialism was as much a faith as for revolutionary Marxists.

The ensemble of these views, shared in different degrees by many practical politicians, is known as "reformism" or "revisionism." It revised the old belief that socialists could come to power only in a general cataclysm and by violent means. In Sweden and Norway, parliamentary tactics proved useful for the socialists as a party and for the workers. With one million members, the SPD was the strongest party in the German Reichstag and in the International. It polled one-third of the vote in 1912 and was flanked by millions of "free" trade-union members (smaller unions led by liberals and Catholics). In the south some liberal princes or legislatures made it possible for socialists to play a part in local politics.

As the labor movement was becoming a lobby for working-class interests, the Socialist Party was in danger of losing its militant appeal. At its Dresden congress of 1903, Bebel pronounced his anathema on "revisionism" in all its forms. The party could not abandon its revolutionary ideology without losing its effectiveness and cohesion as a movement. Yet the truth was that the German workers, and their mighty organizations—with a bureaucracy, a treasury, buildings, and so forth—had much more to lose than just their chains, *pace* the *Communist Manifesto*.

In France, socialism was divided into an orthodox Marxist party under Jules Guesde and the "possibilists" under Paul Brousse and Alexandre Millerand. When the latter joined the radical cabinet of Pierre Waldeck-Rousseau in 1899, the party expelled him and then all socialist groups were united in the SFIO (Section Française de l'Internationale Ouvrière, significantly omitting the terms "socialist" and "democratic"). Millerand went on to become President of the republic in 1920—as a candidate of the Right. He grew so reactionary that the Radicals forced him to resign in 1924. When Aristide Briand joined the cabinet in 1906, the SFIO expelled him, too.

The syndicalist distrust of parliamentary representatives and professional labor leaders proved justified when the various fatherlands called on them for co-operation. The Webbs defended England's rule over uncivilized peoples, and Gustav Noske proclaimed that the socialists wished to give Germany a better army. The Italian party had to expel Leonida Bissolati and Ivanoe Bonomi, who supported the conquest of Tripolitania and Cyrenaica. Bebel himself declared: "If it's war against the Czar, I shall shoulder a gun even in my old age." The decline of internationalism can be read in the resolutions of the International. In 1907, at its Congress in Stuttgart, it flatly declared that the workers of the world would respond to war with a general strike.

Five years later, at Basle, it adopted much milder language, over Lenin's and Rosa Luxemburg's protests.

To run ahead of our story, nationalism proved stronger than internationalism. When war came, Karl Kautsky meekly declared that the International was an instrument of peace and therefore could have no policy after peace had broken down, a sophistry which could not conceal the fact that the International had broken apart indeed. In France, Jules Guesde, who once had condemned all collaboration with bourgeois parties, now joined the government of National Unity, the Union Sacrée. Some old radicals and syndicalists, like Gustave Hervé and Georges Valois, turned ardent patriots and, ultimately, fascists. Mussolini, a radical whom the Left wing had installed as editor of *Avanti*, betrayed all his former convictions and comrades, founded *Il Popolo d'Italia*, and agitated for Italy's entry into the war. Marcel Cachin, who was to become a French communist leader in the 1930's, was the messenger who brought Mussolini the money from the Allied propaganda funds.

In Germany, Friedrich Ebert, as chairman of the parliamentary group, declared on August 4, 1914, a day of infamy for socialist internationalism, that "in the hour of danger the nation's poorest son will not leave the fatherland in the lurch." Ludwig Frank, a young Jewish deputy in the German Reichstag, enlisted on the first day of the war and died with the illusion that "In the trenches we shall lay the foundation of a new society." Similar sentiments prompted Charles Péguy to volunteer for the French Army. The war seemed to be offering workers and socialists the opportunity to obtain the recognition that had been the movement's real aim all the time. As early as 1902, Hjalmar Branting had spoken of the Swedish workers' desire for full citizenship; now he proclaimed a temporary truce in the class war. In 1916, Thorvald Stauning joined the Danish cabinet "to defend Danish neutrality." Neither country was then in danger of being attacked.

This, however, is only one side of the story. Eduard Bernstein, Kurt Eisner, and other Right-wingers joined the Left in denouncing the war. In England, Ramsay MacDonald and Bertrand Russell went to jail. In France, Jean Jaurès was assassinated on the first day of the war. Though later on reformism came to be associated with patriotism, and radicalism with pacifism, it is noteworthy that in 1914 some outstanding reformists remained internationalists.

The deepest rift occurred in Russian socialism. The Social Revolutionaries were a radical populist party which had developed from Slavophile and anarchist traditions. The Social Democratic Party, founded by Georgy Plekhanov in 1898, was a clandestine sect; it had to hold all its conferences abroad, and its intellectual leaders devoted much of their time to vilifying and expelling each other. In 1903, at its London congress, the party split into a majority (Bolshevik) faction under Lenin and a minority (Menshevik) faction under Julius Martov and Plekhanov. The issue was whether the party should be open to all or, as Lenin wanted, only to committed militants working under an iron discipline. The significance of this split will become apparent in the following chapter.

The First Russian Revolution

WHEN Nicholas II ascended the throne in 1894, Russia was well on her way to joining the West. The able Finance Minister Sergei Witte contracted loans from France, invited foreign capital to exploit the rich timber, mining, and oil deposits, built the Trans-Siberian Railway to open up the East, and bought the most modern equipment for Russia's young steel industry. It is true that a price was paid for rapid modernization. Half of Russia's sugar and a great part of her wheat harvest were sold on the London market at greatly reduced rates, while the Russian masses often went hungry. In response the peasants rioted. The workers, who were concentrated in large factories, organized underground unions; the students were restive. Liberal petitions threatened the public order. Inevitably, the modernizers thought, Russia also would imitate Western constitutionalism.

The Social Revolutionaries counted on something at once more dangerous and more benevolent. The Slavonic soul of the Russian peasant, his ancient village community, the *mir*, his traditional spontaneity, would enable Russia to eschew the painful way of Western capitalism and materialism. The Marxists, by contrast, felt that, like all Western nations, Russia had to go through all stages of democracy and capitalism. Hence, the next revolution on their agenda was not socialist but bourgeois-democratic, where the workers would not collaborate with a liberal government.

In contrast to the Social Revolutionaries, who were activists, the Marxists therefore fell easily into economic fatalism. Their trade unions, as Lenin pointed out, were more interested in becoming legal than in promoting the revolution. Condemning their "economism" and "abstentionism," he designed a strategy to transform the bourgeois revolution into a dictatorship modeled after the Jacobins in the French Revolution. Such a plan required adroit maneuvering and strictest party discipline. Lenin insisted that the party be an "iron cohort" of "professional revolutionaries," an order rather than a mass party. The Mensheviks, who actually were the majority, as well as Leon Trotsky, Rosa Luxemburg, and other Leftists, rejected this elitist concept and hoped to build Social Democratic organizations along Western lines. But when the revolution came, all factions were utterly unprepared for it.

Nicholas II, a weak and not very bright monarch, lived in fear of revolution. He dismissed Witte, whose modernism frightened him, and, under the influence of the bigoted Constantine Pobedonostsev, he gave all power to Viacheslav Plehve, the

46

Minister of the Interior, who allowed the *Okhrana* (political police) to rule by terror. Plehve was assassinated by Social Revolutionaries after the outbreak of war with Japan in 1904.

The following year, Russia's Navy and Army suffered stunning defeats at Japanese hands. The Czar's cruel system stood revealed as ineffective. Prisoners of war returned full of revolutionary élan. The liberals shouted for reforms. On January 22, 1905, "Bloody Sunday," the priest Gapon, a well-intentioned servant of the Czar, marched with a few hundred petitioners to the palace in St. Petersburg. The troops fired. Hundreds were wounded, seventy killed. Attempts to restore order served only to escalate the terror. In February, Grand Duke Sergei was assassinated. A Congress of County Councils (*zemstvo*) called for the convocation of a Constituent Assembly. Riots and mutinies filled the summer months. Sailors seized the armored cruiser *Potemkin* and threw their officers overboard (the greatest Soviet movie of the 1920's deals with the episode). Workers in St. Petersburg, Moscow, and elsewhere elected councils of deputies (*soviets*—the first of their kind). Strikes, demonstrations, and rioting culminated in October in a ten-day general strike. On October 30, the Czar published a manifesto granting a constitution. To split the liberals, he also recalled Count Witte to office. The "Octobrists" declared themselves satisfied with the manifesto. But when the "Cadets" (Constitutional Democrats) and their allies won the elections, the Czar went back on his word and sent the Assembly (Duma) home twice.

But unlike the French National Assembly of 1789, the Duma did not constitute itself as representative of the nation. No civil war ensued between the Crown and the people. Instead, a great wave of strikes swept over Poland; the St. Petersburg soviet, under Trotsky's direction, staged a general strike. These outbursts of "permanent" revolution frightened the bourgeoisie. Better an autocratic Czar than social revolution.

Meanwhile the Czar had called on an able tactician and moderate conservative to head the government. Peter Stolypin tried to satisfy the demand for agrarian reform and at the same time to wean the nation away from its political ambitions. He used military power to suppress the revolution while carrying out some of its aims. His farm reform had three objectives: to break up the village community, to create a peasant class of free owners, and to improve productivity. Two and a half million peasants elected to secede from their communities. Another two million were given ownership by a decree of 1910. (Another three million already owned their allotment in 1905.) With the purchase by peasants of land from the nobles, the state, and the royal household, a class of prosperous *kulaks* had emerged by 1917.

The Social Revolutionaries proposed to nationalize the land and to give it to individual peasants for use on the basis of family needs. The Mensheviks proposed to "municipalize" the big estates. Lenin adopted the Social Revolutionary slogan of "land distribution," and he kept his word in October 1917. But there was the question of what to do with the big estates.

The first Russian Revolution left a deep mark in the West as well. Once more there was hope; there was heroism and a legend. The mass strikes unleashed new waves of labor action in many countries. The First International had been buried under the ruins of the Paris Commune; the Russian Revolution revived the fervor of European workers and gave the Second International a new myth: that war would be answered by revolution.

Fissures in the Structure

THE European system excluded not only the poor; it exploited the peoples overseas. But the superiority of Europe could no longer be taken for granted. The British had won the Boer war only by dint of an effort that a mere colonial expedition should not have required. The Germans had to murder masses of Hottentots to keep their South West African colony. The Riff-Kabyles resisted the French "civilizers." In China, the Boxers had been beaten by a joint expedition, but the United States now posed as the guardian of the Middle Kingdom. Worse still, Japan, not even a white nation, struck into the arena of world politics.

The "white man's burden" became heavier and its rewards more doubtful. Instead of providing the metropolis with wealth, the colonies demanded investments, protection, and political departures from the liberal heritage.

The weakness of the empires was as important a source of trouble as their strength. Few "nation-states" were monolithic; most were composed of nationalities assembled in earlier centuries and never successfully welded into citizens' communities. Belated efforts to Russify, to Germanize, to Anglicize, and so forth, the minorities aroused opposition and kindled ethnic nationalism. Some nations ruled over others which lived in dispersion, as the Poles lived in Russia, Austria, and Prussia. The southern Slavs were divided among several small states, Turkey, and the Hapsburg Empire. Czechs, Albanians, Welsh, Irish, Bretons, Lithuanians, Latvians, Estonians, Icelanders, Norwegians, Basques, and Catalans did not possess autonomy.

Of all these, only Norway succeeded in severing its ties with the Swedish Crown by amicable agreement. The Balkan Slavs and Greeks had to fight against Turkey in 1912 to liberate their countrymen from Ottoman domination, but then fell out among themselves over the distribution of the spoils. As a result, Albania was created, and Serbia and Greece received shares of Macedonia which the Bulgarians claim as their ethnic patrimony.

Austria-Hungary, the Hapsburg dual monarchy, held many Slavs who were irresistibly drawn to their free brothers. But they were also separated from each other by history and religion, the Croats and Slovenes being Roman Catholic; the Serbs and Bulgars being Greek Orthodox, inclined toward Russia. The 10 million Bohemian Czechs applied the mulish methods of passive resistance for which they have become famous, and their deputies in parliament used inkpots, desk tops, and trumpets to obstruct the normal conduct of business. *The Good Soldier Schweik*, Jaroslav Hašek's World War I satire, has become a symbol of the immovable meek.

The Magyars were ruled by the big landowners and a top-heavy bureaucracy that made up in patriotic ardor for what it lacked in efficiency; Budapest's desire to rule over Slavs was matched only by its dislike of being ruled from Vienna. Crown Prince Franz Ferdinand, who passed for a liberal, toyed with the idea of changing the dual monarchy into a triple monarchy, giving his Slav subjects self-government.

In Russian Poland, too, the foreign ruler seemed incapable of granting civil rights. Having failed to "buy" the Polish middle class with economic opportunities, after 1905 the Czar fell back on his old alliance with the landowners. Thus, the Polish people were exploited jointly by Russian and Polish masters; no basic reforms were even promised.

The one nation that fought for its independence and, indeed, seemed on the way to getting it was Ireland. As we have seen, the Irish Members of Parliament, ably led by John Redmond, had helped the Liberals pass their budget, social legislation, and the Parliament Act. Prime Minister Herbert Asquith was pledged to grant home rule and would have forced it through the House of Lords but for the war and a Conservative conspiracy to keep Ulster under the British Crown. The Protestant majority of Northern Ireland, led by Sir Edward Carson, armed itself against independence. Their threats made the achievement of a free Ireland doubtful, and then the war intervened to stop all further developments.

All these rumblings under the rafters did not make the empire-builders any more cautious. On the contrary, to obviate the disintegration of their empires, the rulers felt compelled to adopt even more arrogant language in world politics.

CHAPTER 12

The Road to War

IN 1903, Serbian officers—members of the Black Hand, a Pan-Slav conspiracy—
assassinated King Alexander Obrenovich, an Austrian puppet, and put Peter
Karageorgevich, a liberal and patriot, on the Serbian throne. His Prime Minister
was Nikola Pashich, a peasant leader whose appeal transcended the country's borders:
Serbs, Croats, and Slovenes under Hapsburg and Ottoman domination hoped that he
would unite the southern Slavs. Pan-Slavs in St. Petersburg applauded, and the
Vienna court remembered how little Piedmont had grown into Italy by taking Venice
from the Hapsburg Empire. Austria, therefore, sought, and at first obtained, assurances
that the Czar would not support the drive for a "Greater Serbia."

In 1908, however, Austria annexed the provinces of Bosnia and Herzegovina, which
it had occupied since 1878. Having obtained no "compensation," Nicholas II felt
humiliated in the eyes of Pan-Slavs. In the Balkan wars of 1912 he sponsored a
Greater Bulgaria. But his protégé was defeated; Austria established the puppet state
of Albania, barring the Slavs from the Adriatic. The Czar sat uneasily on his throne;
his military attaché in Belgrade openly fomented anti-Austrian agitation. Not to be
bested, the Vienna government decided on a gesture of provocation. On June 28, 1914,
Serbia's national holiday, Archduke Franz Ferdinand and his wife were sent to visit
Bosnia. On that day, in Sarajevo, both were shot dead by Gavrilo Prinkipo, a Serbian
student. These shots loosened the avalanche that was to bury old Europe.

Since the Black Hand was involved, the Serbian Government was prepared to
make amends and accepted other points of an Austrian ultimatum, but it could not
allow Austrian police to operate on Serbian soil. Austria, however, decided to wipe
out Pan-Slavism once and for all; a quick little war against Serbia might bolster the
shaky prestige of the Hapsburg monarchy. But the Czar, unable to swallow another
humiliation, ordered partial mobilization and thereby set in motion the infernal
machine of the treaties. If Austria was threatened by Russia, Germany had to
mobilize; if Russia was threatened by the two central powers, France had to mobilize,
threatening Germany with a two-front war. To avoid this, Germany's former Chief
of the General Staff, Count Schlieffen, had designed a strategic master plan: Should
Russia order a mobilization, Germany must not wait for the Franco-Russian alliance
to come into play but must strike first, not into the immense spaces of Russia, but
quickly and ruthlessly at northern France, where that nation was most vulnerable,

violating Belgian neutrality to achieve maximum surprise, and rushing toward Paris with overwhelming power. There Germany would dictate the peace before the Russian steamroller had gathered momentum or the British made up their minds whose side they were on.

But the Schlieffen plan backfired. Nothing could help the British make up their minds as fast as the presence of a German force on the Channel coast. Once mobilization had begun on the Continent, the system of alliances and pledges drove the powers inexorably toward war. With hindsight, many believe that England could have urged moderation on the war hawks in Berlin and Vienna with the blunt announcement that she was committed to the defense of France. As it was, not even Prime Minister Asquith knew how far the British and French commanders had gone in planning their joint defense.

By contrast, Kaiser Wilhelm supported Austria to the hilt. Aware of the risk he was taking, he asked the Czar by telegram not to mobilize fully—a last chance to inhibit the chain reaction. But a Crown Council in St. Petersburg was told that half-mobilization was impossible. Although fully on notice that it gambled with the life of the monarchy, the council professed that it was tied to the wheel of fate: Austria had to mobilize to prevent the Hapsburg monarchy from falling apart; Russia had to mobilize to prevent the destruction of Serbia, which might unleash a Pan-Slav revolution in Russia, while Germany had to help Austria to prevent the loss of an ally. For the same reason, France had to support Russia. Germany had to attack Belgium to prevent intervention by the British; the British had to intervene because they had to prevent being prevented from intervening. The alliances and the staff preparations did not deter but precipitated the aggression.

In all capitals, the leading statesmen felt inexorably driven into a war that at least some of them knew might become "European" in scope; but they all accepted it as the verdict of fate. Once the engines of war were underway, they had to go to their somber destination. "I did not want that," said Wilhelm II naïvely, unaware that he was pronouncing a terrible self-indictment. The Russian Foreign Minister Sazonov later admitted that since the first Balkan crisis he had lost control over the southern Slav unrest which, after all, he had helped to foment. Sir Edward Grey later wondered whether it was really necessary "to assume that everything everywhere that Germany wanted was dangerous to us." Similarly, Germans later on wondered why their statesmen had interpreted every move by every other power as "encirclement." Germany's clumsy attempts to break out of the imagined "encirclement" seemed to justify the attempt to contain her. Once engaged in such an acceleration of mutual suspicion, no one could escape its vortex. The *Daily Mail* put it succinctly: "A mistaken course of policy has led us to the terrible conflict—in which we are now engaged." Indeed, Liberals and Labourites who had opposed the war before August now professed that they were in it.

Was the war actually inevitable? Four areas of friction might have become causes of war sooner or later: Russia's desire to have an outlet into the Mediterranean, the threat of South Slav nationalism to the Hapsburg Empire, the French desire to reconquer Alsace-Lorraine, and British jealousy of Germany's naval program. To begin with the last, the Liberal cabinet loathed the naval race, which deprived it of funds to carry out its social program; it had sent Lord Haldane to Berlin to negotiate a moratorium, but Germany's price was dissolution of the Anglo-French Entente.

The Alsace-Lorraine question had degenerated into an issue of French domestic politics rather than of international policy. The apostle of Franco-German understanding, Joseph Caillaux, had failed. The chauvinistic Raymond Poincaré had become Premier in 1912 and President in 1913; he and Georges Clemenceau, the old radical and anti-militarist, were trying to outjingo each other.

The paradox of the Dardanelles question is that it was neither Germany nor Austria that barred Russia from the Mediterranean, but England. However, Pan-Slavism entangled the Czar in its quarrel with Pan-Germanism, and these national movements threatened to destroy both the Romanovs and the Hapsburgs. The monarchs, therefore, found themselves unable to yield on this issue; some of their ministers knew that Europe could not survive the war into which they were leading her, but none was able to let go of the tiger's tail.

If guilt has to be assigned, we must name Count Berchtold, Austria's Foreign Minister, who deliberately designed a policy to humiliate the Czar and the King of Serbia; Alfred von Kiderlen-Wächter, the German Foreign Secretary who failed to stop him; Poincaré and the Russian Ambassador in Paris, Alexander Izvolski, who as Foreign Minister in 1908 had been duped and who fomented the South Slav unrest to avenge himself. Russian Foreign Minister Sazonov and British Foreign Minister Grey, who allowed things to drift, may have one excuse. No one in August 1914 could think in terms of a "world war," a war for survival, or any fundamental change in the relations of the European powers. At worst, they felt, the war might drag on for ten months. Certainly few thought of four years of war.

But we must not look for guilty individuals. Rather, a new spirit was asserting itself. This spirit accepted war as a way of life and rejected the idea of a "concert" that had ruled Europe for a hundred years. It even looked forward to a new society that would emerge from the trenches. A world was breaking down. In the last analysis, World War I was due neither to diplomatic mistakes nor to economic or military rivalries, but to the uneasiness of a ruling class that could no longer control society and its ideas. War—a beautiful, invigorating, holy war, *frisch und fröhlich* to the Germans, *revanche* to the French—seemed to solve many problems, personal as well as public, for some people who felt that peace was onerous.

Not everyone was sure that the soldiers would be "home by the time the leaves fall." Péguy felt that "a new age has begun." Sir Edward Grey said on that fateful day, after he had handed the German Ambassador his papers: "The lamps are going out all over Europe; we shall not see them lit again in our lifetime."

Part I has answered a question that historians have been asking ever since 1914: Was the world that perished in the World Wars really a beautiful garden the statesmen ought to have saved?

We have shown that it was both beautiful and sick. While all forces—those of the *status quo* as well as the lower classes, the minorities and ethnic groups—were looking toward the future, their combined labors helped to undermine the stability of the system and eventually to shatter its peace. In Part II we shall see that the most advanced minds were prescient of the crisis; in Part III we shall watch the crisis break out.

PART II

The Crisis of the European Spirit

CHAPTER I

The Cultural Rebellion

AFTER the proverbial lightning has struck, those with the benefit of hindsight may ask whether the sky had indeed been blue. Imperialistic conflicts were not just the machinations of some interested parties but grew out of an unrest of the European mind to which the novelist Stefan Zweig referred as "an excess of energy, some inner dynamism that had accumulated in forty years of idle peace." The same drive and unrest that had given Europe mastery over so many tradition-bound nations also upset the equilibrium of forces in Europe and the moral balance of Europe's masters. War, revolution and anarchy, dissipation, and the conquest of the unknown fascinated the sons of the class that had equated success with comfort, peace, and progress. They adored doom; they savored the morbidity of Richard Strauss's early operas and the decadence of Oscar Wilde's bittersweet aphorisms. Writers deplored the loss of the old aristocratic values and denounced the bourgeoisie as unpoetical, insensitive, indecorous, unchivalrous, not fit to sing about. Bohemians found the middle class prurient, greedy, and ugly. New voices were heard, calling the new century to a merry war against nineteenth-century narrowness, academic sterility, Victorian fussiness, and bourgeois utilitarianism. Just before the turn of the century, the German comic-strip artist Wilhelm Busch had good-natured fun with hypocrites and squares; the poems of Joris Karl Huysmans had dazzled and shocked the bourgeois by flaunting their secret vices before them; now Bernard Shaw brought the same message home with sharp wit, André Gide scorchingly.

None of these attacks on hypocrisy and rigidity was yet seen as a threat to the social order. Some old institutions had come apart and old beliefs had become unserviceable, but the old unity of culture was not shattered. In a nostalgic vein, Thomas Mann described the downfall of an old patrician family—his own, in his novel *Buddenbrooks*. But there was no apocalypse in the novel, no ferocious mob bent on avenging injustice, merely a sweet-scented decline and a touch of decadence; a sensitive young boy, the artist of the family, is a pathetic victim of a life he cannot control.

In his poem "The Second Coming," W. B. Yeats expressed the same general idea in different terms:

> Things fall apart; the center cannot hold;
> Mere anarchy is loosed upon the world, . . .

The best lack all conviction, while the worst
Are full of passionate intensity.[1]

Previous centuries had lived by and for ideas. But Yeats now—anticipating existentialism—would "no longer permit life to be shaped by a personified ideal; we must serve with all our faculties some actual thing." The boundaries of faith and morality had crumbled. "Do away with all moral restrictions!" exclaimed the poet Gabriele d'Annunzio. And eventually, sex was allowed out of the underground literature into the open and was given high literary form by D. H. Lawrence. New values and new sensibilities were to be explored.

Yet those who so fervently asserted their freedom from inhibitions and ideas were not free from an obsession with newness for its own sake. "*Il faut être rigoureusement moderne*," Rimbaud had said. In H. G. Wells's *A Modern Utopia* (1905), the perfect state never stays fixed but is kinetic and subject to further revolution. To be modern, explained the poets of the age, means to reject all traditions and also to refrain from creating new ones. "No good poetry is ever written in a manner ten years old," said Ezra Pound.

The bourgeois loved to be tickled or even kicked, though not spat at. While the bohemians were slapping his face, he accepted their antics in good humor. Everyone wanted to show how naughty he could be, at least vicariously. Shaw's *Don Juan* found the best people in Hell. If it had become unfashionable to believe in God, it was smart to flirt with the Devil.

It was part of the market psychology that aesthetic and intellectual wares of increasing sensationalism had to be offered. This was the way shown by newspapers, by the cinema (in 1904 England already had 3,500 theaters), by spectator sports, peep shows, fashions, and the extravaganzas offered in department stores. The poets and artists who thought they were escaping bourgeois materialism hardly realized that they were merely fulfilling it. The German historian Karl Lamprecht showed that the materialistic age had to be followed by a sensualistic culture (sociologist Pitirim Sorokin later called it "sensate"). This culture might look down on its predecessor's crude utilitarianism, but it was even farther removed from idealism. The Impressionist painters had re-created the fleeting character of all sensations; with the Postimpressionists the sensation became an end in itself. "Not the fruit of the experience, the experience itself is the end," Walter Pater ecstatically explained. In the same vein, Oscar Wilde praised the new French "novels without a plot . . . trying to realize all the passions" and the Imagist metaphors, "as monstrous as orchids and as evil in color." Arthur Symons and Aubrey Beardsley published *Savoy*, a magazine of the sensational, the morbid, the exotic, and the bizarre.

This decadence, which mistook sensibility for feeling, experience for substance, and violence for manliness, was greeted by Symons as "a new and beautiful and interesting disease." Violence, in fact, eventually became the last frontier of fastidiousness:

---

[1] Copyright 1924 by Macmillan Publishing Co., Inc., renewed 1952 by Bertha Georgie Yeats.

André Gide's Lafcadio asked for "a gratuitous act," and a young dandy shot a stranger on Montmartre for kicks. Thomas Mann said that "gestures alone are understood, not ideas." Rudyard Kipling exalted the life of the soldier. The Surrealist André Breton called for "any kind of revolution that will take the bourgeoisie away," and Joseph Conrad wrote: "In the destructive element immerse." The sophisticated, steeped in a *fin de siècle* boredom rather than the exhilaration of opening a new century, had come to an impasse. Poet Paul Valéry opined: "*Le monde est fini.*" In disgust, Oscar Wilde sighed: "I wish the whole globe were finished." And soon T. S. Eliot was to charge that the world was coming to its end, not even with a bang but with a whimper.

The music of the age reflected these moods—impressionistic in Claude Debussy, temperamentally brilliant and sensual in Maurice Ravel, brooding and boundless in Gustav Mahler, resigned in Arnold Schönberg, apocalyptic in Stravinsky.

Similarly in painting, Expressionism, Futurism, Cubism, and Fauvisme[2] proclaimed in ever more intensive disharmonies that the world was falling apart. All lamented the loss of a unifying idea, bore witness to a culture deeply at war with itself, doubted its values, and jeered at its certitudes. The gods had fallen, as Nietzsche had proclaimed.

Charles Péguy deplored the vanishing of great myths: "We are the last generation with a republican mystique. After us begins the world which we shall call modern— the world that tries to be clever." From this terrible perspective, the writers fled into a new hero worship, exalting vitality, courage, nobility, and deprecating the bourgeois paradise of calculated happiness. Werner Sombart, then still a socialist and a historian of capitalism, exclaimed that people were losing their ability to love. But in the satirical play *Re Baldoria* (*Le Roi Bombance*), Filippo Marinetti charged that the socialists were just as materialistic as the bourgeoisie and that a revolution was likely to end in the satisfaction of the palate for some rather than in freedom and poetry for all. Loss of poetry, or in Max Weber's words "the world's demystification," was the crime of the bourgeoisie.

But one could not simply retreat into poetry. The old, false idealism of his predecessors was barred to the modern poet. Hugo von Hofmannsthal, politically reactionary but modern as a critic, explained why contemporary poetry was incapable of synthesis; it lacked the magic of harmony and must reflect the dissonances of modern life. A poet with any passion, he said, reacts against his age.

Many reacted violently. Their magazines now had names such as *Action, Storm, Revolution*; we find artists suffering nervous breakdowns and voicing death wishes, or volunteering for the war. So too did the heroes of literature—Hermann Hesse's Demian and Thomas Mann's Hans Castorp, for example—faithfully reflecting the mood of their authors' youth.

---

[2] The *Salon d'Automne* of 1905, in which Henri Matisse and Georges Rouault first exhibited, is usually considered the birthplace of modern art. Wassily Kandinsky started abstract art in Munich as early as 1910; but since most abstract artists came to be recognized only in the 1920's, their socio-historical significance will be discussed in Chapter 3 of Part V.

"Enthusiasm, greatness, heroism—once upon a time the shadows of these gods were visible. Today they are puppets. War has left, and eternal peace is its pitiful heir," said *Die Aktion* (1911), whose editor, Franz Pfempfert, was a pacifist.

It did not really matter what war or which revolution. While many writers inclined toward anarchism, Marinetti and his group of Futurists were ardently nationalistic; they combined the worship of modern technology with a fervent love for the primeval, the primitive, and the destructive. Their "Manifesto" of 1909 praised aggressiveness, the anarchist's destructive deed, and the *vivere pericolosamente* which Mussolini was to adopt later on as his motto. It declared that the motor car (model 1909) was more beautiful than the Greek *Nike*. It called war "the hygiene of the world," and it promised to destroy libraries, museums, and academies. The European spirit was running amuck. In previous crises people appealed to ideas or to something in man that was "better"; now the decay itself was the object of cultural exploration and adoration.

Lytton Strachey averred that he "preferred anarchy to the Chinese Empire." He belonged to the brilliant group of intellectuals who for a time gathered in Bloomsbury. They were all upper-class agnostics, brought up in the belief that modern Cambridge embodied the peak of civilization, derisive of the age of the masses, contemptuous of practical socialists such as the Webbs and critical of "materialists" like H. G. Wells, John Galsworthy, and Arnold Bennett, writers who belabored "unimportant social facts" instead of describing the ever-changing impressions of the mind. This illustrious circle included Bertrand Russell, who then was working on his *Principia Mathematica*, George Edward Moore, the philosopher of ethical relativism, Leonard and Virginia Woolf, their friend Victoria Sackville-West and her husband Harold Nicolson, Lytton Strachey, E. M. Forster, John Maynard Keynes, the Sitwells, Rose Macaulay, and Katharine Mansfield. Totally dedicated to mutual praise of one another's works, they relished destroying the reputation of others.

A parallel movement in Germany, ribald, defiant in its use of eroticism to castigate middle-class morality, united Arno Holz, Frank Wedekind, Richard Dehmel, Gerhart Hauptmann, Christian Morgenstern, and a few minor writers. In Munich and Berlin a satirical and bawdy cabaret sharpened the accents already set by Aristide Bruant and Yvette Guilbert in Paris.

All these manifestations of disgust were spoken, written, sung, and painted fifty years before the "angry young men" or today's student rebellion, and they sprang from a similar source: boredom with an affluent society, revulsion against the fathers' middle-class values, but also a feeling of newness, the exuberance that comes with the ability to do what has never been done before, the joy of enlarging the frontiers of freedom, of testing the limits of censorship, of challenging the restrictiveness of "good taste." Often a provocation is staged not because what it says needs to be said but because it has not been said before or because it displeases the authorities. In other words: The rebellion often is on the level of pranks ("happenings"), and it relies on vagabonds, saltimbanques (see Picasso's blue canvasses), whores, bohemians, and beggars—the outcasts of middle-class society—rather than the workers, who, after all, are part of the system.

The writers who took part in this rebellion against middle-class values probably mistook a literary for a social revolution; but the Futurist critic Paul Arca reassured the bourgeois in *Athenai*: "Don't expect the marauding attack of barbarous arsonists in the museums and libraries. . . . Our only concern is to shake the young intelligentsia loose from pedantry, imitation, sentimentality; to instill in it the love of intuition, spontaneity, passion, subversion, danger, and action." In Gerhart Hauptmann's *Rats* the twin themes of literary and social revolution are treated almost as one: hypocrisy in art is doomed for the same reason as hypocrisy toward the poor. But Hauptmann was to turn soon thereafter to romanticism; the entire movement, which had *épaté les bourgeois* for fifty years (ever since Flaubert created the phrase), never got near to overthrowing them. For, as we shall see, the artists were closely connected with the culture against which they thought they were protesting. They were both its product and its counterpart.

CHAPTER 2

Mass Culture and Middle-Class Culture

MOST inventions that form the physical basis of our present culture were made before this century began: for example, the linotype, mass-circulation papers, motion pictures, the radio, the phonograph, the motor car. But it took about a generation before they significantly changed the quality of life. At the beginning of the century, most people were hardly aware of the great opportunities that lay ahead through mass production of cultural goods. But some intellectuals began to deplore the deterioration in public taste. They feared a sort of cultural Gresham's Law: cheap, mass-produced articles would drive out the tasteful products of ancient handicraft. This was an optical illusion. True, mass production spread *kitsch* throughout the world: pipes with bowls shaped like Bismarck's head, beer mugs that played "London Bridge Is Falling Down," oleographs of battle scenes, ashtray replicas of the Fontana di Trevi—horrors still to be found in antique shops. But later on good art also was reproduced, and well-designed utensils and decorative articles were manufactured for the mass market. *Kitsch* became the forerunner of taste. Far from leveling down quality or homogenizing taste, the market demanded a great variety of style, new techniques, new points of view.

Nowhere is this development more apparent than in the history of the motion picture, the most characteristic product of our age. Precisely because it must sell in a mass market, this industry has constantly invented new forms of expression. As early as 1906, Charles Pathé, a great showman, screened a film with a train moving rapidly toward the spectator. He brought the documentary to the masses and marketed the first trick films (cartoons), Emile Cohl's "Marionette" series, and the first social reportage, Louis Feuillade's *On Strike* (1912). He quickly proceeded to the horror film and also staged the great pageants—*Les Misérables, The Last Days of Pompeii,* and *Quo Vadis?*

The movies have instructed people who do not read and taught viewers how to see with a more discriminating eye. In the beginning, it is true, they were mostly thought of as entertainment for the lower classes. Words and commentary were projected on the screen or spoken by a master of ceremonies, and most theaters had a pianist who pounded out the *Ride of the Valkyries* to accompany the chase after the criminal or tinkled schmaltzy melodies while the heroine abandoned herself to a strictly clocked interval of kisses. The technique of dead-pan silence, on the other hand, was used in slapstick and in the first satirical films. An American director, Mack Sennett, who became Charlie Chaplin's teacher, brought meaning to the comic film. His short grotesques gave a topsy-turvy view of the world, with mayhem resulting from good intentions.

Most movies, of course, were either sentimental or adventurous, and virtually all had happy endings. The seamstress married the millionaire; the villain was caught. Since, as every schoolboy knew, adventure was to be found in the Wild West, the sheriff, the rustler, the gold digger, and the covered wagon were as familiar to Europeans as to Americans. Later on, of course, critics would condemn these movies as escapist. But the early movies became a true cultural institution precisely because they offered ordinary people a glimpse of a never-never land in which true love and courage were tested and rewarded. They projected the little man's dreams of a better world; there is an element of protest in every Wild West story. Likewise, the adventure story that schoolboys used to read in installments had moral pretensions. Thus, *Frank Allen the Avenger of the Disinherited* was a sort of Robin Hood who robbed because he hated the Establishment. A similarly primitive anarchist was Fantômas, the hero of a monthly serial that Feuillade made into a serial movie. The character was so successful that Fantômas clubs were founded; Max Jacob and Guillaume Apollinaire were members. Edgar Wallace, who became a best-selling writer of whodunits in the 1920's, also had a moral purpose; in *King of Souls* he even preached metempsychosis.

Pulp magazines and B-pictures, the successful detective story, the gothic and horror novel have hardly changed since their invention, except for a few technical tricks. Science fiction, by contrast, has acquired both sophistication and vulgarity. In *20,000 Leagues Under the Sea* Jules Verne was intent upon testing a scientific assumption. Later on the genre was to degenerate into pure adventure. Women's magazines still preferred the tearful love story, preferably involving a high-born personage who got into trouble or a low-born one who attained honors and riches.

But the dreams fulfilled in this literature were rather unsophisticated and appear silly to the modern reader. Later on, Wagnerian fantasies of primeval grandeur were grafted upon purple scenes of Oriental splendor, with orgies of incest and opium thrown in for good measure. Utter refinement of vice had been shown by a twenty-year-old woman writer, "Rachilde," whose "works," *La Marquise de Sade* and *Monsieur Venus*, were passed around secretly. A child star, Polaire, was shown in a movie based on Colette's sentimental *Claudine*, the story of a schoolgirl who attracted the lecherous interest of middle-aged gentlemen. Pierre Louys published the novel *The Adventures of King Pausole* (1901), which inspired Marinetti's satirical play, *Re Baldoria*.

The "revue" or variety show, with its inevitable cancan dancers, also appealed to erotic interests. The cabaret attracted some of the greatest songwriters of the time, who usually performed their own songs. This art was still reserved for the connoisseurs. The masses had the operetta and its hit songs—schmaltzy, or saucy, and military. The phonograph made them popular. This instrument, still a novelty and a luxury, catered to the vulgar as well as to the most refined tastes. A list of early collectors included many modern artists and *avant-garde* people. The tone quality of early recordings was poor, but everybody could now hear Caruso. Movies and records brought the greatest, and the worst, actors and singers to the masses. In the theater they had been legendary figures; now they were seen, heard, and owned. The newspapers built up stage "personalities"—truly a mass culture.

Modern art was collected and modern plays seen only by an elite. But the mass of the educated representing the predominant culture were not the audience that supported any new style. Rather, they followed the advice of academic teachers who told them what they might safely admire. They bought sets of classical authors in gilt-edge editions, learned to appreciate classical paintings, saw the approved plays after consulting the reviews, took subscriptions to the nine Beethoven symphonies with an instructive introduction, or, if they were very modern, to a Wagner cycle. In all European countries theater and opera were—and are—state-supported; they are public functions for the perpetuation of that which has been found good and beneficial —and the new, of course, was suspect. Empress Auguste Victoria personally intervened to prevent the staging in Berlin of Richard Strauss's *Rosenkavalier*; the director of the National Gallery there was fired when he acquired some canvasses by contemporary artists.

Museums multiplied; adult education was introduced; "appreciation of the classics" began. Ladies' clubs wandered through forests of Greek plaster casts; eager students tried to apply Renaissance models to the design of modern living. With a piano in most middle-class homes, especially those with marriageable daughters, music was a status symbol. Family magazines, art histories, popular science books, as well as the voluminous, profusely illustrated encyclopedias—the perfect wedding or first-communion gift—reduced the art and wisdom of the centuries to a treasure house of cultural wares; the classical authors almost literally dissolved into so many quotations gathered by Bartlett or Stevenson for use in after-dinner and commencement speeches, and editorials were expected to contain a good number of such gems.

Thus, we observe a stream of popular mass culture that rises from *kitsch* to dream, and an elite mass culture that freezes art into ritual. The one mildly challenges existing values; the other tries to stabilize them.

CHAPTER 3

The Creators of Modern Art

WHAT we call "modern art" is now more than two generations old. It had been fully developed in all its phases before World War I; its fathers—Cézanne, Gauguin, and van Gogh—were born in the mid-nineteenth century. Their themes were the abstract, the exotic, and the subjective. Gauguin said that "the idea of beauty is the great mistake in Greek art." The Impressionists nevertheless had tried to depict nature in a beautiful way. *Art nouveau* at the turn of the century no longer claimed to represent nature as it is perceived but tried to bring to light some inner beauty or truth. It still idealized its subjects. But the slogan *L'art pour l'art* liberated the artist from the tyranny of beauty. The work should be true, honest, sensitive, sincere. When François Mauriac in 1929 wrote the epitaph on his generation, he said: "It suffered from one fatal disease. It was incapable of insincerity, and therefore it could not live any longer by values that had gone by in the 1880's." Even the serene impressionistic sensualism of Monet (who lived to 1926) would no longer do. With Georges Seurat and Paul Signac, the painting became autonomous as it were; the viewer had to find the synthesis in himself. Yet the canvases were still "imitative."

A bold departure was needed to make the painter sovereign. Cézanne went beyond the superficial aspect, showed how the world was structured, and experimented with spatial relations. After him came the Cubists, who completely broke with the tradition that a painting must borrow its structure from the visual. Rather, they built from an inner vision, telescoping many views of the subject in juxtaposition and super-imposition. Or they would present a problem such as motion by analyzing the various stages of an action, taking the given world apart, and putting it back together as they saw fit. The movement, started casually by André Derain, Georges Braque, and Pablo Picasso in 1908, was taken up seriously by Albert Gleizes, Francis Picabia, Juan Gris, Marcel Duchamp, Fernand Léger, and Robert Delauney. As early as 1911, their works filled a room at the Salon des Indépendants and created a scandal. But eventually, Cubism turned into a mere game for academic formalists who repeated themselves. Only Duchamp and Picasso went on to create ever new styles and to invent new approaches.

Whether the painters knew it or not, the parallel between their theories and the new philosophies of Ernst Mach, Henri Bergson, and Schiller is striking. Their apologist Apollinaire (Guillaume de Kostrowitsky) offered explanations such as: "We do not know all the colors; each of us invents new ones. Every god creates in his

65

own image; so do painters; only photographers manufacture duplicates of nature. Truth cannot be compared to reality since it never changes. Resemblance no longer matters, it must be sacrificed to truth." The artist's intuition claimed to be closer to "the ultimate" than our everyday human experience and the surface concerns of our civilization. Jean Arp wrote for the Dada exhibition of 1915: "These works are constructed with lines, colors, surfaces, and forms. They strive to surpass the human and achieve the infinite. They negate man's egotism." As a demonstration, Picasso reproduced some of Poussin's paintings in his own style to show that their artistic verities were eternal, quite independent of the "content" and of contemporary ideals of beauty.

The Cubist movement may have had its greatest influence not on painters but on the following generation of architects. The severe lines of buildings and furniture, the deliberate attempt to remain functional and "tectonic" found support in Picasso's designs. The new architecture started with the so-called house without eyebrows built in Vienna by Adolf Loos; its style excluded all superfluous elements, above all, the luxuriant stucco work that graced façades of the preceding period. All falseness, all pretense, all elements that were not structural had to go. A building had to proclaim its function and the location of its essential elements to the viewer. Iron girders had to be visible. Flying buttresses on neo-Gothic cathedrals were as contemptible as hairpieces on women, palm trees in drawing-rooms, or rhetorical phrases in poems. Loos himself also belonged to the "life reform" movement and agitated for "truth in living." After him, the Bauhaus architects met with sympathetic response in the youth movement and among the new poets.

Soon the architects found that the new building materials permitted a revolution in style. Department stores were built with glass walls. Colorful apartment houses, airy factories, noble bridges, functional railway stations were pleasing to the eye and put new materials to proper use. Eventually, the possibilities of structural steel defied all traditional rules. For the first time since the thirteenth century, architecture once again seemed to deny gravity. It lifted roofs so high that they seemed to float, put up walls that seemingly did not enclose but flew open, curved bridges that did not squat but leaped.

New developments in the novel and in music offer themselves for comparison. In 1911, Arnold Schönberg published his first twelve-tone composition, a form in which each of the twelve notes of the chromatic scale must appear and reappear in sequence, thus subordinating invention to construction. Work under this arbitrary rule, which challenges the composer's ingenuity, can easily degenerate into mere mathematical games; few composers have succeeded in writing twelve-tone works that appeal to the layman. Among the exceptions were Anton von Webern and Alban Berg. Twelve-tone music is the sharpest departure from romanticism, sentimentality, and subjectivism. To this day it has eluded the masses.

The Expressionist line leads from the Dutchman van Gogh to the Norwegian Edvard Munch, the Swiss Ferdinand Hodler and Paul Klee, the north German Emil Nolde, the Russians Marc Chagall and Chaim Soutine, and the Austrian Oskar

Kokoschka. Nolde, a brooding genius who was wedded to the demons of racism, staged the revolt against French Impressionism and its "German satrap," the Jew Max Liebermann. He saw Expressionism as a renewal of the great Gothic tradition. In 1906, he joined *Die Brücke* (The Bridge), founded in Munich by three painter friends: Ernst Ludwig Kirchner, Karl Schmidt-Rottluff, and Erich Heckel; Christian Rohlfs, Max Pechstein, and Paula Modersohn-Becker also joined. Franz Marc, whose serene animal compositions did not quite fit the anguished mood of *Die Brücke*, formed *Der Blaue Reiter* (The Blue Rider) with Wassily Kandinsky.

The 1920's were the great era of the German Expressionists, even though by then the founders had done most of their significant work or were dead. They achieved international recognition only after World War II, when Kokoschka and Beckmann were still at work. In the meantime, an ironic fate had befallen Nolde and his neo-Gothic sculptor friends Wilhelm Lehmbruck and Ernst Barlach: Hitler declared them "degenerate" and outlawed their works. The same misfortune struck the poet Gottfried Benn, an army physician who combined anarchistic with strongly national-istic tendencies, like the Futurists in France. He saw Expressionism in paint and word as a "mutiny with ecstasies, eruptions, and hatred." His brutal description of bloody corpses made him one of the vanguard poets to come out of World War I. When the Nazis acceded to power, he expected them to make Expressionism the official philosophy of the Third Reich, was quickly disabused, and ended in deep alienation after having announced the "New Ice Age." The generation of his grandchildren revered him as survivor of a great revolution.

While Expressionism was very much a German movement, it was not intrinsically nationalistic. Other practitioners of the style, such as the playwrights George Kaiser and Carl Sternheim, leaned strongly to the left; Expressionism's philosopher, Ernst Bloch, became a Communist; its greatest novelists were Robert Musil and Hermann Broch, both Austrian Jews, and its greatest musical spokesman was the Russian Igor Stravinsky. His disharmonies shriek with the same anguish that cries out in Soutine's bloody carcasses, in Edvard Munch's somber lyricism, and Rouault's raw violence, or in Georg Trakl's and Georg Heym's poems.

Through its nervous lines and stark colors, Expressionism tries to evoke highly personal and intense responses. Henri Matisse started a parallel movement in France: *Les Fauves* (The Wild Beasts). Following Gauguin's barbarous and evocative style, this group revived primitive art techniques in an effort to lift primeval instincts out of our unconscious. They spread gaudy colors over large canvases or, like Georges Rouault, encased mythical figures in black outlines as in stained-glass windows. Out of these movements came the Italian *pintura metafisica* and French Surrealism, but neither escaped the danger of degenerating into a playful academism. Chirico later repudiated his early canvases.

The same might be said of abstraction in painting. Kandinsky exhibited the first purely abstract painting in 1912. This one was still full of emotion; later abstrac-tionists fell into a purely decorative mannerism. Mondrian tried to reduce his intense feelings to purely geometrical, almost decorative patterns.

Although Cubism, Expressionism, and Abstractionism started as expressions of unrest and of discontent with academic standards, no style or technique is revolutionary *per se*. Nor does it challenge society on its political level. The new art simply *reflected* the artists' artistic problems. They could no longer find meaning in the old notions of nature, beauty, matter, feeling, form—notions that somehow seemed necessary for the bourgeoisie. If this was a coincidence, the alienation of the artists from bourgeois society was not, and they now proceeded to show that the world of the middle class was not what it seemed. This was the meaning of Picasso's programmatic *Les Demoiselles d'Avignon* (1907) and of Otto Dix's and Oskar Kokoschka's cadaverous bankers. Gottfried Benn summed it up devastatingly: "There will never again be art such as it existed during these last five hundred years. Expressionism was its last form. Our situation is final, critical, terminal. Our task is to transform this generation into a new Europe. . . . That which is being formed now cannot be art; it must be a new breed."

Vanguard art challenges both the older (patrician) and the modern (mass) conceptions of culture. Creative works no longer conform to a style; as each artist claims the right to turn the theater into a vehicle for personal expression, artists renounce the right to be the nation's myth-makers. Although their personal story might be most relevant to their age, they have made themselves irrelevant to its specific culture or threaten it with "crisis."

Official art was still classicist, romantic, and, at its best as at its worst, decorative; but Impressionism continued to be the strongest force for many years. Utrillo, Monet, and Renoir in their old age went on repeating and renewing their beautiful style just as Richard Strauss kept repeating himself in ever new ways. In Russia, Expressionism was considered "modern" until the 1950's, but the Moscow and Leningrad museums show that bold collectors bought the best of modern French art before the revolution.

In one field of art, the audience gratefully followed the creators of modern style, and this is not accidental. The dance is neither a ritual of Western culture nor an article of mass consumption. Its development was left to the discriminating taste of the few who cared. As a result, Rudolf Laban, Isadora Duncan, Sergei Diaghilev, and other modern dancers were received enthusiastically by the new audiences; moreover, they were able to share their triumphs with the *avant-garde* in music and painting. Diaghilev commissioned Stravinsky, Debussy, Poulenc, Prokofiev, Milhaud, and Respighi to write ballets. His dancers were Anna Pavlova, Tamara Karsavina, and Vaslav Nijinsky; his designers, Utrillo, Picasso, Braque, and Matisse.

The decade before World War I was deeply devoted to music, both as an expression of the new sensibilities and as a cult of the classics. Brahms, Puccini, and Debussy still were "safe," as it were; but the daring ones went to hear the works of Strauss or even Gustav Mahler, whose bold colorations exhausted the last possibilities of the Impressionist medium. The following quotation, from a program note to Strauss's *Don Juan*, makes clear how intimately Impressionist painting meshed with the epigones of Wagner in music:

In the case of tne coloring by groups [of instruments], individual tone values assume significance. By isolating the individual color [*Farbe*, meaning here: timbre] substances, the artist gains an ever-changing pattern of extremely differentiated compositions. Just as the quiet harmony dissolves into an abundance of melodious events, so the unity of the color plane is dissolved into several substances ... the color [timbre] becomes flexible, elastic, it breathes; the constant change of instruments results in a constant change of the picture.

Beethoven and Brahms still could build ideas without reference to the particular timbre of the instruments; Debussy and Strauss could not. Whereas in classical painting the stress is on composition and design rather than on color, an Impressionist painting cannot really be appreciated in reproduction because every nuance of coloring is of prime importance. Likewise, in Impressionist music, the melodic tension is submerged in the rich coloring. The daring dissonances of modern music, it has been said, originally were not meant to be dissonances; they occurred because the composer had to sacrifice harmony to his various other intentions and interests— the mixture of sounds, the sensation of shifting values, the pleasure of vanishing points, shading, rhythm, movement.

In 1908, Arnold Schönberg, whose *Transfigured Night* had provoked a scandal in 1900, began to compose atonal music—that is, music that no longer conceived of dissonances as deviations from tonal harmonies but allowed the music to float without any base tone to which it must revert or from which it is supposed to depart. The break-through came with his *Pierrot Lunaire*, followed by Alban Berg's *Altenberg-Lieder*. It is noteworthy that atonal music, which became fashionable in the 1920's, was fully developed before World War I. The parallel to "relativity" will be developed in a later chapter, after we have followed similar trends in the humanities.

CHAPTER 4

Literary Perspectives

IN the beginning of the century, the literary scene was dominated by stars now eclipsed. Anatole France passed for the new Voltaire, Romain Rolland for the successor of Zola. Pierre Loti and Pierre Louys were wrestling for Flaubert's crown. The Catholic convert Paul Claudel charmed the faithful with his mystic drama *Partage du Midi*. In England, two great expatriates, Joseph Conrad and Henry James, were still writing, and two new ones, T. S. Eliot and Ezra Pound, had arrived. In Germany, the older naturalists were being challenged by men like Richard Dehmel and Gerhart Hauptmann, both of whom combined social themes with a new romanticism. A new generation of playwrights, poets, and novelists promised to become one of the most fertile in modern literature: in England, D. H. Lawrence, Virginia Woolf, E. M. Forster; in Ireland, James Joyce, W. B. Yeats, Bernard Shaw; in France, Marcel Proust, Georges Duhamel, André Gide, Jean Cocteau, François Mauriac, Saint-John Perse, Roger Martin du Gard, Jules Romains, Colette; in Germany, Thomas and Heinrich Mann, Hermann Hesse, Alfred Döblin; the Scandinavians, Sigrid Undset, Knut Hamsun, Selma Lagerlöf; the Spaniard, Blasco Ibáñez; the Russians, Dmitri Mereshkovsky, Fyodor Gladkov, Maxim Gorky—a remarkable assortment, especially if we remember that this was an age of fast living, in which people apparently had no time to read long stories. Yet some of these authors were to write *romans fleuve* (stream novels) of many volumes in the 1920's. And although social concerns were supposed to be dead, a good many stories dealt with social questions. Galsworthy's play *Justice* helped bring about prison reform; Shaw's *Major Barbara* obliquely attacked the institution of property. H. G. Wells wrote to change the world, and Arnold Bennett's *Old Wives' Tale* almost accidentally bears witness that the world had to be changed. Frank Wedekind and Walter Hasenclever brought generational conflict to the stage. Carl Sternheim satirized middle-class servility; Heinrich Mann's *Small-Town Tyrant* has already been mentioned. His brother Thomas was to be haunted all his life by the problem of the artist in middle-class society. Galsworthy's *Forsyte Saga* (begun in 1906) followed the fortunes of an English middle-class family.

Yet Balzac's mantle did not fall on socially engaged writers but on such writers as Marcel Proust and James Joyce, who had found new concerns in the works of contemporary philosophers and psychologists: Freud, Strindberg, and Bergson became their teachers. Their works breathe an eroticism so far unrecorded in modern literature. For the Germans, Richard Dehmel, for the French, André Gide, and for the English, of course, D. H. Lawrence, opened new dimensions of humanity.

More important, however, is the second line of influences, which affected not the manifest content of artistic creations but rather the method, the mode of looking at the world. Prompted by the philosophy of Bergson, and perhaps in pursuance of principles tested earlier in poetry, the writers now tried to re-create their "stream of consciousness." Marcel Proust pieced his world together out of fleeting memories; D. H. Lawrence disparaged ideals and concepts and, instead, exalted "the immediate present." In James Joyce, finally, the technique of free association achieved its supreme triumph. All these writers show that each man's world is really his very own.

Related, perhaps, to the free association technique was a tendency on the part of some of the new novelists to display either indifference to chronological sequence or rebellion against the tyranny of time in the ordinary, middle-class sense. It was an impulse similar, perhaps, to that which had prompted painters to reorder space. The new novelists used the technique of "remembrance," of flashbacks or dreams. In short, they deliberately refrained from telling a story as it happened and instead rearranged reality in order to create a work of art out of personal experience. It was a new type of novel in which the plot, even the hero, was not very important; the story, not told coherently, was presented in small remembered bits. Fleeting impressions comprised the total image: a cup of tea, a smell, reawakened rare moments of bliss. These moments were presented, not as reality, but as reflections in the person's consciousness. Experience is not what occurs but what it is shaped into. The parallel with Cubism's reconstruction of reality is obvious.

Some of the new writers won fame immediately; others were recognized later. André Gide, as reader of *La Nouvelle Revue Française*, rejected Proust's manuscript. Apparently Proust's concern was not his. But, on the whole, movements that fought each other on matters of style, philosophy, and justice made common cause against the "philistines." From Montmartre to Chelsea, from Schwabing (Munich's artists' quarter) to Rome (where young artists still had to make their pilgrimage), they were joined together across nations and religions. Max Scheler, the philosopher, has said: "Feelings which all of us now perceive within ourselves had to be forced out of the terrible silence of our inner life by a new breed of artists."

The philistines reacted to this rebellion by calling it effeminate and irrational. Reason, calculation, purpose are manifestations of the male principle; so are industry, capitalism, the state. The rebels mocked these sober institutions and utilitarian virtues. The German satirist Gustav Meyrink had great fun with the *Useful Mr. Smith* of his sardonic tales; but even innocuous writers thumbed their noses at the Establishment by describing the delightful pranks of rogues. And while the grave bourgeois anxiously asked what might be the purpose of all this worship of unreason, they were answered: To give unreason a chance.

The risk that literature might divorce itself from society in this process was gladly incurred. Art could become obscure and esoteric, or it could be irreverent and irrelevant. To Thomas Mann (whose *Confessions of Felix Krull, Confidence Man* was conceived before World War I and finished after World War II) we owe the following naughty statement on the artist's position vis-à-vis society:

> The artist is a good-for-nothing, an irresponsible fellow who merely tries to give pleasure through his antics and will do nothing for the state. He may even be subversive, but in reality is very childish, inclined to exaggerate, and somewhat seedy. Society should treat him with quiet contempt.

With his well-known irony, Mann added:

> He refuses to improve anybody, or to improve the world for that matter. It is very unfair to scold him for that. A work of art may have moral consequences, but the artist cannot undertake it for that purpose.

CHAPTER 5

The Emancipation of the Senses

THROUGHOUT the Age of Enlightenment, an undercurrent of sentimentalism, romanticism, and anti-rationalism had accompanied the discoveries of science. Rousseau rebelled against Voltaire, and Rahel Varnhagen coined for the younger romantics the motto: "Hail to you, dear senses!" In the nineteenth century, reason won and relegated feeling to the arts, the senses to the underground. However, at the turn of the twentieth century, after two generations of sobriety, the pendulum again swung away from analytical thinking. The anti-rationalistic rebellion erupted on three levels. The needs of the body began to be seen as normal, not sinful. There was a Nietzschean change in values, and a change, too, in the theory of knowledge. "We must numb our reason and sharpen our sensibility:" this was André Gide's program in his first work, *Cahiers d'André Walter*, modeled after Goethe's *Werther*. On the first page he put in capital letters: SPONTANEOUS LIFE, INTUITIVE KNOWLEDGE, FAITH.

Before the turn of the century, Krafft-Ebing and Havelock Ellis dared to write about sexual pathology. In 1900, Freud published *The Interpretation of Dreams*, but it took ten years to sell 800 copies of this seminal work. Four years later *The Psychopathology of Everyday Life* followed. The eventual impact of these works can be compared only to that of the works of Copernicus, Newton, and Darwin. They shocked their contemporaries no less than the theory of evolution, and the professionals rejected them almost unanimously.

Meanwhile, D. H. Lawrence's novels were urging readers to face what he called the knowledge of the blood: "My great religion is a belief in the blood, the flesh, as being wiser than the intellect." In *Ann Veronica*, H. G. Wells pleaded for a love that was frankly physical.

The cult of the body, the affirmation of Eros—it had not yet been reduced to sheer sex—was part of a wider, more general reorientation of the entire value system. Civilization no longer was thought of as the enemy of the instincts but rather as their counterpart, or even as their transformed, spiritualized self. Freud explained how, through the mechanisms of repression and sublimation, which he described for the first time, art, the sciences, law, and society arise out of our animalistic endowment, not just in opposition to it. Freud was the first to deal frankly with sex as a prime force in human life; he called it by its name and legitimated it. In this way he restored unity to man, whom Victorian morality had divided into an upper, acknowledged, and a lower, disowned, part. But those who came after Freud went farther. All instincts were deemed healthy; to suppress them was to lose one's humanity. By suppressing humanity, society became the enemy of the individual. D. H. Lawrence widened the concept of instinct to include sociability:

> What ails me is the absolute frustration of my primeval instincts. . . . I think societal instinct is much deeper than sex instinct—and societal repression much more devastating. There is no repression of the sexual individual comparable to the repression of the societal man in me, by the individual ego, my own and everybody else's.

D. H. Lawrence and the followers of Nietzsche took the side of the "instincts," of "blood" or "life." Freud still stood on the side of "civilization" and remained a rationalist. His Swiss disciple Carl Jung broke with him over this issue in 1913. He felt that the sexual libido was only one of many instinctual resources, and he hailed these resources as wholesome, even necessary, for the preservation of human society. Jung also denied that a life of the instincts was destined to destroy society. On the contrary, his concern was to cultivate those traits in our psychological heritage that increased social cohesion. Man was a social animal; there never was a "social contract," but there had always been social myths. Freud in his later work felt impelled to recognize a "collective memory;" Jung postulated the "collective subconscious," a racial memory embodied in tribal myths and "archetypal ideas."

In his later writings Freud relied heavily on the exciting discoveries of modern anthropology. The serious study of magic as a protoscience had already been begun by Edward B. Tylor and James Frazer. The latter's *Golden Bough* (1890) traced religion to magic sources, but the implications went farther. Observations of savage behavior convinced Lucien Lévy-Bruhl that logical reasoning as we know it was not the only mode of thinking available to man. Primitive men, he asserted, live by a prelogical type of associative thinking, *"perceptions collectives,"* which they believe help them to make rain, to assure fertility to the soil and prosperity to the tribe. Back in the nineteenth century, Bachofen, Schopenhauer, and Eduard von Hartmann had claimed a special place for the "unconscious" and had studied Oriental philosophy to discover mystical sources of truth. In a different context, I already have mentioned William James's religious philosophy: that it is not the belief itself that satisfies the religious urge but the experience of believing. When modern poets and publicists call for "faith," they do not bother to say what one should have faith in, or why; they extol the *ability* to believe, to feel, to react. In the same vein, Sorel's "myth" was to move society out of its middle-class sterility to unknown destinies.

Sorel's teacher Henri Bergson was no activist and had come to his own notion of myth by a different road. Studying man's perception of time, he remarked that what we really know is only what is given to our immediate experience. We are not aware of the sequential passage of distinct seconds but of "duration." Similarly, the Gestalt psychologists later were to insist that we do not hear a succession of musical notes but a melody. Analytical research can never yield anything but dead skeletons of reality: truth is perceived by intuition, which Bergson defined as "intellectual sympathy" and for which he claimed a "supra-intellectual insight" greater than analytical and discursive language are able to give.

Paradoxically, Bergson was one of the greatest practitioners of discursive language. Like Freud and Nietzsche, he was not "anti-intellectual," but he felt that he had discovered forces greater than the intellect could handle. In *L'Évolution Créatrice* (1907), he identified that force as *élan vital*, a phrase that promptly became fashionable among the literati, as did Shaw's "life force" and Nietzsche's "wisdom of the body," which may mean something very similar.

Bergson's emphasis on immediate experience paralleled the development of modern art and literature. In the works of Proust, Lawrence, and Joyce, as well as in modern painting, reality was shown to be a thing of the mind once again.

To an age steeped in the mechanical sciences and a deterministic view of nature, these ideas came like a fresh breath of freedom. Man was no longer the creature of his environment; the world was a creation of man. As early as 1895, the chemist Wilhelm Ostwald had published his lecture *Overcoming Scientific Materialism*. Though Wilhelm Wundt's dated work on psychology remained the standard textbook until and beyond World War I, Pierre Janet had published his more modern *Pathological Psychology* in 1882; others, too, had started to undermine the mechanistic views of the nineteenth century.

Using the Latin word for "life," the German biologist Hans Driesch set forth the theory of "vitalism;" he pointed out that organic matter is not subject to the same laws of cause and effect as dead matter, which obeys the principles of mechanics. Living beings are "attuned" to an environment rather than subject to its whims; they are functional and seek a "form." In his *Science and Philosophy of the Organism* (1909), Driesch reintroduced Aristotle's term *entelechy* for the mysterious force that causes two whole starfish to grow out of one egg that has been cut in half.

The geneticist Hugo de Vries replaced Darwin's theory of adaptation with a theory of mutation—a sudden, arbitrary leap toward new forms which shows that nature is not fatalistically bound by cause and effect as the nineteenth century believed. Helmuth Plessner speculated about the freedom of organic matter to create spontaneously, and Frederik Buytendijk observed that organisms do not simply "adjust" but produce adornments, such as antlers, which may not have any useful function at all. Albert Vandel found in organisms an *intelligence spécifique* whose tools are the instincts.

The theory of mutation had two important corollaries, one being that nature, contrary to the Latin adage *natura non facit saltus*, does indeed make leaps—or, rather, that evolution occurs by leaps only. If applied to history, this dialectical law seems to point to a future of wars and revolutions. The other corollary, that only mutations, not acquired characteristics, are inheritable, was more to the liking of conservatives. Theodor Boveri showed that chromosomes were the carriers of all transmittable traits. The political implications of this finding, which Soviet scientists since have vainly tried to disprove, are enormous. It lends support to the science of eugenics, which unfortunately has been discredited by its crude Nazi practitioners.

At this point, there occurs a curious inversion of the idea of freedom. It might be assumed that the liberation of the senses and of the hidden resources of life, like the emancipation of workers, minorities, women, and youth, served to enhance democracy. However, once we free the irrational forces within us, we cease to be free. We discover that they rule us. Instead of emancipating the subconscious, we are dethroning reason, the "I" of the responsible person. "We must not be free from our race," said Maurice Barrès, the French chauvinist writer. The triumphant chant "rationalism is dead" is directed against the ideas of 1789 and of democracy. By appealing to instinct, soul, and tribal consciousness, the obscurantists, racists, chauvinists, and militarists justified oppression and destruction. There was no arbiter to tell a good "will to power" from an evil one. Man's fate, they said, is "tragic" because, by following his instincts, he comes to grief. Philosophies of doom and doubt, of strife and war, began to infiltrate the cheerful illusions of liberty. At the very moment when Europe seemed to be at the height of her power, some people questioned her cultural foundations. This new spirit exploded in the futurist marriage of tribal instincts with modern technology, the nationalist divorce of power from reason, the transformation of patriotism into the glorification of war.

The poetry and music of the age displayed parallel tendencies toward explosiveness: Alexander Scriabin's demonism, Mahler's giantism, Stravinsky's savagery, Ravel's eroticism, Richard Strauss's orgiasticism probe the limits of cultural form. Any step beyond could lead to catastrophe. The "break-through" of which Thomas Mann speaks in *Doktor Faustus*, the work intended as his testament, could lead to adventure and violence. Its price was abandonment of all that European civilization had meant since Socrates. Paul Valéry already was saying that Socrates had been misunderstood, that his message had not been reason but the critique of reason.

CHAPTER 6

Science and Philosophy
at the Crossroads

RARELY had science been so close to popular philosophy as in the nineteenth century. The great biologist Ernst Haeckel summed it all up in his popular *Riddles of the Universe* (1900), of which he knew seven: four were imaginary and three about to be solved. He saw organic and inorganic nature, biology and psychology linked in a beautiful, awe-inspiring chain of evolution in which there was no place for God, soul, miracle.

An alternative view was presented by the neo-Kantian school, which allowed some room for man's feelings, recognized the limitations of our reason, and rejected Haeckel's utilitarian ethics. Above all, they denied that everything can be explained by the law of cause and effect. They opened the door to the workings of accident, reintroduced freedom and irrationality into philosophy, and were glad when new scientific discoveries seemed to confirm their assertions. Modern conceptions in physics, biology, and psychology seemed to increase rather than reduce the number of unsolved "riddles" and to widen rather than bridge the gap between the organic and inorganic, between body and soul. Some even thought that modern science was getting rid of matter (substance) and causality (necessity), the most venerable pillars of old-fashioned materialism.

It was claimed that science had revealed the limits of the scientific world view and had opened new vistas on freedom. The truth was somewhat less sensational. Up to 1900, scientists thought that Newton had spoken the last word on the general structure of the world. Research was expected to fill in some details the way geographers went to unexplored places whose location and borderlines were known. Now it was discovered that whole continents, perhaps entire new worlds, lay hidden behind what was called reality. More disturbingly, some of these worlds did not obey Newton's laws.

The microphenomena inside the atom and the macrophenomena relating to the speed of light required new concepts. Planck showed in 1900 that energy is emitted not continuously but in irreducible "quanta." This was as contrary to common sense as the proposition that water can be drained from a tub only drop by drop. Einstein then showed that it was in the nature of energy to come in discrete packages; scientists had to conclude that Newton's mechanical laws did not apply to the structure of the atom and that nature does make leaps. They had to consider the possibility that the

77

laws of nature might have to be rewritten as often as French constitutions. Already, Marie Curie's sensational findings on radium and radioactivity were shattering another article of faith: that the "elements" were stable and irreducible. What old alchemists had dreamed of was happening right before the scientists' eyes: namely, transmutation. Ernest Rutherford and Frederick Soddy supplied the mathematical formula of the phenomenon; in 1911, Rutherford presented his atomic model, with the electrons circling around a nucleus whose weight had to be a multiple of the helium atom's weight. And what keeps electrons from plunging gradually into the nucleus? Precisely Planck's "quantum," whose multiples indicate the irreducible orbits of the electrons. Any changes that might occur have to be described as a leap from one orbit to the other, releasing or consuming the minimum quantum. Einstein showed that the same principle effectively explained the photochemical effect that had puzzled scientists.

In 1905, Einstein published the *Special Theory of Relativity*, which overthrew accepted views on the nature of light, space, time, and gravity. To understand the philosophical significance of his bold new theories we have to look back for a moment at the popular notion of matter. Before electricity, radiology, and chemistry wrought such fundamental changes in our everyday experience, matter was assumed to be solid, firm material that could be shaped, handled, and moved in accordance with mechanical laws. The clock was the model of the universe. Despite electricity and radiology, it took people some time to learn that some things are not tangible substances, not "things." Even scientists believed, for example, that there must be a "world ether." Since light traveled in "waves," there had to be some medium that was waving, like water or air, and if so, the rotating earth must encounter a sort of "ether wind." But no such ether was discovered in even the most ingenious experiments.

Moreover, two Americans had found that, contradicting all known laws of mechanics, light registers the same speed whether an instrument is moving toward or away from its source.[1] If the speed of light is constant for any observer, the obvious implications were as important as they were difficult to grasp. Without an "ether," through what medium was "gravity" exercising its "pull"? Newtonian mechanics required that action be transmitted in some way, through either impact or pull. But if gravity could be transmitted through emptiness, it had to be a quality of space. Einstein now linked gravity with space; his further conclusions required an overhauling of Euclid's geometrical axioms for space other than the space of our earthly experience. The non-Euclidean geometry was worked out by Hermann Minkowski. Henri Poincaré, the French mathematician, now repudiated the former view in mocking words: "The complicated structure [James] Maxwell ascribes to the ether made his system strange and repellent. One could almost believe one were reading the description of a factory, its cog-wheels, drive-staffs, etc."

---

[1] When a whistling locomotive approaches, passes by, and disappears, we hear its pitch rise and then drop.

Planck's discovery of the "elementary effective quantum" and Minkowski's geometry of the time-space continuum rescued the scientists from the mold of nineteenth-century mechanistic views. As Copernicus had "simplified" our conception of the universe, twentieth-century physicists provided a more elegant, aesthetically satisfying world view, and soon philosophers were to say that truth is merely an aesthetic satisfaction. Poincaré said just that.

As further experiments and observations became known, other well-worn conceptions went by the board. According to classical mechanics, light had to be either waves or corpuscles; now it was shown that in some aspects light behaves like waves, in others like matter. Since both propositions could not be true simultaneously, classical physics had no answer to the riddle. But once physicists had given up their preconceived notions of common-sense physics, it became possible to think of light as just a convenient term for a complicated formula. Likewise, matter now was seen to be an abstraction entirely in our minds. Matter, Bertrand Russell quipped, is a formula for describing something that happens where it is not.

The philosophers greeted the new attitude of science with enthusiasm. It confirmed the neo-Kantian doubt about the "thing-in-itself" and the material substratum of experience. Francis H. Bradley had argued, in *Appearance and Reality* (1893), that what we know is "relationships between terms" only. The empirio-critical school, founded by Ernst Mach and later developed by Vienna's neo-positivists, insisted that there was nothing to know in metaphysics and ontology, that questions about the true nature of the thing-in-itself, or matter, or reality, were "metaphysical"—a polite way of saying: irrelevant nonsense. Long before the new discoveries had confirmed their approach, they told scientists to stop asking "What is it?" and to ask instead "How does it work?" Science, they claimed, can proceed without the unnecessary hypotheses of matter, causality, or even reality, just as a hundred years earlier Laplace, in answer to Napoleon's question as to why he had not mentioned God in his system, had said: "I don't need this hypothesis." Similarly, Bergson and the pragmatists argued that "science consists of conventions; its laws are the work of the scientists; they do not teach us the truth but serve as a rule of action."

Ironically, many contemporaries did not recognize these ideas as revolutionary and disturbing but interpreted them as retreats into idealism and subjectivism. One who was moved to denounce the "new subjectivism" was Lenin, who worried that the proletarians might stop fighting for change in the material world if they were told that matter did not matter. The Marxists, almost to a man, remained wedded to the old middle-class notion of nature, Newton's mechanical laws, the reality of space and time, the thingishness of things. Yet the new developments confirmed what Marx had always maintained: that our views of nature were entirely a product of the society we live in, and that after Hegel the bourgeoisie would not produce another great system of philosophy. For nearly everyone agreed that the new science made philosophy almost impossible. Ontology and metaphysics were dead. Ethics had fallen to the relativists; the theory of knowledge had broken apart into the methodology of so many individual sciences, as Ernst Cassirer showed in *Substance and Function* (1910). Philosophy, which had once been the queen of sciences, now became the handmaiden of researchers. It no longer gave the sciences unity and purpose. Ethics also was no longer derived from ideas but from facts. The relativistic ethics of George Edward Moore, who belonged to the Bloomsbury circle, dealt with practical morality but had nothing to say about eternal principles.

Copernicus, Darwin, and Freud expelled us from the paradise of naïve faith in the uniqueness and greatness of man. Nietzsche had shown the relativity of ethics. Ideas no longer were seen to be enthroned over human existence in eternal majesty. Already some radical thinkers were drawing conclusions that deeply affected our understanding of mankind in its historical development, its purpose and meaning. While the general public blissfully assumed that in God's world all trends point upward, some doubts had been voiced as to whether the best of all possible worlds was good or lasting at all.

Most disturbing among the new sciences were psychology and sociology, which now began to attract the interest of the intellectual elites. In France it was Émile Durkheim, in Italy Vilfredo Pareto, in Germany Max Weber who asked searching questions about the nature of society. In their search for a scientific view of man, they lost that trust in history's meaning that had held society together in the nineteenth century. "Relativism" was no longer satisfied with questioning a particular set of values; it began to ask whether there could be any value in having values.

CHAPTER 7

Undertakers of Western Civilization

THE philosophical confusion was reflected in the social and political sciences. The more one learned about the forms of human organization, the fainter became the hope that man might ever govern himself. Liberal theory had assumed that men in their mutual relations follow their best interests. Now historians, sociologists, and psychologists began to question this. Graham Wallas, a Fabian, maintained that men form their opinions according to patterns they are not conscious of and follow habit rather than reason. His book *Human Nature and Politics* (1908) implied that people can be swayed by demagogues even against their interests, and that good men may be elected for bad reasons. Contrary to liberal thinking, mankind was not marching toward a more rational and democratic society. In his oft-quoted *Psychology of the Crowd*, Gustave LeBon drew on his observation of mass movements during the Dreyfus agitation and on experiences of the labor movement. His avowed purpose was to disparage democratic mass organizations; but the new Right put his shrewd observations to profitable use in its own propaganda. The patriotic fervor that broke loose in all countries on August 1, 1914, vindicated the most saturnine theories of mass behavior; military psychologists, propagandists, agitators, and advertisers quickly learned to apply them.

Irrationalism in politics, ignored or deplored by the Left, was praised as a virtue by the new Right, which stressed organic structures, "roots," inherited values, and traditional masters. German sociologists revived the distinction between "culture" and "civilization," the former referring to the web of human, religious, and emotional ties that make an "organic whole" out of a nation and give meaning to its history, the latter referring to the material goods, the artificial and merely "mechanical" devices serving utilitarian purposes. These ideologies became powerful tools of anti-democratic propaganda and a challenge to the liberal conceptions of Western civilization.

Since Western civilization thought of itself as the apex of historical development, its philosophers had held that history was rational and morality commensurate with reason. Historians had always denied this, but the new philosophy turned the denial into an attack. Vilfredo Pareto showed that the ideas by which men pretend to live are mere "derivations," more or less accidental and arbitrary rationalizations of actions that well up from much deeper sources. Like Nietzsche and Sorel, Pareto held that democracy and rationalism were aberrations; progress was an illusion; humanitarians were fit to be exterminated. Effectiveness alone counted; survival value was the only yardstick; no ideal had eternal value.

In a suggestive way, Pareto's work shows the connection between moral relativism and positivism. Liberal theory had come to a sad end and was turning into its opposite: from indulgence to arbitrariness, from freedom to power, from democracy to elitism. If no truth was certain and morality could not be founded on reason, one social system was as good as the other. If time was an illusion, no one could say what progress was.

Progress, the most self-evident of liberal assumptions, is absent from Pareto's system. He believed that after the "foxes" (the financial wizards, the liberals) had ruled long enough, the time would be ripe for the "lions" (the aristocrats) to have their turn once again. In a much subtler way, Max Weber dropped the notion of a linear development in history and at the same time asserted the return of the irrational. The world, he found, was being robbed of its magic by ever-increasing skills in the mastery of nature and even of society. The old sentimental values were being lost, the "cultural" goods were neglected; in their place, big bureaucratic organizations were installing a rational regime. Even the revolutionary organizations, he foresaw, would fall under this law. His friend Roberto Michels, in his classic *Political Parties*, showed how the machines were winning out over idealism. At the end of the process, when everything had been "rationalized" and everyone was bored, Weber expected the "charismatic leader" who would reverse the situation, appeal to the people's instincts, and fire their enthusiasm. This cycle would recur with clockwork regularity on all continents and in all civilizations.

Finally, Oswald Spengler worked out such a historical cycle in his monumental *Decline of the West*. He, too, predicted "the age of the Caesars" to follow the age of democracy and mass gratification. The book, written during World War I, was the most thorough attack so far on Western values and prejudices. Not only did it deny that our achievements and our ideas were evidence of any significant advance over earlier ages, but it revealed that they were mere replicas of phenomena that earlier civilizations had produced in their declining phases. The end would come for the West as surely as it had come for all preceding empires.

Spengler taught that the era of individualism, freedom, humanitarianism, and methodical doubt had been ephemeral and would be superseded by an age of new collectivism, based on a revival of faith and reliance on force. Readers rejoiced at the pageant of *Götterdämmerung* and the prospect of a new barbarian conquest. Whether one liked it or not, Europe had only two alternatives left: a new Caesar or complete breakdown.

War came, and Europe got both—breakdown and totalitarianism. Nietzsche's and Spengler's imagery of bloody redemption was to be played out in the trenches. German officers read Rilke, that most ethereal, sweet, esoteric poet: "How can we rise if we give our strength to the wretched and oppressed? Let the lazy scoundrels perish. Let

us be hard, terrible, and inexorable! A few great, powerful, divine men will build a
kingdom with their strong, lordly arms on the dead bodies of the weak and crippled"
(*Die Apostel, Erzählungen und Skizzen aus der Frühzeit*). We find similar sadistic
fantasies in Hofmannsthal and in James Ensor's paintings. It was not the war that
caused this breakdown of Western Christian culture; rather, the elite already had
abandoned Western values and therefore the war became possible. Many, in fact,
thought that war was the only way out of the Western "crisis." Georg Heym, the
young poet, wrote: "If only there were a war, even an unjust one. This peace is so
rotten and filthy."

European culture had reached and perhaps passed a culmination point. A revolution in the arts, sciences, and philosophy was in the making, a revolution that would
also free destructive forces and suicidal ideas. The cultural crisis was not the product
of the war but its cause; the war was not an interruption of the cultural revolution
but its manifestation. As Alban Berg was to write in August 1914: "If the war were
to end today, we would be back in the old rot. . . . However fervently I wish for peace,
I cannot ask for fulfillment of this wish now."

The first two parts of this book have shown that the war of 1914 really should not
have surprised contemporaries. The crisis was in the air—not because European
civilization was at its end, but because it was laboring toward a break-through. It
had reached a pinnacle from where it either had to plunge down or take flight to new
heights. Its progress was intimately connected with the crisis.

On the other hand, it is obvious that the broad masses, even the educated masses,
were quite unaware of this crisis. The new art, the new philosophy, the new science
were known only to the experts, and even they were hardly aware yet that their new
discoveries had universal significance. Each was pursuing a revolution in his own
field—a social, a national, an artistic, a scientific revolution. When the war broke out,
to everybody's surprise, European culture and society broke apart because they had
ceased to provide a unifying mold.

PART III

Wars and Revolutions
(1914–23)

CHAPTER I

War as Revolution

WHEN Lord Grey, that fastidious Edwardian gentleman, deplored that the "lamps are going out all over Europe," Lenin exulted at "the beginning of ten years of wars and revolutions." He fully expected to see Europe ravaged and the banner of socialism planted on the ruins of capitalism. Others, too, experienced a revolution, although not the one Lenin predicted. War itself was a revolution that turned European society over to the new Caesars and remade its civilization in the image of their war machines.

Executing the Schlieffen plan, the German armies invaded neutral Belgium, swept through northern France, and got within fifty miles of Paris. There, General Joseph Gallieni mobilized the taxis for troop transport—a first in warfare—and threw all his reserves into the battle. He stopped the Germans at the Marne river, and then both sides dug in. The trenches were quickly extended north and south until there was one long front from the Swiss border to the Channel coast.

In the West, the war of movement was over. For the next four years the adversaries spent themselves in vain attempts to breach the enemy lines, stubbornly hitting them with ever increasing firepower or trying to exhaust their reserves. It was a war without strategic concepts, a mere test of which side could wear the other down.

The German people were not told about the Marne battle; they did not realize that the Kaiser's war plan had failed. Instead, they were told that they had won a great victory at Tannenberg on the Eastern front. Indeed, when the Russian steamroller moved into East Prussia, the German leaders panicked and sent two divisions (which might have decided the issue in the West) to the defense of that province. The German battle plan was designed by a genuine military genius, Erich Ludendorff; but since he was not a nobleman, a safe nonentity, Paul von Hindenburg, was pulled out of retirement to take nominal credit for victories in the East. Ludendorff annihilated the Russian Army, took 92,000 prisoners, and drove the enemy into that vast arsenal of Russian defense: space. His Pyrrhic victory forced the German Army to spread itself thin in the occupation of most of Poland, there to dig in for another trench war.

Until then, wars had been the business of kings, and only recently had the rules on sparing the civilian population been strengthened. It was standard doctrine that would-be combatants collected war chests in time of peace; once these were exhausted, the war had to be ended. This time, however, the war began only after, by the old rules, the powers should have made peace. The Germans were deep inside enemy lands everywhere and confident that no allied force could beat them. At that point, England and France decided to win the war by starving the enemy. The British Navy blockaded the German coastline. The Germans, on their part, used submarines to choke England's supply lines. Airplanes and zeppelins were sent over the cities to scare the populations. For the first time in modern history, civilians became a strategic factor in a war. The enemy held them as hostages; their governments called upon them to endure austerity while outproducing the enemy. Most countries had to ration essential foods, later even clothing and shoes. The rations eventually fell below subsistence levels; the hinterland suffered real hardship. The war, it was believed, would be won by the side that kept its nerve a week longer.

Called to the Western front, Ludendorff laid siege to Verdun, where every fort and bunker was to produce its own epic; he managed to kill 300,000 Germans and 400,000 French. Marshal Philippe Pétain, the stubborn defender of the fortress, coined the slogan "They shall not pass" which was to gain fame once again in the Spanish Civil War; but in neither case was it a substitute for strategy. French manhood was sapped there for a generation. The British had the unenviable task of defending the northern flank of France. In the lowlands of Flanders, where water was seeping into the trenches, General Douglas Haig proved a veritable Colonel Blimp, sacrificing 400,000 men to win a few square miles of soggy terrain. Siegfried Sassoon, who was there, sent home this angry poem:

> Young smug-faced crowd with kindling eye,
> Who cheer when soldier lads march by,
> Sneak home and pray you'll never know
> The hell where youth and laughter go.[1]

But the war had three historic consequences: socially, psychologically, and politically. Firstly, it completely reshuffled the classes. The movie, *La Grande Illusion*, shows how an aristocrat, a bourgeois, and a Jew are thrown together. All war poetry praises the army as a great equalizer.

Psychologically, the war brought a new attitude to soldiering. It was neither glorious nor honorable. Valor was rewarded with death. The best learned how to beat the system. The cavalry, once a noble service, had to dismount. Every patriotic cliché revealed its emptiness. The draftees developed a new ideology of unemotional, un-rhetorical soldiering—a grim philosophy of comradeship for those who had accepted trench warfare as a way of life and an unspeakable contempt for those who had not experienced the "front spirit." Politically, this led to a most undesirable consequence.

The German attacks were carried out by tactical elite divisions, "storm troops," whose assignment was to pierce the enemy line so that infantry could then pour through the gap. In practice, this tactic failed to win battles; on the contrary, it

---

[1] From *Collected Poems* by Siegfried Sassoon. Copyright 1918 by E. P. Dutton Co. Copyright renewed 1946 by Siegfried Sassoon. Reprinted by permission of The Viking Press, Inc.

ground the best units to pieces and left the survivors psychological wrecks who could not find their way back into civilian life after the war. The specialist in total destruction, a dehumanized activist complete with gas mask, hand grenade, and submachine gun, became the terrible symbol of patriotism. He was glorified in Filippo Marinetti's war poems—not as a heroic human being but as an automaton gone berserk; he also was celebrated in the precision prose of Ernst Jünger, himself a shock-troop leader who was to become the prophet of the totalitarian mind.

Here, in the trenches of World War I, out of the union of bestialized man and deadly machines, arose the fascist superman. Another Fascist of the first hour, Colonel Giulio Douhet, recognized the exhilarating possibilities of "liberating" warfare from its latter-day dullness if only the joyous offensive were conducted with modern weapons, the airplane and the tank. He was joined by the English staff officer John Frederick Charles Fuller, an early prophet of the new war of movement that became reality in World War II. In 1914–18 the new weapons were not yet deployed strategically but were used only as tactical support, which was nowhere decisive. Airplanes did reconnaissance and occasional strafing. Their dogfights made fascinating copy; as an air ace, Hermann Göring became a national hero before joining the Nazi Party.

Nor was the use of poison gas, outlawed by The Hague Conference in 1899, decisive. Gas could screen a retreat or smoke out a dugout, but it was undependable in large offensive operations and therefore remained of minor consequence.

The Allies achieved great tactical surprise with their first massive tank attack in 1917. But their leaders had not realized the strategic possibilities or the logistic requirements of mechanized warfare. Hence, although all the weapons of World War II were available in World War I, this was not yet a total and totally mechanized war. Its principal feature was the enormous expenditure of firepower; its actions therefore are generally referred to as "battles of matériel."

On the German side, as it became clear that the war could not be won, the command resorted to increasingly frantic measures: poison gas, tightening of the blockade, eventually unrestricted submarine warfare, which meant that ships were sunk without providing for the rescue of civilian passengers. In due course, the sinking of the liner Lusitania brought the United States into the war in April 1917.

For a hundred years Europe had not seen a war in which both sides fought "for survival." Now the war seemed to be writing its own law, and society had to adjust to its demands. It was no longer a test of human valor but a war of production in which human beings counted only as cannon fodder or as producers of war machines. Fuller and Ludendorff also recognized that to wage total war a government needs economic self-sufficiency, absolute political authority, and spartan discipline—"total mobilization." Ludendorff fulfilled his program by taking all power in Germany to himself, dismissing chancellors and browbeating the frightened Kaiser.

In the Entente camp, the civilian governments assumed an almost similar authority. Economic controls became necessary the moment it was clear that the war would last long. The free sale of gold was suspended first; prices rose, and merchandise

World War I Europe

disappeared. To avoid black marketing, the people demanded rationing. Soon governments had to organize production and supplies, freeze prices and wages, allocate raw materials, even nationalize munitions industries. Neutral Sweden had to ration food. Britain's Ministry of Munitions operated 250 factories; the Ministry of Food bought 85 per cent of imported foodstuffs; the railroads were nationalized; the government spent 50 per cent of the national income. When enlistments fell off, the "un-English" system of conscription was adopted. In the last year of the war, the Labour Party drew the consequences from this experience and published a new program, *Labour and the Nation*, calling for total planning of production and distribution, for national minimum income, democratic control in industry, and nationalization of the Bank of England.

The German experience was even more harrowing. The blockade caused wholesale slaughter of the pig population; cows lost half their normal weight. Eight hundred thousand persons died of malnutrition. The "hunger winter" of 1917 saw the people reduced to their last reserves. Long lines formed outside every shop; whatever was available was *ersatz*—substitute shoe leather, substitute coffee, honey, butter, even meat (whatever that may have been). Had not Walther Rathenau organized the supply of raw materials, the German economy might have collapsed after the first winter. Free enterprise could not sustain a war of that dimension. Production and distribution were so thoroughly regulated that the Austrian socialist Karl Renner exclaimed: "Socialism wherever our eyes can see!" What the war economy proved, of course, was the superior expediency of dictatorial government under conditions of extreme stress. People cursed the bureaucracy but blamed their hunger on the enemy and got used to the idea of a "Prussian socialism," which ideologists like Spengler and Jünger were to substitute for the democratic variety. If the states could conscript 13 million men for military service, there was no reason that they should not conscript others for labor service, and money for forced loans. The war changed the social structure radically: the rich and the poor met in the trenches; the aristocracy was decimated, and many commoners were promoted to officer rank. The whole population took part, either directly or vicariously, in gross brutality, gross amusements, gross experiences, gross chauvinism. Not the "foundations of a new society" but the foundations of the garrison state were being laid in the trenches. Not the spirit of capitalism but the independence of the spirit was being destroyed.

A "national community" was being created in each fatherland. In France it was called *Union Sacrée*, in Germany *Burgfrieden*. The Kaiser, who once had called the socialists "punks without a country," now declared that he knew "no parties, only Germans." The political representatives of labor forgot the resolutions adopted at international congresses and either bowed to necessity or tried to convert it into opportunity. War, it seemed, made people of all classes into brothers. In France, old radicals turned nationalist; Albert Thomas, the trade-union leader, and Jules Guesde, once an orthodox Marxist, joined the government, as did Arthur Henderson in England. In those hours of patriotic panic, when the mobs were shouting for traitors' blood, no labor leader wished to expose his organization to the charge of giving aid and comfort to the enemy. And so even the pacifist members obeyed when the caucus of the German Social Democrats decided to vote for war appropriations on August 4, 1914.

An unspeakable delirium of chauvinism had seized the warring nations. German schoolbooks were purged of foreign words; St. Petersburg was renamed Petrograd (now Leningrad); food shops in New York's German neighborhood were looted; children contributed their savings for "war loans;" women exchanged their gold wedding rings for iron. Professors exhorted their students to die, if necessary, and published vituperative open letters to their equally chauvinistic colleagues on the opposing side. Preachers told their flocks that war was a sacred institution: "*Gott strafe England!*" prayed the Germans, while the British God was expected to punish the "Huns." The war was among other things also a propaganda war. No government had ever before organized, as Britain now did, a Bureau of War Propaganda. Its aim was to tell the world that England was fighting the good fight for democracy; that German soldiers had killed babies in Belgium; that the Germans were on the point of starving to death.

Paradoxically, the war brought equalitarian, populist, and even democratic tendencies to the fore. In France, Aristide Briand, the "apostle of peace," tried to reconcile all parties. When he failed, and after others had tried in vain, Georges Clemenceau, ex-Communard, eventually instituted a new kind of Jacobin dictatorship; the "new Carnot" alone had enough authority to focus the nation's will on victory, to subdue strikes, to suppress mutinies. In England, David Lloyd George led a coalition government. He believed, like Clemenceau, that war was "too serious a business to leave it to the generals." Even in Russia, the great offensive of 1917 could not be mounted until Alexander Kerensky, the would-be Jacobin, had taken over. In Germany, the Kaiser hoped to prolong the agony of defeat by admitting members of the Reichstag majority into the cabinet. The bloodier the war grew in its final phases, the more it needed to be "democratic." The British coalition cabinet gave the franchise to men without property, bachelors, and women over thirty. Education was promised to all up to the age of eighteen. Trade unions in all countries accepted the wage freeze but won recognition as bargaining agents; they established grievance procedures, won arbitration, and, not least important, obtained draft exemptions for their members in vital industries.

The war also accelerated women's rise to equality. They took responsibilities and assumed positions that formerly had not been considered suitable for their sex—as welders in munitions factories, managers and administrators, streetcar conductors, and so on. They now were given the suffrage.

Still more important, the governments had to call on minorities and dependencies to help them win the war. Ireland and India were promised home rule. Black soldiers fought on all fronts. Canadians, South Africans, and "Aussies" played a major role on the battlefields, in war councils, and in diplomatic conferences. If the prize of the war was supremacy in Europe, the price of victory was diminished power on the world scene.

The greatest change, however, was to be found not in any specific institution or relationship but in the attitude to war itself. Up to 1914, peace had been considered the normal thing, war the exception, even an anomaly. The Left had assumed that people prefer making money to destroying property. Wars, it was thought, were forced on reluctant nations by Machiavellian princes and munition-makers. Now war appeared as a condition of human existence, and demagogues could use the war fever to wrest power from the liberals.

Italy, for example, could have stayed out of the war. In return for her neutrality, Premier Giovanni Giolitti even hoped to obtain from Austria the Brenner boundary and the city of Trieste. But diplomacy could not bring glory; only war could! The nationalist mobs in Rome rejected the deal as base. Mussolini's toughs, now organized as Fasci d'Azione Rivoluzionaria, threatened "either war or revolution." Although the parliament favored neutrality, mass demonstrations forced the government to join the Entente in May 1915.

In October 1917, the Italian front collapsed at Caporetto; 800,000 men were lost or went over the hill, like Hemingway's hero in *A Farewell to Arms*. To redeem their honor, the Italian nationalists now made exorbitant territorial demands. A Fascio di Difesa Nazionale, formed of nationalists and revolutionists, tried to keep the government war-minded even after victory. In March 1919, Mussolini issued a program calling for the annexation of Fiume and Dalmatia, for progressive taxation, expropriation of war profits, nationalization of war industries, a minimum wage, and workers' participation in management.

The strange mixture of chauvinistic and socialistic, of radical democratic and nationalistic slogans, reflects the Jacobin temper of the masses. Some began to see the war as a means of social progress or as an expression of a higher, mystical community. It changed the citizen's conception of his place in state and society, destroyed old world gentility, shattered the sweet illusion of peaceful advance, dispelled the dream that conflicts can be resolved by arbitration, tore to shreds the self-image of a society that had been at peace with itself. It yanked entire populations from their moorings, rent the values by which people lived, and perverted their ideas about man, world, and the future. The revolutions that followed only confirmed the collapse of the old order. "Total mobilization" opened the way for bolshevism and fascism and a reversal of all the old traditions of Europe.

CHAPTER 2

The End of the Dynasties

WHEN people realized that the war was not merry, honorable, or glorious, unrest spread among both civilians and soldiers. From the outset, small groups of pacifists and revolutionary socialists had opposed the war policy of their respective parties. On May Day 1915, Karl Liebknecht staged a one-minute demonstration on Potsdamer Platz in Berlin. In July, 200,000 miners went on strike in South Wales. Sixteen thousand persons in England claimed conscientious objector status, and 1,300 went to jail. In France, Clemenceau quelled a mutiny in blood.

A number of prominent writers came out against the war, including Aldous Huxley, Herbert Read, Lytton Strachey, Robert Graves, the Sitwells, Siegfried Sassoon, Bernard Shaw, H. G. Wells, John Galsworthy, and Arnold Bennett in England, Henri Barbusse and Romain Rolland in France, Alfred Döblin, Hermann Hesse, Stefan Zweig, Leonhard Frank, and Heinrich Mann in Germany. Döblin's *Three Leaps of Wang-lun* and Barbusse's *Under Fire* were published during the war. So were Stefan Zweig's *Jeremias*, Franz Werfel's translation of Euripides' *The Trojan Women*, and Romain Rolland's *Clerambault*. D. H. Lawrence noted that "the well-bred, really cultured classes were on the whole passive resisters; they shirked their duty." Draft dodgers, teen-age boys taking fathers' places, and war profiteers became stereotypes of popular literature; a wide gap opened between soldiers and the "home front."

Movingly the problem of early sex has been treated in Raymond Radiguet's *Le Diable au Corps* and in Ernst Glaeser's *Class of 1902*.

For over a decade, an enormous literary output worked over the experience of war[1] —the feeling of futility, of being cheated and exploited, of pity for the victims, and, above all, of comradeship and respect for the enemy. Almost nowhere do we find an attempt to expose the political causes of war.

---

[1] The best-known works are Arnold Zweig's *The Case of Sergeant Grischa* (1927); Erich Maria Remarque's *All Quiet on the Western Front* (originally not meant as an anti-war novel, but attacked by the Nazis because it honestly reported that war is hell and that not all Germans were heroes); Leonhard Frank's *Der Mensch Ist Gut* (*Man Is Good*) (1918); Ford Madox Ford's *Parade's End* (1924–28); *Verdun* (1939), the last volume of Jules Romains' *Men of Good Will*; Roger Martin du Gard's *Summer 1914* (1936); Aldous Huxley's *Crome Yellow* (1921); Ernest Hemingway's *A Farewell to Arms* (1929); Ludwig Renn's *War* (1928); Theodor Plievier's *The Kaiser's Coolies* (1930); and two poems—Siegfried Sassoon's "Dreamers," and William Butler Yeats' "An Irish Airman Foresees His Death."

This is even truer of the films, the most notable of which were *Verdun*, *All Quiet on the Western Front*, and *La Grande Illusion*. In these films war is seen as the outcome of blunder and stupidity, as an ugly fate, as hell. The disgust cut across party lines. There were conservatives and liberals among the anti-war writers, and two of the best films, *Westfront 1918* and *Kameradschaft*, were made by Georg Wilhelm Pabst, who later collaborated with the Nazis.

Among the socialists likewise, reformists and revolutionaries united in condemning the war. In 1915, Bernstein and Kautsky, the old adversaries, joined hands to change their party's war policy; two years later they founded the Independent Social Democratic Party (USPD). The great mass of Socialist workers and their representatives wished to end the war, not to use it as a peg for political revolution. Even the East European monarchies might have survived with moderate reforms had they but known how to end the war. But in 1915, a small number of internationalist and revolutionary socialists from many countries met at Zimmerwald, Switzerland, and adopted Lenin's formula to convert the imperialist war into a civil war.

The first government to collapse under the stress of war was that of Czar Nicholas— if that arbitrary mixture of bewilderment, corruption, and despotism could be called a government at all. Decisions were made by favoritism rather than by deliberation. The uneducated monk Rasputin, a mystic who had promised to cure the Czar's hemophiliac son, ruled the imperial household; he was killed by high-ranking army officers, but incompetence and indecision continued. Mass desertions and surrenders decimated the Russian Army, strikes paralyzed the war industries, and the police were no longer considered reliable. In February 1917, strikes and mutinies forced the Czar to abdicate; on March 12[2] the Duma declared the monarchy abolished. A provisional government under Prince Lvov, with Professor Paul Miliukov as Foreign Minister, decided to continue the war and promised to convene a Constitutional Assembly at a later date. It also confirmed the Czar's secret treaties on war aims— notably the conquest of Constantinople.

But the Russian peasant, the *muzhik*, was interested neither in Constantinople nor in constitution. He wanted land and peace. In Petrograd and other places, deputies from army units and factories began to meet as *soviets* (councils) of workers and soldiers. Acting as a rival government, they issued or authorized licenses for production, supply, and transportation; they also demanded the resignation of Miliukov and of War Minister Alexander Guchkov.

A new government, formed in May, included the young Social Revolutionary Alexander Kerensky. With the masses moving rapidly to the Left, Kerensky became head of the government in July. Meanwhile peasants began to seize and divide the land in tumultuous actions. Kerensky called a Constitutional Assembly, but he also continued the war and admonished the peasants to wait for a farm law. His rhetoric could not contain the revolution that was pressing on. A great offensive staged by General Alexei Brusilov against the Austrian positions failed because too many soldiers

---

[2] Our time. By the old calendar, the revolution is still referred to as the February Revolution.

went home so as not to miss the land distribution and others mutinied when their officers used the knout to enforce discipline. Nevertheless, a Bolshevik uprising in July 1917 failed, and Russia seemed on her way to join the West.

The Russian Revolution gave the Entente powers a propaganda advantage. Now democracy was fighting autocracy on all fronts. While Germany tried to establish puppet governments in Poland and the Baltic countries, Austria's Slavs moved for independence. Thousands of Czechs deserted to the Russians and fought as a Czech legion against the Hapsburg monarchy. In Paris, a Czech council under Eduard Beneš called for the liberation of all oppressed minorities. The Allied cause acquired the halo of a holy war; when the United States joined the fight against tyranny, resistance against continuing the war diminished in France. Leaders of the Socialist International persuaded the Mensheviks to stay away from a planned meeting with German socialists in Stockholm.

In Germany, meanwhile, first the "Independents" and then even the majority of the Reichstag showed increasing reluctance to vote further war appropriations. Riders attached to appropriations bills insisted that the war aim was "peace without annexations." In July 1917, the Kaiser pledged to carry out electoral reforms in Prussia. But the metal workers went on strike in Berlin. The Italian Maximalists also called strikes to end the war. In France, the old syndicalists stirred up labor unrest. Eventually the British Labour Party also came out for a negotiated peace and withdrew its representative Henderson from the coalition cabinet.

While the workers' parties sought an end to the slaughter, the Pope and Austria's new Emperor, Karl, were seeking a negotiated peace. But the chauvinistic governments could not let the German militarists off cheaply at this stage. They needed a victory to fulfill all the promises they had made to win allies. Secret treaties had been concluded assigning Constantinople to Russia, Syria to France, Mesopotamia to England, the Aegean area to Greece, the Dodecanese and southern Anatolia to Italy, Transylvania and the Dobruja to Rumania. Moreover, in an ambiguous declaration, Lord Arthur Balfour, the British Foreign Minister, had recognized Palestine as a Jewish "homeland," while at the same time the Arab sheiks were promised independence from Turkey. A British intelligence officer, T. E. Lawrence, in his gallant campaign of liberation became a hero to two nations. His romantic account of his adventures, *Seven Pillars of Wisdom*, was to win world acclaim.

The Germans, too, knew how to play this game. They gave Poland independence, prepared to organize the Baltic states as their satellites, and promised Texas, New Mexico, and Arizona to the Mexicans. A German submarine set Sir Roger Casement, the Irish nationalist, ashore on the Irish coast to incite an uprising, but he was apprehended and hanged. Ukrainian separatism likewise was encouraged, and finally, the master coup—the German command arranged for a few dozen Bolshevik and Menshevik leaders, including Lenin and Martov, to travel from Switzerland to Petrograd to foment revolution in the enemy's rear, an operation that succeeded only too well. In November 1917, the Soviet Congress seized power in Petrograd. Bolshevik government took Russia out of the war, giving the Kaiser a breather.

These events forced a new Allied move in the propaganda war. To win the support of democrats and oppressed peoples, Woodrow Wilson issued his "Fourteen Points" in January 1918, promising freedom to all peoples within their ethnic boundaries, but also, somewhat at variance with this principle, "adjustment of colonial claims" and access to the sea for Poland and Serbia. After the Bolsheviks had published the secret treaties found in the Czar's archives, Wilson also promised to end secret treaties, naval and other arms races, tariffs, and colonialism. The Allies recognized the Polish and Yugoslav councils that were being formed and promised a fair peace with democratic institutions.

The war-weary Reichstag majority adopted a resolution calling for "lasting reconciliation among peoples" and barring "violations of territory and political, economic and financial discrimination." The Independent Socialists and the shop-steward movement in the Berlin metal and construction industries started active preparations for revolution.

In September 1918, Turkey collapsed; Bulgaria followed in October, and now Emperor Karl, who had ruled Austria and Hungary since November 1916, could not save his throne. Czechs and Yugoslavs declared their independence and the Hungarians, in a vain attempt to save themselves, severed their union with Austria. On November 3, Karl accepted the Allied armistice terms; a week later, he left his country forever. The Hapsburg Empire, once world-wide, had ended.

Despite its victories, and although its troops still occupied enemy countries, the mighty German Army had lost the war. Since September, Ludendorff had pressed the Kaiser to offer an armistice. Hoping that a parliamentary government might be received more kindly in the Western capitals, he invited Prince Max of Baden, a known liberal, to form a cabinet with members of the majority parties—including the Center, the Progressives, and for the first time the Social Democrats.

Instead of accepting Prince Max's offer of a truce, Wilson hinted that he could not deal with the Kaiser; nor did the Allies care to negotiate as long as German armies occupied French soil. Hard-pressed, the Germans nevertheless retreated in good order, leaving total destruction behind them. Early in November, the German Navy Command issued a desperate call for a "last battle." The sailors refused to obey the order and, hoisting the red flag, occupied Kiel and marched on Berlin. At the same time, a Bavarian "People's State" was proclaimed in Munich.

On November 9, 1918, the Socialist ministers informed the Chancellor that the Kaiser had to go. Prince Max put the government into the hands of Friedrich Ebert, a Social Democrat; but the masses wanted no legal transition, no trace of the monarchy. This was to be a revolution. Soldiers elected their "councils." Soon all executive power was handed over to the Council of People's Commissars composed of three Social Democrats and three Independent Socialists. A Congress of Workers' and Soldiers' Councils was convened in Berlin. In contrast to the Russian model, however, most delegates were moderates. Shouting Karl Liebknecht down, they refused to play any revolutionary role and voted to call for a Constitutional Assembly. Thereupon the Independents, anxious to remain in contact with the revolutionary masses in the big cities, withdrew from the government while the majority Socialists became the prisoners of the forces of "law and order." They made a pact with the military to bring the troops home in good order and to assure an orderly transition from the monarchical to the republican powers. Moreover, instead of forming republican militias, they hired "volunteer" formations under mercenary leaders to protect the young republic from the revolution.

Meanwhile, Hindenburg had urged the new government to accept any armistice conditions. Later, the German Right was to claim that the German Army, "unbeaten in the field," had been "stabbed in the back" by a traitorous revolution. Actually the country was exhausted; the front could no longer be supplied with ammunition, food, and transportation; the army units were depleted; soldiers went AWOL. Morale and the economy collapsed before the military admitted their strategic defeat. It is curious, therefore, that Ebert, far from boasting that he had brought the slaughter to an end, later sued the "calumniators" who charged that he had betrayed the Fatherland.

As a result of the war, those most responsible for it ceased to rule their countries; their system was discredited and broken. Instead of monarchical governments, parliamentary democracy emerged everywhere. Moreover, the old empires had been dismantled, at least in Europe; in their place, nations that had never known sovereignty and unity now constituted themselves as states. Boundaries were to run along ethnic lines more faithfully than ever before, although some of the new states still encompassed more aliens than they could absorb: Poland, gathering in territories that Russia, Prussia, and Austria had annexed in the eighteenth century, also acquired Ukrainians, Jews, Germans, and Russians. The Baltic states were to be free within their ethnic borders. The old kingdom of Bohemia and Moravia became a Slav republic with German and Hungarian minorities. Serbia, doubling her territory at Austria's expense, became the "Kingdom of Serbs, Croats, and Slovenes." Rumania acquired Transylvania and Bessarabia with nationally mixed populations. Austria and Hungary remained truncated and helpless. Greece, which had joined the Entente much against her will, found herself a republic and claimed Turkish as well as Bulgarian territory. Germany, much reduced in territory and power, was for a long time to struggle over her social constitution. The greatest change occurred in Turkey, which left Europe to become a modern republic, and in Russia, where for the first time in world history a socialist party took over.

CHAPTER 3

The Bolshevik Revolution

WHEN Lenin arrived at the Finland Station in Petrograd, in April 1917, he surprised the workers who had come to greet him. Instead of telling them how best to exploit their new freedom and consolidate the republic, he explained that they had won nothing worth having, that the republic was a middle-class swindle, that the democratic revolution must soon be followed by a proletarian, socialist one. They should, he told them, continue to fight against the war, for distribution of the land, against the bourgeois parliament, for seizure of power by the soviets. Russia was the weakest link in the chain of imperialism; if the chain broke there, it was certain to break everywhere. Trotsky also shared this internationalist perspective.

Of course, this might help the Germans; we now know that the Bolsheviks had received money from Ludendorff. But Lenin's business was the Russian Revolution; getting rid of the Kaiser was the business of the German workers. To those who found his logic flawed, Lenin answered: "I am a Russian, therefore I am for the defeat of the Russian government." If the Kaiser thought that he was using Lenin—well, in the end we shall see who had been using whom.

Even the Central Committee of the Bolshevik Party was not prepared for this. Faithful to their Marxist timetable, Leo Kamenev and Joseph Stalin, the leaders who were not in exile, had not placed a socialist revolution on the agenda and had condemned distribution of the land (the slogan of the rival Social Revolutionaries) as a petty-bourgeois illusion. Lenin, interested in revolution rather than orthodoxy, picked the slogans that promised to be most embarrassing to the new republican government: peace, bread, land, all power to the soviets. He foresaw correctly that the government, which was not much more than a receiver-in-bankruptcy of the Czarist mess, would disgrace itself and that its successor must be either the counter-revolution or a new Robespierre who could lead the revolution toward the "democratic dictatorship of workers and peasants." In the famous "April theses" Lenin outlined the strategy for revolution: Bolshevik domination of the soviets and prevalence of the soviets over the government.

Lenin's hand was greatly strengthened by the admission of Leon Trotsky to the Party and its Central Committee. Trotsky had been chairman of the St. Petersburg workers' soviet in 1905. His experience enabled him to guide the new soviet on a radical course. The All-Russian Congress of Soviets, in which intellectuals dominated

the workers and soldiers, was assembled in June. In July, Kerensky called for a
Constituent Assembly and Lenin, to forestall it, staged an uprising. But the soviets
failed to respond; isolated, the Bolsheviks were defeated and driven into exile. From
Helsinki, Lenin sent his credo, *State and Revolution*. In this famous pamphlet, he
promised to destroy the existing state machinery and put in its place an organization
entirely responsive to the wishes of the masses. Not surprisingly, he failed to mention
the soviets, which had left him in the lurch, as the proper organ of revolution. In
August, he wrote: "The soviets are a stage which the revolution already has left
behind." He had lapsed into that "putschism" that Marxists everywhere condemned.
His party was small, sectarian, and divided. In March, it probably had no more than
37,000 members, at the time of the uprising perhaps 200,000; it held only 13 per cent
of the seats in the All-Russian Soviet Congress.

In September, however, General Kornilov presented Lenin with a boon. Threatening a counter-revolutionary coup, he marched on Petrograd and compelled Kerensky
to call on all forces of the Left to defend the republic. The government armed the
workers' militias and released the Bolshevik leaders from jail. Kornilov was beaten,
but the workers now had arms. Once more, the Petrograd Soviet, housed in the
Smolny Institute, became the center of revolutionary activity. A left-wing faction of
the Social Revolutionaries joined the Bolsheviks in working for an end to the war,
distribution of the land, and overthrow of the government. In the countryside the
peasants seized the lands; the soldiers deserted; the front crumbled; the government
grew virtually powerless. In Petrograd, Bolshevik workers demonstrated before the
seat of the government. The cruiser *Aurora* in the port of Kronstadt fell into Bolshevik
hands. On November 7, the Bolshevik Red Guards, with the help of an insurgent
regiment and the *Aurora*'s guns, defeated Kerensky's forces (in line with the old
calendar, the event is still called the October Revolution). In Moscow, too, the
insurrection was successful. The Bolsheviks and left-wing Social Revolutionaries
formed the Council of People's Commissars (revolutionary government) in the name
of the soviets and issued a series of basic decrees calling for: nationalization of the
land and its distribution among those who till it; equal rights for women; self-
determination and the right of secession for all nationalities; and nationalization of the
banks and of large industrial enterprises.

The Council of People's Commissars also called on all governments to stop the
war immediately and unconditionally—an appeal obviously directed, over the heads
of these governments, to the war-weary masses.

Although in fact it was the Bolsheviks who had seized the levers of power, they
made their revolution in the name of the soviets. Theoretically, these organs of labor,
soldier, and peasant power should have been the ones to organize an administration.
This, however, was not feasible. In fact, power was badly splintered, and whichever
party was locally strong claimed to be the soviet or refused to co-operate with central
authorities. The nationalities seceded, and soon there were independent governments
in Finland, Poland, in the Baltic provinces, the Caucasus, and even in the Ukraine.
"White" Army units still held large areas of the country; few thought that the soviet

government was definitively established. Even the Bolsheviks did not yet believe in soviet power but allowed the elections for the Constituent Assembly to go on as scheduled in November. To their consternation, they received only 25 per cent of the seats against 60 per cent for the Mensheviks and Social Revolutionaries. Had the Bolsheviks been able to co-operate with the other socialist parties, Russia might have gone peacefully toward socialism.

Since the election had revealed the weakness of the soviet idea outside the two big cities, Lenin took three steps of great consequence. He formed the Special Commission for Combating Counter-revolution (CHEKA), a ruthless police force under Felix Dzerzhinsky. He dissolved the Constituent Assembly by armed terror (January 1918). He concluded a separate peace with Germany—the Treaty of Brest-Litovsk, signed in March 1918.

These measures caused vehement dissension inside the Bolshevik Party and the government. The Social Revolutionary commissars quit in disgust, leaving the field to the Bolsheviks. The Treaty of Brest-Litovsk was harsh and it did not even bring peace, since the Germans, hard up for grain, intervened in the Ukraine. Fortunately for Lenin, the treaty lapsed when Germany broke down in November 1918.

For reasons of security, the capital was moved to Moscow, where Lenin built a strong nucleus of power. The measure soon acquired a symbolic meaning, too: Soviet Russia was leaving Europe, and her government assumed the Asian features of a police state. The enemy was Western and Russian liberalism; freedom was declared "a bourgeois prejudice." Elections to the soviets became a farce. Urban districts elected five times as many deputies as rural districts for the same number of voters. Having gained a majority of the Soviet Congress in July 1918, the Bolsheviks denied the opposition the floor; Social Revolutionary, Menshevik, and Democratic representatives were arrested, their organizations harassed.

The Social Revolutionaries returned to the old method of direct action. An attempt on Lenin's life failed, but it was answered by the official proclamation of "red terror" on September 2, 1918. Civil war broke out and raged throughout the country for three years. The CHEKA shot thousands, while Trotsky assembled a Red Army, using 30,000 former officers as cadres. The White Army included groups of regional separatists, from the former propertied classes, the military, the Cossacks, and other reactionary elements of whom Trotsky said that they had nothing behind them but a hostile rear. The peasants, indeed, feared nothing so much as the return of their former masters. In addition, the generals made the mistake of appealing to foreign powers—Germany first, and later the Entente—so that the Bolsheviks could pose as defenders of the national territory against foreign intervention as well. On government posters of that period the counter-revolutionary generals—Wrangel, Kolchak, Denikin, Yudenich—appear as dogs led on a leash by Western capitalists.

Indeed, the enemy now was the West. The Treaty of Brest-Litovsk had given the Germans valuable territory and had freed entire armies to fight on the Western front. Now the Bolsheviks repudiated the Czar's debts, canceled the licenses of foreign mining and timber companies, expropriated factories and commercial property. All this, and the revolutionary, socialist character of their government, the wanton execution of the Czar and his family, as well as other horror stories now spread by refugees, persuaded the Western powers to intervene. Moreover, some 30,000 Czechs were trapped along the Siberian Railway. Unable to reach their port of evacuation to join the Allies, they seized power in the area where they were stalled—an almost satirical comment on the political situation in Russia. Power was scattered among many local forces; some received aid from foreign governments.

While the Germans tried to organize the Ukraine as their grain basket, the British and French secretly agreed to share valuable assets and strategic positions in case Russia should fall apart. Each sent a small expeditionary corps to their assigned area, under the pretext of "fighting Bolshevism" and supporting a White general who operated in that part of the country. But the French Navy in the Black Sea mutinied, and the British expedition to Archangel had always been half-hearted. Actually, the Western governments expected Bolshevism to fall of its own cruel weight, and old-line diplomats also assured their allies that the Bolsheviks could not maintain themselves in power for long—an estimate they shared with most Bolsheviks, so that Lenin had to write a reassuring article. In fact, his government's writ went no further than its armies. Secessionist regimes had established themselves in Lithuania, Latvia, Estonia, and Finland. In the Ukraine an independent parliament, the Rada, governed under Menshevik leadership; similar governments had taken power in Georgia, Armenia, Azerbaijan (they even applied for a U.S. protectorate); Poland was ready to go to war against Moscow; Cossacks ruled part of southern Russia, with the Hetmans Simon Petlura and Paul Skoropadsky outstripping all previous counter-revolutionary regimes in vindictiveness and bestiality.

In other parts, non-Bolshevik revolutionary forces—Mensheviks, Social Revolutionaries, anarchists—held sway. Peasant militias fought against the Whites and the foreigners but also against the Bolsheviks. The most important of these peasant leaders was the anarchist Nestor Makhno, who vainly tried to come to friendly terms with Lenin. His guerrilla force held out for several years in the south.

Even where the Moscow government had established its jurisdiction, the situation was anarchic. Essential services of a national administration, such as justice, were superseded by terror; mail and railroads simply ceased to function. Since the peasants withheld food deliveries, workers' companies went out into the villages and seized the stores. Industrial production was maintained only by stealing available raw materials. Factories whose owners had fled were nationalized. Before they realized it, the Bolsheviks had created a totalitarian system of war economy, later called "war communism." Driven by their failure to enlist voluntary co-operation, they had no choice but to "flee forward" into dictatorship.[1]

But Bolshevism had one asset: it was the only national, patriotic force. Despite the famine and the many enemies they had made, despite foreign intervention and a full-

---

[1] The term "dictatorship of the proletariat" originally did not mean a form of government, but the social content of popular democracy.

fledged war with Poland, Lenin and Trotsky, creator and leader of the Red Army, prevailed. One after the other, the generals were defeated. The foreign expeditionary corps went home in 1920.[2] The Red Army drove the Poles from Russian soil and advanced toward Warsaw; but it found no sympathizers among the Poles, and when General Pilsudski counter-attacked with French help, he conquered a large part of White Russia. By the Riga Treaty, concluded in 1921, Pilsudski retained much territory east of the ethnic line.[3]

Although the Bolsheviks had won in Russia, the world revolution was contained. Under French sponsorship, a *cordon sanitaire* was built along Russia's western boundaries. It consisted of Rumania, which was given Bessarabia; Poland, which held 3 million Byelo-Russians; Lithuania, Latvia, Estonia, and Finland, all of which had beaten back the Bolsheviks with the aid of German mercenaries, the most reactionary element to emerge from the war. Lenin's hope that the revolution could be carried to other countries at the point of the bayonet had been deflated. Nor had independent revolutions elsewhere checked the capitalist powers. The mutiny in the French Navy collapsed; the Spartacus uprising in Berlin and the two Soviet republics, in Bavaria and in Hungary, were bloodily suppressed. The outlook was gloomy for world revolution. Since all previous experience suggested that a revolution that does not spread in scope—does not become "permanent," to use Trotsky's term—must fall to the forces of counter-revolution or Bonapartism, the fate of Bolshevism was hanging by a thread.

With the civil war over but famine still stalking the land and the people now clamoring for their rights and for the benefits of the revolution, Lenin faced a problem no Marxist timetable had foreseen: The Communists held power in a backward country with no chance of building socialism. Should they retreat toward parliamentary democracy, or toward greater dictatorial rule? Back to capitalism, or on to a new type of planned economy? The sailors in Kronstadt felt that the time had come to carry through the socialist revolution; Mensheviks and anarchists as well as a good number of loyal Bolsheviks felt that the dictatorship had done its job and should start to "wither away," as Lenin had promised in *State and Revolution*.

Lenin agreed that the situation required a retreat from war communism. In his pamphlet *On Taxation in Kind* (1921), he introduced the New Economic Policy (NEP). Requisitions were to be stopped, small-scale capitalism would again be permitted; peasants would have to surrender part of their product but would be allowed to sell the larger part. It is true that the state retained the so-called economic command posts—that is, control of the banks, foreign trade, and big industry. But a free market was once more permitted, and Trotsky earnestly admonished the Party and the workers that, if they wanted farm products, they had to offer the peasants

---

[2] The Japanese remained in Vladivostok until 1922, then withdrew under U.S. pressure. Soviet historians report only that the United States intervened against Communism.

[3] The line had been established by Lord George Curzon. According to this impartial arbitrator, one-third of Poland was populated by White Russians and Ukrainians.

manufactured articles at reasonable prices. "Let's turn our face toward the village," was his new slogan while, paradoxically, he also proposed to "militarize" the trade unions. Nikolai Bukharin, who also had started out as a "Left Communist," now came to be the main theorist of a "Right" turn. He revived the slogan addressed to the peasants by the French revolution of 1830: "Get rich!" At the same time, Lenin tightened the dictatorship.

All this provoked a serious crisis in the Party. The first great purge, "purification of the Party," was ordered to weed out all who had doubts about the wisdom of the leaders or who were found wanting in zeal for the dictatorship. The Kronstadt sailors, aided by others, arose and were bloodily suppressed by Trotsky. The Russian Revolution had had its "9th Thermidor"; Trotsky, its Carnot, also became its Barras.

With his usual frankness, Lenin called the New Economic Policy a retreat. The *kulaks* (those owning a horse and employing a laborer) were to develop a strong farm economy. The "NEP men"—small merchants, honest salesmen, and manufacturers— reintroduced the spirit of capitalism, and with them came speculators, con men, and fixers. Even in the state enterprises, managerial powers now returned to engineers, accountants, or anyone who had experience and knew the business. These changes are dealt with in many Soviet novels of the period, such as Ilya Ehrenburg's *Michael Lykov*, Fyodor Gladkov's *Cement*, and the satires of Mikhail Zoshchenko. No doubt the Soviet state incurred a certain risk in giving economic power to a class that was hostile to the ruling party. Lenin candidly stated that the Soviet economy consisted of small-scale capitalism, co-operative and state enterprises, and very little socialism. He even invited foreign capitalists to acquire "concessions."

Foreign Minister Georgi Chicherin offered the moribund capitalistic economy the great Russian market as a way out of the post-war recession. He also began to seek diplomatic recognition for the Soviet government, beginning with the Baltic states. Lloyd George, always practical and optimistic, hoped to find more than an accommodation: he was convinced that the Bolshevik state had come of age and would be reintegrated into the family of nations. But Chicherin laid down conditions. Russia would repay private loans contracted before the war, but only if she received a new loan. He would not pay any part of the Czar's political debts. This was a political point of honor, but poor diplomacy: the bonds were largely in the hands of France's little pensioners. No French government dared to cancel these loans; therefore, no deal was possible on Lenin's terms. However, if not reconciliation, there could at least be coexistence. Dogmatists might ask whether a socialist state can survive in a capitalist environment. Lenin answered soberly that the main purpose of world revolution from now on was the preservation of that first socialist country. He called the new state of affairs "peaceful living together."

Within four years the Bolsheviks had evolved from a revolutionary party to one whose prime concern was to remain in power, and all its decisions were justified as "necessities of state." When some old Bolsheviks—A. G. Shlyapnikov, T. V. Sapronov, G. Myasnikov, I. G. Medvediev—asked for more democracy within the Party, Lenin prohibited all factions. The Communist Party had to be as monolithic as its state. The trade unions were turned into government organs, and the practice of self-accusation for deficient performance, inadequate Party loyalty, or ideological deviations dates from that time. The police and the Party Control Commission became all-powerful; the Soviet state began to look like its predecessor, Czarist absolutism— only more so. Western ideas and democratic practices became suspect; all contacts with Western socialists were broken off and the Party's Marxist traditions were drastically revised. Abandoning social democracy, Lenin now taught that Russia's dictatorship was the only way to socialism, and revived the old term "communism." In 1919, his foreign partisans assembled in Moscow to found the Third, or Communist, International (Comintern) and elected as its president Grigori Zinoviev, an unconscionable adventurer who played with the lives of thousands of Western Communists. At its second congress, the Comintern laid down twenty-one conditions which established the mastery of the Russians over the Communists abroad. On a world-wide scale, the division of the labor parties now was irremediable. Unlike the French Revolution, which appealed to its friends abroad but got into trouble with their rulers, the Bolshevik Revolution shut itself off from its well-wishers but lived in peace with its enemies.

As a consequence of their isolation, the Russian leaders now had to look to their national traditions for their means of survival. Today, more than fifty years later, we can see that the Bolshevik seizure of power was not the opening of a world-wide socialist revolution, but the first in a series of national revolutions against the international rule of Western capitalism.

CHAPTER 4

European Revolutions

WHEN Walter Gropius, founder of the Bauhaus, came home from the war and watched a mob in Berlin hooting at army officers, he realized that more than a war had been lost. A world had come to an end. It was then that he discovered his "social responsibility as an architect." The upper class could no longer take its superior position for granted but had to justify it by constructive work.

The society that emerged from the war, therefore, was not, as Walther Rathenau cynically remarked, merely a new set of supervisors. The old aristocratic-military castes and their state had collapsed. The middle class now ruled Europe. Many countries saw at least some measure of land reform, some redistribution of property, and new opportunities for the poor to climb the social ladder. Minorities and oppressed nations achieved statehood. Women were given new roles in social life. Education was greatly democratized. The trade unions won bargaining rights. Socialists and former workers occupied board and cabinet seats.

A radical change seemed to be sweeping people's attitudes toward new ways, new ideas, new expressions. Men who had lived in the trenches could not simply go back to the mores of pre-war society. Relations between young and old, between sexes and social classes had to fit some new rules of freedom and dignity. This feeling appears even in the hit songs and dances of the years 1919–21, with their mocking exuberance and occasionally defiant hedonism.

The soldiers, invited to return to pre-war normalcy, found that no country had much normalcy to offer. Lloyd George's promise to make post-war England "a home fit for heroes" was quoted only in derision. Many a parlor anarchist now became a parlor Bolshevik, and was taken more seriously than the old-style bohemian. He had about him an air of being in step with history. Everyone found some icons to smash or some new religion to escape to.

Bewilderment and lack of bearings were the hallmark of the years 1918–19. Hermann Hesse deemed Europe finished and fully expected "chaotic, anti-Christian and anti-intellectual Asians" to take over; following Dostoevsky, who only then came to be appreciated in the West, Hesse saw the danger that "the unpredictable man of the future has the capacity for anything—good or evil." E. M. Forster, afraid and dismayed, confessed that he was unable to write while the world was changing so fast.

Rathenau told his friend Count Kessler that "at night I am a Bolshevik, by daylight not quite yet." Many expected an anti-capitalist revolution as an answer to the postwar crisis, and the Russian example seemed all the more persuasive since it combined the European ideology of socialism with the Asian appeal of the "savage" savior. Had not the light come from the East so often before?

German nationalists, who had fought the world war for "Culture" against "Civilization," now turned to the primitive, mystical, terrible East for revenge and salvation. Lenin's emissary, Karl Radek, jailed in Berlin, received in his cell editorialists and bankers as well as such luminaries of Wilhelminian society as General Kurt von Schleicher and Walther Rathenau, and assorted national revolutionaries from Turkey and elsewhere. Many Germans expected an alliance between the Russian and the German revolutions: their humiliated, blockaded, impoverished, and defeated nations might form an alliance of the losers and disinherited against the victorious and arrogant Entente powers.

A national revolutionary war, however, was the last thing the majority wanted. Even the Independent Social Democrats, though revolutionary, desired peace above all. Only the small Spartacus group around Karl Liebknecht and Rosa Luxemburg formed the Communist Party of Germany (KPD), called for a German Soviet Republic, and prepared an insurrection. *Agents-provocateurs* incited some hotheads on January 15, 1919, to seize the newspaper buildings in Berlin; no general strike or other mass action accompanied the amateurish putsch. After some inglorious shooting, the insurgents surrendered. Rosa Luxemburg and Karl Liebknecht, who had vainly tried to avoid the trap, were apprehended and murdered. Four days later, on January 19, the German voters quietly elected a Constituent Assembly, which met in Weimar, Goethe's town. The majority was composed of Social Democrats, Center, and Democrats (the former Progressives)—the parties of the Peace Resolution.

Abortive, too, was the attempt of Kurt Eisner, an Independent, to build a radical democratic state government in Bavaria. He was assassinated in plain daylight as he was entering the State House. Aroused by the provocation, his followers proclaimed a Bavarian Soviet Republic, probably banking on the radicalized peasants and Bavaria's anti-Prussian feeling. They also had the support of anarchists and idealists such as Ernst Toller, Gustav Landauer, and Erich Mühsam. But the Communists overthrew this soviet, organized a terror regime and launched a hopeless war against federal troops. The "white terror" which followed was most cruel and opened the door to the racists.

The following year, a German Kornilov gave radicalism another chance. A Pan-German leader, Wolfgang Kapp, conspired with the commander of an army district, General Walter von Lüttwitz, to seize the capital. Their putsch, most amateurishly staged, collapsed within a week because other army units and the civil service refused to join. The government called for a general strike to defend the republic. But, as in Russia, once the workers had seized the initiative, they fought on. Red militias were formed, expecially in the mining districts; the action, however, came to nothing. The Red Guards were disarmed; thousands were sent to jail. Disappointed and betrayed, most of the Independent Socialists agreed, at their Halle Congress in 1920, to merge with the Communists.

That same year, the French socialists decided, at their Tours Congress, to join the Comintern. The Bulgarian and Italian socialists already had done so in 1919. In the summer of 1920, north Italian workers seized the factories; red banners and pro-Russian slogans filled the streets. But the revolutionaries had no idea what to do with the occupied plants; they failed to take over the government or even to reorganize it. And so the movement petered out. But it had grave consequences for Italy. The frightened bourgeoisie was now willing to surrender power to Mussolini's terror squads.

One more country—defeated, frustrated, landlocked Hungary—saw a revolutionary attempt. After the demise of the Hapsburg monarchy, the liberal Count Michael Karolyi was made Premier in the hope that he might obtain more lenient peace terms. When that proved an illusion and, even worse, when he undertook to distribute land, he was dismissed. In a series of reshuffles, the Premiership ultimately fell to one Bela Kun, a journalist who had been captured by the Russians and had returned as an agent of Lenin. He proclaimed a Soviet republic, nationalized the land, and declared war on Czechoslovakia and Rumania. His was the first of many attempts to exploit nationalism for the Communist cause. Defeated, he was replaced after six months by the reactionary dictatorship of Admiral Miklos Horthy.

Bela Kun fled to Moscow to direct from there the antics of the West European Communist parties. His emissaries often had little knowledge of the country they were assigned to and led the local Communists into irresponsible actions. Thus, a mysterious messenger appeared in Germany in March 1921 and ordered German workers' militias to seize the Leuna chemical plant. The workers were crushed in the battle of Mansfeld, and white terror drove the Communist Party underground. Paul Levi— Rosa Luxemburg's disciple and successor, who had opposed the uprising—was expelled for insubordination. The guerrilla leader Max Hölz spent several years in a Russian jail and later drowned in a Russian pond. Levi later charged that the uprising, coinciding with the NEP and Kronstadt, had been concocted as a diversionary maneuver in the power struggle between the Russian leaders.

Outside Russia, the capitalist system had remained intact, largely because the socialist leaders did not know how to exploit the revolutionary possibilities. By their own choice, they installed themselves in the democratic systems where their enemies agreed to share power. Dogmatism and sectarianism isolated the Communist workers from those who preferred democratic ways, and this split had two historic consequences: It drove the Social Democrats into self-defeating coalitions with middle-class parties, and it drove the Russians deeper into that isolation which transformed the Soviet into a totalitarian system.

But labor was not the only force to claim the heritage of the European system. We have seen that to be successful, Lenin had to satisfy the peasants. The nationalist forces that emerged from the ruins of the Hapsburg Empire also tried to ally themselves with the landless villagers. Hence the new Czech republic distributed 4.5 million acres of arable land—bought cheaply from the fleeing German owners—among

650,000 settlers and thereby accomplished a social and national revolution. In Rumania, King Ferdinand, and even more his son Carol, tried to undercut the established parties by encouraging nationalist-agrarian agitation. The country had been doubled in size, but half of it belonged to German-Austrian and Magyar big landowners: Ferdinand now distributed the surplus land among 1.7 million families, while the big owners retained only 7 per cent. But lack of capital prevented the new settlers from prospering or improving their productivity.

The greatest peasant leader, himself a peasant, emerged in Bulgaria. During the war, Alexander Stamboliski had opposed Bulgaria's alliance with the Central Powers; he continued to lean to the East even after the Bolshevik revolution. When he came to power in 1919, he fought illiteracy, taxed the rich, distributed all land over seventy-five acres (especially crown land and lands belonging to opposition leaders), and instituted a national labor service. He tried to end the quarrel with his neighbors over Macedonia and met with the Yugoslav peasant leader Stephen Radich; he proposed a "Green International" to co-ordinate the economic policies of all agrarian states and to unite all European farm organizations. Unfortunately, he was consumed by hate of the cities and especially of intellectuals. He closed the universities and abolished freedom of the press; his henchmen, uneducated peasants, persecuted his enemies ruthlessly and enriched themselves shamelessly. He suppressed the terroristic Macedonian Revolutionary Organization (IMRO) and in 1923 was murdered by army officers, most likely IMRO sympathizers. He was succeeded by the bloody, reactionary dictator Alexander Tsankov.

The revolutionary dictatorship of Stamboliski shows certain features that later came to be labeled "fascist": deliberate anti-intellectualism in a democratic guise; violent egalitarianism which cloaks corruption and despotism. But unlike fascism and its later imitations, Stamboliski's Peasant Party was neither militaristic nor chauvinistic, and though it harassed the opposition, it retained parliamentary institutions. After the Russian Revolution, it established the only plebeian dictatorship to stay in power for as long as four years. Inexplicably, the Communists failed to support it; they did stage an uprising against Tsankov, which was bloodily suppressed.

In the Baltic states (Latvia, Estonia, Lithuania), which had been under the political domination of the Czar and under the economic domination of German aristocrats, and to some extent also in Poland and Finland, agrarian reform had the twin aims of national and social renovation. These goals were shared by all parties and were never repudiated, even when the democratic regimes were overthrown and reactionary governments took their place.

Even Poland, where the gentry ruled the countryside, had its agrarian reform. A law of 1919 limited the land one man was allowed to hold to 150 acres in fertile areas, more in woodland and meadows. Since many impoverished nobles were prepared to sell their land, 8 million acres of poor land passed into peasant hands before 1939. Although smallholders eventually owned 80 per cent of all arable land, they were even worse off than their neighbors in Rumania.

Poland was the first country to witness a new type of movement which soon was to be known by its Italian name, fascism. In many countries it arose out of a disposal problem. Army officers and storm troopers or other people who had been uprooted by the war; small shopkeepers and impoverished noblemen who could not cope with the post-war depression united with the military, the big landowners, and the extreme Rightist parties in an intensely chauvinistic, usually anti-Semitic and anti-intellectual movement led by a charismatic personality. Though its origins were often revolutionary and the leaders frequently had emerged from pre-war socialist parties—as was the case with Hervé, Pilsudski, and Mussolini—the movement was always anti-labor and in its final effects counter-revolutionary; or perhaps we should say that like its predecessor, the regime of Louis Napoléon, it took the place of a revolution that had been aborted. Wherever socialist or agrarian revolutions had failed, this nationalistic and militaristic movement imposed its own know-nothing revolution.

The one country where the traditional power of the gentry threatened the political balance of the new democracy, Germany, saw no agrarian reform. Failure to modernize these estates was to be a cause for the fall of the republic. In Germany as in Italy, Poland, Hungary, and elsewhere, the big landowners were able to lead an agrarian, anti-democratic "front," and they found allies among the alienated students who engaged in militant action against the liberal state and the Social Democratic parties.

The intense class war in northern Italy, the unsolved agrarian problem in southern Italy, and the war veterans' frustration helped Fascism get into the saddle in Italy. The returning soldiers found neither jobs nor respect. They blamed Freemasons, liberal parliamentarians, and corrupt draft dodgers; they were ready to follow any leader who promised action, adventure, and grandeur. *Vivere pericolosamente*, to live dangerously, was the slogan of Gabriele d'Annunzio, the poet who had scandalized pre-war society with his spectacular love affairs. In 1919, he told the "*Arditi*," the daring ones, to don black shirts and to seize the city of Fiume, which the Paris Peace Conference had denied Italy. There he installed a theatrical regime worthy of Garibaldi, an act of defiance against big-power dictatorship.

Black shirts also were worn by Benito Mussolini's "Fasci di Combattimento," who constituted themselves as a "Fascist Party," and its goon squads, the Squadre d'Assalto (SA). *Fasces* were the rods which the police carried in ancient Rome. Black shirts, reminiscent of Garibaldi's "red shirts," also were worn by railway mechanics. In its original program of 1920, Fascism was still revolutionary. It demanded partition of big estates and abolition of the monarchy, but also pensions for veterans and war victims and a curb on all powers not derived from the state. The Fascists at that time were a blend of anarchist militancy and soldierly nationalism. Their leader, Mussolini, hated the Roman Church, the police, the law, the rich, the well-bred. In the past, he had worn his hair long, washed and shaved rarely, raved against authority and public order; his recent conversion to patriotism and monarchy could not make the ruling class forget that he was a plebeian, a rabble-rouser. But the liberals, just emerged from the harrowing experience of factory occupation, agreed to place the Fascist goons on their electoral list. Moreover, some intellectuals were attracted by Mussolini's rhetoric, his pseudo-anarchist exhibitionism, his phony promise of class reconciliation, his revolutionary aestheticism which temporarily could seduce even Toscanini and Puccini. His glittering ambiguity attracted millions who hardly knew what he stood for. In the election of 1921, the Fascists obtained 22 seats, and when several liberal governments broke down one after the other, the foolish, weak, and frightened King, afraid of letting socialists into the cabinet, called on Mussolini to save the monarchy. Although the deal probably had been worked out between the army, the Fascists, and the liberal-conservative-clerical majority, 30,000 Fascist militiamen were allowed to stage a "march on Rome," armed with sticks and revolvers, on October 28, 1922. Mussolini himself arrived in a sleeping car from Milano after the army had refused to face the marchers down. The march thus having conveniently led to the capitulation of the conventional powers, King Victor Emmanuel III handed Mussolini the reins of Italy's government.

This operetta aspect of the Fascist seizure of power has overshadowed both the revolutionary origins of Fascism and its potential for evil. Liberals tended to view Mussolini as a buffoon who took power merely to act out his petty daydreams; they underestimated his sense of power, and when he refused to play by parliamentary rules, they complained, like the Austrian generals about Napoleon, that he had beaten them unfairly. The Marxists, on the other hand, also failed to recognize the inner dynamics of the Fascist movement and saw Mussolini as nothing but "the running dog of monopoly capital."

Liberalism apparently had exhausted its opportunities. Unable to cope with the grievous social problems, unwilling to attack the privileges of landlords and industrialists, the former Premiers Giovanni Giolitti and Antonio Salandra had offered Mussolini coalition arrangements. But if they thought to save their skins, they were sadly mistaken. Mussolini was no simple-minded watchdog who let himself be put back on the leash after having sicked the villain. He fully intended to play the role of the savior into which they had cast him. He understood the state Italy was in and exploited his opportunities. Far from being tools of big business or of the landed aristocrats, his thugs were frightening them. It is true that many sons of the ruling class, rather than fight the thugs who were muscling in, decided to join them; but it soon became apparent who was using whom in this alliance. Anticipating Perón, Nasser, Sukarno, Fanon, Lin Piao and similar ideologists of subsequent decades, Mussolini spoke of "proletarian nations," and prepared their attack on Western capitalistic democracy.

A curiously intermediary type of national revolution appeared in Turkey. The Peace Treaty of Sèvres not only stripped Turkey of all her outlying possessions but temporarily even dismembered the Anatolian homeland. However, an officers' revolt, led by Kemal Pasha (who soon was to be called Ataturk, "father of the Turks") tore up the treaty and deposed the Sultan. He also abolished the caliphate and yanked the veil from women's faces and the fez from men's heads. Established as the Nationalist Party, the reformers reorganized the government and started an industrialization program. Ataturk allied himself with Lenin, defied the imperialists, drove the rapacious Greeks and Italians out of the country, and won a new peace treaty at

Lausanne (1923), which left Anatolia intact but called for an exchange of populations: 1.5 million Greek-speaking and Greek-Orthodox people had to leave Turkey, a similar number of Turks had to leave the Balkan Peninsula. The Greeks were settled in Macedonia, while Bulgarian-speaking Macedonians were transplanted to Bulgaria, where they became the nucleus of IMRO.

Kemal Pasha was the first of those modernizing dictators who, in the twentieth century, played the same role for the underdeveloped countries that enlightened absolutism did for some nations in the eighteenth century. His party promoted industry and secularized the state; it was intensely nationalistic and, in the name of national unity and progress, suppressed the labor movement and the minorities. In a concerted action, Lenin and Kemal subdued the Caucasus republics.

Independence movements tend to get radicalized. At first, the Irish fought for autonomy within the British Empire. We have seen how World War I had aborted home rule; then the radical Sinn Fein ("Ourselves Alone," reminiscent of *Italia farà da sè*) went so far as to accept German help. The execution of Sir Roger Casement inflamed nationalist militancy. In 1918, Sinn Fein proclaimed an Irish Free State, elected Eamon de Valera President, and organized the Irish Republican Army (IRA). For three years, its 5,000 militants fought the British Black and Tan police to exhaustion. When the IRA was down to a few hundred men, England agreed to a compromise: an Irish Free State was to be recognized as a self-governing dominion under the British Crown; Ulster (the four northern and predominantly Protestant counties around Belfast) was to have home rule—that is, a parliament and government of its own, with representation in London but without a foreign policy and defense establishment of its own. Sinn Fein refused to accept this solution and continued fighting even against the Free State. Its leader, de Valera, had to wait another nine years, until he became Prime Minister, to lead Ireland out of the British Empire.

The Easter uprising of 1916, though small and inglorious, has become Ireland's national legend. But its historical significance is elsewhere. Its strategy has become the model for many a national revolution in the twentieth century: launched by a tiny minority, which has no chance against the might of the established power but is capable of provoking it into such repressive measures that it eventually antagonizes the entire population, these desperate actions not only have been successful in ultimately achieving their objective, they also have made the point that no society can base its legitimacy on the sole ground that it provides a living for everybody, and no political system can guarantee safety to its citizens if a determined minority refuses to accept it.

CHAPTER 5

The New Order of Europe

"WORLD POLITICS" before 1914 meant the maneuvers of five or six European powers to shift the balance in their favor without upsetting it. As we have seen, this system was so unstable that the very attempt to stabilize it, by means of two alliances, brought on its collapse. After the war, one of these powers, Austria, no longer existed. In its place, new states had arisen: Czechoslovakia, a larger Rumania, and the Kingdom of Serbs, Croats, and Slovenes (later called Yugoslavia). Russia, Germany, and Turkey were, at least for the time being, not capable of exerting much influence; Italy hardly counted; even the two surviving empires, the British and the French, had been greatly weakened. France had been bled white on the battlefield; England's overseas wealth had been drained.

They had won the war only with the help of non-Europeans. United States influence was decisive at the peace conference. South Africa's General Smuts, through adroit maneuvering and substantial aid to England, had earned a place at the table. So had the Canadians and the Australians. India had been promised home rule, and the promise of sovereignty had won Arabian princes over to the Allied side. The former Turkish dependencies were placed under the protection of England and France, but only as "mandates" from the League of Nations and with the proviso that they should be led toward full independence soon. The German colonies were placed under "B" mandate, with no indicated term for self-administration. The mandate system was an indication that the moral climate had changed; the powers no longer dared annex these countries outright.

Colonialism in its old form became untenable in India. The massacre of Amritsar (1919) not only stirred the fighting spirit of the Hindus but the conscience of England as well. As early as 1918, Lord Chelmsford had written to the King: "We have here an educated class 95 per cent of whom hate us." E. M. Forster wrote of the ramifications of this problem in *A Passage to India* (1924). When home rule was denied, Gandhi's campaign of nonviolence put the British Empire to shame; after Beatrice and Sidney Webb, the Fabian apologists for colonialism, came John Strachey, the descendant of a viceroy, who hailed *The End of Empire*. Britain's Government of India Act of 1919 heralded a revolution as world-shaking as the Russian Revolution.

England's relations with her empire underwent a fundamental change. The Imperial

Conference of October 1926 gave the dominions complete equality and sovereignty; the only link between the members of the British Commonwealth of Nations (as it was now called) was allegiance to the Crown and (informally) to the pound sterling. The Statute of Westminster (December 1931) legalized all the changes that had occurred in the dominions' status. The following year, at Ottawa, England even agreed to imperial preferential tariffs, which so far she had refused to accept. The Irish problem was quiescent until Eamon de Valera, elected President in 1932, led his island into a quixotic trade war with England.

While colonial policies continued, notably in black Africa, imperialism no longer was taken for granted. Some colonies were now talking back to their metropolis. The war had freed them from commercial and financial dependence, while England had been unable to export. Moreover, England had to sell many of her overseas assets. The United States had become, from an underdeveloped debtor country, the world's greatest producer and creditor; President Wilson had become the world's moral leader. Largely on his word had the German Reichstag pressed for an armistice. His "Fourteen Points" renounced secret diplomacy, promised the reduction of armaments, prophesied independence to the captive nations; the idea of a League of Nations conjured up a vision of an authority above the sovereign states, which would help them to live under a new international law. Woodrow Wilson did fight at the Peace Conference for his conception of a world parliament or permanent conference which was to guarantee peace and work out a code of conduct. The central instruments proposed for the league were Articles 10 and 16 of its Covenant, which made all nations jointly responsible for each member state's integrity and independence, and obliged them to take joint action against any aggressor. This Covenant was made part of all the peace treaties that ended World War I: Versailles for Germany, Trianon for Hungary, St. Germain for Austria, Neuilly for Bulgaria, Sèvres for Turkey.

Unfortunately, the U.S. Congress repudiated the President's internationalist idealism. It rejected the peace treaties, partly because they were indeed so harsh as to promise more instability rather than stability, but largely because of the obligations which the Covenant would have placed on the United States. The Congress and the American voters were loath to become guarantors of the victory they had paid for so dearly.

Not apparent yet in 1919 was another failing of Wilson's idealism. In promising each nationality its own territory, he ignored the crazy quilt of Europe's ethnic map; or, like other humanitarians, he may have been blind to the injustices inherent in the cause he championed. By giving millions of Germans, Hungarians, Jews, Turks, Russians, and Bulgarians to Poland, France, Yugoslavia, Rumania, Italy, Greece, and Czechoslovakia, he violated his own principle of national self-government. Moreover, the desideratum that states should be ethnically homogeneous clashed with the common-sense rule that a state must be viable as an economic or political unit. The former Hapsburg lands, for example, ought to have organized a Danube Federation around that great trade artery. Instead, they were apportioned among five successor states, none of which could live autonomously. Trieste, a natural port to the

Mediterranean for Austria and Yugoslavia, had been promised to Italy, which had no use for it.

Another incongruity was the status devised for Danzig, an old Hanse city at the mouth of the Vistula. Since the river now became Poland's artery, the port should also have been given to Poland as the gate to that nation's developing trade. Instead, out of respect for both the ethnic principle and Polish security wishes, Danzig was made a free city, cut off from its hinterland, a festering sore that aroused German chauvinism every time its name was mentioned. Poland built its own port of Gdynia opposite Danzig, and to connect it with the landlocked body of Polish territory, a fifty-mile-wide "corridor" had to be driven through German-speaking country, separating East Prussia from the rest of Germany. The Poles made no effort to reconcile the Germans to this inconvenience but turned the corridor into an offensive and humiliating nuisance; Poland also took from Germany part of the coal basin of Upper Silesia and the Polish-speaking province of Poznan; from Austria she took all of Galicia, in the Carpathian mountains, with its ethnically mixed population; Pilsudski, we saw, conquered a large part of Byelorussia and helped himself to Vilna, the old Lithuanian capital. As a result, the Poles came to constitute a minority in their own country—in the name of ethnic justice. Likewise, in doubling her territory, Rumania acquired Ukrainians in Bessarabia and Hungarians, Germans, and Jews in Transylvania. When Greece took southern Macedonia and western Thrace, as we saw, the Moslems had to leave, but the new "Kingdom of Serbs, Croats, and Slovenes" also included Albanian Moslems and Bulgarian-speaking Macedonians. Italy got the strategic Brenner Pass, and with it the Germans of South Tyrol (which it renamed Alto Adige). France took back Alsace-Lorraine, the two provinces which speak German but feel French and which had been separated from France in 1871. Czechoslovakia encompassed the old kingdom of Bohemia-Moravia; but now instead of the Germans, the Czechs were the ruling nation. The more backward Slovaks took second place, but they still looked down on the Magyars and Ruthenians incorporated in the new state. The 3 million Germans in the Sudeten area were to be the dynamite which blew up the state in 1938.

Austria was left a landlocked rump, forbidden to join the German Reich, which was the only alternative to joining a Danube Federation. *Anschluss* (merger with Germany) was the political dream of a majority in both countries; but the statesmen in Prague, Belgrade, and Bucharest were determined to prevent any resurgence of Hapsburg or German power in Central Europe. They formed the Little Entente, under French sponsorship and with French aid. Poland also became a client state of France, for she lived in fear of both German and Russian designs to recoup their lost territories. The Baltic states, too, had to be propped up against the Soviet Union, since the fear of Bolshevism was never far from the minds of the peacemakers in Paris.

The Europe they designed was not a happy family trying to heal the wounds of the war, but a continent split into the vanquished and those who had taken the loot. The League of Nations, as a result, was a victors' club: Germany was not admitted until

1926, and Russia was not invited until 1934. The peace indeed bore the seeds of another war. The post-war economic arrangements in particular must be called unwise even in the light of the knowledge then available. In *The Economic Consequences of the Peace* (1919), John Maynard Keynes quite accurately predicted that Germany would be unable to pay the reparations demanded of her, that the successor states would be dependent on foreign subsidies, and that the dislocations of world trade and finances would lead to overproduction and underconsumption.

The Germans always referred to "Versailles" as the "dictated peace." By the treaty, Germany admitted that she bore sole responsibility for starting the war. To atone for this guilt, she was temporarily deprived of four-fifths of her coal fields, two-thirds of her iron ore, one-tenth of her industries, and obliged to pay an indeterminate amount in reparations. This was fixed in 1920 at $33 billion: $11 billion for damage done to property and $22 billion representing the debts which the Allied governments owed to the United States.

At the time, this was considered a staggering sum. Such a drain on the German economy was supposed to prevent any resurgence of German power. At first, Germany paid in kind, through deliveries of coal, railway stock, machinery, cattle, and other goods. This gave a boost to German industry and made French, Belgian, and English workers idle. Moreover, the Germans got rid of their obsolete equipment, built modern new factories, and outproduced the Allied countries' old-fashioned plants. Reparations turned out to be good business. But when gold payments later were substituted for payments in kind, Germany had to earn dollars through exports; industrial competition therefore grew still sharper.

In 1923, the first post-war boom ended; a slight recession jolted Europe's economy. Chancellor Wilhelm Cuno used this opportunity to announce that Germany was unable to transfer the reparations payments. Against British advice, French Premier Poincaré thereupon marched into the Ruhr basin to seize the mines as "pawns." The German government promptly called on the population for "passive resistance." It paid compensation to striking workers and idle factory owners, printed paper money until the dollar was worth 4 trillion marks, wiped out the savings of the German middle class, and brought the nation to the brink of suicide. Nationalists, monarchists, National-Bolshevik and Communist leaders, German and Red Army officers plotted revolution and counter-revolution as well as a revolutionary war against the West. Lenin's lieutenant Karl Radek made overtures to the German Right, stirring once more the cauldrons of German nationalism, and the Soviet Army (then under Trotsky) appeared to have its own forward policy in Germany. The Rhineland threatened to secede and in Bavaria nationalists of various hues and the army were racing for a chance to overthrow the Republic.

Cuno eventually had to resign; his "resistance" was broken off. The new Chancellor was Gustav Stresemann—once an annexionist but now striving to overcome wartime mentality and to lead Germany back into Europe. Poincaré, who sought to prevent that, did not survive Cuno for long; he, too, had ruined his country's monetary standard. The new Premier in Paris was Édouard Herriot, a Radical who was convinced that a new approach had to be sought. British and American statesmen were working hard to avert the double threat of further revolutions in Central Europe and of Red Army intervention. They offered a new approach to the reparations problem and termination of the Ruhr occupation. At this moment, the German Communists were ordered to form coalition governments with the Socialists in the two states of Saxonia and Thuringia, to prepare for co-operation of the local police with the Red Army, and to strike for revolution on the anniversary of the Russian October. Hitler and Ludendorff also used the confusion to stage their farcical beer-hall putsch in Munich.

Stresemann formed a cabinet of "broad coalition" including Right and Left liberals, the Center, and the SPD. It first dealt with the revolutions: suspended the Constitution, deposed the Socialist-Communist state governments in Saxony and Thuringia, happily quelled the separatist and Nazi putsch in Munich. Then the Socialists were booted out of the coalition; a conservative government was allowed to take the credit for stabilizing the currency and restoring the Constitution (though civil rights still were denied to Communists). But Stresemann stayed on as Foreign Minister.

In 1924, the American general Charles Dawes proposed to lend Germany enough money so that she could pay $600 million in reparations annually. The plan was adopted but soon was found to be unworkable. Another American, Owen Young, in 1929 had the total debt reduced to $20 billion, to be paid in dollars over a period of fifty-eight years. The Young Plan, too, was to be financed by American loans; in addition, German concerns and municipalities borrowed considerable amounts in the United States so that in effect a monetary circuit was established: Germany received loans from the United States and paid reparations to the Allies, who in turn repaid their war loans to the American bankers. The result was that German public debts to Allied governments were transformed into German private debts to American bankers. When the system broke down in the Great Depression and President Hoover had to declare a moratorium on all war debts (1931), Germany had paid $9 billion and borrowed $8 billion; the United States had received $2 billion and was still owed $20 billion. In the end, all debts had to be canceled, since neither principal nor interest could be collected.

But the political consequences were disastrous. In Germany, the names Dawes and Young became symbols of German enslavement by international finance. Both the Communists and the German Right charged that the Versailles Treaty had dishonored and humiliated Germany, that German proletarians—in the sweat of their brows—had to produce the tribute money paid to Wall Street bankers, that international finance had made Germany into a colony. The republican parties adopted this "policy of fulfillment" because they felt that Germany had to work her way back into the family of nations. But in adopting this policy of honor, the German moderates laid the republic open to chauvinistic attacks.

The peace, therefore, was full of conflicts and problems. Some countries were now condemned to defend the *status quo* and others were fighting for its "revision." Among the latter were, of course, Germany, Austria, Turkey, Hungary, and Bulgaria, all of whom had lost territory, but also Italy, who thought she had been cheated, and Soviet Russia, who, apart from losing territory, was excluded altogether from the concert of powers. Again and again, these states tried to form a sort of "losers' club," a rival to the victors' club that the League of Nations was turning into. In all these countries, strong feelings of nationalism came to be identified with rejection of the liberal system and of Western values.

Significantly, the radical Right in these countries saw fit to co-operate with the Soviet Union in frustrating all attempts to build a new European system. The Red Army and the German Army maintained intimate contacts during the Polish war, and in 1922, the Treaty of Rapallo sanctioned a friendship which opened the way for clandestine collaboration: since the Treaty of Versailles barred Germany from building submarines and military aircraft and from producing poison gas and tanks, Russia allowed Germany to build such factories on Russian territory, to train crews, and to consult with Russian officers. But the Germans used Russia only to balance Western power. Stresemann's main effort was directed at the West, and his goal was not to overthrow but to stabilize the international system. By October 1923, the world revolution was over. A new European balance was being sought and built when elections in three countries produced left-of-center majorities during the next twelve months.

Summing up Part III: We have treated the years 1914–24 as a decade of crisis and revolution. The world war itself signified the breakdown of European civilization, and at the same time it produced new forms of social life: comradeship, sacrifice, economic planning, democratic rights for labor, women, youth. The aristocracy lost its pre-eminence. Empires tumbled down, nationalities emerged, new states came into being. The regime of property was deeply affected—first by wartime controls, then by agrarian reform, inflation, the impoverishment of the middle class, and the war veterans' occupational problems.

The new classes also shook up the political party system. Nearly all countries in Eastern and Central Europe underwent revolutions. Only in Russia was a socialist government able to hold out, but at the price of domestic dictatorship and international isolation. In the other countries the revolution was followed by severe repression or even counter-revolutionary and intensely nationalistic, militaristic regimes whose chauvinistic rhetoric threatened international peace.

By 1924, however, serious efforts were being made to liquidate the heritage of the war and to establish a new international order. As we shall see in Parts IV and VI, however, the revolution had only been arrested; none of Europe's problems had been solved. The crisis of European society was continuing even during the brief period of apparent peace and prosperity. If before 1914 Europe had lived in the seeming security of a balanced system of states, there now were nations divided by ideology and experience, classes and minorities that renounced allegiance to the flag, and economic problems defying solution.

If, nevertheless, we call the decade that followed a "Periclean Age," we do so because of its extraordinary fertility in ideas and movements born from this very crisis—as, one should never forget, the original age of Pericles also was a time of great trouble. Europe nearly succumbed to the same fate that overcame Athens twenty-five centuries earlier.

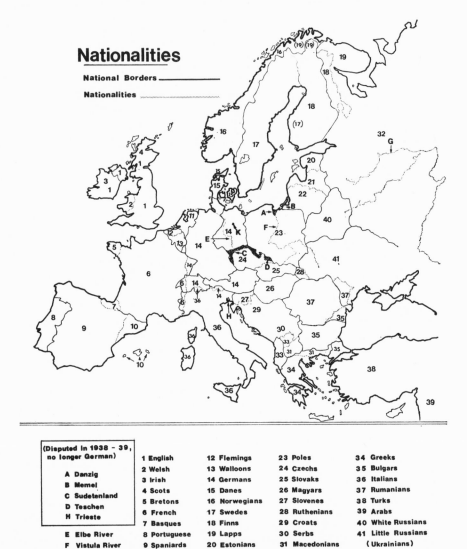

Nationalities

National Borders _____

Nationalities ꞏꞏꞏꞏꞏꞏꞏꞏꞏꞏꞏꞏꞏꞏꞏꞏꞏꞏꞏꞏꞏꞏꞏꞏꞏꞏꞏꞏꞏꞏꞏꞏ

(Disputed in 1938 – 39, no longer German)			
A Danzig	**1** English	**12** Flemings	**23** Poles	**34** Greeks
B Memel	**2** Welsh	**13** Walloons	**24** Czechs	**35** Bulgars
C Sudetenland	**3** Irish	**14** Germans	**25** Slovaks	**36** Italians
D Teschen	**4** Scots	**15** Danes	**26** Magyars	**37** Rumanians
H Trieste	**5** Bretons	**16** Norwegians	**27** Slovenes	**38** Turks
	6 French	**17** Swedes	**28** Ruthenians	**39** Arabs
E Elbe River	**7** Basques	**18** Finns	**29** Croats	**40** White Russians
F Vistula River	**8** Portuguese	**19** Lapps	**30** Serbs	**41** Little Russians
G Volga River	**9** Spaniards	**20** Estonians	**31** Macedonians	(Ukrainians)
K Berlin	**10** Catalans	**21** Letts	**32** Great Russians	
	11 Dutch	**22** Lithuanians	**33** Albanians	

National Borders and Nationalities, 1918

PART IV

The Periclean Age of Europe (1924–33)
1: Politics

CHAPTER I

The Thirty Years' Peace[1]

EUROPE was scrambling out of the crisis. As in ancient Greece, international affairs were part of domestic politics in all Western countries. The Left was for peace and conciliation and against military expenditures and imperialism; the Right was chauvinistic, militaristic, and empire-minded. It also was anti-Russian, at least in propaganda, while the Left kept hoping for a mellowed Communism and was mindful of the large Russian market. Soviet Russia was too weak to challenge the West directly for her defense, so Stalin candidly told the Fifteenth Party Congress (1927) that Russia counted on dissension among Western governments and their fear of Communist revolution. Western moderates held that peace with the Soviet Union, European unity, and social progress were the best insurance against both revolution and reaction. In the minds of conservatives, by contrast, tensions abroad and a strong defense establishment also seemed to be guarantors of the class structure.

By a happy coincidence, the men who had come to power in 1924 were all convinced that the policies of fear had to be discarded, that Europe had to be given a new structure, and that the nightmare of the past ten years must not be repeated. With the Ruhr conflict settled, the currencies stabilized, and the Communist threat checked, the war's legacy was gradually being forgotten; people began to look to the future with more hope than had seemed possible in a long time. Aristide Briand, a former syndicalist and wartime Minister of the Interior, now devoted himself to achieving European reconciliation. Ramsey MacDonald, jailed as a war resister, now headed the first Labour administration. Gustav Stresemann, one-time trustee of the annexionist German Association of Industrialists, now supported a constructive European policy. Édouard Herriot, leader of the French Radicals and a scholar, preached the new gospel of collective security. What changes! What hopes! Would Germans and French be able to forget their centuries-old feud? Stresemann, responding to a British initiative, offered a German pledge to renounce the rhetoric of "revenge" and to abide by the *status quo* if England would guarantee it. MacDonald would have liked to include the Soviet Union in a European security system, but his minority cabinet was overthrown, and the Tories returned to power with a strongly nationalist and anti-Bolshevist platform. Prime Minister Stanley Baldwin and

---

[1] Concluded 446 B.C., broken by Sparta in 431 B.C.

Foreign Secretary Austen Chamberlain hoped to build a European system without the Soviet Union. In October 1925 they met with Stresemann, Briand, and Mussolini at the Swiss resort of Locarno. There they concluded treaties which became the foundation of a new period of peace, and Germany was invited to join the League of Nations. The Franco-German border was to be guaranteed by Great Britain and Italy. This was the closest any treaty ever came to the essence of collective security; the "Spirit of Locarno" was often invoked as a symbol of peace. Moreover, to allay Russian suspicions of encirclement, Germany was exempted from Article 16 of the League of Nations Charter, obliging members to lend assistance to a League war. Stresemann also signed a treaty of friendship and neutrality with Russia before he took Germany's seat on the League's Council, in September 1926.

But Germany did not conclude similar pacts guaranteeing her eastern and southern borders. To secure these, France therefore concluded conventional alliances with Poland and Czechoslovakia; she also built a series of fortifications running from the Swiss to the Belgian border—the Maginot Line.

The era of good feeling thus was hedged in with military pacts. Disarmament conferences droned on and on. The United States, England, Japan, France, and Italy agreed to stabilize the tonnage of their major warships at the ratios of $5:5:3:1.67:1.67$; this stopped the arms race but did not reduce armaments. Russia's Maxim Litvinov proposed total disarmament; Germany, deprived of heavy arms by treaty, demanded equal rights. Other "revisionist" nations (Italy, Turkey, Hungary) also filled the Disarmament Conferences of 1930 and 1932 with their demands for deeds. The French countered with a proposal to create an international police force; for them, the principle of "security" was paramount—and history was to prove them right all too soon. In 1933, Germany resumed her liberty and the Disarmament Conference had to admit failure.

Meanwhile, the American Secretary of State, Frank Kellogg, and Briand appealed to the powers solemnly to renounce war as an instrument of national policy. Virtually all powers signed in Paris on August 27, 1928, though some had reservations. The Soviet Union signed with her neighbors the "Litvinov Protocol" of February 1929, banning war between them. Unmistakably a climate of mutual understanding began to spread through the world—or at least through Europe, for civil war was raging in China, and France was fighting colonial rebels in Syria and Morocco. Chamberlain, Herriot, Briand, and Stresemann established a working relationship almost tantamount to a directorate of Europe. The Allies abandoned their military control of Germany in 1927; the Young Plan of 1929 ended financial control. Allied troops evacuated the Rhineland in 1930.

True, the same Baldwin government that had done so much for peace in the West raided the premises of Russia's trade agency in London and again severed diplomatic relations with Moscow; when MacDonald returned to power, in 1929, he was to resume them.

Although the Russians feared it as an instrument of the *status quo*, the League of Nations was a weak instrument of peace. Under the unanimity rule, neither its

Council nor its Assembly was capable of decisive action. Its authority was limited to the few fields in which a climate of world opinion was stronger than the interest of any particular government. It could deal with problems of health, with the traffic in drugs, slave labor and women, with obscenity, prisoners' rights, and refugee relief. For these and similar purposes its able Secretary General, Sir Eric Drummond, assembled and trained an international civil service which later was to become the nucleus for the much broader operations of the United Nations. But its Commission on Minorities could not remedy the manifold grievances of oppressed nationalities; it could only bring them to public attention, hoping thereby to restrain the oppressive governments. Through its affiliate, the International Labour Office, the League promoted sixty-seven conventions for the protection of workers, women, and children, for fair labor practices and factory conditions, for social security and welfare legislation.

The League's supervision took some of the hardship out of the exchange of a million Greeks and Turks. Polish and Rumanian Jews, White Russians, and Mensheviks who fled to the West received "Nansen passports"—a paper of limited usefulness but, in the light of the horrors to come, of no small account.

But on the great questions of peace-keeping, the League was less effective. The World Court could adjudicate only those disputes that the litigants agreed to bring before it. The Council dealt with forty-three political disputes, of which it was able to settle twelve; another twelve were left unsettled, while nineteen were settled outside the League. In four great cases where Article 15 was invoked against aggression, the League acted with diminishing effectiveness.

When Mussolini occupied Corfu, in 1923, the League helped to bring pressure on him to evacuate the island. When he attacked Ethiopia, in 1934, the League ordered economic sanctions against the aggressor but was unable to prevent his victory. When he invaded Spain, in 1936, the League did nothing. When Japan invaded Manchuria, in 1931, the League condemned the method but recommended the formation of an autonomous state "recognizing Japan's interest." The League also recognized Pilsudski's seizure of Vilna, in 1920.

The question was where to start: to bury quarrels between particular nations first, or to create great instruments of arbitration? French statesmen argued that the powers did not quarrel because minorities were oppressed but that minorities felt oppressed because outside powers encouraged them to fight for autonomy; they also argued that the arms race did not create tension but rather was its result. According to this view, security itself had to be guaranteed before one could think of disarmament. An international police and airtight collective agreements had to precede any specific measures of appeasement. In other words, the League could not do big things because it was unable to agree even on small matters, and it was helpless before small problems because it had not provided for over-all security. Hence one had to look for alternatives to the League.

One such alternative was a confederation of the Continent: a United States of Europe. The idea of Pan-Europe was suggested by Count Coudenhove-Kalergi, a man of multi-national ancestry. His plan excluded the Soviet Union and the United

Kingdom, the one because its economic system could not be integrated into capitalistic Europe, the other because its imperial obligations would not permit it to adjust to a common tariff, a common farm policy, and so forth. All the other nations of Continental Europe were to be united first by arbitration treaties, which eventually would lead to a permanent alliance and a customs union; realistically, each nation was to retain its sovereignty and constitution within the federation.

In 1930, Briand, following up on an idea of Herriot, tried to give this vision a diplomatic body. An informal "memorandum" invited the powers to establish a "European conference" with a permanent secretariat and executive organs. The proposal was lame and legalistic. If Europe was ever to live, it had to have a flag before it had an army. Europe never was a geographic entity. It was an idea: Christianity, the Occident, Humanism, Progress, Freedom.

Ever since the French Revolution "Europe" had been the ideal of democrats and liberals, a weapon against nationalism and militarism. Before World War I, the educator Friedrich Wilhelm Foerster, the painter Franz Marc, the writer Romain Rolland, and others published the magazine *Neues Europa*. Its editor was A. H. Fried, president of the German Peace League. During the war they considered themselves "underground Europe" and remained in touch with such like-minded spirits as Stefan Zweig, Franz Pfempfert, Frans Masereel, Henri Barbusse, and Bertrand Russell. After the war, the International League for the Rights of Man, the Socialist International, and the Freemasons gave warm support to Briand's policies.

The Social Democrats of all countries were the most devoted spokesmen for European reconciliation; they supported all initiatives to reduce tensions and to increase confidence. For that they were often ridiculed as dreamers or vilified as lackeys of cosmopolitan Jewry and as traitors to the fatherland. The Communists, on the other hand, fearing a united, potentially anti-Bolshevist Europe, denounced the socialists as "social imperialists."

But few socialists and radicals were prepared to give the League teeth. When the case arose, they voted for sanctions only with great reluctance; in Left labor circles the suspicion never died that the League was a victors' club or, in Sir Stafford Cripps's words, "an international burglars' union." Pacifists in all countries denounced warlike capitalists, anti-Soviet interventionists, and, in particular, the "merchants of death," the unholy alliance between munitions-makers, the military, and governments. These attitudes, and concern for the defense needs of the Soviet Union, prevented the radical Left from developing a positive theory of collective security; later, they prevented Western governments from arming against fascist aggression.

The idea of transnational solidarity, expressed in novels and movies too, had become so attractive that even the chauvinists of all countries tended to unite. Fascists in the 1930's developed a strong esteem for each other; party lines crossed border lines, with a fascist international opposing an anti-fascist peoples' front. Ideologists like Ernst Jünger and Henry de Montherlant even spoke of "the comradeship of the trenches" and appealed to the "combat soldiers of the war" on both sides.

The chauvinistic undercurrents, which remained strong throughout the period, were to grow predominant during the Depression. The new national states, founded on intense hatred of their former masters, sought remedy in protectionism or in projecting hostility and anxiety *vis-à-vis* their neighbors, or they would stir bitter rivalry between ethnic groups. Whenever calamity befell a country, either the government or the opposition found it expedient to blame it on foreigners: to "export the domestic worries."

The new trend toward nationalism is poignantly illustrated also by the sudden rise of Zionism precisely in those central and southeastern European countries whose new republican structures were opening great new opportunities to the Jewish intelligentsia. Even though their interest in the Jewish religion was waning, young Jews in growing numbers started rejecting "assimilation," and prepared themselves to go home to the land of their ancestors.

Historically, nationalism grew in a democratic climate; but in the twentieth century it was promoted by protectionist interests, especially agrarian and big industry, whereas the banking and trading interests as well as the workers (that is, the liberal-labor coalition) were free-traders and internationalists.

CHAPTER 2

The New Social Structure

THE revolutions in Central Europe did not touch the regime of property as such; nevertheless, they shook the old class structure profoundly. The First Estate no longer was considered privileged by birth. It no longer owned a state's administrative and military machinery. The state itself no longer was sacred. As landowners, the gentry were to be no more than one among several economic classes seeking to promote their interests. Some of the new states even expropriated land. In Czechoslovakia 4.5 million acres of land were distributed; in Rumania, 17 million, but none in Poland (except in Poznan, where Poles supplanted Germans).

The East European gentry had been bled in the war. Now they suffered from the general decline of agriculture as an industry, but they could still use their former prestige to commercial advantage. Though the German Constitution abolished all titles of nobility, a particule "von" or a military rank still was a social asset. A certain Harry Domela, who resembled the Kaiser's grandson, was able to milk "society" for years before being unmasked. A referendum to expropriate the princes who had ruled the twenty-five German states before 1918 failed in 1926.

In France, where the aristocracy no longer had any power, it still commanded respect. Its way of life and values were still admired. In Italy, Fascism degraded the political status of the southern landowners but left their economic and social power intact. In Spain, the aristocracy retained both its economic and its political power. The British Parliament of 1911 had deprived the Lords of their absolute veto; an Act of 1923 required the Prime Minister to have a seat in the House of Commons. In the public services, the old squirarchy was being supplanted by career men whose title to office was education rather than birth. In republican Germany and the Hapsburg successor states, the virtues and vices of the service nobility were passed on to the middle-class state employees. Kafka's novels owe their popularity in no small part to their truthful reflection of the nightmarish experience of bureaucracy. Sociologists began to study the danger of the "termite state."

Meritocracy, technocracy, bureaucracy, and plutocracy ruled in France. Ninety per cent of the Conseillers d'État and other high functionaries came from the École des Sciences Politiques; they usually married into wealthy families or were rewarded, after retirement, by directorates in banking and industry. The army officers came from the École Polytechnique, politicians often from the École Normale Supérieure (a teachers' college), or from the law schools. The lower civil servants, having the right to organize, forced the government to accept the merit system as the basis for promotion. While this led to excesses of the bureaucratic mentality (a satirical film, *Ces Messieurs les Ronds-de-Cuir*, was popular in the 1930's), it assured France of a stable civil service in the midst of her merry-go-round cabinet changes.

In almost all countries, political leadership now passed to people trained in law schools or holding advanced degrees. New men of power rose also from the ranks of business and labor: Walter Rathenau in Germany, Louis Loucheur in France, Stanley Baldwin in England were industrialists turned statesmen. Representatives of industrial associations easily found their way into politics. Such was the background of the liberal Gustav Stresemann and the conservative Alfred Hugenberg in Germany. In France, René Meyer, André François-Poncet, and more recently Georges Pompidou may be mentioned as examples of men who came to politics through their industrial and banking connections.

For the first time labor leaders achieved social recognition. It is true that among them we now find, next to those who rose from the ranks, intellectuals and other defectors from the ruling class. Émile Vandervelde, Walter Citrine, Stafford Cripps, John Strachey, Rudolf Hilferding, Otto Bauer, Léon Blum, Alvarez del Vayo, and Hendrik de Man were intellectuals. On the other hand, those with a working-class background, such as Arthur Henderson, Friedrich Ebert, Indalecio Prieto, Léon Jouhaux, often rose to a conception of statesmanship that transcended their social and political origin. Some simply adapted themselves when their party rose to power; others defected from the ranks of labor to join the establishment, like Ramsay MacDonald, Philip Snowden, Pierre Laval, Aristide Briand, August Winnig, and Gustav Noske, the self-styled "bloodhound" who restored power to the officers in the republic. A broad stratum of political and administrative functionaries thus was being added to the ruling class; socially they rank with professional men, industrialists, and financiers, well above the old middle class.

War and inflation also had eroded the morality of the industrial and commercial classes. The very notion of property, so central to middle-class values, withered along with currency values. Young men saw that quick, speculative profits created new fortunes while honest tradesmen lost theirs. The prescriptions of Polonius no longer held as a rule to live by. The thrifty saw their life savings melt away, while the borrowers got rid of their debts easily. Speculators, manipulators, con men, or people who simply had taken advantage of the emergency situation now were invading the fashionable spas, occupying the gambling tables in once aristocratic casinos, buying furs and jewels for their wives and mistresses, and behaving as though European opinion had never distinguished between self-made money and inherited wealth. Since many of the "new men" were foreigners or Jews, anti-Semitism grew among the traditional classes in many countries.

Finally, the fall of the monarchies and the decline of the aristocracy robbed the middle classes of an element that had underpinned their own status. A middle-class society can exist only as long as it is in fact in the middle. Only as long as they recognized their betters could they expect deference from their inferiors. Now inferior people claimed that everybody was equal, and some even rose to leading positions. New forms of wealth were being created and were widening the gap between big and small enterprise; people with neither education nor pedigree suddenly became "directors" and "councillors" in title-minded societies. Old property was being challenged by new enterprise, a status elite by a functional elite. The *nouveau riche* was despised and ridiculed by the educated as the bourgeois had been at the court of Louis XIV. A Berlin magazine gave a prize for the best suggestion as to what "Raffke" (a mythical member of the *nouveau riche*) says in front of the Rome Coliseum: "Don't build if you don't have the money."

In Eastern Europe a new bourgeoisie developed as natives began to replace the Germans and Jews who had monopolized the professions and commerce before World War I. They were joined by the younger sons of peasants whom the homestead no longer held. This new middle class was weak, opportunistic, and corrupt. It never imitated the civic virtues that in Western and Central Europe had made the middle class the backbone of the modern state. Nor did most civil servants in the newly rising countries make up in honesty and zeal for what they lacked in education.

Even Western Europe witnessed some fantastic careers: Hugo Stinnes, the German industrialist who amassed steel mills, shipping companies, movie studios, newspapers, and other enterprises and who died broke; Ivar Kreuger, the Swede who built an empire on his match monopoly and who ultimately shot himself, buried under a mound of forged bonds; Sir Basil Zaharoff, of indeterminate nationality, who supplied arms to any government and any insurgent force. Yet despite such "new men," on the whole the banks, the big industrial and commercial concerns were in the hands of the great European families who had owned them before the war—the Krupps, the Neuflizes, the Lazars, the Rothschilds, the Schneiders, and others. The wealth of these families was still increasing. While, in manners and law, society was becoming more democratic, economically speaking the top 5 per cent were as remote as ever from the rest of the population. In England, one-tenth of 1 per cent owned one-third of all assets, and 1 per cent owned another third.

One category of "person," the corporations, had only recently been acknowledged as responsible before the law. More and more, the owners of a concern came to be removed from actual influence; the real powers of decision were concentrated in the hands of managers, who had no significant personal means but who commanded great authority in the name of "the company" or even "the economy." Some of these managers held directorships in a dozen different companies. They had, and still have, command of millions of pounds, marks, francs, and florins that were never theirs, and they act on behalf of hundreds of thousands of employees as though they were trustees of communal institutions.

It was natural that this new power should first emerge in the new industries—electrical engineering, chemistry, and also in the new commercial banks which financed big industrial mergers or bold colonial ventures. It also dominated the entertainment industries. Walter Rathenau coined the phrase, often quoted by anti-Semitic agitators, that the world was ruled by four hundred people who knew each other and had to agree with each other to make it run smoothly. This small group of people have been identified with the two hundred shareholders of the Banque de France or its forty directors, with the directors of the four big banks in England and the four big "D-banks" in Germany. Other men who became influential in this period as presidents or chairmen of corporations were Sir Alfred Mond (first Baron Melchett, of Imperial Chemical), known as the promoter of "Mondism," the method of settling industrial conflicts through direct contacts; Hermann and Dietrich Schmitz (I. G. Farben); Carl Duisberg (Deutsche Metallgesellschaft); Alfred Hugenberg (Raiffeisen-Genossenschaften); Arthur Silberberg (potassium); Achille Fournier, who joined the Schneider family as the children's tutor and became director of the Le Creusot mills; Giovanni Agnelli of Fiat.

As Hobson and Hilferding had emphasized, the pre-war economy had been dominated by "finance capital." In the 1920's, the banks still commanded political influence, but inflation had freed industry from their tutelage. Many concerns were able to finance their expansion out of profits, and their cartels protected them from price fluctuations and competition. In 1923, there were 1,500 cartels in Germany; in 1931, 2,500. Britain's Imperial Chemical, Germany's I. G. Farben, and France's Kuhlmann group collaborated in the European Dyestuff Cartel, which in turn was connected with DuPont in the United States. In England, the Unilever concern enjoyed an unobtrusive monopoly.

Small businessmen might remain independent producers but they lost power to the corporations; many who technically were still counted as employers became in fact appendages of the corporate economy as subcontractors or franchise carriers. For those who lost out in the competition, new opportunities were opened in the expanding service industries and in semi-professional or professional occupations. The social services, advertising, sales promotion, travel, and recreation employed numerous people with education and connections but without capital or skill. These were referred to as the "new middle class," though many of them came from the old middle class. The middle ranks of civil service and of management, too, considered themselves "middle class" and tended to vote conservative, except in France, where historic reminiscences, anti-clerical sentiments, and civil service unions kept them Radical.

A new dimension of the salariat appeared when office work expanded in government and business. Young middle-class women who formerly would have stayed home until marriage now found employment in the growing administrative and sales staffs and there mingled with the daughters of workers for whom office work meant social advancement. Although poorly paid, they became pioneers of the consumer mentality and would not be confused with the working class. Salaried employees now accounted for an increasing proportion of the total labor force, while in the most industrialized countries the percentage of production workers was stagnant at best.

The most promising opportunities for working-class sons were to be found in the lower civil service, which raised their social status and job security. But, of course, individual mobility was limited. Only 6 per cent of the higher civil servants in England had working-class parents. So did 25 per cent of the salaried employees in private business.

The first sociological essay on the salariat was written by Siegfried Kracauer in 1930. The status symbols of the new middle class are the monthly salary, the paid vacation, the business suit, the job description specifying contacts with people rather than with goods, and the different style of life. Although a white-collar employee may earn no more than a worker, he spends more on dress and home, less on eating, drinking, and entertainment; he sends his son to high school, and his general outlook on life and society is conservative. He struggles against being pushed down into the proletariat. Though in some countries unions are available for salaried employees, they reject the class concept and their politics are conservative.

While all these shifts brought rising expectations and new opportunities for talented individuals, "self-made" men were rarer in Europe than in America. As a matter of fact, social mobility was less a new development than a new article of faith. The upper classes accepted, nay recommended, it as an alternative to revolution. The German socialists, forgetting their class program, launched a program of educational reform under the slogan: "Gangway for the talented!" "Equal opportunity" was understood to mean the replenishment of the upper classes by co-optation; in no European country, even today, does it mean de facto equal education for all. In France a rigorous system of examinations allowed, and still does, talented students to obtain scholarships—but, in practice, many a worker cannot afford to keep his son in school for extended periods.

The traditional two-track system of German education now was slightly amended. Lower-class children still went to grade school until the age of fourteen, but now their transfer to secondary schools was facilitated, and in some grade schools "extension classes" prepared talented pupils for university. But higher education was open to only a small contingent of workers' children.

In England the poor went to elementary school until the age of fourteen, the middle class to grammar school or dame school until sixteen or seventeen, the upper class to "public schools" until eighteen. But in 1918, H. A. L. Fisher, as president of the Board of Education, instituted in each district secondary schools to which children might transfer at the age of eleven, and technical schools which they could enter at fourteen. Scholarships permitted the talented to attend schools whose curriculum was no different from that of the coveted "public schools." These, however, continued to model themselves after Plato's Republic, teaching comradeship, self-discipline, cleanliness, sports, and homoeroticism. The universities of Oxford, Cambridge, and Dublin still were considered in a class by themselves; but the "red-brick universities" in the provinces began to acquire better teachers and in turn assured the secondary schools of higher standards.

Every country had some experimental schools, usually very expensive. But too many elementary school teachers still relied on the rod; English grammar schools banned it only in 1971. But the curriculum grew a little more modern in the 1920's. Textbooks became somewhat freer, exams less rigid, and discipline more relaxed. In many classrooms history ceased to be a dry recapitulation of dates, kings, and battles; civics classes allowed for some discussion. Though never "progressive" in the American (Deweyan) sense, European schools began to make concessions to life. The 1920's were an age of psychology and of attempts to "understand"—hence sometimes of permissiveness in education. New types of schools substituted science and modern languages for Greek and Latin. Nevertheless, the old French *lycée* and German *Gymnasium* still carried prestige; their students still had a better chance of becoming great scholars or high-ranking civil servants.

A. S. Neill founded Summerhill, Paul Geheeb the Odenwaldschule, Gustav Wyneken the Schulgemeinde Wickersdorf, Bertrand and Dora Russell their free school—all model establishments for liberal education where the development of character, free expression, and independent judgment took precedence over book learning and discipline. These extremely progressive schools, however, recruited their students from the new liberal meritocracy and, for all their prestige, were elite schools and contributed little to democratic education.

A great new venture was the nursery school. Society seemed to take the education of young children away from uneducated mothers. Day care centers and kindergartens were opened for the children of the poor, relieving working mothers of some home duties and giving their children more opportunities to develop their potential. The Montessori method became popular. Psychoanalysts, anthroposophers, and others vied to test their systems on young children. A stirring movie, *La Maternelle*, called for a more personal relationship between teacher and child.

On the Continent, all universities now were open to women. Female students were admitted to Oxford in 1919. As a class, women undoubtedly gained greater freedom and equality than any other class. They now mixed freely with men, danced with abandon. Girls could invite guests into the house without parental permission, attend parties without chaperones, and even smoke—though not yet in public. Women proclaimed their new freedom in short dresses and bobbed hair. Fashion itself went democratic. The invention of synthetic fibers, particularly rayon, and of new dyes helped to spread new fashions among all strata of the population. Ready-to-wear manufacturers began to copy the styles of famous Paris designers; and the fashion industry learned to adapt the new styles to a growing market.

The flapper, boyish in appearance, a little forward in manner, and independent in work, became the fashion ideal. Unfortunately, peace took women's jobs away and war had decimated the ranks of prospective husbands. Trade unions strongly resisted equal employment. Women therefore strove to enter the professions, art, and politics. The Sex Disqualification Removal Act (1919) in Britain prohibited discrimination in many professions. But in factories and offices women still received, on the average, one-third less pay for equal work; in executive positions, in politics, and the ministry they remain grossly under-represented to this day.

In the home, meanwhile, technology was producing another revolution. Gas ranges, central heating, electric light, hot water, and in the later 1920's, electric appliances, liberated housewives from many chores. Furniture, too, became simpler and maintenance easier. Households grew smaller. Butlers, governesses, and sometimes even maids were dispensed with. More married women took salaried jobs, though not as many as in the United States; their place no longer was exclusively in the kitchen. Early marriages and the growing availability of birth control methods changed the structure of the family, de-emphasizing its patriarchal character.[1] All this affected the old authoritarian, paternalistic practices in politics and economics as well.

Social pressures toward equality were further strengthened by the new technology in consumer goods. Many articles that had been luxuries now became accessible to the lower classes. Although the automobile was to remain a status symbol for two more decades, in the long run, technological progress proved to be an enemy of class barriers. Radio, for example, never had been restricted to an elite. Standardized production methods and mass-distribution industries also helped to equalize life styles. Although Europe never went in for modern merchandising to the extent of America, her industry, too, adopted the new philosophy that demand must not merely be satisfied but created. From cigarettes and lipsticks to soap powders and mechanical toys, products were urged on the people; the mass market fostered a measure of uniformity of tastes and habits.

In 1930, José Ortega y Gasset described "mass man" as a "spoilt child," uninhibited in the expansion of his desires, ungrateful to the past, irresponsible to the future, drifting in the winds of any current fashion. Ortega's fear of socialism and of workers blinded him to the benefits of mass culture: upgrading of the common man, equalizing of opportunity, broadening of the cultural community. He saw the "revolt of the masses" only in terms of Roman paupers who wanted a free ride and were forever eager to overthrow established government and to hail new Caesars. Some of his political observations were more relevant to the condition of Europe. The politicians were catering to a mass market, or trying to manipulate it. Advertising, whether political or commercial, appealed to the most vulgar taste. In the past, fads and fashions had been cultivated by a limited public; now they were taken up by vast numbers who found self-confirmation in the fact of their size.

Ortega formulated a sort of Gresham's law for civilization: Undeserving people demand equal rights. "The mean souls know that they are mediocre, but they are impertinent enough to proclaim the rights of meanness. . . . The masses want to destroy everything that is distinguished, talented, noble. He who is not like them and does not think like everybody else is threatened with extinction. Once a nation was subtly put together with elites and mass, today there is only mass."

Similarly, Martin Heidegger's elitist and esoteric philosophy, published in 1927, spoke with contempt of "everyman" and common sense. Alexis de Tocqueville, who had denounced this threat to Western civilization a hundred years earlier, now

---

[1] On the other hand, younger mothers meant an increase in the birth rate, whose previous decline had worried nationalist politicians.

achieved a new popularity among the elites. Likewise, Hendrik de Man and other proto-fascists deplored "mass culture."

The passage of forty years has shown us that Ortega was wrong. The masses have not destroyed high culture but rather have appropriated it. His strictures against liberalism, democracy, and socialism, consumer culture, and mass society, were unfair at the time they were published. Before mass unemployment reduced them to paupers, workers in the modern industrial states were trying hard to be everything Ortega said they were not: articulate rather than amorphous, autonomous rather than Caesarian, rising to a place in society rather than living off its charity.

Organized labor never aspired to become part of the middle class but thought of itself, its relatives, neighbors, and sympathizers, as "the people." Its spokesmen addressed it as the class whose interests coincided with every man's striving for equal rights and economic security. In most states it was the largest, though by no means the most powerful, pressure group. Wherever its representatives were in government, they increased public services, built houses, sought wider state powers to regulate the distribution of income, enlarged public enterprises, increased welfare payments. But nowhere did labor in the 1920's develop economic policies designed to avert a depression or to plan for the future. It largely confined itself to "welfare politics" which would protect and, if possible, extend the workers' share in the national product. For the first time people realized that the wage level was a political issue. Rudolf Hilferding, at the German Socialist Party congress in Heidelberg, 1925, coined the term "political wage."

During the revolutionary period the workers had won the right to elect shop stewards; the trade unions were made agents of collective bargaining; grievance procedures were established; wages rose considerably above the pre-war level, especially for unskilled workers; in most Western countries the eight-hour day and five-and-a-half-day week became either rule or law. The International Labor Office in Geneva exerted pressure on all governments to limit the employers' arbitrary power, protect the rights of individual workers and of their unions, extend social security and welfare measures. Despite serious reverses in some countries and lags in others, despite severe setbacks in actual wage income during the Depression, the working class as a whole was improving its material condition and its status in the social and political structure of most European countries.

This general observation, however, is subject to three grave qualifications. Since the European economy was undergoing a structural crisis, the prosperity of workers in new industries was offset by unemployment in some old industries. Moreover, new labor-saving techniques checked the further growth of the industrial labor force, while the farm crisis drove peasants to seek employment in the cities. When the Depression came, both peasants and workers were hard hit, and competition for the fewer jobs was intense. Thirdly, fascist and conservative governments tried to make their national industries competitive by deliberately depressing the wage levels.

European farming was on the decline. During the war the peasants had prospered. Inflation had permitted them to pay off their debts. But then low-cost producers overseas began to pour their grain and meat into the European markets; the dreaded "scissors"—rising prices for goods the peasant buys, falling prices for what he produces—cut the lifeline of those who could not modernize. For a farm to be profitable, both its size and its operating capital had to increase.

Only in the most advanced countries, like Denmark and the Netherlands, did the peasants respond resolutely and effectively to their dilemma, abandoning traditional methods and turning themselves into modern capitalistic farmers. They also adapted their operation to special markets: truck gardening, converting imported grains into dairy products, meat, and eggs, standardizing their products and co-ordinating their output with the demands of processing and packaging plants. In the Scandinavian countries these problems were solved with the help of co-operatives and under the guidance of Social Democratic governments. In Italy the Fascist government sponsored the packaging of tomatoes and citrus fruits. But the French and German winegrowers, truck, and dairy farmers never organized. Unable to raise capital or to change their tradition-bound ways, they frequently burst out in senseless revolts against tax collectors, warehouses, and land-registry offices.

In most countries the peasants had been considered a bulwark of conservatism. They obeyed the lord of the manor and the priest as though the Hussite and Peasant wars had never been fought; their enemies were middlemen, usurers, liberals, free-traders, innovators, Jews. In northern France they had been anti-Dreyfusards; in Germany they looked back to the good old days of the Kaiser. Even where they prospered, they resented the unrest the cultural revolution brought into their lives. Their ideologists castigated the rootlessness, elegance, and education of urbanites.

Further east, landlessness and backwardness were the problems of the rural masses. In a small country like Hungary, 2 million farm laborers owned not a square foot; another million were "dwarf holders" whose main income was from wages. In Rumania, where (apart from Russia) agrarian reform had gone farthest, 75 per cent of the farm population did not produce enough for their own consumption. The yield of their land was half the West European average, and they lacked the capital to improve it.

Land reform was based mostly on political and nationalist factors, to a certain extent on social factors, but not at all on economic reasoning. It was designed to stave off Bolshevism, to break the power of the squirarchy, to improve the ethnic balance, to get a clamorous opposition off the street; but it failed to establish the prosperous communities of medium-sized farms which conservatives consider the backbone of a modern state. Before 1945, only a quarter to a third of all farms in East European states were over fifteen acres—barely affording a subsistence. The 1.7 million Rumanian ten-acre settlers soon found that without cattle and implements they could not live on their small plots. The National Peasant Party under Julius Maniu, which in 1927 obtained 75 per cent of the vote, disappointed the rural poor. Anxious to attract foreign capital and to promote the consolidation of farms, Maniu allowed the settlers to sell their plots, which the previous liberal administration had forbidden. By 1940, the magnates and usurers had repossessed a third of the land.

In Croatia, where the peasants felt exploited by the Serbs, the peasant leader Stephen Radich led a fierce movement but had no program. At one point he even went to Moscow for the inaugural ceremony of a proposed Peasant International. He was assassinated in 1928 before agrarian reform had gotten under way.

In three eastern countries where large estates predominated, the magnates resisted modernization and instead demanded subsidies and tariffs. Their prestige in the villages and political pull in the conservative parties allowed them to speak in the name of "agriculture" or "the peasants." But the social policies designed to "keep the peasant on the soil" benefited the big estates and ruined the small farms. They actually depopulated the countryside and drove the uprooted away from the land, thus defeating the social philosophy of conservatism.

Lack of capital and ignorance of the market economy deprived the peasants of their share in the short-lived prosperity. From the mid-1920's on, agricultural prices began to decline while interest rates and taxes remained high. Big estates and small farmers were united in asking for protective tariffs, subsidies, the cancellation of debts, the extirpation of usurers. Nationalist agitation gave voice to their resentment of domination by the city, by the liberal state, by Jewish middlemen. Neither liberals nor Marxists offered programs that made sense to the peasants. When ownership of land no longer provided security, the liberal state met with crisis in Central and Eastern Europe, but not in the northern and western countries, where the Left showed the farmers a way to efficiency and new markets.

CHAPTER 3

Experiments in Democracy

NOT even in Periclean Athens were the masses as involved in politics as in the European democracies of the 1920's. Party membership ran into the hundreds of thousands or, in the case of labor, even millions; meetings drew huge crowds; arguments were heated; the turnout in national and local elections was high; many issues that had not been political before were now politicized.

An important new development occurred in the mode of representation. In republican theory so far the state was composed of individuals who had concluded a social contract. As a result of the post-war revolutions, the contract was to assure equal rights to all. Under the rule of formal democracy, however, the poor were far from equal. "The law in its majestic equality," said Anatole France, "forbids the rich as well as the poor to sleep under bridges, to beg in the streets, and to steal bread." Hence, rights now were given also to associations that represented the citizen in his economic, ethnic, and philosophic concerns. Ever so grudgingly, the former ruling classes had to accept these deputies as partners in government. In "pluralistic" democracies different parties represent distinct interest groups and more or less frequently exchange government benches for opposition seats, and vice versa.

Parliaments and constitutions were the ultimate sources of pluralistic rights. Revolutionary parties might advocate a different "system," but they, too, learned to use the parliamentary order as a suitable framework for political action and in fact collaborated to make this system workable. Their rhetoric formed a strident contrast to their conduct, and even their extra-parliamentary actions, such as mass meetings and protest marches under police supervision, merely provided organized outlets for frustrated indignation. Only their ideologies were apocalyptic, and they expressed the resentment of the unrepresented.

The parties representing pressure groups can be aligned on an ideological scale from Left to Right. The socialists, allied to labor unions, represented the workers. The liberals represented the upper middle class. In some countries, the Catholic or Christian Social Party was strong among the petty bourgeoisie and the peasants. In others, these classes followed the Peasant Party or the agrarians. The conservatives, who represented big industry and finance, big landowners, and pensioners, also had a following among church-going peasants and salaried employees. The percentages varied, however, from country to country.

Both in government and as opposition, the Social Democratic (labor) parties had become reformist and parliamentary, working for the improvement of the system, not against it. In the poorer areas they still preached the Marxist ideology of class war, and their youth groups also cultivated revolutionary theory. But they proved themselves in municipal administration and reform, in progressive approaches to education, health, welfare, and culture. They tried to widen the public sector of the economy, especially in public utilities and transportation.

In Germany and in the Scandinavian countries, Social Democrats were frequently part of the government; in England they twice won a plurality. Their showpiece was the city of Vienna with its public housing, its welfare institutions, its child care, its schools and cultural activities. In 1920, Hjalmar Branting opened a five-year reign of socialist reform government in Sweden. Denmark followed under Thorvald Stauning in 1924. Dutch and Scandinavian farmers shed the old peasant traditionalism and adopted a resolute program of modernization in coalition with either socialists or others. Thomas Masaryk and Eduard Beneš, as leaders of a reformist peasant party in Czechoslovakia, tried to make farms large enough and farm work efficient enough to sustain the peasant population.

In the Balkans, modern farm policies were hamstrung by domestic and foreign bankers, in Germany by the *Junkers*'s political influence. The impoverished small peasants often turned their wrath against usurers, tax collectors, the city. A know-nothing, populist movement in a rural area is described by Hans Fallada in *Peasants, Bosses, and Bombs* (1930), a complement to his world-wide success, *Little Man, What Now?* (1932). Both describe the frustrations that led to the Nazi tide and similar movements in other countries.

In Catholic countries Christian-Social parties appealed to the peasants and the small bourgeoisie with slogans that were both anti-capitalist and anti-socialist. In France, the Church tended so far to the Right as to be identical with the conservatives. In Austria, the Christian-Social Party looked back to the good old Hapsburg days; it was led by an able, ruthless prelate, Dr. Ignaz Seipel. In Italy, Pope Pius XI helped Fascism by repudiating the courageous priest, Don Luigi Sturzo, and his Popolari, who might have stopped its advance.

The German Roman Catholics were represented by the Center Party, which during the monarchy had been in opposition and became the backbone of all republican governments until 1932. But the leaders of its democratic and labor wing soon were displaced by conservatives; only in the state of Prussia did it continue its coalition with the socialists and liberals. On the federal level it participated in right-wing coalitions, and its Bavarian sister party, strongly entrenched in farm areas, was frankly monarchist.

In 1931, on the fortieth anniversary of the encyclical *Rerum Novarum* and in the depth of the Great Depression, Pope Pius XI published his own encyclical, *Quadragesimo Anno* (*In the Fortieth Year*), which brought the social teachings of the Roman Catholic Church up to date. He admitted that many socialists came close to Christian views and that the prevailing distribution of wealth was unjust. He reaffirmed the right of workers to organize and to have a share in management, but his solution was "corporatism," the peaceful co-operation of management and labor in industrywide syndicates. To contrast them with Mussolini's corporations, the Pope pointedly called for "free corporations." He came out for state ownership of large enterprises, but on the whole preferred small business.

A wide range on the Left-Right spectrum was covered by parties sailing under the labels of liberalism. Herbert Asquith was an old-style liberal, David Lloyd George a social liberal or radical. In France the two wings of the Radical Party were led by Édouard Daladier and Édouard Herriot, respectively. In Germany, Stresemann headed the right-wing "People's Party," Friedrich Naumann and Hugo Preuss, the father of the Weimar Constitution, staked vain hopes on the "Democratic Party." The liberals everywhere were still the party of free trade, of the old middle class, of free-thinkers and dissenters, of professors and writers; but in most countries their days were numbered. Liberal speakers seemed to exude that quaint nineteenth-century air of rhetorical idealism which Thomas Mann captured so well in his portrayal of Settembrini in *The Magic Mountain*. As an economic philosophy liberalism was dead. John Maynard Keynes proclaimed the end of *laissez faire*. "There is no compact conferring perpetual rights on those who have," he wrote. "The world is not so governed that private and social interests always coincide."

As a political and cultural philosophy, however, liberalism outlived its economic theories. Especially in France, the Parti Radical continued to consider itself the heir to the ideals of the Great Revolution. Though rather conservative in economic matters, it retained its hold on the hearts which, as the saying went, beat on the Left while the wallet was carried on the Right. Heavily seeded with Freemasons, and part of nearly every cabinet, it remained the largest party in France. But in England and Germany the liberals declined rapidly during the early 1920's. In Spain and Italy they had destroyed themselves by misrule.

Parties on the Right, variously calling themselves conservative, moderate, Christian, or republican, appealed to traditionalism and nationalism. They also had considerable following among women and, during the 1920's when the Left seemed "old," among young voters who resented the state's subservience to business interests. They professed an idealistic philosophy and reprimanded the workers for, as François-Poncet, himself a lobbyist for the Schneider-Creusot interests, put it, the "sordid materialism of their demands." Monarchical and dictatorial regimes seemed to them more virtuous, while republics were ridden by scandals. Democracy, they felt, was essentially corrupt; its "system" ineluctably brought to the fore the worst elements, often foreigners and Jews.

As ill luck would have it, the wife of Berlin's democratic Mayor Böss had received from a Jewish contractor a mink coat, which the Right portrayed as a national disgrace. A few years later the municipal pawnship of Bayonne, in southern France, was milked by an immigrant from Odessa, Alexandre Stavisky; attempts to hush up the embarrassing affair involved high-placed republican politicians.

Traditionalists seem to feel that scandals have more philosophical significance than the bread-and-butter issues of pluralistic politics. Their own economic interests are usually dressed up in high-sounding patriotic principles or in abstractions like "the economy" (meaning big business) or "sound money" (meaning high interest rates). These principles are invariably those of the French Comité des Forges, the British National Industrial Council, the German Industry League. The farm lobby and similar influential bodies, too, are linked with these parties through personal and financial ties. Strangely, half the English farm laborers also tend to vote conservative. For Toryism projects the image of hierarchy in which each finds his niche, or of a master whom the lowly can trust.

In times of crisis, the image is reversed, the master is a devil, respect turns into hate. Unable to understand social forces and unwilling to be disillusioned, the little man suspects foul play—a sinister plot by foreigners, Wall Street, the Freemasons, the Elders of Zion, or the Pope. At this point the Right loses its most active followers to the extreme Right, which is militantly anti-democratic, anti-Semitic, and anti-capitalist, and may even become revolutionary and pseudo-socialist.

On the far Left, the Communists claimed to be Marx's true heirs. In Germany and France their strength lay in the metal industries. In England they had sympathies among the miners, but during the Depression they came to be the party of the unemployed and the intellectuals. Their function in society was to provide a subculture for the alienated, a counter-religion for the nonbelievers, a counter-establishment for the dissenters. A small but vociferous group of artists and writers sympathized with their fight against militarism, colonialism, fascism, and bigotry, so that in the 1930's the Communists' influence in the press extended far beyond the narrow cadres of their party. The German *Weltbühne*, which frequently sympathized with Russia and radical causes, was widely quoted although it printed less than 10,000 copies. With seven thousand members, the British Communist Party had a book club enrollment of forty thousand. In all Communist parties the membership turnover approached 50 per cent yearly.

The mass parties of Europe were an invention of the Left. The leadership controls the deputies and also, at least in normal times, has the lower ranks well in hand. When insurgents grumble over "bossism," "party loyalty" usually carries the day, and splits usually end in disaster for the anti-organization man. It was especially the rank and file that have insisted on conformity; they were the organization, and they defended a system that was their life and their guardian. The socialist worker or trade unionist would spend his evenings in the "People's House," attend meetings, study the party's literature, canvas the neighborhood. As long as this "self-activity" continued, the worker had the feeling that he was involved in the nation's affairs. In the Depression, he even might put up with a wage cut as long as his consent was obtained and his representatives had legal channels to voice his grievances.

As long as they had this political contact, the masses defended the republican institutions and, even though they might receive less in material benefits, remained devoted to democracy emotionally; while the bourgeoisie, which enjoyed many advantages, was prepared to discard it.

It was the democrats who had reason to complain. Administrations were staffed by traditionalist civil servants, and the courts were run by staunch reactionaries. Especially in Germany and Austria, they returned blatantly biased verdicts. Enemies of the republic were protected; its defenders, as well as Communists, of course, were severely punished on technicalities. Hitler's sentence for high treason was a year's detention in a fortress—a gentlemanly confinement—while detractors of the army were given years at forced labor, or life sentences.

Often a Leftist government found itself confronted with a strike of big businessmen who refused to buy its bonds or "lacked the confidence" necessary to have the wheels of industry turn. In coalitions, the labor ministers always were at the mercy of their liberal partners. Thus, when Ramsay MacDonald became Prime Minister in 1924, his Labour Party had only 192 seats and the Liberals 158, against 257 Conservatives. This government raised unemployment benefits from 15 to 18 shillings and started slum-clearance. But it was overthrown, and the Conservatives launched an insidious scare campaign against the Bolshevik bogey. The yellow press published a forged letter, allegedly written by Grigori Zinoviev, then president of the Comintern, instructing the Communists to infiltrate the Labour Party. As a result, panicky Liberal voters deserted their party, which was never to recover. Labour, though gaining a million votes, lost 41 seats, while the Tories obtained 412 seats.

Class war now stalked England. Winston Churchill, at the Exchequer, pursued a policy of deflation, restored the pound sterling to its pre-war parity, and secured high interest rates for the bankers; yet exports and employment declined. England's low-yield coal mines, especially, were not competitive; Prime Minister Baldwin—who owned 100,000 shares of mining stock—supported management's decree to cut wages and lengthen the work day. On May 1, 1926, the owners declared a lockout; two days later the Trade Union Council called a general strike. The lines were drawn. With the help of OMS (a volunteer strike-breaking organization) and the army, Baldwin forced the Trade Union Council to capitulate after nine days. The miners continued to stay out for another six months and then surrendered unconditionally. Baldwin rammed through Parliament a vindictive Act forbidding secondary strikes, strikes against the government, and political contributions by trade unions. But that did not reconquer any markets for British coal.

Fortunately, labor found other employers more responsible. In 1928, Sir Alfred Mond began to hold "conversations" with the union leaders, Ben Turner, Ernest Bevin, and Walter Citrine. These approaches led to a shorter work week and a general rise in wages, notably in new industries. The policy, denounced by the Communists as "Mondism," was destined to substitute conciliation and collaboration for militant class conflict. Direct negotiations between industry and labor leaders were "industrial democracy," as the Webbs had foreseen it, but a far cry from the "participation" or "Control Councils" the socialists desired.

In 1929, Labour was given another chance. Its mandate was to nationalize the mines, to establish a national health service, to provide substantial subsidies for slum clearance and construction, to aid the farmers by creating marketing boards. But it had to contend with a depression more serious than anybody had foreseen. To overcome the deficit, the City called for "heroic measures," notably a substantial cut in unemployment benefits. The Depression was still seen not in terms of people and idle production capacity but solely in terms of the bondholders' security. A flight from the pound sterling brought the government down in August 1931. Labour was not to be trusted in troubled times.

Now MacDonald turned against his party and defeated it at the head of a "National Coalition" with Conservatives and Liberals. He cut unemployment benefits, though not unemployment. For the first time in exactly one hundred years, England again had a tariff on grains; food prices rose. MacDonald devalued the pound sterling and tried to solve England's problems by retreating into the empire, through subsidies, preference tariffs, and the "Buy British" campaign. After beating his former party in another election, he was duly booted out by his new friends—the tragic caricature of a labor leader who aspired to be a statesman but whose vanity buried his generous impulses. The leadership of Labour fell to the uninspiring Arthur Henderson, a former iron worker, and later to Major Attlee, who held the party together in the face of mounting dissent by idea men like G. D. H. Cole, Harold Laski, and Stafford Cripps.

The economic crisis was less severe in France, but the political climate was stormier. Forty-three cabinets ruled France between 1918 and 1940. Nine of them were of the Left or Center-Left; nineteen were distinctly Right. The Radicals were part of all of them. Often elected in left-wing landslides, they slid back to the Right; financial interests saw to that. In 1924, after the disastrous Ruhr invasion, the voters repudiated Poincaré's nationalism and gave power to Herriot and Briand, internationalists who promised tax reforms and sought reconciliation with Germany and Russia. But in 1926, the financial community refused to buy government bonds. Herriot, weeping, resigned, and Poincaré again formed the Cabinet of National Union; he obtained the powers that had been refused to Herriot, raised the value of the franc from 2 to 4 cents, and in the 1928 elections won a majority. In 1932, the mood of the voters turned Left once again, and two years later, when Camelots du Roi, Jeunesses Patriotes, Volontaires Nationaux, Croix-de-Feu, and other fascist leagues, in the pay of well-known industrialists like Coty and Hennessy, threatened a coup, and a reactionary Premier, Gaston Doumergue, proposed to convert France's ceremonial Presidency into an authoritarian executive, the republican forces organized to resist. This was February 1934, a year after Hitler had seized power across the Rhine, and Frenchmen were not disposed to be ruled by men of his ilk.

All through the post-war period, the lot of the French peasant and worker had not improved. There was little in the way of social security. The trade unions, all but powerless, were divided into Socialist, Christian, and Communist organizations. The two Marxist parties had condemned themselves to sterile opposition and therefore lost able politicians to the Radicals, who could offer them interesting careers. Léon Blum, leader of the Socialist Party (SFIO), found it impossible to support even the Leftist governments of Herriot and Joseph Paul-Boncour in 1932. But in February 1934 the entire Left joined forces to save the republic, and the parliament itself was able to foil the anti-democratic plans. The next elections brought to power the Popular Front, which will be discussed in a later context.

The Scandinavian countries had been spared war and inflation, and they had not engaged in the arms race. Their budgets were sound; their homogeneous distribution of wealth permitted them to maintain harmony among the classes. In 1918, Thorvald Stauning had joined with the Radical Liberals to form a coalition government; in 1924, he headed the first Danish socialist government. Beaten at the polls in 1926, he returned in 1929, again in coalition with the Radical Liberals, whose agrarian program he fully supported.

In Sweden, Hjalmar Branting passed a comprehensive body of social reforms between 1920 and 1926. In 1932, the socialists returned to power under Per Hansson's leadership. He fought the Depression with Keynesian weapons, using large-scale public-works programs and also bolstering consumer income with generous unemployment benefits. Both Denmark and Sweden strongly supported co-operatives, put a floor under consumer earnings, provided effective health insurance, expanded public services, planned efficient state enterprises, made judicious use of progressive taxation and flexible finance policies.

Norway's Labor Party held power only briefly in 1927–28. It had to overcome strong pro-Soviet and syndicalist traditions within its ranks. But eventually, all Scandinavian socialists adopted the "Folkhem" theory of the Swedish thinker Nils Karleby— namely, that a socialist economy was developing imperceptibly within the framework of the existing society as more factories were being run by the state, business was being regulated, workers were acquiring personal security and representation in the councils of management. Stark class differences were being smoothed over by wise social policies and co-operation between labor and management.

Even in Finland, where the proximity of the Soviet Union and the resentments of the Baltic barons posed special problems, the crisis was overcome by constitutional means. An agrarian law of 1922 broke up the large estates; but the conservative, militaristic Baron Karl von Mannerheim, a national hero in the 1918 war against Bolshevism, never accepted either democracy or farm reform. In the 1930's, the semi-fascist Lapua or Lappo movement demanded strong measures against the small Communist Party, abducted the President, and terrorized the population. President Pehr E. Svinhufvud, though himself a staunch conservative, foiled the reactionary coups and began a policy of close collaboration with the other Scandinavian governments. His successor, Kyosti Kallio, outlawed the Lapua movement and led a socialist-agrarian coalition, which later fought bravely against the combined Nazi-Communist assault. Finland and Switzerland, incidentally, offer unique examples of nations with substantial minorities and no record of major ethnic conflicts.

Czechoslovakia, the last of the great democracies in this brief survey, was torn apart by national strife from its very inception. The Slovaks were the minor partners, culturally and economically backward; devout Catholics, they were unhappy when the enlightened leaders made John Hus a national hero and founded a national church. The country also encompassed Hungarians, Poles, Ruthenians, and, above all, 3 million Germans who lived in the most highly industrialized areas, bordering on Germany, along the Sudeten range; hence they were called Sudeten Germans. The Czechs admittedly were taking revenge on these Germans for every indignity they had suffered at their hands under the Hapsburg monarchy. A thorough-going land reform divided the estates of former German landowners among 650,000 Czech settlers; along with these settlers came Czech schoolmasters, postmasters, stationmasters, and so on, all preferably with large families to insure a rapid de-Germanization of the schools. The policy exacerbated the centuries-old hostility between the two nationalities. Virtually every party was split along national lines; only the Communists were united and therefore appeared to be the strongest party.

Nevertheless, thanks to its enlightened policy of social reform, the nationalist-agrarian-socialist coalition under the leadership of Thomas Masaryk and Eduard Beneš held the state together until German separatism found active support in the Reich. A patriotic youth organization and a lively athletic movement supported the state and gained international respect. Beneš was a leading figure in the League of Nations and an architect of the Little Entente between Prague, Belgrade, and Bucharest. France supported the alliance, and Schneider-Creusot was the majority shareholder in the Skoda munitions plant. Czechoslovakia was too much a creation of revenge and fear to succeed; her market was too small, her security too precarious.

Democracy still lived as a great idea, and those who enjoyed its benefits no doubt felt that, for all its faults, it was the best of all impossible systems. But the great idea no longer inspired the masses as it had in the nineteenth century. They had the vote now but could not use it for their betterment. Democracy had given the people neither power nor food—and therefore not even equality. In some countries not even formal democracy survived. During the Depression, both England and France had resorted to government by decree. Right-wing academicians began earnestly to speak of a "crisis of democracy"—a crisis which their co-religionists had done their best to bring on. In Germany and Austria the tragedy of democracy was played out in full view of the world.

In discussing these countries, one can make two mistakes. The tragic end of these democracies seems to place the historian under obligation to look for some basic defect which made their fall inevitable, or he may compare the sad reality with the high hopes of 1848 and 1918. We must evaluate not an imaginary republic but the political choices of men in the most trying crisis.

CHAPTER 4

Weimar and Vienna— Two Splendid Failures

THE Weimar Republic was born out of two defeats: the collapse of the Reich and the abortion of the *Räte* (Councils) revolution. It was a compromise from its very beginning. Both the Right and the Left considered it a half-way house—the ones on the way back to the old pageantry of kings, armies and civil servants, the others on the way toward a socialist, or at least radical-democratic, republic. The radical idea was embodied in the Constitution, the most advanced any country had enjoyed since 1792. It even provided for a social-economic chamber and ascribed to the government an obligation to serve the welfare of the people. It was the first constitution to make collective bargaining a fundamental right; that is, it recognized the pluralistic character of the new state. As its flag it adopted the black, red, and gold under which the students had fought the princes in 1848, a declaration of liberal democracy.

For this very reason, the industrialists and agrarians hated the republic. They wanted a strong, reliable, authoritarian government that could keep the masses in awe and respect. Instead, the Reichstag was a market place for pressure groups. Governments changed often; the party leaders were power brokers. Also, the army— symbol of past glory—was placed under civilian control; and the republic was tainted with the humiliating Versailles Treaty. It paid reparations to the Allies; it tried to reconcile the West. The former upper classes were irked because in politics, administration, in business and the professions new people achieved leadership, some of them from humble origins, some of foreign stock. The "Jew Republic" enjoyed no authority among the educated classes, in whose eyes it lacked legitimacy. At election time and in parades, the Rightists displayed the imperial black, white, and red instead of the new national flag.

Workers, on the other hand, would complain that the "Socialization Commission" came to nothing, that the Shop-Steward Act of 1920 emasculated their controlling power, that the old imperial civil servants, judges, and army officers were still running the state and were in a position to frustrate progressive legislation or to pervert the law. The penalty for assassinating republican statesmen—Erzberger, Rathenau, Eisner—was a few months in jail, and Ludendorff continued to receive his pension after he had led a putsch. Left writers were given stiff sentences for exposing the Black Reichswehr (clandestine army units training in violation of the Versailles Treaty). The workers called the state a bourgeois republic and marched under their own red flag.

Each party had its militia. The Right launched the "Steel Helmet," the Communists had the "Red Hundreds" and later the "Red Front Fighters," the Social Democrats the *Reichsbanner*, the Nazis the brown-shirted SA (Storm Troops) and the black-uniformed SS (Defense Corps). Their frequent street brawls took dozens of lives yearly, not counting those whom the Nazi *Feme* executed as "traitors."

Nevertheless, the republic overcame its birth defects, its lack of legitimacy, and even the militancy of the class wars which never subsided throughout its life. The economic foundation of political compromise was laid in 1920 when an Agreement to Co-operate (*Arbeitsgemeinschaft*) for industrial peace was concluded between trade-union leader Carl Legien and industrialist Hugo Stinnes. In 1927, at its Kiel convention, the Social Democratic Party substituted "economic democracy" for Marxism. Under sophisticated arbitration machinery, real wages increased 60 per cent over their pre-war levels, and the working week was reduced to forty-four hours. Social insurance, welfare, and public health were greatly improved. In the big industrial states, Prussia and Saxony, socialists and republicans formed coalition governments which reformed education, brought the utilities under public control, republicanized police and administration, and enlarged the public services. Big industrial cities like Berlin, Hamburg, or Chemnitz had socialist majorities which provided welfare aid, psychiatric counseling, birth-control clinics, experimental schools, progressive theaters, adult education, magnificent recreation facilities and, above all, that fervent intellectual climate for which the Weimar Republic has become justly famous. It was this climate of innovation that united writers of the Left and of the Right, and it can be said that both Bertolt Brecht, a Communist, and Gottfried Benn, a monarchist, belonged to the Weimar Republic despite their political opposition to it.

The universities and the professions were overwhelmingly anti-republican, but some of the most significant, world-famous intellectuals rallied to the republic: Thomas Mann, Max Weber, and the historians Hermann Oncken and Friedrich Meinecke. The latter told his students: If we cannot have what we would love best, then let us love what we have. Eventually this advice was taken by some opinion leaders and representatives of the bourgeoisie, too. Thus Dr. Stresemann was able to lead his former National-Liberals (reborn as People's Party) from monarchist nostalgia to co-operation with the republican parties; he served as Foreign Minister to his death in 1929. Elements of the Youth Movement also became converted to republicanism, and eventually even the Nationalists (formerly the monarchistic Conservatives) decided to "operate on the basis of accomplished facts." As a matter of practical policy, they provided occasional votes for the passage of constructive legislation and promised their bewildered followers that they were "conquering the state from within."

In 1925 President Friedrich Ebert, a Social Democrat, died. To succeed him, the republican parties agreed on an unattractive Catholic, Wilhelm Marx. The Rightists rolled out a national monument, Field Marshal Paul von Hindenburg; the Communists, on Stalin's orders, presented their own man, Ernst Thälmann. Thanks to this diversion on the Left, Hindenburg won a plurality of 14.7 million against 13.8 million for Marx and 1.9 million for Thälmann. When the Kaiser's general took the oath on the Constitution, the republic seemed to be assured of stability and respectability; temporarily the nonconformists on the Right were silenced—though not for long, we shall see.

It has been said that the state of Weimar was a republic without republicans. The Independent Socialists and the Communists between them mustered 18 per cent of the vote in their best year. Monarchists, nationalists, and racists, added up despite their deep differences, never achieved 30 per cent before 1930. But even counting all the disaffected on the Right and on the Left, these two camps could never form a majority. They were fighting each other in streets and beer halls. At the worst point of the Depression, in 1932, the Nazis and their allies won 43 per cent, the Communists 18 per cent of the electorate. At all previous times, the moderates had a majority. The (Catholic) Center Party and the two liberal parties could form a coalition either with the Social Democrats or with the conservatives. Yet by their nature such coalitions produce compromises rather than policies.

To complete the picture, the two workers' parties between them never got more than 45 per cent of the vote, and there never was a chance for socialism by ballot. Had they been united in decisive action, their influence might have been greater; but there was no chance of united action even in the face of common danger. A Social Democratic police commissioner in Berlin was responsible for the killing of thirty-three demonstrators on May Day, 1929. The Communists worked in tandem with the militarists to destroy republican institutions; they even joined the Nazis in a referendum against the Prussian government.

It was a picture of confusion—no one had a policy, no policy had a majority. When the Depression came and 3 million were unemployed by 1930, the social insurance scheme ran out of funds, and only seven years after the worst inflation in history, no one dared to suggest deficit financing. The Social Democrats proposed taxing the rich; their liberal coalition partners would rather cut unemployment pay. Over this, the Social Democrats quit the cabinet; by the rules of the parliamentary game, a right-wing coalition should have faced the music.

This time, however, the nationalists refused to play the game. Their new leader was Alfred Hugenberg, a press and movie tycoon, a monarchist and chauvinist, who saw an opportunity to weaken parliamentary government. He allied himself with the fanatical adventurer, Adolf Hitler, to form a "patriotic front" of all the disgruntled and perplexed who blamed Germany's misfortunes on the republican party system, the Versailles Treaty, and the world conspiracy of Jewry. His strategy succeeded only too well: In the September 1930 elections Hitler, "the drummer," won 2 million votes away from Hugenberg's own party. In addition, generously financed by big industry, he mobilized 3 to 4 million who had never voted before: idealistic youths who yearned to give their life for Führer and Fatherland, déclassé army officers, bankrupt shopkeepers and dispossessed peasants who hated Jewish politicians, department stores and bankers, and also many jobless to whom the possession of an SA uniform and boots meant the restoration of their manhood.

After this election, any workable majority would have had to include either the Social Democrats or the Nazis. Chancellor Heinrich Brüning, a Catholic conservative and at heart a monarchist, decided to rule without a majority by emergency decree. Using residual powers of the President, he sought to diminish the role of the Reichstag. To the socialists he said: "The alternative to me is a coalition including the Nazis." What that meant could be seen from their misrule in some smaller states. The republicans had much to fear. Above all, they wanted to preserve the form of parliamentary government even while the Chancellor and the President were eroding its substance. By granting emergency powers, the timid socialist leaders allowed the Reichstag to abdicate, and at the same time it shared responsibility for Brüning's unpopular policies. His deflationary measures only increased unemployment. Had the republicans known that the Depression would run another three years, that unemployment figures would double, and that the Nazi vote would rise to 37 per cent, they might have allowed a Rightist coalition to ruin itself. For all practical purposes, the republic was dead when the republicans hid behind an authoritarian president. In April 1932 they reelected Hindenburg with 19.3 million votes against 13.4 million for Hitler and 3.7 million for Thälmann.

What they thought they were preventing they brought to pass. The senile Hindenburg, who was run by a reactionary camarilla, fired Brüning and, after a series of unspeakable intrigues, delivered the government into the hands of Adolf Hitler, as head of the strongest party in January 1933. The cabinet included Hugenberg and other conservatives who made sure that the economic departments, foreign affairs, and defense were in "safe" hands. But the Nazis staged big parades and styled the change of government into a "national uprising." On February 27, the Reichstag building went up in flames, providing a welcome pretext for a rule of terror. Even so, although the republicans could hardly campaign in the elections of March 1933, the Nazis won only 44 per cent of the vote. They gave themselves a majority, however, by ejecting the Communists from the Reichstag. Thus Hugenberg, who had hoped to use and either tame or dismiss Hitler, was duped too.

The Weimar Republic had been a noble experiment in pluralism and should not be judged by the ultimate victory of its enemies or the faint-heartedness of its leaders, but by the achievements which it bequeathed to posterity. It planted the seed of equality and social justice; it gave birth to a cultural life unequaled in any other nation during a comparable period. At no other period had political life been more intense, and shared by such numbers. Perhaps the tensions under which it lived contributed to the intellectual and artistic effervescence which has given the Weimar Republic its great name.

Could it have been saved? The inglorious exit of its defenders stands in stark contrast to the gallant resistance offered a year later by the workers of Vienna and of Paris, and three years later by the Spanish republicans. The Weimar Republic was sick and paralyzed; its governments could not act decisively in crisis, nor could the people act to save it: with 6 million unemployed, the trade unions could not contemplate a political strike. Social Democrats and Communists were fighting each other instead of the common enemy. Greater was the guilt of the willful men who unscrupulously destroyed a state to vent their private grudges and who deliberately fomented resentment in order to further their plans. Especially the scheming General von Schleicher and Hindenburg's friend von Papen hoped to use the Nazis—but they were deceived deceivers. Schleicher, the "political general," had hoped to establish an authoritarian regime, based on the army, trade unions, and disaffected Nazis.

If comparison can serve as an answer, we must admit that greater militancy on the part of the republicans did not prevent the collapse of a neighboring republic. Austria, a rump left after the dissolution of the Hapsburg Empire, with a capital too big for the country's shrunken size, adopted a constitution modeled after the Swiss example: home rule for each of the seven rural provinces, which were Catholic and conservative, and for Vienna, which was socialist and whose upper middle class contained a large percentage of Jews. Most Austrians had abandoned the dreams of empire and sought *Anschluss* with Germany, but the Versailles and Saint-Germain treaties forbade any act of self-determination. In 1931, Germany and Austria planned a customs union, a step that might have bolstered the prestige of both republics sufficiently to save them from the Nazi onslaught. But the Western powers foiled the project.

The domestic policies of Austria were dominated by the intrigues of Monsignor Ignaz Seipel. His Christian-Social Party formed coalitions with agrarians, nationalists, and fascists, and when he failed to gain a majority he conspired to rule dictatorially or to call back the Hapsburgs.

The bane of Austrian politics was the militias and their silent civil war. On the Right were the veterans' leagues and the Home Defense League (Heimwehr), financed and supplied with arms by the Central Federation of Industry; on the Left was the Socialist Protection League (Schutzbund). Both stressed military training, and their mutual provocations sometimes ballooned into street battles and murder. In 1927, a Vienna court acquitted three nationalists who had confessed to the murder of two socialists. That same week Leftists in all countries were protesting the execution of Sacco and Vanzetti in Boston; barricades went up in Paris. In Vienna, the Palace of Justice was burned down; the police killed ninety-eight rioters.

The socialists never recovered from the repression that followed, but remained in sterile opposition. Their program, adopted at Linz in 1926, committed them to democratic methods; but in contrast to their German comrades, Austria's Social Democrats were averse to coalition governments and friendly to the Soviet Union. This made them immune to Communist competition, but they developed Marxism in their own way. Hugo Breitner, an excellent administrator and finance expert, turned Vienna into a model city of social progress, with public housing and progressive education. The socialist youth groups were animated by a spirit of militant humanism. Its socialist culture made Vienna the mecca of all progressives.

Yet with all their intellectual superiority, the Austrian socialists lacked the will to power. When Austria's central bank failed and capitalism seemed near collapse, the wily Seipel offered them a coalition; but the socialist leader, Otto Bauer, said: "We should not be receivers in bankruptcy." Dazzled by his own brilliant analysis of the Depression, Bauer failed to see the real danger, namely that the Heimwehr leaders were slipping away from Seipel's control and began to play Hitler's or Mussolini's games—for pay. A playboy adventurer, Baron von Starhemberg, was wrecking the Republic.

To prevent a Nazi takeover, the diminutive Chancellor, Engelbert Dollfuss, suspended the constitution in 1933 and, inspired by the Pope's encyclical *Quadragesimo Anno* and Mussolini's *Carta del Lavoro* (see next chapter), began to establish a corporate state. In February 1934, Dollfuss and the Heimwehr suppressed the Schutzbund, deposed local socialist administrations, jailed the mayor of Vienna, and forced the socialists underground. The Karl-Marx-Hof, Vienna's proudest housing project, and other developments in the workers' districts were shelled and damaged. Three hundred died in street fighting; nine Schutzbund leaders were hanged. Four months later Dollfuss was assassinated by the Nazis. His successor, Kurt von Schuschnigg, was unable to reconcile the socialists. When Hitler, in 1938, summoned him to Berchtesgaden and ordered him to appoint a Nazi Police Minister, no one was left to defend Austria's sovereignty.

CHAPTER 5

Experiments in Dictatorship

AFTER Mussolini was given dictatorial power on October 28, 1922, he promptly appointed Fascist prefects and subprefects, gave quasi-police status to a Fascist militia, vilified the opposition parties, and pushed through parliament an electoral law that assured two-thirds of the seats to his party. During a twelve-month period, two thousand crimes of murder, assault, and arson were laid to his SA. The homes of Benedetto Croce, the philosopher, and Francesco Nitti, a former Premier, were destroyed; so were the Socialist Party offices in Ancona, Milano, Genoa, and Livorno. The great maestro Arturo Toscanini, at first a supporter, had to leave the country.

After the 1924 elections, which gave the Fascists two-thirds of the vote, a young socialist deputy, Giacomo Matteotti, stood up in parliament to expose the fraud and denounce the terror. He was assassinated the next day. An outraged country demanded punishment of the murderers; but two of them were released immediately and two others given light sentences. The opposition parties left parliament in protest and constituted themselves as *Monte Aventino*, in remembrance of the Roman plebeians who had entrenched themselves there to wrest their rights from the patricians.

Then Mussolini took the final step to government by goons. On January 3, 1925, he assumed responsibility for any violent act done by the storm troops, changed the rump parliament into a Fascist chamber, suppressed all independent newspapers, and dropped his nationalist coalition partners. As secretary of the Fascist Party he appointed a former bank clerk, Roberto Farinacci, a brutal terrorist and advocate of strong-arm tactics. Henceforth podestas (mayors) were appointed rather than elected; an obedient Grand Council was placed above the Chamber of Deputies and the Senate. The despotism of a rapacious clique was being transformed into the dictatorship of one man, and his party was turned from a mob into the all-pervasive instrument of a ubiquitous state. All other parties were dissolved, their ministers dismissed. A secret police, OVRA, won power over the life and liberty of every citizen. In 1926, an Act for the Defense of the State gave special tribunals license to deport any suspect.

Despite its revolutionary phraseology, its emphasis on youth and action, Fascism did not touch Italy's class structure. The King, the landowners, and the industrialists applauded when the Squadristi vented their sadism on trade unionists, beat up Freemasons, and purged socialist organizers with castor oil.

Mussolini's young followers had believed in his idealism, perhaps even in his "socialism." They thought of Fascism as a movement against the "materialism" of both the upper and lower classes.

Having first betrayed the socialists, Mussolini now had to repudiate these discontented, resentful followers or to convert them into watchdogs of his regime. A Fascist militia was created—as much to discipline the Fascists as to intimidate their enemies. The Fascist Party was subjected to a severe purge, in which every member's ranking was determined by his loyalty and merits. Quoting the party program of 1920, or even owning a copy of it, was prohibited. All Fascists and militiamen had to swear an oath of obedience to the Duce, the title Mussolini now affected. To assure a steady supply of obedient Fascists, the party created the youth organizations, Giovani Fascisti and Avanguardia; the latter recruited its members from the Balilla, a sort of Boy Scouts, which was compulsory for all boys under fourteen.

The state was to be the master of all Italians. It controlled all their activities from cradle to grave, at work and at leisure. The government's Opera Nazionale Dopolavoro was in charge of leisure-time activities. Every thought was predigested. Independent parties and labor unions were outlawed; any independent university teacher was considered an enemy of the state. Deputies were elected on a single list compiled for the whole kingdom by the Grand Council of the party. The voter had the choice of voting either yes or no, and few were brave enough to stay away from the polls. Even these deputies could ask none but approved questions. Since Mussolini had reserved the right to promulgate laws without its consent, parliament had become nothing more than a claque for his speeches.

In 1926 Mussolini promulgated the *Carta del Lavoro*, his most original creation and the foundation of the "corporate state." Both employers and workers in each of six large industry groups were to form a *sindacato*, or union, the only recognized representatives of every person in that industry, with the sole right of bargaining for all. Nonmembers had to pay dues, too, a practice unheard of in European free trade unions. In each industry, syndicates of employers and employees formed a "corporation" which was responsible for labor peace. Actually, the organizers on both sides were government-appointed; their collective agreements usually resulted in wage cuts. Strikes were forbidden.

Mussolini had fought for a high exchange rate for the lira, which cost Italian industry valuable export markets and forced it to reduce prices and wages. Since the latter fell more rapidly than the former, the Fascist regime was unpopular among the workers, and its consumer industries became vulnerable in the Depression.

Other classes fared better, at least in the beginning. Farmers were given instruction, marketing organizations, and modern equipment. Settlers could buy land with long-term, government-backed loans. A large swamp area near Rome was drained. Tourists had the benefit of better hotel service and trains that ran on time.

In surrendering to the usurper, Italian society took its cue from the Vatican, which was hostile to the secular state in general and to Italy's liberal state in particular. The Curia reaped its reward in the great Concordat of 1929. The ex-anarchist and atheist, Mussolini, became the savior of capitalism, of monarchy, and of clerical power in Italy.

Pope Pius XI, who liked mountain climbing, no longer was "the prisoner in the Vatican"; he recognized the State of Italy and received 750 million lire as compensation for the former Papal State territory. He remained "sovereign" only for the Vatican and its gardens. The Concordat made Catholicism the state religion of Italy, gave the church a monopoly on marriage registration, and made religious instruction compulsory in all schools. Later, Mussolini tried to interpret this last clause in the narrowest possible way, claiming that the child belonged to the state first and had to learn the old Roman virtues. He meant to make Italy great; therefore he needed soldiers and a war-minded nation. All the pageantry and panoply of his regime were military. To boost the declining birth rate he whipped Italy's families into a "battle of the cradle." He called on teachers to wage a "battle against illiteracy." To make Italy self-sufficient, he called the peasants to the "battle of the grain." But he also developed hydroelectric power and fostered industries like rayon and automobiles. Illiteracy declined to 10 per cent. Italy produced the best racing cars in Europe, and on the reclaimed marshes, Mussolini settled farmers, and malaria was wiped out.

The price Italy paid for domestic peace was high. Freedom was suppressed; political life was nonexistent. Thinking was a luxury only a brave man could afford. Philosophers and scientists fled this atmosphere; great writers (Ignazio Silone), statesmen (Carlo Sforza), artists (Arturo Toscanini), and scholars (Giuseppe A. Borgese) lived in exile. Official art was as academic-heroic as in all dictatorships. For recreation, Italians had parades; for comedy, a buffoon playing the role of Prime Minister. For expression, the inane *Du-ce-Du-ce-Du-ce* yells of the crowds and martial phantasies about the Mediterranean, Italy's *Mare Nostrum*. A second-rate Hegel scholar, Giovanni Gentile, gave Fascism a hand-me-down Spenglerian philosophy.

Educated people tended to dismiss Mussolini's antics as a show staged for the masses. They did not yet recognize Fascism as a new political philosophy but mistook it for another, if perhaps harsher, form of military dictatorship. The term "fascism" at the time was applied generically to terroristic and unconstitutional regimes like those of Tsankov in Bulgaria, Pilsudski in Poland, Svinhufvud in Finland, Primo de Rivera in Spain, Smetona in Lithuania, King Alexander in Yugoslavia. It makes more sense, however, to reserve the term for the more totalitarian regimes that mobilize all citizens' bodies and souls for a supreme national effort. A milder form, called clerico-fascism because of its Roman Catholic inspiration, ruled in Austria under Dollfuss and in Portugal under Salazar. The other regimes, which have made no effort to integrate the nation and to force every citizen into its organizations, are only military or police dictatorships, with no deep roots in the country.

Even Italy did not become totalitarian until the latter 1930's. Fascist leaders muscled into the ruling class, exalted by Mussolini as "hierarchy," but left both nobility and capitalism intact. This gave some plausibility, at the time, to the Communist theory that fascism is nothing but the "running dog of monopoly capital."

The regime that came to rule in Austria in 1934 called itself a Christian guild state. Its ideology had been formed by Othmar Spann (a romantic conservative who felt that history had been in error since 1789) on the basis of *Quadragesimo Anno* and the *Carta del Lavoro*, on nostalgia for the Catholic monarchy, and on Austrian patriotism. Frankly promoted as an alternative to National Socialism, Dollfuss's and Schuschnigg's "Fatherland Front" was perched precariously between underground Nazis and underground socialists.

In Spain, too, a military coup was staged to save the monarchy from crumbling. In 1921, the army in Morocco was routed by Riff Kabyles under the Berber leader, Abd el Krim. To end the outcry for "responsibilities," General Miguel Primo de Rivera seized power in 1923 and dissolved the Cortes. His slogan was "Nation, Church, and King;" his program was borrowed from Spanish critics of parliamentarianism—whether radicals like Joaquín Costa or elitists like Antonio Maura and Ortega y Gasset.

Republicanism was the "cause" of the middle classes and of the regions. Primo de Rivera suppressed the parties and tried to hold the middle class in check by arousing in their back *sindicatos libres* (free trade unions). He also tolerated the socialist UGT (Unión General de Trabajadores) as long as it refrained from political action, and made its chairman, Francisco Largo Caballero, a councilor of state. His Finance Minister, José Calvo Sotelo, even tried to tax the rich and pioneered in a scheme of pre-Keynesian economics, financing an ambitious "Ten Year Plan" of public works—roads, electrification, railway expansion—through an "extraordinary budget." His state monopoly for oil did not mind buying Bolshevik naphtha, thus antagonizing Shell and Standard Oil interests. Conservative politicians and business thereupon joined intellectuals, students, lawyers, disgruntled artillery officers, and air pilots in opposition to the dictator. When the peseta fell in the Great Depression, Calvo Sotelo's schemes collapsed—and with them the dictatorship.

Primo de Rivera's regime was not totalitarian. It had no mass following. Despite his efforts to convert the dictatorship into a civilian regime, despite his copying of the Fascist Grand Council and the *Carta del Lavoro*, his was basically a military government which kept a precarious balance by playing off one class against the other. Despite its violent attacks on parliamentary government and "bossism"—the infamous cacique system—the regime should be called reactionary rather than post-liberal.

Even less than Primo's dictatorship can the one of Professor Antonio de Oliveira Salazar be called fascist. The parliamentary Republic of Portugal suffered from corruption and bossism still worse than the Spanish monarchy. In 1926, when labor unrest aggravated the apprehensions and the value of the escudo dropped to 4 per cent of par, an army coup overthrew the republic. After some infighting among the military, General Antonio de Fragoso Carmona emerged as dictator. He got himself elected President in 1928, but was unable to cope with the ills of the country; he then called on Salazar, an unassuming professor of economics who once had aspired to the priesthood. As Minister of Finance, Salazar imposed an austere regime of regeneration on Portugal, saved the currency, and inspired business with confidence. For all practical purposes, he was dictator by 1930 and became Premier in 1932. He called his regime Estado Novo (New State) and allowed only one party, the National Union.

In 1933 he promulgated a constitution. Heads of households who had a certain level of education got the right to choose deputies from a list of candidates prepared by the ruling party. Even this assembly had no rights, since the President alone could appoint and dismiss ministers. Presidential elections were a farce. For himself Salazar asked neither honors nor publicity; but his regime was one of stagnation and repression. The sources of its strength were continued friendship with England and its overseas empire.

In Poland, democracy succumbed to a combination of military and agrarian reaction. The first Premier, Ignace Paderewski, a great pianist but poor politician, withdrew from the government after the state had been launched on its tragic career. The Polish leaders were more intent on annexing minorities than on building them an enduring home. Head of state was Marshal Josef Pilsudski, formerly a socialist, now a conservative landowner and patriotic demagogue. He soon grew tired of parliamentary dissensions and withdrew into the Ministry of War.

It is true that political life was floundering in the proverbial Polish confusion. The fifteen parties in the Sejm overturned governments at a rate of three a year; a socialist President was assassinated after a week in office. Eventually, Ladislav Grabski formed a nonpolitical cabinet of experts. It stabilized the zloty and launched a land reform which promised to transfer 500,000 acres each year to the peasants, on easy terms to be guaranteed by the state. During this period, 8 million acres of land changed hands; the share of 16,000 big estates was reduced from 80 per cent to 20 per cent of the plowed acreage. But when Vincent Witos, leader of the Peasant Party, was elected President in 1926, Pilsudski struck against the republic. At the head of his "legionaries" he forced the Sejm to make him President, then handed the office to his friend Ignace Moscicki. The subsequent governments were all military. Though the Sejm was not officially abolished and elections continued to be held, members of the opposition were arrested, the press was censored, and the "colonels" governed by decree. Pilsudski ruled through a combination of intimidation and repression, with sporadic outbursts of despotic "corrections" of the government routine; but he never tried to substitute one-party or one-man rule for the kaleidoscope of multiple parties for which Poland is famous. On April 23, 1935, however, parliamentary elections were officially replaced by a system of corporate nominations and appointments to a parliament which itself was only a cover for military government. On Pilsudski's death, on May 12, 1935, Marshal Edward Smigly-Rydz assumed power but had to balance precariously between the pro-German officers and the democratic parties.

Similarly, the Horthy regime in Hungary did not abolish the parliament and it outlawed only the Communist Party, but it was essentially a police regime. It assumed fascist traits under Gömbös in the 1930's. The Eastern monarchies in Bucharest, Sofia, and Athens were constitutional in name but for all practical purposes dominated by strong men, like Bratianu and Venizelos, usually heading corrupt machines.

The last dictatorship in this brief survey is that of Yugoslavia. Once the "Kingdom of Serbs, Croats, and Slovenes" had been unified, its ethnic groups discovered their differences. The Serbs are Greek Orthodox and use the Cyrillic alphabet; the Croats and Slovenes are Roman Catholic and write in Latin script. Moreover, the state included Bulgarians in Macedonia, Montenegrins, and some Albanians—"poorly baptized Turks." Its Serb Premier, Pashich, tried to give the country a centralist administration which many resented as being "Great Serbian." In the Skupchina (parliament), representatives of regional interests frequently used the obstructionist tactics they had learned in the Austrian Diet. After the Croatian peasant leader Stephen Radich was assassinated in 1928, King Alexander took all power to himself, revoked the constitution, dissolved the parties, redrew the borders of the provinces, and renamed them so as to erase the traditional ethnic divisions. He christened the kingdom "Yugoslavia" (South Slavia) to emphasize its unity. As his Premier he appointed the former chief of the Royal Guard, General Peter Zhivkovich. A new constitution gave the King power over the courts of law and the right to appoint half the Upper Chamber.

But terrorism seemed to thrive on persecution. The Italian-sponsored Ustasha in Croatia, the Bulgarian IMRO in Macedonia, the Moslems, and the Communists found new recruits among students. In 1934, Alexander was assassinated in Marseille, while visiting the French Minister of Foreign Affairs. The assassins were members of the Ustasha and probably in the pay of Mussolini.

The great variety of dictatorial regimes reflects the gamut of the socio-economic systems in which they operated. But they all had in common the basic characteristics which Marx and others had found in Bonapartism. A dictatorship becomes possible when, in a situation of violent internal strife, the contending classes hold each other in check. It suppresses political liberalism but gives free rein to the capitalist economy or even helps to expand it by means of public funds. It must represent the masses vis-à-vis the capitalist interests and increase the welfare economy; it must provide patriotic outlets for the social and economic frustrations of the masses. It is militaristic and imperialistic.

Let us now turn our attention to a dictatorship that was built on other premises.

CHAPTER 6

Socialism in One Country

LENIN's death after a long illness, on January 21, 1924, coincided with the end of the world revolution in Europe and with the first successes of the New Economic Policy in Russia. He left to his intimates a "Testament" in which he adjured them to remain united and not to let any single man—least of all Trotsky (Leib Bronstein) or Stalin (Josef V. Djugashvili)—assume a position of leadership. Yet the following years developed into a struggle of leadership between these two—one a brilliant writer and speaker, the gallant organizer of the Red Army and, next to Lenin, the best-known man in the Communist world; the other a plodding and plotting bureaucrat who quietly built the obscure post of Secretary General of the Party into the most powerful political machine of all times. The old Bolsheviks were all suspicious of Trotsky and feared that, like the great French Revolution, theirs might also fall into the hands of a strong man. Stalin therefore was able to form a "troika" with Kamenev and Zinoviev, the head of the Leningrad Party organization, the most proletarian and "Leftist" in the country, and also president of the Communist International (Comintern).

Trotsky attacked the triumvirs on two counts: they were allowing the Party to become bureaucratized and they sacrificed the world revolution to narrow state interests. In January 1925, he was deprived of his army post, but he continued to fight for his theory of "permanent revolution." Trotsky denied, and Stalin affirmed, that "socialism can be built in one country, even though it be underdeveloped and surrounded by capitalist hyenas." Trotsky placed the world revolution ahead of all other interests; Stalin asked the Communists abroad to subordinate their interests to those of the Soviet Union. At the Fourteenth and Fifteenth Party Congresses, in 1925 and 1927, Stalin formulated his policy of coexistence (*sosushchestvovanie*) and supplemented it with the theory of "relative stabilization of capitalism." Communists now replaced the tactics of splitting the labor movement with the "united front" tactics. They abandoned the Red Trade Union International and rejoined the "reform" unions of the Amsterdam International, the British Labour Party, even Chiang Kai-shek's Kuomintang, sports and other fraternal organizations. In every possible way they tried to establish themselves as junior partners of the labor movement and of "progressive" forces in the world.

This reorientation was accompanied by a violent upset in the leadership of the

Communist Party. Both in Soviet Russia and in the Third International, the "Leftists" were being replaced by "Rightists." Stalin used the occasion to rid himself of his two colleagues. Zinoviev had to yield the Comintern presidency to Nikolai Bukharin, a former Leftist who now pleaded for further concessions to the peasants. The Russian Party was subjected to an iron discipline. At the Fifteenth Congress Stalin demanded the complete submission of all dissidents, renunciation not only of their right to disagree in public but of their right to an opinion of their own. Zinoviev and Kamenev recanted; Trotsky, who remained adamant, was expelled from the Party and banished first from Moscow, then from the country.

Stalin told the Congress: "We have maintained peace with the surrounding states despite enormous difficulties and provocations. The relations between the USSR and other countries are based on the assumption that coexistence between opposite systems is possible." Finally, "Our policy is based on give-and-take. If you give us credits, you will receive a certain part of the pre-war debts." Indeed American, British, and German firms were building power dams and steel mills in Soviet Russia. The German Army (evading Versailles Treaty restrictions) built airplanes and submarines, manufactured poison gas, and trained pilots—all on Soviet soil. But no big settlement was forthcoming, and Russia's industrial development was stalled for lack of capital.

At that time the Soviet economy showed a wide variety of enterprises. The great industrial trusts were in the hands of the state and often were managed by non-Communist engineers who had become reconciled with the revolution. But apart from social-welfare measures (such as nurseries for the children of working mothers) not much socialism was to be found in those factories: neither did the workers share in management decisions nor did they have the right to strike. What there was of planning consisted simply of crash programs, such as bringing electricity to the countryside and increasing the power supply. The completion of Dniepostroy was celebrated as though power dams were the invention of socialism.

The NEP allowed small businesses to function in local trade and some consumer industries. Though their flexibility was indispensable to supplement the socialist plan, NEP men were constantly harassed and prevented from expanding.

In the agricultural sector, the vast majority of holdings were in the hands of peasant families. Those who owned a horse and a cow and employed a farmhand were called *kulaks*, rich peasants; though by Western standards they might at best be described as "medium-sized," the Left considered them natural enemies of the Soviet rule. The regime encouraged the formation of co-operatives (*artels*, which preserved individual property) and collectives (*kolkhozes*, where most of the land is common property and work is directed by an administrator). There were about 50,000 farms of these two types, encompassing 4 million out of a total 25 million farm families. Finally, the highest form of farm organization, the *sovkhozes*, or state farms, few in number, were run on completely industrial lines.

Under this system the Soviet economy was developing slowly; the "scissors" between farm and industrial prices was closing a little, supplies were somewhat improved and in some sectors surpassed pre-war output. The peasants could keep a large part of the harvest. Then suddenly, in 1927, Stalin switched signals. At the Fifteenth Congress, the same that expelled the Left opposition, he introduced a resolution which for all practical purposes adopted its program, and announced a "Five Year Plan for Industrialization." The following year, 1928, this plan was published. It projected enormous increases in industrial production and a counter-attack against the *kulaks*. Class war was renewed in the countryside; the 5 million "village poor" were urged to force all farmers into the *kolkhozes*. In 1929, the pace of both industrialization and collectivization was accelerated.

Indeed, by 1932, 60 per cent of all peasants had lumped their holdings together, but at what cost! Stalin had misjudged the Russian peasants' attachment to property. Rather than surrender their cattle to the *kolkhoz*, they slaughtered 10 million cows, and in the collectives they continued to obstruct the plan. By 1933, Russia was suffering a severe famine; the Red Army first had to feed its new recruits before it could begin their training. Furious, Stalin tried to whip the recalcitrant peasants into submission. Hundreds of thousands were sent to Siberian concentration camps; no one knows how many died.

Instead of accelerating Russia's development, the "general line" actually retarded it. Leaders like Bukharin who had been identified with peasant interests, or Tomsky who presided over the trade unions, or Rykov and Kalinin who had grass-roots support in the Party, warned that the experiment would not succeed or would force the hierarchy to tighten its control beyond imagination. This is what actually happened. The Party was superseded by its inner apparatus, which now began to depoliticize the bureaucracy. Whoever represented a stratum of the people, an ideology, an interest, or whoever was not fast enough in changing his views as the "line" was being changed, had to go and, in addition, to take the blame for failure of the program he had opposed. This is the law of dictatorship: In liquidating oppositions left and right, the bureaucratic center comes to rely on an ever-narrowing group of functionaries who are less and less in touch with the people and increasingly base their decisions on the leader's whims and on the self-propelling consequences of his policy. The "second revolution" was to destroy the economic independence of classes and the ideological independence of Party members who might challenge the domination of the apparatus and of Stalin.

The rationale for this effort, however, was "rapid industrialization." The policies of reconciliation with European labor had not worked. The Soviet Union was isolated not only from the capitalist governments but from the workers in the West as well. A change of strategy suggested itself in Stalin's paranoiac mind: Russia was backward; her steel output and hence her defense industries were lagging behind the hostile West. Stalin promulgated the slogan "Catch up with the West and overtake it!" That necessitated huge investments, and the funds had to be squeezed out of the peasants and workers. The state, needing grain for export, had taken the old landowners' place.

The first Five Year Plan and the farm collectivization were to pull Soviet Russia up by her bootstraps and put her defense apparatus on a par with that of any potential aggressor. For ten years Russia was to be on a war footing, with martial law ruthlessly invoked against recalcitrants. All energies were to be bent toward this great effort, which was comparable in history only to the work of Peter the Great. The rate of investment, originally planned to be 625 million rubles yearly, soon was raised to 1.3 billion and eventually to 3.4 billion. The Five Year Plan was to be fulfilled in four years, in specific sectors even faster. Russia was to be changed from a peasant country into a modern industrial state. National pride was whipped into competition with the West. Victories were celebrated when the production of pig iron reached that of France, then that of Germany. Technology took priority over socialism. The system of equal wages was abandoned; skills were rewarded; teamwork was stressed; piece wages assured the principle "To each according to his deserts." By half time of the Second Five Year Plan, a Donets miner, Alexei Stakhanov, produced 102 tons of coal in a day; at once "Stakhanov teams" rushed into work in all industries.

The Five Year Plan was not a well-balanced program of development but rather a crash program, ballyhooed by every propagandistic and coercive means imaginable, to achieve certain defense goals irrespective of costs. Neither human suffering nor economic waste were allowed to stand in the way of "Russia's second revolution." When the war came, the Soviet economy was achieving its Third Plan period and producing 15 million tons of pig iron (three times as much as in 1918), 18 million tons of steel (four times as much), 166 million tons of coal (five times as much), 31 million tons of oil (three times as much), 48 billion kilowatts of electricity. No doubt, without Stalin's revolution, it might have produced more houses, shoes, textiles, and so on, but it might have fared even worse in the war than it did.

To explain the need for more sacrifices, Stalin cited the threat of foreign intrigue and blew up the intervention scare into a national paranoia. An intense campaign against "foreign spies" swept the country. One conspiracy was discovered in the Donets Basin: an "industry party" allegedly had been formed to overthrow the government at the behest of Poincaré or Chamberlain. Returned émigrés "confessed" that they had engaged in subversive activities and sabotage.

The Russian xenophobia had unfortunate consequences for the European labor movement. The Communist International was used by the Kremlin to blackmail the Western governments rather than to promote the cause of socialism. At their Sixth World Congress, the Communists were told that their "main enemy" was not the bourgeoisie but the Social Democrats, who indeed were Western oriented.

When the Great Depression broke out, the labor parties were divided and paralyzed. On the extreme Left, people looked to Russia, the great example of a different way, or even to the Red Army as the expected liberator; the moderate Left anxiously clung to the crumbling ramparts of formal democracy. Neither designed a common-front strategy to defend the interests of all workers, to ward off the fascist danger, and eventually to overcome capitalism. The Communists directed their propaganda against democracy and especially against the "Social Fascists"—meaning the Social Democrats. They collaborated with the Nazis in destroying the republican institutions of Germany; their Party egoism rejoiced when their numbers swelled at the expense of the hated socialists, while, in fact, the defenses of democracy were cracking and the terrorists of the Right were preparing to take over.

CHAPTER 7

The Great Depression

IN the ten years that followed the war, yearly per capita income rose from $250 to $293 in England, from $178 to $199 in Germany, from $161 to $188 in France. It fell from $109 to $96 in Fascist Italy, and it rose from $368 to $541 in the United States. Although income was unevenly distributed and millions remained unemployed, the pre-war peaks were exceeded everywhere. New industries provided a higher standard of living with serially constructed houses, new industrial designs, electrical appliances. England's overseas investments had once more risen to £3 billion and in 1929 yielded £212 million; her empire trade rose to £770 million. Savings account deposits in Germany rose to 9 billion reichsmarks in 1929, after having been wiped out completely in 1923.

Some German industries were surging ahead so dynamically that even the ensuing Depression could not check their upward trend. Electrical consumption doubled every ten years; rayon production rose from 10,000 tons in 1913 to 91,000 in 1927 and 400,000 tons in 1937. The number of registered motor vehicles increased from 1,213,000 in 1922 to 8,381,000 in 1937.

But not all changes were to the good. Old industries declined; new producers in overseas countries began to compete with the former monopolists. World trade no longer expanded; protectionist policies in some countries restricted it still more. At the same time the European peasants were being ruined by low-cost overseas producers.

A change, little understood at the time, occurred in the role of government both as a consumer and as a manager of the economy. Public consumption developed faster than private consumption as states and cities had to build roads, transport, and recreational facilities, hospitals, schools, parks, public utilities for rapidly growing population centers. But neither governments nor the public were prepared to recognize that new responsibilities also required a new approach to public finance. Instead of creating capital resources for their new activities, governments withdrew money from the private sector. Instead of stimulating over-all consumption, the welfare tasks curtailed capital formation. Nor were public authorities equipped to provide substitute financing when the circulation of money in the private sector slowed down for whatever reason. The body economic grew faster than its circulatory system.

The most important change, however, occurred in the shop. The old patriarchal relationship between owner-employer and worker yielded to the new businesslike attitude of management and union. Though most workers still were employed in small family enterprises, the 500 largest corporations of Europe now owned half of all manufacturing assets and employed a third of the industrial labor force. Even medium-sized enterprises (in Europe 50 to 500 employees) had to resort to the ruthless labor-saving methods which then were called rationalization. Assembly lines, speed-up, mechanical equipment, weeding-out of unproductive workers, time clocks, modern cost-accounting—all the new methods were allowed to override the old personal relations between employer and employee.

At first, rationalization provided jobs as industry invested huge sums to build machine tools. For many years this wave of new investment, combined with the con-sumer boom in home appliances, created and sustained prosperity. But, eventually, labor indeed was "saved," that is, unemployed. A documentary of the time proudly showed a blast furnace worth a million dollars that was serviced by just one worker, or a "mechanical miner" capable of doing the work of fifty men. When the laid-off workers failed to find jobs in new or expanding industries, a vicious spiral of growing unemployment would be started. Even at the height of prosperity, in 1928 and again in 1938, England had an irreducible minimum of 1 million jobless; in Germany, almost 2 million were jobless in 1928.

The new equipment increased output and at the same time reduced the income to buy it. Much of the investment turned out to be "misplaced," not by an error of judgment but because there was too much capital seeking an outlet, too little purchas-ing power seeking goods, and not enough credit facilities to mobilize future income nor fiscal policies to offset the lack of private liquidity. The whole system was inflexible. The old monopolistic practices, which had secured a steady market for the established suppliers, no longer worked. The new products glutted the market at the very moment when "sound financial practices" and technological unemployment curtailed consumption.

Besides, structural imbalances jolted European industry. People were not able to leave obsolete jobs (or, as in northern England and Scotland, distressed areas) fast enough. Government efforts to sustain employment in such industries and areas often proved counter-productive. This was true especially in agriculture. Attempting to keep as many people as possible on the land, governments subsidized the inefficient European farms—and only succeeded in pushing overseas farm prices even further down. Contrary to previous experience, the price index had kept declining throughout the boom.

Finally, some accidental, nonsystemic conditions touched off the crisis of con-fidence that shook the vulnerable world economy. The reparations, as we have seen, created a "transfer problem" on foreign exchange. The international debt structure was dangerously unbalanced, and America's protectionist policy had resulted in a depletion of Europe's gold reserves; a speculative boom was straining the limits of liquidity. Any of these or other external causes could set off a depression because the basic economic relations were maladjusted.

On October 24, 1929, the world was alarmed by the collapse of the New York stock market. Sensible investors had felt for some time that the shares were overvalued. Discovery of a big stock swindle, however, set the selling wave rolling; the "crisis" (as Europeans called it more aptly) spread rapidly throughout the world. By the summer of 1930, order cancellations and loan recalls had reduced the volume of trade in virtually all countries; bankruptcies and unemployment increased, prices and sales volume declined. Where cartels upheld prices, production was cut sharply and many workers were laid off; in other industries, which had to reduce prices to stay competitive, wages were cut ruthlessly. As incomes declined, taxation, rent, and debt service became more burdensome. The peasants, whose obligations remained fixed, were hit the worst by falling prices. In some areas, outraged peasants met the tax collectors with pitchforks and avenged foreclosures with arson.

Misery, despair, hunger, suicides, instability, insecurity, loss of confidence in the system's functioning, eventually the decline of public morality, degeneracy of political strife, and fascism were the fruits of the Depression. Between 1929 and 1932, industrial production fell 16 per cent in England, 28 in France, 33 in Italy, 47 in Germany. World trade in food declined 11 per cent, in raw materials 19, in manufactured goods 40. Unemployment affected 4 per cent of the labor force in France and Switzerland, 6 in Italy, 8 in Denmark and Sweden, 12–13 in Belgium and England, 17 in Germany. Many more worked only part time, and wages were declining.

The governments looked on with much hand-wringing and little imagination. Since their revenues were falling, their automatic reaction was to reduce the budget; since they were losing foreign trade, their remedy was to depress the price and wage level, eventually to devalue the currency, or to raise the tariff walls, or all three. But since these measures were taken competitively by all the governments, the effects canceled each other out, and the spiral of contracting exchanges went on and on for four long years. During all those years, in contrast to earlier depressions, none of the built-in stabilizers came into operation. The decline in wages, costs, and interest did not encourage the start of new ventures, nor did the decline of prices open up new markets. The closing of marginal plants did not rid the overcrowded industries of their surplus production problem. The unemployed received some compensation, but budgetary difficulties soon forced governments to cut the dole rates. With incomes declining, dwindling tax receipts forced further budget restrictions; instead of starting public-works projects, governments allowed the spiral to keep tightening.

In part, the trouble was political. When the German Government, hit hardest by unemployment, proposed to spend some billion marks on relief measures, it could not borrow on acceptable terms. The capitalists denied the republic their "confidence" and demanded that the Broad Coalition be dissolved. The same happened to Herriot in France. Likewise, the British Labour government had to resign when industrialists persuaded the Exchequer that wage cuts were a remedy for the Depression.

A political event also precipitated the collapse of Europe's financial structure. When in March 1931 the German and Austrian governments tried to form a customs union, angry French creditors withdrew their funds from the Austrian Creditanstalt, which promptly closed its doors and pulled two of Germany's four leading banks down with it. In July, all German banks were closed and the government instituted the control of foreign exchange. Marks could no longer be converted into other currencies without permission; payments on reparations were stopped. When President Hoover announced a "moratorium" on all debts between governments, dollar loans were withdrawn from British and French banks. France had enough gold to withstand the run; but on September 21, 1931, the Bank of England stopped paying gold for notes and allowed the pound sterling to find a new level.

It was the end of an era that had been ruled by the gold standard, an era where "safe as the Bank of England" meant the height of confidence, where the pound had served as an international measure of value. In the preceding decade, England had made great sacrifices to restore and maintain this guarantee of international monetary discipline which encouraged free trade and enforced the automatic adjustment of the balance of payments. With the gold standard abandoned, England gave up free trade and fenced her empire off from the rest of the world. It now was everyone for himself; other countries were forced either to follow England's lead in devaluing their currency or to institute controls which then had to be drawn tighter and tighter. The last effort to rebuild an international monetary order was torpedoed by President Franklin D. Roosevelt at the World Economic Conference, which took place in London in 1933. It took twenty-five years for all Western currencies to become freely convertible again.

The simple system of multilateral exchanges in a homogeneous world market now yielded to a complicated pattern of separate and bilateral arrangements. The British Empire withdrew into its own system of empire preferences. Some countries, like the Scandinavian, which depended on the British market, followed the pound into a "sterling bloc." Creditor countries, like Switzerland, tried to secure the debt service by earmarking the deficit of their trade balance for that purpose. Countries with currency controls like Germany tried to barter their products and to sell in the hard-currency markets to build up their reserves.

Most imports were controlled by quota and payments were no longer made to the foreign supplier directly but into a state exchange fund which reimbursed national exporters. When their claims became negotiable, the discounts had the effect of a devaluation. It was as though the government were creating a black market for its own currency. Hjalmar Schacht, the president of the German National Bank, in particular achieved mastery in this technique.

Thus, the age of *laissez faire* came to an ugly end. International co-operation, international division of labor, the world market, free price competition yielded to manipulated, subsidized, supervised, and regulated markets. But economic nationalism was unable to stop there. To save foreign exchange, governments had to control national production and consumption and to take over the bankrupt enterprises. Soon the Fascist government found itself owner and manager of most of Italy's big corporations; the Spanish and later the Nazi governments created monopolies for gasoline and rare metals.

The European tradition was not averse to intervention or public ownership anywhere. Railways and communications had been government-operated since before the turn of the century; most municipalities owned their utilities and local transportation systems. Neville Chamberlain chartered the British Broadcasting Company and the Central Electricity Board, and the Baldwin government enacted more social legislation than Labour had done. Conservatives favored welfare economics and protectionism; all governments recognized their obligation to create employment. Now the Russian example prompted Hitler to promulgate a Four Year Plan; even in traditionally individualistic Belgium and France people spoke of an *économie dirigée*. Most governments sought to boost purchasing power by a combination of public works, welfare payments, and governmental credit expansion.

The Nazi government had its own device to eliminate unemployment and its discontent. Young men and women were summoned into the labor service; a mass army was set on foot; industry received huge orders to equip these armies and to build strategic roads. It also used tax credits to stimulate replacement of industrial machines. In contrast to the republican governments, the Nazis were able to borrow enough money to finance their ambitious programs. By 1936, Hitler had reduced unemployment from 6 million to 2 million. Some economists think that the Depression had run its course by 1932; but Hitler also absorbed some structural as well as cyclical unemployment.

In England the recovery was slow. There, too, unemployment declined to 1.5 million in 1939. Four "special areas" were designated in 1934 in which old staple industries, coal, cotton, and ship-building, had suffered most. Partly by spending 2 billion pounds, some improvement was becoming visible by 1936. Thereafter the arms race helped to accelerate recovery. An area most grievously afflicted was the Highlands; but a scheme to build factories there was defeated by Scottish deputies who feared to disturb the Loch Ness monster. The building boom in the southeast and the planned development of the London area helped to absorb many who left the north.

Only in France did the Depression linger on. The Popular Front government devalued the franc and began a program of public works; but since it did not enjoy the support of the capitalists, recovery in France also had to wait until more conservative governments started rearming.

In other words, the Left either had no program for combating the crisis or was prevented from carrying out measures that smelled of democracy and social progress. Capitalism was saved not by welfare economics but by practices and controls that might have been even more repugnant to its classical philosophers; moreover, the arms race and a good measure of economic nationalism contributed heavily to the volume of orders.

Most important, investors' morale was influenced by political developments. The Depression had brought to power governments that guaranteed an end to social experiments and labor power. The dreaded revolution, which Marx had predicted as the inevitable result from such a deep depression, had not come. Instead, fascism had been established in Italy and Germany and was on the march in Eastern Europe.

A Conservative and long-time critic of *laissez-faire* economics, John Maynard Keynes, provided the ironical rationale for these new policies. In his *General Theory of Employment, Interest and Money* (1936), he showed that it did not matter whether the pump of recovery was primed by the opening of new goldfields, the plunder of Indian treasures, the building of pyramids, the creation of public works for useful purposes, or by "burying pound notes and then digging them out by financially sound enterprise." He became the herald of enlightened fiscal policies, designed to expand circulation when men and equipment were underemployed, or to brake the speed of turnover when full employment was straining the institutional ligaments of the system. His theories were implemented successfully by the socialist governments of Sweden and Denmark, with ambiguous results by the New Deal in the United States and the Popular Front in France, and most vigorously by the totalitarian dictators in Germany and Italy. The full-employment slogan was soon to be taken up by the Left in England and America; but, basically, Keynesianism is neither Right nor Left. It is a theory of economic management, not of revolution. Keynes became the successor of Montagu Norman as governor of the Bank of England. In France, a Popular Front government took the Banque de France out of the hands of "the two hundred families," but the much demanded "structural reforms" came to nothing.

Since the crisis of capitalism also appeared as a crisis of liberalism and of democracy, the moderate Left was paralyzed. The radical Left waited for the revolution and meanwhile exhausted itself in gestures of despair. Hunger marches went from the mining districts to London. One of them brought with it a petition carrying a million signatures: Abolish the Means Test (the degrading inquiry into the resources of welfare families). Such demands show how low the morale of the unemployed had sunk, how sadly they were lacking political ideas and leadership. Was it any wonder that the pied pipers of nationalism and imperialism were able to lure them with promises of greatness and foreign adventure? In England, the Beaverbrook and Rothermere press campaigned for a United Empire Party. France and Spain were on the verge of civil war. In Germany and Italy, ultra-nationalist governments were preparing for the "explosion" everyone expected.

This will be seen in Parts VI and VII. But before that, we shall look at the ideological situation that prepared the way.

Summing up Part IV: We have stressed the difficulties of the modern state after the old symbols of authority have collapsed. The revolutions had created new types of state: total dictatorships and pluralistic democracies. Only the former could appeal to a sense of "national purpose"; the latter were proud of precisely the opposite: the blossoming of many forces whose conflicts exposed the system to unbearable stresses. All problems were in the open. Governments were asked to assume more responsibilities than ever before, while at the same time they commanded less prestige and legitimacy. Class antagonism and ideological conflict claimed every citizen's attention. Political life became polarized; never before had so many people been involved. Even the fascist leagues were examples of this militant participation.

We have to distinguish between two crises. The one, economic, ought to have ended the capitalist system but did not. The other, political, nearly killed parliamentary government. The masses of Europe were not mature enough to deal rationally with tough problems. They did not have the benefit of great leaders, and they had lost the cultural mold that makes political differences negotiable. For the cultural crisis of the West now was approaching a climax. This is the subject of Part V.

PART V

The Periclean Age of Europe (1924–33) II: Culture

CHAPTER I

Life and Expression
in the 1920's

COMPARE any paintings or photos of the pre-war decade with any of the period between the two world wars. The striking difference in styles reveals a new attitude toward technology. Although few basically new inventions were being made in the 1920's, the earlier ones were accepted, developed, and applied in a thousand new ways. Every week new products appeared on the market, new processes were patented. New highways carried millions of motor cars; workers learned to process man-made raw materials; engineers designed rigorous job descriptions and work schedules, culminating in the inexorable flow of the assembly line. Just as in the factory the worker no longer had a choice of operations, so consumers were educated to buy packaged and branded goods. Household articles no longer sought to imitate works of art but took the bare, "streamlined" shape of technical efficiency.

Twentieth-century people created for themselves an environment which, perhaps for the first time, seemed entirely man-made and controllable. Systematic efforts brought the new conveniences to remote villages, assuring for the first time total participation in the culture. By the end of the 1920's, Europe was covered with a network of radio stations, some powerful enough to reach neighboring countries. The telephone spread to middle-class homes. The weekly visit to the movies became a habit for many low-income families.

Industrial materials were made to specifications: glass that did not break, steel that did not rust, rubber that did not lose its shape under heat, paints and dyes that did not fade, fibers that resisted tearing. Coal was being displaced by oil as a fuel, but it became the base of paints and fibers. Electricity replaced the unsafe gas light.

The chemical and electronics industries transformed our consumption patterns. The first sound track was produced by Lee de Forest in 1923; the first full-length "talking picture" was made in 1928. Television was invented simultaneously by Vladimir Zworykin and P. Nipkow in 1924 but did not come into practical use before World War II. Telephoto and color photography, invented by Americans in the same period, was adopted by the news media at once. The Germans began working with acetylene fibres (invented 1895); in 1932, Hermann Staudinger published a fundamental study on polymers on which the development of artificial fibers was to be based. Synthetic resins were invented in 1931.

The quality of housing was radically improved by city planning, new standards, and new building methods. Slum-clearance projects were underway in every major city. Subsidies were granted to builders who conformed to improved standards. Wholesome "settlements" or garden cities arose. Lower-middle-class families moved into the new developments; former slum-dwellers began to enjoy such modern amenities as gas ranges, electric light, and private bath and toilet facilities.

Some of the new amenities accelerated women's emancipation or changed the structure of family life. Tempting new gadgets changed buying habits and financial ethics. Though "being in debt" was still considered unrespectable by proper middle-class families, the installment (hire-purchase) plan now made it possible to buy household appliances that formerly had been out of reach.

With all this new technology, the city began to invade the countryside. Overcrowding forced the upper classes to seek refuge in nearby suburbs. The radio and motor car reversed the trend which railway and modern marketing techniques had adumbrated but not completed. Instead of depopulating the country, city life now came out to it. With the automobile, rural settlements could be as close to their markets as the big centers. In 1922, England had a million cars; seven years later, twice as many. In 1923, many cities were served by air express in almost all weather conditions.

The public eagerly took part in this orgy of technological progress. Car races and similar competitions kept public enthusiasm at a high pitch; new "world records" or "firsts" were set every year. Perry Thomas drove a car at 176 m.p.h. in 1926; H. O. D. Segrave achieved 231 m.p.h. in 1929 and also set a speedboat record. The *Europa* crossed the Atlantic in four days seventeen hours. In 1927, Charles A. Lindbergh crossed the Atlantic in a single-seater. (Actually the Atlantic had first been flown by two RAF officers who had not made a point of alerting press photographers.) Hugo von Eckener crossed the Atlantic in a Zeppelin; this clumsy vehicle was soon discarded as impractical, but the excitement it created was incomparable.

There was plenty of adventure in the new technology. The Italian Umberto Nobile flew to the North Pole in a semi-rigid airship and had to be rescued by the Norwegian explorer, Roald Amundsen, who perished in the attempt. Flying was a new experience vicariously shared by all. Fusing men with machines to conquer new frontiers, racing-car drivers and air pilots seemed like modern centaurs. Their exuberance has been exalted by Antoine de Saint-Exupéry and André Malraux. Filippo Marinetti called for a completely "mechanized poetry." A school of proletarian poets also sang of exalted harmonies between man and his machines, about creativeness and productivity. "I am the camera eye, the mechanical eye," said the first Soviet moviemaker, Dsiga Vertov. "I am the machine which shows you the world as no human eye can. I liberate you from human inflexibility." His film *Donets Basin Symphony* (1931) glorifies technology.

Unfortunately, neither mechanization nor speed liberated mankind from the lash of competitive labor; rather, both acted as stimulants to higher speed, increased productivity. Fusing man with his instruments is merely a subtler form of subjection than exploitation by capitalists; and it was precisely in Russia that the machine was deified. There, instead of man gaining the mastery over his inventions, the iron commands of industrialization seemed to triumph over man even more harshly than in the West. But the mood was world-wide. Techniques were praised not as means to an end but as beautiful in themselves. Whatever could be had to be invented; whatever advance progress demanded would be consummated, no matter what its human cost. "Rationalization" in industry assumed that the replacement of men by machines makes the production process more rational. Social costs—measured in terms of unemployed human resources, of crowding and loss of community values—were not included in the balance sheet. Man simply had to bow out where the machine claimed superiority.

Oswald Spengler advised the young generation to accept technology as its "fate," even though he deplored the new, soulless culture. Others seemed to endow the wonders of techniques with the soul that they themselves had lost. Still others revolted. Aldous Huxley wrote the bitter satire, *Brave New World* (1932), a mock Utopia which anticipated the total dehumanization of men in a culture entirely dominated by efficiency calculations. Even before him, Eugene Zamyatin had published *We*, a negative Utopia in the same vein, denouncing the mechanical life of an all-too-imminent future.

Painters, too, protested the dehumanization through technology of man and of art. They deliberately destroyed the images of the human environment, dissolving them into geometrical shapes or showing man as a wretched animal incapable of living up to his own better self. Giorgio di Chirico, Picasso, Léger, and Duchamp, each in his way, have struggled with the problem of lost roots, reducing the human form to mechanical symbols. None of them succeeded in integrating the machine into man's experience. Often the viewer is not sure whether he sees an exaltation of technology or a mockery of it, submission to the demands of mechanical necessity or protest against it, presentation of a god or of an outrage. In Juan Miró and Paul Klee, irony obviously prevails over awe. Others, alas, succumbed and retreated into madness.

In 1923, Abel Gance produced the film *La Roue*, for which Arthur Honegger wrote the music—later used in his train-locomotive orchestra suite *Pacific 231*—showing machines, parts, and instruments as though they were living beings, an orgy of reified montage, the first of many more in the same vein, especially in Russia. More ambivalent, Fritz Lang's monumental film *Metropolis* (1926) showed the enslaved masses marching to work, all in step, into a factory that has the looks of a Moloch. In René Clair's *À Nous la Liberté* (1931), the workers are like robots, and assembly-line work is likened to the work of a prison gang. The same theme was taken up by Charlie Chaplin in *Modern Times* (1936). The sequence of these four films is interesting. Gance and the Russians accept the mastery of the machine; Lang seems to believe in the idea of a technological utopia; René Clair rebels against this idea; Chaplin, completely disillusioned despite the New Deal ideology, shows the crack-up.

However, the greatest protester against the machine age was a little animal that seemed to defy the laws of mechanics: Walt Disney's Mickey Mouse. Popular all over Europe, as well as in the United States, this fantasy was a projection of the little man's dream—to be able to escape from the big monsters, to be able to grow or to shrink as the situation required, to be resurrected after being utterly crushed, to succeed by doing the improbable and irrational. Other cartoon films in the same vein followed, but later the whole genre degenerated into mere adventure and fantasy play.

Jazz, making its appearance in European coffee houses at about that time, may have played a similarly liberating role. It came as a symbol of youth and its new attitude toward life. The plaintive sound of the saxophone (tentatively introduced by Meyerbeer, Berlioz, and Massenet, but rejected by opera audiences), the syncopated rhythms, the use of drums and other percussion instruments seemed at once archaic and modern, exotic and futurist. Lascivious like the tango and stirring like the revolution, jazz offered precisely the ambiguity of choices which that society liked to maintain. It was African and American, simultaneously primitive and mechanized. Conservatives discovered in its beat the irresponsible defiance flaunted by left-wing radicalism, while Moscow condemned it as the putrid flower of decadent capitalism— and both probably were right. Recording companies and *avant-garde* journalists hailed it as the music of our age; but the music critic of the German left-wing *Weltbühne* called it "the spasms of our age" and then wondered whether he was not mistaking the birth pangs of a new age for spasms. What kind of age? "One that must constantly reassure itself that it is an age and has a rhythm."

The new technology changed the relationships between work, play, and dream. At first, people accepted progress as an opportunity to realize their true dreams. The eight-hour day, the forty-four-hour week gave them leisure to cultivate their little garden plots, to go hiking and fishing, to read, to play. Sports, both active and spectator, became a major pastime. If work had grown mechanical and monotonous, play grew less ritualistic. The right to leisure and pleasure came to be looked at as the inalienable right of all citizens, at least in the West. Johan Huizinga was to write *Homo Ludens* (*Playful Man*) which, pursuing ideas of Romano Guardini and Leo Frobenius, took issue with the philosophy of *Homo faber*, man the maker: man is himself, he argued, not when he toils but when he plays, an idea familiar to Schiller, Coleridge, and later Marcuse.

But twentieth-century sport was not idleness. Much of it was work, and competitive —truly the obverse side of the coin of industrial society. The bicycle riders who undertook the *Tour de France* or, in the Berlin Sportspalast, the *Sechstagerennen* had to work hard and were exploited commercially. Nevertheless, the awakened interest in world records, prize fights, and championships was evidence of a yearning for heroes who earned their wreaths through personal valor. The tennis champions Bill Tilden and Suzanne Lenglen, the amazing Finnish runner Paavo Nurmi, the heavyweight fighters Jack Dempsey, Gene Tunney, Max Schmeling, Jack Sharkey, and Primo Carnera became the envy of every schoolboy; Lindbergh's solitary flight across the Atlantic proved that the age of chivalry was not dead yet. People swam the English Channel to gain world fame; soccer teams were goodwill ambassadors. Governments encouraged these activities, provided facilities, created national symbols, and surrounded leisure activities with a patriotic aura. In Fascist Italy the state even organized all the leisure-time activities of its subjects: Dopolavoro saw to it that the citizen continued to be useful in his leisure time. Under fascism, sports were government-directed. In republican Germany and republican Czechoslovakia they were patriotic exercises based on individual prowess. In Western and Northern Europe they were entirely free; nonetheless, events like a prize fight or endurance test united the nation across class lines. While some sports, such as tennis, remained the province of the well-to-do, most sports were democratic. The fittest have a chance, regardless of birth or money, and everybody can watch, bet, and comment expertly.

Equally democratic were fashions, with their emphasis on the youthful, sporty look. There was an air of adventure as well as relaxation about the young men in their baggy sweaters and fedoras that seemingly defied the formality of the old society, a hint of a certain anti-establishmentarian intellectualism in their heavy, horn-rimmed glasses and long hair worn combed back instead of parted. In the later 1920's, men tried to look rakish, martial, or up-and-coming, never mature and settled. Beards and mustaches were dropped. Age had no advantage.

Women were supposed to be slender, athletic, and trim; those who did not look naturally youthful watched their figures by doing calisthenics. Matrons were not considered attractive. Legs were to be seen. In the early 1920's, designers began first to deny femininity, replacing the hour-glass figure with the boyish, lean look. Emancipated women were supposed to be comrades, not wives. But soon the repressed sexuality returned, bringing in a new fashion which emphasized women's frailty and whimsicality. High heels and short, tight-fitting skirts made it difficult to run after a bus or board one. By way of compensation, women could now clothe their legs in beautiful rayon and begin a new type of flirtation.

The Depression years brought an emphatic change in fashion. The trend toward youth, primitivism, abstraction, and geometric design was suddenly abandoned. Women were urged to look feminine yet matronly, conservatively bourgeois, not to say Victorian. Street dresses still were short, but evening gowns came down to the ankles. Make-up, nail polish, elaborate coiffures, and ornate jewelry seemed like a retreat from the recent fashion revolution, from the equality and ease in social relations. The new fashion seemed to deny the Depression; society was trying to convince itself that nothing had changed since before the war.

Four revolutionary developments revamped the image of woman: the bobbed hair, the raising of the hemline from ankle to calf to knee, make-up, and the freedom to smoke in public. Each of these four innovations was frowned upon by employers. In *The Long Week-End* (1941), Robert Graves traces the acceptance of any daring innovation in fashion: from brothel to stage to bohemia to society to society's maids to millgirls to suburban housewives. He might have added that they also followed a West-East course: from America, the land looked on by most Europeans as the home of freedom, to England, to France, to Germany, and regions farther east. Travelers brought cocktails, chewing gum, and the new music and dances to Europe.

The speed with which these innovations followed each other was symptomatic of the restlessness of the period, of its craving for the novel, of its determination to prove that it was alive and enjoying itself. In the later 1920's, night clubs flourished in the big cities. An air of rakishness was fashionable in high society, and the lower middle class imitated it. Plunging necklines and bare backs became evening styles. From memoirs we gather that at some house parties in London, Paris, Berlin, and elsewhere, attended by high society and some literary and theater people, clothes were shed altogether. The police often staged drug raids in night clubs; and if we can believe Maurice Dekobra's, Pitigrilli's, and Joséfin Peladan's novels, drugs were easy to come by. Society wanted its kicks. It also wanted to be shocked. Josephine Baker, dancing in a topless banana-leaf G-string, startled night-club audiences; her jazz drummers stirred them with vibrant rhythms—pleasurable sensations, a mixture of thrills, excitement, and embarrassment.

As society grew bored, it began to lament its hangover, as did T. S. Eliot in "The Love Song of J. Alfred Prufrock" and "The Waste Land," or Bertolt Brecht in the decadent songs of *Mahagonny*. Sardonic works like André Gide's *The Counterfeiters* (1926), Aldous Huxley's *Point Counter Point* and Evelyn Waugh's *Decline and Fall* (both 1928) vividly show the disenchantment with a society that had come to equate freedom with a lack of values and scruples.

The hit song of the 1920's suggests instant love and often alludes so directly to its consummation that parodies quickly substituted lewd and obscene words for the ambiguities that the original covered up with schmaltz. Radio and phonograph assured the new hit rapid acceptance. But in contrast to racy folk songs, the hit songs dared not be too disrespectful. They had to be acceptable to stage and movie producers. Though they might be erotic, they were not to question the established order of the world.

The mass entertainments reflected the search for sensuality and sensation. Sex was no longer relegated to the back streets but, literally, allowed into the limelight, at least for those who could pay. A new kind of show—the lavishly produced revue, with new, sophisticated lighting and stage effects as well as coveys of subtly undressed girls —conquered the stage. These eye teasers appealed to audiences less refined than those who had once supported the ballet; for that very reason they demanded more refined stage effects designed to make visible that which earlier audiences had been content to imagine—but also to conceal that which still was left to the imagination. The most famous of all the shows touring Europe in triumph were the Tiller Girls. In Paris, the Moulin Rouge and Folies-Bergère catered to the tourist trade, and the ageless Mistinguett (born Jeanne Bourgeois) visited all world capitals with her show.

It is difficult to define the term sexual license. There had always been license for the man, provided the woman was of a class lower than his own. Women were supposed to be chaste not only in body but in mind, but this was not true in high society. Novelists tell us that only the middle-middle class was virtuous, not the rich nor the poor. What was new in the 1920's was men's attitude not toward sex but toward women of their own class, and women's feelings about themselves. They refused to remain objects of sexual exploitation. They demanded companionship, reciprocity. They felt that their worth increased if they were to give freely what hitherto could be had only at a price. Many a "free marriage" united couples more solidly than any formal ceremony could have; from America came Judge Ben Lindsay's proposal to legalize "companionship marriages." Though Europe never reached the high divorce rates of modern America, divorce, at least in Protestant countries, was becoming easier. While society did not yet accept it lightly, still it no longer considered divorce a disgrace.

Reformers everywhere tried to ban the double standard from marriage; but although relations between the sexes were becoming more honest, men still enjoyed sexual freedom while at the same time guarding their wives' honor. French juries continued to acquit murderers who had caught their spouses *in flagrante*. Italy, Spain, and other Catholic countries, but not Austria and Bavaria, maintained the "double standard" of morality for men and women.

In every country except Russia, reformers kept hammering at the one closed door to sexual freedom: birth control. Only the rich could control the size of their families; the poor died as the result of illegal abortions. (To this day, legal abortions are severely restricted in many countries.) In the 1920's most countries allowed abortion only if the mother's life was in danger, not even in case of rape or if the child was a likely victim of a congenital defect. The established Churches also frowned on contraceptive practices.

However, techniques of both contraception and abortion were widely known, especially in the larger European cities. Some communities stretched the law to the limit; a number of socialist mayors opened clinics for both counseling and treatment. "Sex reform," as it was called, consisted mostly in education and publicity; doctors wrote "how to" books, and pioneers openly defied the law. Marie Stopes, a physician, wrote *Married Love* and opened a clinic in London; her campaign eventually forced the Anglican Church to permit the use of contraceptive devices by married couples. A French woman writer, in a book of the same title, proclaimed that "my body belongs to me."

Equal freedom was demanded for deviates and abnormal practices. In the 1920's, when morality on the whole had become "relative," upper-class deviates also found it easier to admit their affliction or even take pride in it. Havelock Ellis's *Studies in the Psychology of Sex*, Edward Carpenter's *The Intermediate Sex*, Magnus Hirschfeld's *Geschlechtskunde*, and André Gide's confessions were widely read. In Paris, the Boulevard Montparnasse was an open market for male prostitutes; Berlin had dance halls frequented by male and female homosexuals. In many youth movement groups homosexuality was almost a mark of distinction. Contemporary novels also suggest that incest and bestialism, the most ancient taboos, were turning into acceptable topics of conversation.

The supreme vices were thought to come from the Orient. Secret cults and strange drugs were tried by the upper class; and, for the first time, the general public participated in them vicariously through pulp magazines and pseudo-literature whose ornate style suggested perverse practices.

CHAPTER 2

The Lively Arts—Popular Culture

BEFORE there was art there was kitsch. As a rule, history books do not give recognition to the so-called popular arts; they record only that which promises to last—highbrow culture. Only when the house collapses on the culture priests' heads does the historian register, with unwilling pen, the barbarians' invasion. But it was precisely in the 1920's that some art historians began to point out that the peasant who came to Florence failed to admire Michelangelo's David but knelt before some shockingly crude canvas of Hell; one knew that amateur quartets in Hickstown did not play Stravinsky. When studying publishers' records, we see that the works of Stefan George, Marcel Proust, and James Joyce together did not reach even 1 per cent of the reading public.

What did the others read, recite, and sing? Limericks, probably, and their equivalent in other languages—but folk songs too. What is worth recording about them, however, is not ideas but styles. A history of the minor arts must concentrate on the performers who in their own time were in public view, no matter how commonplace and inferior they may have been. Since it is personalities that are being merchandised, the public character of these performers is often the cultural message. As archeologists explore the garbage dumps of past civilizations, the history of culture must peruse literary trash, examine best-seller lists and hit-record sales. This is history not of what is memorable but of what was being experienced; its subject has been called popular culture. It includes popular literature, most movies, radio, television, folk songs, women's magazines, juvenilia, comics, pornography, dance music, mystery novels, advertising, and of course the penny papers, the tabloids.

What was new in the 1920's was the fact that these media were no longer looked down on as products of an inferior culture but were allowed to enter the mainstream of public life. Though the McLuhan revolution proper may not have occurred before the middle of the century, its coming was signaled early enough by sociologists, literary critics, and politicians. Hitler remarked in *Mein Kampf* that people do not think in concepts but in images; advertisers deliberately substituted pictures for words; Siegfried Kracauer and Rudolf Arnheim, the first regular movie critics, observed that the film follows laws other than those of the theater. Illustrated magazines of the period still featured mostly pictures that tried to tell a story; but in political posters symbols came to predominate, and advertisers preferred images for ready identification. Outdoor advertising also changed the visual experience of city life; it overwhelmed the pedestrian with pictures and lit up the night with illuminated signs. Political and commercial advertisers seemed to rely on behaviorist psychology, too; they tried to impress on the public a name rather than a reason.

While the eye was thus being besieged by visual stimuli, the ear was being caught—or assaulted—by another one-way communication: the radio. Again, it was found that, to be effective, this new medium had to appeal not to the listener's critical powers but to his willingness to submit to the magic of the voice. Even the most superficial book contains the seeds for discussion; but even the most profound broadcast leaves the listener in the position of a passive, captive receiver of messages. The culture of the book, which had ruled Europe for five hundred years, was being assailed both by the new techniques and by the new masses for whom these media meant their first participation in culture of any kind. Society at large was becoming receptive to the new media.

Literary critics promptly began to complain that the mass media did not require active involvement, that should mass media style be carried over into encounters between people, conversation might grow barren; they observed, and advertisers knew, that people like to repeat readily available, prethought, preformulated, pre-packaged standard phrases. Instead of learning about the world from a teacher, the critics said, people would tend to confuse things heard on the radio with personal experience and take them as their frame of reference. Knowledge thus gained might be deceptive. With reference to documentary films, it was pointed out that a "candid" picture may lie. While the details may be accurate enough, the viewer may not know that the total picture was edited; he cannot differentiate between the important and the trivial, between "fact" and the camera view.

The mass-circulation magazines imitate this film technique. By reporting on the private lives of the great, they give the "little guy" the illusion that he is privy to their secrets. Socrates becomes a pal, with his worries and failings. This peeping-Tom view of history replaces analysis by consumption of a pseudo-experience. The interviewer goes straight up to the maker of history and gets the inside dope from his own mouth. Moreover, the magazine format reduces important and significant events to the same size as trivia. You get a visit with Einstein, an explanation of Turkish farming, a sports event, and the story of a new perfume in the same issue, set in the same type, with the same sort of pictures.

The difference between high culture and its vulgarization became blurred when illustrated magazines began to discuss theological issues or to educate their readers in the pleasures of visiting a museum; when publishers gave the same jackets to great classical works, to modern *avant-garde* experiments, and to mere entertainment or outright trash; when newspaper stories spread esoteric knowledge about Joyce or Kafka—and advertised them as geniuses with reputations outshining that of Aeschylus.

The movie may bring esoteric works of art to the masses—which does not neces-sarily mean down to their level. Anticipating later developments, Kafka's *The Trial*, Dostoevsky's *Crime and Punishment*, Schnitzler's *Miss Elsa* have been rendered faithfully and artistically. On the other hand, Toulouse-Lautrec, Michelangelo, and van Gogh have been bowdlerized in cheap, exploitative films, and *The Blue Angel* became a world success precisely because of the qualities Heinrich Mann repudiated.

But most movies were entertainment. Pictures were technically imperfect and artistically on the level of pulp literature. Adventure film and comedy were the subjects most likely to attract crowds. During World War I, Charlie Chaplin introduced a new dimension: significance. Mary Pickford and Gloria Swanson were seen in the first full-length films. In the 1920's, the new medium was used in strange new ways to illustrate man's bewilderment. The first great documentary was *The Wonders of Skiing. Nanook of the North, Trader Horn,* and *Chang* showed life in faraway countries through stories about natives.

Few critics had yet recognized the movie as a new and special art form. Today it may be trite to say that the silent movie relied on visual devices to make its point; then, talking pictures had to find their own laws of presentation and perception. Sacha Guitry was a great actor and comedy writer of the time; his films, nothing more than photographed stage plays, were boring. However, one did not go to the movies to see a "good" play or to be edified. One went to be entertained, to be thrilled, to be excited by the extraordinary beauty of Greta Garbo, to be horrified by the frightening imagination of Fritz Lang or Alfred Hitchcock, the hideous face of Lon Chaney.

The movies as an art form are a product of the industrial age. They require the co-operation of author, director, photographer, set designer, engineers, actors, editor, and all the other contributors listed in the credits.

No doubt the movie homogenizes experience, and its economics tempt producers, who after all are responsible to stockholders, to look for the widest audiences with the least differentiated taste. Ricciotto Canudo called the movie industry an "image factory;" Upton Sinclair angrily and analytically labeled it a "dream factory."

The films of the 1920's reflected the wish-fulfillment dreams of the time: every youth a Rudolph Valentino (*The Sheik*) or Douglas Fairbanks (*Robin Hood, The Thief of Baghdad*), every girl a seductive Marlene Dietrich or a demure Mary Pickford. The romantic love story assured people that all's well that ends well, that love conquers all. In subtler ways, the archetypal characters of Harold Lloyd, Charlie Chaplin, and Buster Keaton proclaimed the same faith in survival. Their creations often are morality plays that verge on satire; they also illustrate the little man's bewilderment in a strange and cruel world. Weird visions of alienation in the modern world appeared in *The Cabinet of Dr. Caligari* (1920), *Dr. Mabuse* (1922), *Metropolis* (1926)—expressionistic films exploring previously untouchable themes. The German horror film mixed Jungian psychology with symbolist techniques and sensational, often topical subject matter. Surrealistic montages projected images of anxiety or of man's bondage to fate and instincts; but often expressionism merely provided thrills, as did the first *Dr. Jekyll and Mr. Hyde* (1920) and the first *Dracula* (1922). Scandinavian directors (thirty years before Ingmar Bergman!) used a similar vocabulary in erotic films of great frankness, such as *Vampire, Satan's Book, Dies Irae, Eroticon.* Friedrich Murnau (*Tabu,* 1931) was the supreme master of imagist horror pictures.

Movie makers soon learned to develop pictorial images and symbols to point up new significances; thus, Marcel L'Herbier treats the Paris Stock Exchange as a mysterious animal in *L'Argent* (1928). Others were carried away by the technical possibilities of the film, reveling in brilliant detail even if they had no story to tell. Jean Epstein presented *Coeur Fidèle* (*Faithful Heart*, 1923), consisting of nothing but moods and dramatic impressions, a technique that Marcel Carné was to develop in *Quai des Brumes* (*Port of Shadows*, with Jean Gabin, 1938). The art movie sought to create visual poetry. Soon a *cinéma pur* was experimenting with things like pots and pans doing eurythmics. Fernand Léger (the painter), René Clair, and Henri Chomette produced fantasies that were forerunners of Disney's *Fantasia* (1940). The art film relied heavily on technical expertise and artistry in the limited sense as practiced in the circus. On a still lower level, the film developed the star, or diva, system, creating the cult of the photogenic individual.

But the public wanted stories, entertainment, and thrills. Its tastes were catered to by the French *Pathé-Cinema*, the German Universum Film AG (UFA), which fell into the hands of the reactionary tycoon Alfred Hugenberg, and also by the European producers who flocked to Hollywood. The German film companies produced sweet pageants, light comedies, historical kitsch, and patriotic gore, but also a handful of masterpieces by Fritz Lang (*M*, 1930) and G. W. Pabst (*Kameradschaft* [*Comradeship*], 1930). Ernst Lubitsch, who also started with UFA, was to make *Ninotchka* (with Greta Garbo, 1939). He always managed to convey his contempt of authority, while Pabst and Lang were political weathervanes. They had connections with Leni Riefenstahl, Hitler's film director. Lang's wife, Thea von Harbou, wrote scenarios reflecting totalitarian and nationalistic attitudes: man's surrender to the mechanics of big organizations, his submission to a strong, if insane, leader's will (*Metropolis*); reduction of humans to architectural ornaments; cultist use of Teutonic legends (*Die Nibelungen*); fascination with fate and with hollow grandeur. Such treatments were not confined to Germany, though. Abel Gance also combined expressionistic horror techniques with chauvinistic propaganda and a Napoleon cult. Russian films, of course, always stressed patriotic themes, and barracks comedy was popular in all countries.

In the 1920's the French, despite their early pioneering, had only a few great film directors. René Clair discovered the musical grotesque in *Sous les Toits de Paris*, *Le Million*, *À Nous la Liberté*, and *Le Dernier milliardaire*. His satire was hard-hitting. Like Chaplin and Brecht, he compared capitalist society to a prison or a gangster club. Jacques Feyder (1888–1948) also put the film to political use. In *Les Nouveaux Messieurs* (1929) he satirized trade-union leaders; in *La Kermesse Héroïque* (1936) he debunked war and heroism. (Ironically, he accepted Nazi help in producing this film.)

The great star, or perhaps the great myth, of the 1920's was Greta Garbo, first seen in Mauritz Stiller's *Gösta Berlings Saga* (1924) and then in Pabst's *Die Freudlose Gasse* (1925). Her haunting beauty seemed to hold a promise to a jaded generation that somewhere in the world romance was still possible.

Strangely, the great films of V. I. Pudovkin and Sergei Eisenstein, widely admired for their technical innovations and their monumental view of simple people and of masses, found no imitators in the West, where these films were generally confined to invited audiences. Except in the big cities they were not shown in public theaters but in clubs or specially hired halls.

Although a few great stars were truly international, most art films with world-wide appeal were the distinct products of a particular country, seen in other countries only by select audiences. Some great movies were pointedly made as joint ventures: *Comradeship* exalted the solidarity between German and French workers during a mine disaster; *Verdun* and *La Grande Illusion* meant to overcome the spirit of war. But the great majority of movies distributed internationally were of the "Western" adventure type.

The heroes of pulp magazines also acquired fame in many countries. Arsène Lupin, Raffles, Sherlock Holmes were read in serials. Movies brought world-wide audiences to Dr. Fu Manchu and Tarzan. The decline of the species is exemplified by Superman, who is no longer a human insurgent but an omnipotent savior whose intervention is ardently desired by the little man. Such leader images, especially when accompanied by sadistic fantasies, may have contributed to the Nazi mentality.

No cultural history would be complete without a chronicle of crime. Surely there are fashions in crime. Society sympathized with underworld characters, especially when their stubborn use of defendants' rights drove the judge crazy. It enjoyed mock-affectionate skits about mass murderers. It tolerated homosexuality, adultery, crimes of passion. It laughed about impostors. It took a fervent interest in juvenile delinquents and applauded the play *Revolt in the Reform School*, followed by numerous movies about prison riots. Humanizing the prisons was a liberal cause; crime prevention became a serious subject among social workers.

The detective story indicates increasing sophistication in reader attitudes toward the police and crime itself. In times of conservative tastes, the hero is the detective; in revolutionary times it is the criminal. Sir Conan Doyle, the inventor of the imperishable and imperturbable Sherlock Holmes, was an archconservative. So was his most successful follower, Edgar Wallace, whose inventiveness thrilled the 1920's. Both start from the premise that the criminal is a misfit and that violation of the proper code of behavior is easily spotted by application of strict logic: since the world is rational, order will be restored by the power of reason.

During the 1920's, crime stories tended to depict the police as both stupid and overly assiduous, yet nevertheless the master detective seemed to be in full command of society's resources. The problem of eliminating evil was a ritual of purgation. With the apprehension of the criminal, the *status quo* was restored. Dorothy Sayers, an eminent practitioner of the art, wrote that the reader must become convinced that the bigger problems of hunger, maladjustment, hate, and politics can be solved and resolved in the manner of *Death in the Library*. This rationalism, no longer fashionable in serious literature, was still practiced by the popular writers of the 1930's: Agatha Christie's Hercule Poirot, was the owner of those famous "little gray cells"; and

Georges Simenon's Inspector Maigret even was a representative of authority. Phillips Oppenheim was another master of the genre.

But the detective story not only assures us that crime does not pay; it also admits that crime has its satisfactions. Whether the popularity of the thriller contributed to the decline in morals or was its mere symptom, no doubt it foreshadowed the breakdown of inhibitions and of authority which came to plague Europe in the 1930's.

In the past, criminals had been "the underworld," the paupers (undeserving poor), the scum that was kept at arm's length, and in turn had done everything to stay invisible; theft and robbery were the most common crimes. Now the gambler and gentleman con-man or blackmailer began to assume an almost heroic stature; the outlaw turned into a noble Robin Hood. In times of war, depression, and inflation, to defraud the government or to flout the law became a game.

There were twice as many indictable offenses as before the war; frequently the offenders were juveniles, even children. To stay out of jail seemed to be a question not of guilt or innocence, but of luck or of having a good lawyer. With the courts overloaded, governments found it necessary to liberalize criminal codes. The public did not yet side with the criminals, but it began to see that criminals were human beings, too. With the revival of Dostoevsky and the romantics, young people more and more tended toward the belief that society itself was to blame for crimes that unhinged it. Two famous best-sellers, Jakob Wassermann's *The Maurizius Case* and Franz Werfel's *Nicht der Mörder, der Ermordete Ist Schuldig*, deal with the ambiguity of justice and morality. A generation gap was to open between those who still believed in order and those who had no experience of it.

With Bertolt Brecht's *Threepenny Opera* and the films Marcel Carné directed in collaboration with Jacques Prévert, a new anti-hero appeared: the downtrodden outlaw, the deserter, the desperado, the lonely outsider, the dropout. Originally mistaken for a rebel, the character so often portrayed by Jean Gabin (*Quai des Brumes*, *Le Jour se Lève*, and so on) is rather a disillusioned innocent who, though resigned to perpetual defeat, accidentally exposes society for the things it has done to him. In *Forbidden Games* (1952) René Clément was to go even further in revealing the cruelty of society by opposing to it the naïveté of innocents or by letting innocents do innocently what society is doing guiltily.

In the 1920's and 1930's, the mystery story became increasingly "realistic"; that is to say, both detective and criminal appear as human beings engaged in combat. Though their psychology is still rudimentary, the novels of Dorothy Sayers and Agatha Christie no longer present the hero and the villain in stark black and white. After World War II, Margery Allingham made it a law that even in thrillers the criminal has to be human. Up to World War II, crime and spy stories were written mostly for relaxation. Eric Ambler used it to convey his personal sense of threatening cataclysm. Today, espionage serves the brutalizing commercialism of Ian Fleming as well as the highly sophisticated message of John Le Carré (*The Spy Who Came In from the Cold*) or Len Deighton (*Funeral in Berlin*).

Serious authors such as G. D. H. Cole, Sidney Webb, Cecil Day Lewis (Nicholas

Blake), and John Stewart (Michael Innes) have also written crime stories for relaxation, or have used them for serious discussions of important issues.[1] Chesterton's novels and tales deal with the idea of universal guilt. Brecht built a theory of the crime story on the premise that the gangster is the prototype of the capitalist. Since he saw Nazism as the political arm of monopoly capitalism, the equation "Hitler = gangster" was in his eyes not a moral judgment but social analysis. The same idea underlies his play, *Der Aufhaltsame Aufstieg des Arturo Ui* (*The Resistible Rise of Arturo Ui*). But Brecht was wrong: Fascist regimes suppress private criminality because the state claims a monopoly on criminal behavior. Hitler went as far as to discourage publication of detective stories because "there is no such thing as a socialist crime novel."

A similar pride in the state's virtue has thus far prevented the crime story from flourishing in the Soviet Union and its satellite countries. The criminals in popular novels and on the stage are capitalist spies or, if Russians, sons of decadent *émigrés* and asocial characters. They must conform to the type of the "negative hero" prescribed by "socialist realism." Russian movie houses, however, screen Hollywood Westerns.

W. H. Auden has suggested that thrillers are unpopular with bloody dictators because such work permits the reader first to identify with the criminal and then to see the guilt removed from himself. Dictators must insist that everybody is guilty. The newest trend in detective stories is away from thrillers that are, as it were, intelligence tests, and toward novels of adventure which put raw courage above brains. The classical detective plot has been dissolved into a series of sado-masochistic episodes, or been supplanted by science fiction stories which serve the same purpose. Movie and television adaptations of this species in particular show a world made up of disjointed happenings, of irrational, arbitrary, cruel decisions by inscrutable powers —in brief, the rule of evil. Reality is seen as a horror story full of scandal, hypocrisy, and absurdity. As a result, the reader no longer can help the detective in setting the world right again. As a mere voyeur, he must accept the shocking activities of reprehensible agents who are directed by secret powers of evil. These trends have been greatly intensified by the invasion of American comics, movies, and thrillers; but the Europeans are by no means novices in the genre.

As a rough indicator of change in public mentality, we might list the qualities of a popular hero in 1900, in 1930, and in 1960. In the beginning of the century, he definitely belongs to the upper classes or even to nobility; between the two wars he is an entertainer or sports champion; today he must belong to a minority or be an underdog. The anti-hero in cartoon literature was a toughie two generations ago, then a noble outcast or enemy of society; today he may be wealthy. The personal characteristic most appreciated by our grandfathers was dashing bravery; by our fathers, cunning efficiency; by us, cool.

---

[1] More recent examples are: Hans Habe's *The Net*, Alain Robbe-Grillet's *Les Gommes* and *La Maison de Rendez-vous*, Jean Cayrol's *Midi Minuit*, and Michel Butor's *L'Emploi du Temps*.

CHAPTER 3

Literature, the Arts,
and Society Between the Wars

SPENGLER has suggested that every civilization can be summed up in some characteristic art object. As the Eiffel Tower and Albert Hall are symbols of the late nineteenth century, so Erich Mendelsohn's Einstein Tower in Potsdam (near Berlin) and Le Corbusier's apartment houses in Marseille betoken the twentieth. Sober but sweeping, clear lines suggest the purpose of the building and exhibit its structural elements, characterizing the new "functional" style. Just as in a poem by Auden there is not one superfluous word, the very form of a Bauhaus chair precludes ornamentation. At least that was the theory. And indeed wrought-iron gates ceased to imitate vegetation; but automobiles lent their "streamlined" forms to refrigerators and other implements which do not move. The new idea of modern design spread from the Bauhaus in Dessau to all of Europe. Its director, Walter Gropius, at first strongly influenced by Frank Lloyd Wright, departed vigorously from his "organic" style to create a purely urban environment. When Gropius, László Moholy-Nagy, and Ludwig Mies von der Rohe came to the United States in the 1930's they in turn influenced American architects. Le Corbusier stayed closer to Wright. The Bauhaus style might more appropriately be called analytical rather than functional. Its designers paid only superficial attention to utility; they were obsessed with pure form. Proportion and clarity expressed the idea, as in a Mondrian painting. Nonarchitectural associations were undesirable. After Freud revealed that balconies symbolized breasts, they became suspect to modern architects.

Paris still was the home of the *avant-garde*. In England the Post-Impressionists did not become respectable until the late 1920's; even in the 1930's the general public had not accepted them. When Jacob Epstein exhibited his "Genesis" in 1931, no paper would publish a full-length picture of it. Some of his earlier sculptures had been vandalized.

In painting, by contrast, the subconscious, the nonobjective, the nonrepresentational became the cause of the *avant-garde*. Surrealism tried to combine art and revolution. Introduced by André Breton and Philippe Soupault in 1921, it used psychoanalysis, hallucination, and automatic writing in an attempt to awaken the nonrational, noncognitive sensibilities. The Surrealists felt they were, or pretended to be, in thralldom to their material, and they forswore any endeavor to manipulate it. Fortunately they did not stick to their prescription but produced superb poetry and canvases which showed them in full control of their talents and materials. Their publications contain contributions by Francis Picabia, Louis Aragon, Max Ernst, André Breton, Paul Éluard, Ivan Goll, Comte de Lautréamont, Apollinaire, Robert Delaunay, Jean Painlevé. Like Dada, they mistook for revolution any unusual method of surmounting banality, dullness, middle-class mores, realism, intellectualism, Western civilization, fatherland, and humanity. Their hates were exquisite; they turned nihilism into totalitarian terror, read each other out of the movement, and caused disturbances during each other's performances.

Inevitably the Surrealists were drawn to the Orient and even more strongly to Soviet Russia. In 1930, Aragon and Jacques Sadoul went to Moscow and came back denouncing Freud and Trotsky; with Henri Barbusse they organized the Writers' Congress Against War and Fascism. Aragon beat up the editor of *Nouvelles Littéraires*, who had used Mayakovsky's suicide to decry the lack of freedom in Soviet Russia. He also wrote a poem calling for the assassination of cabinet members and socialist leaders. When he was indicted, Breton cited in Aragon's defense the *Surrealist Manifesto*, which absolved the poet from all responsibility for the products of his unconscious. Later on, Breton grew critical of the Soviet Union and of Communism; but he went on demanding "absolute revolt, total insubmission, formal sabotage."

In a thousand ways Surrealism demonstrated its disdain for the bourgeoisie. But the bourgeoisie digests nothing as readily as revolutionary art. Soon Surrealists produced putrid literature for a putrid bourgeoisie which apparently interpreted Surrealism to mean that nothing in this world is sacred, solid, or ideal: a class of *nouveaux-riches* without morality found itself legitimatized by an art which had ceased to idealize man.

Soon after the war, the discovery of new forms grew more important than the primary emotion. Once Georges Rouault had shown his revulsion from the war in the stark outlines of his barbarian king, lesser artists expressed lesser emotions on lesser subjects with the same vehemence. They were more interested in vehemence than in its cause. Expressionists, Futurists, Constructionists, Abstractionists used any kind of feeling as a pretext for experimenting with new modes of representation. This holds true for great painters no less than for minor ones. Picasso was long obsessed with the problem of showing motion. But the lesser ones mistook his technical efforts for the essence of art; they, too, experimented with new forms—less happily because they had less to say.

The wealth of new forms in twentieth-century art should not mislead our judgment. Far from indicating a new freedom, they rather reflect an almost Byzantine competitiveness. The artist has to justify himself before the court of public opinion by a new invention. Everything has to be tried out. Each year galleries must show new techniques, make new materials available for artistic expression—just as poets year after year find new words to use poetically, and composers more daring progressions capable of sustaining a musical structure.

Modernism thus presents itself in many facets; not a few of the new artists led themselves, each other, or their public, to believe that new forms amounted to new ideas, that sensationalism amounted to liberation, agitation to revolution, a chamber of horrors to a depiction of anxiety. Unfortunately, pretense was so easy that a highly talented painter like Salvador Dali preferred to make his reputation as a charlatan, a modestly endowed painter like George Grosz could be hailed as a great cartoonist because of the dogged one-sidedness of his caricatures, and a speculator like Giorgio di Chirico could pass off his metaphysical charades as profound (he later revealed that the dealers and critics had taken seriously what he had meant as a joke and went on to produce mediocre nineteenth-century academic canvases).

Nevertheless, there remains an extremely rich variety of expression: Beckmann's frightening intensity, Soutine's shrieking bodies, Munch's agitated lines, the tortured people of Kokoschka and Kirchner, the sensitivity of Miró, Nolde's bright melancholy and Klee's dream world, Mondrian's reductionism and Modigliani's sensualism, the structural analysis of Braque—each symbolized another phase of the soul-searching, frustrated mood of the period. Most of these masters had begun to receive recognition before the war and, in the period between the two wars, were the established leaders of the new style. The themes common to all of them are doubt, skepticism, an often lacerating self-analysis, defiance, alienation. To be sure, Monet still produced serene landscapes, Maillot perfect, undistorted figures, Bonnard comfortable interiors, Chagall canvases full of naïve joy, Derain flower fantasies, and Miró mocking humor.

Some of these older masters had created a "style" that they now continued to exploit in academic fashion. Chagall and Braque continued to produce the Chagalls and Braques that had once made them famous; Max Liebermann and Lovis Corinth continued an honest German naturalism. Monet pushed French impressionism to its outermost limits; Matisse still was placing odalisques before colorful wallpapers. The Secession and the Independents had yearly exhibitions of the same kind of new canvases. And the middle class adopted the new styles with the earnestness of students learning a new language. People's tastes indeed improved greatly. On the wall a reproduction of van Gogh's "Sunflowers" now took the place of the neoclassical girl with the half-open bodice; the graceful head of Nefertiti pushed the bust of Richard Wagner off the piano.

In music, too, we have this dichotomy. One line was started by Igor Stravinsky and found its greatest triumph in Béla Bartók. Both tried to exploit every shrieking disharmony in the romantic-naturalistic vein. The new, sophisticated audiences were devoted listeners to Oriental rhythms and the syncopes of jazz. Students bought the latest Gershwin records; Kurt Weill and Maurice Ravel enticed, tickled, and frightened their public with weird and vulgar sounds; Ernst Křenek created a sensation with the jazz opera *Jonny spielt auf*.

Looking at concert and opera programs, however, one finds a preponderance of the well-established classics; even Debussy, Mahler, and Sibelius were considered moderns. The opera theaters performed Gilbert and Sullivan, Leo Fall, Franz Lehár,

Jacques Offenbach, Johann Strauss, Alexandre Lecocq, and musical comedies along with the well-worn classical repertory. But thanks to state or municipal subsidies, European producers also presented modern operas, notably Moussorgsky's *Boris Godunov*, Puccini's *Tosca* and *Madame Butterfly*, Richard Strauss's *Rosenkavalier* and (more rarely) *Salome* or *Elektra*—works that belong to the pre-war period and are still repertory pieces the world over. Musical life was not "contemporary," as at the times of Mozart or even of Verdi. The connoisseurs' interest concentrated on the performers: indeed, with recordings of past performances now setting increasingly rigorous standards, perfection and virtuosity had to improve in each new generation. Great interpreters like Schnabel, Casadesus, Serkin, Toscanini, Weingartner, Beecham, Ansermet, Furtwängler, Walter, the Budapest String Quartet, Casals, Landowska, Chaliapin, Melchior, Flagstad were known far beyond the circles of their devotees. The great festivals of Bayreuth, Salzburg, and the like drew ever growing crowds.

Truly contemporary music that was not popular music, however, had to struggle hard. The public found atonality bewildering and did not recognize the new sound effects as the logical consequence of Post-Impressionistic techniques. Great works like Stravinsky's *Histoire du Soldat* (text by Ramuz) and *Oedipus Rex* (text by Cocteau), Hindemith's *Mathis the Painter*, Béla Bartók's orchestra compositions were rarely performed before World War II. Carl Orff was able to create a public for himself with the *Carmina Burana*, and the French group of "The Six" (Milhaud, Tailleferre, Poulenc, Auric, Duruflé, Honegger) had an appreciative audience. But Alban Berg's *Wozzek* and *Lulu*, almost the only great operas then written in the twelve-tone idiom, were not heard publicly until the 1940's.

Theater audiences were more receptive to contemporary plays. In Europe the stage has always been a public forum, and the public loved lively debates; it also loved the exciting innovations—the flashback, the use of lighting to create illusions of time and space, the extension of the stage into the orchestra, the theater-in-the-round, the revival of the Greek chorus. All this denied the traditional covenant that the audience was listening in on an actual conversation. Pirandello reversed the direction of communication in the theater. Instead of holding up a mirror to the audience, his actors looked for an audience that would reflect them. Older dream-plays, by Calderon, Grillparzer, Kleist, Strindberg, were revived; Henri-René Lenormand's and Brecht's new ones cast fresh doubt not only on established truths but on the assumption that truth—or, for that matter, man—can be known.

Experiments with other theatrical forms also served special causes. Erwin Piscator introduced the turn-table stage for the anti-war play *The Good Soldier Schweik*, based on Jaroslav Hašek's World War I classic. Brecht experimented with the epic drama and the didactic oratorio, then with the political musical. Sean O'Casey experimented with Expressionist plays, as did Auden later. T. S. Eliot and Yeats sought to revive the verse play. Cocteau and Picasso staged a ballet which created a scandal, and revived ancient myths creating even greater scandals. Paul Raynal's *Le Tombeau sous l'Arc de Triomphe* (*The Tomb Under the Arc de Triomphe*), which contrasted soldiers with civilians, chided the dishonesty of his age. Jean Sarment, like Pirandello, shook the public's faith in truth, identity, and romantic idealism. Marcel Pagnol's *Topaze* shows how circumstances shape man. His trilogy of the Marseille waterfront—Marius, Fanny, César—became a stage and movie classic. Jules Romains wrote a biting satire on the medical profession's commercialism and the public's gullibility in *Doctor Knock*. Louis Jouvet who played the title role later made the comedy into a successful movie. Romains was less convincing in *Le Dictateur*, a strange play reflecting the ambiguity of his politics. Jean Giraudoux attacked militarism in *Tiger at the Gates* (1935). G. B. Shaw, still the greatest international playwright, had no great success after *Saint Joan* (1923).

Yet the age found its most lasting expression not in plays but in novels. Twentieth-century writers delved deeply into the unconscious mind and into "racial memory." They painted large canvases of their society, experimented with new forms, and contended with new modes of perception.

This is no chronicle of either the "firsts" or the "best." A history of the public mind must emphasize the popular authors of the 1920's and 1930's. Nor is it possible to deal with all the varieties of the new novel. Limitations of space confine this survey to three or four trends of historical significance.

The first of these is the psychological novel, which sowed many of the seeds for the development of Western consciousness. The second is the *roman-fleuve*, the crowning achievement of the realistic novel and fulfillment of promises since the novels of Stendhal and Balzac. Finally, the existentialist novel, which explored the totalitarian moods of the 1930's and, as a footnote, the war novel.

The psychological novel encompasses the unique achievements of Marcel Proust and James Joyce. Each in his own way unlocked realms of the preconscious mind, played with the concepts of time and memory, and gave man a new understanding of himself. Proust's *Remembrance of Things Past* (1905–22) deals with the nature of memory, experience, and time itself. In Joyce's *Ulysses* (1922) we follow the wandering of one Stephen Dedalus, student, and Mr. Leopold Bloom and his wife Molly through one day of their lives. We are made privy to their innermost thoughts and dreams, which seem to present themselves in an illogical, unorganized sequence. But soon we become aware that this "stream of consciousness" is a technique to reveal not only the character's inner self but the true structure of the experienced world. What Joyce describes is an intricate pattern of symbols, images, reflexes, desires. "Life is not a series of gig lamps symmetrically arranged; but a luminous halo, a semi-transparent envelope surrounding us," said Virginia Woolf, whose imagination ran in the same vein. Her perception dissolved the world into impressions.

In these writers the decadence found its culminating achievement. After them, the psychological novel no longer presupposed a fixed universe of experience and reference; each writer created his own universe and tried to be original by creating a technique of his own, symbolizing each individual's unique approach to the world. Many of the new writers no longer composed their novels in the traditional way, with a coherent plot and recognizable characters, but instead organized their novels around an experience as it presented itself to the consciousness irrespective of time sequence and characters.

Simultaneous with the great experimenters, the realistic novel of manners also reached a peak—at least in sheer volume. Here, too, the author is carried into social ramifications and psychological depths which swell the novel into the *roman-fleuve*, the multivolume cross-section of society. Roger Martin du Gard wrote the eight-volume *Les Thibault*, Georges Duhamel ten volumes of *Chronique des Pasquier*, Jules Romains *Les Hommes de Bonne Volonté* (twenty-seven volumes). Ford Madox Ford looked back on the war in *Parade's End*. John Galsworthy's massive *Forsyte Saga* showed the passion behind the façade of respectability. Romain Rolland's *Jean Christophe*, written before World War I, achieved world fame after it through its pacifist message and warm humanity.

Next to these great witnesses of contemporary conflicts we should place Hermann Hesse (*Steppenwolf*, 1927), André Gide (*The Counterfeiters*, 1926), François Mauriac (*The Vipers' Tangle*, 1932), Aldous Huxley (*Point Counter Point*, 1928)—all famous in their day for the incisive honesty of their confessions. They were the great moralists of the age, merciless in their skepticism and self-laceration.

Two Austrian authors whose fame came posthumously ought to share honors with them. Robert Musil's *The Man Without Qualities* is truly an inventory of his "age without quality"; Hermann Broch's *The Sleepwalkers* is an incisive criticism of his society. But the honors went to another German author, whose vast erudition, urbanity, and intelligence impressed his contemporaries: Thomas Mann. After a decadent and nationalistic debut, he became the foremost writer of the Weimar Republic and later, during the Hitler period, the spokesman for German exiles. But he is a witness rather than a creator of the modern consciousness. The novel that more than any other reflects all the themes of the period was Mann's *The Magic Mountain* (1924), the story of a young man who spends seven years in a tuberculosis sanatorium in the Swiss Alps. There he meets a cross-section of European society—rotting inside, like their society—and we are spared no detail of a pretty lady's pulmonary tissues. Two antagonists, the liberal-democratic rationalist Settembrini and the fanatically totalitarian anti-rationalist Naphta, have a running debate on Europe's future; the hero, like Europe, is torn between a longing for death and a love of life.

Naphta shares traits with both fascist and Bolshevik intellectuals, nationalists and technocrats, worshippers of the mass as well as elitists, Dionysians and Jesuits, aesthetes and terrorists. Settembrini is an old-fashioned liberal and humanist, a wind-bag and bleeding heart. While Naphta destroys himself, Settembrini clearly is living in a past irrevocably dead, and all the other protagonists are going toward their deaths, Thomas Mann, however, does not analyze the crisis; he simply accepts it as given. The debates between Naphta and Settembrini are purely ideological, related neither to living persons nor to social structures.

Twenty years later, in *Doktor Faustus*, Thomas Mann again used the symbolism of disease, syphilis this time, to describe the hubris and fall of Germany. In his *Joseph* tetralogy, Mann evoked the Biblical epic for the comfort of his fellow exiles. Broch, too, retold a great myth in exile: *The Death of Virgil*. All these works, including Musil's, no longer are novels in the traditional sense. Joyce and Proust had exhausted the means of story-telling. As early as the end of the 1920's, *avant-garde* critics predicted that the novel had nowhere to go. After the careful and detailed exploration, in many volumes, of an individual's memory, of a family's history, of a society's destiny—what was left to say? Sociology and psychology had become sciences. Marxists pointed out that the novel was essentially a bourgeois form of expression and that in its declining phase this society no longer was able to produce a vigorous self-portrait. Facile parallels were drawn with Hellenistic society or Byzantium, whose monuments testify to their academic sterility, decadence, and fear of doom.

Refutation of these theories came in a spate of books that fulfilled these very predictions. The novels of James Joyce, Franz Kafka, Louis Ferdinand Céline no longer depend either on plot or on character; both are deliberately blurred. The action is absurd; the language is that of dreams; the imagery leans heavily on symbolist poetry and abandons all rational structure. In this first period of the anti-novel, however, there still was discernible development, even if circular.

Nothing happens in Céline's novels. The writer merely spews forth his hate of the world, his despair of mastering its challenges. In powerful, earthy language he laments the apocalypse—but an apocalypse without subsequent salvation. This apparently was the first generation whose writers did not even pretend that they were describing darkness only to lead the reader toward the light. They knew no light, and yet they continued to write.

The protagonist of Kafka's novels generally is an individual in impotent conflict with unknown, immovable, unreachable powers. He is charged with a crime and made to feel guilty though he never learns what law he has broken. Or he is hired without being told what he is to do, or he presents a petition and is given the run-around, or he is supposed to meet someone whom he cannot meet. There is never any development. The protagonist learns that nothing he might do can change his condition or the council of those in power—perhaps they cannot change it themselves, as is hinted in a superb, brutal anticipation of the annihilation camps, where in the end the executioner himself mounts the scaffold.

The power of these novels lies in the fact that no solution is ever offered. The reader is left bewildered, helpless, and exasperated, but his condition has been brought home to him with an urgency previously known only in Kierkegaard. Some interpreters see Kafka's novels not as an indictment of bureaucracy but as a pious rejection of the world itself.

The third trend that can easily be discerned is the vitalist and existentialist literature. The novel had proceeded from romanticism to realism, naturalism, and decadence in a fairly unbroken line. Vitalism was both rebellion and new beginning. It brushed aside reflection, psychology, even the individual, in favor of action, myth, and imagination. Among its masters were Knut Hamsun, D. H. Lawrence, T. E. Lawrence, Jean Giono, Ernest Hemingway, André Gide, Gabriele d'Annunzio, Gerhart Hauptmann, and André Malraux. Their heroes are vagabonds, adventurers, rebels, even terrorists and criminals; their world is a chamber of horrors and the only way out a meaningless death. Their view of both individual and society is deeply pessimistic but—life goes on, and the hero picks up his burden.

These writers were strongly influenced by Nietzsche and Bergson. Their "Dionysian" spirit was rebelling against the "Apollonian" fetters of the classical tradition. They were pursuing "life" as opposed to "culture." They wrote from the viewpoint of the Id which makes us want to act out, which drives us to risk the extreme situation, the borderline of experience.

It was obvious that even the best of these writers, who personally hated war, could lead heedless youths to believe in the redeeming value of war, to a desire to extinguish the self in favor of the race, to blood worship. The great liberation of the senses, therefore, eventually resulted in surrender to their tyranny. In *Lady Chatterley's Lover* (1928), Lawrence contrasted the vitality of natural man with the impotence of the upper classes. In *The Plumed Serpent* (1926), he despaired of Western man completely. The same "life force" is exalted in Bernard Shaw's *Back to Methuselah* and, more playfully, in *Man and Superman*.

These same writers helped create the myth of the hero, which then began to assume anti-democratic, anti-humanist significance. To be engaged, never mind for what cause, became the watchword. *Vivere pericolosamente*, Mussolini's maxim, could be the caption over the life and work of T. E. Lawrence ("of Arabia"), André Malraux, Ernest Hemingway, Henry Miller, and Antoine de Saint-Exupéry. Their fame was intertwined with their lives. They were activists; they had braved danger. Europe longed for heroes who also were literate. Action, it seemed, was the road to self-knowledge; the full life, earned through the full death, led to full understanding. Those who could not achieve this intensity relapsed into mediocrity. "You had faith, a challenge, you were prepared to do deeds," cried out Hermann Hesse in *Steppenwolf*, "and then you discovered that society did not ask for deeds and sacrifice, that life is not heroic poetry but a drawing-room." Malraux called his major novel *Man's Fate*. His people, like Hemingway's, live on the brink of death and encounter themselves in the experience of life's absurdity. Though a man of deep convictions, Malraux sought political action for the sake of the experience rather than for its goal—also for comradeship, and for a leader's sake. He admired T. E. Lawrence, Trotsky, de Gaulle.

The same image of a centaurlike existence—fighting, writing, enjoying art, heightened by an exotic setting—is projected in T. E. Lawrence's autobiographical *Seven Pillars of Wisdom*. Saint-Exupéry similarly converted adventure into an exploration of the universe and his inner self. Both were shadowy figures, soldiers of fortune.

Not since Byron had literature been so close to politics and to action. Malraux and Orwell fought in the Spanish Civil War; so did Ludwig Renn and Gustav Regler. Hemingway and Arthur Koestler were there as reporters. Sartre, Vercors, and Camus together with many writers, joined the Maquis during the war. Carlo Levi and Silone were in the anti-Fascist underground. Their writings reveal the bitter experience of men who were prepared to give their lives but later found that they did not know what they had been fighting for. What remains is a memory of the good fight against evil and of the friendship of comrades who were shoulder to shoulder with them at one time but may no longer be.

Reluctantly I include in this group Ernst Jünger, the bard of the World War I commando troopers, the pioneer of "total mobilization," the visionary of the sexless, soulless subject of the termite state. Himself a troop leader who was unable to find his way back into civilian life, Jünger exalted the selfless hero without regard for human beings and values. In razor-sharp, crystal-clear, and all but mythical language Jünger celebrates a great renunciation of humanity. Next to Sorel's, Jung's, and Heidegger's, his was the most telling attack on the spirit of 1789. The attitude he championed required complete surrender of man to the machine. To be sure, in Jünger's mind that machine still was subordinated to an idea—that of the Fatherland; hence he fell out with the Nazis, who wished to exploit that same machine for purposes of sheer power.

The German, French, and Italian Futurists created a chauvinistic war novel that might be called contemporary, cool, and totalitarian. Besides these books of some literary value, there flourished a low-grade output of patriotic trash, which glorified army life and the various fatherlands in print and film. They must be mentioned only because of their number, which unfortunately was far greater, and in some countries far more influential, than the famous great anti-war novels. To name only a few authors, there were Hans Carossa, Gottfried Benn, Rudolf Binding, Werner Beumelburg, Gustav Frenssen in Germany, Henry de Montherlant in France, Filippo Marinetti in Italy. Hans Grimm's *A People Without Space* dealt with life in Germany's former African colonies, an area of little economic interest that was cherished as a symbol of former greatness.

Most of the "modern" writers were on the political Right and openly attacked the values of free intellect. But the Left led so vigorous a counter-attack in the 1930's that to this day the general public's image of literature in the inter-war period is dominated by the writers of little magazines like *Die Weltbühne* in Germany or *New Signatures* in England. One of the contributors, Louis MacNeice, said in his book *Modern Poetry* that "unlike Yeats and Eliot [we] are emotionally partisan. . . . The poetry of Auden, Spender, and Day Lewis implies that they have desires and hatreds of their own and, further, that they think some things *ought* to be desired and others hated." These men, to whose ranks we may add André Gide, Bertolt Brecht, Alfred Döblin, Andersen Nexö, Christopher Isherwood, Louis Aragon, Paul Éluard, André Breton, and Federico García Lorca, were on the Left. But it would be unfair to say that Ezra Pound, Céline, Marinetti, and others on the Right did not hate. Also, it is true that to this day *The Waste Land* is quoted more often by the Left.

Only a few writers were decidedly left-wing and outspokenly political. Moreover, in most cases, style and perception were not related to the overt content (or even the intention) of a work of art. A more frequent charge was that most of the literati did

Lifetimes of the Great
Synopsis of Contemporaries

1850 1860 1870 1880 1890 1900 1910 1920 1930 1940 1950 1960 1970

Sigmund Freud 1856—1939
Max Planck 1858—1947
Henri Bergson 1859—1941
Gustav Mahler 1860—1911
Aristide Maillol 1861—1944
Max Weber 1864—1920
Richard Strauss 1864—1949
Vassilij Kandinskij 1866—1944
Marie Curie 1867—1934
Luigi Pirandello 1867—1936
André Gide 1869—1951
Henri Matisse 1869—1954
Marcel Proust 1871—1921
Thomas Mann 1871-1950
Bertrand Russell 1872—1969
Arnold Schönberg 1874—1951
Hermann Hesse 1877-1962
Albert Einstein 1879—1955
Paul Klee 1879—1940
Oswald Spengler 1880—1936
Angelo Roncalli 1881—1963
Pablo Picasso 1881—1973
James Joyce 1882—1941
Igor Stravinsky 1882—1969
Franz Kafka 1883—1924
Walter Gropius 1883—1969
Edouard Le Corbusier 1887—1965
Martin Heidegger 1889—date
Ludwig Wittgenstein 1889—1951
Louis-Ferdinand Céline 1894—1971
Paul Hindemith 1895—1963
Bertolt Brecht 1898—1956
Henry Moore 1898—date
Federico Garcia Lorca 1899-1936
Jean-Paul Sartre 1905—date
Samuel Beckett 1906—date
Albert Camus 1913—1960
Aleksander Solzhenitsyn 1918—date
Harold Pinter 1930—date

not take a more active part in partisan affairs. In 1942 Orwell, recalling the 1920's, observed:

> Look at the writers who begin to attract notice ... Joyce, Eliot, Pound, Huxley, Lawrence, Wyndham Lewis. Your first impression ... is that something has been punctured. ... The notion of progress has gone by the board. They don't any longer believe that ... men are getting better and better by having lower mortality rates, more effective birth control, better plumbing, more aeroplanes and faster motor cars. Nearly all of them are homesick for the remote past. ... All of them are politically reactionary. ... None of them cares twopence about the various hole-and-corner reforms ... such as female suffrage, temperance reform, birth control.

The new poetry reverberated with the sounds of contemporary civilization. Although it rarely imitated the rhythm of the machine or the precision of science, it took the environment as its measure of beauty; it trembled with the nervous tension of our society; it agonized over the dilemmas of power. Poetic language appropriated all the words of technology; it embraced the foul language of the slums; it utilized the everyday language of life in the big cities, of business, of physiology. Auden succeeded in merging the imagery of the old and the new "as the hawk sees it or the helmeted airman." Poetry has grown contemporary in diction, in subject matter, and in rhythm. Auden, Spender, Brecht, Léger (Saint-John Perse), and C. Day Lewis left the ivory tower, the formalistic experiments, the *avant-garde* posture, and frankly placed man in his new environment. More important, this new poetry no longer tried to seduce, to soothe, to interest man, but to bring home to him the meaning of his daily experience, to awaken and disturb him. Brecht and Aragon did so frankly in the service of the Communist Party, occasionally at the expense of their art. Louis Aragon tried to write his novels, *The Bells of Basel, Residential Quarter*, and *Les Communistes*, according to the precepts of socialist realism. Paul Éluard remained a Communist to the end of his life (1952), but he wrote no Party poems and was no commissar.

The poetry of politics was itself a symptom of the crisis in European culture. The writers doubted their calling and found no meaning anywhere. The Left seemed to offer plagued consciences a chance to prove their commitment. Of these attempts Walter Benjamin wrote: "The capitalist apparatus of production and publication has an astounding capacity to assimilate revolutionary themes. ... Revolutionary hack authors serve it without changing it. ... They are making misery into an article of artistic consumption. They even transform revolutionary reflexes into articles of entertainment."

This vanity fair of left-wing opinion in high society, a movement which was perhaps both radical-democratic and decadent, was attacked by the Nazis as "culture Bolshevism." It undermined the ruling class's self-confidence as Beaumarchais's had done at the court of Louis XVI. In a whirl of pleasurable self-laceration, middle-class society was dancing toward its death, as Eric Charell's film *Der Kongress Tanzt* illustrated so naïvely.

By the early 1930's the center of Europe's cultural life beyond any doubt had shifted to Berlin. Established and aspiring writers, painters, and composers flocked there not only from other German cities but from Rome, Vienna, and Prague and even from London and the United States. Theatrical innovations, first performances of modern music, *avant-garde* movies, new fashions, high society—all this was in Berlin. Berlin was the market place for the taste of the age, the transit point for Soviet literature to the west and English literature to the south. The city radiated liberalism. International film and theater hits were made by Berlin audiences. Much of this activity was due to the energy, sensitivity, and judgment of Jews, for better or worse the most up-to-date, concerned, and liberal part of the population. Their prominence in the arts and professions, in journalism and communications, gained the Nazis many votes from jealous competitors. In the provinces, Berlin was the symbol of the new Babylon, the meeting place of everything sick, decadent, negative, or *avant-gardist*, of every vice, cynicism, and nonconstructive criticism—in a word, of "culture Bolshevism." Berlin was at the core of every doubt in the Western world's solidity. "Red Berlin" had its political cabaret, its left-wing boulevard paper, its dissenting weeklies, its *avant-garde* stage, its folk singers or their equivalent. Naughty Berlin had its cocaine peddlers, nude parties, sensational murders, crime syndicates; literary Berlin had student cafés, subversive lectures, psychoanalysis, Oriental cults; political Berlin had party militias, a largely helpless government, an unpopular Reichstag, satirical papers. Beside the financial, commercial, and industrial center that was Berlin, it also was the vice capital of Europe, the hotbed of political intrigue, the *avant-garde*, and the dregs of society.

CHAPTER 4

Soviet Art and Literature

As in the West, Expressionism, Cubism, and Futurism seemed to be associated with revolution in Russia, too. Soviet artists brought *avant-garde* ideas mainly to two media: the political poster and the "agit-prop" play. Both required sharp contrasts, stereotyped characters, ritualistic or symbolic use of figures in prescribed patterns. From this came the highly stylized "proletarian theater." Its director, V. E. Meyerhold, tried to liberate the actor from his psychological knots and make him into the instrument of a social message. His experiment was hailed in the West as a new departure; later, Brecht developed the epic drama that sought to keep the audience from identifying with the characters. Meyerhold discarded the curtain, flats, and decoration. His students, Vertov and Kuleshov, transposed constructivist theories to the screen and developed the techniques of the "camera eye" and montage. In the art of film the Russians were innovators without followers, however.

The revolution did not change Russia's traditional arts. The ballet did not try to become proletarian. Moscow's most accomplished stage director, Constantine Stanislavsky, merely intensified the "method" of Western psychological realism. Russian poetry remained in the hands of the Imagists and Symbolists. Alexander Blok, Boris Pasternak, Vladimir Mayakovsky, Boris Pilnyak, and Anna Akhmatova rallied to the revolution, but their efforts to pour proletarian wine into the Formalistic or Expressionistic bottles of Western decadence were not appreciated by the Soviet government. Trotsky criticized them in his pamphlet *Literature and Revolution*.

He also deprecated the pathetic attempts of *avant-garde* intellectuals to create a culture for the new ruling class—the so-called *proletkult*. Meyerhold's cultish conception of the theater lent itself to a pseudo-proletarian monumentalism with baroque visions of moving masses and gigantic battles, of man acting with machinelike precision, of parading troops, or of automatons speaking like men. Although the style called itself *proletkult*, it was Western, pre-revolutionary decadence, full of Freudian and other symbolism. Like the Italian Futurists, it used human forms in pictorial patterns.

Perhaps satire was a more congenial expression of revolutionary attitudes. After all, as Trotsky pointed out, revolution was a permanent process; much that was old-fashioned remained to be criticized. Much that had been hidden now became overt. Thus, Mikhail Zoshchenko has one of his heroes rejoice that the revolution has given him electricity instead of his old candlelight—only to be repelled by the shabbiness of the walls it reveals. Ridiculing the government's crash program to overcome illiteracy, the author says in praise of a village: "Wake any citizen up in the middle of the night, and he will sign his name."

Some of the early Soviet writers expressed their disappointments in bitter confrontations. The problems of the NEP are candidly discussed in Fyodor Gladkov's *Cement*; Constantine Fedin's works offer an unvarnished view of the complexity of Soviet life; Leonid Leonov's *Thief* shows the conflict between personal ambitions and the Party line. Trotsky called for freedom of art and, as the most realistic art form, recommended novels and stories. But he declared that the Imagist Vladimir Mayakovsky was Russia's greatest living poet and had no objections to Ivan Katayev's fantasies of sophisticated escape.

After the revolution had settled down and its government had shored up its power, the saga of the civil war became the great theme of epic story-tellers. A great pageant of Russian peasants, Cossacks, revolutionary militia, marching armies, and fleeing women unrolls in Isaac Babel's *Red Cavalry*, Alexander Fadeyev's *Nineteen*, Mikhail Sholokhov's *And Quiet Flows the Don*, Dmitry Furmanov's *Chapayev*—all of which later on were made into films. These novels do not spare us the savagery of the civil war. Like the American Civil War literature, they cannot avoid the genre character of the historical novel; they freeze the revolution into a series of heroic murals; they transform it into patriotic history and avoid problems which concern the Soviet citizen.

The next generation of novelists, however, those who emerged in the 1930's, speak of a different Soviet reality—the collectivization of farms, the building of factories, the construction of dams. The real hero in these novels is the work to be done, not the men who do it and suffer doing it.

It was Gorky, the author of revolutionary works like *The Mother*, who advised Stalin to urge "realism" on Soviet writers. But the literary commissars turned "socialist realism" into a grotesquely sterile formula: predictable good guys battle with the opponents of collectivization; enemy agents embody the depravity of the West; the man in the leather jacket saves society from falling apart and gets the girl. The poets praised productivity, collectivization, dedication to the fatherland, the wise leader who was planning a great future for the Russian people, the building of socialism, and the reshaping of the minds of political prisoners.

Such stories, fed to the Soviet presses by the thousands and made into hundreds of undistinguished movies, provoked underground reaction: oblique satire by exaggeration or evasion by means of elaborate descriptions of nature. But Soviet literature in the 1930's and 1940's is bureaucratic even when it attacks overzealous bureaucrats. The writers were afraid of expressing individual feelings, conflicts, and doubts; even style was dictated. Criticism was no longer the expression of a personal opinion but the verdict of appointed judges. The Writers' Association was the instrument of surveillance and admonition.

Under this overanxious care, Soviet art lost ground even in the one field where it had been pre-eminent: the film. The first Russian movies, received in the West like a revelation (Sergei Eisenstein's *Potemkin*, 1925, and *October*, 1927), showed startling use of symbols, exciting deployment of mass action, bold sequences. But when Eisenstein made *The General Line* (1929) in response to Stalin's Five-Year Plan, the result was deplorable. In the 1930's he fell out of grace with the dictators of Soviet art. Only outside the Soviet Union was he able to create another great film, *Que Viva Mexico!*, which was financed by Upton Sinclair and produced in Mexico. In 1938 Eisenstein once more became a Soviet hero, for now his mythological style was in line with the government's needs. *Alexander Nevsky* deals with the defeat of the Teutonic Order 1242 at the hands of a Russian prince. It is bloody patriotic trash.

Vsevolov Pudovkin gained fame through *The Mother* (1926), which also uses the montage technique; but, in contrast to Eisenstein, he used professional actors and demanded total expression from them. His *End of St. Petersburg* (1927), in direct rivalry with Eisenstein's *October*, also shows his more subjective approach; and *Storm Over Asia* (1928) was totally Expressionistic. A more lyrical talent was Alexander Dovshenko, whose *Earth* (1930) made the theme of collectivization more convincing. But his later productions were "socialist realism."

Despite the general mediocrity of Stalinist art, a few directors in the 1930's succeeded in making minor masterpieces, each within his own narrow genre. Thus, Ivan Pyriev excelled in the field of comedy; Grigory Alexandrov made dreamlike, playful, nonsense films; Alexander Ptushko directed fairytale films, for instance *The New Gulliver*; Nikolai Ekk made educational history with *The Road to Life* (1931), which showed the transformation of juvenile delinquents into members of a commune.

Stalin feared, despised, and respected the intellectuals. In the end, through his attempts at regimentation, he destroyed them. Mayakovsky, Sergei Yesenin, and Marina Tsvetayeva took their own lives; Pilnyak, Sergei Tretyakov, and Babel died in prison camps; Alexander Voronsky and I. Lezhnev perished no one knows where; Mikhail Bulgakov was forbidden to write; Meyerhold sought work in America; Anna Akhmatova was slandered; Boris Pasternak and others had to prove their usefulness by doing translations. Even in death, Gorky was made to serve the state: his sickness was the pretext for a savage purge of "cosmopolitan" doctors.

Yet, for all their misfortunes, Soviet writers managed to find ways of expressing the aspirations of the human heart; they remained the educators of their contemporaries.

Alexei Tolstoy and Ilya Ehrenburg may be cited as examples. Both had emigrated but returned in the early 1920's, and both went rather far in compromising with the regime. Yet both through their writings conveyed a sense of personal dignity and of remembering their contacts with independent writers and artists. Tolstoy had to rewrite his *Peter the First* twice before it satisfied the censors; and still it reflects the tension between the demands of the state and the individual. When Eisenstein tried something similar in his film *Ivan the Terrible*, the Party condemned the film as "too formalistic;" it also deplored Eisenstein's failure to show the dread Czar as a determined fighter for industrial progress. Made in two parts (1944, 1946), the complete film could not be shown until 1958.

CHAPTER 5

Science, Philosophy, and Religion Between the Wars

THE first two decades of the century had brought decisive original breakthroughs in knowledge and theory: in relativity, psychoanalysis, genetics, quantum physics, and atomic science. The science of the 1920's and 1930's systematized our widening knowledge of the universe, pierced outer space with larger telescopes and electronic devices, pried the atom open with ingenious new apparatus, and started to unravel the secrets of life. A vast collective research enterprise was under way. Science was entering the industrial age. Its progress was no longer ignited by the flash of a solitary genius but the co-operative effort of many workers in many fields of experimentation and exploration. In 1921, Niels Bohr began to invite his colleagues James Franck, Max Born, Oscar Klein, and others to regular meetings at which they mapped out plans for further research into the structure of the atom. The most prominent scientists in each field became heads of institutes with many assistants. The great experimenter no longer had to waste his time with technical details, but could divide the work as efficiently as in a factory. He also had at his command comprehensive manuals and encyclopedias of all other sciences, and his apparatus was developed through systematic collaboration of many experts. In the most advanced countries, councils of scientists advised the public on the needs of research and worthy projects.

All these aids, which were not available in the past, changed the methods of scientific research. Well-financed institutes were able to "order" the solution of a problem, giving due consideration to the probable time required.

One science helped the other. "Electronic optics," introduced in 1927 by Hans Busch, made possible the construction of high-power microscopes, the study of crystals, metallic surfaces, and the human cell. New clocks used the electric properties of certain metals. Ultrasonic waves could be generated with the help of crystal properties. Starting from experiments with X-rays and cathode rays, Ferdinand Braun and Lee de Forest developed their "tubes," which became the source of our electronics industry, radio, and television. The cross-fertilization of science and technology was systematized. Discoveries led to new instruments, new instruments to new discoveries. The invention of the electron counter (Geiger, 1928) would benefit atomic science and later atomic industry.

One result of this co-operation was the new atomic science. In 1919, Ernest Rutherford for the first time changed one element into another—proving that man could match nature. In that same year, Francis Aston found isotopes; in 1932, James Chadwick explained them by discovering the neutron, an H-nucleus without electrical charge, and Carl Anderson found the positron, a positive opposite to the electron. Harold Urey made "heavy water," deuterium, which is not found in nature. In that same fertile year, John Cockcroft produced the first nuclear reaction by bombarding lithium with protons. Ernest Lawrence invented the cyclotron, which became the tool for all subsequent nuclear research. The neutron has enabled physicists to build new elements and, above all, to manufacture radioactive elements with radiation suitable for medical and research purposes.

Enrico Fermi enlarged our world by "postulating" the neutrino and by proving the existence of "anti-matter"—that is, nucleons with a reverse spin. In 1938, Otto Hahn and Fritz Strassmann proved experimentally Einstein's prediction that enormous energy is released when atoms are split. Moreover, when uranium of atomic weight 235 was bombarded with neutrons, it disintegrated into nuclei of lesser atomic weight and gave off more neutrons, which again could be used to bombard other U-235 atoms. This was the much-sought chain reaction. The process might explain the phenomenon of "new stars," which had long puzzled astronomers. It also made possible the A-bomb and H-bomb. European scientists who came to America enabled this country to take the lead in atomic research, and to build reactors that one day might replace other sources of energy.

Much more important than this expansion in width of our knowledge was the cumulative effect in depth of the new techniques of investigation. The more scientists learned, the less were they able to fit all their discoveries into a unified world view. As we have seen, they had long ago abandoned the quest for the "what" and contented themselves with the question "how." They now abandoned seeking a single cause for a single effect and put their laws into the form of statistical averages and probabilities. They had come to accept the idea that it does not matter what matter is; now they were able to state lucidly why the old, comfortable notions of space, time, light, and matter had become unsatisfactory and yet could not be replaced by new ones. The radiological discoveries forced physicists to rethink their fundamental assumptions, and a wit at the Max Planck Institute near Berlin had put up a sign reading: "Look out! Danger of falling matter! Temporarily closed because of radical renovations."

Max Born, Louis de Broglie, Werner Heisenberg, and Erwin Schrödinger developed the equations that took the place of matter and are known as quantum mechanics. Bypassing the question whether light is the emission of corpuscles or the propagation of waves, these equations fitted either simile—and neither was more than a simile, de Broglie suggested in 1923. Heisenberg contributed (1927) the famous "uncertainty relations" setting a limit to our knowledge of what went on inside the atom. He showed that an observer may determine with desirable exactness either the position or the speed of a subatomic particle, but never both at the same time.

These developments profoundly shook the notion earlier scientists had entertained about cause and effect. Until then, the skeptical view was a pastime of philosophers; now scientists seemed to confirm that an understanding of this notion was neither attainable nor even desirable. Einstein felt that "reality" is not what we see or ascertain as experiential data but an "intellectual construction" needing constant confirmation. Differing from others, however, he felt that by means of a "universal field theory" he could save the notion of causality and some of the certainty of classical physics (1929). He pursued this goal to the end of his life.

Nineteenth-century science still believed that the true secret of nature was known, if not to man then at least to God. The new science of the twentieth century rejected all "metaphysical" questions, all attempts to relate our common-sense experience to some reality behind appearances, all illusions of finding eternal principles which might be independent of our own creative intelligence. A "theory" now was conceived of as a policy rather than a creed; a "law" was a pattern and no longer a determining cause. No great system like the imposing structures of classical science and philosophy could be built on such assumptions. Instead, each of the sciences now developed its own methodology and logic; general philosophy, no longer the mother of all sciences, was being reduced to logical-linguistic analysis, techniques of cataloguing the universe, and other exercises in clarification. The unity of science was in doubt. But where did that leave the humanities? Modern science called for a revolution in education and public philosophy, but the masses would not hear of fundamental changes. Meetings were called to question the theory of relativity. Freud's views were pilloried before large audiences; they were also defended. Theories that must be baffling to common sense were discussed in mass-circulation magazines and newspapers: that the world was neither finite nor infinite but ever expanding; that it may be no more than 13 billion years old; that scientists no longer knew what matter was; that the senses could not be trusted to convey a true or even an approximate picture of the universe. Science, which had unseated philosophy after the latter had ousted religion, now in its turn seemed unable to answer fundamental questions.

If science no longer provided the model for the behavioral sciences, the latter now were free to develop their own methods and to arouse interest among laymen. Anthropology, ethnology, culturology, sociology, psychology, mythology flourished and branched out into many schools, some of which lent themselves to popularizing. People read the disciples of Frazer, Spengler, Toynbee, Freud, Westermarck, Durkheim, and other authors who originally had written for scholars only. Gestalt psychology opened a new understanding of perception; Alfred Adler's analysis of inferiority complexes and Carl Jung's psychology of archetypes, spin-offs from Freud's psychoanalysis, gained a large popular following; social psychology established itself on the borderline between psychology and sociology. Existentialism put up its tents in an area between psychology and philosophy with Karl Jaspers's *Psychology of World Views* (1919). Similarly Max Scheler and Karl Mannheim, starting out from quite different premises, developed the "sociology of knowledge."

In his two great addresses of 1919, *Science as a Calling* and *Politics as a Calling*

Max Weber had set the tone for the decade: "Science is forever neutral to values"; the scientist must know that salvation is not the fruit of knowledge. Max Scheler, who had been seeking a "normative ethics," ended his search in 1926 with the lament that "we are the first people who do not know what man is and know that we don't know it." He asked: "Does the increased awareness of man's nature mean that he knows better where he stands? Or is it merely an ever-growing illusion?" George Edward Moore also ended his most diligent search for an ethical system with the resigned statement that philosophy cannot prescribe.

Through Moore's friends, the mathematical philosophers Bertrand Russell and Alfred Whitehead, the London school of neo-Positivists was connected with the like-minded "Vienna Circle," whose leaders were Moritz Schlick, a fierce fighter against metaphysics in all its forms, Right or Left, idealistic or materialistic, and the icy Ludwig Wittgenstein. The school, which also sailed under the flags of "logical positivism" and "empirical philosophy," included physicists like Philipp Frank and Hans Reichenbach, economists like Otto Neurath and Ludwig von Mises, logicians like Rudolf Carnap and Karl Popper—situated on all shades of the political spectrum. Most of them later found asylum in the Anglo-Saxon world and rallied around the Chicago School of Scientific Philosophy or the British School of Linguistic Analysis, whose leader now is Alfred Jules Ayer. With Wittgenstein's *Tractatus Logico-Philosophicus* (1922) philosophy seemed to have come to an end; his conclusion was that one must not speak of that which one does not know. With that, philosophy had reached a metaphysical nadir. Its last refuge was smoked out ruthlessly by the phenomenological method, invented by Edmund Husserl for the purpose of finding once more "the things themselves," cleansed of all contingent impurities. He called this method "reduction," for it was to strip our perceptions of everything accidental and to "reduce" all notions to pure intuition. He believed that this phenomenological reduction or *Wesenschau* (intuition) opened new ways of knowledge, baring the true experience behind all experiences. Of those who were stimulated by Husserl's initiative, Max Scheler was able to explore the forms of sympathy; Alfred Schütz analyzed the structure of society. Independently, Karl Jaspers founded existentialism as a new philosophical anthropology, and warned his students not to pursue the elusive goal of philosophical systems (*Welsensschauungen*). Knowledge, these philosophers, psychologists, and sociologists showed, depends on the human "perspective," and no science can claim to guarantee the truth. In Scheler's hands, finally, sociology developed a radical, self-lacerating relativism which cast doubt on all previously accepted values.

It is almost ironical that this radical skepticism became the basis of a radical turn toward faith or, in many cases, of a substitute faith supported by the flimsy claim of intuitive understanding and empathy. Starting out from Dilthey's philosophy of life or from Bergson's analysis of nonrational phenomena, pseudo-philosophers like Ernst Krieck and Ludwig Klages reached for the forbidden fruit of mystical meaning. Nikolai Hartmann offered a new ontology. In *Time and Being* Martin Heidegger took a deliberate "leap" into speculative fields where intuition once again could seek for "pure being" and ask primary questions. He tried to turn philosophy back toward the pre-Socratic search for the myths humanity must live by. His philosophy, which claimed to take the place of bankrupt school metaphysics, was both anti-rationalistic and anti-humanist. It had its roots in a tradition of heterodox thinkers, from Tertullian and Pascal to Kierkegaard and Nietzsche, an undercurrent which surfaced in the first quarter of this century, and then burst upon a desperate student generation with the vehemence of an earthquake.

Existentialism denied that men understand each other and the world they live in, or that life has meaning, or that striving for happiness makes sense. The philosophers had explained the world so as to make it a more hospitable place to live in. Existentialism, on the contrary, bade its adepts to be strangers in the world. This was the message of Kafka's *The Castle*, of Camus's *The Stranger*, of Sartre's *Nausea*. Every existentialist work could carry the motto propounded in Sartre's *No Exit*: "Hell is other people."

Heidegger hoped to revive ontology, which had been believed dead. Carl Jung stressed the importance of mythical thinking in the genesis of human attitudes. In contrast to Freud, who still felt that irrational motivations had to be studied and mastered by reason, Jung took a positive view of the collective soul and built his therapy on recognition of its myths. Many post-Bergsonian, post-Nietzschean, and post-Freudian thinkers elsewhere fell into the same trap: They assumed that what is there must be exulted in. Heidegger's idiosyncratic, obscure language added to the awe this wisdom inspired.

The philosophical consequences of the crisis (described as such by Husserl and Jaspers) were still in the realm of academia. But there were others. When Lord Carnarvon died of a mosquito bite shortly after removing Tut-ankh-amen from his pyramid, Conan Doyle declared that an "elemental" had avenged the desecration of the ancient tomb and that a curse lay on everybody connected with the expedition. Some of its members did indeed die a natural death some time afterward, and millions of people eagerly believed Doyle's assertion. There were other indications, too, that superstition and magic beliefs found an audience in the twentieth century.

The Depression brought increased interest in faith-healing and other quackeries. A man in Berlin cured everything, from melancholia to appendicitis, with applications of cottage cheese; he even published a weekly paper. A shepherd could diagnose diseases (even pregnancies) by looking at a patient's hair through a magnifying glass; he made a fortune with "natural medicines." Dietary fads were the rage.

Small wonder that the Catholic Church could not lag behind. After due deliberation it recognized the stigmata of two Theresas, one in the Bavarian village of Konnersreuth, the other at Lisieux in France. Both women performed miraculous cures and were beatified. In times of distress people turn to more palpable beliefs than the pale theology that liberalism is able to offer. A visit to Lourdes moved the Jewish poet from Prague Franz Werfel to write *The Song of Bernadette*. Conversions to the Roman Catholic faith astounded a world that had seemed to turn its back on religion altogether: Evelyn Waugh, Raïssa Maritain (wife of the Thomist philosopher); Sigrid

Undset, whose trilogy *Kristin Lavransdatter* makes use of Scandinavian folklore; Werner Bergengruen, who published *The Grand Tyrant and the Tribunal* during the Hitler years and *Dies Irae* (sonnets about the Germans' affliction and guilt) after Hitler's fall. Graham Greene expounded Catholic ideas in his novels *The Power and the Glory* and *The Heart of the Matter*; Alfred Döblin, whose *Berlin Alexanderplatz* as both novel and film had been the most radical attempt of humanistic realism, and who had flirted with utopian communism, converted to Catholicism after his return from exile.

The greatest Catholic writers of the period are Paul Claudel, François Mauriac, and Georges Bernanos. T. S. Eliot, who in poems like "The Hippopotamus" had mocked the church, now opened and closed "The Waste Land" with passages from St. Augustine and joined the Anglican Church.

A reactionary trend made inroads in the Anglican Church when, in 1927, the new prayer book was proposed. An outcry against its "Roman" tendencies did not stop the Lords from adopting its idolatrous features, but it was rejected in the Commons, largely by Scottish, Irish, and Dissenter votes. No one thought it odd that a matter of theology should be decided by political log-rolling.

Modern religion, where it has not become shallow by efforts to reconcile faith with the progress of science, tends to become mystical or fundamentalist. Rejecting the liberal theology of the preceding era, it denies that man can do anything to save himself. If we read Kafka's *Castle* and *Trial* as theological allegories, the same message comes through even more poignantly. Not only is man born with guilt, but like Job he does not even know what he is guilty of, and nothing he does can bring him face to face with his accuser. He can neither exculpate nor purge himself.

Forsaken by those who had so long presumed to be the counselors of his conscience, Western man looked around for aid and comfort. Traditional religion was unable to help; it had not been designed to deal with the modern problem of an existence that seemed to be absurdly meaningless. Liberal religion had accommodated man's conscience with respect to society but not with respect to himself. In this situation, two heroic efforts were made to give man's soul once again an anchorage outside himself—one by the Roman Catholic Jacques Maritain, the other by the Protestant theologian Karl Barth. Maritain provided a modern canon of orthodox Thomist philosophy; Karl Barth renewed Calvin's and Kierkegaard's somber faith—namely, that man's salvation did not depend on his own efforts and certainly not on his ability to perform God's work on earth. Transcending "modernism," both these writers castigated the sentimental moralism of liberal theology: sin is ever present; the world is a putrid, malodorous place; God is forever hidden; even in his symbolic revelations he appears as the "wholly Other."

Karl Barth issued the anguished cry of "crisis theology" and poured scorn on the illuminists and liberal theologians who lived in the comfortable illusion that man can find repose in a God whom he understands. On the contrary, he asserted, only the utter despair over the abyss that separates man from God is comfort, and all attempts to ascribe human reasonableness to God are blasphemy. Obviously, this theology was suitable for a time when men had grounds to ask whether God had used reason in creating this sorrowful world. Barth rejected science, progress, reason; despising those who sought an easy religion, he said: "To be religious is to be torn, discordant, restless." His followers Friedrich Gogarten, a conservative German pastor, and Emil Brunner, a Swiss, have further pursued Barth's quest for a nonhumanist religion of "experience."

Heidegger was an unbeliever, Barth a Protestant, Kafka a Jew. The Catholic novelist François Mauriac was equally obsessed with original sin. His novels are populated with characters who must bring grief to each other. One of his most gripping novels, *The Kiss of the Leper*, tells us by way of a parable that every kiss may be that of a leper. The true hero of much Catholic literature in this century is depravity, man's helplessness to redeem himself. The century that finds it so difficult to believe in God certainly believes in the Devil. The same Manichaean streak that we found in much of the century's philosophy and poetry also is present in its theology and psychology. Sensitive men become brutalized because they cannot stand the strain of our world's paradoxes. Many suffered an intellectual failure of nerve and surrendered to various authorities—the church, the state, a leader. This will be treated in detail in the following chapter.

Summing up Part V: The culture of the 1920's, great and exciting as it was, cannot be called classical in the sense of a confident, normative achievement. It was experimental, self-doubting, and deeply divided, a culture on the point of suicide or regression.

But also a culture of high achievements and great hopes. The very tension between promises and frustrations may have been the spring that activated the subtlest minds and excited them to highest artistic expressions. Obviously, the gap between highbrow and low-brow culture was widening; so was the communication gap between the humanists and the natural sciences. Still wider was the gap between those who saw the solution in better rational control and those who surrendered themselves to irrational cults, to tribal myths, or to charismatic leaders. There was no longer one European culture holding society together; there was no mold in which statesmen could have shaped the international and economic crises. The question was whether European culture would break down in a new barbarism or whether it could break through to higher ground.

The Periclean age was one of crisis. On all levels—economic, social, cultural, and intellectual—society was exploding.

PART VI

The Eclipse of Europe
(1933–45)

CHAPTER I

Failure of Nerve

In his *Five Stages of Greek Religion*, Gilbert Murray says that after a period of enlightenment, human progress, and democracy, sometime between the third century B.C. and the first century of our era, there occurred a general breakdown, a failure of nerve characterized by pessimistic, other-worldly philosophies, a loss of self-confidence and human pride, a regression from science and a conversion to revelation, a turn toward asceticism and mysticism. This collapse of humanism was accompanied by indifference to the welfare of the city and surrender to imperial conquerors. Despairing of their abilities, in quest of salvation, people prostrated themselves before the altars of strange gods and before the thrones of godlike dictators who promised release from civic responsibility. The Hellenistic empire experienced a political and cultural crack-up.

The second quarter of our century witnessed a similar failure of nerve, loss of civic responsibility, cultural self-doubt and philosophies of despair. It is true that romantic protests against the Age of Reason had never quite subsided, but now they assumed a new urgency and scope. The attack on civilization was no longer nostalgic but radical. What man had lost, it seemed, was not this or that value of the good old times but his identity as a member of a tribe, nation, or race. Western civilization, it seems, had been misled in developing the proud, independent individual at the expense of "rootedness" (an expression used by mystics like Aldous Huxley and Simone Weil, but also by the German "blood and soil" poets who nurtured the Nazi philosophy). Carl Jung's discovery of "archetypes" and of the collective unconscious influenced poets like W. B. Yeats and Gottfried Benn. Writers like D. H. Lawrence, James Joyce, and Knut Hamsun also were concerned with myths new and old. In Part V, we have dealt with these writers in a literary context; we shall now consider their politics.

Hamsun's symbolic novels castigated the materialism of civilization, our illusions of progress, the mass culture of our cities, our faith in technology and free enterprise. His success in Germany was partly due to his hatred of the "Anglo-Saxons": restless and busy, greedy and sensationalist, the hero of *August World Skipper* tries to get rich through speculative ventures and ends by being pulled down into a precipice by a herd of stampeding sheep he had bought for gain. Jean Giono's *The Great Herd* is a strong statement of anti-war and anti-capitalist sentiments. Regrettably, Giono's pacifism led him to collaborate during the Nazi occupation of France. Hamsun also ended as a friend of Hitler. More virulent still is the contempt of humanity pouring forth from the pages of Louis-Ferdinand Céline. In *Journey to the End of the Night*, he used foul language and slang for the first time in higher French literature; his world is vile and repulsive, full of corruption, crime, and meanness. In later books Céline spewed hatred against Jews, democracy, capitalism. During the war he collaborated with Hitler, and after the war he wrote a moving account of flight and the onset of madness during his last years.

A deep pessimism pervades these writers' works. They show evil and frustration not as obstacles or as challenges to mankind's self-improvement, but as examples (or perhaps as similes) of man's utter inability to redeem himself. Man is seen as a paradox, his existence as absurd, his efforts as vain. Such pessimism is usually associated with conservative views in politics and religion. Reason's claim to discover solutions for the plight of mankind is considered shallow, incompatible with an "organic" view of society. Words like "organic," "integral," "whole" were used as positive epithets in contrast to "inorganic," "fragmented," "analytical," which implied undesirable traits, inferior philosophies, and even unwelcome people who held such views—democrats, Jews, urbanites.

In contrast to old-fashioned conservatives, these new skeptics did not think that happiness could be attained through a return to the past, nor did they think that was desirable. Some sought salvation in new cults: surrender of the self to a leader, a return to tribal myths. In *Intellect as the Enemy of the Soul*, Ludwig Klages urged awareness of the racial consciousness; Symbolist poets revealed exciting ways of reliving ancient myths. Man, it seemed, could be whole again if only he would trust the voice of collective memory and renounce the pretensions of individualism, intellectualism, and progressivism.

The attack on the values of the Enlightenment found more ammunition in the new philosophies of history. From Spengler to Toynbee, comparative studies of civilization seemed to show that progress was a myth, that modernism was just one phase in an ever returning cycle, that the Occident was withering, and that its current decline paralleled the fate of all previous civilizations. Its time was running out, and its aspirations were revealed as no more valid than those of its predecessors. On the contrary, Paul Valéry asserted, they had led mankind astray from the true sources of life. Count Hermann von Keyserling announced the new rise of the East; Spengler proclaimed a new age of the Caesars; Toynbee foretold a new religion. Superstition was rife among the uneducated; the educated became adepts of Hinduism, occultism, mysticism. Where psychoanalysis was used as a philosophy rather than as a psychiatric method, it bore a suspicious resemblance to the erotic mysteries of the late Hellenistic world.

Oriental cults had been the rage in decadent Europe even before the war. The philosophies of India made converts in the English-speaking world. Krishnamurti and Radhakrishnan were taken up at the universities. Fuller, the first tank strategist and later member of the British Union of Fascists, became a propagandist of Yoga. Professor Cyril E. M. Joad wrote *Counter-Attack from the East*. John Middleton Murry and Katherine Mansfield fell in with Russian mystics.

Hugo von Hofmannsthal confessed that he was seeking "not freedom but belonging. . . . It is impossible to live without a wholeness you believe in." According to this view, the individual is worthless in himself and must become part of the source of life or of being or whatever. The great discoveries of the Gestalt psychologists and of anthropology were harnessed to the bandwagon of "holism"—a popular-science philosophy substituting mysticism for exactness. Similarly, Husserl's phenomenology and Jaspers's existentialism were misappropriated to replace experimentation by vision. What to them had been a serious (and rigid, not to say arid) effort to understand the condition of man's experience of himself now became a fashionable, facile method of dismissing theory.

The philosophy of existence as understood by the public is hortatory rather than analytical, and therefore hard to describe in objective terms. Poetic, unsystematic, and anti-systemic, deliberately reminiscent of Nietzsche, it seemed to mobilize human resources inaccessible to traditional reasoning. Scheler said that such a philosophy cannot be grasped in analytical terms, or understood by those who view it with skepticism. To be appreciated it has to be accepted; the learner has to surrender himself to it. Here existentialism forsakes what Western philosophy had tried to achieve since Socrates—intersubjective validity—and returns to the Oriental tradition of orphic, mystic, introspective meditation. An act of faith alone can open the floodgates of the new ontology. Jaspers has admitted that to rise from mere "being-there" to existential being one needs something similar to grace; to experience transcendence requires the gift of being able to have such experience. Not only that; to understand Heidegger and Jaspers it is necessary to accept their system of values, and even their quaint language. What philosopher before Heidegger has placidly used deprecatory terms—anyone (*das Man*), gossip (*das Gerede*), curiosity (*die Neugier*), inauthenticity (*das Uneigentliche*)—as ontological categories? Philosophy no longer discusses dispassionately the conditions of knowledge; it is resentful, angry, "engaged," and tries to "engage" its followers. Sartre, patently influenced by Heidegger, blandly dubs as "inauthentic" attitudes he does not approve of and enjoins his readers to become "authentic"—that is, to conform to his own notions of what man should be.

Not bound by the principles of reason that were supposed to hold society together before Nietzsche's world-shattering discovery of God's death, the existentialist hero acts without interest and idea, for nobody's benefit and for no superior cause. He has no bearings in a universe filled with anonymous powers; his social environment is not structured and therefore appears to him as "mass" society. Feeling forlorn, he must consider the whole world his enemy. No wonder that his primeval experience is dread, anxiety, guilt, and that the prime mover in his world system is a hypostasized nothingness which "nihilates" the comfortable assumptions of existence in a civil society.

Heidegger, following Kierkegaard, made the important discovery that man is indeed possessed by irrational fear and may act out of the wanton desire for nothing-ness. He also took from Freud (or from St. Paul and St. Augustine) the insight that in admitting original sin we may be able to live with it, nay, even to go out into the world and act without being inhibited any further by guilt feelings. Existentialism here reveals itself as a Manichaean religion, recognizing that man must do evil in order to live.

Heidegger was a Nazi when he published *Being and Time* (1927). Six years later he helped Hitler subvert the university and personally ousted his former teacher, Husserl, a Jew, from his chair. Nazi intellectuals hailed his philosophy as an instrument to destroy the ideologies of liberalism. Heidegger, in turn, hailed Hitler's movement as the embodiment of that "being unto death" which was to "liberate" Western man from the fetters of the Enlightenment. In seizing the presidency of Freiburg University, Heidegger dedicated it to "knowledge service" (*Wissensdienst*), which he placed in a highly suggestive parallel to labor service and military service. Truly too much "engagement!"

Obviously I am not dealing here with the professional aspects of these philosophies, whatever their merit, but am using them as samples of public political psychology. Scheler's sociology, we saw, had questioned specifically the values of middle-class democracy. Almost prophetically, he pointed out that his own philosophy coincided with the "self-liquidation of parliamentary democracy." Indeed, the Marxist critic, George Lukács, has described this late German philosophy as the "Ash Wednesday of a parasitical subjectivism which must incessantly criticize a world which is its basis and yet is breaking down. Nothing is firm any more, nothing is reliable. The solitary 'I' in the midst of a desert stands awed in anxiety and sorrow." The anti-democratic intent of existentialist philosophy—noticed already in Scheler—can be pursued from Nietzsche to Jaspers and Heidegger. Jaspers's personal kindness, his honesty, and his Jewish wife saved him from falling into the Nazi trap; but intel-lectually he belongs with the philosophers who were not content to look at democracy with dispassionate skepticism. In all his publications before 1933 he leveled vicious, often demagogic, attacks against "the masses" and "democracy." This is especially true of his memorial essay, *The Contemporary Condition of Mind* (1932). The negative traits of that which Jaspers derisively calls "the world" he always finds in a democratic society.

Shocking as such pronouncements may sound coming from the lips of philosophers dedicated to the pursuit of pure being, they were not isolated occurrences. Since the beginning of the century, many Western literati had debased their art in the service of the nation, the race, the state, the monarchy, the church.

In opposition to these writers on the Right, Julien Benda published his famous indictment *The Treason of the Intellectuals*, perhaps the last great manifesto of liberalism. He maintained, as did Max Weber before and as Karl Mannheim was to do a little later in *Ideologie und Utopie* (1929), that the intellectual's special role is the search for truth, independent of any outside allegiance; he added that therefore intel-lectuals must at all times embrace the cause of freedom. Those who support a cause antithetical to freedom betray a sacred trust. Unfortunately, Benda was mistaken on one fundamental point. He thought that his audience consisted of intellectuals who had abandoned reason and surrendered themselves to the passions of the age. Such an appeal might have made sense to the older generation of romantic conservatives—even though they might have rejected it—for they spoke the same language of humanism as the liberals. The new nihilists, however, were a different breed. They had surpassed humanism; they had not rejected reason but exhausted its possibilities. In fact, they had come to irrationalism as the ultimate conclusion of traditional reason.

Nor were these new antihumanists simply intellectuals who happened to be chauvinists. In fact, they did not plead for the victory of this or that fatherland, but felt that they had come to the end of the road as intellectuals and hence had to become warriors (for obviously, the choice of becoming middle-class citizens was not to be contemplated). Perhaps mankind could find a way out of this rotten civilization by means of a great cataclysm, a war, or a revolution, any of which might bring out the heroic virtues of man. Following Nietzsche, Charles Péguy and Rilke, now Marinetti, Gottfried Benn, Ernst Jünger, and Gabriele d'Annunzio looked forward to a new race of warriors to save mankind from intellectualism. At the end of his life, W. B. Yeats joyously welcomed World War II—"that horror that might save civilization." Jünger rejoiced at the spectacle of seeing "mind destroying itself"; they all worshiped Nietzsche, the scourge of Christian and middle-class morality. The Russian poet A. Blok repudiated the mission to civilize Asians and embraced barbarism. During the Ethiopian war Marinetti raved about the beauties of destructiveness, and extolled the superman "perfected with gas mask and submachine gun" who was bringing a new civilization not to the savages but to his own kind. Both he and Jünger took special pleasure in seeing man joined to technology in the grotesque self-immolation of the species.

Nihilism had long been a philosophy posing as social revolt. It now turned into a disease posing as a philosophy. The new barbarians used the symbol of the soldiers who, on returning from the trenches of World War I, found civilization disgusting, hated the civilians whom they had protected with their lives, despised ideologies, and trusted only their own kind—from either this side of the trenches or the other. The soldiers' anti-civilian mood appears in Sassoon's *Counter Attack*; Robert Graves expressed it by saying that "this ragtime f——g peace" followed "this bloody f——g war."

It was not merely that so many ex-servicemen were incapable of readjusting to civilian life. But for centuries the soulless routines of middle-class life had been compared unfavorably with the posture of the fighter who risked his life to prove his valor: "On the battlefield a man's a man" (Schiller). In the 1920's, men donned trench coats to show their aversion to middle-class values. In the 1930's they marched with Hitler's Storm Troopers, Degrelle's Rexists in Belgium, de la Rocque's Croix de Feu in France, Corneliu Codreanu's Iron Guards in Rumania, Gyula Gömbös's Arrow Cross troops in Hungary, Primo de Rivera's Falanges in Spain, Prince Starhemberg's Heimwehr in Austria. Wearing brown, black, silver, and other colored shirts, and boots to pound the pavements of middle-class cities, the new barbarians exalted the spiritual value of a warlike nation that would not bow to the dictates of money.

"A long period of law and order, such as our generation had experienced, produced an actual craving for the abnormal, a craving stimulated by poetry"—thus Jünger's comment on his first encounter with a trench piled high with corpses. To him, war was the supreme proof of human freedom, the great releaser of human valor, the destroyer of all false civilization, the loosener of the full potential of human creativeness and destructiveness. All conventions and moral excuses ceased to exist when man experienced that great sensation of annihilation, the complete eclipse of the self in an ecstatic act of complete bestiality.[1]

Few of those who committed the "treason of the intellectuals" have conceded that fascism profited from their philosophies of despair. At worst, they admit, they were misinterpreted. The intellectual's plight is that he must follow his ideas even to absurd conclusions. Some, who had come to doubt the values of Western culture, drew the conclusion that they must destroy it. The heritage of Greek, Roman, and Renaissance civilization was wasted by its very heirs, not by outsiders. Not knownothings but intellectuals had immolated its spirit.

No wonder the bewildered crowds now turned to new creeds, sought shelter in totalitarian movements, and surrendered their critical will to the charisma of a strong leader, a Duce, Führer, even a Croat *Poglavnik* and a Rumanian *Conducator*.

---

[1] In fairness we should add that Jünger later on became horrified by the forces he had helped to unleash. His symbolist novel *On the Marble Cliffs* was an attack on Nazi barbarism in thinly veiled language, the only such book to appear in spite of the censor.

CHAPTER 2

The Rise of Integral Nationalism

IT may seem strange that a society that relied so fervently on technology and rational organization for the conduct of its daily life should put such stress on passions and instincts in justifying its political choices. The ideological "superstructure" sometimes seems to be built in contrast to rather than as a complement of its social base. Early in the century, thinkers like Rathenau and Sorel had combined technocratic ideas with a romantic belief in myth.

For technocrats can only administer. They need legitimation and loyalty, a firm framework of political authority in which they can operate. Spengler's prescription was "Prussian socialism," a combination of the old caste society with modern mass technology. Max Weber had called for the "charismatic leader."

During World War I, German army officers charged with "moral mobilization" had studied the techniques of mass manipulation and thought control. Following Gustave Le Bon, their post-war successors taught the method to a mesmerizing rhetorician and built him up as a "leader." Hitler was a born propagandist, and he has described his techniques candidly. He noted that a lie told often enough and reaffirmed brazenly, despite all proof to the contrary, will finally be believed. What he had in mind probably was not lies but "myth" in the sense of Sorel. He used such archetypal myths to build a philosophy for the Nazi movement. The German people were called to rule the world; a Jewish conspiracy had deprived them of their victory in World War I; a secret world government now ruled them through the instrumentality of the republic; to be resurrected, the German people had to follow a leader who spoke from the heart of its racial heritage.

Hitler identified urban civilization and commercialism with "the Jew"; virtue and power he attributed to the peasant and warrior of Germanic stock. The task was to call on "the blood" and return to "the soil"; if there was not enough soil, geopolitics told the Germans how to conquer more *Lebensraum*. "Blood-and-soil" literature inundated the German book market in the 1920's, coinciding with a revival of romanticism and a new interest in the Middle Ages. All this was thrown into the murky brew of Alfred Rosenberg's *Myth of the Twentieth Century*, a book more often quoted than read.

Likewise, Mussolini promised to restore Rome's greatness; dreams of the glorious

Louis XIV animated the Camelots du Roi; Macedonian terrorists remembered the "Greater Bulgaria" of the Middle Ages. In contrast to ordinary nineteenth-century patriotism or even chauvinism, these new movements endowed the national rebirth with quasi-religious significance. Like Emperor Barbarossa who was to emerge from his mountain, the leaders were seen as saviors. The Pan-Slavs had viewed Moscow as the "Third Rome," chosen as God's instrument for a sacred mission. Dostoevsky's German translator, Moeller van den Bruck, wrote a pamphlet, *Das Dritte Reich*, prophesying a great resurgence for Germany. Stefan George, the poet, picked up the word and built on it a myth of the ideal state. ("Reich" in German means empire as well as kingdom in the religious, apocalyptic sense. The number three also is sacred.) One of George's disciples then wrote a book, at once scholarly and edifying to believers in a "secret Germany," about the splendid empire of Frederick II, Barbarossa's grandson and the Anti-Christ. Nothing less than the Second Coming was expected.

Mussolini cultivated similar fantasies. He tried to appear as a new Caesar. He restored the Imperial Forum and the emperors' villas which tourists visit today; he built the stadium in that extravagant neoclassical style which seems to be the hallmark of dictators. Hitler was to surpass it in the grandiose pageants of his party conventions, and still more in the plans for a world capital he held ready for the day after victory. (Mock-ups of these buildings have been reproduced in Albert Speer's *Erinnerungen* [*Inside the Third Reich*].)

Yet it was not the romantic memory of lost empires that turned people toward the new Caesars but their promises of a revolution, their new attitude toward old institutions, their claim to represent the people as parliamentary parties no longer did. Julius Caesar himself, the archetype of all dictatorial leaders, had been an associate of the rebel Catilina and his populist party, an archenemy of the capitalistic senators, who assassinated him. Many of the new leaders—Mussolini, Paul Déroulède, Gustave Hervé, Georges Valois, Doriot, Déat, Oswald Mosley—had begun their careers in the labor movement, usually on its radical wing. Hitler himself substituted the unwieldy name "National Socialist German Workers' Party" for the dynamic "German Racist Party" when he became its leader. Just as in the nineteenth century a tribune of the people had to be anointed with democratic oil, so in the twentieth century "socialism" was invoked to counterfeit the people's will.

It would be more correct, however, to speak of a militaristic populism. But Hitler's lieutenant Gregor Strasser used the term "anti-capitalism" when he proposed a common front to Communists and socialists. The small shopkeepers and craftsmen, unable to cope with department stores, banks, big enterprises, "anonymous" capital and joint-stock companies, saw capitalism as a conspiracy against their security. Expressing this backlash, Nazi and fascist leaders abounded in anti-capitalistic rhetoric, promised to "break the thralldom of interest," vituperated against usury, supported direct action against foreclosures, and occasionally even led strikes. They were forever ready to attack "irresponsible capital." Hitler made the distinction between "parasitic" (Jewish, cosmopolitan) capital, which he proposed to abolish, and "creative" capital, which he supported and which supported him. To be sure, when asked what he would do about the banks, he answered: "I don't have to nationalize the banks since I nationalize the bankers." His socialism consisted mostly in rhetorical devices like "workers of brain and brawn" or "workers of all classes"; to him, socialism was the achievement of a mysterious "race community" where all Germans were brothers.

Mussolini, likewise, said in his *Carta del Lavoro*: "Work in all its forms, technical, intellectual, and manual, is a social duty." He abandoned the word "socialism" and adopted the more fitting symbol of the *fasces*. His programmatic article in the *Enciclopedia Italiana* declared that "this is the collective century and therefore the century of the State" and "fascism accepts the individual only insofar as his interests coincide with the State's."

Statism or collectivism also was the ideology of German militarists. Ernst Jünger and General Ludendorff called it "total mobilization." In *Der Arbeiter* (*The Worker*), Jünger even projected the development of a new "type"—completely devoted to the job, contented but soulless, devoid of any trace of individuality, even of sex. What these ideologists of fascism offered was a socialism of the barracks, both in conception and in the style of execution.

By his own words, Mussolini offered a "totalitarian" state, neither socialist nor liberal nor capitalist. Because of this ambiguity, the Fascist and Nazi deputies refused to sit on the extreme right of the parliament, where one would have looked for them. They meant to be both conservative and revolutionary. In fact they were neither; they stood outside the traditional Right-Left line-up. In Germany, the radical wing of the Nazi movement called itself "National-Bolshevik." Others have spoken of a "Jacobinism of the Right." Hugo von Hofmannsthal and Hermann Rauschning dreamed of a "conservative revolution"; Hans Freyer called it "revolution from the Right." Rauschning—a conservative who served Hitler as district leader for Danzig—later indicted Nazism as "the revolution of nihilism." But the name that describes these movements best is "integral nationalism," the term coined by Enrico Corradini at the turn of the century. Words such as "integral" and "organic" were sacred to Othmar Spann, Rudolf Smend, and other Germanic philosophers.

Corradini was dissatisfied with parliamentary monarchy. He redefined nationalism in a radical, Jacobin way, sought contacts with revolutionary syndicalism, raged against a bourgeoisie which was essentially cosmopolitan, and called on Italy as a "proletarian nation" to arise against the "mercantile nations," their international system, the gold standard, and free trade. Before his own conversion, Mussolini charged that Corradini's "national revolution" would leave the army, the king, the church, the landlords, and the capitalists where they had been. When he had the chance, Mussolini himself also substituted the pageantry of a "national revolution" for the toilsome fight to achieve specific social aims. Italy's "integral nationalism" was to become the model for the "national-revolutionary" movements in the Third World, for Peronism, and for Arab socialism.

Charles Maurras, no longer read today but influential in his time, used Corradini's ideas to marry royalism with ochlocracy. In his paper, *Action Française*, he polemicized against the capitalist exploitation of labor and the legalistic fetters of "bourgeois democracy," and he tried to adopt Proudhon as his patron saint.

In 1925, George Valois split away from the Action Française to found Le Faisceau. He hoped to win disappointed syndicalists and Communists, but attracted mainly war veterans. Failure later drove him toward the extreme Left. His lieutenant Marcel Bucard, however, spurred by Hitler's success, renewed the venture in 1933. In 1934, Jacques Doriot split from the French Communist Party and founded the Parti Populaire Français (PPF), which attracted many intellectuals, and led them first into neutralism and then into collaboration with Hitler. In a similar way Marcel Déat defected from the Socialist Party (FSIO) and founded his own Rassemblement National Populaire. He used both the themes of the necessary revolution and of European peace to disrupt the united front against fascism; during the war he became a collaborator and argued that Hitler was an heir of Robespierre.

In England, too, Sir Oswald Mosley's "New Party" grew out of the labor movement. When Mosley got disenchanted with "the meaningless slogans of nineteenth-century socialism," he made a pilgrimage to Rome and founded the British Union of Fascists, whose members donned black shirts and beat up Jews. During the war, those who had not fled to Germany were taken into custody. At one time, Mosley had attracted able men like Harold Nicolson and John Strachey, but his preachment of hate and violence lost him many of those who at first had flocked around him.

Integral nationalism, fascism, National Socialism, and similar movements in other countries reveal themselves as pseudo-democratic, pseudo-socialist, populist parties drawing into their ranks a motley crowd of victims of capitalism—the many who find in the "national community" a substitute for genuine equality and in national greatness a vicarious compensation for their own misfortunes. This radicalism also attracted alienated students who rejected their parents' middle-class values. Although the workers derided them as *fils à papa* or *señoritos*, one cannot doubt the sincerity of their desire to identify with the disinherited. Some of the most incisive studies of social conditions in Hungary and Rumania were made by people who later were convicted as fascist collaborators. The Iron Guard actually helped people by setting up neighborhood projects, building roads, schools, and hospitals. Fascism on the rise is always populist.

Nonetheless, the main target of all integralist, nationalist, and fascist movements was not capital but organized labor. Their main recruiting ground was among the middle class and in the traditionally conservative districts; their militancy was directed not against the establishment but against the Social Democratic and Communist workers and their unions. Their terror tactics in the workingmen's districts was a measure of their failure to convert proletarians into fellow patriots. But the terror also was designed to win over those whom they called riff-raff, and it was partly successful. The Nazis were able to gain a foothold among the unemployed.

The Nazi Party attracted few trade unionists, but a quarter of its members described themselves as "workers." The storm troops included thousands of the unemployed or unemployable for whom wearing a uniform was the only symbol of self-respect still available. These *lumpen*-proletarians were joined by *lumpen*-bourgeois and *lumpen*-aristocrats who either had lost status or were in danger of losing it and were full of resentment against those who had arrived. While Karl Marx had offered them only the dire verdict that they would be pushed down into the proletariat, Hitler assured them that there was a way out: neither Communism nor capitalism but the German uprising.

Hitler, Goebbels, and Göring never spoke of "revolution," they said "uprising." Franco's counter-revolutionary pronunciamento also was called *levantamiento* or *alzamiento*. Mussolini substituted "action" for revolution. But all totalitarian movements project the image of liberation. Like New Left and Third World ideologies of the 1960's, they perceived only dimly who was to be liberated, and from what. The imagery of this liberation goes back to Richard Wagner's Siegfried (allegedly modeled after Bakunin). The proletarian nature-boy slays the treasure-guarding dragon. In diluted form, we find the myth again in Superman, Tarzan, Li'l Abner, and Frank Allan, Avenger of the Disinherited. The enemy also was seen not in specific institutions but in the personified abstraction of "the Jew" or "the Freemason" or "the City." The little man who was being crushed by the anonymous power of invisible institutions was told that the leader, the dragon-slayer, would crush these powers.

Jewry was the threefold enemy: socially, in terms of status; in business; and as the image of a counterfoil. In Central and Eastern Europe, Jews were middlemen, cattle traders, bankers, shopkeepers; they also were conspicuous in the professions. The proportion of Jewish politicians, lawyers, doctors, entertainers, writers, journalists, and so on, was far greater than their share in the total population. They were concentrated in the big cities, and they owned department stores and apartment houses. Petty-bourgeois and peasants vented their anti-capitalist resentment against Jewish traders; the upper class, fulminating against the social mobility of Jews, accused them of being "pushy." In Eastern and Central Europe, anti-Semitism was the stock-in-trade of right-wing parties; Jews tended to be liberal and radical. In France, anti-Semitism had often appeared in symbiosis with the unorthodox socialism of artisans and craftsmen. In Italy and Spain anti-Semitism was no issue; some of Mussolini's lieutenants were Jews.

There is more to anti-Semitism, however, than economic rivalry and fear of social displacement. The Jew was an archetypal figure of hate and shame who seemed repugnant to many pious Christians. Historical conditions have made him a migrant, barred from taking root in most countries. Since his contacts with the rest of the population were limited to business, he acquired the reputation of being materialistic. Because an alien minority is always suspected of sinful practices, the majority project their own vices on it. Hence the stereotype of the Jewish rapist, the bloodsucker, and other anti-Semitic cartoon types. Eventually the Jew had to stand for everything people did not like in their civilization. A monument to this myth was Julius Streicher's sick and obscene paper *Der Stürmer*.

Where, as in Italy and Spain, anti-Semitism could not become a political dogma, the Freemasons had to fill the role of the bloodsucking plotter. But invariably fascism needs an archenemy who is at once inferior and powerful. At all times and in all countries, Know-Nothing movements have exploited the little man's rage against the dark powers that seem to stifle his virility. Unable to cope with the real sources of his misery, he lashes out wildly against representatives of the "system" and dreams of the "night of the long knives." His quasi-religious fanaticism degenerates into sadistic delusions of power.

Fascism is essentially a religion of resentment. It appeals to the "little man" who in Fallada's novel asks "what now?" without ever being able to supply the answer. Democracy often does not work for him, or it works in ways not obvious to him. In his experience, it is always the others who pull the levers of power: they are organized; they have the money; they know how to use the law. In other words, he does not enjoy his independence and would rather surrender it to a fatherly government which promises to place "order" or the interest of the "national community" above private (namely, other people's) interests. The mingling of classes in the army, the party, the labor front, the leisuretime organizations becomes a substitute for democracy. Big Brother is, through some mystical communion, acting from the deep fount of the people's consciousness.

Fascism finds a psychological foundation in the craving to obey a leader's will, to extinguish personality in the great stream of nation or race, to renounce reason, to surrender to a dynamism of power. Erich Fromm has spoken of the *Escape from Freedom*, the abdication of personal responsibility as all burdens of decision-making are shifted onto the leader. Whereas Marx said that the proletarians must make their revolution themselves, fascist leaders assert: "I will do it for you." Whereas democracy calls on people to have confidence in themselves, totalitarian parties say: "Have confidence in us."

Ernst Nolte rightly speaks of an "epoch of fascism" comprising the second quarter of this century, a time when social and economic systems that may have had different origins in different countries converged toward a typical model of totalitarian state, complete with leader cult, monopoly of party, militaristic ideology, intensely nationalistic policies, often racial arrogance and anti-Semitic propaganda. This type is distinguished from ordinary reactionary, conservative, military, or police dictatorships by its pseudo-democratic, pseudo-participatory features, the close rapport between leader and people, the virtual integration into the state of the entire population, and in most cases the plebeian, mob character of the new elite.

It will not do, therefore, to call fascists and Nazis the mercenaries of capitalist or conservative reaction. Few healthy businesses and few true conservatives supported either Hitler or Mussolini. Nor will it do to explain the Nazi movement as the resurgence of a supposed Teutonic will to world domination. The parallels in Italy, Rumania, Bulgaria, Finland, and elsewhere are too close to allow any charge that Germans had a monopoly on madness. Fascism was populist, anti-parliamentarian, anti-liberal, anti-conservative, anti-cosmopolitan, anti-humanist, anti-rationalist; but, above all, it was apocalyptic, a Jacobinism of the Right.

The most systematic interpretation of Italian Fascism has been given by Giovanni

Gentile, Mussolini's Minister of Education and a student of Benedetto Croce. Starting out from Hegel's assertion that the state is the reality of the moral idea, he declared that the highest development of the state represented the totality of human progress, that no one dared stand in the way of the further development of the state. Its power was the glory of man's achievement; the individual must serve it. True freedom lay in submission to the state. Though the individual could not be free, the state must be free.

Hitler did not deify the state in this fashion. He saw the state as a mere tool and envisaged a nation transcending the boundaries of any country. He said he envied the Jews who were not confined by national borders; he hoped to give the German people a similar opportunity to rule over other nations. He always cultivated the "Germans abroad" (*Auslandsdeutsche*) and he picked "Nordic" individuals in other countries to serve as satraps for the ruling nation. The ideological instrument of this power dream was race. The "Nordic" were called to be warriors and leaders; other races were fit only for subordinate, manual, and menial work. This doctrine was taught at German universities even before Hitler came to power. Eugenics was practiced by the Nazi state through the Nuremberg Laws of 1935, which excluded Jews from contact with Germans, through special advantages given to couples of "Nordic" heritage, through a program of sterilizing or killing the mentally retarded, and through the genocide inflicted on foreign workers and conquered peoples during the war. That Hitler was fanatically dedicated to the race doctrine cannot be doubted in view of his extermination campaign against Jews, gypsies, and other nations, although Albert Speer and Hermann Rauschning assert that Hitler considered his race doctrine merely an instrument of domination. This can surely be said of the cynical Dr. Josef Goebbels, the genius of mass propaganda, but not of Heinrich Himmler and Reinhard Heydrich, the elite-guard leaders, who tried to make their troop into a core of selectively bred super-Teutons.

Note: The most notorious backers of Hitler were not German—Sir Henry Deterding of the Royal Dutch and Shell Oil Company, and the electronics concern Phillips. The Schroeder Bank in Cologne was instrumental in making his match with the German industrialists; but even Jewish houses, like the Darmstädter Bank, paid him "insurance money." Other contributors were Bechstein, the piano manufacturer, Thyssen, the steel king, and Kirdorf, a coal syndicate executive.

CHAPTER 3

The Age of Fascism

WHEN Mussolini staged his political shows, Europe thought him a joke and a freak. His imitators were taken even less seriously. Hitler, with his Chaplin mustache and ham actor's forelock, was considered the hireling of some bankrupt corporations. After his surprise victory in the September 1930 elections, a liberal paper ironically pitied him: Now he must decide whether to join a coalition and betray his hoodlums or stay with them in the wilderness. Hitler was forced to choose the latter alternative—and went on to victory. When power was handed over to him in January 1933, his party chiefs, like Mussolini's chieftains ten years earlier, ravenously fell upon the spoils, purging Jews and republicans from the civil service, ousting them from universities and editorial offices, from management positions in industry and finance. Nor did Hitler, like Mussolini, wait several years for the opportunity to drop his conservative allies, Hugenberg's Nationalist Party. He created the opportunity. The Reichstag was dissolved, and during the election campaign the SA (storm troopers) had license to rough up opposition leaders. On February 27, the Reichstag building went up in flames, and Hitler promptly issued a Decree for the Protection of the State. Despite the terror, the Nazis received only 43.9 per cent of the vote. By arresting the Communist deputies, however, Hitler assured himself a majority in the rump parliament. The intimidated deputies gave Hitler dictatorial powers for four years and thenceforth were called to further sessions only to sing the national anthem. To shift the blame for the Reichstag fire from themselves, the Nazis staged a show trial where a pyromaniac Dutchman, Marinus van der Lubbe, admitted having set the fire. A co-defendant was the Bulgarian Georgi Dimitroff, Moscow's secret emissary in the German Communist Party; his able defense made him an international hero of anti-fascism. The Russians later exchanged a spy for him and made him head of the Communist International.

Once in power, Hitler brooked no resistance or reservation. Hugenberg had to surrender the economic departments. The trade unions were taken over by the Nazi Labor Front. The nationalist "Steel Helmet" was merged with the SA, the independent youth leagues amalgamated with the Hitler Youth. Professional brotherhoods, those of lawyers, actors, writers, doctors, and so forth, were organized into Reich Chambers under Nazi chairmen who had power to issue and revoke licenses. The Protestant Church was placed under a Reich bishop. Newspapers, publishing houses, broadcasting, and the movie industry were thoroughly reorganized. Every bride had to buy a copy of *Mein Kampf.* A secret state police (Gestapo) persecuted all enemies of the regime. An elite corps, the black-uniformed SS (*Schutzstaffel*) struck terror into recalcitrants. All state (*Länder*) governments were "homogenized" with the new administration; few institutions escaped this process of "co-ordination" (*Gleichschaltung*). The exceptions were some offices and businesses that commanded respect abroad. Such were the Foreign Office and the *Frankfurter Zeitung*, which, almost alone among German papers, was allowed well into the war years to cultivate its old bourgeois values. Only two institutions were able to preserve a measure of independence: the army and the church. At least for a while, they gave shelter to persons who had reservations about the "New Germany."

Hitler at first dealt gingerly with the old ruling classes. He pretended to persecute only "Bolsheviks," and the Right winked at his loose interpretation of the term. Of 225,000 political prisoners more than 200,000 belonged to communist, socialist, and republican organizations. These, as well as many common criminals and Jewish detainees, were kept in concentration camps, often after they had served regular prison terms. Parties of the Left were driven underground.

Open resistance soon was no serious threat to Hitler's regime. A greater challenge to his ulterior purposes arose from two factions in his own government: on the one hand, the fanatics who had believed in the second half of the National Socialist label; on the other hand, the traditionalists who had hoped to use Hitler and then to dismiss him. The first were concentrated in the SA, whose leaders, moreover, were challenging the army's supremacy. The second were entrenched in business, in the army, and in the churches. Instinctively Hitler did what every dictator must do from time to time. He purged the Right and the Left deviationists simultaneously and lumped them with criminals and "homosexuals." On June 30, 1934, the SS descended on "traitors" and "conspirators"; Hitler's oldest friend, Captain Ernst Röhm, and his old benefactor, General von Schleicher, were killed. Franz von Papen narrowly escaped, to be made ambassador to Austria and later to Turkey. It is from that day that we must date the era of European fascism.

As in all totalitarian states, the machinery of government became a strictly technical instrument of administration; the law was no longer the basis of the state. All power lay in the hands of Hitler and a few supreme subleaders: Martin Bormann, chief of the NSDAP organization; Heinrich Himmler, chief of the SS; Hermann Göring, who was responsible for the four-year autarky program, for the Prussian state government, and for the air force.[1]

It is remarkable how many respectable people rallied to Hitler after the bloody coup. The mayor of Leipzig, Carl Goerdeler, later a hero of the Resistance, became Hitler's Price Commissioner; Hjalmar Schacht, the financial wizard, organized the

---

[1] While the power of the Propaganda Minister, Dr. Josef Goebbels, was most visible, there is little evidence that he took part in the highest decision-making councils. Neither did the army: it was told when to strike.

German economy for him as an instrument of domination of Europe. The army forgot the murder of one general and the vilification of others when Hitler gave it the most formidable defense budget ever heard of. After old Marshal Hindenburg's death, on August 2, 1934, the army officers swore fealty to the Führer's person, and most of them kept their oath ten years later, when they might have saved Germany's honor by overthrowing Hitler.

Nevertheless, the officers' corps tried to remain a closed club and became the center of all schemes against the upstarts and dilettantes who now were running Germany. When Göring tried to undermine the army's morale with shabby intrigues, he was only half successful. The Foreign Office, on the other hand, was superseded by a parallel staff under Hitler's confidant Joachim von Ribbentrop, a former wine merchant, who eventually also assumed the title of Foreign Minister.

There remained only one force with independent spiritual authority: the churches. The German clergy were traditionally conservative and patriotic. Although they prayed for Hitler during his wars, still they would not allow storm troopers to become bishops. Hitler, on his part, would gladly have avoided a *Kulturkampf*.[2] His first diplomatic act was to conclude a concordat with the Vatican. But his anti-religious, anti-clerical lieutenants tried to control the Catholic hierarchy and the monasteries' assets. When these attempts turned into persecution, Pope Pius XI had to publish an encyclical in the German language: *Mit Brennender Sorge* (*With Burning Concern*, 1937). Individual churchmen also resisted Nazi orders, but they remained isolated. Bishop Clemens von Galen of Münster stands out as a martyr against such opportunists as Theodor Innitzer, Archbishop of Vienna, and Eugenio Pacelli, Pope Pius XII himself, whose usual excuse was that they were preserving the church as an independent organization[3] and appreciated the fascist protection against a Bolshevik takeover.

The Protestant Church was more vulnerable. It had always been essentially a German church; but when the Nazis tried to rename it "German Christians" and to take over its administration, a minority of pastors formed the Bekennende Kirche (Witness-bearing Church). Their spokesman, Martin Niemöller, a former submarine commander and ardent patriot, was put in a concentration camp; another member, the young theologian Dietrich Bonhoeffer, was executed. Provost Heinrich Grüber in Berlin also suffered for his convictions. But there was not among Protestants the same widespread hostility to the Nazi state as among Catholics.

The Nazis' plebeian manners gave offense to the educated and aristocratic circles that at first had acclaimed the overthrow of the republic. Oswald Spengler, once the ideologist of a "Prussian socialism"; Ernst Jünger, who had exalted "total mobilization"; Gottfried Benn, who had celebrated "German Art"; the Expressionist painter Ernst Nolde, who had felt so "Nordic"; Thomas Mann, who at first felt that a writer

---

[2] The term Bismarck used when he tried to "nationalize" the Roman Catholic Church—and failed.
[3] The cost of its preservation was described by Rolf Hochhuth after the war in his controversial play and book *Der Stellvertreter* (*The Deputy*).

cannot live away from his language; the actress Marlene Dietrich, who had first thought it possible to do business with the Reich Chamber of Culture; Stefan George, who had created the myth of the Third Reich; the steel tycoon Fritz Thyssen, who had financed Hitler's campaigns—they all fell out with the totalitarian claims of the Nazis, were silenced, or had to go abroad.

Not everyone who muttered disagreement within the safety of his four walls can be counted among the resistance fighters. But there were groups, such as the Kreisau Circle around Helmuth von Moltke, a scion of military heroes, where dissenters discussed Germany's future after Hitler. The talks were inconsequential; the participants were executed along with those who took part in the abortive putsch of July 1944.

Three groups whose suffering was not brought on by any political underground activity on their part were the Jews, the gypsies, and the Jehovah's Witnesses. By contrast, the Italian Fascists maltreated their enemies but did not go out of their way to destroy inoffensive minorities. Not until Italy had completely fallen under the Nazi sway did Mussolini, too, adopt this characteristically totalitarian trait.

In possession of all power, Hitler assumed the title "*Reichskanzler und Führer*" and set out to execute his program. He promulgated the Nuremberg Laws, placing the Jews back into medieval isolation and announcing Germany's claim to racial domination of Europe. On July 25, 1934, his Austrian minions assassinated Chancellor Dollfuss and put Europe on notice that Hitler purposed to change its map.

Having exported its ideology and its murderers, fascism was to export its wars. But for the time being it exported people. Those who were threatened because of their convictions, those who were barred from employment, those of Jewish ancestry, were forced to seek asylum in foreign countries. Since Jews had been prominent in the professions, this emigration deprived Central Europe of outstanding scientists, philosophers, musicians, writers, poets, actors, journalists, critics, doctors, stage directors, lawyers. They gained influence on public opinion in the West; they found employment at the universities and in the arts; they helped to put Western science and technology ahead of Hitler's. Germany's science, by contrast, suffered from censorship and lack of communication. The level of literacy and of critical thinking declined. Not since Louis XIV expelled the Huguenots had a country so mutilated its human resources. In a rage of anti-intellectualism and anti-humanism, the Nazis burned books by Jewish and Leftist authors, purged from libraries and museums whatever they deemed "un-German," and banned modern art, which they thought "decadent."

Even Hitler's severest critics do not dispute his success in reorganizing the German economy; the secret of this prosperity, however, was the total subjection of all business activities to the demands of the state. Franz Neumann has suggested the term "command economy" for this typically fascist form of control, and Hilferding has pointed out that in its last stages the Nazi economy was no longer governed by the laws of the market.

Tearing up the Treaty of Versailles as he had promised, Hitler ordered general conscription and engaged in a feverish program of rearmament, which also helped to overcome unemployment. The army was equipped with the most modern weapons; defense industries were given massive orders; a network of heavy-duty superhighways was built. Göring created the most modern air force of the day. A four-year plan was launched to make Germany independent of fuel, metal, and rubber imports and to gear the economy for a major war. Synthetic rubber (*Buna*), fiber, and other materials were invented. Foreign trade and foreign exchange were subjected to rigid controls. The farm economy was regulated down to the most minute detail. But since true self-sufficiency could be obtained only by considerable belt-tightening, the Nazi economy would eventually have to conquer *Lebensraum*.[4]

Like Italian Fascism, German Nazism has tried to shape the life of its citizens, to model their minds, and to fill their souls with its images, myths, songs, symbols. The individual was to be submerged completely in the "national or race community." He was to work, to feel, to fight, to die for the Führer. His leisure time and his vacation were organized for him, either by party work or by a movement such as Kraft durch Freude (Strength through Joy), as in Mussolini's *Dopolavoro*. The monopoly of information, the regime's most fearful weapon, pictured the world for him as the camera does for movie goers—with the difference that no exit is possible for the population of the totalitarian horror chamber. While the governments were thus transforming humans into robots and soldiers, they were also subjugating the arts and sciences to their will.

At the same time, an important change took place in Italy. The Depression had forced the government to take over nearly all of the largest corporations. World-famous firms like Fiat, Montecatini, Olivetti, Snia Viscosa, Pirelli, and Edison were put under the financial supervision of a national Istituto di Ricostruzione Industriale. This was a far cry from nationalization, but it made the Fascist state directly responsible for the entire economy. Independent firms could obtain no credit. The Banca d'Italia controlled all banking and investments. Since the state had become the biggest employer, even the sham "corporations" of the *Carta del Lavoro* appeared as too independent; all industries were assigned to a number of "departments" which simply decreed wages and prices. When the state proved not equal to dealing with these problems, Mussolini decided to export his troubles. Conquest was his remedy for the damaged reputation of Fascism, war his answer to unemployment, glory his substitute for fulfilling promises.

Across the Adriatic, Albania by that time was financially dependent on Italy. Mussolini hoped to expand his influence along the coast, into Austria, Hungary, and Bulgaria, the "revisionist" states of Southern and Central Europe. Since these countries also were lying in Germany's path of expansion, Mussolini could hardly have

---

[4] Through shrewd barter agreements and the use of soft debts, Schacht also managed to make the Balkan economies so dependent on German goods that the "economic space" had practically been conquered without war.

cherished his emulator, who was a rival and many times stronger to boot. Was their growing friendship, then, one of those rare cases where philosophical affinity prevailed over divergence of interests? In the beginning, ideology did not unite the dictators but rather set them against each other. During the Dollfuss crisis of 1934, Mussolini sent troops to guard the Brenner Pass. But he could not be satisfied with the modest role of a defender of the *status quo* under British tutelage. He was thirsty for glory, action, and empire. The rhetoric and style of Fascism were incompatible with Mussolini's earlier assurance (to Emil Ludwig) that "Fascism is not for export." Now he financed the Heimwehr in Austria, the Arrow Cross in Hungary, the Spanish monarchists whom he also supplied with arms, and the Croatian Ustashi.

Late in 1935, Mussolini invaded the Biblical kingdom of Ethiopia, which had defeated an Italian army in 1896. There was not much to gain there. The country's natural resources were (and still are) undeveloped, and Italy had no capital to export. Faced with brazen aggression, angry world opinion forced the League of Nations to adopt economic sanctions against Italy. However, since oil was not included in the embargo, and England failed to close the Suez Canal to Mussolini's troop transports, his tanks and airplanes easily overcame the poorly armed Ethiopians. Thus, in one act Mussolini proved that the League (that harebrained scheme of liberal dreamers) was ineffective, that collective security (that chimera of old-style conservative diplomats) was an illusion, that the *status quo* was not sacrosanct and the Western powers were not credible.

Moreover, since Germany had not observed the embargo, the ideological affinity between the two dictators now could become effective. Both were intent on changing the map and felt that their common enemies were the "haves"—the powers defending the *status quo*. Soon they were to form an "Axis" around which world politics was compelled to turn from 1936 to 1939.

Neighboring Yugoslavia now was squeezed between its archenemy, Fascist Italy, and the rising power of Germany. Schacht's techniques of money management already were pulling the Yugoslav economy into the German orbit and weaning Yugoslavia away from France and the Little Entente. At the court of Prince Regent Paul, the councils were divided between a pro-Russian and a pro-German party. Prime Minister Milan Stoyadinovich tried to achieve a rapprochement with the fascist powers and even to imitate their corporate one-party system. He formed the Yugoslav Radical Union (JRZ) and a state-run trade union (Yugoras), but was unable to overcome the Serbs' allegiance to their democratic parties or the Croats' adherence to regional autonomy. All opposition parties united under the leadership of the Peasant chief Vladko Machek and received 44 per cent of the vote (1938); when Machek joined the cabinet, Croatia was granted some "autonomy" but neither self-government nor democracy. Instead, a safe JRZ man, Ivan Shubashich, was appointed governor, while the Croatian Peasant Party was infiltrated by fascists, the country was being steered into the Axis camp, and Ante Pavelich, the future Führer (*Poglavnik*), was organizing his murderous Ustashi.

Hungary was the country where the *status quo* was defended by an informal coalition from the conservatives of Count Bethlen to the Social Democrats, while all the destitute and frustrated classes, from the academic proletariat to the farm laborers, looked to the extreme Right for necessary reforms. General Gyula Gömbös, Horthy's Minister of Defense, came to power in 1932 and shocked the establishment by refusing to name a single magnate to a cabinet post. He was supported by Mussolini, who even persuaded him to mute his rabid anti-Semitism. Gömbös's successors after 1936 grew increasingly more pro-German and anti-Semitic; extremist National Socialist groups exerted increasing pressure to distribute land, to reconquer territory lost in World War I, to act strongly against Jews and usurers. The most militant fascist movement was the Arrow Cross under Ferencz Szalasi, an inspiring patriot and terrorist who was jailed several times for subversion. When the Germans occupied Hungary, however, he protested vehemently.

In the Balkan Peninsula, a thin veneer of constitutionalism barely disguised various forms of dictatorship. General Metaxas held the reins of Greece's government tightly and professed a Hitlerite ideology. In Bulgaria, a fascist-oriented Officers' League seized power in 1934, but the wily King Boris III was able to wrest it from them to keep Bulgaria neutral in the coming war. Rumania's King Carol, too, proved himself as his country's foremost politician and held the fascists at bay, for seven years, through absolute rule. But, economically, the Balkans were already prisoners of Dr. Schacht's *Grossraumwirtschaft*, and the political influence of the Axis was evident in the departments of government, in the press, and in the streets.

While similar to the Hungarian Right in social and ideological make-up, the Rumanian Legionnaires (later called Iron Guards) had distinctive national traits. Their leaders were two university professors, Corneliu Codreanu and Alexander Cuza. Their ideology was Christian, but they preached and practiced murder as a political method, and they were militantly anti-Semitic. Codreanu, often jailed, was finally shot by the police in 1938. When the Legion took revenge on the Minister of the Interior, hundreds of their own were executed in retaliation. From then on, it was open warfare between the King and the Iron Guard. In 1940, General Ion Antonescu, a puppet of the Germans, took power; King Carol followed his Jewish mistress into exile. Antonescu appointed Legionnaires to the cabinet; but, like Hitler, he had no use for idealists and dismissed them soon after. The Iron Guard answered by massacring thousands of their enemies and Jews, but finally were defeated and fled to Germany. Antonescu hung on as dictator for several years.

A different mixture of aristocratic, intellectual, and socialist impulses helped create the Falange Española, which originally consisted of the personal followers of José Antonio Primo de Rivera, the late dictator's son. In 1934, these elite terrorists merged with the pseudo-Christian and pseudo-syndicalist Juntas de Ofensiva Nacional Sindicalista (JONS), whose confused program was violently anti-bourgeois, anti-capitalist, anti-Marxist, and anti-liberal. In the 1936 elections, the combined party got only 40,000 votes; but it claimed strong influence among students, and workers considered it a dangerous enemy. Falangists indeed had helped the police in beating down the Asturian miners' uprising in 1934, and they were to play a part in the generals' pronunciamento of 1936. José Antonio was executed by the republicans, while the generals banished his lieutenants from power. In 1937, after subduing half of the Iberian Peninsula, Francisco Franco ordered the fusion of the Falange and the monarchical, traditionalist Requetés into the Falange Tradicionalista y de las Juntas de Ofensiva Nacional-Sindicalista. To preside over it, he appointed his brother-in-law Serrano Suñer, a partisan of Germany but a traditionalist in general outlook. He jailed its left-wing leader Manuel Hedilla Larrey, of working-class background, but allowed his pseudo-socialist phraseology to survive. The Falange never played the role of the fascist party, but was a docile organ of the military state. Hence one cannot describe Franco's dictatorship as fascist or National Socialist in the specific sense of these terms. Many of the true fascists joined the enemies of his regime. Thus Dionisio Ridruejo, who in 1936 composed the Falange's anthem, has become a leader of Acción Democrática and regrets having helped what he now calls a rigid oligarchy into power.

The "tradicionalista" in the party's name represents the Navarrese Carlists' contribution to the Franco regime. This regionalist group was reactionary but by no means fascist. Neither should the Irish Legion, which fought on the Spanish rebel side, tempt us to label the Irish Free State "fascist." Eamon de Valera, President since 1932, used the British Empire's difficulties to sever all ties with England. Renamed "Eire" by the Constitution of 1937, the island was priest-ridden, backward, and reactionary. During World War II it remained neutral, but it was careful to avoid any identification with the pagan regime in Berlin. In 1948 it became an independent republic.

After the tragic, we must mention the infamous. Knut Hamsun's compatriot Vidkun Quisling gave his name to an ignominious species. His Nasjonal Samling (National Union) was an obscure movement with a murky ideology. He hoped to unite the Nordic peoples and he hailed Hitler as the instrument of the divine will. Apart from some abject lick-spittles, Hitler found no other confederate in Norway.

Elsewhere, willing opportunists did Hitler's business. Such was the case of Father Josef Tiso in Slovakia and of Léon Degrelle in Belgium. In the early 1930's, paid by Mussolini and taking his cues from the Austrian and Italian models, Degrelle started a Christian-Socialist movement among Belgian youth and named it after their publishing house, Christus Rex. In the days of Belgium's constitutional crisis such an adventure was bound to succeed, at least temporarily. Rex attacked all political parties, but especially the conservative leadership of the Catholic Party, adopted the broom as its emblem, published 200,000 copies of Le Pays Réel (The Real Country) daily, and filled the largest meeting halls. In 1936, the Rexists elected twenty-one deputies and twelve senators; they forced the government to denounce the alliance with France. A fascinating orator and shrewd tactician, Degrelle supported the strikes and social reforms of 1936 and concluded an alliance with Flemish separatists. Had he tried a coup then, he might have found support in the army and in parts of the business community, perhaps even at the court. Some influential people were already seeking an accommodation with Hitler; after Munich Degrelle became their spokesman. But the people did not want surrender; in 1939, only Degrelle and three other Rexists were re-elected. When a year later the Nazis occupied Belgium, they did not even try to use him as a quisling; he had no choice left but to enlist in the Legion of Walloon Volunteers to fight Hitler's war in Russia. He hoped to return as *Gauleiter* of Belgium, or perhaps of a revived Burgundy, ignorant of Hitler's promise to Himmler that his SS-State would be located at that very place.

If Degrelle was despicable, how is one to describe socialists who left their party because it was not sufficiently patriotic, and who subsequently hailed Hitler? The Belgian socialist Hendrik de Man, who earlier had taken part in the German youth movement and who in the early thirties had stirred his nation with the idea of a planned economy, greeted the occupation of Belgium in 1940 with these words: "War has brought the downfall of the parliamentary regime and of capitalist plutocracy in the so-called democracies. For the working class and for socialism, the collapse of this decrepit world is not a disaster but a liberation." Likewise, Jacques Doriot, mayor of the workers' suburb of St. Denis, split from the Communist Party to found the fascist Parti Populaire Français.

Some Frenchmen like the syndicalist Ganivet became Hitler's collaborators, paradoxically, through love of peace. We have already found in this company the film director Jacques Feyder and the novelist Jean Giono. Others hated the republic so bitterly that they found Hitler preferable to war, and the Nazis were able to use some ideological affinities with the extreme Right for their propaganda in France. But the bulk of the demonstrators and veterans who in February 1934 overthrew a republican government should not be called fascist. The Croix-de-Feu was a patriotic, reactionary veterans' league; its leader, Colonel François Casimir de la Rocque, came out for nothing more specific than Work, Family, and Fatherland. His actions contributed to the fall of the republic in an indirect way, however. They undermined what little confidence the French people had in the authority and legitimacy of their government. The more militant and openly fascist, pro-German and pro-Italian groups on the extreme Right could not have operated with such impunity had Frenchmen looked at the republic as the instrument of the national will.

Especially after 1936, when the Popular Front came to power, its enemies held every type of calumny, sabotage, and terrorism justifiable in venting their wrath against "the system." "Cagoulards" (hooded men) planted bombs in stores and banks or tried other means of making public life unsafe. The leader of this terrorist gang, Eugène Deloncle, probably was in German pay and during the occupation became an open collaborator. Others posed as pacifists and accused the government of preparing an ideological war against Hitler; anyone who stood up for collective security and international law was smeared as a hireling of the Jewish-Bolshevik conspiracy. The mass-circulation magazine *Gringoire*, in particular, carried viciously anti-Semitic stories—all in the name of peace. Here was a new quirk in nationalism. Those who had traditionally waved the flag and sounded war whoops now were the peace-lovers. They professed that they would rather be Nazis than dead.

The Action Française had 60,000–70,000 members, as compared to the French Communist Party's 40,000 and the Socialists' 150,000. But Colonel de la Rocque's Croix-de-Feu (later the Parti Social Français) leaped from 500,000 in 1935 to 2 million in 1938.

Antonio Salazar, Portugal's dictator, had been indoctrinated by Portuguese disciples of Charles Maurras, who propagated the teaching of "Integralismo Lusitano" at the universities. At Coimbra the Centro Académico de Democracia Crista developed in protest against the professors' liberal legalism. Besides Salazar, Dr. Gonçalves Cerejeira, the Cardinal Patriarch, General Santos Costa, leader of the nationalist army officers, and Professor Mario de Figueiredo, a cabinet minister, belonged to this movement. The integralists were violent in word and deed; although monarchists, they called for an "integral remodeling of society" and often were called Jacobins of the Right. They exalted the beauty of nature and execrated "demo-liberalism"; they praised the virtues of municipal autonomy but rooted for a strong state; they were anti-Semitic and imperialistic.

In its symbolism the Estado Novo vainly tried to imitate the fascists. It had a Legião and a Mocidade (Boy Scout) organization; it introduced the Roman salute, deprecated pacifism, liberalism, and capitalism; it sent 20,000 volunteers to aid Franco. To hold a job in the civil service, or even in business, one had to belong to the Legião. The political police, trained by Nazis, survived their mentors. Political "justice" was meted out by special Tribunais Plenarios Criminais.

Finally, let us look at the East. After Pilsudski's death, in 1935, and under the impact of Hitler's successes, Poland tried to save herself by mimicry. The generals who acceded to power sought popular support through a "movement" that was organized by Colonel Adam Koc and called Camp of National Unity. It was chauvinistic, anti-Semitic, and hostile to the minorities. But it advocated land distribution. When Koc grew more rabidly fascist, he was replaced by a more moderate man, but promptly formed his own "Young Poland." The colonels who ruled Poland in her last days found themselves wedged in between fascists abroad and at home. Loathing Russia and suspicious of democratic movements, however, they were unable to form coalitions with any forces at home or abroad that might have defended Poland's freedom.

In neighboring Lithuania, Antanas Smetona had been the virtual dictator since 1923. In 1934, he suppressed an uprising by his former ally Augustine Voldemaras. Soon he outlawed all parties except the Nationalist Union, but he was unable to unite the country when its existence was threatened by both Poland and Germany. Latvia, too, had a semi-fascist coup in 1934, executed by Karlis Ulmanis. Only in Estonia did the tide run the opposite way: a new constitution restored democracy just before the country was engulfed in World War II.

To sum up, fascist and fascistoid movements had arisen in many countries, partly as the lunatic fringe of the Right, partly as splinters of the extreme Left. They were different from ordinary conservative groups in that they refused to work within the system and proclaimed a revolutionary alternative to both capitalism and socialism. Called to power, the leaders soon rid themselves of their socialist following, but in dealing with the old establishment they maintained their revolutionary style.

Coming to power as a minority party, the fascists first did not overthrow the old ruling classes, but they made all the established elites subservient to their own political purposes. They superimposed a political elite on state and society, subjected business and civil service to the goals of national mobilization, and converted trade into an instrument of conquest. Like the Japanese Co-prosperity Sphere, the German *Grossraumwirtschaft* became the underpinning of a large empire in which other nations were to be the scullions.

After the Nazi conquest of power, terroristic methods also came to be applied to foreign affairs. Fascism became an "export article" to the extent that conspirators abroad were in the pay of the revisionist powers. The various dictatorial movements, which in ideological leanings and social content may have been far apart, came to be part of a world-wide movement and began to revolve around the "Axis" that Berlin and Rome were then forging.

CHAPTER 4

The Popular Front and the Spanish Civil War

DOMESTIC and foreign affairs were strangely intertwined in the 1930's. Every time a dictator won some success abroad, democrats experienced it as a setback for liberty in all their countries. Every blow to collective security was also a threat to the labor movement's security and to civil rights at home. The Right in France openly rejoiced when Hitler or Mussolini humiliated the French Government, which they considered Bolshevist.

The international civil war reversed the roles of Right and Left with respect to national defense. Traditionally anti-militarist, the Socialists and Communists now wanted to pit power against the fascist threat. The switch was not easy. The Labour Party maneuvered itself into the pathetic position of asking for resistance against the dictators while rejecting the defense budget. On the other hand, to stop Hitler one might have to conclude an alliance with Stalin, whose bad reputation and unscrupulous tactics might taint any cause that appealed to his helping hand—or with the French military, whose anti-republican traditions had never waned.

In 1934, French Premier Laval went to Moscow and concluded a reinsurance treaty. Stalin also undertook to come to the aid of Czechoslovakia if and when France did likewise. To make the alliance believable, Stalin suddenly abandoned his anti-Western, anti-capitalist militancy. He told the French Communists to stop undermining their army, which now had become an ally of the proletarian fatherland. He ordered a complete turnabout in Comintern policies. Instead of destroying bourgeois culture, the Communists were to "inherit" it; instead of condemning and vilifying Social Democrats and bourgeois radicals, they were to conclude electoral alliances with them and, wherever possible, to support their governments. Dimitroff first called this "the tactics of the Trojan horse," as though it were a maneuver to infiltrate democratic organizations; but the Western Communists jubilantly fraternized with socialists and democrats. For the call for a united Left had surfaced spontaneously from the masses.

The Popular Front was created in February 1934 in response to the threat of a fascist coup in Paris. The victim of that attempt, Édouard Daladier, though himself a man of the center, acquired a mystique of the Left. Trade unions, intellectuals, artists, anti-clericals, anti-royalists, Communists, Socialists, Radicals—a great movement rallied behind Daladier to confront Colonel de la Rocque's "fascists." Mammoth demonstrations demanded an alliance with the Soviet Union, "structural reforms," and a renewal of democracy. With such a program, Communists, Socialists, and Radicals in Spain and in France formed electoral alliances which won majorities in February and July, 1936, respectively.

After its victory, the Popular Front in France formed a government, which the Communists supported without participating in it. Its leader was the socialist Léon Blum, a writer of note and a well-loved leader, but not a tough fighter. Daladier became Minister of War; Pierre Cot, a Radical with close ties to the Kremlin, was made Minister of the Air Force. For the first time the Communists joined a parliamentary coalition—not to promote a revolution, though, but to prevent one. To their dismay, a wave of sit-down strikes swept the country. The workers understood the Popular Front as a mandate to rebuild the economic system. Millions of French workers for the first time were given the benefits of collective bargaining and firm contracts. Blum persuaded workers' and employers' representatives to work out a general accord; two weeks later the Chambre wrote into law the forty-hour week and two-week paid vacation. Later, a "Wheat Office" was created to subsidize the farmers.

These reforms were followed by the nationalization of the Banque de France and the defense industries, the establishment of a social-security system, and a reversal of fiscal policies. Great public works were to provide employment for all. In neighboring Belgium a similar strike movement coincided with Hendrik de Man's strong agitation for a "Plan" and a restructuring of the kingdom's society and state. Similar reforms were being prepared in Spain.

All seemed to be going forward. The Left took hope that it was on the offensive again and would be able to build defenses against aggressive fascism. Then the blow fell. Abetted by financial interests in London and with the active support of Hitler and Mussolini, the Spanish generals struck out against the government of the republic. The ensuing civil war had world-wide repercussions which led to the dissolution of the Popular Front. The old powers had no confidence. French finances were harassed by machinations on the London Stock Exchange; the franc had to be devalued. Eventually an insidious campaign of the French Right, peasant and middle-class protests against rising prices and wages, the growing disenchantment of the radicals, dissensions over the Civil War in Spain—all this combined to bring the Popular Front to an inglorious end in June 1937.

To understand the Spanish Civil War, we must go back to the municipal elections of 1931, at whose outcome King Alfonso fled and a republic was proclaimed. Liberal intellectuals like Manuel Azaña, Niceto Alcalá Zamora, Alejandro Lerroux, and Indalecio Prieto—that is, a freethinker, a Catholic, a former syndicalist turned conservative, and a socialist—tried to reconcile conflicts which for decades had striven to come out into the open. Among these were: harsh poverty and a rigid class division; illiteracy and superstition; various freemasonries which considered themselves above the law; a reactionary class of big landowners, and 3 million landless farm workers inclined to anarchism; an oppressive, superstitious clergy which supported the rich and was itself a major shareholder in many industries; an indolent, conspirational officers' corps; serious regional conflicts. The Basque provinces and Catalonia, industrially the most advanced, were fighting for the right to use their own language in their schools and courts. On the other hand, the old Kingdom of Navarre and other provinces were still clinging to the traditions of the Carlist pretender.

Azaña as Premier pushed through the Cortes a number of reforms which the local authorities found difficult to enforce. Estates of over fifty-six acres were to be divided up. But the state had no money for compensation; apart from some violent seizures by the workers themselves, only a few thousand acres were distributed. The republic scared the rich but disappointed the poor. Church and state were to be separated and religious orders were to be dissolved; but for all practical purposes the power of the Roman Church remained unbroken and the faithful were alienated. Education was taken out of the hands of the clergy; but since the state had neither money nor trained teachers, many children went to private schools—or to none. The army was greatly diminished in size, but officers continued to conspire. Thus, General Franco was given the Moroccan command and General Mola the command of strategically important Burgos; General Sanjurjo was made police commissioner of Barcelona, where in 1932 he staged a pronunciamento. The republic did not dare to abolish the reactionary Guardia Civil; it merely recruited a rival police, the Guardia de Asalto. The forces of the Right and Left were fighting a see-saw battle for preponderance in the republic.

By 1933, the republic had not satisfied the Left, while the Right was rallying for a showdown. The Catholic Premier, J. Gil Robles, hoped to wear the Left out with legal repression. In 1934, the miners in Asturias rose under the slogan, "Proletarian Brothers, Unite!" Regionalists and syndicalists in Catalonia and socialists in Madrid joined the insurrection. They were beaten. Thousands were jailed, including the socialist leader Largo Caballero, the Catalan leader Luis Companys, and many anarchists and trade unionists.

The Popular Front promised to free the prisoners. In this hope the anarchists, for the first time in their history, took part in an election, thus assuring the Left's victory. But they did not wait for the formation of a government to open the jails and to close the convents; they occupied the fields and the factories and drew the socialists into a vast wave of direct action. Azaña, having been elevated to the Presidency, appointed a cabinet slightly to the left of center but with no Socialist or Communist in it, while Largo Caballero, now the leader of the socialist left wing, engaged in a revolutionary propaganda which earned him the name of a Spanish Lenin. The Communists were over-anxious to avoid even the appearance of revolution. Moscow wished to establish diplomatic relations with Madrid and negotiated an agreement to supply naphtha to the Spanish Petroleum Monopoly—reason enough for Shell and the London press to believe every atrocity story spread by Spanish monarchists.

The City openly supported an anti-republican conspiracy. On the Right, the legalistic Gil Robles lost his influence to the monarchist Calvo Sotelo. The forces were being polarized. Plans were laid for a typical Spanish "pronunciamento ' an army coup supported by the Carlists, the church, the monarchists, the small Falange, and financed by Mussolini and mining interests in London.

Civil war already was raging in the streets of Madrid. The Falange shot Lieutenant Castello of the Guardia de Asalto; two days later his comrades shot Calvo Sotelo after he made an incendiary speech in the Cortes, and thereby precipitated the Pronunciamento. On July 18, General Franco started the uprising in Morocco. Using Italian transport planes and pilots, he moved his foreign and Moorish mercenaries over to the mainland. Army and Guardia Civil joined the insurgents; the Guardia de Asalto, Navy and Air Force remained loyal to the republic. But not trusting the government, which indeed was wavering, the people of Barcelona, Madrid, Valencia, Santander, Bilbao, and Malaga rose up in arms, first in defense of the republic, but soon to overthrow the local authorities, to expropriate factories, to occupy land, to throw out or kill their oppressors. People were executed summarily wherever their opponents seized power locally. Thus Spain's most remarkable poet, Federico García Lorca, was killed by the fascists.[1]

Prevented from negotiating with the rebel generals, the government was forced to lead in a fight it could not evade. But in many places socialist or anarchist unions were in charge of military operations and security, and soon also of production, distribution, and transportation. Hastily formed militias held the actual power; some nationalized, others socialized, and still others municipalized the services. In Catalonia a large coalition of Leftists, including winegrowers, regionalists, socialists, Trotskyists, and anarchists, formed a revolutionary *Generalidad* and socialized all industry. In the Basque provinces, on the other hand, Catholic republicans formed an autonomous government, and their clergy supported it. Everywhere else the church sided with the rebels, along with a large part of the civil service and the upper classes.

While the government had lost all authority, the large and powerful trade unions—the socialist UGT and the anarchist CNT—organized the defense of the republic. In September, Largo Caballero formed a left-wing government which at last gave recognition to the actual distribution of power in the country; it also included two Communists. In November four anarchists, too, entered the government. Spain had acquired a revolutionary state, which now proceeded to give itself an army and an administration. This was contrary to anarchist theory, but the enemy was at the gates of Madrid. There Franco's mercenaries were stopped by gallant defenders.

The rebellious generals realized that their pronunciamento had failed. They had provoked the revolution they were pretending to forestall. Unable to conquer Spain, they took the fateful decision to call in foreign armies: a German air squadron and four Italian divisions. On the other side, volunteers from many countries came to the aid

---

[1] The majority of Rightist civilians who were killed by the loyalists died in the first days of the insurrection, during the sweeping counter-coup; by contrast, many thousands of loyalists were killed by the military in the weeks and months following the conquest of each province. Perhaps 100,000 were murdered without the law; 100,000 died in battle, and 600,000 were wounded. About 300,000 loyalists emigrated after the war, and the prisons were filled for years with victims of repression and vengeance.

of the republic, many of them veterans of World War I and of anti-fascist battles. The Russians also sent tanks, aircraft with pilots, and staff officers. The Spanish Civil War turned into a rehearsal for international war.[2] At Guadalajara, in March 1937, Italian anti-Fascists beat Mussolini's troops. An irate Duce swore that he would see Franco through to victory. The League of Nations and a farcical "Non-Intervention Committee" were unwilling and unable to stop the aggressors.

Thanks to Soviet military aid and the volunteers, the Communists gained ascendancy in the republican army and government. They felt that the Spanish Republic could be saved only if the democracies interposed their own power against the fascist intervention. Stalin hoped to win England and France for such a coalition; he therefore had no use for a revolution in Spain and discouraged the socialist and anarchist experiments. He also demanded the suppression of the Trotskyist militias. In May 1937, a pitched battle erupted in Barcelona between Communist-led republican forces and the revolutionaries. Largo Caballero had to resign and was replaced by a right-wing Socialist, Dr. Juan Negrín, who worked well with the Russians. Although the Leftists continued to serve in the cabinet, for all practical purposes the Communist line prevailed; the revolution was stopped and a modern army was organized.

But the hope for intervention by Western powers had never been realistic. The Popular Front government in France, torn between its pacifist inclinations and its sympathies for the republic, between its fear that England might leave it to face Germany alone and its efforts to unite the big powers, accepted the principle of non-intervention, looking the other way when Czech, Mexican, and other black-market arms were smuggled across the Pyrenees to the loyalists. Moreover, Léon Blum's cabinet ran into financial difficulties. Blum was unable to hold the coalition together or to overcome the hostility of the stock exchanges. After a year he was replaced by a sound though corrupt Radical, Camille Chautemps, followed later by Daladier, whose policies ran counter to the domestic and foreign aims of the Popular Front.

The British monarchy, meanwhile, was absorbed in a bizarre affair which deeply affected its subjects. King Edward VIII, who had acceded to the throne early in 1936, was fond of a twice-divorced American woman. Had she merely been his mistress, the Conservatives might not have objected; but since he intended to marry her, Prime Minister Stanley Baldwin forced him to abdicate. The King became the Duke of Windsor; he and his Duchess enjoyed immense popularity throughout the world as living proof that romantic love was not dead.

Baldwin also had to resign, however, and was replaced by Neville Chamberlain, who promised to give England both a comprehensive social-insurance system and peace. He tried to save the empire by making concessions to the revisionist powers, a policy that came to be called appeasement. He offered Hitler the Portuguese and Belgian colonies; he fired Anthony Eden, the Foreign Minister who was a defender

---

[2] The German Air Force destroyed the Basque city of Guernica. (Picasso's angry "Guernica" canvas is in New York's Museum of Modern Art.) The Italian forces grew to a total strength of 80,000, one-fifth of the entire rebel army. On the republican side there were 2,000 poorly camouflaged Russians and 45,000 international volunteers—the famous International Brigades

of the League of Nations and an enemy of Mussolini. Chamberlain hoped to separate Hitler from Mussolini and to keep fascism the internal affair of each country. Educated to look at Continental dictators as mere blackmailers, he could not understand that fascism and revisionism had become world political forces and that Mussolini was driven by his rhetoric to become Hitler's partner and to strive, though with totally inadequate means, for hegemony in the Mediterranean.

Over these intrigues, the Spanish Republic was allowed to succumb. The Russians stopped sending supplies by early 1938, while Mussolini's "volunteers" continued to pour into the country. In January 1939, Barcelona fell and Madrid was isolated. A coup ended the futile resistance on March 29, 1939. In its last year, the republic had been a mere shell of Communist rule.

Hope was dead once again; it had not been killed by its enemies alone. It had been dealt a deadly blow by its alleged friends.

Franco showed no mercy to his adversaries who had fought so bravely. His regime combined all the worst features of all the reactionary regimes in Spain's past. Landlords, the military, and priests once more ruled over a hungry people. No reforms whatsoever mitigated his somber dictatorship. It took thirty-three years, a full generation's time, until once again a Madrid theater was able to stage even a nonpolitical play by García Lorca. The gloomy War Monument in the Sierra proclaims the vindictive spirit of the regime.

CHAPTER 5

The Moscow Trials

THANKS to the help it had lent the Spanish Republic, the Soviet Union was a hero of the Left. But it dealt a rude blow to the Popular Front when some of its most famous leaders were indicted in Moscow for treason, sabotage, and subversion. In a series of show trials the defendants accused each other and confessed that they had been spies in foreign pay, that they had conspired to overthrow the Soviet government, that they had planned to cede Russian soil to the fascist aggressors. In a truly Kafkaesque ending, their prosecutor, Genrikh Yagoda, ultimately found himself in the prisoners' dock confessing to these same crimes. Old Bolsheviks, high and low functionaries by the thousands, were purged; the concentration camps were filled as rapidly as their inmates died—the victims of hard labor, malnutrition, and unspeakable cruelty. Having liquidated the Communists, Stalin ruled with the secret state police (GPU, later renamed NKVD); his henchman Nikolai Yezhov gave his name to this eerie episode: *Yezhovchina*.

The rationale for the terror was the danger of war. Russia was transformed into a besieged fortress; all resources were strained for defense. Enormous investments had to be made in heavy industry while the workers could not be given consumer goods in return. Canals and roads were built with slave labor recruited by the all-powerful GPU. At the same time the nation was spiritually mobilized to defend the fatherland. Textbooks were rewritten; Marxism was abandoned: Not socialism but "Mother Russia" dominated Soviet propaganda. Peter and Catherine the Great, Suvorov and Kutusov, Alexander Nevsky and other heroes of the great Czarist past were celebrated in novels and movies. Russia needed patriots, not Communists; hard taskmasters, not anti-fascists.

The Party bureaucracy was destroyed. Of 1,966 delegates to the Seventeenth Party Congress, no fewer than 1,108 were arrested for "counter-revolutionary activities"; 70 per cent of the members of the Central Committee were denounced as enemies of the Party. But the real enemy was ideology. The Spanish Civil War had taught Stalin that Russia could expect little help from foreign democrats, socialists, and even Communists. The purges liquidated the ideologists who still pinned their hopes on anti-fascist brotherhood.

In the great revelation at the Twentieth Party Congress twenty years later,

Khrushchev was to describe some of the horrors that shook Russia, and especially its ruling party, during those years of collective self-flagellation:

> When Stalin said it was necessary to arrest this man or that one, there was no gain-saying; everybody had to believe that the man in question was an enemy of the people; those responsible for the security of the state fell all over themselves to prove the guilt of the accused with falsified documents. What proofs were there? The "con-fessions" of the arrested people—and the justices accepted these in all seriousness. And how come that a person admits crimes he cannot have committed? There is only one way: physical torture until the loss of consciousness and intellectual breakdown. This was the method by which the confessions were obtained.

No one went to bed confident that his clear conscience protected him from being rudely awakened. Anyone could be accused of any crime. Not only was the accused declared an enemy of the state, but his relatives and all his associates had to fear for their lives.

The riddle of the *Yezhovchina* will never be completely solved. Most Western writing[1] on the subject has concentrated on the moral and psychological problem of the "confessions." But the real riddle of the trials is not the question *why* the defendants confessed but *what* they confessed. It would seem that the rudiments of a conspiracy did exist, given Stalin's ruinous course and his betrayal of Marxism. People in high places undoubtedly were looking for a successor. Although no one knows to what lengths the opposition was prepared to go, they must have considered the military consequences of a coup. Would it invite a Nazi attack?

At the trials, the defendants took upon themselves all guilt for defeatist thinking and proclaimed, within hearing of the German Ambassador, that Russia was now united and capable of protecting herself. At the same time they told the Russian people that whoever had speculated on Stalin's fall was a traitor to his country. The old Communists, who had sacrificed all their principles to stay in power, paid one last service to their Party by sacrificing their honor on the altar of unity. In a totalitarian regime, dissent is treason; betrayal of the leader is a crime to be atoned for by death. The person and policies of the leader were identified completely with the country's survival.

There is, however, a different theory. The trials were a discussion of defense strategy; in veiled form some of the defendants' speeches were proposing that Russia should risk war with Hitler even if the price was high. Stalin, we shall see, thought it wiser to seek an accommodation with the fascists. The German ambassador in Moscow reported that some of Stalin's intimates seemed eager to revive the Rapallo policy and were unhappy that Foreign Minister Litvinov made anti-fascist speeches in the League of Nations. Their opponents, however, may have speculated that war with Hitler might be a blessing in disguise. Could not the inevitable setbacks of Soviet

---

[1] The psychological problem of the trials has been examined by Charles Plisnier in *Faux Passeports*, which unfortunately has not been translated into English. The book has been eclipsed by Arthur Koestler's *Darkness at Noon*, which misses the most relevant political points.

arms provide an opportunity to overthrow Stalin and to rescue Bolshevism on a reduced territory?

For the moment, Stalin tried to win approval in the Western democracies. It is ironic that just at this time, when his power became absolute, he promulgated a constitution, complete with civil rights, representative bodies, and legal safeguards. Soviet Russia was to appear like a "regular" state worthy of being allied with the capitalist republics of the West. Mock elections were held, while Stalin ceased to consult even with the members of the *Politburo* and no Party Congress was convened.

Trotsky has charged that this façade concealed a dictatorship of the bureaucracy, and that the "bureaucratic degeneracy of the Soviet state" corresponded to the decline of the Party. Likewise, in a secret "testament" that was circulated underground, the Kremlin's top economist, Eugene Varga, accused the "bureaucratic oligarchy" of securing a privileged status for itself in the beginning of the 1930's. The instrument of its domination was "nomenclature": the establishment of lists of selected individuals who reserved for themselves all policy-making positions, the highest salaries, the dachas and official automobiles, "envelopes,"[2] tennis courts, swimming pools, food not to be found in ordinary shops, the secrets of state, and the power over the other people. Varga described the minds of these rulers as "petty-bourgeois"; in Marxist fashion he saw the restoration of class differences in the Soviet Union as a counter-revolutionary development, a return to capitalism, the domination of a new bourgeoisie.

Indeed the new Code of Laws reflected the needs of that new class. The family was restored to its place as the foundation of society, abortion was forbidden, divorce made more difficult, and family property protected. Yet, Stalin's concern for his administrative personnel did not create a "soviet bourgeoisie"; nor did his call for higher productivity result in technocratic rule for industry. Engineers, too, were purged. Khrushchev told the Twentieth Party Congress that when a functionary was called to his superior, he never knew whether it was to give advice or to be sent to Siberia. Is this how a ruling class lives? If there was a "soviet bourgeoisie" at all, it was a service class. The regime remained arbitrary, personal, and totalitarian. It was neither "Right" nor "Left" but opportunistically open to all possible courses. It had no need to follow anti-fascist or any other ideology and took its bearings exclusively from the interests of the Russian state. On this level, Stalin could deal with other totalitarians.

Walter Krivitsky, an intelligence officer who defected, assures us that as early as 1934 Stalin had decided to come to terms with Hitler. Ostensibly, Foreign Minister Maxim Litvinov was seeking security arrangements with the West; but during the 1937 trials both fascist and democratic countries were impartially denounced as patrons of the "diversionists." Western consulates were closed in 1938; the end of the trials coincided with a wave of unofficial anti-Semitism, a surge of Russian chauvinism, and the persecution of all who remembered Lenin.

The regime emerging from the terror, therefore, was one of total mobilization; its

---

[2] The custom, inherited from the Czar's bureaucrats, of buying favors.

economy was defense planning, its ideology nationalist, its politics totalitarian. The *Yezhovchina* was nothing less than counter-revolution, white terror. Stalin had broken the continuity with Lenin by physically exterminating his comrades, by ideologically making a mockery of Marxism, by institutionally transforming Party rule into his personal dictatorship. The Marxian class diagram does not provide categories to describe Stalin's revolution, a national, totalitarian, patriotic mobilization which changed the Bolshevist into a fascist pattern of institutions, ideology, and action. It was a revolution conducted precisely against the tendency of *embourgeoisement* among the Party and state bureaucracy members. Twenty years after the October Revolution, Russia was ready for her Napoleon.

With totalitarian rule now installed in so many countries, war was becoming unavoidable. The very attempt to avert it only precipitated its coming. The following chapter relates the destruction of European security; but in order to understand how it came about, we must return to the year 1933.

CHAPTER 6

The Collapse of the European System

POLAND'S Marshal Pilsudski was the first European statesman to recognize the danger of Nazism. Immediately upon Hitler's ascent to power, he created an "incident" in Danzig to test the firmness of his Western allies. When France seemed reluctant to humiliate the German dictator then and there, Poland decided to seek better relations with her dangerous neighbor. From then on, European security and the *status quo* were under constant attack. Germany slammed the door on the Disarmament Conference and the League of Nations. Instead of condemning Hitler, the Pope hastened to conclude a concordat with him. Having thus been made respectable, Hitler was able to sign a nonaggression treaty with Poland (January 26, 1934).

This was the first dent in France's formidable system of alliances. She had sponsored the Little Entente (Yugoslavia, Czechoslovakia, and Rumania) and the Balkan Entente (Turkey, Greece, Rumania, and Yugoslavia); she had an alliance with Poland and, under the Locarno system, a guarantee by England and Italy of her boundaries. Presently she strove to strengthen this system further by composing her differences over Africa with Italy and by sponsoring the Soviet Union's admission (September 18, 1934) to the League of Nations.

It was now a race between the forces of collective security and the *status quo*, on the one hand, and lawless revisionism and opportunism, on the other hand. In July 1934, when the Nazis tried to seize Vienna, Mussolini marched his troops to the Brenner Pass, and when Hitler began to rearm in March 1935, England, France, and Italy met at Stresa (April 1935) to confirm their common interest. On May 2, 1935, France and Russia signed a treaty of alliance, and Stalin told the French Communists that henceforth they would have to be good patriots. Under Russian sponsorship, the left-of-center parties in several countries began to form anti-fascist alliances. The Popular Front was to provide an ideology for collective security and League of Nations legality.

Yet this united front was poorly assembled and divided by conflicting interests. Only two months after Stresa, England signed a naval agreement with Hitler. Mussolini wanted Ethiopia as bounty for his help in defending the *status quo*, and France's Premier Laval and England's Foreign Secretary Samuel Hoare allowed him a free hand in Africa; but a wave of public indignation burst upon the diplomats. The people recognized what the statesmen refused to see: that peace is indivisible and collective security dare not tolerate exceptions. The anti-fascist militancy of the Popular Front and the fiery rhetoric of Litvinov and Beneš at the League of Nations eventually forced the powers to repudiate the foul deal and to adopt sanctions against the aggressor. It was the first, and for thirty years the only, example of such an international action; alas, it failed to stop aggression, because it was only partial. Even the Soviet Union sold its naphtha for use by Mussolini's airplanes and tanks. In 1936, Italy's King was proclaimed "Emperor of Abyssinia."

With collective security discredited, Hitler now sent troops into the Rhineland, demilitarized under the Versailles Treaty. Today we know that the German generals had advised against the move and that decisive action in London and Paris might have given them an excuse to depose the dictator. In the absence of any resistance, Hitler found his prestige enormously enhanced. The European system being deflated, the Western democracies were unwilling to use their strength while they enjoyed military superiority. They confirmed the low opinion fascists of all countries had of parliamentary governments. The helplessness of Western civilization found expression in a popular song, *Tout Va Très Bien, Madame la Marquise*.[1]

The Spanish Civil War gave another demonstration of irresolution on the part of the democracies, and of increasing boldness, nay insolence on the part of the dictatorships. At first, Hitler had hesitated to be drawn into the conflict. But when he saw that the governments in London and Paris were afraid of him, he took sadistic pleasure in exposing their weakness. Mussolini did not conceal his intervention but openly decorated "volunteers" of the Spanish war. The dictators now co-operated to change the map, to increase their influence, to spread their ideology. In June 1936, Mussolini handed the office of Foreign Minister to his son-in-law, Count Galeazzo Ciano, who was fanatically anti-British and hoped to convert the Mediterranean into an Italian lake while Hitler was upsetting the *status quo* in the North. In October the two dictators announced that they had formed an "Axis," around which world politics was to spin henceforth. In November this was followed by the Anti-Comintern Pact between Germany and Japan, to which Italy acceded a year later.

The international war became quite ideological. Fascist propaganda attacked the democracies because they were either "capitalistic," "decrepit," or allied to "Communists." The European Left, in turn, tried to link its national aim—defense of the *status quo* against the revisionist onslaught—to its socio-political aspirations: the rise of populist and democratic forces to combat the danger of fascist reaction. But the defenders of democracy were not backed by the full power of their countries. The Tory government in London secretly, as was soon to be revealed, sympathized with Franco; the Popular Front government in Paris was being eroded from within. Before Madrid, Franco boasted that in addition to the four columns besieging the

---

[1] In which the butler advises his mistress that the master perished in the flames of the mansion while "everything is going very well."

city he had a "fifth column" inside which would open the gates for him. In every country a "fifth column" was working for the victory of fascism even if this were to endanger national security. Conservatives who remained patriots on the other hand did not care to be found in the same camp with either the Russians or their local "Reds."

The fascist, revisionist states now called all like-minded nations and parties to rally for a great redistribution of the earth. Hitler wanted the return of all territories that had been taken from Germany at Versailles (though for the moment he assured France that Alsace-Lorraine was not among his demands); his Austrian partisans agitated for *Anschluss*. Mussolini asked for Nice and Savoy, Corsica and Tunisia; he also established good relations with Arab nationalists in Palestine and Egypt who agitated against the British Empire. Hungary had lost territories to Czechoslovakia and Rumania; Poland had claims against Czechoslovakia and Lithuania. In Yugoslavia the Croats were encouraged to fight for independence; in Belgium the Germanic agitation aroused the Flemish against the dominant Walloons; in Brittany a Celtic group tried to foment separatism. Germany's and Italy's intervention, by land, sea, and air, in the Spanish Civil War assured the world that this dynamic new force was not to be stopped by the niceties of conventional diplomacy. In March 1937, Yugoslavia thought it wise to compose her differences with Italy. When France sent her Foreign Minister on a tour through Eastern Europe, he came back empty-handed.

In February 1938, Hitler called the Austrian Chancellor Kurt Schuschnigg to his Eagle's Nest at Berchtesgaden and ordered him to appoint Nazis to his cabinet. Since Mussolini no longer protected Austria's independence, Schuschnigg yielded on March 11, and German troops marched into Vienna. A week later Lithuania bowed to a Polish ultimatum.

The Czechoslovakian quadrangle in the center of Europe now was surrounded on three sides by Germany. Moreover, the country's most highly industrialized parts along the Sudeten mountain range, adjacent to Germany, were populated by German-speaking people; Hitler's lieutenant Konrad Henlein had organized these "Sudeten Germans" into a fifth column, ready to explode the Czech Republic. Foolishly, Neville Chamberlain, the British Premier, encouraged Hitler's expansionism toward the Balkan Peninsula; perhaps he speculated that in the pursuit of hegemony there, Germany would eventually clash with Russian interests, as had happened before World War I. Hence, instead of defending the bastion of Western security in Central Europe, Chamberlain did his best to destroy it and to smooth Hitler's drive toward the East. The *Drang nach Osten* announced in Nazi propaganda must have appealed to the influential Soviet-haters in London who formed the so-called Cliveden set (named after Lady Astor's estate where it met). It included Sir Basil Zaharoff, the munitions-maker; Sir Henri Deterding, of Shell Oil, Montagu Norman, of the Bank of England; the editors of *The Times* (London) and *Observer*; also, members of the influential Rhodes Circle and of Chatham House with their publications, *Round Table* and *International Affairs*. These organs produced a steady flow of adverse information on the League of Nations, on France, Spain's legal government, and the Soviet Union, as well as friendly comment on Germany's grievances and Hitler's moderation and power. They all agreed that the peace of England should not be sacrificed for the defense of small countries or dubious principles. Their opponents called them "appeasers," because they nursed the illusion that Hitler's appetite would be satisfied if just one more of his demands were fulfilled. David Low has portrayed this climate of opinions in numerous biting cartoons.

Encouraged by Chamberlain's "observer," Lord Walter Runciman, the Sudeten Germans escalated their demands, and Hitler rejected all concessions the Czechs offered. The German generals were dismayed. How would they ever get rid of Hitler if England practically urged victory on him? The chief of staff, General Ludwig Beck, sent an emissary to Downing Street, promising to arrest Hitler should his boldness lead to war. Instead of heeding this advice, Chamberlain flew to Berchtesgaden, armed only with an umbrella and inexhaustible good will. He granted all of Hitler's demands only to be presented, nine days later, with a new ultimatum: Hitler wanted no plebiscite but immediate occupation of the Sudeten area.

It seemed that over a mere question of procedure the world would have to go to war. Gas masks were being distributed in the capitals; mobilization orders went out; the British Parliament went into session—when, dramatically, a messenger appeared to tell Chamberlain that Hitler had agreed to a conference. The frightened members of Parliament broke into cheers. On September 29, 1938, Hitler received Mussolini, Daladier, and Chamberlain in Munich. Without asking for Czech consent, the powers decided that 15,000 square miles of their territory with 3 million inhabitants were to be occupied by the German Army within ten days. Arriving in London, Chamberlain announced to a cheering crowd that he was bringing them "peace in our time." But the Czechs were not even allowed to remove their property from the surrendered land; their strategic fortifications were now in Hitler's hands. Already he was asking for Danzig—as his "last demand."

French Premier Daladier rightly felt that he had suffered an ignominious defeat and was prepared to resign. But the crowd at the airport in Paris cheered him for breaking France's word. The prospect of war had paralyzed all minds; people did not want to "die for Danzig" or any piece of sovereignty hundreds of miles from their borders. Léon Blum admitted that on the morrow of Munich he heaved a "craven sigh of relief."

The relief was not to last long. Like jackals, Hungary and Poland helped themselves to pieces of Czechoslovakia; the Slovaks were encouraged to demand first autonomy and then independence. Finally, on March 15, 1939, Hitler occupied rump Bohemia-Moravia, while Hungary seized Carpatho-Russia and Italy prepared for an invasion of Albania.

Seeing that he had been deceived, Chamberlain reacted with surprising determination. England and France now undertook to guarantee the independence of Poland, Turkey, Greece, and Rumania. They accelerated their arms program, but Hitler, with considerable lead-time, was able to increase his advantage. As early as November 1937, according to Colonel Friedrich Hossbach, he had told his general staff that the German superiority over the Western powers would reach its peak in 1939. Chamberlain's policy forced England and France to accept war with Germany at the least favorable moment. Yet between March and August 1939, he did nothing to forestall Hitler's expected attack on Poland.

There was only one way to deter such an attack. France, England, and the Soviet Union could have announced jointly that they would defend Poland even against her will. Stalin demanded the right to pass through Poland and Lithuania if he was to save them. But Poland feared being rescued by the Red Army more than being swallowed by Hitler. Nor was such a risk acceptable to the other Baltic states or to the influential circles in London and Paris. Chamberlain did not use his powers of persuasion in Warsaw and Kaunas as he had done in Prague six months earlier. Fear of Russian preponderance in Europe, therefore, prevented the conclusion of a collective security pact that alone could have made that fear unnecessary. Russia's small neighbors were allowed to voice apprehensions that prevented England from pressing for an alliance. Negotiations in Moscow were carried on with the greatest deliberation.

Meanwhile, Stalin had not depended on a successful outcome of these negotiations. Ever since March 1939, he had sent signals to Berlin indicating that ideology need not impede coexistence. After Prague, Hitler tuned down the anti-Bolshevik propaganda while Stalin fired Litvinov, a Jew and a champion of the League of Nations. An agreement was concluded to exempt the two heads of government from mutual recrimination. Economic questions were being discussed as openers; and on May 20, Stalin's new Foreign Minister Vyacheslav Molotov asked for "political conversations." He expected Hitler to offer him what the Western powers stubbornly refused: a free hand in the Baltic states. On August 20, Hitler telegraphed a message to Stalin; the answer set him to pounding the wall: "Now I have the world in my pocket!" The next day a shocked world learned that Foreign Minister Ribbentrop was flying to Moscow; on the 23rd, a partly secret treaty was signed giving Russia the northern tier of the Baltic states, Bessarabia, and western Poland up to the Curzon Line (p. 103), while Germany received Lithuania and western Poland. Stalin had abandoned every Communist principle, stabbed his Western comrades in the back, and unleashed the furies of a second world war.

The fateful pact—limited to a month within which Hitler had to act—made war a certainty. Stalin had temporarily diverted the fascist onslaught from himself. If England and France were to honor their word to Poland, he could watch the Western imperialists and fascists destroy each other. If not, he had won at least a buffer zone to delay Hitler's attack on the Soviet Union.

Hitler, in his turn, hoped for a quick war. He went through the motions of offering the Poles a deal, but gave them no time to answer. Instead of negotiating, he dispatched his armies against Warsaw, exclaiming: "Now I hope no son-of-a-bitch will propose another conference!"[2] He expected the decrepit democracies to accept the *fait accompli*

---

[2] A. J. P. Taylor's lament that war broke out because someone failed to ask for a twenty-four-hour delay, giving Poland time to think it over, is unworthy of a historian. Hitler did not want a peaceful settlement. Taylor lets the cat out of the bag by suggesting that Poland might have been compensated by territory in the Ukraine! Ingenious!

he had created and was astounded when Chamberlain now refused to sit down with him to endorse the conquest. "Negotiations only after the German Army has returned to its bases," was the Prime Minister's message.

The war the appeasers had striven to avoid was on. Hitler was not satisfied within the German boundaries of 1939, nor even with the hegemony over Eastern Europe, which he could have achieved without war. Appeasement had failed because Hitler needed more than local successes. He needed war, glory, conquest, a dynamic image of irresistibility. It is futile to interpret Hitler's action in terms of traditional power politics. Appeasement only had increased his appetite for war. Albert Speer, his architect, Munitions Minister, and friend, says in his memoirs that "it was part of [Hitler's] dreams to subjugate the other nations. France, I heard him say many times, was to be reduced to the status of a small nation. Belgium, Holland, even Burgundy [of course, the Nibelungen kingdom!] were to be incorporated into his Reich. The national life of the Poles and the Soviet Russians was to be extinguished." The aim had rung out in the Nazi marching song "Today We Own Germany, Tomorrow the Whole World." But to realize that dream, Hitler needed a spectacle of military prowess: a quick, glorious, though small and comparatively cheap war.

The Western powers were woefully unprepared for that war. Despite feverish armament efforts after Munich, their armies were technically and numerically inferior to the Axis forces, their strategy was defensive, and, above all, their spirit was not attuned to the age of total war. (In his biting cartoons, David Low has created a mythical "Colonel Blimp" who still sees the world in the light of the colonial wars; our cut shows him sitting with Prime Minister Chamberlain on top of the volcano, both blissfully ignorant of the danger they are in.)

CHAPTER 7

The Second World War

WHEN Hitler's mechanized armies smashed Poland's meager defenses, even those who had never doubted the outcome were amazed at the precision and power of the German advance, the reward of careful planning and timing. Within two weeks, 500,000 Poles were incapacitated; the Germans lost only 45,000 men. On September 17, Stalin seized Byelorussia to the Curzon Line; Hitler annexed the parts that had belonged to Germany until 1918 and established a protectorate over the rest. Latvia, Estonia, and Lithuania were forced to sign nonaggression treaties with Stalin and to give him bases. Similar demands were tendered to Helsinki. The Finns accepted part of them. But on November 30, the Soviet Army attacked the Karelian Isthmus. It met with heroic resistance. After a long, painful winter campaign, Russia's greater resources finally overwhelmed the Mannerheim Line. In March 1940, Finland sued for peace. It had to yield territory, but it kept its independent government.

In the West, the armies so far were confronting each other without doing anything much; the French spoke of a *drôle de guerre*, a phony war. But Hitler kept his soldiers on the move. In a daring air and sea maneuver, he occupied Denmark and Norway in April 1940. A British expeditionary corps failed to hold northern Norway. King Haakon VII went to England, while Quisling ruled Norway as the Nazi satrap. The Danish King stayed, but the Danes refused to play the role of "Nordic brothers." They helped Jews to escape to neutral Sweden.

The campaigns in Poland and Scandinavia confirmed the views of Colonel Charles de Gaulle and General Douhet that mechanized armies were strongest in offensive operation. Surprise, according to Clausewitz, can overwhelm superior forces. By contrast, the French generals had learned the lessons of World War I too well. Over-aged and civilian by temperament, they had placed reliance on the Maginot Line, a continuous series of fortifications that would have been impenetrable to the armies of 1914–18. Neither the politicians nor the generals understood the significance of high mobility and concentrated firepower. They were afraid of airplanes carrying poison gas and fire into the cities; hence their concern was to keep this kind of terror away from the population. Hitler realized that modern aircraft and armored tanks had turned war once more into an art. Once again, the battle was to be a great game of thrust and riposte; the campaign was conceived as the movement of a great mass toward strategic goals; war was liberated from the sterile doctrine that defense was the stronger position. The German staff saw the chance of destroying the enemy army in a vast enveloping movement.

On May 10, 1940, Hitler's bombers attacked Rotterdam; airborne divisions landed at strategic points, throwing the unsuspecting Dutch into paralysis. At the same time, led by dive bombers, the armored (Panzer) columns swept through southern Belgium, annihilated opposing forces of the French, English, and Belgians near Sedan, then advanced toward the Channel port of Abbéville in a great encircling movement. The British Expeditionary Force was caught in northern France and Belgium between gigantic pincers; superior German forces squeezed it against the sea. With heroic efforts, mobilizing the entire air force and every available vessel large and small, the British managed to extricate 340,000 men from the pocket of Dunkirk, but left behind them incalculable quantities of arms and ammunition.

Meanwhile, on May 10, Chamberlain had resigned and his opponent, Winston Churchill—the last Victorian, a lifetime maverick but always a staunch defender of King, country, and empire—had assumed power at the head of a broad coalition that was determined to win the war. He promised not peace but "blood, toil, tears, and sweat." To a whole generation he became the living symbol of England's will to survive.

Belgium's King Leopold surrendered on May 28; Hitler's forces drove freely into France. There was no resistance. A month after he had launched his campaign he entered Paris, from which the frightened population was fleeing in panic (shown in the film *Jeux Interdits, Forbidden Games*). The government—now under Paul Reynaud, who vainly appealed to Churchill for air support—fled to Bordeaux and there decided to resign. Reynaud, Georges Mandel, and a few traditional patriots went to Africa to found the "Free French" army. The venerable—though senile—Marshal Henri Philippe Pétain formed a new cabinet for the purpose of surrendering to Hitler. General de Gaulle, catapulting from near anonymity, went to London and began a radio campaign summoning Frenchmen to resistance.

On June 21 a German general dictated the surrender terms in the same railway car where twenty-two years earlier Marshal Ferdinand Foch had humiliated the German Army; France was divided into an occupied part, encompassing Paris and Bordeaux down to the Spanish border, and a southern part whose capital was to be Vichy. There Pétain had himself proclaimed chief of state. He removed the name "republic" from official papers, replaced the motto *Liberté, Égalité, Fraternité* by *Travail, Famille, Patrie*, abolished trade unions and the forty-hour week, and called on Pierre Laval to conduct the day-to-day operations. Laval, a former radical who had moved far to the Right, confessed himself a "disciple of Briand," who had sponsored Franco-German friendship. He hoped to save as much as possible of French independence by co-operating with Hitler, at a price and in a most mulish way: he found endless subterfuges in complying with German wishes and proved himself a wily politician and schemer. But this dangerous game of collaboration dragged him deeper and deeper into the mire of subservience. He had to give Hitler material aid, had to extradite German anti-fascists, had to round up French laborers for shipment to German factories to take the place of Germans who had been called to arms—although he managed to deliver fewer workers than Belgium or Czechoslovakia.

The shame of this collaborationist regime was compounded by its ideologists. Charles Maurras exclaimed that "our worst defeat had the happy result of ridding us of democracy." Déat and Doriot exulted; the Communists offered to testify at the trial of Léon Blum, the "war criminal," and *L'Humanité* carried anti-Semitic material. Pétain announced "a new order based on social hierarchy." Roger Martin du Gard said that he preferred Hitler to war; even André Gide hesitated before joining the Free French in Africa.

Céline was a victim of his paranoic anti-Semitism. Drieu la Rochelle and Henry de Montherlant were dazzled by the vision of a new, well-ordered Europe.

In the beginning, the occupation was bearable. People had little to eat, fuel was scarce, and the prisoners of war did not return. However, few arrests were made, and fraternization was encouraged, especially with intellectuals. A new call for peace went out to England. But Churchill answered in the rolling phrases which were to be the signature of this war: "We shall fight on the beaches, we shall fight on the landing grounds, we shall fight in the fields and in the streets, we shall fight in the hills, we shall never surrender. . . . Our Empire beyond the seas, armed and guarded by the British Fleet, [will] carry on until the New World steps forth to rescue and liberate the Old."

The British destroyed the French Navy at Oran and remained masters of the sea. Air attacks prepared the invasion of England. The city of Coventry was razed; air bases and port installations were bombed; London was subjected to haphazard destruction. But the Royal Air Force defended the country; every night Spitfires and Hurricanes rose to meet the invading Messerschmitts. By October, Göring's Luftwaffe had lost 1,800 planes; the RAF, 900. Germany was short of pilots and had lost the "Battle of Britain"—the last battle where chivalrous man-to-man fight still was decisive. Churchill gravely acknowledged that "Never in the field of human conflict was so much owed by so many to so few." A movie, *Mrs. Miniver*, told the world how housewives, too, became heroes of this war.

After a year of war, Hitler ought to have been satisfied. His troops held the ramparts from the North Cape to the Sahara and were plundering the stores of Paris, Copenhagen, Oslo, The Hague, and Brussels. He ordered King Carol of Rumania to yield Bessarabia to Stalin, Transylvania to Hungary, and southern Dobruja to Bulgaria. An Iron Guard cabinet under General Ion Antonescu ousted the King and then joined the Axis.

And yet, Hitler had only come up against new frontiers and difficulties. Franco refused to declare war against England. Germany had to occupy the Vichy part of France, too. More troubles arose in the East. Disregarding the nonaggression treaties of the preceding fall, Stalin annexed the three small Baltic states, abducted their presidents, and gave them Soviet constitutions.

In negotiations with Hitler, Molotov asked for a seat on the Danube Navigation Commission and for preponderant influence in Bulgaria. Hitler, trying to turn him away from the Balkans, offered Russia the Straits, the Persian Gulf, and the Indian

Ocean. But as early as July 1940, he laid plans for an invasion of Russia; in September, he strengthened the Anti-Comintern Pact militarily. In December, he started military and diplomatic preparations for "Operation Barbarossa," the attack on Russia.

In March 1941, Bulgaria and Yugoslavia were asked to join the Anti-Comintern Pact. When King Boris pledged that he would not take part in any war, German armies occupied Bulgaria. In Belgrade, Prince Regent Paul signed the pact; but anti-Nazi, pro-Russian army officers proclaimed young Peter II King and called on the nation to defend its independence.

Hitler quickly decided to expand his Balkan operation. German armies overran Yugoslavia and Greece in three weeks of April. A breathtaking air maneuver took Crete in May. Yugoslavia was divided up between Germany, Italy, Hungary, Albania, and Bulgaria. Croatia became a puppet state under the *Poglavnik* Pavelich and the Ustasha. Rump Serbia was placed under the caretaker government of its last Minister of War, General Milan Nedich, a Serbian Pétain. First since the Armenian massacre, the Ustasha government practiced genocide. It sent Jews and Serbs to concentration camps or killed them, and forced Orthodox people to convert to Roman Catholicism. This took place with the blessing of Archbishop Aloys Stepinac of Zagreb, and the Pope granted Pavelich an audience.

The very swiftness of the German victory allowed parts of the Yugoslav Army to hide out in the woods. Later they were joined by Serbs who fled from the Ustasha assassins and by others who did not care to be deported to German labor camps. General Draja Mikhailovitch, an ardent Serb patriot, collected them in a guerrilla force, which took the traditional Serbian name of Chetniks; he prudently husbanded his forces against the day when an Allied landing would unleash a general uprising. Until June 22, 1941, the Chetniks received no help from the Left; only after Hitler had attacked the Soviet Union did the Communists launch their partisans. Then, however, they were more daring, more ruthless in sacrificing lives, more useful in diverting German forces from the Soviet front, and also more effective in giving the Yugoslav people pride and identifying them with the anti-fascist cause. They also appealed to all Yugoslavs, not only to Serbs. Their leader Josip Broz, known under the name of Tito, had gained experience in the Spanish Civil War and in previous underground work. He appealed to patriotism and won the peasants' admiration, although they suffered from German reprisals. He liberated western Serbia and parts of Bosnia (where Edward Kardelj was put in command) and Montenegro (under Milovan Djilas). His administration was built on Soviet-type *odbors* (people's councils). As rivalry arose between Tito and Mikhailovitch, a three-cornered fight ensued between Communist partisans, Chetniks, and Germans. Driven back into the Bosnian mountains, Tito nonetheless increased his force to 150,000 and formed the Anti-Fascist Council of National Liberation of Yugoslavia (AVNOJ). When the Italians later surrendered, Tito obtained their arms. On recommendation of his envoy, Fitzroy MacLean, Churchill recognized the AVNOJ as Yugoslavia's government. In November 1943, Tito informed the Big Three Conference at Teheran that King Peter was deposed, his cabinet in London illegal, and Mikhailovitch—who had joined in a

German attack on him—a traitor. Mikhailovitch had maintained himself by maneuvering and compromising, had collaborated with generals of the Nedich government, had negotiated with Hungarian, Rumanian, Bulgarian, Albanian, and Greek nationalists. The Allies had to drop him if they wished to be received in Yugoslavia as liberators.

Atrocities occurred on all sides in the horrible Balkan war. Djilas, who later was to be the spokesman of the anti-totalitarian forces, purged Montenegro so ruthlessly that the Chetniks joined with the Italians to oust him. When the Italians withdrew from Slovenia and Montenegro, the returning partisans executed hundreds of Chetniks. Though Djilas has said that his disgust with Stalin dates back to the early 1940's, at that time he proclaimed Montenegro a member of the Soviet Union.

The Balkan campaign delayed "Barbarossa" by a month; later, too, guerrilla activities were to tie down Axis forces needed elsewhere. But for the moment, possession of this bridge to Africa gave the dictators a decisive advantage. General Rommel was able to rescue the battered Italians in Libya and to push toward Alexandria. His zigzag war along the African coast earned him the sobriquet "desert fox," another of those wartime exploits that lend themselves so readily to fictionalization.

With Europe his from the Dniester River to the Atlantic, Hitler was ready for the great blow which he hoped would again convert the English to his anti-Communist ploy. His Panzer fist hit the unprepared Stalin hard, on June 22, 1941. Within six months he conquered 20 million square miles, captured half a million Russian soldiers, destroyed the central Soviet army but failed to accomplish his strategic objective: the annihilation of the enemy's power of resistance. The bulk of the Russian forces simply retreated into the vast Russian space, as they had done a hundred and thirty years earlier in the Napoleonic war. And while retreating, they destroyed everything the Germans might find useful. The savage strategy of the "scorched earth" slowed the German advance, but Hitler might still have won a political victory had he pushed vigorously toward Moscow. But for economic reasons, instead, he drove toward the granaries of the Ukraine, the industrial Donets basin, and the oil wells of the Caucasus.

Winter that year came earlier than usual, and the Germans had wasted precious time. They were stalled in the Leningrad environs and a hundred miles from Moscow. (The siege of Leningrad has been memorialized in books and films.) They held a line from the northern tip of the Sea of Azov to the eastern tip of the Gulf of Finland; but the main Soviet forces were intact, even capable of counter-attacking. Frost-bitten, mired in mud and snow, the German offensive first slowed down and then stopped. Its lines of communication were over-extended.

In his occupation policy Hitler made the mistakes inherent in his system and philosophy. The Germans had always looked down on the "Slavs" as inferior in mind and morals, hewers of wood and drawers of water. The war gave the SS a chance to plan genocide: to eliminate leaders, to decimate the men, and to hold the women in servitude; to weaken them biologically, to loosen their hold on the land, and to replace them by Germans or others of Nordic stock. For the children, Himmler held that they only needed to go to school for four years and learn to count up to 500, to sign their names, serve their masters honestly and obediently, and praise God for allowing them to be ruled by the great German people.

The Nazi conception of the war was one of enslavement and extermination. Their cruelty reached its peak in the Ukraine. Had they been able to see the Russians as human beings, they might have perceived a great political opportunity; millions of Ukrainian and Russian peasants were prepared to welcome as liberators any enemy of the Bolshevik regime. They were deeply disappointed when they discovered that Stalin had not lied. The Germans behaved like Tatars, murdering, looting, torturing, and raping. Alfred Rosenberg, Hitler's ideologist and a connoisseur of the Eastern scene, said: "We do not come to liberate any Russians; we are carrying out German world politics."

German hubris dug Germany's grave. It aroused the Russian people to resistance. Stalin could issue his call for "scorched-earth strategy": Let the enemy find no house wherein he can hide, no food he can eat, no wood to warm himself, no laborers he can press into work for him, no bridge he can cross, no vehicle or machine, no horse or cattle, not a nail to fix a broken wheel. The Russian people complied almost to a man, and the Germans had to contend not only with an enemy army and an exceptionally hard winter, but with a population bursting with fury.

Favored by nature and aided by the people's zeal, sacrificing all for the fatherland's survival, the Soviet Army was able to protect Leningrad and Moscow during two long winters. In the second summer, the Germans advanced to the foot of the Caucasus and laid siege to Stalingrad, the former Tsaritsyn, on the Volga. The defense of the narrow shoreline, the house-to-house fighting in the ruined city with the symbolic name became another epic of this war. (See Theodor Plievier's *Stalingrad* and Konstantine Simonov's *Days and Nights*.)

There, in November 1942, the Germans met their fate. A giant pincers of fresh Russian troops closed behind the attacker, annihilating twenty-two divisions. Whipped by Hitler's mad orders, 150,000 Germans died in two months of desperate fighting; on January 31, 1943, Field Marshal Friedrich Paulus surrendered with 90,000 men. At the same time, the Russians broke the siege of Leningrad and advanced on the entire, long front.

The Soviet Union could not have turned the tide all by itself. The moment Hitler invaded it, Churchill had offered an alliance. He also met with President Roosevelt to proclaim the Atlantic Charter, which set forth principles of freedom and social progress for the post-war era, but above all ensured that no territorial change would be recognized. Russia's and fourteen other governments also set their signatures to these principles.

As early as September 1940, England had obtained fifty American destroyers to guard the transports of supplies she bought in the Western hemisphere; in March 1941, the American Lend-Lease Act facilitated these purchases. In November, Roosevelt extended a $1-billion credit to the Soviet Union. A steady flow of convoys now crossed the Atlantic, unloaded war materials in England and went on through submarine-infested straits to Archangelsk. Others went around Africa to the Persian

Gulf. By mid-1942, Russia had received 3,000 planes, 4,000 tanks, millions of tons of other hardware, vehicles, and foodstuffs.

Naval engagements between German submarines and American transports had occurred all through 1941. On December 11, Hitler compounded the mistakes he had made about England and Russia by declaring war on the United States. The moment for which Churchill waited had arrived.

Eleven months later, American troops under Eisenhower landed in Morocco, joined forces with the British commander, Field Marshal Bernard Montgomery, who had beaten Rommel in Africa; they ferried over to Sicily in July 1943, and worked their way up the Italian boot. On July 25, Mussolini was forced to resign by an angry *Gran Consiglio*; its members, his own creatures, now were anxious to save their skins, and applauded his arrest. The Fascist Party was dissolved. Marshal Pietro Badoglio, acting head of a provisional government, surrendered on September 3; but Mussolini, freed by a German SS squad, proclaimed a republic in the northern cities still under German control. From Milan he thundered edicts in the old spirit of radical revolutionary socialism, vainly trying to rally the Italian people to his drooping flag. When the German troops in Italy surrendered, in April 1945, Mussolini and his mistress were captured by partisans and killed; their bodies were hanged head down in a public square in Milan.

Mussolini, who originated a world-historic movement, nevertheless was no man of destiny but a political bandit whose tactical intelligence permitted him to exploit opportunities of playing a role. But he ruled Italy badly enough and missed every opportunity for statesmanship. Driven by insatiable egomania, he responded to each challenge by increasing the pressure of violence. Ignorant of the responsibilities of power, he played with its pageantry until its reality caught up with him.

Meanwhile, with Russia bearing the brunt of the war, Stalin demanded the opening of a "second front" that would divert more Germans to the Western defense. The Allies had the choice of invading either France or the Balkans. The latter alternative might have allowed the Western Allies to take Vienna and Budapest before the Russians did. Churchill personally reconnoitered the terrain and had a meeting with Tito, who flattered and probably fooled him. Churchill came away with the impression that Tito might at worst become a little Balkan dictator. Therefore, when Tito voiced strong objections against an invasion of the "soft underbelly," he abandoned the plan. It was one of the most momentous decisions of the war. The Western Allies were to land in France while the Russian steamroller overran Eastern Europe.

All through 1943 the German Army was retreating slowly from Russia. Soviet forces reached the Polish border in January and the Rumanian border in April 1944. On June 6, 1944, the long-awaited D-Day, American and British forces landed in Normandy, secured a beachhead, and poured into France. Paris was liberated on August 24 by the French Forces of the Interior (FFI) and Allied troops; de Gaulle led the victory parade the next day. Most of France was free by the end of the year; but the Germans launched a strong counter-offensive in the Ardennes, the "Battle of the Bulge," in December.

Belying his pretended anti-Bolshevism, Hitler defended his Western positions most strongly, while evacuating Russia and allowing the Russians to come closer to the heart of Europe. During the last months of 1944, while he still enjoyed the use of the Channel coast, he launched 10,000 rockets against London—killing 2,500 people but failing to obtain the expected shock reaction. Far from grinding down the will of the English people, this new and terrible weapon stiffened their determination.

Despite their overwhelming firepower, it took the Allies five more months to break the German war machine in its homeland. On May 1, 1945, Hitler and Goebbels, completely isolated, killed themselves. Even their most faithful followers refused to follow them into death or to take all of Germany along into their doom. On May 7, a group of German generals went to Reims to sign the articles of surrender.

The man before whom Europe had trembled for ten years must be judged neither by his initial success nor by his ultimate failure. There can be no doubt he was a political genius who could galvanize his nation with his own mania. His vision was a Europe under German domination—a schoolboy's vision of a hierarchically ordered empire with himself as the supreme king, and each of his racial brothers permitted to see himself as a knight fulfilling a mission. For ten years, as long as his uncanny eye for the weaknesses of his enemies at home and abroad provided victories for the German people, Germany lived out the fantasy of a continuous festival of liberation. Based on hate, his delusion of power could be realized only in the pageantry of war and in the destruction of everything Europe had stood for in the preceding 500 years. The gruesome monuments of Lidice, Oradour, and Auschwitz proclaim that Nazism was anti-European, a lapse into barbarism. Some reverse Machiavellians now advise us from hindsight that the sacrifice of lives and happiness made in World War II was too high a price for eliminating this evil from European soil. They do not understand the contemporaries' revulsion, the bitter disappointment of all thwarted attempts to coexist with the monster, the failure of appeasement, the final insight that surrender would have meant the end of European history.

CHAPTER 8

The Powers and the Peoples

BY previous arrangement, the Russians occupied Vienna, Prague, and Berlin. Though they had no direct share in the liberation of Yugoslavia, they also were allowed a victory parade in Belgrade. The post-war map of Europe reflected the distribution of military power. Bulgaria, whose King had refused to join Hitler's war, nevertheless was occupied by Soviet troops in September 1944. Eastern Poland was reannexed as soon as the Soviet troops entered it; and when they reached the old Polish territory, in August 1944, a Moscow-trained puppet government was set up, first in Kholm, later in Lublin. In turn, the Western Allies kept Soviet representatives from participating in the surrender of enemy forces on Italian soil and gave them no share in the administration of Italy.

At the Yalta Conference (February 1945), Churchill and Roosevelt recognized the *faits accomplis* in Eastern Europe. Ignoring the Atlantic Charter, the Baltic states and eastern Poland were to be annexed by Russia; German territory east of the Oder and Neisse rivers was to be "administered" by Poland but was also declared to be Poland's compensation for the eastern part she had ceded to the Soviet Union. The rest of Germany was to be divided into three occupation zones. Between the Oder and Elbe Rivers there was to be a Russian zone of occupation; the territory west of the Elbe River was to be occupied by England and the United States. However, out of courtesy, the two then yielded part of their zones to France. All four powers were to participate in the Control Council which was to oversee the administration of Germany.

At the Conference of Potsdam, in July 1945, Russia also was awarded part of the German province of East Prussia with its capital Königsberg (now Kaliningrad), and France the temporary administration of the Saar. The German capital, Berlin, which was now inside the Soviet occupation zone, was to be an independent unit, to be jointly administered by all four powers, yet to be policed in four separate sectors. In consideration of their rights in Berlin, the Western Allies agreed to add two highly industrialized provinces, Saxony and Thuringia, to the Soviet Zone. Similarly awkward stipulations were being made for Austria and its capital, Vienna.

Economically, and especially for reparations purposes, Germany was to be treated as a unit. The powers were to satisfy themselves out of German assets; a low level of production and consumption was set for the German population. Germany was to be demilitarized and kept impotent to rearm herself.

Thus the attempt of one nation to establish itself as the master race came to an inglorious end. Yet, in a most sinister way, Hitler had indeed carried out some of his demopolitical plans. By keeping their young men captive, or by direct methods of starvation and extermination, he had decimated nations whom he considered lesser breeds. Of 8 million European Jews, two-thirds died in concentration camps, were gassed or incinerated. The world was aghast when the extermination camps were discovered. Germans refused to believe that these crimes had been committed in their name. Nowhere and at no time had people been killed on such a vast scale simply for being what they were.[1] Two million captured Russians were allowed to die from starvation, disease, and wretched working conditions. Millions more of Poles, Czechs, French, living in German labor camps separated by sex, also were withering leaves on the population tree. Strictly enforced laws barred German women from any contact with prisoners and foreign workers. But in *Group Portrait with Lady*, Heinrich Böll has told the moving story of love between a German girl and a Russian prisoner of war. Incidentally, soldiers of all nations hummed the nostalgic German lay of Lili Marlene.

As in Russia, the genocide policy backfired in France. When the police rounded up "volunteers" for service in German factories, thousands took to the hills and forests —hence the name *maquis* (bush)—and formed partisan units. Also, after Hitler had invaded Russia, the French Communists rediscovered their patriotism and anti-fascism. They were able to provide the straggling escapees with an ideology and to weld them into a disciplined force. These groups, brought into contact with Gaullist officers and supplied with arms and direction from England, constituted the Forces Françaises de l'Intérieur, paralleling the Free French overseas.

Unfortunately, the Allied leaders had misjudged the political mood of France, and personality differences had alienated them from de Gaulle. Instead of informing him of their landing in Morocco, they had arranged to be met there by Vichy's commander in chief, Admiral Jean-François Darlan. Though Darlan's opportunism certainly saved numerous lives, staunch anti-fascists found a "deal" with this collaborator hard to stomach. He was assassinated and replaced by General Henri Giraud, who had escaped from a German prison camp. A soldier without political guile, this brave man was soon eclipsed by the fame of de Gaulle and the Free French. Together they formed the nucleus of a new, the Fourth French Republic, to which now many were beginning to rally: writers like Albert Camus, Jean-Paul Sartre, André Malraux; politicians like Pierre Mendès-France, Jacques Soustelle, Robert Schuman, Georges Bidault, Vincent Auriol; social thinkers like Raymond Aron and Jean Monnet; military men as well as Communists. United in a Conseil National de Résistance, they vowed an end not only to Hitler but to the financiers who had helped him. When de Gaulle entered Paris, he was able to give the Fourth Republic a provisional government supported by all parties.

---

[1] The extermination of the Jews has been the subject of hot controversy. See Raoul Hilberg, *The Destruction of the European Jews*. Novelistic treatments in André Schwarz-Bart's *The Last of the Just*, and in John Hersey's *The Wall*, describing the uprising of 60,000 Jews in the Warsaw ghetto; see also the Czech film *The Shop on Main Street*.

In Italy resistance fighters arose only after Mussolini had reestablished himself in the north; they fought for power and rank in a future Italy rather than against Mussolini. Among them were the Socialists under Pietro Nenni and the Communists led by Palmiro Togliatti, both of whom had won experience in the Spanish Civil War. There also were old-style liberals and democrats. Alcide de Gasperi tried to convert the former *Popolari* into a modern party of Christian Democracy. Greatest interest was aroused by the new Republican Party, which had been inspired by the underground group of intellectuals, Giustizia e Libertà. Its founder Carlo Rosselli had been assassinated in exile by Mussolini's emissaries; its present leader, Professor Ferruccio Parri, projected the Jacobin image of a guerrilla leader. After many intrigues, all militant groups had joined the CLN (Committee of National Liberation).

Though the partisans demanded abolition of the monarchy, Togliatti joined Marshal Badoglio's cabinet. But after Rome fell, King Victor Emmanuel and Badoglio abdicated. In the Ivanoe Bonomi cabinet that followed, Togliatti became Vice-Premier, while Count Sforza, a pre-Fascist liberal of independent views, was jettisoned. In 1945, Parri formed a republican coalition government with de Gasperi as Foreign Minister: for once, Communists, Socialists, and Catholics were united on a program of radical democracy for Italy, though not for long.

The most successful and the most frustrated resistance movements were those in the Balkans. General Mikhailovitch's Chetniks were completely outmaneuvered by Tito's guerrillas. When the Germans retreated, AVNOJ was practically in possession of all power. The old state was shattered; big-estate owners and industrial managers were discredited as collaborators. Tito was free to nationalize and redistribute any assets that had not been destroyed.

In Albania, likewise, Enver Hoxha led the Communist guerrillas to power. A similar fate might have befallen Greece but for a peculiar episode. When Churchill visited Moscow in October 1944, he made an old-fashioned power deal with Stalin, yielding up to him Rumania and Bulgaria, and in turn getting a free hand in Greece. As a result, when the Germans retreated, Allied forces under General Ronald Scobie occupied Athens; the Communist Party (in the guise of the Hellenic People's Front, EAM, and Hellenic People's Liberation Army, ELAS) followed Moscow's order and joined the government. When, in December 1944, the coalition fell apart, Churchill personally went to Athens and with Stalin's blessing installed Archbishop Damaskinos as regent. But the local Communists did not acknowledge big-power deals and took up arms against the monarchy, although Stalin gave them only half-hearted support.

By contrast, in the Netherlands and the Scandinavian countries, where the society had remained intact, the German retreat was followed simply by the restoration of the old order.

Let us now look at two underground movements that failed. When they divided Poland, both Nazis and Soviets tried to liquidate the cadres of the Polish Army. Four thousand Polish officers were later found in a mass grave near Katyn. A Red Cross committee produced incontrovertible evidence that their burial had taken place while Katyn was in Russian hands. When the Polish government-in-exile, residing in

London, remonstrated, the Soviet government broke with it. The Poles also objected to the transfer of territories agreed to by the Big Three at Yalta. General Wladyslaw Sikorski, the exiled leader, was as intractable as General de Gaulle; he died in an airplane crash, and some have charged that this was no accident.

His successor Stanislaw Mikolajczyk, of the Peasant Party, was not of the same stature, but he fought with equal vigor against the plan to "move Poland to the West." Stalin, therefore, gave all power to the Lublin group and even saw to it that no other Poles could interfere with his plans. A Polish army under General Wladyslaw Anders, assembled on Soviet soil, was shipped at great cost to fight in Italy. An underground army under General Tadeusz Bor-Komorowski, which had been hiding in Warsaw, was allowed to rise against the Nazis in August 1944; but instead of co-ordinating its own operations with the uprising, the Soviet Army was marking time thirty miles outside the gates and did not even permit Western relief planes to land on Soviet-occupied territory. Bor fought for two months, but eventually his fifth column was completely wiped out by the German troops. Then the Russians took Warsaw.

Inside Germany, resistance at first had been conducted exclusively by the Left. Republicans, trade unionists, socialists, and Communists smuggled their pamphlets into Germany from Prague, Paris, and Luxembourg. Later on, the Churches, the nobility, the army, and other conservative circles discovered that they too had been betrayed by the Nazis. Hitler's Price Commissioner Goerdeler, the chief of espionage Wilhelm Canaris, the chief of staff General Beck, the young diplomat Adam von Trott, and other prominent persons began to seek contacts with like-minded persons in the government apparatus and even looked to foreign governments for support. During the war they also made contact with Social Democrats and former trade-union leaders; when the war went wrong, many army commanders joined the conspiracy. On July 20, 1944, Colonel Claus von Stauffenberg set off a bomb in Hitler's headquarters. This should have been the signal for the arrest of all Nazi leaders. But the generals, who had planned foreign conquests so efficiently, now failed miserably.[2] The resistance was suppressed; 5,000 conspirators and suspected conspirators were executed, among them marshals, generals, high officials, clergymen, intelligence officers, bearers of well-known names, even SS commanders, with a preponderance of noblemen.

Since the Allies had adopted a policy of "unconditional surrender," it is doubtful that the conspirators, if successful, could have obtained more favorable terms of surrender. Germany had to go to her ultimate doom. She lost 4 million people after inflicting 40 million deaths on other countries, two-thirds of them civilians wantonly killed in terror raids and retaliatory actions. The list of dead includes 21 million Russians (10 per cent of the population), 375,000 Czechs, 6 million Poles, 1,680,000 Yugoslavs, 160,000 Greeks, 386,000 British, 810,000 French, 88,000 Belgians, 210,000 Dutch. Among the victims were 6 million Jews.

Wholesale destruction of human lives, the killing of hostages, reprisals, and terror

---

[2] Some abhorred the crime of insubordination or would not break their oath to Hitler. In the war-crimes trials later on, they pleaded that they had been mere soldiers taking orders.

attacks on civilians with incendiary bombs and (in the last stage) with rockets and atomic bombs marked World War II as a turning point in history. War was being waged for extermination and survival. Many of its actions were unrelated to military objectives and had turned into sheer acts of savagery. France remembers the killings of Oradour; Czechoslovakia, the destruction of Lidice; England, the bombing of Coventry; Holland, the bombing of Rotterdam; Germany, the burning of Hamburg and Dresden; Japan, Hiroshima and Nagasaki.

Incendiary bombs set the city of Hamburg afire; thousands died of asphyxiation. The Dresden raid has been described by Kurt Vonnegut in *Slaughterhouse 5*. Surveys undertaken after the war have shown that the air raids, terrible though they were, failed to disrupt Germany's production and transportation sufficiently to affect the outcome of the war; nor did they seriously undermine the population's morale. Yet, terror tactics were used as a weapon on both sides. Originally, "strategic bombing" had definable industrial targets; when it turned into "carpet bombing," the strategic purpose was lost, and blind fury was unleashed on the enemy population.

No war before this had uprooted so many people. Fifty million became displaced persons: rounded-up, expelled, forced to flee, drafted for labor service, held as prisoners long after the war. Seven million foreign workers were conscripted into German factories. Millions of prisoners never returned home. Ten million Germans went as refugees to the western part of Germany, partly from East Germany and the Polish-occupied zone, partly from other East European countries.

The material damage was inestimable. Cities had been destroyed, communications disrupted, production facilities razed. The Soviet Union alone demanded $10 billion in reparations; the Western Allies lost 23 million tons of shipping; England counted 4 million homes and $6 billion worth of plant, equipment, and transportation facilities destroyed in air raids.

Possibly still more important were the moral consequences of the war. European civilization evidently was bankrupt; the white man's pre-eminence in the world was gone for good. European history was no longer world history. Europe's technological leadership could no longer be equated with moral or cultural superiority. The soldiers returned from the war brutalized, cynical, shorn of all illusions. In the beginning they might have believed in the ideas their leaders had invoked; in the end they were fighting for sheer survival—little men caught in a big machine of destruction.

Europe had lapsed into five years of barbarism. Her proud industrial equipment no longer served productive purposes; her cultural works could no longer be cited. People no longer counted except as statistics. Their own governments subjected them to severe rationing, the enemy to bombing and reprisals. Civilians were mobilized to work in factories and held as hostages. Women became laborers; mere children were drafted for a last-ditch defense. Total mobilization, total planning, total destruction narrowed the gap between the fascist, Bolshevik, and capitalist systems. In every country the individual will was submerged in the general will to victory.

The machinery of the "lightning war," of course, was the proper symbol and instrument of these developments. The precision of large troop movements; the close co-operation between air force, artillery, tanks, and vehicles in a panzer division; the rapid decisions; the enormous quantity of material that had to be pinpointed—all this made the machinery of destruction in war look so much like the machinery of production in peace that the weirdest visions of brainless, mechanized worker-soldiers seemed to have come true.

World War II brought mankind close to the nightmare of 1984. Hitler could be defeated only with the weapons he had chosen.

Leadership fell to the two nations which still believed in their mission; the United States in the West and the Soviet Union in the East. Both assumed responsibility for a new organization of peace. But no longer did they conceive peace as a concert of powers. Rather, each saw itself as hegemon in its part of a divided Europe; each was armed with an idea; each was contemptuous of the European nations that had been unable to contain the aggressor in their midst. Europe had been the center of the world; she was now ruled by the two powers that had been on its periphery. She had generated attitudes and ideas which for centuries had revolutionized the world and conquered continents; now she received guidance from her one-time disciples. Once she had provided the capital and the technical know-how for the industrialization of the world; now she had to ask America for help and advice in rebuilding her capacities. She had been used to call on her colonies for the replenishment of her resources and for the display of her power; now she was confronted with national revolutions in her colonies.

Those who surveyed the prospects of reconstruction in 1945–46 did not express much hope for a return of Europe to power and influence. Replacing the broken windows alone, one expert opined, would take Europe ten years. To find new ideas and inspirations, others felt, she would have to look abroad. No one at that time dared to think that either the *status quo* could be restored or a new start be made from "point zero."

PART VII

*A Divided Europe
(1945–58)*

CHAPTER I

Heritage of the War

THE end of the war did not mean a return to normality. People were suddenly poor; there was nothing to buy—or rather, only those with connections lived well. On the Continent, money would not buy much; cigarettes were the general currency. The quality of life kept deteriorating even though reconstruction had started.

It was not just buildings that had been destroyed. The fabric of society, geared to the needs of the war, had come apart. In the occupied countries, cheating the government and sabotage had been patriotic acts; after liberation, it was difficult to readjust to the concept of law. Even in England public morality was low. Victory did not taste sweet.

The cheers of victory faded quickly; everyday reality was bleak. Films like *The Bicycle Thief, Open City, Shoeshine, General della Rovere* give us a glimpse of how people felt, how survival depended on little things. People dug out of the rubble in bombed cities and stole from each other to furnish makeshift rooms. Millions of displaced persons, prisoners, refugees, foreign workers, expellees, hungry people, and adventurers were on the road in search of a better place or just some place to live, looking for lost relatives or for a new life. There also were the millions who, rather than return to Russia, preferred to stay in refugee camps.

What mattered above all was to have survived. Thornton Wilder's *The Skin of Our Teeth* enjoyed a tremendous success all over Western Europe.

The struggle for survival went on in many different ways. "Hitler is gone—and its just another Tuesday," said a German anti-fascist. The end of the war, which everyone had looked forward to, was not the end of worry, and the celebration lasted just one day.

The first thing the British did after the war was to turn their great wartime leader out of power. Though they still admired Churchill, they wanted a different government—one that did not remind them of war, glory, and despair. Longing for a different England, they made the sober, unassuming Clement Attlee Prime Minister and gave his Labour Party its first solid majority.

In France, too, the emphasis was on change. De Gaulle came sparkling with the charisma of a wartime leader—as the man who had been right and who had stayed pure. But with him came a group of new men who nationalized public utilities, banks, mines, airlines, and factories like the Renault automobile plant, whose owners had worked for Hitler. They purged collaborators and put Pétain and Laval on trial. Local mobs cut off the hair of women who had fraternized with German soldiers. And the Communists used the opportunity to pin the "collaborationist" label on their republican rivals.

The new French Government established a comprehensive social-security system and a four-year plan of reconstruction. Socialists, Communists, and the new Mouvement Républicain Populaire (MRP) each polled a quarter of the vote; together, they were able to form a coalition government. They wrote a constitution denying de Gaulle the dictatorial powers he craved; the military budget they allowed him was much smaller than he deemed necessary—so in January 1946, when he threatened to resign, they did not dissuade him. He then founded the Rassemblement du Peuple Français, which for years conducted obstructionist policies.

Czechoslovakia gave the Russian liberators a rousing welcome and reestablished its statehood under a National Front government composed of Communists, Socialists, Popular Democrats, and Popular Socialists. The Germans were expelled and Czechs settled in their stead—a major population shift for a small country, that gave rise to an important social reorientation. The Rightist parties and collaborators were ruthlessly purged, and anti-Communist leaders arrested. In May 1946, the Communists polled 38 per cent of the vote; their leader, Klement Gottwald, became Prime Minister. Jan Masaryk, son of the revered founder of the Czech state, was appointed Foreign Minister; Eduard Beneš was elevated to the Presidency—a ceremonial post. Beneš, the martyr of Munich, had always been pro-Russian; but when he tried to resume leadership in his country, he found himself obstructed by the Soviet Army and Czech Communist militants. Barred from traveling, unable to protect his friends from vile calumnies, and handicapped by age and poor health, he had to let things drift.

In Italy, the Parri government with the Resistance halo soon yielded to the general longing for order and normality—much to the dismay of the intellectuals who had hoped for a moral rebirth, and of a large part of Italy's working class, which had been stirred up by Mussolini's revolutionary manifestos. Neither had found new leaders yet. The literature of the transition period reflects its worries, hesitations, and doubts, and offers no clear vision of the future.

Austria suffered under a triple pressure. She had been "liberated" from a prison she had enjoyed all too conspicuously; her liberators made little haste to relinquish the pawn they were holding. The proverbial Austrian merely transferred his servility from one master to four. The hypocrisy of the Viennese petty-bourgeois has been exposed by the satirist Helmut Qualtinger (Herr Korl) and in Orson Welles's film *The Third Man*.

Germany more severely than any other country smarted under self-inflicted wounds and under the blows she had deserved. The country was occupied by five nations, of which at least three were taking revenge for savage acts of racial arrogance. The Poles expelled Germans from their occupation zone; the Russians allowed their soldiers to loot and rape; the French followed a policy of malevolent neglect. The British were coldly correct and as austere as fairness would permit; the Americans came with the idea of "reeducation." The Morgenthau plan to turn Germany into pasture was never realized, but all occupation powers dismantled valuable machinery and removed equipment, either to rebuild what Germany had destroyed elsewhere, or to still their fear that Germany would rise again. The supply of consumer goods continued to shrink; by the winter of 1945-46, scarcity was universal.

Supplies from UNRRA (United Nations Relief and Rehabilitation Administration), contributed mainly by the United States, helped Europe over the hump. Of the $1 billion distributed in Europe by the United Nations, more than half went to Germany; a good part of that disappeared into the Soviet-occupied areas and further east. Since the Russians did not provide for the countries they had overrun, some of those who nominally belonged among the victors were worse off than the defeated Germans.

To restore order and to assure minimum nutritional standards, the occupation powers in Germany decreed the harsh but necessary measures which their governments did not dare introduce in their own countries. Starting June 10, 1948, a currency reform wiped out nine-tenths of all wealth; everybody had to start from scratch and to work for cash. This gave Germany a headstart for recovery. Even the dismantling of outmoded equipment, the cities in rubble, and the breaking up of cartels turned out to be blessings in disguise. Germany entered postwar competition with brand-new modern machinery, with newly planned cities and well constructed roads, with a disciplined labor force and a new crop of managers who had gone to the cruel school of "point zero." This was especially true of the expellees and the refugees, who first had to build new homes.

The problem, however, that nagged thoughtful Germans was not of a material nature. Germany had to find a new identity, but she was not allowed to make a revolution. Had she purged herself, had German tribunals judged the Nazis for crimes committed against the German people and against the world, had German action committees taken over the newspapers, had German parties created a new administration, there would have been no need for every German to carry the entire burden of guilt. Instead, an international court was set up at Nuremberg to try the war criminals. Though its sentences were just, it failed to convince Germans who knew about Russian war crimes, the destruction of Hamburg and Dresden, and the atomic bomb (see the film *Judgment at Nuremberg*).

In the American zone, Germans had to fill out detailed questionnaires about their political connections, military service, and so on. The procedure was laughable. Hans Globke, the commentator of Hitler's Nuremberg Laws, became the right-hand assistant to Chancellor Adenauer; General Reinhard Gehlen, who had played an important part in military intelligence for the Nazi state, was to provide the same services to the Federal Republic and probably to the United States. The parlor Nazi Ernst von Salomon published a scathing indictment of Allied policies in the form of an ironical novel, *Der Fragebogen* (*The Questionnaire*).

The pre-Hitler leaders were either over-age or tarnished by previous failures. Some of the exiles found it difficult to communicate with a people whose wartime experiences they had not shared. An attempt to reintroduce pre-Hitlerian literature met with dubious success; Brecht's *Threepenny Opera* and Kurt Tucholsky's *Rheinsberg* offered too slight a fare for a nation that had just been confronted with films from the extermination camps.

Some new voices and some old ones, however, tried to give new directions to the German people. The playwright Carl Zuckmayer came home from America and talked to German youth about its future. Hans Werner Richter, a new novelist, began to publish *Der Ruf* (*The Call*) even while still a prisoner of war in the United States; in 1947, he founded "Group 47" with other German writers who were hoping and groping for new, radical approaches to social life, literature, and politics. Thomas Mann wrote the allegorical novel, *Doktor Faustus*, a profound, soul-searching, searing interpretation of German history. The philosopher Karl Jaspers spoke nobly of Germany's need for self-purgation. The historian Friedrich Meinecke interpreted the German past as a "tragedy." Kurt Schumacher, a religious socialist, emerged from the concentration camp emaciated and broken in health, but wearing a martyr's crown and speaking with great authority in the name of "the other Germany." Konrad Adenauer, who was to be Chancellor of the Federal Republic, spoke of Germany as part of a new Europe; so did Ernst Jünger. But the most widely quoted author was one whom few Germans had known in his lifetime: Franz Kafka, who had divined and anticipated the horrors his contemporaries were to experience.

The question which was most urgent for Germans but which in fact concerned all Europeans obviously was whether they would find a way out of Kafka's world. Would they, as the Germans put it somewhat ambiguously, *die Vergangenheit bewältigen*— which may mean either "come to grips with the past" or "overcome the past"? Of necessity, such a task required a new moral philosophy, different from the academic philosophies of pre-Hitler days. Three new approaches offered themselves: Christianity, Marxism, and existentialism. Traditional Christian consolations made no sense to people who had faced Hell and did not aspire to gain Heaven but who just the same wished to find meaning and sense in life's absurdities. Not the methodical Thomas Aquinas but the tormented St. Augustine, not the Sermon on the Mount but the Book of Job, not the serenity of Boethius but the anguish of Kierkegaard came to be the inspiration of the theologians.

At the same time the churches turned to social and political activism. Christians abandoned their other-worldly aloofness and turned from a Sunday religion to a workaday faith, from sermons to action. The old conservative Christian parties steeped themselves in this new spirit of social Christianity. In France, Dominican fathers went out into factories and villages to live with the people as "worker-priests." Martyrs like Dietrich Bonhoeffer, active resisters like Provost Grüber who had braved the Nazis became saints of this new movement among Protestants and Catholics alike. Even though the Catholic hierarchy lagged behind for another twenty years, the rank and file was seething with new ideas. Young Christians went to Israel to work in communes.

Marxism had become the state religion of the Soviet Union; it had fulfilled a quasi-religious function also for Western workers, who had looked at *Das Kapital* much as a

Christian looks at the Bible. In the 1940's, a young generation of students began to discover a different kind of Marxism: the critical philosophy of the activist, humanist "young Marx." But ironically, in those post-war years when a Marxist revolution seemed to be on the agenda, the Communist parties missed their chances. Marx slept in the sarcophagus of orthodoxy and did not emerge until the student revolution of the 1960's awakened him.

Existentialism underwent an even greater transformation from the ontological trembling of petty-bourgeois helplessness to the radical posture of the "great refusal" which sustained resistance fighters during the war. To a new generation, existentialism now appeared as a new ethics of responsible action, a justification of man's "authentic" responses to conventional attitudes. Sartre's plays and films, Camus's gripping novels reflect movingly the intellectual's situation among the ruins of his world. There were no firm foundations, no assurance of a future, no certainty of coming through; and yet man had to find the source of hope within himself and to create himself the world in which he wished to act. In the legend of Sisyphus, Camus saw the exemplar of human existence: Knowing that his task is futile, Sisyphus nevertheless chooses to shoulder his burden, thus asserting his freedom and his humanity.

The intelligentsia was ashamed of the passive role they had played before the war; now they were looking for commitment to public causes. As the French existentialists said, they were seeking "engagement." Like the Group 47 in Germany, the French intellectuals tried to make themselves politically effective. Under the leadership of Sartre, David Rousset (who wrote *L'Univers Concentrationnaire*, a record of the time he spent in a German concentration camp), and others, they founded the Rassemblement Démocratique Révolutionnaire. As a political party it was a dismal failure; as a public gesture it pointed to things to come twenty years later.

CHAPTER 2

The Partition of Europe and the "Cold War"

FOR all practical purposes, the Yalta Conference had settled East Europe's fate. Stalin was to occupy and incorporate into the Soviet Union Byelorussia, Bessarabia, Carpatho-Russia, the small Baltic states plus Königsberg, one-tenth of Finland including the Isthmus with the strategic Mannerheim Line, the island of Hango at the mouth of the Sound, the Porkkala base near Helsinki and eastern Karelia. Poland was to be "moved westward." Rumania and Bulgaria were to be in the Soviet sphere of influence, that is, they were to be governed by "democratic governments friendly to the Soviet Union." To Stalin this meant that it was his right to appoint such governments. In Bucharest his Foreign Minister, Andrei Vishinsky, personally installed a front non-Communist, Petro Groza, at the head of a Communist-dominated cabinet; in Sofia, Dimitroff set up a Fatherland Front in which the Communists increasingly controlled the other parties. In Poland, the Lublin group co-opted members of the London group, but Mikolajczyk and his non-Communist colleagues found so many obstacles in their way that they were officials in name only. In Czechoslovakia, the National Front government welded six anti-fascist parties and popular organizations into a unitary slate, which then proceeded to "win" elections. In East Germany and Hungary, the Communists had no following and depended on a Popular Front government to assure the transition to Communist rule.

Agrarian reform became the vehicle for the Communist ascent to power. Vacated estates of Germans and collaborators were distributed among the landless. The power of the Magyar magnates and the Prussian *Junkers* was broken. In Rumania (which now again included Transylvania), Poland (in possession of new territory), and Czechoslovakia (again in possession of the Sudeten region), entire provinces became available for new settlers and provided the Communists not only with vast sources of patronage but also with an opportunity to build, in virgin territory, a new apparatus of Party government. In the cities, the technique of seizing power followed a well-planned, step-by-step pattern. First, pressure was brought to bear on the Social Democratic parties to form a United Proletarian Front with the Communists or even to merge with them. Even though the Communists were the junior partners numerically, their closeness to the occupying power, their greater discipline, cohesion, and zeal usually gave them the ascendancy in the alliance. Social Democratic leaders who resisted the merger exposed themselves to considerable danger. Two spokesmen of the Yiddish *Bund* were shot in Moscow; sixteen other Polish leaders who had gone there for negotiations were arrested and sent to Siberia. In East Germany and in West Berlin, dissenters were abducted.

With these and similar methods the Communists brought under their discipline such socialist leaders as Fritz Ebert, son of the late German President, and Zdenek Fierlinger in Czechoslovakia. Then this Socialist-Communist workers' party proposed a Popular Front, United Front, Fatherland Front or National Front to the other parties. The Communists thus tripled their leverage, using first proletarian unity and then national unity as a transmission belt of power. Such states where Communists rule by proxy or in coalition were dubbed "people's republics," although the Western press referred to them as simply "satellite states."

For, meanwhile, the first shot of the so-called cold war had been fired in San Francisco at the founding session of the United Nations. There, in April 1945, Soviet Minister Molotov declared that the Western powers had helped Hitler to invade Russia. Even earlier, though little noticed at the time, the French Communist Party had published an open letter repealing the wartime truce between the classes and calling on all sister parties to resume the fight against capitalism.[1]

Tito, too, shed his Popular Front image as soon as he found himself in control and began a spirited attack on the Western powers and their friends in Yugoslavia. General Mikhailovitch was executed and Yugoslavia declared a socialist republic. Tito's artillery shot down American planes, and he openly supported Greek guerrillas under General Markos Vafiades who opposed the return of the King and of his pro-Western government.

The satraps who came to take power in Warsaw, Bucharest, Sofia, Prague, Budapest, and Berlin, respectively, were Boleslaw Bierut, Ana Pauker, George Dimitroff, Klement Gottwald, Matyas Rakosi, and Walter Ulbricht—not underground fighters but Muscovite *apparatchiks* of the most dogmatic stripe.

In the West, meanwhile, subtler means had been used to insure the opposite result. The Communists were accepted or even invited into governments, provided they abandoned the committees and other Soviet-like instruments of rule they had founded and dominated in the Resistance period. In West Germany there was no need to give Communists any share in administration since the occupying powers worked hand-in-glove with Catholic and corporate powers. By the time the Big Three met at Potsdam (July–August 1945), the Continent was divided roughly along a line that ran from Trieste on the Adriatic Sea to Lübeck on the Baltic—not only for police and military but for political purposes, too. At Potsdam, Stalin surprised his partners by asking for Libya and Tangier. But Harry S. Truman, who had taken Franklin D. Roosevelt's place, did not share his predecessor's confidence that he could handle Stalin, and began

---

[1] Since recently a school of "revisionist" historians has been trying to lay the blame for the cold war on President Truman, it is meet to remember that these dates antecede his accession to power.

to distrust his intentions. The British elections, which interrupted the Conference, also replaced Churchill and Eden with the Labourites, Clement Attlee and his Foreign Secretary Ernest Bevin, a trade-union official and stout anti-Communist who felt that Russia's advance in Europe must be checked.

The confrontation at Potsdam only confirmed Stalin's belief that the Soviet troops had to stay in Central Europe; their lines of communication to Germany and Austria justified continued occupation of Eastern European countries, too. Western statesmen in turn doubted that Stalin would ever abandon these pawns, or even feared that the Red Army was poised to conquer the rest of Europe. Although they concluded that under such conditions they could not abandon their German foothold, the Western diplomats were less than circumspect in negotiating a new *status quo*. Instead of insisting on a package deal for all of Europe, they first agreed to confirm the changes that had occurred in the East. Peace treaties were signed with Finland, Bulgaria, Rumania, Hungary, and Italy. Tito received Istria with Fiume, but not Trieste, which Italy claimed. (For this loss Tito blamed Stalin's "big-power solidarity" with the imperialists.) Rumania received Transylvania from Hungary, but had to yield the southern Dobruja to Bulgaria, Bessarabia and part of Bukovina to the Soviet Union. But numerous conferences of foreign ministers brought no agreement on Germany and Austria.

Each side still hoped to change the boundary lines in its favor. In 1946, East and West fired more verbal salvoes. In February, Stalin warned that another world-wide depression and armed conflict was in the making; in March, Churchill, speaking at Fulton, Missouri, in Truman's presence, added the term "iron curtain" to our political vocabulary, and Stalin answered by comparing Churchill to Hitler. At the United Nations, Molotov rejected the American plan for joint control of nuclear energy, while England and America backed Iran's demand for withdrawal of Russian troops from Tabriz and helped Turkey to resist Soviet demands for a new Statute of the Straits. In July, suddenly, Molotov announced an about-face in Soviet policy toward Germany. Instead of being partitioned and penalized, Germany was to be united and neutralized. Secretary of State Byrnes followed suit in September with a declaration that Germany was to be reunited and rebuilt. Both East and West were now wooing the Germans, each protesting that the other was preventing what both feared—that they might have to leave the country and lose control. Each side was building up a state on its side of the Elbe.

An article in *Foreign Affairs* (July 1947) signed "X" (George Kennan, the State Department's top Soviet expert) explained that it was U.S. policy to "contain" the Russian advance in Europe; this was to be done by building independent states along the Soviet border. In criticism of this essay, Walter Lippmann wrote the series of articles that gave the cold war its name. (This may be the place to recall the meaning of a much-abused term: "Cold war" signifies a diplomatic and propagandistic power play, short of the use of arms, for preponderance in Europe. It does not apply to other areas, where the war may be "hot," and it implies recognition of existing borders.)

Meanwhile, the Greek Civil War went badly for the royalists. The British had to leave. In March 1947, Truman announced the "doctrine" that America must "help free people to maintain their national integrity" everywhere; Congress voted a $400-million grant to Greece and Turkey. Secretary of State George Marshall, following up in June, launched the great plan that bears his name. The United States was offering generous aid toward the economic recovery of Europe with the explicit purpose of saving her from Communism or Russian dominance, or both.

Stalin considered this a challenge. With his satellites he refused to accept Marshall Plan help or to participate in any joint European planning. French and Italian Communists fomented demonstrations and strikes in order to paralyze the effort. In response, the Communist ministers were eased out of the French and Belgian governments. England, France, Belgium, the Netherlands, and Luxembourg formed a defensive alliance, Western Union, on March 17, 1948.

A trade and financial war ensued. Eighteen Western countries founded the European Recovery Program (ERP) to implement the Marshall Plan; the East launched its rival Molotov Plan. In Belgrade, the European Communist parties founded a new international organization, the Communist Information Bureau (called Cominform) under the leadership of the most orthodox member of the Russian Politburo, Andrei Zhdanov. It announced a new era of international class war and the formation of two irreconcilable "camps." In May 1948, Valerian Zorin, a Soviet Deputy Foreign Minister, personally directed a Communist *coup d'état* in Prague. With that, Czechoslovakia disappeared behind the iron curtain.

Now the Western powers decided to organize their part of Germany. A radical currency reform was to sever economic ties between the Eastern and Western zones, and initial steps were taken to form a government in West Germany. To foil Allied plans, Stalin declared a blockade of all land communications with West Berlin (June 1948). The Socialists of that city had resisted the pressure to merge with the Communists and to annex Berlin to the Russian-occupied zone; their leader, Ernst Reuter, a former Communist, was elected mayor. When the Russians denied him access to the City Hall, which was in their sector, he moved his offices to the American sector, declared the Western mark legal tender for the three Western sectors of Berlin and made his besieged city the outpost of freedom in a totalitarian environment. Accepting the challenge of the blockade, the 1.8 million West Berliners became heroes of the non-Communist world. Supplies—food, drugs, machinery, even coal—were flown in by airplanes on a minute-by-minute, precision-planned schedule, the magnificent airlift. For a full year the undaunted Berliners held out on their slim rations, until Stalin lifted the blockade. On the same day, May 23, 1949, the German Federal Republic was founded and Bonn became its capital. The Russian zone of Germany then also declared itself a nation.

A year later, the Federal Republic (FRG) was integrated in the Western and the German Democratic Republic (GDR) in the Eastern defense systems. The iron curtain had been riveted down along the Elbe River. On April 4, 1949, Western Union was enlarged into the powerful, fifteen-nation North Atlantic Treaty Organization (NATO): the original five members (England, France, and the Benelux countries) were joined first by the United States and Canada, together with Norway, Denmark, Iceland, and Portugal, then by Greece and Turkey, and eventually by two former enemy states, Germany and Italy. Stalin had not been able to halt any of these developments, but he had held on to his own gains and split Europe in two.

The once mighty continent thus had been transformed into ramparts of the two superpowers. Perhaps some Western leaders had counted on the power of America to push the Soviet influence out of Europe again, but when, in September 1949, the Soviet Union exploded its first atomic device, the balance of power was stabilized. Europe's nations were trapped in a contest that forced each of them to seek protection in one of the two "camps" or "blocs." In the process, the division of Europe came to be accepted, and the polarized parts had to coexist with each other. Thus "cold war" became the premise of "cold peace." New diplomatic techniques had to be developed to keep conflict within circumscribed limits. The hegemonial powers used tension to keep their satellites in line. Paradoxically, if they wished to reduce the risk of war, they had to enforce respect of the dividing line, with a solid front on either side of it, and with no no-man's lands tempting either side's cupidity. The cold war, therefore, reversed all traditional notions of diplomacy. "Tension" became normal; "relaxation of tensions" meant the unleashing of unpredictable developments, creation of con- tested areas, and uncertainty—risks which in an atomic age should not be taken. A fluid situation is less easily controlled than one with definite, agreed-upon boundaries. Although the guns were pointed toward each other, both sides understood that they were not to be fired. Cold war was another name for coexistence or, as the Russians call it, competitive and antagonistic but peaceful coexistence.

For many Europeans, however, the division did not mean security but dependence. They did not accept that reconstruction had to be based on political stability. And radicals argued that, by way of backlash, anxiousness to preserve the *status quo* in Europe helped conservatives in the super-power countries, helped militarism and chauvinism, and helped Zhdanov in Moscow and McCarthy in Washington.

CHAPTER 3

The Reconstruction of Western Europe

THE Marshall Plan put Europe on her feet again. Never before had a nation defended its own interest in such an enlightened and generous action. America needs a strong Europe to share the burden of collective security. No security without reconstruction; no reconstruction without security. The Americans provided the capital to prime the pump, and the shield. The Europeans had the know-how, manpower, and facilities. The plan provided an ambience of international exchanges, a world market for the free-enterprise system in which the Allies on both sides of the Atlantic knew how to work. For the first time, the Western leaders regained confidence that their system had a chance. Hence, a comparatively mild injection of funds—$10 billion over three years—produced miraculous economic results.

Recovery was not the only purpose of the European plan; the other was reform. During the war, Europeans had learned how to use government direction to stimulate and co-ordinate private enterprise. Lord William Beveridge had in 1942 published his great plan for full employment and social welfare. Now, in Sweden and elsewhere, the disciples of John Maynard Keynes developed techniques of maintaining boom conditions; in France, Jean Monnet agitated for "*Le Plan*." Eugene Varga, the top economist of the Comintern, was so impressed that he cautioned the masters of the Kremlin not to speculate on an early breakdown of capitalism.

The very destruction and dislocations of the war, he pointed out, had laid the foundations for a long boom. Reconstruction was combined with the complete revamping of production and distribution. Every problem was turned into a new start, every drawback into an asset. Displaced persons, a willing source of labor, needed housing, furnishings, tools, clothing, and food. Demand was likely to exceed supply for some time to come; with the Marshall Plan credits, private enterprise was able to plan ahead. Moreover, the war had shaken up management and removed traditional institutional or personal obstacles to better adjustment.

The combined effects of skillful manipulation, new leadership, and transatlantic co-operation gave the recovery a dynamism which quickly (around 1950) carried production indexes to their pre-war levels and in the subsequent boom years far beyond. Annual growth rates of 5 or 6 per cent or more were the rule; some countries at times even achieved 8 or 10 per cent. By 1960, many countries produced twice as much as before the war, and consumers had 50 per cent more goods and services at their disposal than in the best pre-war days.

	Growth Rates* 1950–68	Index of Industrial Production (1938 = 100)			
		1948	1952	1958	1968
United States	2.0	241	297	331	612
West Germany (FRG)	5.0	51	115	189	469
France	4.0	104	133	190	474
Italy	4.8	101	149	232	575
Netherlands	3.4	112	153	212	684
Belgium	3.1	122	137	157	302
Great Britain	2.2	112	126	150	226
Austria	4.9	92	167	256	524
Sweden	3.5	142	155	191	399
U.S.S.R.	6.9	173	226	433	863
Czechoslovakia	4.7	142	206	321	475
East Germany (GDR)	7.5	71	173	263	385
Yugoslavia	14.0	148	182	342	607

* Real per capita increase per year, in per cent of GNP.

N.B.: Differences in statistical methods and territorial changes tend to distort the basis for comparison. The Soviet and East European figures appear to be deliberately inflated. Eastern plans provided for impressive increases in mining, steel, and similar productions, which were given extra weight in computing the indexes. SOURCE: United Nations.

Having provided for economic health, the statesmen of Western Europe gave their half of the Continent a political structure. In May 1949, ten countries formed the Council of Europe: England, France, Belgium, the Netherlands and Luxembourg (the original Western Union) plus Ireland, Italy and three Scandinavian countries. NATO established headquarters in Paris and envisaged the creation of a unified command. The first SACEUR (Supreme Allied Commander in Europe) was Dwight Eisenhower. Though the General was well liked in Europe, however, national pride resented the prominent role of Americans in shaping Western strategies, and no nation was yet prepared to give up its cherished sovereignty. On the contrary, France, Portugal, and Belgium shamelessly used the NATO shield to bolster their colonial empires.

Further integration, therefore, had to wait for another emergency or was smuggled in by the economic back door. In 1950, a European Payments Union was created, with the Bank for International Settlements in Basle as its instrument. In that same year the French Foreign Minister, Robert Schuman, proposed a European coal and steel cartel. The idea was realized in 1952. The six nations which later formed the Common Market (the Benelux countries, West Germany, France, and Italy) created their first supranational venture, the European Coal and Steel Community (ECSC). In addition, these six countries agreed to form a European Defense Community (EDC).

Nothing could have promoted European unity so effectively as an integrated army. The idea came to fruition in a roundabout way. The Korean war found the Western defenses woefully inadequate; with America's forces pinned down in a remote part of Asia, Europe seemed unprotected. Since the NATO partners were contributing far less than they had agreed to, the only way to plug the gap in the NATO defenses seemed to be the rearmament of Germany. However, no one wished to revive the German Army. French Premier René Pleven therefore suggested that German regiments might serve in Germany under Allied army commanders. This gave birth to the draft EDC treaty, initialed in May 1952.

To Stalin, this seemed a powerful threat, and he tried everything to dissuade the Germans from joining. He offered to negotiate about the reunification and neutralization of their country—an idea that appealed to many, especially on the Left. But German and French nationalists did not like the idea of a European army either, and a coalition of Rightists and Leftists scuttled it in the French parliament in 1954. The idea of serving in the same army with former enemies was repugnant to many deputies.

But those who objected to German regiments, alas, got in their place something still less desirable: an independent German army. Under United States pressure, the Paris Treaties of October 23, 1954, gave Germany and Italy full sovereignty, had them recruit armies, and received them as partners in the revived and renamed Western European Union; this whole setup was placed under the NATO umbrella to keep the German rearmament under control.

This bold action jolted Stalin's successors in the Kremlin into a new diplomacy. Austria, which for ten years had languished under a burdensome occupation, was evacuated in return for a promise of strictest neutrality. Finland, likewise, got the occupied base of Porkkala back, but had to extend her Treaty of Friendship with the Soviet Union. Despite these demonstrations, and despite desperate attempts by the German Social Democrats to block ratification of the Paris treaties, Germany and Italy became members of NATO in May 1955.

Meanwhile, the European Coal and Steel Community began to develop a dynamism of its own, pushing toward more extended co-operation. Particularly the French Minister of Planning, Monnet, and the German Foreign Minister, Walter Hallstein, ably supported by the Belgian socialist, Henri Spaak, had great visions of a United States of Europe that would abolish individual sovereignties with respect to finance, commerce, currency, social legislation, and defense. The Council of Europe was won over for the project; as early as March 1957 the six ECSC countries signed the Rome treaties creating the Common Market, or European Economic Community (EEC), and the European Atomic Co-operation Agency (Euratom).

The EEC is more than a customs union. It plays an important role in directing the flow of investments, in balancing price levels in the member states, and in co-ordinating their social legislation. Its "Commission" is not composed of delegates of the member countries but is a truly technocratic body with vast powers to intervene in the member states' economies. Its first president was Hallstein. The founding members were Germany, France, Italy, Belgium, the Netherlands, and Luxembourg —usually called "the Six." Austria, which would have liked to join, was prevented by a Russian veto. England and three Scandinavian countries decided to maintain the sterling club and the Commonwealth orientation; these countries later (in 1960) formed the European Free Trade Association (EFTA), a much less integrated community. Portugal, Austria, and Switzerland also joined EFTA, while Finland, which would have liked to form a trading area with the other Scandinavians, was kept isolated by another Soviet veto.

The output and trade figures for EEC, EFTA, and the Communist areas show growth rates varying from country to country, apparently unrelated to economic systems. West Germany, which had chosen a showcase model of *laissez faire*, achieved the same index as France, which had adopted planning; England and Belgium advanced at the same slow pace, though one was guided by socialists and the other by traditional coalitions.

Perhaps the conditions of recovery should be studied in each country separately. No doubt England's structural difficulties and her stubborn defense of the sterling empire provided a less favorable climate than the radical relief from all mortgages in defeated Germany. In France, by contrast, the recovery was weighed down by pension claims, pre-war debts, and reluctance to devalue the currency drastically.

The EEC countries had a total trade volume of $8.2 billion in 1953, half of it with each other. In 1969, this had risen to $56 billion, of which $36 billion were traded inside the Common Market and only $3 billion with Eastern Europe. The EFTA and other European countries started out from approximately the same dollar amount, but increased their total to only $28 billion, half of it inside EFTA. Eastern Europe had a trade volume of $5 billion in 1953, 80 per cent of it inside its area; this rose to $22 billion in 1969, $16.5 of it inside the area. The figures show that the Common Market countries were stronger to begin with and were able, through their association, to intensify their relations, to increase their exchanges, to reap the benefits of an international division of labor. Power tends to attract more power, and quite naturally Western Europe's internal trade was matched by a $60-billion exchange between the Common Market and the non-Communist rest of the world, while Eastern Europe's imports and exports to those countries increased to only $7 billion and the exchanges between Eastern and Western Europe reached $9 billion.

What all this amounts to is an economic division of the world that follows, intensifies, and perpetuates its political division. The ideological polarization was total. On one side, Communism was reduced to Stalinist orthodoxy; on the other side, "free enterprise" became an article of faith so strong that it could override all respect for the West's other ideological prop—democracy. The alliance also supported the monarchy in Greece, the dictatorship in Portugal, and the colonial empires of several members. It supplied the French Republic with arms and funds against Arab and Vietnamese insurgents. With few exceptions—as in Belgium, whose Socialist Premier Spaak was a strong supporter of European unity and of NATO—U.S. policy favored conservative parties. In the case of England, it placed difficulties in the way of Clement Attlee's Labour cabinet.

No doubt it was unfortunate that Europe's recovery was linked so intimately with the polarization of the world and that the cause of European unity, an old socialist idea, was identified with conservative policies. The undisputed success of these policies was in no way predicated upon the cold war or on anti-Communism. The Left needlessly disengaged itself from this success, largely for reasons of party politics, and thereby deprived itself of the opportunity to link the cause of Europe with social reform.

In November 1954, reacting to the foundation of the Western European Union the previous month, Moscow was host to a Security Conference with seven other Eastern governments. In May 1955, following the final integration into NATO of West Germany, Moscow's bilateral alliances with the people's democracies were replaced by the Warsaw Pact, a multilateral defense treaty "on friendship, co-operation, and mutual assistance." Like NATO, the Warsaw Pact was given a unified command, under Marshal Ivan Konev. The treaty entitled member troops to occupy any member country. The (East) German Democratic Republic was admitted in January 1956.

Thus the "balance of terror" rent Europe in half. Neither side could destroy or absorb the other; neither side dared to leave much uncommitted territory in-between. Both found security in polarization.

CHAPTER 4

The Soviet Empire

BY the peace treaties Stalin had regained millions of people whose ancestors had lived under the Czars. Once independent nations had joined the family of Soviet peoples, counter to Lenin's treaty of 1921, which had granted them freedom "in perpetuity."

The nationalities thus incorporated into the Soviet Union were assured "sovereignty." The Karelian Soviet Republic was created for the Finns, the Moldavian Soviet Republic for the Rumanians of Bessarabia; Byelorussia (White Russia) and the Ukraine were dubbed "independent" to assure them seats in the United Nations. Lithuanians, Estonians, and Latvians would be "autonomous" within the framework of the Russian Soviet Federated Socialist Republic, though thousands of them had been transplanted to Siberia.

Beyond the borders of the Soviet Union there now extended the satellite empire. Central Europe was given transitional regimes under the eye of the Red Army. In Hungary, the Small Peasants Party had a majority. Its leader, Ferencz Nagy, first tried to co-operate with the Soviet authorities; but in June 1947 he was forced to yield the Premiership to a more pliable person. At the same time, the Socialists had to merge with the Communists and with a phony National Peasant Party into a "Left bloc." In August 1948, all parties merged into the Hungarian Independent People's Front, and the government fell into the hands of the bloody Matyas Rakosi, who proposed to purge both non-Communists and his personal enemies among the Communists. Cardinal Joseph Mindszenty was sentenced to jail for life; the Communist Foreign Minister Laszlo Rajk was shot as a Titoist.

In Bulgaria, the brave Nikola Petkov, leader of peasant resistance during the war, refused to join the Fatherland Front; he was vilified in parliament, arrested, accused of dealing with the enemy, and sentenced to death. The lesson was not lost on less stalwart characters, especially some Social Democrats in other countries. Grotewohl and Ebert in Berlin, Fierlinger in Prague, Cyrankiewicz in Warsaw were persuaded to lead their organizations into a United Front. Some liberals and anti-Catholics also agreed to play the unity game. Those who refused were "exposed" as Nazi collaborators. This is how Stalin politically secured his newly won empire.

A great political bonus fell to the Communists through land reform. Large estates were divided; where small farms were the rule, as in Rumania, a harsh law decreed further subdivision to a maximum size of ten acres. Although these farms were less efficient and later had to be collectivized, for the moment the reforms brought support for the Communists. Drawing on the experience of the Soviet party, the European Communists hoped to retain power through the judicious manipulation of the social imbalance.

In Czechoslovakia the Communists obtained only 38 per cent of the vote in 1946. But despite the bitter memories of Munich, the electoral terror, and the effective use of patronage, all forecasts indicated that in the elections scheduled for the spring of 1948, the Communists would lose. To avoid this, Prime Minister Gottwald fabricated a constitutional crisis, forced non-Communist ministers to resign, and then accused them of treason. Workers' militias controlled the streets and demanded a Communist government. Jan Masaryk, who refused to yield, was defenestrated, and the party's "action committees" installed a terror regime. It was the first application of the Communist doctrine that, once in power, a Communist government cannot be overthrown by legal, parliamentary means.

After the experience of the war, security may have been Stalin's prime motive for acquiring this huge glacis. But there were economic dimensions to the Soviet empire as well: Russia exploited the satellite economies for the reconstruction of her own economy, and tried to prevent the independent economic development of the occupied areas, some of which were technically more advanced than the Soviet Union. In January 1949, the Soviet Union, Bulgaria, Poland, Rumania, Hungary, and Czechoslovakia founded the Council for Mutual Economic Aid (called Comecon in the West) with extensive powers to intervene in the economic planning of each member country. Instead of receiving Marshall aid, the East European satellites had to give aid to the Soviet Union. Their production plans were geared to its economic needs. The favorite form of industrial colonialism was the establishment of a "mixed company"—that is, an enterprise in which Russian and national authorities held equal shares of the capital stock but whose manager invariably was a Russian. Thus, from Manchuria to Austria, control of mining, timber, transportation, and industrial facilities passed into Russian or Communist hands. In trading satellite products for satellite goods within the empire as well as for foreign goods outside it, the Soviet Union continues to earn a middleman's profit, buying cheaply and selling dearly.

Satellite products also were used in the international black market of arms and ammunition. Thus, Czechoslovakia supplied arms to both sides in the 1948 Palestine war and to Nasser in the big 1955 deal. The cotton Egypt delivered in exchange for these weapons later was resold in the same markets that had formerly been Egypt's customers.

Industrial development was one of the issues that prompted Tito's secession. Stalin tried to channel Yugoslav investments into industries that export raw materials to the Soviet Union; Tito desired a balanced development. After Yugoslavia gained her independence, her industries developed, while older industrial countries like East Germany and Czechoslovakia stagnated during long years of Soviet exploitation. The Russian masters were poorer than their subjects, and the call to "catch up" reflected a painful experience. Russian soldiers, administrators, envoys had seen that in the capitalist West proletarians were not starving but owned watches, lived in separate one-family apartments, and used modern appliances. Some Soviet scientists began to write favorably about Western philosophy and science. Thereupon a campaign was launched to show that Russians had invented the dynamo, radio, phonograph, and a thousand other things.

Imitation of the West was not confined to useful implements, however. Artists and writers began to experiment with Western styles. Expressionism and even abstract art could be seen, secretly of course, in Moscow lofts. Still worse, the young people were flocking to American movies; jazz records became a major black-market item. Such signs of "moral decline" indicated danger to the stability of the state.

A vigorous counter-offensive was launched by Zhdanov, the most influential member of the Politburo after Stalin. In the style of biblical prophets, he campaigned against "bourgeois culture," its slaves and dupes among Soviet citizens, against the depravity of even looking at it. These blandishments, he said, were the work of evil agitators, spies, agents of the international bourgeoisie. He also used this chauvinistic propaganda to purge his rivals, whom he charged with being un-Russian, rootless intellectuals. Jews, traditionally the most Western-oriented and least patriotic Soviet nationality, were singled out for attack as "cosmopolitan."

Possession of an empire breeds an imperialistic ideology. On the first available occasion, Stalin assured the Russians that their army had beaten Hitler single-handedly and that world history knew no greater people. Mindful of the centrifugal tendencies among the national minorities, he declared the Great Russians to be the empire people, the backbone of all the subject nations. The new national anthem extolled the Great Russians as "marching out front." The literature of the period combines pride in the Russian people with contempt for lesser breeds and fear of antipodes. For fear is a corollary of imperialism. Imaginary dangers were conjured up, enemies were seen everywhere. Encirclement, Stalin said in answering a question about the empire's vast expanse, is not a geographical but a political notion. He might have said that it was a state of mind. Those who did not share his claustrophobic feeling, those who might even have welcomed foreign influences, were guilty of the crime of xenophilia. The concentration camps were being filled. Police Chief Lavrenti Beria ruled over many millions of slave laborers, reminiscent of Ivan the Terrible's private state. Unable to put all his subjects into concentration camps, he threw a quarantine belt around them.

Also like the paranoiac Ivan IV, whom he exalted, Stalin projected his fears onto the world political theater. The cold-war atmosphere was created before the cold war was launched. Instead of enjoying peace and free communication with her former allies, Russia remained in a state of siege. Neither the Soviet Army nor the defensive spirit was demobilized. The cold war was a way of sealing Russia off, of having peace with a wartime spirit, of preventing pent-up tensions from turning into centrifugal forces. Deliberately, the lure of the West was transformed into hatred against it. Zhdanov obtained a free hand on the ideological front. Strict rules were laid down on how Soviet writers should write, musicians compose, geneticists interpret mutations, physicists deal with mc^2.

Intellectuals are dangerous. They must be watched, but they might also be bought. In the satellite countries, the Communists made great efforts to woo them. Writers, artists, actors, and scientists were treated like members of a ruling class; they received larger rations, better housing, and, above all, captive audiences. Book production in most socialist countries, even in backward Albania, increased more rapidly than any other sector. But the price extracted from intellectuals was ideological war with the West.

CHAPTER 5

Tito's "Special Way"

EVEN in 1948, Stalin's empire was not as homogeneous as it appeared to the outsider. Nor was Stalin's hold on his subjects as secure as he would have liked. In the Kremlin, two factions were fighting each other. The militant, revolutionary Zhdanov spoke for the expansionist wing; the accommodating, bureaucratic Georgy Malenkov led the isolationists. Zhdanov supported the impatient satellite leaders who were caught between the Soviet Union's demands and the backwardness of their countries; for them, world revolution was the only way out. They also had national grievances: Tito was angry because Stalin had given Trieste to Italy and Carinthia to Austria; Dimitroff wanted Greek Macedonia, with the port of Salonika, for Bulgaria. Both therefore aided the Greek insurgents, whom Stalin had abandoned. They also planned to create a Balkan federation which, together with Poland, might stand up to the Soviet Union and perhaps even attract the Ukraine. They were sternly rebuked in Moscow. Dimitroff, a sick man, gave in. Tito did not.

Of all the Central European leaders, Tito alone had an independent power base. He did not owe his victory to the Red Army, and he had built his party in his own image. He forbade Yugoslav Communists to report to the Soviet Ambassador on deliberations in their Central Committee; Stalin took the view that no Communists anywhere in the world could have secrets from him.

This was not Tito's first insubordination. During the war he had refused to work along with the King (see Sartre's play *Les Mains Sales, Dirty Hands*) and had opposed Churchill's project of a Balkan landing. He had tried to provoke a third world war, shooting down American planes. To Stalin, this independent leader seemed as dangerous as the old Bolsheviks he had killed in the 1930's. When Molotov called him a "*Bukharinist*," Tito knew he was marked for the executioner and refused to go to Moscow. Thereupon the Balkan satellites, in February 1948, declared a blockade against Yugoslavia, and the Cominform expelled the Yugoslav Communist Party.

Refuting the myth that he was fighting "Communism," President Truman offered Yugoslavia arms and credit. Tito received a billion dollars in goods and weapons and concluded alliances with the Turkish and Greek governments (which latter he had tried to overthrow). Belgrade became the mecca of disaffected Communists and left-wing Socialists who had been waiting for a signal to rise against both capitalism and Bolshevism.

Tito, however, did not give that signal and repudiated the idea of "Titoism." On the political plane he accepted help from anybody who would respect his independence. But ideologically he remained a Leninist; the Party dictatorship remained as absolute as before. His new friends could not induce him to release Archbishop Stepinac from his prison or to permit non-Communist parties, or even factions inside the Communist Party.

Titoism is not a heresy but a schism, to borrow the language of the Roman Church; it is not a new development in Leninism but can be reconciled with the main body of Soviet thought. Tito discouraged the attempts of his home-grown idea men, Mosche Pijade, Dedijer, and Kardelj, to become the apostles of a Marxist reformation. He was less interested in contacts with dissident Communists in other countries than in alliances with non-Communists in the Third World (next chapter). His was a strictly personal power play.

Elsewhere, Stalin contrived to do what he had planned to do to Tito. Dimitroff was called to Moscow, where he conveniently died—of natural causes, it is said. Zhdanov, too, died, and in the wake of his demise the Leningrad organization was thoroughly purged. Nor did Zhdanovists and potential Titoists abroad long survive. Traicho Kostov in Bulgaria, Rudolf Slansky in Czechoslovakia, Rajk in Hungary, all of them heroes of the Communist movement, confessed to deviations and were executed. Even in France some of the more intransigent leaders were fired. The Greek Communist Party expelled its heroic guerrilla leader, Vafiades. A little later it was the turn of Ana Pauker and Vasile Luca in Rumania, of Wilhelm Zaisser and Paul Merker in East Germany—all powerful men as long as they were tuned in to the Russian wavelength, all Stalin's valued henchmen once, all dropped overnight, often for no apparent reason. Some, like Slansky and Rajk, seem to have been Zhdanov's men; others, like Kostov, were accused of being nationalists. In Poland, Wladyslaw Gomulka, who also had the reputation of a "national Communist," barely escaped execution after being demoted from leadership.

Having defied Stalin, Tito had to give his nation a model of socialism they could support. Collectivization was stopped. A new law created workers' councils in every factory and industry. The councils elected and supervised the boards which were to set the policy for each production unit; but the day-to-day operation was to remain in the hands of a manager who was to be appointed by higher authorities: plant managers by the Industry Board, industry managers by the Government Planning Board. The ministries which formerly had controlled all sectors of industry were replaced by co-ordinating councils composed of regional representatives; these were to concentrate on planning. Thus a balance was struck between central control and regional, local, trade, or plant initiative, between authority and checks, competence and control. Moreover, workers were given responsibility for making their industry profitable, for sharing the profit and allotting part of it to investment, and so on. These reforms were only the prelude of the "market socialism" advocated by the Polish economist Oscar Lange and the "new model" applied in the satellite economies fifteen years later.

In 1951–52, agricultural controls were relaxed as well. Prices were allowed to find their own level. In 1953, peasants were allowed to withdraw from collectives; a majority availed themselves of the chance. Of 3 million hectares that had been collectivized, only 1 million, or 10 per cent of all arable land, was still under state or collective management by 1955. But all holdings in excess of 10 hectares (25 acres), or 15 hectares in rocky areas, were subject to confiscation.

In 1953, Yugoslavia adopted a new constitution. The Lower House was to be composed of 282 deputies elected nationwide and 70 elected by the Assemblies of the six federated republics. A Chamber of Producers was to unite delegates of two categories of workers: collective and co-operative farmers, and industrial and white-collar workers. Candidates were to be nominated in open meetings, but voters could select secretly from the list so collated. The Assembly elects a Federal Executive Council and a President—a farcical provision as long as the Party (renamed "Communist League") holds all real power.

Much of all this, of course, remained theory. But some intellectuals took the theory seriously; the first was Milovan Djilas, a veteran guerrilla from Montenegro and a vice-president. Having criticized the bureaucratic degeneration of the Party, he was expelled and sentenced to seven years in jail; he rose to international fame through his books *The New* [Ruling] *Class* and *Conversations with Stalin*. Djilas's fate dramatized the bitterness of the conflict between the old Party cadres and the centrifugal forces Tito could not master.

It was precisely the "new class," the Communist hierarchy, that felt threatened by any genuine and democratic movement. To keep the Communist bureaucracy happy, Tito not only had to stop the democratization process but after Stalin's death eagerly seized the chance of a *rapprochement* with the Soviet bloc. He supported Khrushchev during the Hungarian crisis of 1956. He sent Professor Mihajlo Mihajlov to jail for publishing a critical diary of his journeys to the Soviet Union. In 1961, Belgrade was host to the conference of nonaligned nations, and soon Tito made himself independent of U.S. arms aid. He restored to the Party, instead of the voters' meetings, the right to nominate candidates to the Federal Assembly. He bore down heavily on "cosmopolitan," Western ideologies.

The main advocate of a return to Soviet-style politics was Vice-President Alexander Rankovitch, chief of the UDBA (secret police) and friend of the Soviet KGB. It was said that he waited for Tito's retirement to seize the reins of government and that his bugging devices reached into Tito's palace. This probably contributed to his overthrow in 1966; simultaneously his hardcore veterans were purged from the Party and the police. But this was not to be Tito's last change of direction. He constantly wavered between support of the Party and impatience with its inefficiency, bureaucratism, and favoritism. Like Pilsudski and Stalin, he kept the system in rotation and renewed the guard, relaxing and tightening the reins, giving in to popular demands and condemning them.

CHAPTER 6

The "Third Force"

A VIGOROUS foreign policy enhanced Tito's prestige. Together with Nasser and Nehru, he envisaged a "third force" beholden to neither of the two blocs. As "positive neutralists," they developed a world political dynamism that occasionally boosted their influence beyond their real power.

Nor were they alone in seeking a way out of the cold war. De Gaulle, while in power, had maintained good relations with the Kremlin and strove to prevent France from getting entangled in an anti-Communist front. His successors in office helped found NATO, but dragged their feet in negotiations for European unity. De Gaulle's former lieutenant, Mendès-France, as Premier in 1954 aborted the EDC plan. Nationalists in all countries, afraid to lose their cherished sovereignty, were equally averse to the idea of Europe and to the American hegemony. Had not the danger of a Communist takeover been so clear and present, many more might have objected to the alliance and the cold-war ideology. In Germany a movement against EDC, inspired mostly by Nazi veterans and other Rightists, promoted the slogan "*Ohne Mich*" ("Count Me Out," reminiscent of the Italian "*Nè Me Frego*"). In Italy a neo-Fascist paper, *L'Uomo Qualunque* (*Everyman*), had a tremendous success. In England the old empire fanatics felt that the alliance would reduce them to the same level as Germany and France; unwilling to be America's junior partner, they felt that the British talent for diplomacy and compromise could avoid the confrontation policy that threatened to leave England with little room for maneuver.

More vocal and more embarrassing to policy-makers, however, was the left-wing opposition, which could not forget Hitler and World War II. Jews and radicals feared nothing so much as a revival of German nationalism; an alliance with the German Army was repugnant to them. On the other hand, they still gave credit to the Soviet Union for her wartime sacrifices; many of them refused to believe that Stalin could have imperialist designs on any country. They supported the Soviet demand for "banning the bomb," for the abandonment by all powers of foreign bases, for the withdrawal of all occupation armies. They considered the Marshall Plan a U.S. scheme to dump its surplus goods, and engaged in demonstrations against NATO.

To exploit these sentiments, Stalin launched a "peace offensive." Picasso designed a dove as its symbol; a "Peace Congress" in Paris assembled delegates from fifty nations. French longshoremen refused to unload American cargoes; French wine drinkers and culture snobs staged a vigorous campaign against Coca-Colonization.

Intellectuals in all countries, but especially in France, also reacted against the impact American culture was now making on Europe. American consumer goods (especially household appliances) and business methods were widely admired, imitated—and scorned. American books flooded the market, and it was precisely the criticism of American culture by American intellectuals that was lapped up and spread in the high-brow magazines. Faulkner, T. S. Eliot, Henry Miller, known to but a few before the war, now became leaders of a revolt against the "air-conditioned nightmare" of a mechanized, soulless civilization. A change in the understanding of critical literature occurred. Older writers like Sinclair Lewis, John dos Passos, and Upton Sinclair had enjoyed great success in Europe during the 1920's and 1930's as critics of a social order or of middle-class values; European writers like Kafka and Brecht also on occasion placed the scene of the capitalistic "Jungle" in the United States. But no one at the time felt that this was "anti-American."

Now intellectuals saw the protest in national terms. Projecting their alienation from their own society onto the screen of a world-wide struggle between "cultured" Europe and "barbarous" America, they gladly quoted American authors to support their fight against "Americanization." Taking sides in the cold war, some, like Marcuse, Sartre, and Maurice Merleau-Ponty, went so far as to denounce democracy and tolerance. Julien Benda had to add a new chapter to his *Treason of the Intellectuals* to denounce Stalin's intellectual lackeys in the West. Camus fell out with Sartre over the question whether a French Socialist had the right to condemn Soviet concentration camps.

Most intellectuals, however, and in the beginning Sartre himself, tried to maintain a "neutral" stance in the cold war. They even spoke of a "third force" in politics, culture, and social ethics. They wanted neither American capitalism nor Stalin's collective prison but a just and democratic order that was not beholden to any big power or bloc. This was the position of Camus, as editor of *Combat*, and of his successor Claude Bourdet; of Hubert Beuve-Méry at *Le Monde*, the distinguished Paris daily read the world over; of Kingsley Martin of *New Statesman and Nation*; and also of the *Observer* and the Socialist press in most countries.

Initially, the third-force concept was a purely intellectual one. Soon it found institutional substance in Tito's efforts to build a coalition of neutral states. Looking at a globe, it was a tempting vision that the red area in the East and the blue area in the West could be separated by a gray, neutral strip of territory starting up north in Sweden, winding through Germany, Austria, Switzerland, and Yugoslavia, leaping across the Mediterranean to the new states of Africa and the Near East, and ending far south in India and Indonesia. This conception seemed to grow both more urgent and more plausible when the Soviet Union exploded its first atomic bomb. Now the world faced the problem of living with dual control of destruction. As anxiety increased and, with the start of the Korean war, the blocs grew more intransigent, more people found merit in the idea of interposing a "neutral zone" and of "disengaging" the armies at the point of friction. Prime Minister Attlee thought it good politics to fly to Washington to implore Truman not to use atomic bombs in Korea.

Such sentiments were reinforced by some structural and accidental features of European politics. Protestants in Germany, Sweden, and elsewhere resented the conservative, Catholic leadership in the EEC. Socialists criticized the coal and steel community as a capitalistic cartel. Indeed, the governments in Bonn, Paris, and Rome were conservative: Konrad Adenauer had been mayor of Cologne at the time when the steel and coal barons ruled the Rhineland; Robert Schuman was closely associated with similar interests in France; and Alcide de Gasperi so outwitted the Italian Socialists that their leader, Pietro Nenni, once a right-winger, found no pillar to lean on except the Communists. The Europe that tried to be born had all the ugly features of Restoration; it earned the epithet "Carolingian" because it left the "pagan" half out in the cold: Adenauer has even been accused of lacking interest in the provinces under Soviet control because their reintegration would have shifted Germany's religious and political balance back to Protestant and Socialist majorities.

The Socialists indeed had taken a back seat in European politics and blamed their misfortune on the cold war. The German leader, Kurt Schumacher, was a martyr and a fanatic. Intellectually, he towered above the organization men; but he was sick, bitter, and irrational. He refused to recognize the partition of Germany and adopted the pose of an all-German patriot. When the Federal Republic was founded, he fought against every step in its formation, and even more doggedly against NATO, in which he felt Germany would provide only the infantry. Adenauer, he felt, was sacrificing German unity to American cold-war strategy; he went so far as to call him "Chancellor of the Allies," an appeal to the nationalists. He persuaded socialists throughout the world to support a program of German neutralization and unification.

After Ernest Bevin's untimely death, the British Labour Party, since 1951 once again in opposition, also returned to its traditional pacifism. Out of power, the radicals usually gain influence in the party, and they had a superb spokesman in the personable, popular Aneurin Bevan, ex-leader of the Welsh miners, efficient Minister of Health in the wartime cabinet. To a generous man like "Nye" Bevan there could be nothing more attractive than a scheme that seemed to be fair to Germany without being unfair to those who still were suspicious of her.

Moreover, if Germany was neutralized and troops could be withdrawn from both sides of the Elbe River, then the Soviet armies might eventually leave Central Europe and restore freedom to the Czechs, Poles, and the Balkan nations. After Stalin's death the Tory minister, Anthony Eden, proposed a similar scheme: thinning out the occupation forces. Predictably, he failed. For why should Moscow buy it if the implications were so profitable for the West? At a later stage, after the loosening of the Soviet empire, Poland's Foreign Minister Adam Rapacki tried again. He proposed to "denuclearize" Central Europe with a view toward subsequent withdrawal of troops. Interestingly, the Russians rejected the proposal to even discuss the two phases simultaneously.

Whether or not the Left's foreign policy program was realistic, it seemed to provide an alternative to the sterile cold-war ideology, and it saved the Left from its sterility in domestic affairs. The visible improvement of living standards in the Western countries forced the Left to fight over small side issues. Since it could not propose revolution at home, it projected all frustrations and dissatisfactions, as well as all hopes of a better future, onto the international screen. There, the mirage of goodwill and reconciliation afforded them a focus for all the anxieties of the atomic age. Farther to the Left, of course, there lurked the old dream of a world no longer ruled by power. Europe's imperialism had had its time; it had defeated itself. The next stage of history was the retreat of empire.

Capitalism and liberalism were now considered obsolete in many intellectual circles. As Heinrich Mann (who died in East Germany) had written in self-criticism: "Liberalism and a narrow kind of humanitarianism helped us to tolerate capitalism while the system was still possible, brightening it up so that we could still afford flights of conscience and human love." Thomas Mann, too, went to Weimar for the Goethe Bicentennial and pleaded for reconciliation of East and West, in the name of culture. There, with the brutish Ulbricht on the dais, he reminded his audience that, as early as twenty years before, he had exclaimed: "Would that Karl Marx had read Hölderlin!"

CHAPTER 7

End of Empire

THE war in Asia had ended the myth of Europe's superiority, and eventually the Caucasians lost confidence in their destiny. Over Churchill's protest, England finally, in 1947, fulfilled her thirty-year-old promise to give independence to India and Burma. She also gave up the mandate over Palestine and allowed the State of Israel to emerge.[1] France also had to relinquish her mandate over Syria and Lebanon; a date was set for the evacuation of British troops from Suez, and the Italian colonies became independent. When the United States released the Philippines, it also forced the Dutch to give freedom to the Sunda Islands (Indonesia) and supported Ho Chi Minh's bid for Indochinese autonomy.

Contrary to popular belief, the loss of empire was not the cause but the effect of England's post-war poverty. To finance her military expenditures, England had sold £13 billion of her overseas investments. The total yield in 1938 was £175 million; ten years later, they brought only £75 million in devalued currency, but cost £200 million to protect. Sir Stafford Cripps, Labour's dour Chancellor of the Exchequer, harshly told his compatriots that they had to tighten their belts. Overseas military expenses constituted one-third of the deficit in England's balance-of-payments; she could ill afford such luxury.

The Commonwealth was transformed into a club which no longer carried the British name in its title. The Prime Ministers of the former dominions and crown colonies continued to meet every year, but they designed no joint policies and were no longer held together by the British Navy.

Club membership still had a few economic advantages. Empire preference gave English workers cheap food imports and assured English manufacturers, bankers, shippers, and insurance carriers profitable markets. Paradoxical situations developed later when the African states insisted that England assert her sovereignty over Rhodesia—to protect the black majority against their white rulers—or when England had to admit West Indian and East Indian subjects whom the newly independent governments were expelling. France also founded a "Commonwealth of French [-speaking] Nations," which however was not conceived as a community of equals.

---

[1] The occupation powers in Austria and Germany had a "disposal problem," as many surviving Jews refused to go back to their native countries in Eastern Europe.

A projected Council of State was to include delegates, with equal rights, from the colonies and metropolitan France. For a long time, incidentally, the post of Minister of Colonies had been held by an African. This window-dressing scheme was accepted in sub-Saharan Africa but challenged in the Maghreb and in Vietnam. The young Sultan and the Istiqlal Party in Morocco, Bourguiba's Neo-Destur in Tunisia, Messali Hadj's Mouvement National Algérien (MNA) fought for Arab autonomy. In Vietnam, Ho Chi Minh harassed the French for six years, draining their forces until in 1954 he achieved the symbolic victory of Dien Bien Phu. At the Geneva Conference, Premier Mendès-France gave up all of Indochina; subsequently he abandoned Tunisia and Morocco, which had long hoped to win their freedom without war. But in Algeria, France's oldest colony in Africa, the republic had extended the franchise to those Arabs who lived under French and Christian law—one out of nine million. Successive governments hoped to hold onto the country where a million French settlers (called *pieds-noirs*) owned land. However, declaring it a department of France did not make it so.

Back in 1943–45, the Arab leaders might have settled for an autonomous Algeria in the framework of the new French Republic. When this was denied and the unfair "statute" was imposed in 1947, bitter fighting ensued and atrocities were committed on both sides. (The film *La Guerre d'Algérie*, though not a documentary, evokes the essence of the conflict.) With Egyptian help, nationalist militants formed the Front de Libération National (FLN) and waged a fierce guerrilla war from bases in Tunisia and Morocco. Its army completely wiped out the socialist MNA and other rival organizations. From 1954 on, its terror dominated the Arab population and step by step managed to involve the entire French army, just returned from its defeat in Indochina. When the Socialist Guy Mollet became Premier in 1956, he tried to compromise, granting the franchise to all Arabs, but was hooted down by the *pieds-noirs* and was threatened with an army coup.

To regain the initiative, Mollet designed a plan to strike at the source of Arab unrest —Cairo. The opportunity came when Egypt's new leader, Colonel Gamal Abdel Nasser, nationalized the Suez Canal. British and French shareholder interests may have been violated; but, more important, the sensibilities of all empire boosters were bruised. Since 1951, England had again been governed by Tories, the empire party. Even though Churchill retired in 1955 after four years as Prime Minister, his successor, Anthony Eden, continued his world political course. He concluded an alliance with Turkey, Iran, Pakistan, and Iraq—the controversial Baghdad Pact.

Guy Mollet and Anthony Eden joined Israel when it attacked Egypt in 1956. They failed, either because of domestic opposition or because the American Secretary of State, striking an anti-colonialist pose, left his allies in the lurch. He not only succeeded in impairing Western imperialism but also opened the Third World to Soviet penetration. For Khrushchev was given all the credit for Nasser's survival. Anthony Eden had to resign and handed the reins of government to Harold Macmillan, an impeccable, unflappable gentleman who had been Chancellor of the Exchequer. He drastically reduced England's defense commitments, abandoned UMS (Universal

Military Service), withdrew British forces from Korea, Libya, and other overseas bases, set a date for the liquidation of all British forces from stations east of Suez, dropped the "Blue Streak" ICBM, but developed nuclear weapons.

Repercussions of the Western defeat reverberated not only in the remote colonies, which now began to stir; they also affected the struggle between NATO and the Warsaw bloc. The empire states had joined NATO in the hope that, despite explicit wording to the contrary, the American umbrella would also protect their overseas possessions. Indeed, U.S. military grants had supported France's war in Indochina, as American credits obviously made it easier for Belgium and Portugal to maintain their empire positions. When the United States did not back the investments militarily, these countries grew less ardent in their loyalty to NATO. But, meanwhile, the Soviet Union was able to pose as protector of national revolutionary governments and movements in the Third World. In 1958, Iraqi generals overthrew their pro-Western King and pulled their country out of the Baghdad Pact.

Guy Mollet was followed by two equally weak governments which could neither end the Algerian war nor save the republic at home. The attempt to maintain the empire killed the French Fourth Republic, which was all too similar to the Third in spirit and structure. After losing two colonial wars, it was mired in a third which unbalanced its budget, undermined army morale, and provoked students to rebellion. While at the top vested interests ruled the administration and the parliament, vast masses at the bottom of the social pyramid were disaffected. While party feuds discredited the republican institutions, a large number of votes were cast in empty protest, either for the Communists or for the freakish shopkeeper, Poujade. These, and the equally unco-operative Gaullists, made it impossible for any government to obtain a majority. Minding the dire lessons of the Weimar Republic, the center parties which otherwise were irreconcilable—conservatives and socialists, clericals and radicals—formed coalitions which by their very terms were condemned to inaction. The resulting *immobilisme* then drove more voters to the extremist parties, and citizens to *incivisme* (withdrawal from political activities). The Communist-led trade unions struck against the government and the war; partisans of the FLN planted bombs in Paris; followers of Poujade refused to pay their taxes.

It should be noted that, despite these frustrations, the Fourth Republic was not all confusion, corruption, and selfishness. Under the surface of political infighting, the economy flourished, cities were being built, families were growing, the population increased. The Schuman Plan and the Monnet Plan stimulated investment and gave direction to industrial development. In the ten years following 1948, factory output increased 50 per cent, farm output 30 per cent. Small shops, which traditionally had weighed the French economy down, now began to merge. By and large, the French people recognized the need for government intervention. The maverick Radical Pierre Mendès-France, first a Gaullist, then a Socialist, and Jean Monnet gave France the Keynesian tools to rebuild her economic life; subsequent administrations obtained special powers to deal with the problems of economic management. At the end of the ten-year period, the French economy was basically healthy and expanding. But the

Fourth Republic was morally undermined; even its defenders were cynical and opportunistic.

The enervating, humiliating war was responsible for wrecking France's stability and security. Half a million Frenchmen were fighting in Algeria. The last government of the republic, in 1958, headed by Pierre Pflimlin (MRP), was ready to negotiate with the Arabs; but the *pieds-noirs*, the army, and some Gaullist politicians, led by Jacques Soustelle and Georges Bidault, staged a coup. The troops in Algeria proclaimed de Gaulle chief of state; in Paris, too, parliament offered him the government. De Gaulle accepted on condition that he be given a free hand. He proposed a new constitution, giving the President the power to appoint cabinet ministers, to dissolve parliament, to rule by decree. The people approved and elected de Gaulle President. He made Michel Debré Premier and Maurice Couve de Murville Foreign Minister. In 1962, Debré was replaced by Georges Pompidou.

The politicians yielded because they knew that only de Gaulle would be able to end the war. When he did, however, he betrayed those who had helped him to power. Army officers and *pieds-noirs* rose against him in 1960 and again in 1961. Now the roles were reversed: The Rightist *Organisation de l'Armée Secrète* (OAS) became the bomb throwers. But de Gaulle used his authority to silence the opposition. He negotiated France's withdrawal from Algeria and the peaceful departure of the French settlers. French capital and know-how was to help the Algerians develop their economy. Especially the Sahara with its rich oil deposits was to be an area of joint exploitation. The *pieds-noirs* were transplanted to southern France and absorbed into French life; they still are a reactionary element in French politics.

Once she had yielded to the Arabs, France could not deny liberty to her black colonies; beginning with Guinea, all of French Africa became free, and de Gaulle reaped the harvest of his good judgment in terms of goodwill among the Third World nations. For ten to fifteen more years, France retained her preponderance in her former colonies, not only financially but politically, too. In neo-Marxist literature, this has often been called "neocolonialism," and eventually the French-speaking Africans parted company with French politics, though not with French markets and venture capital. They retain associate status with the Common Market.

In 1960, Belgium suddenly thrust independence on the Congo, which was not in the least prepared for self-government and soon plunged into a disastrous civil war. British and Belgian mining interests in the Katanga province tried to prolong their hold through the secessionist puppet regime of Moise Tshombe, but failed; Tshombe's mercenaries were defeated by a United Nations expeditionary force—with the United States providing financial, logistic, and political support.

At the same time the South African Union left the British Commonwealth, and in 1963 the Central African Federation broke down after ten years of agony: Northern Rhodesia and Nyasaland became Zambia and Malawi under black leadership, while Southern Rhodesia declared its independence as a republic pledged to uphold white supremacy. Meanwhile, Kenya, Tanganyika (now Tanzania), and Uganda also achieved sovereignty. The Commonwealth became an empty shell, an embarrassment to England, a burden on her treasury. When Labour came to power again in 1964, the government announced its intention to withdraw from all outposts east of Suez; at the end of the 1960's they abandoned Aden and the southern Arabian sheikdoms. The loss of the colonies weakened neither England, France, Belgium, nor the Netherlands. Though individuals or companies may have sustained losses, the countries themselves saved monies and found better use for their energies. England, which had depended most on her commercial and financial preponderance in the Commonwealth, did suffer some setbacks. But the overseas countries were rapidly developing their own industries anyway; the old division of labor between them and the metropolis could no longer be counted upon to feed the latter's staple export industries. A new orientation was imperative, and the somewhat informal EFTA group was no substitute for England's old privileges. The treasury continued to lose gold, and the pound sterling came under attack by speculators.

In August 1961, therefore, Macmillan took the decisive step of applying for membership in the Common Market. The British request was fought violently by ultra-conservative empire fans on the Right and by neo-isolationist Labour representatives on the Left. No longer the head of a mighty empire, Britain did not easily find a role for herself in Europe. Her interests were not identical with those of the Continental countries; her pride would not let her admit that she had become America's junior partner. The truth, however, was brought home to her in a number of humiliating ways. The pound sterling, devalued from $4.03 to $2.80 in 1950, could be defended only by repeated loans from the United States and the International Monetary Fund. Even though England had tested A- and H-bombs, her resources were insufficient to develop missiles of her own. A joint American-British projectile, the Skybolt, however, was abruptly abandoned by President Kennedy after his victory over Khrushchev in the Cuban missile crisis; at the Bahamas Conference, in December 1962, Kennedy forced Macmillan to accept American Polaris rockets and to integrate British submarines into a NATO force. England had detonated its first A-bomb in 1952; France followed in 1960. Both rely on airplanes for delivery, the system that de Gaulle called imaginatively if unrealistically *force de frappe*. But in Part XI we shall see that both countries lacked the economic muscle to stay in the big-power game.

While England on the whole adjusted well to its loss of status, some sections of the public suffered secondary pains. When West Indians, Indians from Africa, and Moslems came to England, race riots erupted in the poorer districts where the new arrivals settled and competed for jobs. A Conservative demagogue, Enoch Powell, stirred up racist feelings which worried his own party. An equally primitive reaction came from an unexpected quarter: the intellectuals, who so far had considered the world their oyster, suddenly expressed resentment over America's cultural imperialism. The idea of empire died hard. But when all the adverse reactions are added up, the British public has come out of the crisis remarkably poised and healthy, firm in its institutions and habits.

With imperialism no longer responsible for some measure of imposed order, the forces of nationalism asserted themselves in the eastern Mediterranean. The Greek Government supported a patriotic movement for *enosis*, or union of Cyprus with Greece. In 1959, Britain granted independence to the island but stipulated that it must remain neutral and that its Vice-President must be of Turkish origin. Cyprus's President, Archbishop Makarios, suspended constitutional guarantees and either instigated or tolerated a pogrom against the Turkish minority. When the communal riots threatened to get out of hand, the Greek and Turkish governments had to step in as protectors of their respective kinsmen; and since both countries were NATO members, the issue created a crisis in the Western defense community, too. Makarios, seeing a chance to play an independent role on the world stage, sought Soviet aid to protect Cypriot independence and became active in Third World politics. The Western powers lost prestige and their alliance was weakened. All Greeks who were dissatisfied with the *status quo* found themselves in natural opposition not only to their government but to NATO as well. The weak Greek monarchy, in turn, growing more dependent on U.S. support, became increasingly alienated from its own people and eventually, as so often before, became dictatorial. Mired between the forces of social change and the mindless nationalism of backward peoples, the West became responsible for a regime in Athens that satisfied no one.

In summarizing Part VII, we may marvel at the resilience of Europe's economic forces and deplore the price she had to pay in terms of political partition and loss of sovereignty. More ominously, another rift began to develop between the governments willing to pay the price for stability and prosperity, and a swelling undercurrent of opinion which felt that the *status quo* was unsatisfactory and that the governments represented conservative interests. Parliamentary parties, trying either to profit from these resentments or afraid to lose contact with the masses, made themselves the mouthpieces of this impatience with the *status quo* and assumed a stance of defending European independence against American presumption. (Parallel developments in the East will be discussed in Part VIII.)

Opposition to the *status quo*, whether social, racial, religious, tribal, or national, thus took the form of resentment against the United States and NATO. Europe had recovered from the war under U.S. tutelage, but the restoration had been linked up with the ideology of anti-Communism. Now, however, on both sides of the iron curtain the national forces asserted themselves again. The American and Russian empires had given Europe stability by dividing it between themselves, so that at best Europe could find its unity only by first redefining its diversity. The second post-war decade, therefore, was to bring profound changes—not all of them for the better—in the self-understanding of the European nations. There was not yet a clear idea of a European future. The nations that had abandoned imperialism fell back on old-fashioned nationalism and defined their own identity in hostility to their protectors rather than in a sense of their own future. We shall pursue this process first in the East.

PART VIII

Eastern Europe After Stalin

CHAPTER I

The Thaw

On March 5, 1953, the old tyrant who had brought misery and greatness to the Soviet Union was dead. Stalin's stubborn deviousness, his ruthless crudity, which had been the basis of his success, had helped to give the Soviet state a bad name all over the world. His death afforded the successors a golden opportunity to repudiate that which was odious without giving up his heritage. He had ruled Russia brutally; he had conquered recklessly, but the blood shed in his wars and purges had written a heroic chapter in Russian history.

Who was this recluse whose enigmatic personality has been the subject of so many books? A Czarist police agent, whom history turned into the executor of its will according to Marx? A great patriot, whom bad luck compelled to become a mass executioner? A wardheeler, whom circumstances catapulted into the role of statesman? Or an adventurer, scheming to subjugate the world to his *idée fixe*?

His was a sinister greatness; destiny availed itself of his wiles. He was Right or Left as it seemed necessary, conciliatory and even "democratic" or intransigent and stubborn, whichever suited his political purposes. To call him a Communist is an insult to a great idea. He used Communists to undermine an enemy government, but he abandoned them to persecution whenever they disturbed his friendly relations with a foreign country. He withdrew from world politics when Soviet Russia was too weak to participate; he threw its weight into the balance when he saw a chance to make it felt. His main obsession was the capitalistic power of the Anglo-Saxon democracies, and he used Japanese, Italian, and German fascism to free himself from their ever-threatening encirclement; he turned intervention (which he always believed imminent) into successful counter-attacks. The reconquest of former Russian territory, the control over satellite governments and neighboring countries, the support of colonial revolutions, alliances with smaller nations, and diversionary actions elsewhere testify to his resourcefulness. But he never exploited to the full, perhaps never even fully understood, the vast increase of power the Soviet Union had gained under his leadership.

From a patriotic point of view, his great merit was to divorce the Soviet Union from the fate of international Communism, to subdue the brother parties to the imperturbable will of the Kremlin, and to liquidate the doctrinaire Communists at home who would place the interest of the idea above the interest of the state. But while ruthlessly rooting out Communists, he never forgot that the Soviet state had been created by a revolution; he knew that Communist Party rule would perish unless revolutionary activities kept its domestic enemies at bay. The totalitarian state was not the instrument of any single class, least of all the proletariat, but not of the bureaucracy either or of any single person. The man who concentrated all power in his own hands was himself the instrument of the policy he had foisted on a reluctant people: self-sufficiency, headlong industrial development, total mobilization.

Of Stalin it has been said that he had to invent himself. Not a genius, he had to be an oracle; not a thinker, he had to be a dogmatist; not a statesman, he had to be a tyrant; not a leader capable of being loved and loyally supported by admiring followers, he had to kill those he could not control. Unable to enjoy the power that haunted him, he was forced to remake it every year. No divergence could be tolerated; no ruling circle could establish itself against the rest of society. His cronies were all in the same prison; a slip of the tongue could be fatal. Without explanation or apology, even without being guilty, a man could be devoured by the merciless machine if his profession, class, group, nationality, or belief was earmarked for purging.

For, contrary to most dictatorships, the system was based, not on a group of little tyrants but on the institution of revolving elites, with each taking turns at being the instrument and the victim of terror. All power groups were involved in this game—the factions, the Party bureaucracy itself, the state bureaucracy, the police, the army, the managers, peasants, workers, and so on—and one man, chained to it, was turning the gigantic wheel.

This infernal machine had an ideological complement: the hostility of unknown, mysterious powers abroad. The nightmarish vision of encirclement built a moat around the socialist fortress, making it impregnable to outside attack but also preventing those inside from leaving it.

Having made Russia great but unhappy and dreaded, Stalin could render his country no further service except by his death which opened the way for a new start. The incipient purge did not come to pass. The Party announced that one-man government would be followed by "collective leadership." Prisoners were released from the isolators. Writers were allowed some leeway. Everybody breathed more freely, and consumers were promised better supplies.

This new era generally is known as the "thaw," so called after the title of a novel by Ilya Ehrenburg. It was a brief respite from dictatorship while Soviet society groped for a new formula of power relations. No one believed that a pluralistic form of government would emerge from the inevitable disputes. Four elites were bidding for the heritage of total dictatorship: the state police (originally Cheka; then GPU, NKVD, and finally KGB), the economic and state managers, the army, and the Party. They were represented by four very different men: the dreaded Beria, the efficient Malenkov, the popular Marshal Zhukov, and the humble Khrushchev. The police contender was summarily liquidated, possibly murdered by his colleagues in the Politburo. The army leaders had against them the same fear of "Bonapartism" which had felled Trotsky and which reflected the force of the three bureaucracies in Party, state, and economy.

The managers had their chance first, in the person of Premier Malenkov. His regime, which lasted from March 1953 to February 1955, might be described as a bureaucracy trying to replace a personal by an administrative dictatorship and appealing for popular support to consumers, managers, the cultural elite, and the citizenry at large. Its great symbol and device, which was to be the cause of its fall, was the separation of state and Party functions. Malenkov, a typical *apparatchik*, staked his future on the state administration, into which, enlisting the managers' help, he expected to integrate the centrifugal forces. Placed before the choice, he decided to be Prime Minister rather than Party Secretary. His scheme was to functionalize the state, to build a stable bureaucracy, and to let technocrats rule and manage. Instead of disappearing, the heavy-handed bureaucrats were to become the instruments of a new start in Soviet life.

Hence, Malenkov's reforms were merely administrative. The Soviet people were not given a voice in the management of their own affairs. But the managers were. Soviet democracy, which formerly had been confined to but a handful of people in the Politburo, now was extended to hundreds; the Politburo changed its name to the less terrifying one of Presidium.

Malenkov also hoped to expand consumer industries and to put a brake on heavy industry and defense production. He expressed his anti-militarism by asserting that in a war Soviet society would suffer just as badly as the capitalists. Up to then dogma had required that in a war only capitalists die; the new Soviet elites thought otherwise. They were longing for some relaxation of the tension that had been Stalin's method of ruling them. They wished to enjoy the fruits of all the sacrifices they had made. Having restored pre-war production levels in their country, they now saw many new possibilities, and intended to use them.

In the satellite countries, a first "thaw" had in fact occurred in 1952 when the "Muscovites," leaders who had come from Moscow after the war, had been replaced by Communists who had stayed in their countries throughout the war. Now a second change of guard brought to power still more "national" Communists, and the most hated Stalinists had to relinquish their offices. Thus Imre Nagy became popular in Hungary, Gomulka rejoined the Central Committee in Poland, Gheorghe Gheorghiu-Dej had to share power with others in Rumania. Generally, as in the Soviet Union, the office of Prime Minister now was separated from that of political boss. A general "liberalization" of the Soviet system seemed to be in the offing, promising both internal reforms and a relaxation of Moscow's hold on the satellites, possibly even a general "disengagement" in Central Europe. Excited by these forecasts and encouraged by obvious uncertainty in the leadership, workers in East Germany, Poland, and Czechoslovakia started riots in June 1953 and wrested concessions from the puppet regimes. But the West failed to help with political initiatives[1] and allowed the revolutions to be repressed.

---

[1] It seems that Beria might have agreed to a retrenchment in return for security. An offer of mutual withdrawal might then have been effective. But could it have saved his life?

Malenkov apparently was unaware that Stalin's gaze was not the only thing that had been glacial and that the thaw was unfreezing many more relationships than had been anticipated. The dynamic Soviet society was bursting at its seams. Malenkov told people to wait but offered nothing to assuage their momentary unrest. Moreover, Soviet foreign policy had come to a complete standstill.

In February 1955, Malenkov had to admit publicly that he was "inexperienced in matters of administration"—he who had been Stalin's right hand in running the war! He ought to have admitted that he was inexperienced in the art of politics. His rival Frol Kozlov criticized Malenkov's "bad style of leadership," his attempts to solve by administrative measures problems that called for political answers. He failed because the functioning of even a totalitarian dictatorship depends on political, not administrative, skill.

If the Soviet Union needed a politician, it had a master of the craft in the person of the First Secretary of the Communist Party. Nikita S. Khrushchev had clung to his post by inclination and shrewdness. He knew that neither police nor managers nor bureaucracy could rule the Soviet Union. The only alternative to Party rule was a military dictatorship. Malenkov's successor, as Premier, was indeed a general. Was Bulganin merely a stand-in for Zhukov? Bold action alone could avert the danger of Bonapartism. If the Party wished to regain the trust Stalin had squandered in its name, it had to repudiate his excesses, his "personality cult," his cruelty, his arbitrary rule, the terror. This was done at the Twentieth Party Congress, in 1956, first by Anastas Mikoyan and then in Khrushchev's "secret speech," which divulged and condemned Stalin's cruelty, his arbitrary, tyrannical methods, his system of terror.

The speech was a tremendous gamble. By purging the Party of its past mistakes, Khrushchev brought the centrifugal forces back into the power structure of the Party state and placed himself in line to succeed Stalin as dictator of the Soviet empire. He crushed the old Stalinist terrorists by debunking and demoting their leader's image. He offered the managerial elite relief from its heaviest burden, insecurity of person. He promised a rule of law and recognition of the new forces that were claiming their share in the nation's leadership.

The Congress also repudiated some old Leninist dogmas: that war was inevitable; that Communists in Western countries cannot acquire power by parliamentary means; that the Russian way was the only right way to Communism. Together, these new insights came to be known as "revisionism."

CHAPTER 2

The Khrushchev Era

RUSSIAN and Soviet history had arrived at one of these Hegelian thresholds where quantity turns into quality. The aims of Soviet policy changed along with its style and techniques. A society that was growing more complex required subtler methods of planning than the crude ordering of percentage increases in production. The network of industrial relations had to be integrated; more people had to concur in decision-making, more factors had to be considered. The Party hierarchy, the military, engineers, administrators, and economic managers had set themselves apart from workers and peasants and emerged as a "state bourgeoisie" which saw the world outside as a field for expansion, as an opportunity for the display of power. The perquisites of this elite were multiplying. They had seen the loot coming in from the conquered areas; they knew what it had contributed to their task of reconstruction. The world market had to provide the coveted consumer goods which were their incentives.

The "toiling intelligentsia" were now entitled to apartments still denied to the lower classes; they participated in important state functions, mingling with the mighty; they sent their sons and daughters to choice schools, spent their vacations in protected resorts, paid no more than 17 per cent taxes, and rode in official cars. But these managing classes did not look at life from the consumer's point of view. They conceived of themselves as leaders, organizers, producers, innovators, builders, planners, and explorers. They had a mission: to catch up with the West and overtake it. Many were young because Stalin's purges and the war had opened careers for them early in life.

Contrary to Western expectations, Soviet society had now achieved material progress within the confines of its system. Despite the bureaucratic bungling, the terror, the frequent zigzags, and the sheer stupidity of Stalin's planning, his industrialization program had, after all, been successful by Russian standards, his state had become the accepted reality, and no one could think of alternative methods to achieve results. Even in agriculture, the one field where basic reform might have permitted a great leap forward, the regime still found it safer to put up with occasional shortages than with free peasants.

By 1950, total industrial output allegedly was twice the pre-war level, though not yet for consumers. Ten years later it had again doubled and just about reached the halfway mark to America's level. Khrushchev predicted that in another decade the Soviet Union would overtake the United States. But Soviet expansion ran into the natural problems of rapid growth. Resources become subject to the law of diminishing returns or, as in the case of steel, of limited use. The Soviet planners found that, instead of outproducing the U.S. steel industry, they might better substitute plastic materials for metals. After running hard, Soviet industry still lags behind American; a Soviet citizen's disposable income is much less than half of what an American can consume even if all noncomparable factors are reckoned in favor of the Soviet Union.[1]

Although the Soviet achievement is impressive in view of the low starting level, lopsided development has left the Soviet Union with significant weaknesses. It had to buy its pipelines abroad and receive Western help in setting up large automotive plants. It has invented and produced rockets and sputniks, nuclear bombs, oil-drilling equipment, and first-rate optical and surgical instruments, but the quality of consumer products often leaves much to be desired.

The Russian townsman may not get more food and better services than in Czarist times. But he does own a radio and a small television set which puts him in touch with at least his part of the world; he reads a newspaper; he flies if he has business in the capital; he is looking forward to better housing and, in another ten or twenty years, perhaps a car. He enjoys a first-class education, an annual vacation at a Crimean resort, full medical care, and a pension. Women are freed from many chores of child care because nursery schools are available to all.

Modern life is slowly coming to the Russian countryside. The peasant uses motorized equipment on his land; the young look toward a future of agro-cities and full equality. Again and again, the government has been forced to satisfy the Soviet people's hunger for goods, even at the expense of military equipment, as the intensive power struggle in the Kremlin called non-Party support and "politicking" into the picture.

More significantly, Khrushchev relaxed ideological controls, at least temporarily. Poets were given freedom of expression; Khrushchev personally intervened to permit publication of works by Yevgeny Yevtushenko and Alexander Solzhenitsyn. Having told the leading cadres of the Party the truth about Stalin's crimes, he rehabilitated some of Stalin's victims. When the Stalinist majority in the Presidium challenged Khrushchev's power, he even called on the Central Committee, representing Party democracy, to support him. On this occasion, for the first and only time in Bolshevik history, a lower echelon overruled a higher Soviet authority.

But the "liberal era" did not last long. The concentration camps remained; the rehabilitation of Stalin's victims was stopped. Khrushchev returned to the earlier view that in a showdown with capitalist armies Soviet power would survive, and he

---

[1] Per capita U.S. steel consumption in 1967 was 1,398 lbs.; in the U.S.S.R., 915 lbs. Total production of cotton, wool, nylon, and rayon yarn was 2.6 million tons in the United States, and 2 million in the Soviet Union. The United States had 104 million telephones in use, the Soviet Union 10 million. The 180 million Americans lived in 53 million dwelling units, the 217 million Russians in 17 million (1960 census figures).

accelerated the arms race. Consumers again had to take a back seat. The army was modernized, motorized, and equipped with automatic weapons. The rocket program was pushed vigorously toward spectacular victories of Soviet over American technology. In quick succession—from August 1957 to September 1959—the Soviet Union tested its first intercontinental missile, launched the Sputnik, and landed the first rocket on the moon.

On the strength of these successes, Khrushchev was able to dismiss Defense Minister Zhukov, the popular marshal who might have become his rival, and later also Bulganin, the Chairman of the Ministerial Council. Once again the posts of Party chief and head of government were in one hand. In 1959, Khrushchev told the Twenty-first Congress that the Soviet Union was entering the state of Communism, where according to Lenin the state was to "wither away" and each was to be given according to his needs. He lashed out against the bureaucrats and even against the Party, which he tried to transform from a workers' vanguard into a people's party. He divided the country into self-governing districts, called *sovnarkhozi*. This ought to have encouraged local initiative but failed to, because people had grown so used to being ordered around. Unlike Tito's, the reforms of Khrushchev were mostly of an administrative nature and did not reach down to factory and village level. Even so, thousands of managers acquired some veto power over decisions they were supposed to carry out.

As a result, the Party, which knew how to organize people, and the bureaucrats, who knew how to administer things, were constantly at war. To arbitrate between them, Khrushchev had to perform a balancing act which required all his skills and all the histrionics of his exuberant nature. Even had he been less ambitious, circumstances would have forced him eventually to take decisions into his dictatorial hands and to subdue the Party that had elevated him. His own "personality cult" was well on its way.

Like Stalin before him, Khrushchev became an oracle making pronouncements on matters outside his competence, from the planting of hybrid corn to the correct taste in paintings. Once again, the leader's rage at the sight of some new-fangled creation could send the luckless artist home to destroy or conceal the evidence of his boldness. Having first lifted the ban on free artistic expression, Khrushchev soon returned to Stalinist orthodoxy. The thaw was freezing over for a second time as a new dictator tried to secure his rule.

But, for all his efforts, Khrushchev never enjoyed as solid a control of the Presidium as did Stalin. He often found it necessary to call on the "people" against bureaucrats and bosses; eventually he had to turn against the Party itself. He split it into two sectors: agriculture and industry; he packed its meetings with "experts" in various fields who were not necessarily members; he announced a "Chemical Party Congress," thus giving the Party a specific assignment on an economic and technical matter devoid of ideological significance; he exhorted the Party henceforth to exchange places with the industrial and administrative managers. He took the great risk of offending the sensibilities and traditions of these faithful organizers of power.

Naturally they began to resent it and to conspire against his schemes—"hare-brained schemes," the outraged bosses were to call them when they finally deposed him.

Khrushchev's earthy personality, his predilection for proverbs, and his common sense will not soon be forgotten either in Russia or abroad, nor will his erratic decisions, his threats of atomic destruction, his gambling with the security of mankind. The next chapter will discuss his foreign policies. Suffice it to say here that he was humiliated by Kennedy and that under him the Soviet Union's rivalry with the People's Republic of China became exacerbated ideologically and irremediable politically.

These setbacks, combined with his dictatorial manner and his domestic zigzagging course, but above all his growing antagonism to the Party cadres, made his overthrow inevitable. Like Malenkov, he had underestimated the Party's strength. Mikhail Suslov, its ideologist, Leonid Brezhnev and Nikolai Podgorny, the organization men he had made, all turned against him. Surprisingly, a vote in the Presidium was sufficient to transform the mighty Khrushchev into a nonperson in one day in October 1964.

CHAPTER 3

The Politics of Coexistence

THERE is a widely held misconception that Stalin's foreign policy was as aggressive as his domestic policy was repugnant. But he told the *New York Times* shortly before his death: "I continue to believe that a war between the United States and the Soviet Union cannot be considered inevitable, that our countries can live in peace in the future." He would have been satisfied, as he told President Truman at Potsdam, to divide Europe between the two big powers. His conception of coexistence was passive, negative, isolationist, and exclusionary. The new collective leadership after his death used the same term, "coexistence,"[1] with a new slant. In keeping with the thaw, they tried to project an image of de-Stalinization and reconciliation. Psychologically and diplomatically, they wished to break out of the besieged fortress. Where Stalin had acted on the principle, "Whosoever is not for me is against me," they declared, "Anyone who is not against me will be counted as a friend."

The plan for this diplomatic revolution was implemented in 1955. In February, Bulganin and Khrushchev flew to Belgrade and apologized for errors which they ascribed to Beria. They did not succeed in bringing Tito back into the Party fold but established warm state-to-state relations. Austria was granted the peace treaty for which she had been waiting ten years. The Russian troops evacuated her territory in return for heavy payments and a tight guarantee of her neutrality.

When, despite these Russian maneuvers, Germany joined NATO, the Soviet leaders frankly admitted their defeat, invited Chancellor Adenauer to Moscow, resumed diplomatic relations, and, as a token of goodwill, released German prisoners of war whom they had held for ten years.

In January 1956, Soviet troops also left the Finnish base of Porkkala, but Finland had to renew the "Treaty of Friendship" for twenty years and practically concede to the Kremlin a veto on her foreign policy.

Coexistence was, for the Soviet leaders, the confirmation of the *status quo*. But they no longer saw this situation as defensive. Their strategists had made a new appraisal of their strength on the world theater, of their military capabilities, and of their atomic power. They saw the power balance shifting from the West to the East.

---

[1] For this purpose, Lenin had used the Russian term *mirnoye sozhitelstvo*—peaceful cohabitation; Stalin and Khrushchev called it *sosushchestvovanie*—existing together.

They no longer needed to fear America's atomic bomb; their air force could deliver telling blows on European targets, which, to quote Khrushchev's cynical word, made "hostages" of Rome, London, Paris, Oslo, and other NATO capitals.

An atomic stalemate had superseded the American monopoly. Dulles had warned that at the slightest provocation he would unleash NATO's "instant massive retaliation," but he could not threaten any offensive. Having promised, before the 1952 election, to "roll back the iron curtain," he now acknowledged the "balance of terror" by which the American power, even though superior to Russia's, was paralyzed. Since Western Europe was so much more densely populated and its industry so much more vulnerable, the Soviet retaliation need not even be as massive as America's. Nor did Western Europeans cherish the prospect of being "liberated" after incineration, and even less did they wish to be the theater of war in a showdown between the super-powers. Their own efforts to gain a voice in world politics remained feeble.

Soviet strategists hardly needed to fear the token thermonuclear weapon England acquired in 1955, or the *force de frappe* outfitted by de Gaulle in the 1960's. The Red Army now had a capacity for "lightning war"; its military journal openly discussed "preventive war."

Having diagnosed the weakness of the Western overseas positions, the Soviet leaders now encouraged the colonial peoples to rise against foreign domination. In announcing "coexistence" at the Twentieth Party Congress, Khrushchev explicitly reserved the right to support "wars of liberation."

Late in 1955, Bulganin and Khrushchev made a triumphant tour through Afghanistan, India, and Burma. They supported these countries' "neutralist" attitudes and praised the spirit of Bandung.[2] The return visits of Nehru, Tito, the King of Afghanistan, and U Nu of Burma brought in their wake other visitors the next year: the Shah of Iran, Sukarno of Indonesia, Ho Chi Minh, as well as political leaders from five European states. While Western diplomacy was standing pat for the defense of the *status quo*, the Soviet Union appeared to be the friend of all colonial and ex-colonial nations that still harbored resentments against their former masters or were acquiring new grudges against America's tutorial attitude. A first great success came in mid-1955: the arms deal with Nasser, which led to the Suez war of 1956, the reversal of the power balance in the Near East, and the alignment of the Soviet Union with Arab nationalism.

The new outlook also permitted more flexible tactics to the Communists in several countries of the West. In France, they became the major parliamentary opposition party. In Italy, they worked in close alliance with the Nenni socialists. In the under-developed countries they established close links with national-revolutionary movements, and even governments.

---

[2] At the Bandung (Indonesia) Conference, in April 1955, Asian and African statesmen called for an end to colonialism and affirmed a neutral attitude in the cold war. Six years later, during a "Third Force" conference in Belgrade, Khrushchev exploded a fifty-megaton bomb, breaking a self-imposed "moratorium," yet the delegates exonerated him on the grounds of "self-defense."

CHAPTER 4

Crisis of Empire

THE overthrow of Stalin's image in the Soviet Union brought in its wake the demolition of his statues in the satellite countries; a wave of criticism and discontent swept away the authority of the Moscow-appointed leaders. Warsaw students met in the "Club of the Free" and the "Crooked Circle," Cracow students in the "Basement," Lodz students in the "Front," Budapest students in the Petöfi Clubs, named for the Byronic poet slain by Russians in the Hungarian revolution of 1849; they published magazines such as *Pro Postu*, which dared to say what was wrong with Communism. Adam Wazyk's *An Ode to Adults* put the finger on the sensitive nerve of freedom denied to Poland. By the middle of 1956, the people were discussing issues they had not dared to mention for years.

Poland was the first country to explode. Demonstrations demanding social, political, and national liberties began in the fall of 1956. Party Secretary Okhab himself and the Stalinist "Natolin" group now proposed to co-opt into the Politburo his former enemy, Gomulka; the veteran Party worker and resistance fighter whose "nationalist deviation" had landed him in jail under Stalin, now was a welcome front for the power structure. Although a reform group, called the Evolutionists, had reservations about his sincerity, Gomulka was elected Secretary. For the first time, the Polish Communists had a leader who identified with the country.

It seemed that a "Polish October" had come. A national Communist Party was seeking its own road to socialism. The Central Committee also asked for the resignation of Marshal Konstantin Rokossovsky, a Russian who served as Poland's Minister of Defense. The latter promptly surrounded Warsaw with Soviet troops, and Khrushchev came to the Polish capital. Gomulka gave him assurances of his own loyalty and promised that Poland would not leave the Warsaw Pact or Comecon on condition that the Soviet troops were withdrawn to their barracks. He publicly opposed the widespread demands for their total withdrawal. Subsequently he remained a faithful follower of Soviet leadership, since only Russia can protect Poland against German irredentism and only the Kremlin can protect the Communists' hold over Poland. At the time, however, the people greeted their "liberation" with wild outbursts of public rejoicing. The demonstrations continued through the rest of October, and the enthusiasm increased when news from Budapest told of another anti-Soviet revolution.

While in Poland the people came to celebrate the victory which one Communist faction had won for them over another, in Hungary the people themselves arose against their oppressors and staged a revolution of deep significance socially, politically, and intellectually. Student groups had long been preparing their resistance; workers had long been restless. The ferment had seized all Hungarians, in particular the young and the most dedicated socialists. This was no mere rebellion of a disgruntled nation, no mere outburst of the downtrodden, but a movement which entered the stage with mature ideas and with deliberation. It was not anti-Communist in the sense of a reactionary movement; it was a socialist, liberal, humanist movement against Communist and foreign oppressors. From its first day it reinvented the instrument of *soviets* (councils), which every proletarian revolution discovers for itself. Students and workers simultaneously raised the flag of self-government and freedom under Communism. Their militias took arms against the hated AVH (secret police). They demanded freedom and a change of government and system.

Nor was their rage appeased by a mere change of guard. The popular Imre Nagy became Prime Minister again (October 23); Gerö yielded the Party secretariat to János Kádár (October 25), also a martyr of Stalinist persecution and reputedly a friend of Tito's. Yet the revolution continued to broaden and deepen until the oppressive state collapsed and all public buildings were in the insurgents' hands. The Hungarian Army made common cause with the people; even some Russian soldiers expressed sympathy with the movement. As in Poland, Soviet troops converged on the capital (October 24); but in contrast to what took place in Poland, they immediately went into action. Although so far no anti-socialist forces had joined the fighting and Tito condemned the Russian action, *Pravda* justified the intervention as necessary to crush the "counter-revolution." As the revolution spread, however, the Russians felt forced first to withdraw their troops from Budapest to the eastern and northern borders.

Nagy now invited all democratic parties to join his government. Mikoyan and Suslov, hurriedly flown to Budapest, promised (October 29) an early evacuation of all Soviet troops; the following day the Soviet Presidium backed them up with a generous, statesmanlike declaration "on friendship and co-operation between socialist states," assuring the People's Republics of "full equality, respect for territorial integrity, independence and sovereignty, and noninterference in domestic affairs." As soon as the truce became effective (October 30), Nagy announced free elections and the revival of political parties.

The revolution had won. Budapest was free of Soviet troops. After the old Socialists, other parties also dared to reappear. The prisons were opened; even reactionaries and Nazi collaborators like Cardinal Mindszenty were freed, though as yet they did not become active politically. The old Hungarian flag was hoisted.

With this, the Hungarian revolution had overstepped the mark which the Polish revolution had respected. No longer "national-Communist," it lost the support of the "liberal" Communists. Gomulka, Tito, Kádár, and Mao Tse-tung, who had condemned the first Soviet intervention, suddenly faced with freedom inside the Soviet orbit, called it counter-revolution. Nagy was known to favor neutralism for Hungary.

On November 1, fresh Russian troops crossed the border. Having warned Mikoyan of the consequences of this move, Nagy denounced the Warsaw Pact and proclaimed the neutrality of "free, independent, democratic Hungary." But he proposed to negotiate with the Soviet occupation authorities.

Had the Western powers at that point mustered the courage to offer the Soviet government a face-saving bargain—for example, withdrawal of all foreign troops from Central Europe—they might possibly have saved Hungary and gained freedom for all satellite countries. For the Russians apparently were hesitating. Though they accused the Hungarian movement of being "fascist" and "Western-inspired," they could hardly conceal from themselves that the Hungarian people as a whole were behind Nagy and that he was no Gomulka. Nor was Hungary, like Poland, naturally dependent on Russian protection.

When the Hungarian negotiators arrived at Soviet headquarters on November 2, they were treacherously seized and, later on, shot. On November 4, Soviet tanks moved into Budapest but met with fierce resistance. For an entire week, superior Russian forces fought the Hungarian Army, police, and militias. Nagy took shelter in the Yugoslav Embassy, which later extradited him to the Russians and to certain death. Cardinal Mindszenty found refuge in the U.S. Embassy.

As their man to replace Nagy the Russians installed Kádár, a man initially as critical of Rakosi and Stalin as Nagy himself. Like Gomulka, he had a reputation for liberalism and patriotism; he had been a purge victim in 1952. In this crisis he kept faith with Russia and betrayed his fellow Communists. Declaring that Nagy was controlled by counter-revolutionaries, Kádár formed a new, genuinely Communist government and called for Russian assistance. Thus, 107 years after the first suppression of Magyar freedom by Russian troops, he legitimized the second.

One hundred eighty thousand Hungarians fled to the West; many who failed to escape were killed or subdued. The police again ruled with an iron hand. Striking workers were arrested and leading intellectuals were sentenced to long prison terms.

In the aftermath of their October revolutions, Poland and Hungary moved toward opposite ends in the Communist spectrum. Gomulka abolished one freedom after another and was unable to put Poland on an even keel. Her economy was flagging; her standard of living failed to rise. In Hungary, a regime that at first was hated as no other before was able to ingratiate itself with the people, to relax rigid controls, even to grant cultural freedom within limits; living standards were allowed to rise somewhat, and coffee houses began to thrive. Kádár was no less loyal to Russia than Gomulka, but he ruled less obtrusively and did not bother people with ideology. Artists were allowed to express themselves; Jews were not persecuted. The Kádár regime was more like Horthy's, Gomulka's more like Pilsudski's. The mentor of Marxist philosophy, George Lukács, who had taken part in the Nagy government, was pardoned, and his fame as the leading revisionist thinker brought credit to his government.

Khrushchev had not been mistaken in gambling on Gomulka's loyalty. While the people were jubilant over their new freedom, Gomulka was already scheming to restrict it. He gave them elections of sorts—a list of candidates, headed by Communists, from which the voters were asked to strike a given number. Even Cardinal Stefan Wyszynski appealed to their good sense: Elect all Communist candidates or else the Russians will move in. The voters complied and gave Gomulka the farcical mandate to build a non-Russian socialism under Russian bayonets.

Moscow graciously wiped the Polish debts off the slate and allowed the Polish economy a respite. The church also was rewarded. A *modus vivendi* was negotiated allowing it greater freedom than in any other Communist country. The real winners of the October revolution were the peasants, for they were spared collectivization. But the freedom-loving intelligentsia in the cities and the students were soon to be robbed of their gains. Only a year later *Pro Postu* was banned; in 1961 the student club Crooked Circle was dissolved.

Russia's intervention in Hungary provoked a crisis among Western Communists and lost Khrushchev his reputation as a "liberal" in those Western circles where Russophilia was chic. But the Western governments were unable to exploit the Soviet embarrassment. The United Nations Security Council failed to place the matter on its agenda while there was still time to intervene. Secretary-General Dag Hammarskjöld did not go to Budapest to rescue persecuted fighters. Eisenhower published a lame declaration which practically conceded that Hungary belonged in the Soviet orbit and did not demand a withdrawal of Soviet troops; for all practical purposes he had recognized Moscow's conquests in World War II.

Nor was this the time to "roll back the iron curtain," as John Foster Dulles had promised. America's close allies at that point were engaged in the first Suez war— which was universally condemned by the Third World. In the United Nations, Eisenhower joined the majority and the Soviet Union in pressing for withdrawal of the French and British, while Khrushchev, unruffled by the world's outcry against his own aggression in Hungary, publicly threatened to send volunteers to Suez and to atom-bomb London and Paris.

The coincidence that the Hungarian revolution and the Suez war happened in the same week had consequences far beyond the separate significance of either of these events. The Western powers' moral and physical paralysis condemned them to inaction in Central Europe and to defeat in the Near East at the same time and eliminated two of them from the club of big powers. Of the two remaining super-powers, one had just demonstrated that it was capable of ruthless and decisive action; the other had faltered. The Suez war together with the Hungarian debacle marks the turning point for the balance of power. From then on the center of gravity moved almost steadily away from the West and toward the East.

CHAPTER 5

Polycentrism and Revisionism in Eastern Europe

IN the wake of Khrushchev's victories in Poland, Hungary, and the United Nations, "national" Communism turned into a hollow phrase for another decade. Tito received no thanks for the diplomatic help he had lent the Russian intervention.

Even so, the Soviet empire was never to be the same again. Comecon was reorganized to allow the development of the satellite industries, Moscow had to negotiate with its partners, had to recognize their sovereignty, to ask their permission to station troops on their soil. The Soviet Union also supported the initiative of Poland's Foreign Minister, Rapacki, to denuclearize Central Europe, a proposal pointing to the ultimate withdrawal of all foreign troops from Europe. In 1959, Rumania followed up this program with a proposal to conclude a new Balkan Pact prohibiting the installation of rocket bases.

Meanwhile the Moscow leadership had begun to quarrel with Mao Tse-tung. The development of Chinese Communism is not part of this survey, though its end product, the so-called cultural revolution, made an inordinate impression on Western Europe's neoromantics in the late 1960's. Nor had the differences between Moscow and Peking attracted much notice before the formal break in 1961. There were divergences of policy, however. Mao saw an opportunity to harass Western positions in South Asia at exactly the moment when Khrushchev was ready not only to coexist with capitalism but to hold summit meetings with its leaders. He berated Moscow for encouraging "revisionism"—a grave charge among Communists.

A conference of eighty-one Communist parties, held in Moscow in November and December 1960, reached compromise formulas declaring "coexistence a form of class war" and no longer referring to the Soviet Union as the "Fatherland of All Toilers." Two centers of Communist thought were now recognized in the "camp," with a non-recognized Yugoslav variant "number three" outside the camp. The latter continued to inspire dissident movements in European Communism east as well as west of the iron curtain.

In East Germany, the philosopher Walter Harich, the playwright Bertolt Brecht (who died before the Hungarian revolution), as well as some economic experts had started a movement for greater liberalization, for freedom of thought, freedom to elect representatives, and even industrial self-government. In Italy, the leader of the Communist Party himself, Palmiro Togliatti, strove to liberate his Party from the Soviet model intellectually and from "the iron dependence upon the Soviet Union" in matters of policy and organization. Elsewhere, veterans left the Communist Party in disgust and tried to set up new groups with a Titoist or Luxembourgian orientation. Norwegian and Danish delegates took part in the 1958 Congress of the Yugoslav Party, and the Polish ambassador stayed in Belgrade when his colleagues from other satellite states left in protest.

The program adopted by that congress was to be the first document of reform Communism. It recognized the changes that have transformed private capitalism into a new model of corporate, organized capitalism. At the same time it criticized the transformation of the Soviet state into the bureaucratic dictatorship of a new class. It rejected the view that Communists had a monopoly on revolution and that there was only one road to socialism. In its chapter on socialist economy, the Yugoslav program declared that planning was not a sufficient, and nationalization only a temporary, characteristic, but that self-government in industry was essential, as was personal freedom. The Yugoslav philosopher Gajo Petrovic went even further and envisaged the withering away of the Communist Party. His colleague Svetozar Stojanovic proposed specific measures to federalize and democratize the Party.

The crucial question for revisionism, however, was the attitude toward the Soviet Union and its empire. The Yugoslavs felt that the term "coexistence" as used by the Russians posed the false alternative of choosing between two "camps" and actually presupposed and perpetuated this limitation of choices. They envisaged peace not as a balance of two camps but as the breaking-up of blocs and empires. Rumania went a step further and claimed the same right as the Soviet Union to deal independently with Western powers. Just as Yugoslavia had done ten years earlier, Rumania began to resent the one-sided investment programs Comecon tried to impose on her economy for the Soviet Union's benefit. As an underdeveloped country, she was slated to be a supplier of raw materials and foodstuffs; even the few industrial sites she was allowed to develop had to be located near Soviet markets. In the 1960's, Rumania therefore adopted a Six Year Plan of rapid industrial growth and increasing exchanges with the West.

The same tendency was apparent in Poland; she even took a $200 million credit from the United States. Of all the satellite countries, Poland and the DDR have succeeded best in balancing their foreign trade. East Germany's best customer is, for political reasons, the Federal Republic. Poland divides its trade evenly between Eastern and Western markets.

In his domestic policies, too, Gomulka remained flexible. Collectivization was stopped; relations with the Roman Catholic Church were almost cordial as long as Cardinal Wyszynski supported the regime and refrained from consulting with the Vatican. For safety's sake, however, Gomulka also supported an independent Catholic organization, PAX.

Poland has more private enterprises than even Yugoslavia. But her national independence is curbed by geographic factors and fear of Germany, and her cultural renascence has been interrupted by frequent relapses into censorship and repression.

The Rumanian Government has remained more Stalinist in domestic affairs. It nationalized the Roman Catholic Church. The Hungarian minority in Transylvania had at first been given autonomous rights; but in 1960 the region was split up and the parts distributed among districts with Rumanian majorities. In economic policies, Rumania is orthodox. Only 15 per cent of its land is in peasant hands. But under the leadership of Gheorghiu-Dej and his successor Nicolae Ceausescu, Rumania has made herself largely independent of Russian tutelage and has conducted a national foreign policy of her own. She has become estranged from Comecon and the Warsaw Pact; she exchanged ambassadors with West Germany in 1967; her troops did not take part in the 1968 invasion of Czechoslovakia. She did not vote with the Soviet bloc in the United Nations on Near Eastern affairs, and displayed some independence in the 1972 European Security Conference.

Bulgaria saw the return of the Stalinist Vulko Chervenkov, who provided occasional "Chinese" features such as a "great leap forward," but under Todor Zhivkov it veered into a more moderate course while staying close to Soviet policies in both domestic and foreign affairs.

In the arts, too, the climate changed in the satellite countries, though tentatively and with many backslidings. While in the early 1940's their music had to sound Russian and all their literature had to conform to the drab style of "socialist realism," in the 1960's folk music was resurrected; painters were able to discard the heroic style and catch up with modern trends in the West; writers could be realistic (though not satirical); philosophers could once again ask basic questions. As Soviet historians dismantled the Stalin legend, so Polish patriots at last were permitted to remember their sufferings and their deeds in World War II. Rumania, Hungary, and Poland restored to places of honor their classical and romantic literature of the past; for a while, the modernists prevailed in the writers' groups. And all these Communist countries, including Czechoslovakia and East Germany, proudly cultivate the monuments of their national kings.

Though reaction set in again in the mid-1960's, some Polish intellectuals openly quit the Party and the Writers' Union. The Party philosophers, Adam Schaff in Poland and Robert Havemann in East Germany, denied that *partiinost* (Party-think) could be effective and healthy in matters of taste and conscience. They were duly censored; but they had made their point, and the ferment of criticism never settled down again. The foremost Polish revisionist philosopher, Leszek Kolakowski, eventually sought asylum in the West; the Czech writer Ladislav Mnacko went to Israel. East German intellectuals had been fleeing to the West in great numbers—the Expressionist philosopher Ernst Bloch, the critic Alfred Kantorowicz, the novelist Uwe Johnson among them—until all exits were sealed in 1961. The folk singer Wolf Biermann was placed under surveillance and forbidden to perform in public. With few exceptions, the writers who stayed either fell silent or had to write as ordered. As one of them observed: To be relevant, one must be persecuted.

The German Democratic Republic had the most Stalinist, the most bitterly hated, for a long time the least secure of all satellite regimes. One hundred and three thousand East Germans defected to West Berlin in the first half of 1961; in July, the stream swelled to 25,000; during the first ten days of August, to 30,000. The majority of the refugees were skilled workers, doctors, engineers, scientists, agronomists; they were the elite of an elitist society. Not poverty but love of freedom drove them to leave their positions. On August 13, a wall began to go up all around West Berlin, insulating the population of the German Democratic Republic from the West. Many people were shot trying to scale this shameless monument to tyranny.

As a symbol, the Wall testified to the fear of the tyrants. But it has given the East German rulers security. The people in the East, believing that the West failed them politically and ideologically, stopped looking across the Elbe River for leadership. Disappointed, they fell back into political apathy, and their government then turned their bewilderment to advantage. While adhering to a strictly Stalinist Party rule and closest ideological supervision, Walter Ulbricht introduced sweeping reforms in two fields where the apolitical Germans have always excelled: education and economic organization. Higher education was based on a comprehensive track system, giving every student the training that would develop his capabilities to the point where they would be most useful to the state.

In July 1963, Ulbricht announced a "New Economic System" reminiscent of Lenin's NEP. Disregarding the shocked protest of his old-guard bureaucrats, he gave far-reaching powers of decision to plant managers, district and county economic councils, industry cartels, and individual ministries. Instead of detailed production norms that had to be met ton-by-ton, year-by-year, managers were given "target figures," broad guidelines, and "perspectives." The success of a plant was no longer to be measured by the amount of goods it had produced regardless of cost, but by its unit profit. With sound methods of cost accounting, of money incentives for managers and bonuses for workers, the notion of a "socialist market" brought managerial thinking to the stifled economy. Under the guidance of young, enthusiastic technocrats, production soared and made East Germany the most advanced country in Eastern Europe. It is true that the excessive demands of Comecon negated many benefits of power and flexibility after only two years, and that their leader, Erich Apel, head of the Planning Commission, committed suicide. But the bulk of the reform measures were maintained, so that the German Democratic Republic now has the unique distinction of a non-Stalinist economy administered by a Stalinist government, or "revision without revisionism."

The ideas so successfully used in Poland for the agrarian sector, and in the German Democratic Republic for all industry, had been developed earlier by the Polish economist Oskar Lange under the name of "market socialism." They were further elaborated by younger economists in Poland, Germany, and Yugoslavia. Their new protagonists are interested neither in freedom nor in a revision of Marxism or Communism; they simply find that the technical problems of organizing the economy in their own country are very similar to those they can study in books by Western technocrats and economists. A certain "convergence" is taking place on this managerial level, even though the divergence between political philosophies and political practices remains unchanged.

Each of the satellite countries uses a different system of incentives and bonuses to stimulate output and assure a better distribution of the product. Poland allows a large percentage of consumer supplies to go through private hands, but controls enterprise through taxation, rationing, and price guidelines. Eighty-five per cent of the farm land also is in private hands. Hungary gives 10 per cent of the harvest to members of collective farms. In Yugoslavia, most collectives were dissolved and industrial planning leaves considerable discretion to local managers. Yugoslavia still is largely underdeveloped, and her economic record is not necessarily one of greatest efficiency. Yet she is proud that her system of democratic controls sets her apart from the satellite countries.

Eventually, the new ideas were bound to attract the attention of the Soviet economists. Yevgeni Liberman is the exponent of "market socialism" in the Soviet Union. He has repeatedly insisted that his ideas are not "revisionist" in any philosophical sense; that they merely reflect the need for flexible responses to the increasing complexity of highly industrialized systems. He would expand peasants' individual plots, and in the consumer sphere allow prices to find their own level. He proposed decentralized planning along the lines of East Germany and Yugoslavia. But so far he has failed to convince the bureaucracy that such flexibility would not diminish its power.

Soviet peasants, however, were given more latitude in selling the surplus product of their private plots, and a semi-official gray market for secondhand articles has always existed. As an experiment, Khrushchev opened some departments in Moscow stores to a free market in which suppliers were allowed to compete. Aleksei Kosygin, then Vice-President, initiated a liberalization program, beginning with some textile and clothing factories. After he had risen to first place in the administration, he went even further and made the entire textile sector subject to the law of supply and demand. Within the limits of their allocation of raw materials and investment funds, factories now were told to make a profit—that is, to compete in price and quality, to keep strict accounts of costs, and to distribute bonuses or reinvest profits. The Twenty-third Congress, in 1966, adopted this principle for a limited number of consumer industries and consequently refrained from establishing an over-all development plan for the next five or seven years, as previous congresses had done. Needless to say, heavy industry, investment, defense supplies, foreign trade, farm output, and most other economic activities were still being controlled by the appropriate ministries and by Gosplan, the central planning authority. But the reform, timid though it was, gave the green light to bolder experiments in the satellite countries. Notably, the Czech economist Ota Šik, who was to defect after the 1968 invasion, has drawn all the revisionist conclusions of "market socialism."

CHAPTER 6

The Fall of Khrushchev
and the New Party Regime

REWARDING the gigantic effort of a crash program, the Soviet Sputnik opened the space age on October 4, 1957, months before the Americans were able to catch up, and for many years Soviet technology retained its lead. On April 12, 1961, Major Yuri Gagarin became the first man to travel outside the earth's atmosphere.

The effect of these Soviet successes was not merely psychological. Europe was living in the shadow of superior Soviet weapons, which Khrushchev never stopped rattling. The Intercontinental Ballistic Missile (ICBM) also made America vulnerable to atomic attack; its guarantee of European security was getting less believable. Khrushchev therefore felt that the time had come to normalize the situation in Europe. He told the Western powers that they must recognize the partition of Germany and get out of Berlin by June 1959. To obtain a reprieve, Eisenhower invited Khrushchev to Washington and admitted that the situation of Berlin was indeed anomalous. A summit conference was called to Paris for May 1960.

Khrushchev thought he had won. But the Western powers stood firm on their rights. Before the summit opened, de Gaulle told Khrushchev that he had gone too far. Fortunately, an air accident gave the Soviet leader a face-saving "out": Russian rockets shot down an American reconnaissance plane over Smolensk. Pretending great anger, Khrushchev loosened a stream of obscene verbiage, upset the summit, broke off the disarmament negotiations, and made himself a nuisance at the U.N. General Assembly. He revoked his ultimatum, but he also demonstrated that the Western powers could not abrogate the partition of Germany. A wall went up in Berlin, hermetically sealing the East off from the West (Chapter 5).

This was the climax of the cold war—and its turning point. The two Europes were neatly separated. Sooner or later, the Western powers would have to recognize the Russian conquests of World War II. Further pursuit of the cold war had no purpose. De Gaulle, returned to power in 1958, was the first to see that, once the atomic stalemate guaranteed Europe's security, the individual members of NATO gained room for maneuvering. Consequently, he embraced some of the "neutralist" ideology, which recommended him to the Left and to other critics of NATO. This trend met with similar tendencies in the Warsaw Pact countries, which we are going to discuss in the next chapter. The prospect may have made Khrushchev bolder *vis-à-vis* the West just when he needed a victory. For he had suffered reverses in the Congo and in Peking. To regain the initiative, therefore, he decided to gamble once again in the fall of 1962. Renewing his ultimatum on Berlin, he installed atomic rockets in Cuba, probably hoping for some reasonable trade-off. If Kennedy were to withdraw from his outposts in Europe, the Soviet Union might abandon Castro, whose maintenance cost a million rubles a day.

Again, the Russian bluff was called. The missile crisis of October 1962 revealed the basic unpreparedness of Soviet arms. Khrushchev's star began to wane. At the same time his difficulties on the domestic scene increased; he found himself confronted with the choice of either yielding to the bosses and restoring the hated image of Stalin, or destroying the Party. As we have seen, he was preparing a Thermidor, the greatest crime imaginable against Soviet ideology; he was dismantling "proletarian" power, he was debasing the Party. He had broken the unity of international Communism by publicly quarreling with the Chinese. He had provoked defections in the empire and permitted the nationalist deviation in Eastern Europe. Above all, he threatened to take power from the Party bosses.

In October 1964, therefore, the Politburo, resuming its old name and its proper function, deposed Khrushchev from both his Party and state functions, apparently with the support of the army and of the apparatus of heavy industry. The Soviet Union at that point was ruled by a new collective leadership, from which emerged a new troika: Leonid Brezhnev became Secretary General of the Party, Aleksei Kosygin took the title of Premier as chief technocrat and administrator, Nikolai Podgorny officiated as President of the Russian Socialist Federation of Soviet Republics. For a while their power was threatened by Alexander Shelepin, who had his hands in the labor, youth, and police apparatuses, and by Mikhail Suslov, the Party's chief ideologist; the latter lost out in the Czech crisis, while General Andrei Grechko, Chief of Staff and Minister of Defense, supported the troika.

This new regime has not solved any of the domestic problems that brought it to power. But it has stopped the trend toward revisionism, restored the Soviet Army's prestige abroad, opened a new era of world politics for the Soviet Union, and returned to Stalin some of his former glory.

While Brezhnev might best be described as an organization man rather than by his ideological alignment on the Right-Left scale, the Twenty-third Party Congress, in 1966, showed a perceptible shift toward orthodoxy. The conservative forces made further gains when the diplomatic situation tightened and dissent once again looked like treason. Revisionist works already published were not withdrawn from circulation, but no new writings by Vladimir Dudintsev or Solzhenitsyn could be published. When Daniel and Sinyavsky were sent to Siberia, however (Chapter 8), for uttering critical thoughts, many Soviet dignitaries as well as students expressed sympathy for the prisoners. A letter signed by twenty-five prominent people voiced dismay at

Stalin's partial rehabilitation by the Twenty-third Congress. Among the signers were Pyotr Kapitsa and Andrei Sakharov, atomic physicists; Maya Plisetskaya, prima ballerina of the Bolshoi; Innokenti Smoktunovsky, actor; Ivan Maisky, former ambassador; the writers Boris Slutsky and V. F. Tendryakov.

The Soviet authorities could not totally suppress this opposition. They had to release people from prison or asylum because highly placed friends interceded with the government. Most significant, the movement spread to scientists, whose co-operation is essential for defense and development. The culmination of this literature of dissent, so far, was an essay, *Thoughts About Progress, Peaceful Coexistence, and Intellectual Freedom*, by the brilliant physicist Andrei Sakharov, the father of Russia's H-bomb. Many scholars supported him. Still more daring, though politically less sound, was Andrei Amalrik's pamphlet, *Can the Soviet Union Survive Until 1984?* Many young writers for a while supported "civil liberties" demonstrations. A branch of the League for Human Rights was founded. Apparently yielding to pressure from abroad, the Soviet government (and other Communist countries) allowed the emigration of thousands of Jews who for many years had vainly tried to go to Israel.

Since 1968, a semi-legal magazine, *Chronicle of Current Events*, was published in *samizdat* (typed copies) until the authorities found it necessary to crack down on it in 1972. The paper was extremely well informed; its editors obviously were known to the police, but protected by highly placed persons. Likewise, a manuscript purporting to be Khrushchev's memoirs was sold to Western publishers by persons known to be in good standing with the Soviet intelligence apparatus.

When these rumblings of an opposition threatened to spread among the intelligentsia, the authorities started a new propaganda wave against traitors who allowed alien ideas to gain ground in Russia. Once more free thought became dangerous. The Brezhnev-Kosygin team battened down the hatches, brought ideology into line, and once again placed the people on a mobilization diet. A crash program of naval and rocket armament put the Soviet Union on a par with the United States; Khrushchev's strategic goals—coexistence on the basis of condominium, *détente*, and progressive deceleration of the arms race, eventual priority for the consumer industries—were scuttled. Once more the aim was to beat the Americans in the Third World and to push them out of Europe.

Opportunities were provided by a combination of lucky coincidences. President Johnson was bogged down in Vietnam; de Gaulle's vanity destroyed the unity of NATO; a new German administration needed to display progress toward *détente*; Israel stepped into a trap which triggered another Arab *jihad* (holy war) and opened a chance for the Soviet Navy to challenge American power in the Mediterranean. Western Europe's soft underbelly and its oil supply became vulnerable to Soviet maneuvers. From a position of strength Soviet diplomacy was able to demand new negotiations on European security and disarmament.

But it was challenged on its own home ground. The Chinese would not be appeased by Khrushchev's ouster; two attempts to organize another Communist world conclave failed; Rumania, Czechoslovakia, even Bulgaria showed signs of weariness with the Warsaw Pact; eventually the collapse of the Antonin Novotny administration in Prague forced another showdown between the forces of reform and the forces of reaction within the Communist world.

CHAPTER 7

Spring in Prague,
Followed by Winter in the Empire

BUCKING the revisionist trend in the satellite empire, we have seen, there remained two exceptions: Walter Ulbricht in Germany, a petty Stalinist tyrant whose strategic position in the cold war forced the Kremlin to back him to the hilt, and the dour Antonin Novotny in Czechoslovakia, last fortress of an unreconstructed Stalinism. Czechoslovakia was the only Communist country engaged in a regular *Kulturkampf*. It kept Archbishop Josef Beran imprisoned for reasons not connected with any wartime affiliations. De-Stalinization had been slow and half-hearted; but in 1956, Slovaks, Ukrainians, Hungarians, and Germans were given some self-administration, and in 1959, *kolkhoz* peasants were recognized as owners of the land they had brought into the co-operative. Only a quarter of all arable land was in 8,000 *kolkhozes*; 15 per cent of soil under the plow was state property.

Completely subservient to Moscow, Novotny agreed to unfavorable trade terms with the Soviet Union. As a result, the Czechoslovak economy was in permanent difficulties. The government failed to obtain the managers' and workers' co-operation; life was drab. The eternal soldier Schweik reasserted his mulish presence. It was obvious that, to avoid bankruptcy, Czechoslovakia had to seek a basic reorientation in domestic and foreign policies, in economic and administrative routines. Ota Šik pleaded for a "socialist market" to allow honest price relations and sound cost-accounting. But the Party apparatus resisted all basic reforms.

Since 1962, the Slovak intelligentsia was in open rebellion. In 1963, the Central Committee expelled leading Stalinists from its ranks, rehabilitated the martyred Slansky and Clementis, and began to talk of "humanist socialism." Not a single Stalinist ran for office in the Slovak elections of 1964. Eventually, Czechoslovakia, like Bulgaria and Rumania, sought economic ties with the West and even began a *rapprochement* with West Germany.

The Writers' Congress of 1967 criticized the leadership; during the second Suez war the people expressed their sympathy with Israel; on the thirtieth anniversary of Thomas Masaryk's death thousands demonstrated for independence and democracy. In November 1967, a student demonstration, brutally suppressed, triggered a wide sympathy movement, which in January 1968 brought to power a coalition of liberals and Slovaks in the Central Committee. This could not have happened without a nod from Brezhnev, who had abandoned Novotny at the December meeting of the Central Committee. The new Premier was Oldrich Černik, the strongest critic of bureaucratic planning; the new First Secretary Alexander Dubček, a Slovak and a liberal—and also, as was soon to become clear, a democrat and a humanist.

With Dubček stood students, writers, and artists who had long been pleading for cultural freedom, old Communists who were ashamed of their Party's degeneracy and police methods, Slovaks who desired self-government and Czechs who loathed the Russian overlords, economists, and plant managers who despaired of operating under prevailing conditions, reformers in government and Party who were sick and tired of dogmatism. "A radical solution of the present crisis," said the philosopher Karel Kosik, "is possible only if bureaucracy and police are replaced by a socialist democracy. The basis of the present system is the absence of any political rights for the masses; the basis of a future system must be the political equality of all citizens." Michael Lakatos, of the Academy for Constitutional Law, even advocated "pluralism." It was a bloodless, democratic revolution, as the philosopher Ivan Svitak explained, a change in the uses of power without changing the economic foundations of socialism.

Before long the Czechs were able to read in their newspapers what had been going on during the last twenty years: Kafkaesque trials, police murders, Jan Masaryk's defenestration. Soon they demanded free discussion, public debate of issues in a parliament, even legalizing of an opposition party, the right to strike, the independence of the judiciary. The Party adopted an "action program" which could have been written by Tito. Dubček declared that socialism must grant its citizens more personal freedom than do bourgeois democracies. A "Two Thousand Word Manifesto" for free speech received 40,000 letters of support. Ota Šik proclaimed that civil liberties were a precondition of greater productivity.

"Spring" had broken out in Prague. The people of Czechoslovakia were happy; they saw the future in bright colors. There was no retreat from socialism. No collective farm was dissolved; prices were fixed as before; the plan was being fulfilled. Dubček created a market for ideas, not for goods, and he spoke of "socialism with a human face." In March 1968, the National Assembly elected Ludvik Svoboda (formerly commander of the Czech troops in the Soviet Union, but disgraced under Novotny) to the Presidency. *Svoboda* is the Czech word for "liberty."

Word spread through the other socialist countries: We, too, need a Svoboda, a Šik, a Dubček. Even in the Soviet Union people began to look toward Prague. None of this pleased the Gomulkas, Zhivkovs, Ulbrichts, and Brezhnevs. This was indeed revisionism. What if such a regime were to open diplomatic relations with the former enemy (as Rumania had already done)?

Up to that year East Germany, Poland, and Czechoslovakia had formed a "strategic triangle" within the Warsaw Pact. Now Czechoslovakia seemed to revive the Little Entente which once had linked her to Rumania and Yugoslavia—and all three to France. The old-timers spread rumors that Czechoslovakia was in the hands of saboteurs and subversives who were trying to pull her out of the Warsaw Pact and to lead her back into bourgeois democracy and reaction. "Germans," "Jews," "cosmopolitans" were once again denounced as seducers of the Czech people.

Fear gripped the Soviet and East German leaders. Warsaw Pact maneuvers were held in Czechoslovakia during June. Warsaw Pact leaders (all except the Rumanians) met to condemn Czech revisionism and to warn the Czechs that another German invasion was at hand. Specifically, they denounced the abandonment of "democratic centralism" and the disregard of the "Party's leading role." Late in July, the Czech and Soviet politburos met at the bordertown of Cierna. Dubček assured the Russians that his country would stay inside the socialist camp, but on his return to Prague he declared that he had signed nothing. Early in August again, he met the Russians in Bratislava—but only to sign his death warrant. The final communiqué stated that "Socialist countries must come to each others' aid."

On the night of August 20-21, five Warsaw Pact armies (excluding Rumania) marched into Prague—uncalled, for not a single member of the Central Committee would issue them an invitation. Dubček, Černik, and other leaders were arrested and flown to Moscow. There they had to agree to humiliating conditions: the stationing of Soviet troops on their soil; the abandonment of the rehabilitation campaign; the slowing down of economic reforms; the restoration of censorship; the suppression of non-Communist opinions and organizations; the gradual replacement of their own leadership in the Central Committee by Brezhnev's handpicked men.

According to the so-called Brezhnev doctrine, no state that has once been Communist can be allowed to lapse back into a pre-Communist system and no state that is part of the Soviet system of alliances may leave it. "A Communist government is responsible not only to its own people but to all Communist countries and the Communist world movement. Recognizing the Czechs' right to self-determination in this particular situation would amount to the self-determination of its enemies," *Pravda* said after the invasion. In the Communist "camp" all its peoples are prisoners.

At first the invasion was answered by a world-wide cry of outrage. Communists the world over left the Party in disgust, among them the theoreticians Roger Garaudy and Ernst Fischer. But de Gaulle's Foreign Minister, Michel Debré, opined that "one does not close a road simply because a traffic accident has happened." Sixty-one of seventy-five Communist parties whose delegates made a pilgrimage to Moscow absolved Brezhnev of all wrongdoing, and as early as June 1969, one-fifth of the French electorate gave their vote to one of those sixty-one parties.

A harsh winter followed the "Spring of Prague." Dubček and his friends were demoted and eventually retired from political life. In their place Gustav Husak and other men trusted by the Russians took charge. They were not as bad as Novotny; but neither were they as liberal as Kádár in Hungary. Looking for the meaning of the Czech Spring, we read in the sixty-page Action Program of the Czechoslovak Central Committee that the trade unions must be independent; that workers in the factories and peasants in the collectives must have a voice in management; that plants must be able to make decisions and follow the market; that small private enterprise is compatible with socialism; that consumers need protection, too; that no party must substitute itself for administration, management, and social organization; that democracy is essential for the development of socialism; that the right of assembly and coalition must not be abridged; that freedom of worship must be guaranteed; that a freely elected parliament must become the supreme seat of power; that the judges must be independent. For the Communist Party Dubček had advocated secret elections, freedom to organize factions, rotation in office, and control by the membership. But he had not seen the restoration of democracy as a return to parliamentary liberalism. He hoped for a "higher form of socialist development" ending in the withering away of the state and the emergence of "freedom as a social act." Quite naturally, the organs of this freedom were to be, as in Hungary, elected soviets and "committees for the protection of freedom," principles hailed also by the Italian, French, Austrian, Spanish, and Japanese Communists. The Italians alone stuck to their guns even after the invasion.

There is now in Europe a large reservoir of able intellectuals who have adopted a program of humanist socialism. They range from ex-Stalinists like Garaudy and Fischer to the Yugoslav philosophers and to the followers of Luciano Gruppi, who claims the intellectual heritage of Antonio Gramsci and Togliatti, one-time leaders of the Italian Communist Party; from Sartre to Kolakowski; from Dubček to Ernst Bloch. They may not all hold the same tenets, but they are critical of both capitalist and socialist societies. An ocean of blood and tears and a wall of inhumanity and dogmatism separates them from Communist bureaucrats.

The humanist critics of the Soviet government and its puppets are not identical with the technocratic dissidents who wish to improve the functioning of the system without liberalizing its intellectual and political life. Rumania and East Germany have instituted economic reforms going beyond anything Dubček imagined; but in both countries the political dictatorship is as strong and as rigid as in Stalin's time. In Hungary, Kádár has granted a measure of freedom to the intellectuals; life in Budapest has resumed some of its old "Danubian" gaiety, and life in Bucharest reflects the accelerated development. Supplies are plentiful; economic decision-making is relatively decentralized. But of course the greater discreetness of the police and of the Party dictatorship only conceals the iron fist.

In Poland, where economic woes were incurable as long as Russia exacted unpaid contributions for the empire's defenses and her own capital equipment, riots occurred in 1968 after the authorities banned a play by Adam Mickiewicz, a national poet over a hundred years dead, which contained unflattering references to Czarist(!) Russia. While liberalism was suppressed, nationalism was deflected into a channel traditional in Poland: Jew-baiting. Once again "cosmopolitans" and liberals had to emigrate. Power fell to a group of Stalinists led by police chief Mieczyslaw Moczar; they called themselves Partisans, though few of them had been guerrillas during the war.

Eventually the government was forced to introduce reforms. Honest prices were to reflect costs; enterprises had to show a profit—all of which meant, to begin with, a sudden end to subsidies, an abrupt increase in the cost of basic living expenses, the taxation of the poor. Ineptly timed, these decrees hit the Polish people shortly before

Christmas 1970. Food riots immediately broke out in many Baltic cities and in Silesia—that is, in areas comparatively recently settled by Polish immigrants. The regime was shaken to its foundations. Gomulka and his ex-Socialist Premier, Cyrankiewicz, had to resign. They were replaced by a strangely mixed new team. Party leadership fell to Edward Gierek, an ambitious *apparatchik* who had spent many years in France and Belgium as a miner and had later made Silesia into a show-piece of Communist development. The important Ministry of Defense was occupied by his rival Moczar, the Premiership by a technocrat, Piotr Jaroszewicz, a declared foe of "world Zionism." This unstable coalition has granted concessions to the poor and has made more consumer goods available. The riots thus may have limited Poland's colonial exploitation, but the imperialist domination of Polish politics by Soviet commissars continues.

Anticipating the end of the development: It was political necessity that eventually brought relief to consumers in the satellite empire. After the brief Prague Spring, the Kádár regime in Budapest decided to bribe its citizens and gave them goods in return for political apathy. A sort of NEP, the "new mechanics," gives leeway to small shops and private enterprise, permits people to buy or build houses, and tolerates a small "gray market." The example was imitated more timidly by the Husak regime in Prague and the Gierek regime in Warsaw. As a result, supplies have become more plentiful, and the capitals of East Germany, Czechoslovakia, and Hungary now have a decidedly "Western look." Even Warsaw is infinitely less drab than Moscow and Leningrad. Everywhere a tacit deal seems to be consummated: You may withdraw into your private life, provided you let the government do its job; it no longer demands your total engagement.

Obviously, some of the old cadres do not like this course. There is new discussion which often takes the form of reprimand and exhortation. Inevitably, liberal and conservative factions will emerge. Similar splits will develop, or have developed, in the Western Communist parties. Both Maoists and revisionists rejected the Brezhnev doctrine. The French Communist Party was beset by internecine conflict. The Italian Communist Party divided three or four ways, with Giorgio Amendola leading the pro-Soviet wing, Luigi Longo and Enrico Berlinguer holding an opportunistic center, Pietro Ingrao attacking both from the Left, and a Maoist group rallying dissidents around its *Manifesto*. West Germany's revived Communist Party had to contend with a radical student opposition that prides itself on being "extra-parliamentary." The Greek Communist Party lost its most famous member, the composer Mikis Theodorakis. The Swedish Communist Party expelled its leader, C. H. Hermansson.

The final suicide of Communist doctrine came as a result of Israel's Six-Day War in 1967. Anti-Semitism was elevated to a political ideology in the guise of anti-Zionism. Stalin had resorted to anti-Semitic innuendo when he liquidated the "cosmopolitans," the friends of reconciliation with the West. Khrushchev had permitted the publication of writings and cartoons which, masked as anti-religious propaganda, were embar-rassingly reminiscent of Julius Streicher's infamous *Stürmer*. Once again, in the late 1960's, Jews were desperately trying to leave East European countries. After the Czech invasion a pamphlet was printed in Russian, Czech, and Slovak, describing the Dubček "conspiracy" as the work of "international Zionism." This, of course, dovetails with the Communist attacks against Israel. For Soviet strategists tried to egg the Arabs on to a *jihad* and gave them arms to create a "second Vietnam" for the United States in the Middle East. They almost succeeded six years later in the Yom Kippur War.

Of all Communist countries, Yugoslavia had left the Stalinist model farthest behind. But she paid dearly for her relative freedom.

In 1965, Yugoslavia had to refund a loan from the World Bank, which insisted on radical economic surgery: devaluation of the dinar from 1/750 to 1/1250 of a dollar, reduction of costly subsidies to parasitical industries. As a result, the government required strict cost-accounting, shut down marginal plants, restored a free market for most goods, and allowed prices to find their own level. The living standard of the masses was cut sharply, and unemployment was accepted as a regulator of the labor market. Fortunately the continuing boom in Germany and Switzerland absorbed surplus manpower; workers sent their foreign earnings home, learned modern production techniques, and went home to teach others. Also, millions of tourists came to fill the coffers of Yugoslavia's central bank. But the Croatians who earned those dollars were unwilling to let them go for the development of poor Macedonia, or be ruled by Serb bureaucrats. And tribes in a multi-national state, split by language, religion, and history, hardly need issues to feel disadvantaged. Croats, Montenegrins, Slovenes, Bosnians, Albanians, perhaps even Bulgarians in Macedonia, all were waiting for Tito's retirement in order to demand autonomy in a country held together only by his great prestige. Criticism of the federal administration was so widespread and received such open support in the local press that Tito decided to decentralize and partly dismantle the state apparatus, as he had done in the economic sphere. In 1970, a new constitution gave recognition to the centrifugal forces, permitted the country's six federated republics a high degree of self-administration, and also provided for an intricate quota system at each level of administration, which cannot be compatible with efficiency and honesty.

Even though the Party remained the center of power, it was to expose itself to the pressures of economic, regional, and intellectual interests. No wonder Yugoslavia now produced a crop of revisionist philosophers and the university of Zagreb became the mecca of unorthodox Marxists from all over the world. Tito found himself in the position of a leader who is being pushed by the led. The moment the centrifugal forces in the region and the liberal forces in the Party threatened to grow uncontrollable, he drew in the reins, purged the Croat party, removed liberal professors and journalists from their posts, and centralized the Party regime again. Since then, the see-saw battle between conservatives and liberals, centralists and regionalists has never stopped. The constitution is constantly being rewritten.

Tito still holds the country together and finds it difficult to resign. Constitutional arrangements have been made to assure a democratic succession. It is likely, however, that, in the case of Tito's demise, the Party, and within it the orthodox faction, will tighten the reins to save the country from disintegration and foreign intervention.

CHAPTER 8

Some Notes on Soviet Culture

DICTATORSHIPS live by crash programs. They produce outstanding achievements in specific fields, while the rest of the landscape may remain a desert and the majority of the population dissatisfied. Soviet physical science and Soviet engineering were capable of overtaking the West in rocketry and aviation equipment. However, they lag behind in fields the government did not recognize as essential early enough—such as computerization, where experts cannot be trained as the need arises but can emerge only from a generation of scientists, researchers, experimenters, engineers, and users whose ways of thinking have assimilated the conditions and possibilities of the new field. Freedom of communication and freedom of research cannot be replaced even by the most strenuous government efforts. Hence the paradox that, although the Soviet Union is providing the most excellent science education for a great number of students and its institutes turn out more scientists and engineers than most Western countries proportionately, yet it has won few Nobel Prizes and has produced few of the scientific and technological breakthroughs of the century. (Nikolai Basov and Aleksander Prokhorov participated in research leading to the maser-laser principle; Pavel Cherenkov discovered a radiation effect named after him.)

Nonetheless, it would be a mistake to underestimate the Soviet achievements even under Stalin. Either with the help of satellite citizens or through their own efforts, Soviet scientists have reinvented just about every major invention of the West, and they are part of the community of scholars and scientists which gathers in periodic conventions and reads each others' specialized journals. In this connection, it is well to remember that more Soviet scientists understand Western languages than vice versa.

Strangely enough, something similar holds true for the humanities and *belles lettres*. Despite the isolation and the fanatical xenophobia of the Zhdanov period, foreign literature was available to Soviet citizens in excellent translations even then—and alas, some of Russia's most gifted writers were forced to do translations because they could not publish, or could not even write, works of their own. We shall never know how many masterworks have been lost to Russian literature, or what direction Russian literature might have taken had it not been directed. For the dictator not only stifled genius and imagination, he ordered works written to measure; scarce paper was made available to sycophants. Thus a regional writer, Mikhail Sholokhov, whose imagination ran to sentimental populism, set the style which Stalin accepted as "socialist realism," a genre which quickly also spread to film-making and all but destroyed the great tradition of the early Soviet directors. Patriotic themes prevailed; the style had to be more and more heroic, academic, and classical. Twenty-eight offices supervised authors, actors, directors, and producers. Nothing controversial could be printed or shown. In a supreme, almost Kafkaesque irony, Sholokhov himself was to rewrite part of his *And Quiet Flows the Don.*

Conflict was not supposed to be a part of the Soviet experience and hence was not essential for the dramatist. In the pre-war movies, drama had still been provided by the saboteur who had to be foiled. The films of the late Stalin period only knew the collective hero: the coal miner who fulfilled the norm in four-fifths of the time, the *kolkhoz* worker who inspired his colleagues to build an electric plant, the biologist who succeeded in creating new species. Theoretically, socialist realism requires a negative hero to be vanquished by the positive hero; but since no enemy of the regime can be intelligent, the film (or novel) is bound to be one-sided and dull. The best Soviet products, therefore, are one-character films like *The Bespoke Overcoat* (based on a Gogol story) or *The Village Teacher* (1947). Works of art have to show *partiinost, narodnost, typichnost,* and *ideinost.* That is to say, they must be composed from the point of view of the "Party"; they must deal with themes taken from the life of the "People"; they must "typify" that which is best; and they must have a message that conforms with the Party "line."

The form of the film or novel also is prescribed. The story must be comprehensible to simple people, just as music must be based on recognizable melodies. The positive hero, a model for the young reader, must win; the negative hero can never be represented as a genuine product of Soviet life. The treatment must not be realistic but project "ideal types." "Socialist realism" had to consider real that which might be ideal, and to hail as ideal that which was real.

Clever authors beat the system by describing landscapes and objects in most painstaking detail. While in the West *chosisme* meant that writers had nothing to say, in the East they were fearful of saying too much. Stalin's and Zhdanov's pronouncements on literature, art, linguistics, and genetics had to be accepted as gospel truth by people who knew better.

The same scientists who were working on the splitting of the atom were compelled to condemn modern physics as undialectical and unmaterialistic. Trofim Lysenko, who contended that acquired properties can be made inheritable, surprised a biologists' meeting with the announcement that the Central Committee had approved his theory, making a scientific debate superfluous—but later on, the Soviet Union imported American hybrid corn produced by selective cultivation.

After Stalin's death, writers acquired a little more freedom in the choice of subject and manner of presentation. Painters experimented with post-Impressionist styles. Satirical stories began to circulate in Moscow; thousands of youths assembled on Red Square to hear Yevtushenko read his poems. But Boris Pasternak was unable to publish his novel *Doctor Zhivago* in Russia, for indeed it was frankly pre-revolutionary.

It preached love in a time of hate; it spoke understandingly of people in an age of machines and organizations; it was a novel against age and place and society. When Pasternak was awarded the Nobel Prize for this work, he was not allowed to accept it. He died in isolation.

Dimitri Shepilov, who had helped Khrushchev into power and had been Commissar for Cultural Affairs, was condemned and dismissed "for issuing liberal instructions and never mentioning Party loyalty." Ilya Ehrenburg, who showed too much nostalgia for the good old bohemian days in Paris, was under a cloud; Yevtushenko, almost poet laureate in the early days of the thaw, was reprimanded for finding some good things to say about his trip to America.

During the brief period of Khrushchev's "liberalism" the official Soviet Writers' Union became a lively place where factions debated openly. Alexander Tvardovsky published in *Novy Mir* experimental and even critical contributions. In 1962, he carried Solzhenitsyn's *One Day in the Life of Ivan Denisovich*, which raised a storm. The bureaucrats detested the novel's stark realism as vehemently as its sturdy faith in man and its message that life triumphs over chicanery.

The Party Secretary for Cultural and Ideological Matters called a meeting in which he gave the assembled intelligentsia a tongue-lashing. Nevertheless, a zig was always followed by a zag. In 1963, the Soviets stopped jamming BBC and Voice of America broadcasts. Youth unrest was no longer suppressed so severely; young people taped American jazz, danced Russian versions of Western dances, took to wearing jeans and long hair. But as early as 1965, neo-Stalinism put a brake on the new freedom: "hooligans" were arrested; a campaign against "vicious" Western influences was launched. Writers like Valery Tarsis and Sergey Yesenin were repeatedly confined in insane asylums; then suddenly Tarsis was allowed to go to England.

Under the Brezhnev regime, the repressed criticism found clandestine outlets. Shut out by the official publishing houses, Russian writers resorted to self-help and began to circulate typed manuscripts which were copied and recopied to inundate the cities with a voluminous underground literature—*samizdat* (self-publishing). It is in this kind of "edition" that Soviet citizens first made the acquaintance of Solzhenitsyn's great novels *The First Circle* and *Cancer Ward*. Since he received the Nobel Prize in 1970, Solzhenitsyn has been a gadfly of the Soviet conscience. Under extreme pressure, he was forced by the government to emigrate in 1974.

In 1965, Yuli Daniel, a writer, and Andrei Sinyavsky, a critic (Avram Tertz), both friends of the late Boris Pasternak, were arrested, indicted for writing satirically about "socialist realism" and vilifying the fatherland abroad, and later sentenced to five and seven years of hard labor, respectively. Alexander Tvardovsky's play *Tvyorkin in the Other World* was removed from the Moscow stage; the author lost his candidate-membership of the Central Committee, and the editorship of *Novy Mir* magazine, which had published all the poets of the thaw, was put into more reliable hands. Even Konstantin Simonov, a stalwart pillar of patriotic realism, was unable to publish his wartime memoirs.

Russian motion pictures since the thaw have shed the dreary clichés of socialist realism. Nature, human beings, love, happiness, and distress are once again seen on the screen. In the satellite countries, directors have been allowed to produce pictures as good technically, as sensuous in content, and possibly more sensitive in treatment than those of their Western competitors. The Carlsbad Festival is not yet the equal of Cannes; but interesting pictures from Eastern European studios have been shown there for the last ten years, and if movies are any reflection of political conditions, they are indeed encouraging. An East German film tells of a returning soldier who under Russian occupation does not find everything to his liking. A Yugoslav film candidly shows the bleak world of an unemployed man even under socialism. The Soviet director Yuli Raisman admits that misfortune, an unfaithful wife, and the conflict between young and old can spoil the best Five Year Plan. Czech and Polish directors have sent some beautiful films to the West and earned high praise in addition to royalties. Some of them show that under a strait-laced regime frank eroticism may amount to a political manifesto.

Being closely watched by both authorities and public, the East European writer has responsibilities that his Western colleagues may envy. He has to be careful to say no more and no less than necessary to make the existence of his chains known. Any attempt to deny the chains or to overdramatize their clattering would impair his artistic integrity; any attempt to break the chains would endanger his life and his family's well-being. Fortunate were the Germans who could flee to the West and still be creative in their own language. These were not enemies of the regime but Marxists who tried their best to remain in good standing, until they found that it was better to live in a country whose principles they condemned than in a country that followed their own precepts. Rudi Dutschke came to the West to organize the SDS; Herbert Marcuse has shown no desire to go to the East.

In East Berlin, the folk singer Wolf Biermann, professing "to live under the best system but to be unhappy," is under house arrest, but the government turns over to him the royalties it receives from his Western publishers. The life of intellectuals in these countries is exciting and significant, a sort of guerrilla warfare between them and the censors. One satirist explains it pungently in a mock reminiscence of the Stalin era: "What a life we had when everything was forbidden. All I had to do would be to say 'crayon,' and everybody in the audience would nudge his neighbor: 'Did you notice how meaningfully he said crayon?' "

One hope clearly emerges from all these observations. The ice age Orwell prophesied in *1984* is far, far away. Institutions of totalitarian tyranny have proved to be as unstable as those which guaranteed freedom. Even where oppression and conformity have held sway over a long period of time, the spirit of freedom and humanity has always vigorously re-emerged. Eastern Europe still shares the values of our civilization. It has survived Stalinism, as Western Europe has survived fascism and Nazism.

Another observation may be added in summary. There are as many varieties of socialism and communism as there are of capitalism. For many years, a clear division between two types of society seemed to suggest itself, and the cold war seemed to be the consequence of their incompatibility. The Soviet system was "Asiatic," while

European society was free and "open," as Professor Karl Popper has explained. Today, many observers are speaking of convergence. Perhaps one should speak of a variety of patterns that all started from different developments of the European idea. I have devoted considerable space to the peculiar routes the idea of progress took in Eastern Europe. But I have no doubt that diversity conceals unity, and that the tactical alliances which today tie Eastern Europe to the Third World will not obliterate the basic solidarity of the European continent.

This part has revealed modes of operation and patterns of development which are characteristic of totalitarian systems and look strange, or even weird, to us Westerners. Similar patterns had been imposed on Western nations from time to time, however. They are not typical of the East but of a certain period in the history of several nations.

PART IX

Post-War Society in Western Europe

CHAPTER I

The Welfare State

AFTER reconstruction, new people took the helm; new classes were recognized as molders of their own destiny; new parties asserted a claim to participate in public life, or old ones changed their names and aims to keep in step with the times. The war had wrought irrevocable changes. If capitalism still was the prevalent system of production and property still the basis of power, the old *laissez-faire* economy now was checked by government controls and a host of new institutions which the economist John Kenneth Galbraith was to call "countervailing forces." Local and national governments now spent larger shares of national income than before; social services increased; new techniques of economic management have prevented some of the fluctuations that used to make many incomes so insecure.

What had been possible in wartime and had been learned then could be put to better use in peacetime. Monetary controls and fiscal policies now are designed to turn on and off the flow of funds, to direct investment where it is most desirable, to reward or penalize enterprise as the need occurs. The banking system, once autonomous or even defiant, co-operates with, or is directly controlled by, the state.

On this basis, most Western states now set new goals for their economy: to redistribute wealth and to channel economic activity toward welfare-oriented goals. While incomes still are far from equal and class differences have only been mitigated, government action has removed some of the worst obstacles to social mobility. The state provides higher education for all who desire it and a goodly number of scholarships. It places a floor under the income of all families, guarantees either employment or social-security benefits, and provides public housing as well as social and health services.

Expanding the philosophy developed in Sir William Beveridge's wartime reports, the British Government adopted a full-employment policy and used the techniques of economic management which John Maynard Keynes, now governor of the Bank of England, had developed in the 1930's. The government also initiated a reform of the entire social-welfare system.

Thanks to such measures unemployment fluctuates at very low levels (less than 2 per cent) in Sweden, Switzerland, Norway, West Germany, and France; at tolerable levels (2–5 per cent) in England, Denmark, and Belgium; it is still unpredictable (up to 10 per cent in some years) in Italy, Ireland, and Greece. The boom in the most advanced countries helps overcome unemployment in remote, underdeveloped areas as migrant workers from Turkey, Greece, Spain, Yugoslavia, and Italy find training and employment in the North. But although their earnings and new skills contribute to their own countries' development, the discrepancy between highly industrialized and laggard areas may even be growing. There also are pockets of high unemployment in distressed areas of Macedonia, Scotland, and Northern Ireland. In southern Italy a special effort is needed to bring incomes up to national standards. In 1950, a *Cassa per il Mezzogiorno* (Fund for the South) was established with a billion liras to be spent on farm improvement and vital services as well as development loans.

These features have earned the new system the name of "welfare state." The French call it *économie dirigée*, although persuasion and incentives rather than directives and orders are used to arrive at desirable goals. Similar techniques of "market planning" without direct intervention in management decisions were introduced in England, the Scandinavian countries, and the Netherlands.

Yet, the techniques of Keynesian management also created new problems. Where the goals of full employment and welfare are given priority over production and efficiency, inflation will take away some of the gains in money wages. Some countries, such as England and France, have suffered repeated assaults on their currencies; however, the governments have concluded that this inconvenience is more tolerable than the uncertainties of the business cycle: the disturbances it creates are less painful than the problems which the new economy can overcome.

Orthodox Marxists, who had predicted the demise of capitalism, first attributed the post-war prosperity to the backlog of demand. They also charged that world capitalism, led by the U.S. hawks, owed its post-war boom largely to increasing defense orders. But after the war ravages had been repaired, the West European economies continued to prosper under a judicious management of public funds. That showcase of the "capitalist way," the "economic miracle" (*Wirtschaftswunder*) in West Germany—masterminded by Chancellor Adenauer's economic adviser, Professor Ludwig Erhard—depended on shrewdly applied stimuli to the building industries, on fiscal encouragement of investment, on manipulated discount rates, on subsidies to peasants, and on import regulations. Officially, it was called a "social market economy" to distinguish it from classical *laissez-faire* liberalism. That is to say, free competition was encouraged where possible but supplemented by interventionism when and where necessary. The "miracle" was helped enormously by sheer luck, by the population increase, by the radical currency reform wiping out all old debts, and the low value set for the D-mark by the Allies, which gave Germany an export surplus. Nevertheless, in 1966 the miracle began to run out; Erhard, who by then had become Chancellor, immediately lost the confidence of his coalition partner, the FDP (Free Democratic Party, the party of big business). His own CDU (Christian Democratic Union) abandoned him and formed a coalition with the Socialists, whose gifted Minister of Economic Affairs, Karl Schiller, wrought a new economic miracle.

Two lessons were obvious. It did not matter which party provided prosperity and which ideology went with it. And welfare economics now became the common heritage of all parties, so that none of the benefits one party had introduced was abolished when the other party came to power.

A striking case in point is the adoption of economic planning by two dictators of the Right. Spain's INI (Instituto Nacional para Industria, founded in 1941) has played a decisive role in the country's amazing post-war development. During the past ten years, for example, 500,000 homes were built privately, but 1.7 million were constructed with government support.

In France, likewise, recovery depended largely on planning, and when de Gaulle came to power again, he not only continued but expanded state intervention and welfare policies. "Targets" were agreed upon between industry and government in accordance with possibilities and needs. Credits and other encouragement were given to those who complied; difficulties were encountered by those who deviated from the plan, even though the penalties were not as high as they are for an American farmer who exceeds his quota.

Planning is comparatively easy in an industry dominated by a few large concerns. This is notably the case in chemistry, steel, rubber, and electrical supplies. In other fields, too, such as coal, cartels saw to it that the plan was followed. European industry had always been highly organized, with hundreds of price agreements and market quotas regulating output and distribution. Now some important cartels acquired the power of political authority. Under the Schuman Plan, ECSC became a "high authority" with the right to shut down marginal plants, direct investment to the most profitable places, and allocate markets. Its success was stunning.

A third element of planning was state ownership. In most European countries mass transportation, power generation, telegraph, telephone, and radio already were public property. After the war, the coal mines were nationalized in France and England. Electricity either was or soon came into public ownership in France, Germany, England, and, later, Italy. The airlines, much of merchant shipping, and the central banks were state-owned. So were 40 per cent of French and Italian banks, 60 per cent of Italy's steel industry, the most important aircraft factories, and the Renault auto plant in France. Hitler's jeep was converted into the Volkswagen and immediately, under state management, became a world-wide success. As mentioned before, many of Italy's great concerns had come under state control in the Fascist era. In Europe it would have been unthinkable for private corporations to develop and exploit atomic energy, television, or facilities like Telstar.

When the Labour government came to power in 1945, it immediately nationalized steel, coal, transportation, the Bank of England, the utilities and, most spectacular of all, the health services—all told, a fifth of the nation's business. The House of Lords, though it could not prevent the nationalization of the steel industry, delayed it for two years; hence, the public corporation had hardly begun to operate when the Conservatives came back to power and returned the rolling mills and blast furnaces to their former owners. Still, they did not dare denationalize any of the other industries, and despite some grumbling among doctors, they maintained the National Health Service. Every resident, and even every visiting foreigner, became entitled to free medical and dental care, drugs, eyeglasses, even hairpieces if medically indicated. The scheme was financed like a state insurance plan through employee and employer contributions. Doctors were free to join, and by 1953 only 3 per cent were still refusing to participate. Patients are free to choose their doctor. Though there were abuses and the service eventually cost more than initially contemplated, most people, including doctors, now are pleased with it and would no more give it up than the Germans would abandon the health insurance originated by Bismarck sixty years earlier. The Scandinavian countries have similar schemes, but, of course, all must be financed through taxation and contribution.

The Labour government next proceeded to reform the educational system. Already the Education Act of 1944 had abolished all school fees and made schooling mandatory up to age fifteen. Now stipends were made available to worthy students in secondary schools. Half a million pupils were added to the rolls, and 5,000 additional students entered the universities each year. In 1946, the National Insurance Act did away with the humiliating "dole"; instead, every unemployed, disabled, or senior citizen was to receive a weekly payment. Thus the old Fabian slogan "Security from the cradle to the grave" was realized for the first time. Public services constitute 15 per cent of the nation's income,[1] and since wage income was thus released for purchases in the private market, consumer industries also benefited. Living standards have increased proportionately.

The Scandinavian countries had Socialist or Socialist-coalition governments for a long time. Even more systematically than England, they had developed welfare-state goals and welfare-state techniques. In Germany, the tradition of social insurance, health services, and retirement benefits had never been interrupted; but, in addition, a vast new welfare program had to be designed for victims of Nazi persecution, inflation, and war, for the refugees and the expelled. More than 20 per cent of the West German budget is spent for these purposes. France spends 16 per cent of her gross national income on welfare programs and pensions; in addition to other social services, considerable bounties are being paid for children. The result of such policies is a more equitable distribution of disposable income. Economic equality smoothes both class relations and the business cycle; for, according to Keynes, wide differentials between income brackets make an economy more vulnerable to sudden fluctuations.

Public housing is a tool of both social policy and of full-employment economics. All European governments, socialist as well as conservative, used the rebuilding of bombed-out neighborhoods as an opportunity for large-scale town planning, slum clearance, and road construction. Since 1945, England has built 6 million dwelling units, more than half of them publicly financed and planned. This includes two dozen "model towns" of half a million population each, designed for better accommodation, better land use, more park areas, better administration, and also to syphon off the surplus population from the great urban conglomerations. With the farm population

---

[1] Britain spends $285, West Germany as much as $507 per capita per year on welfare. The old-age pension for a single person in England is now £7.50 a week, about half of recognized living costs.

rapidly dropping from one-third before the war to one-fifth after it on the average, and to one-twentieth in the most advanced countries, urban ecology became a prime problem everywhere. Even sparsely populated Sweden found it necessary to plan the living conditions of its working population. Vällingby, nine miles by subway from Stockholm, with a six-acre shopping center and residential subcommunities grace-fully arranged around a lake, has gained world fame. Similar suburbs are radially located along the great arteries. Swedish·communities own the land they develop, and they plan so as to integrate health policy with transportation policy, employment policy, and other factors.

In France, new suburbs have been built partly by private builders and partly by town planners. Called *grands ensembles*, these settlements combine a pleasant layout with great utility. Germany, of course, offered the greatest opportunities for post-war planning; many socialist municipalities, such as Berlin, Stuttgart, Hamburg, and Frankfurt, have shown how much can be achieved with comprehensive planning. There, too, problems of migration, employment, transportation had to be squared with the narrower goals of providing inexpensive, decent housing for millions of people.

In Holland, Austria, Belgium, and France, nonprofit builders and co-operatives have received government loans, tax privileges, land grants, and other public assis-tance. *Avant-garde* architects were engaged to design new cities or districts and blocks—settlements—that were not only aesthetically pleasing but that also provided the social services and sanitary features that so far had been absent from workers' tenements. Planners and designers worked in league with the socio-political vanguard. They all strove for a revolution in man's environment, making it both more humane and more rational.

Before World War II, only 15 per cent of the European population lived in houses built with public assistance. Now, 75 per cent of all new houses received such aid; by 1959, the British authorities owned a quarter of all housing. Even the Greek generals, unimaginative as they are in most other respects, build houses for low-income families and support the farm income.

The purposes of both social policy and a planned economy are served by taxation. England instituted high death duties, which will eventually force the nobility to sell their art treasures and to abandon their castles. In other countries taxation was less progressive; but everywhere its effect was to encourage the transformation of personal businesses into corporations. This form of business organization, in turn, facilitates mergers and intensifies the technological drive toward bigness—and big firms are not only more efficient but they also pay higher wages than small ones. Thus, the various elements of the welfare state's social policies dovetailed with its economic policies and with the general trends in technology and in economic and social thinking: optimal plant size, optimal income distribution, planning for future development and a full-employment policy, welfare services and pensions, state ownership in key industries. While some of these tendencies also had long been basic demands of the socialist parties, they now became standard practice for all governments. When the Tories came back to power, they did not change the Labour government's social policies; indeed in the election campaign they boasted that they had provided more public housing than Labour. In fact, the platforms presented by Butler for the Conservatives and by Gaitskell for Labour were so similar that people were joking about "Butskellism."

Wage policy was a different matter. The Conservatives usually warned against inflation; the Socialists usually preferred the risk of inflation to the risk of unemployment. While nominal wages increased and currencies depreciated, total real family wages increased; mass consumption sustained a prolonged boom. A veritable craving for electrical appliances and motor vehicles swept Europe. The American example, the experience of dwindling money values, a sudden shift away from the old European habit of "save now, buy later," a post-war urge to live it up and enjoy one's income while it lasted—all this may have contributed to a profound change in spending patterns. Television sets became commonplace. The middle classes bought small cars, the young workers motorcycles and scooters. This motorization in turn changed the pattern of travel and entertainment. Two or even three weeks paid vacation for everybody, long weekends, earlier retirement, and the extension of compulsory schooling meant a sudden increase in the number of people who had leisure and were seeking entertainment. New industries catered to these demands.

Travel abroad was one of the great luxuries that up to recent times only the leisured classes could afford. Now Europeans young and old went to see other countries. Their very numbers changed the character of the old resort areas. Many traveled in groups, meeting in youth hostels or trailer camps and learning each others' folk songs and dances. The barriers fell: no more customs inspection, no more visa controls. Road signs were unified; people learned each other's language, ate each other's national dishes, adopted each other's habits, traded and worked with each other so that at least the urban population felt at home everywhere throughout Western Europe. Social legislation was assimilated, migrant workers were employed under equal conditions, side by side with native workers, and wage differentials between rich and poor countries began to narrow.

A final distinguishing feature of the welfare state is the change in labor-management relations. A variety of devices was introduced to give workers or their representatives insight into the problems of the enterprise, and even a share in decision-making, at least in matters concerning personnel. In France, joint "factory committees" were established to adjudicate disputes over working conditions and wages. In Germany, trade-union representatives were admitted to the board of directors of the big steel and coal concerns; the Social Democratic Party is committed to institute full "co-determination" (participation in management) once it gains a majority. In England, too, the nationalized industries have worker representation on the boards. While these institutions often fail to fulfill trade-union expectations and are no serious challenge to management's authority, they may point to more comprehensive democracy in the economy.

Workers are part of the welfare state and benefit from its operation. Their unions are guaranteed a place in the structure of the economy; the Communist-controlled unions in France and Italy have ceased to be revolutionary, and where Communists are mayors, they fulfill the welfare state's purposes and teach the workers how to take advantage of its laws. The old class distinctions are vanishing and workers' children graduate from high school.

And yet, the workers are not full partners of the nation or of "society." Security from cradle to grave, progressive taxation and public housing, planning for full employment, and state ownership in key industries had always been the goals of the socialist labor movement. But as more of these specific programs were being fulfilled, socialists realized that their ultimate goal, social equality, was eluding them. To be sure, there now was an official policy of equal opportunity for all. But a vast majority of students in the good schools still come from well-to-do homes and expect to use family connections in their careers. In government, in the higher civil service, in diplomacy, in banking and industry, on the boards of public corporations, we still find the same family names that had once held a monopoly of these positions. After nationalization, the British steel industry continued to be run largely by its former owners and managers. The Continental cartel bureaucracy, the planners in national offices, the "Eurocrats" in supranational agencies, are drawn from the same strata that had directed individual enterprises.

Despite progressive taxation and death duties, the ruling classes have maintained their leading position in society; despite open admission, only a small percentage of the population attend secondary schools and even fewer institutes of higher learning. Academic fraternities and clubs still are the stepping-stone to desirable careers; education, manners, speech, and life-style determine the company one is admitted to. "Society" sets itself apart from "the people" by having cocktails rather than a glass of beer or "pinard."

Both in Germany and in France, even the leadership of workers' parties had its sprinkling of millionaires. And while no Tory government so far can boast of a trade-union leader risen from the ranks, the Attlee cabinet had just as many Etonians as Churchill's. With all the great changes in the economic structure, the old "ruling class" has simply been transformed into the "Establishment." Progress therefore must be measured not by the attainment of specific goals but by the direction some actual changes indicate. Where before the war 7 per cent of England's higher civil servants had come from working-class families, the percentage rose to 17 in the 1960's. Where teaching and preaching had been almost the only road to middle-class status for a poor youngster, it could now be reached through engineering, economics, the natural or the social sciences. New careers were opening up in middle management and in the technical services. The white-collar or white-smock jobs were the new way of climbing the social ladder. Not by penetrating into jobs formerly monopolized by the propertied classes but by creating new kinds of professions did workmen's sons enter the middle class. Up to one-fifth of the Western labor force now falls into categories which in the Soviet Union are grouped as "technical intelligentsia."

The peasants, traditionally a conservative class, have grown quite modern-minded in Western Europe. Despite subsidies and protective policies, ruthless competition forced more than half of the rural population out of farming. Modern farm machinery and co-operative marketing techniques have transformed many of the old European all-round farms into specialized production units; peasants have turned into capitalist farmers. Even so, the average holding is far below optimal size; too many are even below the minimum considered necessary for sustenance (around 15 acres in most countries). Average farm size is 40 acres in Denmark, 30 in France, 20 in Holland and West Germany, less than 20 in Italy. Moreover, these small farms must sustain too many people. Farm wages, therefore, are low; a farm family's income is typically only half that of an urban worker's. Where a worker makes $3,000 a year and his wife $2,000, the typical farm family has a total yearly income of $2,000–$3,000.

Yet this reduced and exploited farm population now provides most of Europe's food except tropical fruits, vegetable fats, and corn; increased use of fertilizer and of machinery have boosted productivity. Ten years after liberation, French farmers had 250,000 new tractors; motorization became a factor shaping not only their production but their lives as well. Machinery absorbs up to one-sixth of farm expenditure; peasants spend four times more on it than before the war. Farming now constitutes less than 13 per cent of national product in Italy, 8 per cent in France, less than 4 per cent in England and Germany, though still 20 per cent in Eastern Europe.

Farm finances are far from healthy. Government policies of parceling prevent the best utilization of the land. Small farms do not use their machinery fully. To prevent a further exodus from the land, governments shore up prices or pay subsidies, but they are unable to halt the liquidation of unprofitable farms. Yet even prospering peasants are not satisfied and will occasionally riot. The French dairy farmers' strike was started in well-to-do villages.

In northern Italy and France, peasants demonstrated for larger subsidies, against taxation, even against the controls that were supposed to protect them. Discontent in backward areas breeds proto-fascist movements such as Poujade's short-lived protest party in France and the neo-fascist Movimento Nazionale Italiano. In Italy the south, Sicily, and Sardinia are especially vulnerable—or, rather, traditionalism is no longer a reliable safeguard even in those semi-feudal areas. A similar movement, protesting against taxes and adherence to EEC, ended the Socialist hold on government in the Danish elections of 1973.

The Common Market had benefited French peasants at the expense of American exporters and Germany's small producers; it will be even harder on British farmers and consumers. But all governments now recognize that consolidation and modernization are the only way to make Europe's farm economy viable.

Modernization and insecurity are also the plight of small shopkeepers and other parts of the petty-bourgeoisie. No sooner had they seen new avenues in the expanding service industries when this field, too, was taken over by big organizations. The middle classes have not been pushed down into the proletariat, but neither have they been able to defend their economic independence; many shopowners are just outlets or representatives of a concern, and self-employed only in a technical sense. Yet the number of these semi-independent agents is increasing. The post-war expansion of incomes has called for more service industries and other trades which do not produce goods but cater to personal needs. The growth of these services has shifted the balance away from blue-collar to white-collar and smock workers.

Finally we must mention a group which had developed hardly any class consciousness before the 1960's and indeed cannot be called a class. The recent interest in women's rights, however, reminds us that Simone de Beauvoir opened that chapter in European history with her work *The Second Sex* as early as 1949. However, the movement, neither militant nor shrill in Europe, reached for its aims quietly. French women got the vote in 1945; in 1964, they received the right to open bank accounts, own shops, and hold passports without their husbands' consent. But fewer French than American women have jobs and leave their children with a maid; throughout Europe middle-class women prefer not to be employed, and affluent workers' wives are proud to be free from the mill. But their daughters may now go to college and aspire to a career.

Women account for one-third of Western Europe's labor force—a little more in Germany and France, a little less in England. Women usually get 10 to 20 per cent less for the same work; unions therefore discourage their application for jobs hitherto reserved for men.

In upper-class families, a career raises a woman's status. As a result, relatively fewer lower-class women and more upper-class women work than before the war.

In Catholic countries like Italy, Spain, and France, young women still guard their virginity jealously, and three-fourths have their first sexual experience with their husbands or future husbands. In these areas birth control, though practiced secretly, is still surrounded by strict taboos. In France, contraceptives for women were banned by a law of 1920, and it was estimated that the number of abortions exceeded that of births. For the past ten years birth-control clinics have been tolerated by the government, and in 1974 Giscard d'Estaing and his new Minister of Health, Mme. Simone Veil, pushed a modern abortion law through the Assembly.

Until 1971, Switzerland was the only country where women still did not have suffrage. But in many other countries they have made but scant use of their franchise. One or two dozen women sit in the various parliaments, but few ever had a cabinet seat. Women lawyers, doctors, professors, artists, and editors rarely compete on equal terms. In France they account for only 20 per cent of university professors, 18 per cent of lawyers, 9 per cent of doctors. They are less visible in public life, hold few important positions in industry and commerce. By contrast, their contributions are well received in the world of letters. Among European women of note in this generation we may mention the one-time editor of the London *Economist*, Barbara Ward; Françoise Giroud, editor of *L'Express*; Agnès Varda, the movie director; Simone de Beauvoir, writer; Nathalie Sarraute, the novelist; Alva Myrdal, Sweden's ambassador to the United Nations; Hannah Arendt, the political philosopher who made her home in America; Bernadette Devlin, the Irish firebrand. None of them achieved the stature of Selma Lagerlöf, Ellen Key, Colette, Maria Montessori,

Rosa Luxemburg. In 1974, Mme. Giroud was appointed Minister for Women's Affairs in the cabinet of Giscard d'Estaing.

Inevitably, antiquated family laws will eventually be revised even in Roman Catholic countries. Despite fierce opposition by the clergy, Italy now permits divorce. Further progress may follow; but meanwhile a young generation has adopted customs that bypass the old laws. The cultural revolution has freed women from their domestic imprisonment more effectively than any legislator could.

The material condition of people in Western Europe has, by all standards, substantially improved. Life expectancy is rising by two months every year. Birth rates have increased in two countries which formerly suffered from stagnation: France and Ireland. Real wages are going up for persons with skills; in the more advanced countries they are comparable to American wages, and they are far ahead of the East.

Labor productivity is growing at an accelerated rate. During the first thirty years of the century it doubled; by the end of the second thirty years, after a great depression and another destructive war, it had tripled.

If we arrange the nations of Western Europe by their economic strength, we may group them in an interesting pattern. Taking gross national product per capita in 1970 as a rough measure, the average European still produces only half as much as the average American ($3,840). But there are enormous differences:

1. Three countries not affected by the war: Sweden ($2,730), Switzerland ($2,480), Iceland ($2,850).
2. Central Europe: West Germany ($2,400), France ($2,250), Denmark ($2,320).
3. Northwest: United Kingdom ($2,050), Norway ($2,020), Belgium ($1,910), Holland ($1,670).
4. Coming up: Ireland ($1,010), Italy ($1,350).
5. Poor relations: Greece ($690), Spain ($770), Portugal ($430), Turkey ($290).

Our map, however, shows that national averages conceal horrendous inequalities between regions; regional averages, of course, conceal even wider class differences. A closer look at the figures reveals the existence of dire misery in the midst of prosperity. In France, for example, the official minimum wage of 2 francs per hour is paid to 1 million workers, and one-quarter of the population is below the poverty line; a skilled worker makes about 1,000 francs a month, his helper half that much; a civil-service employee draws 1,800 francs, his director, an engineer or executive twice as much. A primary-school teacher may earn 1,500 francs, a *lycée* (high school) teacher 3,000 francs, a professor 6,000 francs. As everywhere, migrant workers are ill housed and poorly protected from exploitation.

It remains for us to identify the ruling class in this new Europe. Old fortunes have been wiped out by two wars, inflation, depression, and taxation. On the whole, income from property has declined from one-third to one-fourth of all income in England, from one-half to one-third in France, from 40 per cent to 30 per cent in Germany. But what mattered was not the decline of property but the decline of its significance.

The old generation of entrepreneurs has been replaced by new leaders of industry

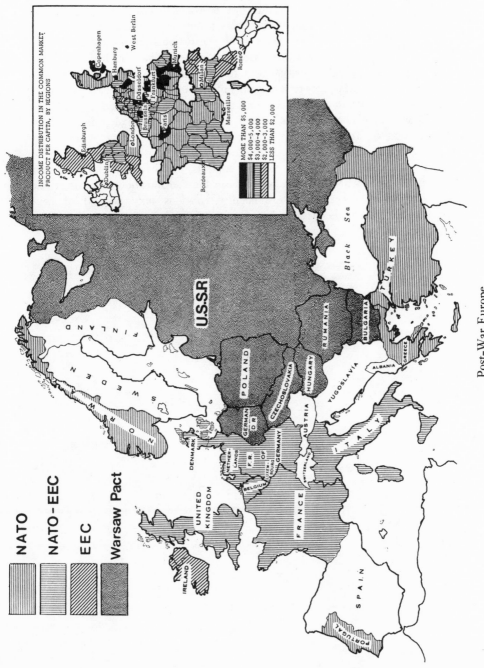

INCOME DISTRIBUTION IN THE COMMON MARKET
PRODUCT PER CAPITA, BY REGIONS

MORE THAN $5,000
$4,000–5,000
$3,000–4,000
$2,000–3,000
LESS THAN $2,000

Edinburgh

Dublin

London

Brussels

Paris

Bordeaux

Copenhagen

Hamburg

West Berlin

Düsseldorf

Frankfurt

Munich

Milan

Marseilles

Rome

NATO

NATO–EEC

EEC

Warsaw Pact

IRELAND

UNITED
KINGDOM

NORWAY

SWEDEN

FINLAND

DENMARK

NETHER-
LANDS

BELGIUM

LUXEM-
BOURG

F. R.
OF
GERMANY

GERMAN
D. R.

POLAND

CZECHOSLOVAKIA

AUSTRIA

SWITZERLAND

HUNGARY

FRANCE

ITALY

YUGOSLAVIA

RUMANIA

BULGARIA

ALBANIA

GREECE

TURKEY

SPAIN

PORTUGAL

U.S.S.R.

Black Sea

Post-War Europe

who are not owners but managers. Not content to direct one company, they are government agents, lobbyists, cartel directors, or association heads, making decisions affecting an entire industry. They are engineers, technicians, accountants, and lawyers, and they identify their interests closely with the national purpose. They think of themselves as a meritocracy rather than as "bosses." They are highly aware of technical possibilities and define success in technological and institutional rather than financial categories. Managers tend to think in terms of "the company," aggrandizing their collective self into a production unit or into a financial power. Especially the transnational conglomerates have created interests that are independent of any human, regional, or even technological purposes. Some of them produce more individually than a good number of countries do.

Because they tend to transcend national interests, they have provoked opposition from many governments. Still more dangerous is the alienation of the directing circles from community concerns in any country. Nations once accused of being "imperialistic" now are helpless *vis-à-vis* a new phenomenon that may, in due course, require new orientations in economic policy.

CHAPTER 2

Technology and Science in the Second Half of the Twentieth Century

WORLD War II ended with the detonation of the first atomic bomb, which opened "the Atomic Age." European scientists had helped to make the experiment a success. Now powerless to order the genie back into the bottle, they thought of means to undo their Promethean crime; one, they felt, was to make the secret available to all nations. Meanwhile, a strong movement had gotten underway to limit or ban and entirely abolish the use and manufacture of nuclear weapons. Marchers demonstrated against the use of British sites for such weapons. The Soviet government supported the effective slogan, "Ban the Bomb," but would not permit verification of such a ban by independent observers on its territory. To circumvent the difficulty, the powers eventually concluded the Moscow Pact of 1963 banning atomic tests in the air, under water, and in outer space (but not underground), which are polluting and can easily be verified. This was followed in 1967 by a pact banning the placing of mass-destructive weapons in outer space, and in 1968 by a nonproliferation treaty banning the transmission of nuclear weapons to countries not yet possessing them. This treaty failed to bar China and India from the "nuclear club." West Germany and Rumania signed it only after being assured that it would not exclude them from competing in the market for peaceful uses of atomic power. For meanwhile, the commercial possibilities and industrial fringe benefits resulting from the development of atomic power began to loom large in the economic prospects of the most advanced countries. These uses range from medical application to biological and industrial research to power plants. England opened the world's first full-scale nuclear-power station at Calder Hall in 1956. By 1967, England produced 16 billion kwh by nuclear energy and Italy 4 billion kwh. In 1957 the Continental Six established Euratom, which built the giant cyclotron in Lausanne. In 1958, the Soviet Union launched a nuclear-powered icebreaker. In 1971, it completed construction of the first commercial breeder reactor.

Another great post-war advance in scientific technology began during the war and for war purposes. The fully automated factory required an "electronic brain," or

349

computer. The theory for such instruments was worked out by John von Neumann[1] and Norbert Wiener. Von Neumann made further contributions in game theory, which is of importance in making strategic decisions; Wiener developed the new science of cybernetics, or the theory of communication and autocontrol. His student Karl Deutsch[2] applied the theory of communications to the study of political bodies, to decision making in large organizations, to international relations and industrial competition. The techniques of systems analysis which sprang from these studies found immediate application first in U.S. business corporations, then in West European countries, and eventually in Eastern Europe and the Soviet Union.

Automation is the logical sequence to mechanization and rationalization—a self-steering or self-governing machine aggregate which can control its output and produce articles "touched by no human hand." Basically, a thermostat or the governor of a steam engine is a "feed-back," the crucial element of all automation. Such automated operations were installed after the war in bakeries and coal mines and in other industries where an electronic judgment can regulate the flow of materials, heat, and so on. Where controls are complex and require adjustment to a preset program, "electronic brains" or computers perform the controlling operations.

Computers are electronic calculators which can be set for various contingencies and, with the aid of a "memory drum" or tape, can store information for later selection and application. Computers may be programmed to respond to certain stimuli, to solve mathematical problems, to select favorable solutions to prepared contingencies (as in a game of chess), and so on. They may solve problems that are either too complex or that require the making of extremely quick decisions such as the steering of a rocket, the logistics of an army in battle, the flow of ingredients in a foundry, the application of game theory to strategic and economic planning, flood control, the working of jet-propelled and supersonic aircraft or of self-steering vehicles, machines, and weapons, and many other techniques.

This "third industrial revolution" produced a new relationship between government, science, and technology. In earlier ages, too, technical progress had been based on scientific insight and in turn had stimulated new basic research. Also, scientists had often enjoyed government grants whose ultimate purpose may have been national mobilization. But at no time before had science depended for such a large part of its activities on the direct interest of industry and government. Even basic research, once the most esoteric preserve of "pure" science, now acquired direct bearing on important assignments in the art of war or in solving advanced engineering problems. The huge sums required to construct a cyclotron or a wind tunnel, the complex organizations necessary to conduct sociological inquiries, the need for teamwork and long-range planning in any modern laboratory experiment, all this gave control over the direction of research to corporations and governments. Of necessity, the questions

---

[1] The contribution of European immigrants to American science and technology can be studied under three headings: refugees from Hitler, the so-called brain drain, and the post-war internationalization of information.

[2] Another European.

were asked by those who financed the projects. The technology which made the new experiments possible also suggested, or even demanded, every next step in research.

The conquests of modern science became available directly and immediately for practical exploitation in the aircraft, chemical, electronics, metallurgical industries and, through immediate feedback, benefited from their advances. The starting time for new discoveries and inventions thus has been shortened. New inventions are first required for the arms race; technological pioneers are mobilized to scan the frontiers of science for new break-throughs. The solutions they find and the supplementary inventions they summon to their aid then find new uses in many nonmilitary and nonindustrial areas and also benefit science, whose solutions for one problem in turn open possibilities for further military-industrial escalation. Varying a famous presidential coining, we may speak of a military (or government)-industrial-academic (or research) complex.

In this manner science has learned more about aerodynamics, thermodynamics, subatomic particles (thirty of which are now known), electrometallurgy, the properties of light (with the discovery of lasers and masers), radioactivity, body poisons, chromosomes, genetics, enzymes, and many other things in the past twenty-five years than in 2,500 years before. Great and important as these acquisitions are, however, they have all been of a more or less practical and empirical nature and "new," most often, just in the methods used. In all sciences, textbooks now devote a good deal of space to discussing methods. On the other hand, none of the recent discoveries has had the shattering consequences of quantum theory, relativity, or psychoanalysis. Science has turned away from the search for universal laws of nature; instead, it offers new hypotheses on any particular problem every ten years.

Just the same, significant new departures were registered or debated in several branches of science, many of them not related to the general advance of technology. Of the great number I shall discuss only two which are of a more philosophical interest: the new cosmology and the new genetics.

In the first half of the century, astronomers believed in the theory of the "exploding world egg." Spectral analysis of far-away nebulae had convinced them that matter is receding at ever-increasing speed. Two conclusions had to be drawn from this observation. At the outer limit, in keeping with the theory of relativity, the continuous expansion of the universe would ultimately reach the speed of light, when matter would be converted into energy; secondly, there had to be a "beginning" from which the explosion started, and the date of that act of creation could be calculated at a dozen billion years before the present era. Recently, however, suns that are much younger, some perhaps just a few million years old, have been discovered; the conclusion seems inescapable that matter is still being created. The universe then would consist of a constant flow of energy or matter originating within the system and losing itself at its outer fringes (to use a layman's coarse simile). This model would contradict the famous principle of entropy, derived from the second law of thermodynamics, that the world will eventually come to a standstill, the much-dreaded "death by stagnation"; cosmology seemed to be promising something more akin to eternal return.

Even more significant seemed the new orientation in biology. In the nineteenth century, progressives knew each other by their benevolent faith in the infinite malleability of the human plasma. If man was to be perfectible, as they believed, they had to assume that civilization, or at least some civilizing influences, could be handed on to future generations. In the biologists' language, this meant that acquired characteristics could be inherited by the progeny. Consistently, the Russian Academy of Sciences believed Trofim Lysenko's fantastic assertions that he could manipulate the genetic heritage of tomatoes. By contrast, conservatives held to the strict view of Galton and Mendel that nature neither changes, except by chance mutations, nor can it be tampered with or improved upon. This view became odious in the 1930's because it was the basis for the fanatical race doctrines of the Nazis. Their unscientific, demagogical use of the biological myth has discredited and stifled also the legitimate, healthy practices of eugenics and population control elsewhere. The charge of genocide has even been invoked to foil attempts at curbing the population explosion in under-developed countries.

But science eventually came into its own. The work of Julian Huxley and Hermann J. Müller, continuing earlier research by Thomas Hunt Morgan, Hugo de Vries, William Bateson, based genetic theory on solid scientific bases. In 1944, O. T. Avery, C. M. MacLeod, and M. McCarry showed that DNA (desoxyribonucleic acid) is crucial for the transmission of hereditary traits; in 1953, F. H. C. Crick and J. D. Watson constructed the model of the "double helix" for DNA.

Cyril Dean Darlington then tried to show, in *Genetics and Man* and later in *The Evolution of Man and Society*, how genetic factors may have influenced human history and the structure of society. At the same time, Konrad Lorenz dealt with aggression as a genetic trait of mankind which has to be domesticated lest it dominate society.

These scientific impulses, coming at a moment when racial strife and the identity search of emerging nations gave such research a political significance, conferred new popularity on anthropology, ethnology, and culturology. It is now pretty much agreed that humanity was not built on one model and is not driven to strive after one ideal but will follow many different paths, fulfill itself in various ways, and offer a multi-colored diversity of achievements and value systems, depending on the interactions between external factors and bio-cultural inheritance.[3] Some scholars feel that in mysterious ways cultural patterns and spiritual attitudes can be inherited as well. It has also been remarked that societies aspiring toward a new type of man favor anthropological theories that may help such endeavor. We still know too little about mutations to say whether the many "small" or the few "big" strides hold the greatest promise for the emergence of new variants in human society. Each culture either promotes or stifles the types capable of assuring it the most favorable development. And vice versa, each culture may either encourage or prohibit the propagation of types that are apt to destroy it.

The social and cultural nature of disease has never been as clear as these days when

---

[3] In this spirit, the Franciscan Placide Tempels published a *Bantu Philosophy* (1928).

health statistics show a remarkable shift away from poor people's diseases, such as tuberculosis, to age-connected ailments like heart failure. In most European countries, infant mortality has been reduced drastically as general hygiene has improved and health services have become available to all. Nutrition standards have been raised. Drugs have been invented to treat diseases hitherto considered incurable. We have antibiotics, vaccines, antihistamines, hormones, cortisone, anesthetics, contraceptives; even some types of mental illness are being treated with drugs. New techniques in surgery and new diagnostic tools have changed the lives of millions and changed the life-style of others. For the first time, war was not followed by great epidemics, thanks to the use of vaccines.

For the first time, also, health is understood as part of national planning. No longer merely a service supplied to an individual, preventive medicine provides for the conditioning of millions for healthy living, the avoidance or prevention of disease. Many doctors would redefine health care in new scientific terms of city planning, welfare service, ecological programs, and national politics. Control of the environment has become a technological necessity and a popular slogan.

CHAPTER 3

The Third Industrial Revolution and the New Class

THE second industrial revolution was connected with the rise of the electrical and chemical industries and with the arrival of the giant corporation and monopoly capitalism. Although obviously such "revolutions" can never be dated very precisely, we speak of a third industrial revolution in the second half of the century, which is carrying the economies of the most advanced countries to still higher levels and permits some less advanced countries to shift directly into high gear, happily skipping the sweat and labors of early capitalism, as described by Marx, or of primitive accumulation by fascist or Stalinist methods. Instant communication, computer programming, market research, international giant corporations may determine a new era of material, technique-oriented civilization. Its characteristic tools are communication and organization, systems analysis—in short, the conceptualization of human interaction. The idea itself certainly is not new; long ago, it had been applied to the use of machines in the shop. It now was extended to the use of organization in business and government, or even in an entire national economy.

Automation, which is only one aspect of this revolution, extends and continues the replacement of human labor by mechanical devices. It consists of four processes: continuous flow or automatic handling operations, whereby the worker is replaced by a machine adjuster; data-processing systems, whereby thousands of recording and processing operations are transferred to an "electronic brain"; feed-back, or self-controlling devices, replacing human overseers; automatic assembly, or the robot factory anticipated in Chaplin's *Modern Times* and René Clair's *À Nous la Liberté*.

Totally automated factories are few in Europe or even in America or the Soviet Union. But feed-back, materials controls, programming, and computers have been introduced in a wide range of processes, notably in the plastic, chemical, and metallurgical industries. New combinations of tools and transmission have been required to make new techniques practicable and profitable. As traditional production methods had to be translated into processes, production for the first time was understood as a process. This new insight not only opened new technological opportunities; it also changed the thinking of those who were engaged in production processes. They conceived of the product no longer as a substance to be handled but as part of a manipulative chain. What really was new in automation, therefore, was not the more or less complete elimination of the human hand but the submission of that hand, if it continued to be needed, to the process, the visualizing of goods moving and machines serving this continuous process.

This new kind of thinking was applied also to the steering of entire economic units; what had been adumbrated during the war now helped to solve peacetime economic problems. The new gospel, coming from America, was accepted only by some pioneers in the advanced countries. "Modernize or perish!" Jean Monnet preached to businessmen, governments, peasants, to all Europeans. Technological advances in the biggest and most highly industrialized countries affect every other country. The "new look" in military power spread from the United States and the Soviet Union to the NATO and Warsaw Pact countries; they learned the techniques of communications control and the game theory.

The new approach also invaded the office and subjected the salariat to the same discipline as the proletariat. In fact, for the first time production of goods and production of less tangible services began to be comparable. "Operators" now service the computerized office machines in much the same way they do the automated lathe. Moreover, in terms of value added and hours consumed, the production of goods proper (manufacture) tends to stagnate, while office work and services tend to expand both in absolute and in percentage terms. In other respects, too, the difference between factory production and services gets narrower: while the latter use more and more machines (accounting machines, multiplying machines, communications equipment, computers—not to mention the punch cards and numbers that nowadays accompany a citizen from cradle to grave), in the factory tools appear to be both more sophisticated and more compact, lighter, easier to handle, housed in more pleasant work rooms and laboratories; often the new, more efficient, and more advanced machines are cheaper than the ones they replace. On the other hand, they become obsolete faster. And of course they require fewer attendants, less exertion, more skill. The proportion between physical labor spent in producing and processing the goods, on the one hand, and white-collar work invested in planning, preparing, designing, supervising, distributing, and accounting for the production, on the other hand, has shifted toward the latter. Reversing a trend that was still conspicuous in the inter-war period, the ratio of fixed to circulating capital ceases to increase. Physically, the average generator of electric power may have expanded tenfold since the war; but the cost of plant per kilowatt-hour has been halved. Better use of materials and their properties, better knowledge of processes result in enormous capital savings. High-grade steel is now produced at lower cost by injecting oxygen into the molten iron, a process first used by Vereinigte Österreichische Stahlwerke in 1950.

The electronics industry has provided European homes with kitchen appliances and television sets; the invention of transistors has greatly reduced the size of instruments while increasing their life and accuracy. Transistors also have made the computers a thousand times more efficient since they were first invented. Computers have greatly changed the rate and direction of further industrial progress. Problems which once had seemed incapable of practical solution, suddenly grew manageable, and the thinking about problems has been changed by the new means.

The greatest progress was registered in all branches of the chemical industry: synthetic and disposable materials, drugs, paints and pigments, detergents, insecticides, fuels, and so on. These developments revolutionized practically all of the other industries and the habits of many consumers. To medicine they gave an entire new pharmacy, plus radioisotopes, and other new inventions. To industry they gave more flexible materials and tools: synthetic diamonds for cutting, rubies for bearings, nylon tires and nylon machine parts, packaging materials and foam rubber, Orlon, Dacron and acrylic fibers that need no more pressing. To farmers, finally, they gave new fertilizers, nutrients, and pest controls.

American methods of distribution came to Europe as well: the shopping center, the self-service store, the supermarket. A poor immigrant boy, John Cohen, made a fortune selling food to England's poor at small markups, founded the Tesco chain, defied the Price Maintenance (fair trade) Law, and was knighted by the Labour government for "services to retailing."

To exploit the new opportunities, management attempts to create and protect its own markets. Technological progress constantly replaces machines and men by new processes; research and development themselves have become great new industries. Finally, this new technology has favored new types of enterprise such as the international combine, the state-owned monopoly, the "chosen instrument," the plan-oriented corporation. Survival was no longer a question of being "fittest" but of being adaptable to the environment of the welfare economy and the various forms of government planning. Though Europe still has an economy of small and intermediate producers, markets are either dominated by a few big enterprises or controlled and regulated by the planners. The government itself, absorbing up to 10 per cent of the national product, has the power to enforce its standards.

Especially since the founding of the Common Market, business can be conducted on a scale comparable to America's and the Soviet Union's. Shell and Unilever have sales exceeding $6 billion; British Steel, British Petroleum, Imperial Chemical, Siemens, Volkswagen, and Philips have gross sales in excess of $3 billion each; the gross sales of Rhône-Poulenc, Montecatini, Nestlé, Thyssen, Renault, Bayer, Höchst, Badische Anilin- und Sodafabrik, AEG-Telefunken, Fiat, Daimler-Benz, British Leyland, Krupp, GEC (the British electrical trust) exceed $1 billion, and each of these companies employs more than 100,000 workers. Each of the four components into which I. G. Farben was divided now has sales exceeding the former I. G. Farben sales total. Others in this category are: British National Coal Board, AKZO Chemicals (Dutch), Companie Française de Pétroles, ENI (Italian, petroleum products), British-American Tobacco, Courtaulds (textiles), Pechiney (metals, France).

Fifty corporations in the OEEC countries have a sales volume of a half billion dollars or more; the total of corporations exceeding a quarter billion dollars is $70 billion. Of the 500 largest firms in the world outside the Soviet Union, England has 55, Germany 30, France 23, Italy 8; together these produce 15 per cent of the world's machinery, automobiles, electronic equipment, and 20 per cent of all chemical and oil products. Many of these firms interlock through joint subsidiaries, cartel arrangements, exchange of shares, and directors; many have American ties;[1] others are state property. Among these are Renault in France; Montecatini, Finsider, Finmeccanica in Italy, and the great petroleum and financial empire, ENI, which the late Enrico Mattei tried to develop as the basis for an independent Italian policy.

The cases of Renault and ENI, to a certain extent also Volkswagen, point up a phenomenon puzzling to both economists and sociologists. These were state-operated enterprises, but the government did not control them. They became the personal empires of their respective presidents or general managers, who used them in the arbitrary fashion of enlightened despotism for policies of their own. Such goals as a new social policy for Renault, the successful marketing of the most popular export car in the world, liberating Italy's fuel economy from Anglo-American tutelage, praiseworthy in themselves perhaps, nevertheless created dubious powers which reversed the relationship between the state and its enterprise. ENI owned a newspaper and influenced the editorial policies of others; it developed and supported the left wing of the Christian Democratic Party; it conducted its own foreign policy; it constituted itself as a lobby in parliament; it milked the public to finance ventures judged worthy by Signor Mattei. No doubt he was as idealistic as Jean Monnet of France; but he was able to say of the kings of Libya and Iran: "I intend to make them my partners in business." Likewise the Volkswagen management told the German Government and people what was good for them.

In setting up her "public corporations," England has tried to avoid the opposite, though technically related danger: not expansion of personal power but creation of a resource which could conceivably render the government financially independent of parliament. Presumably, public corporations are tightly controlled by representation of various public bodies on their boards. In France, the preferred form is the mixed enterprise; but the board members of these corporations are likely to be the same men (or their friends) who also sit in the government's planning and control agencies. They all tend to be graduates of the École Polytechnique or the Institut National des Études Économiques et Financières; they are members of the "Inspectorate" of the Ministry of Finance; they are the people behind the Plan, the National Accounts Office, the Bureau of Forecasts, and the National Planning Commission. And they also sit on the boards of the great banks and private corporations.

Even before the war, this new elite of technical, financial, and economic managers had gained great influence and experience. In the corporations they were wresting power from the shareholders; in cartels and trade associations, the corporation lawyers and managers made decisions which the owners could neither understand nor prevent. During the war, this technical elite grew even more powerful. Civil servants and

---

[1] Among the latter are Olivetti, Rootes, Bull, Simca, Libby-France, Opel, Alsacienne, Agfa-Gevaert. Half of the U.S. involvement in Europe involves five corporations: General Electric, International Business Machines, Chrysler, General Motors, Union Carbide. All told, Americans own more than 1,500 firms in Germany, France, and Italy alone.

managers were called on to run the economy; they fixed prices and production targets, they organized the nation for survival. Nor did they abdicate their functions when reconstruction took the place of war. Nationalized industries and planning enhanced their positions. Industrial managers, public administrators, political organizers, in some countries military men, scientists and trade-union leaders in others, form the leading cadres of highly industrialized societies.

This is especially true of the powerful bankers who guide the destinies of their nations and of Europe as a whole. Hermann Abs rose to the head of the Deutsche Bank in the 1930's, a position he held through three regimes until his retirement in the 1960's. Karl Blessing, head of Germany's Bundesbank, began as an assistant to Hjalmar Schacht, served the Unilever concern for a while, to become the Federal Republic's money manager. Guido Carli provides the same service for Italy. In France, Jacques Brunet and Jacques Rueff, both products of the Inspectorate, control the money supply. At the Bank of England, the exalted position once held by Lord Norman, Lord Keynes, and Lord Cromer is now held by Sir Leslie O'Brien, who worked his way up inside the bank. President of the International Monetary Fund was Pierre-Paul Schweitzer,[2] another former "inspecteur des finances," and Fred Hirsch, a banker.

What is true of bankers and national planners is even more true of the cartel bureaucracy, of international managers, of functionaries in ECSC, OECD, and other agencies of European co-operation. They are now properly called Eurocrats—international men of power. Jean Monnet and Walter Hallstein, the founders of the OECD, and Jean Rey, a Belgian Protestant and present Chairman of the OECD Commission, are perfect examples of this new breed: civil servants of a state they still have to build.

It is true that the nineteenth-century families who rose to economic power have not died out and that big enterprises have also been founded in the twentieth century and even after the war. We can still point to big names such as Weinstock, Agnelli (Fiat), Olivetti, Bercot (Michelin-Citroen), Pilkington, Pinelli, Marzotto, Wallenberg, Brostroem, Springer, Prévost. But the old houses are dying out. The Thyssen and Krupp families have surrendered their shares, and their enterprises are run by able managers. Where industries have been nationalized, their managers often come from middle-class families and engineering or business schools. Finally, the transnational corporations have brought to the top an entirely new crop of business barons who owe allegiance to no state.

In the nineteenth century, capitalists were the leading class because managing was a direct function of wealth. The promoters of individual or national enterprises now are not necessarily wealthy men themselves. Actually, they are seekers of power rather than of wealth. They justify their pre-eminent position neither by birth nor by possession of the means of production, but by their ability to use, to dispose of, and to operate the levers of production, communication, and finance. Often they show political ambitions, too.

---

[2] His reappointment was vetoed in 1972 by the United States.

In connection with this shift from wealth to power, class stops being identical with income. Some people with substantial incomes do not make policy and are economically passive—movie stars, owners of shares and bonds—while actual control rests with executives with significantly lower incomes who technically are "hired" by the shareholders. The trend was first noted before World War I by the Austro-Marxist Rudolf Hilferding and by Max Weber. Just before World War II a French-Italian Trotskyist, writing under the pseudonym "R," denounced *La Bureaucratisation du Monde*. Karl Mannheim, who had fled from Hungary to Germany and from there to England, became one of the most influential analysts of the new ruling class with his *Man and Society in the Age of Reconstruction*. For a wider public, George Orwell showed the nightmare of a totally directed society in his eerie *1984*. (This counter-utopia, a horrifying sequel to Huxley's *Brave New World*, was written in 1948.) Czeslaw Milosz in *The Captive Mind* draws on Soviet examples but actually embraces a much wider range of contemporary experience. Later, Milovan Djilas in *The New Class* accused the Communist bureaucracy of having substituted itself for the old class. These dissident Communists were followed by Herbert Marcuse and Jürgen Habermas, both issued from the Frankfurt Institute of Social Research, as well as by the conservatives, Ralf Dahrendorf and Jacques Ellul, who all see humanistic culture in danger of being stifled by the technocentric mind. For functional bureaucrats have no relationship to the people who make and use their products. They calculate what is good for their organization—whether company, state, or branch of industry—and they believe that they are merely translating the dictates of necessity. Power belongs in the hands of experts, and they think of themselves as servants of their city, nation, or corporation. Dahrendorf therefore speaks of a new "service society" and "service nobility," reminiscent of Hegel's view of the civil service as a "universal estate." Advancement here is by merit; decisions are made according to Max Weber's notion of *Zweckrationalität*[3]—a notion debunked by Habermas as the ideology of the new power elite. Sociology of consciousness and critique of ideology have become special fields of research, pioneered by the neo-Marxists.

Title-conscious Europe indeed expects from its academics more than technical expertise. Wrongly or rightly, it looks to these "mandarins" also for moral guidance, or even for political solutions. But the intelligentsia rejected this mission. Its very mode of operation forbade it to ask for power in its own name. Traditionally it had always served other classes. Its clients had been kings, the Third Estate, and, more recently, the proletarian state. Technocracy has no political philosophy of its own; it is not class-conscious for itself but only self-conscious of its class. C. P. Snow, himself a novelist, scientist, administrator, and politician, wrote a series of thirteen novels about the new breed of masters and their conflicts in *The Corridors of Power*. The

---

[3] "Purpose-oriented rationality" unaffected by personal or other interests. Weber, however, warned the intelligentsia not to lay claim to a superiority it does not have, that of engagement. The scientist can observe and invent, but no science tells him what purpose he should pursue. Erroneously, the public sometimes thinks that knowledge of facts can engender imperatives for action; the scientist knows that commitment never emerges from a test tube or questionnaire.

controversial role that Dr. F. A. Lindemann, Churchill's adviser, played in British war councils provided the background for a widely followed debate on the proper relationship between the "two cultures."

Scientists and scientific manipulators find themselves in commanding roles and in possession of superior insight but without the final power of decision. They are agents, executors of the sovereign's will, which they may influence but not steer. Their position in society thus becomes as ambiguous as that of the bourgeoisie was in the *ancien régime*: status, honor, even power are passing into the hands of people who are not legitimatized by custom or law. They govern though they do not rule; it is only natural that they would like to determine the policy they have to execute. Moreover, this desire is not a purely personal or selfish one. Their ways of thinking and even their moral standards are different from those of the interest groups that still prevail over most areas of life. Their thinking is not capitalistic but technocentric; their ethics is not based on the survival of the fittest but on the rule of rationality in domestic as well as in international affairs. The ideal of competition yields to the ideal of co-operation; the "market" is replaced by the meeting. Especially among the younger generation of social scientists, social workers, educators, pure scientists, and students of the humanities, there grows a new orientation of values. No longer ruled by the performance principle, by the need to excel and achieve, they are informed by a strong revulsion against these attitudes.

CHAPTER 4

The End of Ideology

WHILE the new elites prepared to take Europe's destiny into their own hands and the old classes were reorienting themselves, the political structure of the European states was far from reflecting these changes. The old parties still brandished the ideologies they had developed as spokesmen of various social classes. Interests still were deeply entrenched in the party machines and closely identified with definite ideologies. Historical allegiances still determined the language of party platforms. In their actual practice, however, the parties began to adjust themselves to the new realities. The conservatives accepted the welfare state; the socialists had no intention of going beyond the welfare state.

In Austria the (conservative, Christian-Social) People's Party and the Social Democratic Party had a curious arrangement which lasted through the 1950's to 1968. They formed a permanent coalition, and after each election the cabinet posts were distributed among them in exact "proportion" to the percentage of votes each party had received (hence the system came to be called "Proporz"). The composition of the Swiss Government is also quite nonideological: Socialists, Catholics, and Radicals (that is, conservatives), who as a rule get one-quarter of the popular vote each, are each given two seats in the nine-man Nationalrat; parties polling less than 25 per cent of the vote get only one seat. The merry-go-round of governments in France, Belgium, and the Netherlands amounted to the same state of mutual toleration. *La république des copains* (the republic of buddies), as it was called in France, survived the demise of the Third Republic and was resurrected in the Fourth.

As we have seen, conservatives who followed socialist governments did not reverse, but only revised nationalization and welfare policies; nor did socialists in government subvert the private-enterprise economy so radically that revisions would have been impossible. At the end of the 1950's, the parties even found it necessary to rewrite their programs. This process was slow and relatively imperceptible on the Right, which had always been more pragmatic than the Left; but even there painful splits could not be avoided. For the socialists, revision was a continuation of the tug-of-war which their right and left wings had been carrying on since the beginning of the century. The all-or-nothing philosophy of maximalism still was strong in countries where poverty was most widespread and workers had few rights; gradualism was the order of the day where the socialists were looking forward to a governmental role.

At its congress in Blackpool, in 1959, the Labour Party tried to give itself a new image and made an open bid for the middle-class vote. Hugh Gaitskell wished to get rid of the "working-class" label and promised a "new style" in politics. He also wished to jettison "Clause Four" of the program (drafted by Sidney Webb in 1920), which committed the party to nationalization of all means of production; but Frank Cousins of the Transport and General Workers' Union, along with the Leftist intellectuals, prevented this sacrifice of a shibboleth. Since the personable Gaitskell died prematurely, Labour also had to go into the election of 1964 without "style," but it won nonetheless.

The German Social Democratic Party's convention at Bad Godesberg, also in 1959, went further. It promised to be "a party for all people" and dropped nationalization from its program. It supported "planning where necessary, free competition where possible." It also retired its old leader, Erich Ollenhauer, and promoted the candidacy of Willy Brandt, then mayor of Berlin, for the Chancellorship. Brandt, a personable man of strong human appeal, was representative of that dynamic "style" which at the time was emanating from the young American President. But Brandt had to wait ten more years before he gained the Chancellorship.

Gaitskell's post fell to Harold Wilson, once a leader of the left wing but no prophet of a revolutionary style in politics. Once in power, he renationalized the steel industry, as promised; but in all other respects he conducted his administration in the spirit of Gaitskell's reformism, giving his constituents good technical administration but little political dynamism. His old friends on the Left kept complaining that competence was not enough justification for a Labour government, that its militants needed an ideology as well. And here the core of the party clashed with the bulk of its voters.

More ideology was jettisoned in Germany when the governing coalition of the two Rightist parties fell apart: A "Broad Coalition" on the Austrian model became possible, although Brandt and his CDU-CSU partner Kurt Georg Kiesinger, had little in common. The Kiesinger-Brandt coalition was uneasy, however, and the 1970 election produced a liberal-socialist coalition under Brandt. Although it gave Germany a new foreign policy, the Socialists still were in no position to carry out their minimum demands: democratization of industrial management and socialization of municipal services. The party leadership clashed over this with the Young Socialists and its own left wing. As in other countries and other parties, ideologies refused to die or were revived cyclically after each burial.

In the northern countries, Social Democratic and labor parties had been more successful on a national scale. Though Marxist neither in theory nor practice since the 1920's, they still had to shed that class-party image which had made it impossible for them to breach the ranks of the petty bourgeoisie, the church-goers, and the intellectuals. The Dutch, Scandinavian, and Swiss socialists adopted programs which either repudiated socialist ideology or acknowledged that profound changes within capitalist society by now made it possible for socialists to seek further adaptation rather than abandonment of the free market. Instead, they placed greater emphasis on the liberal heritage of civil rights and humanization of the environment, issues of supreme interest to intellectuals. Not quite by accident it was discovered that Karl Marx, as a young philosopher before he turned into a grim economic determinist, also had devoted much time to these important questions.

This new, humanist Marx appealed especially to the Italian intelligentsia, which was rapidly being alienated from the church. Even in the 1950's a group of young deputies of the ruling Christian Democratic Party pleaded for separation of the state from canonical law, for "integration of the workers into the state," for an "opening to the Left." They were able to have their leader Giovanni Gronchi elected President, but they could not yet elicit any response from the Socialist Party. In 1958, however, Angelo Roncalli was elected Pope and radically steered the church away from his predecessor's doctrines, notably from the anti-Communist, cold-war ideology, toward tolerance, social progress, and respect for the democratic state. He profoundly changed the attitude of many Catholics toward politics and nonbelievers.

This time the veteran socialist leader Pietro Nenni, who had fallen out with the Communists, could not withhold his support from center-left governments, even though that meant parting with some close political friends and especially with workers who still felt that an ideological gulf separated them from all bourgeois parties. But, significantly, he argued that principles must fall silent when in return the coalition partners agree to substantial, specific reforms such as nationalization of the power lines and land distribution. Both Christians and socialists had grown pragmatic. During the 1960's, ideologies played a much lesser part in the lives of nations than in the preceding decade.

The term "end of ideology," coined in the United States, was eagerly lapped up by European sociologists and political scientists, and transformed into a slogan. In the technocentric society, questions are decided by convenience and necessity—if possible, by computers. Professor Helmut Schelsky portrayed the younger generation, roughly those who were under twenty-five in 1955, as "skeptical, depoliticized, and hostile to ideologies," concerned mostly with their own security or advancement within the framework of existing society. This was aptly called "Americanization," for Europeans expect their own kind to be idealistic.

Throughout the 1950's, conservative politicians won elections with slogans like: "You never had it so good"; "Don't rock the boat"; "No experiments." The claim seemed justified by the increasing number of TV sets, cars, motorcycles (or motor-scooters); by the fact that a middle-class style of life was adopted by more and more workmen; by the growing student population; by the shift from country to city, from proletariat to salariat. While income differentials remained steeper in Europe than in the United States, more intermediate strata came to be recognized between bourgeoisie and proletariat; the transitions were getting smoother; the ladder of social mobility seemed easier to climb. The most visible signs of these changes were the increase in high-school enrollment, the general availability of luxury consumer goods, and the leveling of consumer tastes.

Before the war, the percentage of the college-educated nowhere in Europe exceeded

5 per cent. Now attendance in colleges, teachers' seminars, engineering schools, and the like jumped to almost 10 per cent of the eighteen- to twenty-two-year-olds in Denmark, Norway, England, Italy, and West Germany; to 15 per cent in Belgium, France, and the Netherlands; by 1970 it was to reach 50 per cent in Sweden. In 1968, automobiles, more a status symbol than a means of transportation in some countries, were owned by 250 out of 1,000 persons in Sweden, 200 in France, 180 in West Germany and England, 165 in Belgium, 130 in the Netherlands and Italy.

Erich Fromm and others have described man in the late-capitalist civilization as a compulsive consumer. He does not create what he needs; neither does he consume creatively—he just buys his satisfactions. Spectators may be thrilled, but intellectually they remain passive while watching a movie, a sports event, a TV show. The consumer gulps down the picture pages of illustrated magazines, races through landscapes and museums recommended by guidebooks, accumulates a catalogue of restaurants and hotels he has visited; he may even "take in" a lecture or a concert because "culture," too, belongs among the things that increase his status. He surrounds himself with hundreds of gadgets and goods which are substitutes for his personality. If Verlaine had M. Teste say: "To live? Our servants can do that for us," one is tempted to imagine the new men saying: "Our gadgets do our living for us." Achievements no longer are considered the measure of life's fulfillment. Instead, pleasure is usually rated as the highest good. An assortment of goods and sensations can be bought from specialists, such as entertainers, and consumed on the spot.

In the light of our post-war experience it is now possible to see that old-style Marxism was founded on substantially the same notions of value as old-style capitalism: substance, work, conscience, and loyalty to a collective structure. The post-war parties, to a considerable degree, share with the fascists of the preceding period a disbelief in eternal values and ideas, a hedonistic indifference to the transcending issues of man's future. Hence the charge that we are faced not simply with a revolution in values but with a revolt against the very notion of value—or indeed with a cultural crisis.

Capitalism is shedding the last residues of its feudal, traditional patrimony and appears now in its pure form as a culture entirely oriented toward the acquisition and enjoyment of goods, a culture in which the self-seeking individual breaks all ties of family, class, nationality, trade, and religion, to follow his or her personal interests—a culture, finally, where traditional ideas no longer determine the interests of individuals and groups.

The breakdown of ideologies affected equally the conformist and the nonconformist, the establishmentarian capitalist and the critical socialist, the nationalist and the cosmopolitan attitudes. At a moment when, significantly perhaps, everybody was talking about "identity," most people lost their identification with class, church, country, the social structure. The young especially refused to defend the old empires, the old system and its values, and, still more surprisingly, were no longer scared by the system's enemies. The older generation's strong anti-Communist beliefs began to seem hypocritical to its sons. Not the workers, who according to Marx have no fatherland, but middle-class students now denounced their parents' loyalties, the flag, the national anthem, the ideology of Western solidarity and defense.

The seat of "ideological" policies seemed to be Washington, and all those who wished to escape from ideological warfare, both anti-militarists and nationalists, found a common ideology in anti-Americanism. De Gaulle won their admiration in France and elsewhere because his policies were frankly national, self-centered, unideological. Other spokesmen of European stature were Kingsley Martin of the *New Statesman and Nation* and Hubert Beuve-Méry of *Le Monde*. The former was left-wing and iconoclastic, the latter, hand-picked by de Gaulle, was deeply traditionalist. *Le Monde* supplied the European intelligentsia with a steady flow of anti-NATO propaganda and cultural defense against Coca-Colonization. An attempt to unseat Beuve-Méry resulted in the dethronement of the shareholders and eventually in the surrender of all power to the paper's editorial staff. In the end, Beuve-Méry fell out with de Gaulle and supported the student revolt of 1968.

By the end of the 1960's, then, we find a general confusion in the political deployment of masses and leaders. Old conservatives suddenly supported revolution in the streets; old parliamentarians led movements to end parliamentarianism. The parties relinquished their ideologies and were generally held in low esteem, their leaders discredited by scandals or by ineffectiveness. The malcontents either dropped out or formed "extraparliamentary opposition" groups outside the framework of republican politics. Whatever new development was considered significant—the liquidation of the empires, the new orientation in world politics, the realignment of the clergy, the quiet growth of meritocracy, the economic expansion—did not take place within the framework of old-style politics.

CHAPTER 5

The Youth Culture

IN the 1960's there emerged a stratum of the European population which hardly knew the old ideological alignments and did not care to be involved in them. This group was the young, a segment of the population that had never before been recognized as politically relevant. Reversing a trend which had made Europe's age structure top-heavy in the 1930's, the baby boom of the immediate post-war years had boosted the under-thirty to one-third of the population by the middle 1960's. Too young to have absorbed the horrors of war and fascism or to have experienced the cold war on the same level of political consciousness as their parents, they charged their elders with mismanaging the world into which they had been born. Hunger and war, genocide and the atomic bomb, the ideological division of the globe—all that had been brought about by the preceding generation.

Moreover, the new generation grew up in a more permissive and more critical climate. It went to school longer; more students were graduated from college and university. More of them prepared for white-collar jobs and actually obtained positions allowing them to dispose more freely of their time and to earn and spend more money than their parents had been able to do at the same age.

The first generation of post-war students had been earnest and law-abiding, intent only on "making it" in their parents' world. But many found that the positions society had to offer did not satisfy the cultural expectations which their higher schooling had raised. Jobs answered to no calling, work provided no meaning. The younger group, therefore, in rapidly increasing numbers and with still greater frustration, abandoned themselves to the hedonistic climate of the economic miracle. They wanted instant consumption of goods, instant participation in the rites of the culture, instant gratification of their many desires. They were impatient with the prevailing institutions and eager to change those that no longer satisfied their tastes. Society had not grown more demanding, repression had not grown harsher, but sensibilities had been sharpened and the gap between expectations and reality had become wider. The old European credo that ultimately the individual must be the judge of his happiness reasserted itself with a vengeance: as protest, as drop-out, as despair or, in Herbert Marcuse's term, as the great refusal.

The movement progressed in waves of increasing intensity. First came the existentialists in France and Italy and the "angry young men" in England. Later the young people either cynically or voluptuously embraced the century's hedonism, wondering why they should not go all the way doing their thing and living on impulse. These were the "beats," whose gospel came from America; the *Gammler* in Germany; the *gamberri* in Italy; the *blouses noires* in France; the *provos* in Holland; and, in a different mood, the mods in England—an international brotherhood that defied the established order and refused to follow their fathers' ethics, common sense, and occasionally even common decency. Since they did not believe in achieving success and "amounting to something," their style of life occasionally resembled a Franciscan state of poverty, proving that man can be happy without middle-class morality. But others turned to organized banditry as the *Halbstarken* in Germany, teddy boys in England, and similar cousins of the Hell's Angels—drop-outs who would descend on a beach or town for a weekend, terrorize a neighborhood, battle with the police, peddle and take drugs, beg and drink, and try to show in every way imaginable that the Establishment was powerless.

The first movement was humanistic, or rather it tried to salvage some humanistic values out of the rubble of a decadent society; the second movement was entirely anti-humanistic, a product of the decomposition of the old society. The youth culture proper must be distinguished from either, although in its forms and expressions it may have borrowed from both. It was as self-indulgent as the hippies and as irate as the existentialists, but it was mostly nostalgic. It was a desperate attempt to elude adulthood and to prolong the innocent life of youth into the late twenties. Everyone over thirty, everyone who had abandoned Paradise, was an enemy or at best a stranger.

Clearly, "new tablets" were in order, as Nietzsche had told a previous generation; but they were not the tablets of Nietzsche, who still believed in discipline and will power. While all previous revolutionary movements had been puritanical, this most recent one confused sexual and political freedom. But it adopted Nietzsche's elitism, his contempt of the masses, his disdain of social issues. For all its radicalism, this youth movement had no social or political ideology, no reform plan, not even a utopia. Its ideals were frankly the values of the main culture turned into perversion. Its mannerisms in dress, hair style, speech, and musical tastes were able to conquer the commercial establishment it pretended to hate. The new leaders did not live in garrets; they are presidents of multi-million-dollar record companies and perform for mass audiences. Far from achieving any "culture shock," the rock singers have succeeded and have been co-opted by the consumer culture, part of which—a big market indeed —is now the so-called youth culture, with hashish a philosophical ingredient and pop music its poetry.

Perpetual youth had been the dream of many ages. This generation, for the first time, had the means to prolong the years of innocence, not to strive after the model of some achiever but to disdain success and to make poets or drop-outs its heroes. In a decided break with the style of their parents, young people now worship adolescent performers, singers, disk-jockeys, and young music groups. Pop culture began with Daniel Filipacchi's irreverent radio show and the magazine *Salut les Copains*; Johnny Halliday (pseudonym of Jean-Philippe Smet) became the most popular rock star in

France; after him came Gilbert Bécaud; the latest entry, so far, has been Mick Jagger. There will be other groups, each more advanced in the technique of inducing ecstasy and abandon.

European youth did not simply imitate the American subculture; they built on it. The Piper Club in Rome was as original as the Electric Circus in New York. The Beatles in Liverpool were as creative as Bob Dylan. For a long time, the Beatles and Rolling Stones were the most sophisticated *avant-garde* groups in the West, though it must be admitted that they, too, were eclectic in mixing baroque tunes with Indian raga and the most modern techniques of high-brow music. Strangely, this revolution was introduced everywhere by the most establishmentarian of the media—the state-controlled radio.

This music was inspired by political protest only for a brief moment and peripherally. It is nostalgic or sings of a frustration which is purely personal, like "It's a drag to get old." At a psychologists' meeting in Heidelberg, Professor G. Sänger cited the Beatles' *Penny Lane*, the New Vaudeville's *Finchley Central*, and the Rolling Stones' *Going Home* as instances of the old-fashioned longing to go home and find security in the bosom of a family. Like the lyric poets of all ages, rock artists sing of a lost paradise—in this case one where Father does not have to go to the office. In "It's Not Easy Living On Your Own," the Rolling Stones regret that "There is no place where you can call home," but it is not clear why they should be "running like a cat in a thunderstorm." The young man who cannot "make it" in this running then laments his bad luck (in *Painter Man*) and aggressively voices his desire to cop out: "Get off my cloud."

Then the miracle happens. Precisely by getting out they get in. John Lennon has described in fascinating detail how the Beatles were "made." The commercial exploiters just took the nostalgic stuff from them at ever-increasing speed, demanded more, promised to make them rich, set them up as a corporation with affiliates, lawyers, bookkeepers, expense accounts, huge audiences, monster concerts—until the originators of this nightmare fell out with each other, escaped into drugs, yoga, and far-away countries to become poets again. But meanwhile their style had become the fashion which keeps several industries in the black; each singer now has his own corporation for distributing nostalgia and turning protest into merchandise, reproducible at will on records, on radio, in the dance hall, and capable of infinite variations thanks to sophisticated electronic equipment which easily transforms every creative idea into a technological possibility and every emotion into a marketable commodity.

Just the same, this youth culture has made a deep impression, even though it denies any mission and fulfills no prediction. It is not subservient to any party or ideology. It is anti-capitalist but also anti-socialist, if socialism involves party or country; it is anti-bourgeois but neither proletarian nor necessarily aristocratic; it is anti-Establishment but not for any alternative "system." It is anti-war, it is anti-imperialist and anti-political. Occasionally, as we shall see, it emerges from its dreams, gathers around leaders or movements which are not necessarily as romantic as it is, and shakes the Establishment to its very foundations.

Students were in the forefront of the national, anti-Stalinist opposition in Poland, Hungary, and Czechoslovakia, as they were the friends of the Algerian NLF in Paris. They barricaded the London School of Economics and took over several departments at the universities of Berlin, Frankfurt, Regensburg, and Munich. Their powerful student unions—Christian, democratic, and Communist ones—forced radical changes in the curricula of the ancient Italian universities and a thorough reform of education in France. For the first time in history, education has come to be recognized as the business of students. In many instances, unfortunately, these reforms have been used to give power to terroristic groups professing and teaching a special kind of Marxism which cannot tolerate academic freedom. Abuse of these power positions has led to the indoctrination of young teachers and social workers who in turn try to structure their wards away from established society. While the Eastern dictatorships have been able to keep manifestations of a similar estrangement underground, in the West a counter-culture is being educated in opposition to the capitalist welfare state. Though the two kinds of alienation seem to run in opposite directions, both are eating away the civic allegiance of the young generation.

To summarize, a new type of society was emerging in the West. Based on the new technology, it promised to meet all conditions of human happiness under scientific management. The price, however, was the abandonment of ideals and of political visions. Social progress and equality were being approached in a restoration climate. Government and opposition were merging in the swamp of "Butskellism." Meanwhile the real problem remained: that giant corporations freely controlled society's resources but themselves were uncontrolled. The elites of business, administration, and politics tended to merge and to create a new hierarchy of merit which supplanted the old hierarchy of wealth.

Against this nightmare there arose a cultural protest partly in the form of a revolution of style, partly as a tendency of youth toward anomie. Technocentric society finds itself challenged by the youth movement and, as we shall find, by the intellectuals, too.

(*above*) A slum family in the East End of London, 1912; (*below*) tea in the garden in the 1900s

(*above*) Vinogradov's painting of Lenin addressing the Second Congress of the Russian Social Democratic Labor Party in 1903, a typical example of Socialist realism; (*below*) technocrats, social-imperialists, friends of the Soviet Union and founders of the Fabian Society Sydney and Beatrice Webb at their Hampshire home

(*right*) Picasso's painting "Man with Violin," 1910; (*below*) Rouault's watercolor "Les Justiciers," 1913

(*above*) Satirical map of Europe: German view of the European nations at the beginning of World War I; (*below*) wounded British soldiers, victims of gas warfare

(*above*) Rudolph Valentino, the ideal of manhood in the dream factory, in "The Sheik," 1921; (*below*) a scene from "The Miracle": the multitude worships the Madonna

(*above*) A lithograph by George Grosz entitled "The Workers"; (*below*) a still from the German expressionist film "Dr. Mabuse," 1922

(*right*) A British Labour Party anti-war poster; (*below*) a Nazi election poster

Hitler and Mussolini at their first meeting in Venice, 1934

"SORRY, BUT WE DON'T WANT TO BURN OUR FINGERS."

(*above*) A Low cartoon on the Moscow talks in March 1939 (see pp. 249–50); (*below*) a Polish cartoon on the 1939 invasion: "England! You are guilty!"

ANGLIO! TWOJE DZIEŁO!

(*above left*) Albert Einstein, scientist and humanitarian; (*right*) Thomas Mann, "the last of the bourgeois novelists" (G. Lukács)

(*above*) Artists in exile, a photograph taken on the occasion of an exhibition at the Pierre Matisse Gallery, New York, in March 1942; (*below*) Stalin and Molotov at a parade in 1946

(*above*) Refugees leaving Budapest during the Hungarian uprising in 1956; (*below*) the new Coventry Cathedral built to replace St. Michael's Cathedral Church, which had been destroyed by air raids in 1940 and 1941; designed by Sir Basil Spence, work began in 1954 and the Cathedral was consecrated in 1962

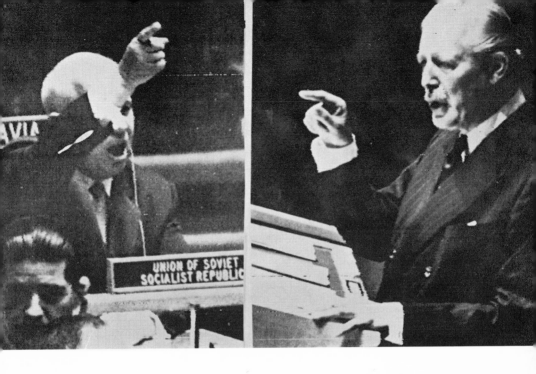

(*above*) Soviet Premier Nikita Khrushchev admonishes British Prime Minister Harold Macmillan during the latter's speech on the break-up of the Paris summit conference at the United Nations General Assembly in September 1960; (*below, left*) German Chancellor Konrad Adenauer; (*right*) General Charles de Gaulle

(*above*) Pope John XXIII pays homage to St. Pius X as the latter's remains are about to leave the Vatican to lie in state in Venice; (*below*) Jean Monnet, "Father of the Common Market," at the center of a group of delegates after the signing of the EEC treaty

Suzy in her tree house: a scene from Fellini's "Juliet of the Spirits"

Zbigniev Cybulski as Maciek Chelmicki in a still from "Ashes and Diamonds"

(*above*) Leaders of the six Eastern-bloc countries place a wreath on the Slavin Memorial in Bratislava during their summit talks in August 1968; (front row, left to right: Kosygin, Zhivkov, Kádár, Brezhnev, Gomulka, Ulbricht, Dubček; Romania was not represented); (*below*) students assemble at the Sorbonne during the 1968 demonstrations

PART X

Culture and Society

Engaged Literature and Its Disengagement

CULTURALLY, the years of dictatorship had been barren. The monumental style Mussolini demanded, the neoclassical giganticism Hitler indulged in certainly could not encourage artists. Emil Nolde painted small sketches of big canvasses that he was not allowed to execute.[1] But judging from what came to light after the war, neither in Germany nor in Italy did many poets or painters secrete subversive poetry or paintings in their closets. Hardly any great novel of manners, no great plaint of doom and decline was waiting after the fall of the dictators. Had the dynamism of the 1920's petered out?

Only among the exiles was there a continuation of the great Periclean age. Thomas Mann wrote the *Joseph* tetralogy and *Doctor Faustus*, Hermann Broch *The Death of Virgil*. Joseph Roth continued to publish until he died of absinthe. Vladimir Nabokov wrote in obscurity in Berlin and was discovered only much later in America. Ignazio Silone divided his talents between political and literary activities. His *Fontamara* and Carlo Levi's *Christ Stopped at Eboli*, Anna Seghers's *Comrades* and *The Seventh Cross* are among the few lasting testimonies of the underground. One might add Arthur Koestler's *Spanish Testament*, a moving account of his experiences in Franco's jail. Another indictment of the Spanish insurgents came from a Catholic conservative, Georges Bernanos, in *A Diary of My Times*. Similarly searing was George Orwell's *Homage to Catalonia*, which castigated the Communist terror in Barcelona. Arturo Barea (*La Forja de un Rebelde*) converted the Spanish Civil War experience into a memoir of human growth.

European intellectuals at that time were not afraid of accusing their own party of wrong-doing. Though most of them looked to Russia as an ally against Hitler and even considered Communism an ideological ally against fascism, André Gide published a critical journal on his travels in Stalin's Russia, and André Malraux did not spare the Communists in his autobiographical novel on the Spanish Civil War, *Man's Hope*. The harrowing experience of former believers disillusioned by the Soviet

---

[1] See Hermann Lenz, *The German Lesson* (1972), a novel (1969) based on Nolde's life and showing the plight of an unrequited admirer of Hitler.

reality has been collected in the anthology *The God That Failed*; contributors were Stephen Spender, André Gide, Richard Wright, Louis Fischer, Arthur Koestler, Ignazio Silone. Of the great European writers only Bertolt Brecht was unable to sever his ties with the Russian Revolution; but his *Galileo* is a horrifying testimony to the price he was paying.

The holocaust was too terrible an experience to produce a major literary work; but we should mention the *Diary of Anne Frank*, a tender self-portrait of a young German Jewish girl, in hiding in Holland, and Schwarz-Bart's *Last of the Just*.

Franz Werfel wrote a chronicle of mass murder in *The Forty Days of Musa Dagh* and later tried to condense terror into human experience in his novel *Jacobowsky and the Colonel*; this comedy of a tragedy was later made into a film: *Me and the Colonel*.

In France, the war produced some moving documents: Albert Camus's *Letters to a German Friend*, Jean B. Vercors's *The Silence of the Sea*, André Malraux's *Days of Wrath*, Jean-Paul Sartre's *The Flies*. Camus, in 1947, set the greatest monument to the wartime experience in *The Plague*.

The fall of Hitler opened the floodgates of a new literary movement. In a strong reaction against its past, Germany threw up its vomit. Starkly realistic, satirical, symbolist, its new writers rejected the restorative mood of official Germany, repudiated all traditions, and despised the present. The young writers of Group 47 proposed to "overcome our past"—not only the recent Nazi past but also the bourgeois-republican past perfect which to them looked so much like the present. In their *Manifesto*, Hans Werner Richter wrote that because "democratic thinking can be transmitted from the top down, not from the bottom up" they had "formed a democratic elite." This elite at once set itself up as martyrs persecuted by the Allied occupation authorities: "We durst not remain silent," wrote Heinz Friedrich after having been silent for twelve years, and proceeded to denounce "not only the patriotic phraseology . . . but likewise the sentimental dulcimers of pseudo-humanitarianism." Alas, they had not overcome the past and were bewildered by the present. Other members of the group were Albrecht Goes, Martin Walser, and Hans Magnus Enzensberger, whose magazine *Kursbuch* (*Railroad Schedule*) was to become the most outspoken critic of the West. However, Heinrich Böll—the left-wing Catholic, author of *The Clown* and *Group Portrait with Lady*, who in 1972 became a Nobel laureate—criticized the group, and Günter Grass, who also fell out with its more radical members, later campaigned for Willy Brandt. Grass's *The Tin Drum*, *Dog Years*, *Cat and Mouse*, and *Local Anaesthetic*—torrential outpourings of a tormented soul, bitter satires full of Olympian laughter in the style of Rabelais, Laurence Sterne, and E. T. A. Hoffmann—strive for what is perhaps the most radical settling of accounts with the past. Among other novelists who contributed to Germany's self-criticism there are, to name a few, Hermann Kasack, Stefan Andres, Alfred Andersch, and Bruno E. Werner.

But soon the past was, if not overcome, forgotten, and writers who dealt with Germany's future or present took on much greater significance. Uwe Johnson, who fled from the East, described poignantly the problem of a divided nation; Johannes

Bobrowski, born near the Lithuanian border, wrote with deep feeling of people living in two cultural environments. Hans Nossack describes a terrible, Kafkaesque world of alienated people.

National misfortune, of course, was not the only concern of post-Nazi literature. As the nation hit its stride, the individual once again confronted his own inner world and the circumstances of his life. Elisabeth Langgässer, a Catholic, wrote of the pilgrimage of modern man in search of transcendence; the Austrian Heimito von Doderer continued the great Viennese novel where Robert Musil had left off; the Swiss Max Frisch and Friedrich Dürrenmatt used German themes to shake the conscience of their own people.

Italy, too, had suffered from a dearth of intellectual stimulation during the years of tyranny. Cesare Pavese had tried to smuggle new ideas into the country by translating English and American authors. Catching up with Western and to some extent also with Russian literature, incidentally, was the first order of business for publishers in both Italy and Germany. The Italian post-war novel proclaimed a humanistic and social realism which reflected the revolutionary possibilities of the immediate post-war years. Pavese and Alberto Moravia presented misery and meanness where they existed. They did not indulge the reader's illusions about mankind. In a gut reaction, Italian writers eagerly turned to themes that were as far removed as possible from the slick drawing-room intrigues or heroic pageants they had dealt with before. Many joined the Communist Party and wrote proletarian novels. Marxist literature was widely read by the cultural elite. The publication of Antonio Gramsci's letters from prison encouraged the belief that Communism was a radical form of humanism; it helped readers see the poetic qualities of the factory worker in the north, the humanity of the down-trodden sharecropper in the south. Vasco Pratolini turned Communist, though in his novels he bravely defends a morality transcending the Party; Elio Vittorini is closer to "socialist realism" in describing the depravity of the ruling class.

Italy's intelligentsia was anti-clerical, anti-bourgeois, and (partly) anti-nationalistic; it also had special problems. How to reconcile Marx with Christ? The revolution with redemption? Some Italian movies contain seemingly irrelevant episodes showing the doubts of a pious man who is attracted to the Communist cause; or they point up striking parallels between Christ's passion and the guerrillas' fight (Pier Paolo Pasolini).

Gramsci had set the example of an intellectual who was faithful to the Party and who yet preserved his independence of mind. Togliatti frankly criticized the Russian Party. But the main reason for the Communists' success among Italian intellectuals was the abyss that separated both from the Establishment. Italy was still too backward, too authoritarian, too superstitiously Catholic to give a home to freethinkers. Her universities still were too reactionary, too inflexibly devoted to routine learning.

To be sure, the best-selling novel in the old Sicilian style continued to be manufactured competently by authors such as the Count of Lampedusa. But the function of the great novel of manners was taken over by the film. A succession of great directors—Vittorio de Sica, Roberto Rossellini, Luchino Visconti, Federico Fellini—

gave the world such outstanding works of social realism as *Shoeshine*, *The Bicycle Thief*, *General della Rovere*, *Open City*, *La Terra Trema*, *I Vitelloni*, *La Strada*, *La Dolce Vita*.

The impact of American realism was not restricted to the occupied countries. England and France, too, underwent the shock of the realism and brutality that had first become manifest in American letters and found that this was just the fare needed after the war. In France, engaged literature was introduced emphatically by Sartre. His own novels, plays, and motion pictures—*Nausea* (1938), *The Roads to Freedom* (a trilogy), *The Chips Are Down*, *No Exit*, *Dirty Hands*—show great virtuosity in using literary and stage devices as well as brilliant mastery of language in order to prove a thesis, usually a doctrine of existentialism or a moral of political philosophy. The characters are constructed to fit the moral; thus, the Communist Brunet is the only fully developed human being in *The Age of Reason*. In Simone de Beauvoir's *roman-à-clef*, *The Mandarins*, exposure of sexual behavior is freely used to discredit political enemies and renegade friends. Sartre severely criticized the literature that preceded existentialism—the psychological analysis of Proust, Joyce, and Mann—and called, instead, for a literature of action. Rejecting determinism, he said that his plays mean to let the audience participate in the free choice which the protagonist makes in a given situation. But his own characters do not seem to be free; they are puppets designed to represent predictable ideas. Sartre's "engagement" was at the service of a party; on the stage it often gives the impression of a propaganda skit.

The cold war extended to the intellectuals. As usual, sacred principles were invoked to justify political choices. Maurice Merleau-Ponty, a philosopher of note though at the time a Communist fellow-traveler, found philosophical proof that terrorism was actually humanism. Sartre fell out with his Resistance friends, Camus and David Rousset, who refused to exculpate Stalin from his crimes. Orwell wrote the satire *Animal Farm* and Czeslaw Milosz *The Captive Mind*. Hannah Arendt equated Stalinist Russia with Hitler's Germany as "totalitarian." Writers concerned with the survival of freedom in such a world founded the Congress for Cultural Freedom; pro-Soviet writers answered by joining the Communist-led "Amsterdam-Pleyel" Movement for Peace. Koestler wrote *The Yogi and the Commissar* and had world-wide success with *Darkness at Noon*. Pro-Soviet writers heard Alexander Fadeyev denounce T. S. Eliot as a "hyena"; anti-Soviet writers assembled in Berlin to discuss the sterility of "socialist realism." Each side accused the other of being corrupt and of substituting political for intellectual values. Among European intellectuals, the Russians had the appeal of "the other" and the primitive, two basic categories in the existentialist universe. Sartre was able to identify his cause with theirs because, like many European intellectuals, he hoped to overcome his own alienation through the victory of Communism. "More than even the two world wars, the great event in [our] life has been to face the working class and its ideology, which gave [us] an irrefutable vision of the world and ourselves," he wrote in *Les Temps Modernes* (February 1956). Sartre invested, consecutively, the Russians, the proletarians, Castro, Mao, and the Third World with this myth of the noble savage.

The lives and works of Malraux, Sartre, and Camus have projected the image of men whose experience was greatly heightened by their intense participation in action and their ardent concern for other people. But these men were engaged on three different sides: for de Gaulle, for Stalin, and for a utopian democracy, respectively. Other writers who also were admired as much for their heroism as for their style were not involved politically but in other ecstasies. Hemingway, D. H. Lawrence, Antoine de Saint-Exupéry, existentialist heroes of an earlier period, had enjoyed being engaged for the sake of experience rather than for any particular cause. What mattered was not the goal or the idea but authenticity and intensity. Words may be empty exercises. In a world that had seen the abuse of all ideals and the destruction of all philosophical systems, no abstract idea could serve as guidance for human behavior; only the most concrete and personal criterion could. Reversing Kant and all previous ethics, Sartre taught that each man should follow the maxim that was right for him even if it was not right for any other man. No man should play a role that had been imposed on him by society. Man should be "authentic." This is what was meant by the felicitous phrases which became widespread: "Existence goes before essence"; "People fight for what they are, not for what they believe," which in turn was a refinement of Marx's famous "Existence determines consciousness"; and "Man makes himself."

Existentialist teachers attacked middle-class values, preached the individual's liberation from the fetters of industrial civilization, and enlarged their social criticism into cultural criticism. Authors like Theodor W. Adorno, Günther Anders, and Herbert Marcuse, who during the 1930's and 1940's had assumed a Marxist stance, now returned to their existentialist origins and castigated the perversion of originality through the devices of "mass culture." Their method, called critical philosophy, uncovered many hidden conflicts and, following Freud, other "discontents of civilization."

But their concern was not academic. They indicted Western, capitalist, and technocratic society as one that necessarily alienates man from himself, falsifies his view of the world around him, and defiles his relations with other men. In his *Eros and Civilization* (1955) and even more in his *One-Dimensional Man—Studies in the Ideology of Advanced Industrial Society* (1964), Marcuse calls for a return to nature and a revolutionary breaking-up of this society. The same general route was taken by Wilhelm Reich in *The Sexual Revolution*.

Cultural criticism found an echo in the literature of the period. In lecture halls, on the stage, in essays and novels, in prose and verse, the intelligentsia was fighting alienation, the bane of industrial society. In the early 1950's a group of young British writers began to sound the discontent with a shrill voice; they quickly were called "angry young men." John Osborne's play *Look Back in Anger* blurted out the impotent rage of a young artist; Kingsley Amis satirized the academic establishment in *Lucky Jim*; John Braine, in *Room at the Top*, wrote of an angry young man who, by trying to fit into the provincial middle class, betrays his own self. Shelagh Delaney (*A Taste of Honey*) and John Arden (*Live Like Pigs*) wrote of people who were not planned for in the welfare state. After the angry young men came the so-called kitchen-sink plays, which dramatized the day-to-day drudgery of life; Arnold Wesker's *Chips With Everything* and *The Kitchen* are characteristic examples. Actually, these young men and women were bored rather than angry, ashamed of having landed a teaching or editorial job rather than being defiant of a society that forced them into these ruts. Most of them were socialists, but their social ideals were not clearly defined, and their personal inclination was not to mount the barricade but to flee to a more private island. This tendency grew more manifest in the protest movement and led its spokesmen from a philosophy of engagement to its opposite. By its programmatic title, though by little else, Colin Wilson's novel *The Outsider* became the most significant work of the group. Its heroes were musicians, actors, writers, sensitive sons of working-class fathers; they aspired to a higher culture but, like their creators, settled in academic routine jobs. Mediocre themselves, they were amazed to discover that the Establishment can accommodate mediocrity at the top. Sons of militants, they had become insiders *in* the Establishment without really becoming *of* it. Hence, Colin Wilson charged that all insiders are hypocrites.

The gesture of defiance is personal rather than social in Camus's *The Rebel*. While his *The Stranger* denounces society's hypocrisy, its author turned away from public causes—not that he grew less concerned, but he came to feel that they were actually private concerns and not responsive to public solutions. Likewise, Kingsley Amis called the Marxism of the intellectuals in the 1930's "romanticism" and defined it as "the irrational capacity to become influenced by interests not one's own." The moment of "big causes," as Osborne's hero, Jimmy Porter, says, had gone. At least for the time being there was no mass unemployment, and the cold war was no emotional substitute for the Spanish Civil War. The hero of modern literature serves no idea. The existentialist Jesus has not come to bring salvation to mankind but merely to assert his own being. The hero of *The Stranger* was utterly unconcerned with the world. The emphatic "engagement" of the 1930's and 1940's turned into disengagement in the 1950's.

The recent history of the European intelligentsia, therefore, may be divided into three periods. Immediately after the war, the intelligentsia sought participation in efforts to remake society; it gave moving expression to the shock of war, to the horrors revealed, to the stark pessimism but also to the desperate determination of the contemporaries.

In the 1950's, after its own solutions had failed of recognition, it bemoaned its alienation, condemned the mass media, deplored the emergence of "two cultures," and withdrew deeper and deeper into its own language and imagery, which made communication with the rest of humanity ever more strained.

In the 1960's, the intelligentsia turned the tables on society. Alienation, boredom, esoteric poetry, the theater of the absurd, black humor, and pop art were exalted; the intelligentsia made ample use of the mass media and adopted their vulgarity although simultaneously it prospered in the exploitation of snob appeal.

The theme of "nausea" originally had been introduced by Céline and Sartre. After the war, it was eagerly taken up by the sensationalist critics who hailed anything that was radically new, then by a generation that no longer would make any compromises with ideology. All *avant-gardists* up to then had maintained that the truth they were seeking, ugly as it might be, was in some way beautiful, or offered a new definition of beauty; or else the satirical, ironical intention was so obvious that by implication whatever was denounced as ugly defined, as its counterpart, the unseen ideal of beauty. The issue could not have been joined more clearly than in this dialogue between Sartre and Maurois: "Does M. Maurois ever go to the bathroom?"—"Yes, but not to write." It was only logical that Sartre's companion, Simone de Beauvoir, eulogized the Marquis de Sade as more forthright than Corneille, more lucid than Pascal, and more pious than St. Augustine. She opened the sluices to a wave of pornographic books which passed for literature in the 1960's, a literature of de-humanization and humiliation, culminating in *The Story of O*, which is depravity without enjoyment. Comparing this output with the productions of two preceding generations, one cannot fail to notice the steepness of the decline. For D. H. Lawrence, sex was still a symbol, a problem, a manifestation of life deeply rooted in the totality of human existence. Present-day sex literature is obsessional. Contrary to the claim of "liberation" made on its behalf, it seems to testify only to bondage.

The new age of "free expression" opened in 1954, when eighteen-year-old Françoise Sagan published *Bonjour, Tristesse*. Two years later, the film director Roger Vadim exhibited an awkward-looking girl who enjoyed—or convinced others that she enjoyed—posing in the nude, and called the picture *And God Created Woman*. In other motion pictures, he exploited eighteenth-century decadence (*Les Liaisons Dangereuses*) and the perverse sensationalism of the Gothic novel (*To Die of Lust*). In 1958, Marcel Carné's *The Cheats* depicted the milieu of the young rich in lurid colors. Its lesson: Those who are not cheats come to grief. The jet set of the 1950's lived by the motto that anything goes provided one can get away with it, and it learned from Brigitte Bardot that the worthiest deed is the unexpected and outrageous. With Pop Art and happenings, we are back at the beginning of the century: the literary *acte gratuit*, played out in black humor and camp, but now and then taking itself seriously and defying public morality and organized society. In Fellini's *La Dolce Vita* (1960), the viewer is supposed to identify with the protagonist's horror of existence.

From criticism and disgust flows the desire to withdraw. Engagement leads to disengagement or, as it is sometimes conceived, to a different kind of engagement—cultivation of the ego and flight into a personal paradise. Alienation was strikingly shown in Ingmar Bergman's film *Persona* as well as in Michelangelo Antonioni's *Blow-Up*, which was youth's shibboleth in 1966. Federico Fellini told a reporter that in *Satyricon* he wished to prepare his contemporaries for "living in a post-Christian time. . . . We are out of Christ. . . . Encolpius and Ascyltus . . . go from one adventure to the other without the slightest remorse, with the natural innocence of young animals. Their rebellion is translated into terms of absolute ignorance and detachment from society."

CHAPTER 2

Further Developments of the Consumer Culture in the 1950's and 1960's

THE mood of an age is determined, not by its philosophers and poets, but by the everyday environment of the people, by the education they get and the work they perform, by the leisure time they can afford and the entertainment available to them, by the heroes they look up to and the villains they look down on, by the tools or instruments they use and the relations they establish with others in the pursuit of their work, and also by the idea of happiness they have formed for themselves and for their community.

Today's popular heroes are no longer the mighty, the builders of empires, the inventors and achievers. Our celebrities are movie stars and singers, "beautiful" people of leisure who profess a philosophy of enjoyment rather than of discipline and toil.

The majority of the people do not participate directly in the activities of the culture elites. They derive vicarious gratification from observing them, talking about them, hearing about them. Modern means of communication have made this second-hand experience a constant and instant accompaniment of daily life. Football players, actors, showmen, and public parasites seem to enjoy the style of life that the ordinary man dreams of, reads about in the slick magazines, sees in movies and newsreels. But the ordinary man is also fascinated by bandits who stole £2.5 million from an English mail train. Though one death resulted from the holdup, ordinary, presumably decent, people donated money for the defense of the criminals, and the students of England's Southampton University elected one of the robbers their honorary president. Television and magazines made the criminals into folk heroes; their wives earned thousands of pounds by letting themselves be interviewed.

The mass media all but idolized the clever Kim Philby (a high-placed officer in the British intelligence service who defected to the Russians), and they cheered when another Soviet spy broke out of a British jail. A little later, *Bonnie and Clyde*, the Hollywood motion picture about a pair of murderers who in real life had been neither romantic nor committed to a cause, became a world-wide success. Sherlock Holmes and Frank Allan were moral characters, helpers to the needy; Ian Fleming's serialized hero, James Bond, is remarkable for his brutality and sexual prowess, for the absence of any subtlety in plot and characterization, for the opportunity he offers the audience to identify with outrageous, often criminal behavior. Thrillers have ceased to be "puzzles for intellectuals"; they are sheer adventure, used to present perversity and depravity. Thus, Raymond Chandler, himself the author of many thrillers, described *The Simple Art of Murder* (1950) as a protest against "a world which is ruled by criminals." Peter Handke gives his murder story *The Peddler* (1967) chapter headings such as "The Unmasking of Law and Order." For indeed, the detectives in modern · murder stories are by no means morally superior to the criminals. Even when they serve society and order, they do so in ways that must ultimately undermine all sense of decency and morality. Yet, the fascist-nihilist heritage is imperfectly disguised here. These are no Robin Hoods but terroristic monsters; their authors seem to revel in the glorification of asocial acts. They confuse freedom with violence, self-reliance with destructiveness. Their ideal of high life and their taste in outlaws confirm the demise of middle-class values. No Samuel Smiles (the British equivalent of Horatio Alger) could be a success today; Peter Fonda is. The popularity of Mao Tse-tung is based not on his true achievements for China but on his alleged dictum that freedom comes out of the barrel of a gun. We are still the heirs of the Romantic age which glorified the outlaw, the vagabond, the criminal—only the intellectual level has been lowered.

A similar point can be made about popular music. The old schmaltz, in Lili Marlene style, still provides hit songs. But the main culture also has absorbed, and in the process has assimilated, defanged, even emasculated, the original expressions of alienation, defection, and protest as they appeared in succession: hot and cool jazz, bop and be-bop, boogie-woogie, rock 'n' roll, and folk rock. All have become objects of consumption, heavily commercialized and sensationalized, exploited by record companies, disk jockeys, and dance hall owners. As the "in" people had to find new assertions of their independence, the music had to grow wilder, the electronic accompaniment louder, the lyrics ever more daring and defiant—without ever sating the taste of the beautiful people for being flailed; we have described a similar process in the development of decadent art early in the century. As the life of a fad or style tended to grow shorter with every generation and the mechanical-commercial establishment consumed the new styles at an ever-increasing rate, the "now" generation had to have its instant revolutions. To remain young, the culture had to produce newness.

Pop music had been commercial from the start, depending as it did on disk jockeys. Its ultimate success came when strip-tease joints around Place Pigalle, which had catered to the tourist trade, suddenly switched to rock groups. Teen-agers now have money; they buy records and clothes; they help determine fashion.

With the trend toward youth, Paris lost her rank as a fashion center. The mod craze came from London. Mini-skirts, wide leather belts, pants suits, Beatle haircuts, riotous color schemes—all originated in the Anglo-Saxon countries. For a while, swinging London deprived Paris of its reputation as the sex center of the world.

In 1947, Christian Dior had introduced the New Look, a feminine fashion which definitely terminated the war mood with its military, angular look. Women were supposed to be as rounded, feminine, lovely as they were in the good old days. Since then, women have grown younger and the hemlines shorter. The mini-skirt rules out age. Collegiate fashion declares wealth, grooming, and neatness obsolete. The female image also changed: from Rita Hayworth to Anita Ekberg and Sophia Loren, to Brigitte Bardot, and eventually to Twiggy. The male idol, meanwhile, evolved from manly types like Humphrey Bogart and Marlon Brando to the boyish, lonely James Dean, who died young, the very young Beatles, and the unheroic Michael Caine.

If the 1920's were called "roaring," what name is one to apply to the 1960's? They did not leave one taboo unviolated, one dogma unquestioned, one custom unridiculed. The distinction between the sexes was all but wiped out both in fashion and in mores, though not necessarily in rights. Some Catholic priests married; saints of a new cult copulated in public. Writers and stage directors forgot the difference between art and pornography. In England, film censorship was abolished and the Lord Chamberlain's powers over the stage virtually ended. In France, brothels were closed, but in Germany and the Scandinavian countries public nudity became big business.

Swedish films pioneered in the representation of love as an animal act. Acres of naked skin came to fill the screen, even where the story did not require it. But in the process, sex lost its Victorian prurience; its "natural" display eventually helped bring about a new attitude toward matters of public and private morality. This was most forcefully shown in the new family laws that came to be adopted in most countries, reflecting more permissive attitudes toward adultery, divorce, contraception, and abortion.

In the midst of debates on the threatening population explosion, the development of an oral contraceptive wrought a revolution in the mores of nearly every country. An undesirable side effect—the substantial increase in venereal diseases—indicated a concomitant increase in promiscuity. There is little doubt that the next generation will be still more tolerant and permissive. The new attitude also benefits people who until recently were considered perverts. Homosexuality has started coming out of the "closet"; transvestism is condoned; transsexual operations are being performed. Entertainment "in drag" can be seen in British workmen's clubs, where Victorianism had held out longest.

Tolerance and permissiveness also determine society's attitude to drugs. Young people have embraced the legalization of hashish (marijuana) as their "cause," and liberals who wish to be up-to-date make a show of their open-mindedness. There is a difference between drug use in the 1920's and in the 1960's: then users knew what they were indulging in, while today they consider the use of drugs a virtue or an assertion of freedom. Vice, it is argued, was for the upper classes; now it is for the people. Then it was bad; now it is good.

The shift in heroes, tastes, and ideals brought to a close a democratic and populist revolution which had started at the turn of the century. Opponents of this upheaval have derided it as "mass culture"; they attribute it not to the deep changes in society but to the invention of mass media. It is noteworthy, however, that Ortega y Gasset wrote *The Revolt of the Masses* in the 1920's and Walter Benjamin *Art in the Age of Technical Reproduction* in the 1930's, when radio was not a mass medium and television did not exist.

Their dire predictions—which merely repeated, incidentally, the strictures against Gutenberg in 1450—have hardly materialized even in our age of much more intensive mass communication. All attempts to manipulate public opinion have backfired, except where a government enjoyed a *political* monopoly of information. Opinion-makers may try to order the flow of communication; but, in the long run, the medium produces channels of information and perception which devalue the monopoly and make it suspect or even counter-productive.

When Orwell wrote *1984*, many people thought that the totalitarian threat might not spare Western society. Sociologists and psychologists, not to mention radical philosophers, have decried the built-in conformism or "one-dimensionality" of industrial mass society. These dangers may indeed exist. But the same technique of mass communication also widens the range of information and the audience's awareness, which, given enough time, learns to distrust and defy the manipulator. The masses who now are gaining access to their nation's culture, consider this opportunity as a lever which will make society more egalitarian and more just.

Wide strata of the population are able to participate in cultural life. For the first time in history, education has become available to a significant population sector. New means of communication have raised the general level of entertainment. Thanks to the mechanical aids of modern technology, music can come into every home. Political debates and educational programs are broadcast over radio and television. Moreover, educational TV now can supplement a much more widespread high school foundation. Most likely, this will lead to some leveling, as curricula are being adjusted to satisfy the needs of the masses and colleges have to jettison some of their elite features. Yet, socially the leveling seems to be "up"—which may displease those who were there first.

Nothing, of course, is easier than to underscore and deplore the decline of standards and the cheapening of taste accompanying mass production.[1] But one need only compare a contemporary record or film with one made twenty years ago to realize our increasing demands on perfection and sophistication. The myth that only the old, hand-crafted products of folk culture had any value is based on faulty memory or on disregard for plain facts. Popular entertainment in the 1960's was of considerably higher quality than vaudeville. World hits like *My Fair Lady* and *Fiddler on the Roof* are better than Lehar's operettas. Millions travel to classical and popular music and film festivals in Salzburg, Bayreuth, Edinburgh, Venice, Cannes, and Spoleto.

Since in Europe public corporations are responsible for educational broadcasts, radio and television provide programs of social and cultural significance, debates, reportages, drama, and opera; even the political cabaret enjoys the hospitality of the

---

[1] Name any year B.C. or A.D., and I will quote an author who deplored it.

air. *That Was the Week That Was, The Establishment, Beyond the Fringe,* and *Hallo, Nachbarn!* were saucy and irreverent—as long as they lasted, for such programs often succumbed to political pressures. Yet, the irrepressible comedians managed to put into song that which could not be spoken. In Paris the political cabaret retains its popularity, and the *Canard Enchaîné* has needled every government.

Television did not bring on the age of McLuhan; newsprint continues to deplete the forests of northern Europe. But the instant reporting of the picture tube did force newspapers to change their formats. The venerable London *Times,* after changing owners, adopted a lighter style and a more appealing make-up. The tabloid spread in quantity and shrank in content; the German *Bildzeitung*—which, in keeping with its name (*Picture Paper*), has little text besides captions—outsells all other German papers. Its publisher, Axel Springer, therefore found scant sympathy with his colleagues when angry students smashed his office windows. Other newspapers, too, increasingly write the impoverished language of radio entertainment, use more magazine-type copy, and carry comic strips. No doubt mass circulation and mass communication tend to cheapen the taste of the audience. The steady stream of make-believe entertainment, of fake experience and prefabricated emotions pouring forth from printing presses in the beginning of the century was to swell into a flood of radio and television communications in the middle 1950's. What is "pretty" and what is "in" is imposed on human minds by a machine producing and changing patterns of thought, patterns of taste, and patterns of attitudes.

These offerings, critics of mass culture charge, require no effort on the public's part. They are manufactured for their entertainment, and most likely deliberately conceived so as to lead the audience away from real experience. Instead of conversation, they get gags requiring no understanding of another person, no accommodation, no conflict, no consideration, no will power. What is being reacted to, and bought, is no longer the content of the communication but the performance. The playwright gets little credit; the actor becomes the glamorous idol. Worse, the idols are manufactured by committees like clothing by fashion designers. Public relations firms and movie companies promote an "image." Consumer culture, hence, is not a culture in the exact sense of the term. Nor is it the culture of consumers, but rather one imposed on them, sold to them, manufactured for them. And yet it is less alien to them than the elite culture they have to learn in school, less alien even than that culture was to its own audiences at the time it was relevant. Nor is this popular culture escapist in the sense that it substitutes sentimentality for bitter reality. Taking sex, dope, or escape itself as its main and most direct concerns, it says frankly what it wants, and it gives its audience satisfaction in the raw.

Europeans like to blame all this on "Americanization." But it is their own creation; America just has been developing it more rapidly. Just as the American musical was an improvement on the European operetta, so the Beatles, in turn, were an improvement on American rock. Western movies and science fiction provided escape for the masses at a time when the European entertainment industries were unproductive; but today, more Westerns are made in Italy and Spain than in California. The similarities and influences across the Atlantic and the strikingly international character of this senescent culture, however, must not overshadow the differences. What appeared to be a mere outgrowth of mass culture and sensationalism in America was interpreted in Europe as a profound expression of a deeply pessimistic outlook on life. Europe did not depend on America, for it had its own traditions on which it could draw after the American impact had perhaps removed inhibitions. Moreover, Europe produced its own answers to the popular culture of America. In Belgium the "singing nun" and in Germany the "singing boy" seemed to restore to post-war society its lost innocence. There were other responses, too, to the new cultural crisis, which we now shall explore in greater detail.

CHAPTER 3

Esoteric Art

IN the early days of fascism Karl Kraus wrote: "*Das Wort entschlief, als jene Welt erwachte*" ("The word fell silent when that world awoke"). Never have poets complained so eloquently about their inability to say anything or to converse meaningfully than after World War II. Paul Celan, whom many German critics consider the greatest post-war poet in their language (he was born 1920 in Galicia, survived a Nazi death camp, and took his life in Paris at the age of fifty), has given frequent testimony of his vain struggle with the "lattice of language" (*Sprachgitter*, which he used as the title of one of his books of verse). Theodor W. Adorno said that music had to abandon all attempt at form or content. Karlheinz Stockhausen invented a music consisting of pauses between single notes; several Italian composers experimented with unstructured noises. Yves Klein painted canvases with surfaces in solid black, or red, or blue; others reproduced a series of prints of the same photo in different colors. Alain Robbe-Grillet wrote a "theory of the new novel" in which he exhorted the writer not to tell a story, to deny the reader any chance to identify with a hero, and instead to describe in minute detail what could be perceived at any given moment. Nathalie Sarraute also renounced message and content to present a world that made no sense.[1]

"It is closing time in the gardens of the West," said Cyril Connolly in the last issue of *Horizon* (December 1949), and continued: "From now on an artist will be judged only by the resonance of his solitude or the quality of his despair." The criterion is sensibility and its presentation, not content. The poets, having no *What* to mold, are concerned with *How*. Are we back in Byzantium? Contemporary English poets are much concerned with counting and scoring devices.

The Romantic poet used to think of his inspiration as the wellspring of his art. Writers now are wordsmiths, craftsmen who merely apply their technical skill to materials they "find"; others produce "under dictation" or by an aleatory process, adding word to word until the pattern emerges; or they experiment, trying out various stories that may fit a character (Lawrence Durrell's *Alexandria Quartet*; *A Wilderness of Mirrors* by Max Frisch). The German poet Karl Krolow admitted that "modern poetry had no alternative but to follow the path from Mallarmé's *Un Coup de Dés*

---

[1] Heinrich Böll has parodied this style in *Group Portrait with Lady* (1972), at the same time showing that the technique is capable of rendering meaningful content.

to Ezra Pound's *Cantos* and Apollinaire's *Calligrammes* to the jests of E. E. Cummings. These writers have raised doubts about the individuality of the poet. His 'participation' in what he writes has been reduced. The distance between poet and poem has been growing." In a much-discussed essay, *Silence and the Poet*, the critic George Steiner has collected similar statements from Eugène Ionesco, Martin Heidegger, Hugo von Hofmannsthal, Rainer Maria Rilke, Brice Parain, Franz Kafka, Theodor Adorno, Arthur Adamov, and Sylvia Plath. Jean-Paul Sartre gave his autobiography the ironical title *The Words*, expressing doubt whether words nowadays do not conceal emptiness rather than communicate content. Malraux declared that "art must exclude everything humanistic. . . . Man is no longer the measure; the artist turns to things, demons, abstractions."

Part of the problem seems to be attrition. Words become trite. Metaphors turn into clichés; emotions become jaded. Writers shy away from using polysyllabic, stilted, or literate language. The passionate periods of a more romantic age sound overwrought to an age that, above all, wishes to be "cool." This is true of literature, music, and the plastic arts. The emptiness of the canvas is presented as "painting" for the same reason that words such as "faith," "fatherland," "tender," "love," "Man," "goodness," and so on, are taboo; but their absence often is the real theme of a work, just as a composer tries to suggest that he is avoiding a conventional harmony or a sentimental melody. Each canvas has to threaten nothingness to the viewer; a piece of music is supposed to shatter the audience's security. Writers, poets, painters, and musicians humiliate the ignorant with plays that mock him and make him listen to incomprehensible verse. There has never been a greater gap between artist and general public—even though, on a different level, there never has been a larger market for commercial art and for art as a commodity.

The artist takes pleasure in representing either emptiness or ugliness. He no longer wants to *épater le bourgeois*; he wants to deter him. He is appalled that art has become accessible to the masses; he flees from slick success among the uninitiated. Art is a sort of *Flaschenpost*, notes sent adrift in a bottle, said Celan; the most profound works of art are devoted to the belief that art is no longer possible. To understand the message, one must have both knowledge and leisure. Art becomes a sectarian cult, a religion for the elite, who thus communicate with those on high and with each other.

Much modern writing and music is Byzantine in its use of allusions and even of direct quotations; to understand it often requires a glossary. Criticism has changed from an evaluation of art into a hunt for nuggets of reference and esoteric hints. Interpretation is no longer left to the scholars of a later generation; it is instantaneous. The enjoyment of art now is found in the solution of hidden puzzles and the deciphering of underlying assumptions—metaphysical, magical, or symbolic of whatever the composer may have in mind. Interpretation, criticism itself, has become an art.[2]

Playfulness and formalism often go together. This is most clearly evident in the

---

[2] Writers like Thomas Mann, Vladimir Nabokov, and Heimito von Doderer contributed to the interpretation of their works by following them up with a volume of footnotes or memoirs.

new music. Following Schönberg and Anton von Webern, the younger composers of twelve-tone music have wandered farther and farther away from expression as it was known before. Olivier Messiaen and René Leibowitz are almost inaccessible to the untrained ear; even more forbidding are the pioneers of "concrete music": Hans Werner Henze, Hilding Rosenberg, Robert R. Bennett, and Luigi Dallapiccola. Nor did in the 1950's and 1960's the surviving masters of the pre-war period—Arnold Schönberg, Igor Stravinsky, Darius Milhaud, and Paul Hindemith—produce any music as stirring and original as the works of their youth.

Yet modern art no doubt does reflect some contemporary reality. Its methods have enormously enlarged the scope of expression. Some of the works it brought forth were monumental, a trend that had begun in the beginning of the century. Some of the new canvases are enormous in size, although their content may strike one as jocular, and some modern authors have become masters of the grotesque, reflecting the cultural climate as they perceive it. Their failure to write great works, they seem to say, is really ours; or it is deliberate, as though they wished to tell us that this is no age to write masterworks. Their sensitivity and penetration, all the artfulness of their presentation, is devoted to the demonstration of our sickness. They are, like the penitent judge in Camus's *The Fall*, accursed magi who suffer from the knowledge that we are damned. They fight for art in a century that either corrupts or kills art; if they seem bizarre, it may be because they have chosen Hamlet's strategy to preserve their integrity. To be sure, such a preoccupation must distort the very thing it is supposed to protect; but the product which thus, like a shield, has been inserted between the artist and society is still art, and some of its manifestations are very powerful indeed—or fanciful, perceptive, inventive, imaginative. The virtuosity of these artists surpasses the technical perfections of all previous ages.

Nowhere perhaps does this tendency appear as clearly as in the so-called art films, a form almost totally new in post-war culture. Dream-like images evoke tribal memories in the viewer's mind; time and space change at will as in a fairy tale. In Alain Resnais's *Last Year at Marienbad*, a room has different furniture for each person who enters it. In Pasolini's *Teorema* a man strips naked in a railway station and then stumbles through a landscape akin to Hieronymus Bosch's idea of Purgatory. The symbolism of Ingmar Bergman's films draws on an almost limitless treasure of pictures and constellations none of which imply reality. This new art cannot be "consumed" or easily assimilated; nor is it mastered once one has learned the "key." It keeps shifting and creates its new language as its previous statements, by now assimilated, are being overtaken.

The psychological novel of the nineteenth century was aware of the complexities of the individual. D. H. Lawrence subsequently proposed to get rid of "the stable ego." But up until the middle of the twentieth century, the hero's physical identity was preserved throughout a novel or film, except where the theme was explicitly a change of personality, such as in thrillers, fairy tales, or science fiction. At least the narrator retained his identity throughout, and readers were confident that the author knew all the secrets of his characters. Even Luigi Pirandello left with the audience a suspicion that he was merely teasing them and that the true identities of his characters could be known.

Suddenly all these assumptions were invalidated, or at least suspended. The author no longer claims omniscience. In the *Alexandria Quartet*, Durrell presents one and the same person in four volumes as four different characters, and fails to make any connection between the four. Even the detective story, whose purpose used to be the uncovering of the villain's identity, now revels in ambiguities, first shown by G. K. Chesterton and more recently in John Le Carré's *The Spy Who Came In from the Cold*.

The East German Uwe Johnson blurs the distinction between his various narrators, so that eventually the author can write only "assumptions" (*Mutmassungen über Jakob*). The Swiss Max Frisch plays the same game. Everybody is acting a role; rare is the man who lives an "authentic" life.

Like Proust, Michel Butor is obsessed with time; like Robbe-Grillet, Nathalie Sarraute is obsessed with thingishness (*chosisme*); like Samuel Beckett, Claude Simon is obscure. Through devices like flashbacks or free association, they all manage to destroy the discipline of their story, the unity of their characters, the sequence of time. Not only character, time, and space, but the coherence of the world and of society has been lost. George Lukács has said that since Balzac the bourgeois novel has done nothing but decline. Since he said this, in 1920, it has abandoned logical sequence. Even the stream of consciousness has been dissolved into fragments of perception. The social novel, the novel of manners, the psychological novel were succeeded by the existentialist novel: the examination of the human condition, full of shame and despair, with corpses agonizing, women retching, boys masturbating, knaves decaying.

All the arts, even motion pictures, have explored nonrepresentational frontiers—alienated states of mind, alienated consciousness of the world, alienated conceptions of the art itself or its means. The philosophy of structuralism has reduced all human experience to certain basic patterns. The *roman nouveau* has banished all feeling and human purpose so that the pure perception of "things" may emerge; but in executing this extreme "thing-thinking" (the sociologist might call it reification), Robbe-Grillet allows his reader to experience his own resignation, as though he were keeping the world at arm's length lest he be overwhelmed by his urge to become engaged, to feel, to act. He has realized this extreme estrangement from people in *Last Year at Marienbad*, the film he helped create. Other artists escape from themselves and others by concerning themselves with the devices of art. This self-reflective activity produces mannerist effects reminiscent of other decadent ages.

In this sphere, an almost euphoric feeling of total freedom is possible for the artist; he can impose his own imagination on his audience. Henry Moore expressed his spirituality through his massive sculptures; Alberto Giacometti imparted his own spirituality through his disembodied figures. But here is the temptation. Some younger epigones who have little to communicate nonetheless offer much to see and touch in the plaster-cast statues, geometric designs, and found-object compositions which in recent exhibitions have mocked art. Talent which does not know where to go is simply a display of muscles; the result is a surfeit of bravado.

All too often this exuberance poses as revolutionary fervor; still more often simple nostalgia is passed off as rebellion. The critic Peter Demetz gave his introduction to post-war German literature the ironical title *Sweet Anarchy* and showed how political Leftism can serve as a "guise for the ballast of inwardness which they [the writers] are unable to throw off." He calls Enzensberger, editor of the radical *Kursbuch*, a "conservative anarchist"; of Peter Weiss he says that the revolutionary ideology protects him from reality like a second womb; the work of Alfred Andersch, whom he admires despite their political disagreement, is dismissed as misunderstood existentialism. While such strictures certainly do not apply to all post-war writers, a good number of them, indeed, would like to give the impression that they have been fathered by Byron out of Rosa Luxemburg—but they inherited from Byron only the limp. Some pose as exiles—which increases their royalties; alienation is made to pay. "Be against!" was the slogan which the German poet Wolf-Dietrich Schnurre issued to his fellow intellectuals; it hardly mattered against whom or what.

Varying a Stendhalian phrase, they write for the "unhappy few."

Nonconformism became a mass cult and had to be manufactured, especially for affluent patrons; hence the need to create ever new fashions of expressing alienation. These were not manifestations of a genuine discontent but safety valves for upper-class alienation; to be out of tune was "in." Once upon a time the Sorbonne taught its students how to have tragic sensibilities worthy of Racine; now it tells them how to feel nauseated. Its method, however, is still the same: the formalization of the right kind of thinking. "Today's philosophy and literature have the function of softening the reader's actual anxiety and revolt by formalizing them. Repeating every day that the reader is distressed, one ends up by tranquilizing him," writes the critic Jean-François Revel.

New movements appeared in all the arts. Luciano Berio, Luigi Nono, Pierre Boulez, and Stockhausen revolutionized the idea of musical composition. In painting, new styles were invented by Yves Klein, Hans Hartung, Wolfgang Wols, Nicolas de Staël, André Lanskoy, Henri Michaux, Eugène Zak, Victor Vasarély—most of them living in Paris but, as in the twenties, speaking many languages. The Americans, notably Jackson Pollock, influenced the abstract Expressionists: Maurice de Vlaminck, Serge Poliakoff, Pierre Soulages. Jean Dubuffet went his own way. In sculpture, Barbara Hepworth and Henry Moore took a new view of abstractionism. The machine served as inspiration to others as it had for Léger and Coates.

In the younger generation the borderlines between painting and sculpture, between art and decorative objects, have disappeared. Any material can be used. No frame confines the picture to any given space; no wall can define it as a two-dimensional window. Size has ceased to be a limiting factor. Some outdoor sculptures rise several stories high. Many of them are pure constructions or give the impression of totem poles; others allow the viewer to imagine that they resemble figures, faces, or instruments. Natural objects, pieces of furniture, plaster casts, bones, hair, felt, metal, blood, nails, bottles, soil, plastic materials are freely used to produce startling effects.

"Action painting" and other experiments no longer can be called art if by art we mean the deliberate disposition of symbols. At the opening of Yves Klein's one-man show, in 1960 in Paris, no paintings were seen. Instead, a few nude women appeared, smeared their bodies with blue paint, and pressed up against the wall. The "painting" thus created was then signed by the artist. The deliberate creation of scandal as a means of promotion, the substitution of a happening for art, the mock-theorizing about the virtues of the new methods, all this was second-hand. Dada was good fun, and in some instances a foundation paid for it.

Stockhausen in one of his scores has the instrumentalists leave the stage (when Haydn invented the joke he did not pretend that it had a meaning), throw apples into the audience, read obituaries, and, in general, encourage the audience to "react." In another, he uses the national anthems of many countries to produce a strange consonance. One critic, after hearing the piece, exclaimed that Bach, Beethoven, and Schubert had not known what music can do.

Electronic music is not necessarily highbrow or even electronic. It sets out to create startling sounds never heard before, with a switchboard mixer modulating the sonorities of voices, instruments, or kitchen utensils. The Pink Floyd, a British rock quartet whose members have studied electronics, convert ordinary schmaltz, pop songs, beat, rock, bird calls, gunfire, jet exhaust noises, and bubbling water into free sequences. They provided the background music for the film *Zabriskie Point* and for Rudolf Nureyev's Proust ballet, *Remembrance of Things Past*.

The claim of "new" composers like Stockhausen, Henze, Boulez, Bo Nilsson, Berio, Henri Pousseur, and John Cage is that they liberated music from all previous conventions and tried to make it a free exercise of the imagination, an improvisation. Nono and other Italians did their best to destroy music as it had been understood before. Of his tone poem, *As A Wave of Light and Power*, Nono said that it expressed the class war against capitalist repression.

Eventually composers shed serialism, that last debt to discipline. They made a virtue of "chance" encounters between sounds and claim that their music not only reflects the reality of the world but that it also corresponds to contemporaneous developments in physics, biology, and the social sciences. One day, perhaps, someone will make the new medium into a vehicle of great ideas. For the moment, its audience is restricted to narrow circles of experts and connoisseurs, on the one hand, and to a sensation-hungry crowd admiring the Emperor's new clothes, on the other hand.

The new movement has invaded even that field which by its very function should have remained immune to it. But there is nothing functional in most "modern" architecture. During the inter-war years, the lines of buildings were severe. The massive or streamlined slabs emphasized structural honesty; the sparing use of material suggested utility, and function. After the war, the new materials seemed to forget that they came from the earth. Design was airy, sprightly, as though deliberately defying structural traditions. Roofs seemed to be floating, supports swirled upward; the building elements seemed to deny statics. Nothing was allowed to rest on a sub-structure; the parts were made to support each other in suspension through tension and pressure. The difference between a Gropius design of the 1920's or 1930's and a

Pier Luigi Nervi design of the 1950's or 1960's is like the difference between the temple of Paestum and the cathedral of Albi. European architects commissioned to build in newly developing countries tended to use buildings to project their fantasies, as Oscar Niemeyer did in Brasilia and Le Corbusier in Rawalpindi.

The need for high-rise buildings, which were almost unknown in Europe before 1939, created new aesthetic problems for architects. They tried their utmost to avoid the "box" look, but the attempt to evade or conceal the obvious often led to bizarre and impractical solutions. Fortunately, the new building materials and the new technology gave architects a wide choice of means and structural ideas. Some startling inventions were suited for churches, railway stations, and government buildings. Berlin wit has given the name "Pregnant Oyster" to a magnificent concert hall.

It goes without saying that model plans could best be tested where entirely new cities were being laid out and architects were not forced to adjust a particular building to a pre-existing environment but were able to plan it as part of an environment consisting of parks, avenues, and other open spaces. The best results were obtained in the forty-mile stretch of Volgograd, once Stalingrad, where the new developments could be so widely spaced as to combine efficiency with hygiene and visual appeal. At Rouen, France, vehicular traffic has been separated from pedestrian traffic, schools, shopping, and recreational areas. On the other hand, the traditional look of the Seine at Paris is being destroyed by new highways and high-rise buildings.

CHAPTER 4

Observations on Post-war Movies

THE film developed from a vehicle of mass entertainment into a new art form. But its nature all but forbids the preservation of a film reel for future audiences; movies are closer to the ephemeral hit song than to the poem that is preserved in books for all eternity. Even great pictures will always be period pieces, easily dated. Hence, although movies have assumed the function of the novel, we must deal with individual films as events rather than acts of creation.

Of course, entertainment and escape continue to be the main purpose of the traditional genres: love story, comedy, historical pageant, and adventure—the last divided into detection (murder), espionage, Western, science fiction, horror, war, and recently pornography. West Europeans loved Hollywood productions, East Europeans the second-hand, West European version of the American product. Films of Karl May stories and a British doctor serial were popular on Czech and Polish television. Russian papers complained that Soviet citizens preferred American make-believe to socialist realism. Yet Moscow theaters had to fill the demand for Westerns.

Vice versa, among the Russian movies it was not the sensitive *The Cranes Are Flying* but the interminable *War and Peace* that achieved popularity in the West; likewise, European movie theaters show the Hollywood pictures that European reviewers condemn.

Obviously, people everywhere still like to see brave men taking the law into their own hands, villains pursued and eventually hanged, the helpless woman protected and won by the virtuous hero. Westerns and socialist-realist pictures follow identical patterns of plot and character construction: good guys versus bad guys, an upright society defending itself against intruders, noble characters among the common herd.

The entertainment that the movie provides for the masses has improved technically, and often thematically, too. Even the German film industry, which was notorious for its conventionality, has made pictures based on Theodor Fontane's *Effie Briest*, Carl Zuckmayer's *Schinderhannes*, Thomas Mann's *Königliche Hoheit*, and Gerhart Hauptmann's *Fuhrmann Henschel*.

We already have spoken of the stark realism of Italian post-war films: *Open City* and *The Bicycle Thief*, made in the ruins of Rome's *Cinema Città*; *Paisà* and *Shoeshine*; Giuseppe de Santis's *Bitter Rice*; Visconti's *La Terra Trema*, which, its clear "Marxist" message notwithstanding, received second prize in the 1948 Venice

393

film festival. Many films of this early period were inspired by the war experience.

Claude Autant-Lara's *Le Diable au Corps* (*Devil in the Flesh*, 1947), based on Raymond Radiguet's novel, skillfully contrasted the pursuit of happiness and the symbols of order and society. In *Tu Ne Tueras Pas*, Autant-Lara attacked the army, the church, and conformism. Later pictures, like Pietro Germi's *Divorce Italian Style* (1962), hit other institutional targets more lightly.

While the East German state movie industry made a business of anti-Nazi films, none of them remarkable, West Germany waited seven years to produce films with critical stories. Zuckmayer wrote the play *The Devil's General*, and Helmut Käutner directed a film based on this true story of the air ace, Ernst Udet. We also might mention some other politically-oriented films with a decided left-wing point of view, such as Resnais's *Guernica* (1950) and *Nuit et Brouillard* (1955, a documentary on concentration camps); Chris Marker's *Cuba Sí* (1961); Jean-Luc Godard's *Le Petit Soldat* (1960, alluding to the Algerian conflict); Francesco Maselli's *Gli Sbandati* (1954, on the Italian Resistance); Lindsay Anderson's *March to Aldermaston* (1959), and also Mario Monicelli's masterful *Organizer* (1964, about a factory workers' strike at the turn of the century); finally, *The Sorrow and the Pity*, the beautifully honest record of the Nazi occupation of France and the French Resistance, by Marcel Ophuls.

Direct criticism of the social and political environment, however, is rarely suitable for a picture that is dependent on mass distribution. The visual imagery of film lends itself better to a different form of social comment: examination of the quality of life, of the human environment, and of manners. In 1959, Luis Buñuel's *Nazarin* won the International Critics' Award, and Resnais made *Hiroshima Mon Amour* (scenario by Marguerite Duras). Miss Duras later directed *La Musica*; Buñuel went on to great triumphs in religious and anti-religious parables, as in *Tristana*, and Jean-Luc Godard became the vanguard of the vanguard.

Godard has identified himself with a cause. The others have touched upon a great number of problems and have used a variety of styles. Truffaut has created the light-hearted horror story *Jules and Jim*, the social-realist *Four Hundred Blows*, the thriller *The Bride Wore Black*, then *Stolen Kiss* and its sequel, *Bed and Board*, and the quasi-documentary *The Wild Child*. Claude Chabrol has made ample use of the new freedom. In *Le Boucher* and the lesbian film *Les Biches*, he has catered to sadistic and lecherous curiosities. Despite their diversity, all these directors are usually grouped under the "new wave" label. What they have in common is the free use of new techniques, a certain disregard for the story line, a love for image, great sensitivity, and an affinity to the *roman nouveau*.

As in the new novels, new techniques were tried in the *avant-garde* movies—partly to express a sense of frustration and alienation in the atomic age, but often simply to play with the effects of new devices. Language was distorted; images were destroyed, sequences cut short. The world was shown no longer as the rationally organized universe the old masters had tried to "imitate," but as an arbitrary assemblage of sensations which accidentally might make sense but generally was absurd. The French motion-picture director Louis Malle, in *Zazie dans le Métro* (1960, after a novel by

Raymond Queneau) and *Vie Privée* (1961, with Brigitte Bardot), offered portraits worthy of Max Ernst. Godard's *Breathless* (1960) showed the gangster-anarchist (Jean-Paul Belmondo) sovereign and despising the world. Paris hailed Belmondo as a latter-day Robin Hood. In a more grotesque way, the same youth rebellion burst out in Lindsay Anderson's film *If. . . .*

Many European and American films addressed themselves to young moviegoers: *Morgan, Blow-Up, The Knack, La Chinoise, Easy Rider, Alice's Restaurant,* and *The Graduate.* The Beatles made a few movies, directed by Richard Lester, which were full of movement and zany humor. No longer need young audiences put up with films made for adult consumption. For the first time they have films they can consider their own. Instead of idolizing the stars, they identify with them.

The freedom of the youth films had been won in the experiments of a decade, notably by Swedish and French directors. Sweden is the only Western country where movie-making is under government control. When in 1963 the number of exported Swedish films dropped from forty to twelve, the ruling socialists decided that the reason was a lack of cultural and social engagement. A 10 per cent tax on all theater admissions is now used to underwrite movies approved of as artistically excellent or socially desirable. Since then, Sweden has produced and exported daring films. The pornographic *I Am Curious (Yellow)* alone brought $2.3 million. But about one-quarter of Sweden's film production is devoted to muckraking and social criticism, mostly of local interest and not suited for export. *Made in Sweden* denounces a concern that had supplied arms to Thailand; *Adalen 31* (also shown in the United States) deals with a strike which was broken but which led to the socialist electoral victory in 1931. *They Call Us Provos* is a Beat documentary.

More than American films, European films are known by their directors. Their excellence is often due to the structure of the European film industry, where the director controls the script or even writes it, and in many cases acts as producer, too. Probably the greatest names are Resnais, Godard, Buñuel, Fellini, Antonioni, and Truffaut. But the most intriguing director of all is Sweden's Ingmar Bergman, who has created new myths and symbols for the "problématique" of his contemporaries. In *Persona* (the Latin word for "mask"), he explored a twofold identity crisis; *Shame* is his unforgettable indictment of war; *The Seventh Seal* is a parable of man's life.

Avant-garde techniques are quickly absorbed and integrated. In this process, years count for decades. In 1958, François Truffaut was banished from the Cannes Festival; in 1959, he was awarded first prize; in 1963, he was a member of the jury. At that time Jean-Luc Godard was thought unacceptable; in 1968, while he was busy building barricades in Paris, the Berlin Senate invited him to its film festival. Claude Lelouch was considered a revolutionary; but *A Man and a Woman* was rightly denounced by the *avant-garde* as a "monochrome of images and music where all conflicts are leveled." In *Grazie, Zia* by the young Italian Salvatori Samperi, the pseudo-radicals finally admitted their impotence and depicted the self-annihilation of their perverse protestations.

The greatest scandal, however, is the facile way in which the industry emasculates the revolution. It simply adopts the new methods of shock and imagination as so many techniques of entertainment. *Breathless* may have esoteric meaning, but on the surface it is sensational. In *The Yellow Submarine*, the Beatles show a mastery of psychedelic effects with a freedom previously unknown, and the anti-war fantasy at the end seems entirely unconnected with the virtuoso performance which the audience remembers.

As a protest against this absorption, a few directors and authors withdrew their films from the Cannes Festival, explaining that this was a class war between producer-proprietors and inventor-workers.

Anxious to bring about a confrontation, the *avant-garde* directors ultimately violate all laws of movie-making. Jean-Marie Straub uses long still pictures to music by Bach with the words, "I rejoice in my death." Godard piles up corpses while a voice utters unrelated nonsense. Godard admits that his aim is, "above all, to destroy the idea of culture, that alibi of imperialism . . . culture, that's war." But even *his* films are questioned by a new generation of nihilists, to whom "a whole arse in the movies is a cloak for the burnt arse in Vietnam." As a climax to the absurdity, the underground film director Hellmuth Costand shows his contempt for society by masturbating in front of the camera. He and his colleagues also use devices of deliberate artlessness to destroy all illusions of a possible culture. The aim of "art" is to negate art, to create scandal.

As a result of these developments, sharp cleavages have appeared between three distinct genres—the popular film which continues to provide vicarious thrills or sentimental gratification, the art film which deals with contemporary problems of perception, and the *avant-garde* film which deals only with itself.

CHAPTER 5

Some Observations on the Stage

IN Europe, where every middle-sized town has its permanent theater (and larger cities also an opera house), the stage has always been more than entertainment and social event. It is a mirror of society, and often its critic. There are, to be sure, light comedies and musicals. But the sprightly wit of Jean Anouilh, Christopher Fry, Marcel Aymé, or Marcel Achard should not mislead us. They are serious. In *The Cocktail Party* (1950), T. S. Eliot tried nothing less, he said, than to save European culture from his barbarian American compatriots; these, however, invaded the European stage and made it truly contemporary. Arthur Miller, Tennessee Williams, Thornton Wilder, Truman Capote, and William Saroyan became popular. And when pro-American feelings turned into hatred of America, European audiences once more applauded authors like Edward Albee and cheered the Living Theater.

In his epic theater, Bertolt Brecht had started a new, didactic dramaturgy. His followers now treated the theater as a communal rite or tribunal, improving only slightly on the Communist "agitprop" techniques of the 1920's. Peter Weiss, Rolf Hochhuth, Conor Cruise O'Brien, and Kenneth Tynan developed the "documentary play," which effectively placed the audience or its most cherished idols in the defendant's dock and satisfactorily solved all cases of political assassination, from Sikorski and Lumumba to the Kennedys and Martin Luther King.

More radical in its implications was the school of Pirandello, which, in contrast to the documentarists, had no social message but continued to assail a more fundamental establishment: the Aristotelian assumptions that the playwright knows what makes his characters tick, that God holds time and space together for the length of the play, and that the spectator has no part in the action.

The principle of contingency, the role of accident, in modern art, has often been praised as "open form." In drama we no longer have guilt and retribution, or cause and effect, but godless pandemonium. The hero acts without purpose; he is heard to say words without much significance. Often he is a repulsive, putrefying carcass with a sick mind and a sickening soul. The cult of the "tragic" which characterized the 1930's was followed by the cult of the "absurd" in the 1940's and 1950's, accompanied by ritualistic professions of "anxiety" and disquisitions on the "human condition."

The existentialist theater is summarized in Samuel Beckett's novella *The*

397

Unnamable: "I can't go on, you must go on, you can't go on, I'll go on." Life is a burden and a riddle. But in contrast to other burdens, this one is carried nowhere; in contrast to other riddles, this one has no solution. Beckett's decrepit stage characters don't know who they are. A happier age, to which T. S. Eliot wished he could return, left the meaning of the world to God. The first age radically to reject God still stands in fear of meaninglessness and death.

This also is the message of Eugène Ionesco and Harold Pinter. Ionesco puts on stage the deep anxiety from which he suffers; he projects his own paranoia onto all of humanity. Pinter refutes Donne: Every man, he seems to say, is an island, fearful of making contact with other men or with time. His people speak in disjointed sentences, which are overheard in bars and trolleycars or public comfort stations. Yet what they say is not heard in context but as the casual eavesdropper might catch it. Pinter puts bits into plays which are as incoherent and enigmatic as the lives of strangers.[1]

Peter Handke tries to "unmask the functions of domination" through clever syntactical juxtaposition. Like Kafka and Beckett before him, he creates tension by withholding information; but—and this is the difference—he hints that even if we knew that which we do not know, we would still think we did not know what we should know. There is no meaning in a play because life has no meaning either; but, as Beckett might add, even of that we cannot be sure. Nor should a play be "realistic" in terms of social or philosophical issues. The playwright is concerned with life's nuances and ambiguities. He does not want to enlighten his audience but to shock them. Pinter once said that his plays should not be performed realistically, as social satire; they should be incoherent, not seek psychological depth, just be "idiotic"— idiocy being a revealing simplification. Ionesco has made similar statements.

Of the seven major playwrights who have practiced the technique of the theater of the absurd, five are in one way or another displaced persons, strangers in their society. Edward Albee is a homosexual, Beckett an Irishman writing in French, Ionesco a Rumanian living in Paris, Peter Weiss the son of German refugees in Sweden, Pinter Jewish. Two other great playwrights, however, are sturdy Swiss: Max Frisch and Friedrich Dürrenmatt.

Peter Weiss tried to be didactic in a new way. His imaginary dialogue between the Marquis de Sade and Marat is surrounded by an almost ghoulish action which eventually engulfs the actors, the audience and actors in the play within the play, and the theater audience.

Dürrenmatt has said that the modern novel should make "structures of human communities" the agent of its action, since the individual is obsolete. He also thinks that modern playwrights fulfill their purpose better by letting ordinary people like secretaries, policemen, con men speak for them. A crime, therefore, is no longer presented to illustrate the complex of guilt and retribution or of responsibility and consequences; do we not know we are guilty anyway? Rather, it is presented to show

---

[1] The same technique has been used most successfully in David Storey's *The Changing Room*, showing people thrown together for a moment's purpose.

the structure of society. The old lady in *The Visit* came to Güllen not to *get* justice but to prove that she could *buy* it. Likewise, in *The Physicists*, the question is no longer, as in classical tragedy, how the community reacts when madmen take over, but how we can guard against the suspicion that we may all be mad. The same proposition is the theme of David Storey's *Home*, and, of course, the suggestion is ever present in Ionesco. Neither the world nor the theater is absurd, but man himself. The plays and movies of recent vintage all show people incapable of communicating with each other and of making sense of themselves. The reason, of course, is the denial of society and of its values. The problem of modern European man—how to live without God— remains unsolved.

CHAPTER 6

Theology Without God

EUROPEAN churches prospered while under the protection of princes, who defended authority, property, and privilege. Later, they obstructed the liberal state and compromised with fascism. The Church blessed those who subdued revolution at home and colonial uprisings abroad. It concluded concordats with Mussolini and Hitler. Even when the Nazis attacked Catholic lay associations and monks, the Roman Catholic Church did not call on the faithful to resist but left the protest to courageous individuals. While Bishop von Galen denounced Hitler from the pulpit, Archbishop Innitzer welcomed the conquering Nazis. It is true that in the encyclicals *Non Abbiamo Bisogno* (1931) and *Mit Brennender Sorge* (1937), Pope Pius XI reaffirmed the Catholic teachings on the relations between state and church, and condemned the breach by Fascists and Nazis of solemn treaties. During the last years of the war, Pius XII (1939–58) also ran diplomatic errands for the Allies and gave shelter to a few hundred Jews. But he failed to protest publicly against the terror, against the extermination camps, and against the war. Not the Pope and hardly any bishops, but simple priests and conscience-ridden laymen acted as "God's vicars" in that great crisis of the faith. Many Catholics, and notably Catholic intellectuals, took a strong stand against fascism and sought to align the church with democratic forces. A. Mendizabal put his pen into the service of the Spanish Republic. François Mauriac became an ardent Resistance fighter. Jacques Maritain addressed a fiery appeal to Catholics to "overcome the dualism between the things of God and the things of the world"; his philosophy of "personalism" had room for "a movement carrying labor toward the social responsibility of its maturity."

Among German Protestants it was mostly the educated and conservative who rallied to the Church Bearing Witness and defended the autonomy of religion against the state. The theology professed by its leaders was often orthodox or even fundamentalist. It was based on the harsh Calvinism of Karl Barth, a Swiss, who called for a "crisis theology." Even a socialist like Paul Tillich, who fled to America, was orthodox in his theology. It is interesting that men of this persuasion who plotted to kill Hitler on July 20, 1944, had made detailed plans which excluded a return to a democratic republic. Likewise, Barth's radical theology rejoiced in the decline of liberalism, proclaimed "the end of modernity," and was generally more sympathetic to a Jacobin state than to pluralism. After the war, Barth even expressed sympathy for the Soviet system. He was "modern" in the sense that he rejected middle-class values.

Pro-Soviet and neutralist ideologies developed in German Protestantism as a consequence of the country's partition. The Soviet-occupied provinces had Protestant and socialist majorities; since Adenauer did not seem eager to reunite with either, the Soviet government was able to use Protestant dignitaries as front men for its "peace" and "unity" appeals to the West Germans. The West German Bishop Hanns Lilje and the East German Bishop Otto Dibelius, Bundestag President Eugen Gerstenmaier, the one-time leader of the Church Bearing Witness Martin Niemöller, the dissident Nazi Ernst Niekisch, and Gustav Heinemann (later President of the German Federal Republic) all were involved in these maneuvers. Protestant politicians, aware of some revisionist feeling among their refugee constituents, were anxious to emphasize the provisional character of the Bonn Republic and to maintain the illusion that Stalin's successors would negotiate about the return of the lost provinces.

Swedish Protestants, too, adopted ideologies suitable to their country's neutral policy. But the bulk of German and European Protestants followed the cold war and "liberation" slogans of John Foster Dulles, himself an Elder in the Presbyterian Church.

In the Catholic Church, meanwhile, great changes had announced themselves during the war. The French Resistance movement was closely identified with de Gaulle's Cross of Lorraine. The church, which came closer to the people than at any time since Napoleon, renewed the traditions of Lamennais, of Le Sillon, and of Péguy. The Abbé Pierre became a leader in the Maquis and after the war helped found the Mouvement Républicain Populaire. Among other things, he led demonstrations which forced the government to underwrite housing for the poor. A group of French Dominican monks exchanged their cowls for blue jeans. But soon, instead of converting the heathen to Christianity, the worker-priests preached socialism and anti-colonialism. In Italy similar ideas were espoused by Danilo Dolci, but they had to wait ten years before obtaining political support. Emmanuel Mounier's monthly Esprit became the leading journal of social consciousness and liberal causes among Catholics.

Eugenio Pacelli (Pius XII), a conservative and an ardent anti-Bolshevist, condemned these deviations in his encyclical Humani Generis. At the height of the Indochina crisis, he dissolved the worker-priest movement. The MRP and the Democrazia Cristiana were turned into the vanguard of the cold war and social reaction. Pius XII, aspiring to sainthood, told of visions of the Virgin, beatified others who claimed to have had miraculous experiences, and admitted new miracles into the canon of the church. In his hope of restoring the church to its former glory and of containing Communism, he clearly appealed to the superstitions and fears of backward peoples; by contrast, he condemned the gnostic and mystic ideas which were taking hold among the most highly educated Catholics. Pierre Teilhard de Chardin, Henri de Lubac, and Yves Congar were attracting attention among laymen; a profound change was taking place in the hierarchy. The conservative Pope clearly had outlived his usefulness; after his death in 1958, the conclave elected Angelo Roncalli, who, as Patriarch of Venice, had known the plight of the poor. He was a man of serene simplicity who believed that the church must keep abreast of contemporary developments and must remember its spiritual mission. John XXIII, at seventy-seven, knew that he had only a few years left, and he used them for a vigorous "updating" (*aggiornamento*) of the church—its hierarchy, its liturgy, and its social teachings. In the encyclical *Mater et Magistra* he spoke of social reform; in *Pacem in Terris* he offered goodwill to men of all faiths and pleaded for peace. He called an ecumenical council (the Second Vatican Council), which convened in 1962 and concluded in 1965, two years after Roncalli's death, with sweeping reforms affecting almost every aspect of the church's life and work: its relationship with other churches, its doctrine, its organization, and the role of priests and laymen. It set in motion an ecumenical movement that may one day reunite the Christian churches.

Many theologians advanced unorthodox ideas, denounced old and sacred institutions of the church as outdated, and even challenged the hierarchy and its dictatorial ways. Cologne's Archbishop Joseph Frings assailed the methods of the Holy Office and obtained the resignation of its chief, Cardinal Alfredo Ottaviani. The Swiss theologian Hans Küng demanded greater freedom for bishops, defended the use of contraceptive pills, questioned celibacy, and put faith above dogma. The Vatican Council revised the church's attitude to Jews and Greek Orthodox Christians, modernized the liturgy, and permitted Mass to be read in the vernacular.

But Roncalli was followed by Giovanni Montini, who took the name Paul VI and set limits to the liberalizing trend. Even though he created the Synod of Bishops, he reasserted the supremacy of the Pope and even his infallibility. He opposed any change in the sexual mores of the faithful and restored some medieval dogmas. Though the Vatican Council had abolished the Index of Forbidden Books, the German bishops refused to give Küng's book *Infallible? An Inquiry* the imprimatur and invoked the 1929 concordat with Prussia (though no such German state exists today) to prevent the appointment of a theology professor who had doubted that Jesus walked on Lake Gennesaret.

Pope Paul's decision to continue the ban on contraception aroused a storm of protests. The Dutch bishops felt that the Pope may not have the right to substitute his own voice for God's. They fought him bitterly on their right to follow their own consciences and to allow their flock to follow theirs. They even raised the question of priestly celibacy.

In one area, however, Paul VI continued his predecessor's policy. The hand of the church now was extended beyond the Iron Curtain to countries like Poland, Czechoslovakia, Croatia, and Hungary, where it counted many faithful. In Latin America, where the church had long been a pillar of reaction in every domain, courageous bishops renewed the social doctrines of Leo XIII, led peasant movements against dictators, and sought good relations with the Communists. Even in Spain, the traditional bastion of orthodoxy, a modernist trend appeared among both priests and laymen.

As an overture to further relaxation, John XXIII had cautiously acknowledged

Poland's new borders in 1962; the following year he received Khrushchev's son-in-law, Aleksei Adzhubei, in private audience, ignoring the Italian Government's pleas that this gesture would help the Communists in the coming elections—which it did. The wives of Communists in the past had followed the priests' rather than their husbands' advice on election day; in 1964, many of them cast their first Communist vote. We already have spoken of the attempts made by Fanfani and other Catholic politicians to draw Nenni into the government. On the Vietnam war, the Vatican also supported de Gaulle's neutralist policies.

Poland and Cuba were two countries in which a Communist government coexisted with the Roman Catholic Church. In 1956, Cardinal Wyszynski had helped Gomulka to stabilize his regime; worship was not interfered with, and church holidays continued to be celebrated as national holidays. But the rapprochement was one-sided. In 1965, when Poland was preparing for the millenary of King Miesko's conversion at the sacred shrine of the Black Madonna in Czestochowa, the Pope proposed to make this a year of pilgrimage for Catholics from all countries; he even offered to come in person. But the Polish Government declined—not politely but with demonstrations, sports contests, and vilifications.

While in the East people looked to religion as a counterweight to the all-powerful state, in the West the power of the Catholic Church declined. Though de Gaulle increased state aid to Catholic schools, they recruited fewer than one-sixth of the children. Laymen were influenced less and less by the church's moral code; where they did maintain separate Catholic associations, these tended to collaborate more and more closely with their non-Catholic counterparts. Thus the Christian trade union (DFTC) and the Jeunesses Ouvrières Chrétiennes went on strike along with the CGT; the Jeunesse Agricole Chrétienne was in the forefront of agrarian unrest, and Cardinal Jean Villot had to rebuke the Jeunesses Étudiantes Françaises for collaborating with Communists. The tradition of Le Sillon proved stronger than that of L'Action Française. The Catholic thinkers who were emerging tended toward religious renewal and liberal social politics.

During the Algerian war, earnest men of the center turned away from patriotic duty and condemned it. Beuve-Méry and Pierre-Henri Simon, both Catholics, used their publicistic influence to arouse French youth against injustice. Mounier's successors at Esprit, Jean-Marie Domenach and Paul Thibaud, published social criticism even under de Gaulle.

From Péguy to Maritain to Mounier, French Catholicism always teetered on the brink of nonconformism. Mounier had fought Franco and spent several months in Pétain's jail. He engaged atheists and Marxists in debate and may be called a Catholic populist. Still farther to the Left, Georges Suffert published Témoignage Chrétien (Christian Witness), critical of both Communism and orthodoxy, but most of all the Catholic politicians.

In Austria, during the 1960's, a dissident Social Democrat, Günther Nenning, took editorial charge of the Viennese monthly journal Forum, originally a CIA publication and converted it into a meeting place of pacifists, revisionist Marxists, left-wing

Catholics, pornographers, and personal enemies of Chancellor Bruno Kreisky. It carried the writings of the Marquis de Sade as well as learned dissertations on dialectics (whether Thomist or Marxist), a hefty section against the Austrian Army, and a good deal of muckraking; but, above all, it served as a "bridge" between the Communist world and those Catholics who agreed to "talk" with it. The *Paulus-Gesellschaft* (St. Paul Society) held a conference at Salzburg in 1965 where such famous atheists as Roger Garaudy and Lucio Lombardo-Radice, assorted philosophers, and French and Italian Communist officials confessed, as abjectly as though on Stalin's orders, that they had not sufficiently appreciated the value of Christian spirituality; Moscow's official Tass called the venture "significant." At that time the old-Hegelian Marxist, Max Horkheimer of the Frankfurt Institute, also rediscovered religion; Ernst Bloch, the Marxist philosopher who had fled from East to West Germany, returned to his first love, mysticism. Kolakowski, the Polish professor who had defected to the West, also tried to link Marxist humanism with gnosticism.

Yet the effort for *rapprochement* is greater from the Catholic side to the Marxists than the other way. The entire relationship between church and social reality is under review, and with it its doctrine on the relationship between faith and world. Earlier, the Jesuits had made serious efforts to reconcile the Biblical word with the findings of modern science. Many believers had stayed within the faith by looking at the old rites and legends as symbolic; now such make-shift adjustments seemed too evasive. Catholic thought had to become philosophical.

Gabriel Marcel sought new inspiration in St. Augustine's tortured vision and rethought Catholic thoughts in existentialist form, as Tillich was doing for Protestant thought. Mounier, on the other hand, developed the philosophy of *personalisme*, which denies the dichotomy between world and man, reason and feeling, truth and beauty, even between God and man—or, rather, he defined the human being as grounded in God, giving him a modern sense of dignity. Much more decisively than earlier Catholic thinking, this philosophy gave the individual and his conscience the certitude of survival in the face of society's demands. But personalism still promised a harmonious solution of the problem of man in the modern world, as Thomism promised reconciliation between man and the universe.

Much deeper and more painful was the experience of a hostile world for the Catholic novelists François Mauriac, Georges Bernanos, Evelyn Waugh, Graham Greene, who show man in all his misery and make him aware of the abyss between himself and God. In their view, man is the eternal battleground between good and evil, and yet there is no way to heaven except through sin. The novelist, or for that matter the philosopher or theologian, can do nothing but make evil perceptible and palpable. After the war, Elisabeth Langgässer and Heinrich Böll joined in this revolt, reacting strongly against the optimistic climate of liberalism, these writers view life as tragic. In stressing conscience, they come closer to Protestantism than any Catholics had been for two centuries.

The Protestant theologians, meanwhile, had learned from Karl Barth to reject

modernism, rationalism, and the liberal attempts to reconcile faith with science or to
seek subterfuges in symbolic interpretation. Barth saw faith as a criticism of the world,
contemporary civilization as a Tower of Babel about to collapse; his preaching had
the quality of the apocalyptic prophets' fire and brimstone, supplementing the
prophecies of doom which in his day were hurled at capitalist society. Rudolf Bultmann
reviewed and developed the Barthian effort to "demythologize the New Testament,"
and he held that "Myth should be interpreted not cosmologically but anthropologically
or, better still, existentially."

In other words, at a time when the natural sciences demythologized cosmology,
theology had to "reinterpret" the Bible's view of nature; now that the social sciences
demythologized man, theology reinterpreted the Bible's anthropology. In both cases
the power of myth was preserved as symbol of the transcendental forces which rule
man and of his need for deliverance from the forces of this world. "The Christian
life means turning away from the world.... This detachment is essentially
eschatological" (Bultmann).

Though Bultmann's attempt to create an existentialist theology failed, his effort
was remarkable because of its radicalism. For the first time a theologian dared to say
that he could not imagine God, and yet assert that he was staying within the faith. His
"theology without God" was accepted by Tillich and Dietrich Bonhoeffer; they in
turn were followed by John Robinson, Bishop of Woolwich, whose book *Honest to
God* provoked an angry reaction in the Anglican Church.

Bonhoeffer became a hero of the resistance in Germany. His martyr's death has
surrounded his words with a halo of supreme significance; his letters have become a
popular book of edification. Like existentialism, the theology of these thinkers defines
God as man's aspiration, not as a force outside man. Like the mystics, they seek
communion rather than a Father in Heaven.

Mystic religion appeared to many to be the way out of the religious crisis of the
twentieth century. But there are great differences among the various prophets of
mystical religion. Martin Buber, who had learned from the Hasidim, was serene and
Spinozistic; Simone Weil, a deeply torn soul, cried out to the unknown God because
her experience of human misery had made her desperate. Ernst Bloch, who had been
an Expressionist in his youth, then a Communist, translated ecstatic religion into
the language of his age. What difference is there between God and Bloch's *Das Prinzip
Hoffnung* (*Principle of Hope*)? He denies God but he respects the place where others
believe God to be.

In contrast to Bloch's ecstasy of experience, the Jesuit Teilhard de Chardin, a
learned anthropologist, projected the vision of a scientific ecstasy, the prospect of
man's further development toward the godhead. Reviving the old magic prophecy
Eritis Sicut Deus, Ye shall be as gods, he speculated about evolution, which he
conceived of as not merely a thing of the past but, more important, as the promise
of the future. In *The Phenomenon of Man*, he mapped out the story of man. The
biosphere (man's environment and natural life) had developed to the point where
the noosphere (man's rational, moral, and artistic life) would take off toward

unpredictable heights—maybe to the perfect perception of God or, more precisely, to his discovery. As a student of Bergson, Teilhard did not hesitate to draw the conclusion that this superior man actually would create the superior God. Instead of seeking God the Creator in the past of the Universe, he looked forward to him; it is no accident that Julian Huxley the atheist wrote the preface, prophesying the eventual achievement of mankind's psycho-social unity.

His brother Aldous, novelist and social critic, also turned to mystic religion as a universal and eternal experience of mankind; later in his life he sought mind expansion in the peyote cult.

The drug experience had smoldered underground in Europe at least since Coleridge's time. Its use in the 1920's generally was associated with vice, high life, and prostitution. As a cult, it did not make proselytes until Americans invested it with the ritualistic and symbolic meanings that it has acquired for the "now generation."

At all times the step from ecstatic religion to charlatanism is a short one. An age on the whole so devoted to science and rationality, and said to have lost all religion, nonetheless produced an outpouring of sects and underground faiths such as had rarely been seen before. Nature healers and various gurus filled lecture rooms and meeting halls in increasing numbers. Especially favored were Oriental mystics; charlatans taught a caricature of Zen Buddhism; Maharishi converted the Beatles and then asked for 10 per cent of their earnings. Astrology flourished among the under-thirty group. Particular fascination fastened on the various saints who imitated St. Francis or lived in "communes." If such communes, in addition to being poor, also engaged in promiscuous sex rites and sponsored "happenings," their appeal was bound to be irresistible.

Perhaps escapes into surrealistic religion fulfill the same function in the West that an increased church attendance fulfills in the East. Both provide a refuge from the demands of society.

CHAPTER 7

The Two Cultures

EVERY age is dominated by some overarching idea, style, or faith, metaphysical and ethical assumptions by which the world and society seem to be bound together. The buildings, literature, and philosophy it leaves to posterity—admittedly after a post-humous process of critical selection—define its spirit as a unit, an epoch with a particular physiognomy in the ages of mankind. Though contemporaries may often be more keenly aware of what divides them than of what they have in common, they are unaware of certain assumptions and supreme values on which they unconsciously agree. We do not know how future historians will assess our culture. So far we cannot affirm that in place of the old beliefs we have acquired the "new" tablets Nietzsche had foreseen. On the contrary, never has the search for meaning been so deeply divorced from the processes of problem solving. Our technology is based on rationality, but our philosophers assert that reason is not commensurable with life, and our poets speak of its absurdity. Our planners promise to build a society that will free man from his material woes, but our moral sense doubts that salvation can be gained just through the proper handling of economic equations.

No previous age had produced so many different philosophies claiming to embrace the whole of human experience and cosmological knowledge, yet their very number testifies how much the goal of unified knowledge eludes us. Moreover, the approaches which hold the greatest promise of such an achievement, the natural and behavioral sciences, are precisely the ones that offer success by piecemeal solutions. We can solve some problems by scientific methods; but even if we were to solve all, we would be still farther away from the over-all goal of harmony, salvation, and reconciliation.

In his pamphlet *The Two Cultures*, C. P. Snow deplored that humanists and technocrats do not even understand each other's language. Nothing threatens the future of mankind so ominously as the pursuit of technical goals that are not informed by human values, or the pursuit of public happiness without regard for the available means. Material means autonomously determining ends will clash with ideal goals which are hostile or indifferent to the material culture.

Our culture is also split into Eastern and Western, where socialist and liberal con-ceptions produce different manifestations in the realm of ideas and of the arts. More-over, for the first time, modern industrial society has created a lower culture that no longer consents to be ruled by the standards of the higher culture, while the *avant-garde* sees itself in rebellion against both the lower culture and the traditional culture. The *avant-garde*, allied with other alienated strata, deliberately creates a counter-culture, rejects the notion that culture must integrate the social structure, and denies the aesthete's conception of beauty. "My art," Jean Dubuffet proclaimed in 1957, "is an enterprise to rehabilitate discredited values." In *Asphyxiante Culture* he wrote: "Now is the time to found institutes of deculture, with especially trained instructors to teach demystification."

Philosophers, sociologists, and psychologists are, of course, always engaged in similar "enterprises," and the sociology of knowledge has deprived all ideologies of their glamour. But it is new for artists to denounce beauty and to claim for art as such a political function. In the *Young Painters' Manifesto* of 1967, Gilles Aillaud warned artists that "the threat . . . is participation in the life of modern bourgeois-technical society." It is obvious that such notions prevent the artist from building monuments that proclaim a "style" or any harmony of this age and society.

Thus having disposed of religion, philosophy, and all ideologies, the great meat-grinder of revolution also had disposed of beauty, art, and the very notion of the ideal. The artists themselves deny society the symbols of certainty and stability, the unity and harmony of an overarching style. They reflect a self-doubt that is not "methodical," that is, constructive, as Descartes suggested in the seventeenth century, but a deep despair, "a passionate unbelief" (to quote Camus), a death wish, a longing for the absurd. Their criticism, if that be accepted as a function of art, does not transcend its object; it does not create "a realm of beautiful appearance" to complement the dreary business of everyday life. It is neither a cult nor an extension of the private personality.

Rather, our literature and philosophy have become a constant exercise in soul searching. Our artists and writers scrutinize "the problematique" of the human situation. In the 1920's and 1930's, we have seen, this endeavor produced weighty works, such as Gide's *Counterfeiters*, Thomas Mann's *Magic Mountain*, James Joyce's *Ulysses*, Paul Hindemith's *Mathis the Painter*, Martin Heidegger's *Being and Time*, Freud's *Civilization and Its Discontents*, Dmitri Shostakovich's First and Fifth Symphonies. It would be hard to match this record by comparable works in the twenty-five post-war years. Günter Grass and Nikos Kazantzakis, Alexander Solzhenitsyn and Max Frisch have given magnificent form to our experience; but whether they are truly great and whether their work will endure we dare not say.

Nor is a list of Nobel laureates helpful. Beginning in 1946, they were Hermann Hesse, André Gide, T. S. Eliot, Bertrand Russell, François Mauriac, Ernest Hemingway, John Steinbeck—all honored for achievements in the previous era; Pär Lagerkvist (Sweden), Halldór Laxness (Iceland), Juan R. Jiménez (Spain), Boris Pasternak, Salvatore Quasimodo (Italy), Ivo Andric (Yugoslavia), Giorgos Seferis (Greece), Winston Churchill, Mikhail Sholokhov, Nelly Sachs and Samuel Agnon (both Jewish refugees to Israel), Miguel Asturias (Guatemala), Yasunari Kawabata (Japan), Solzhenitsyn, Pablo Neruda (Chile)—all clearly chosen for political and geographic reasons rather than for generally recognized merit. The only laureates of the present generation whose work, though controversial, may establish a claim to greatness were William Faulkner, Albert Camus, Saint-John Perse, Jean-Paul Sartre, Heinrich Böll, and Samuel Beckett. None of them has offered a world view comparable to that of the earlier masters; Sartre, who tried, has since revoked his philosophy. He also rejected the prize.

The effect of existentialism has been anti-philosophical. Like Marxism and psycho-analysis, it taught that in the arena of ideas what is proclaimed matters less than who does the proclaiming. All three forsake the traditional approach of ideological contests by immanent criticism and substitute for it extraneous criteria of truth: the socio-logical, the psychological, the existential. The latter provides the broadest, most general, and most philosophical line of attack on traditional philosophy. It may be compared to the Sophist school which preceded Socrates and asked all possible questions in order to show that philosophy was unable to answer them. Existentialists cannot claim that their method answers all questions.

The Marxist school is, if anything, in worse shape. Abandoned by the Social Democrats, asphyxiated by the Stalinists, adulterated by epigones, Marxism in the post-war period has not given new leadership or insight to its Western followers. Its offshoots in China and Cuba are perversions rather than developments of the Marxist idea; in Europe its heritage has long been in the hands of a sterile orthodoxy. Even Lukács, who bravely defended literature against the Stalinist priesthood, could do so only by setting up Molière, Shakespeare, Goethe, and Balzac as models; he was blind and deaf to most modern literature and despised it. Max Horkheimer and Theodor W. Adorno were proponents of the use of Marxism as an instrument to criticize ideologies (including the arts); after their return to Germany from exile, however, they fell into journalistic criticism of Western culture and eventually into obscurantism. Herbert Marcuse, another associate of the Frankfurt Institute, took a couple of additional steps in cultural criticism: in *Eros and Civilization* he used (or, as his colleague Erich Fromm charged, misused) Freudian categories to condemn a civilization that fails to gratify human instincts; in his *One-Dimensional Man*, he condemned all civilization, but in particular the bourgeois-industrial-capitalist one, which forces man to live in the graceless state of alienation. Both Adorno and Marcuse were to fall out with students who took their doctrines literally and sought instant gratification in occupied college buildings.

More serious efforts were made by Erich Fromm, the Yugoslavs Gajo Petrovic and Svetozar Stojanovic, by Iring Fetscher in Germany, Kolakowski in Poland, Agnes Heller in Hungary, and by the Czech revisionists Karel Kosik, Ivan Svitak, Milan Prucha, and Ivan Dubsky to develop the humanist ideas in Marxism. Their endeavors paralleled the Italian trend toward revisionism, which took its cue from the martyred Gramsci. They all fell short of their goal to reconcile philosophy with praxis. On the whole, this literature is eclectic and offers no new understanding of a world which continues to baffle the younger generation.

The popular world view continues to be some form of "scientism"—that is, the belief that somehow the sum of the sciences should yield both guidance and justification for action. The parliaments of all nations appropriate vast amounts for research and development; scientists and experts constantly "counsel" governments; national and international conferences draw scholars together for earnest discussion of problems recognized as affecting all mankind. The progress of knowledge, no longer dependent on the luck of a lonely scholar, is confidently built on communication, organization, and modern equipment. We are penetrating the secrets of space, of subatomic structures, of life, even of the mind. We discover new worlds hitherto unsuspected—new celestial bodies, new galaxies billions of light years away, as well as causes of diseases and genetic agents.

But obviously, those who had hoped (or feared) that the big problems of social and political life might one day be solved by calculation, were disabused. Science does not ask the questions and does not produce, of itself, the criteria of judgment. Crude scientism and pseudo-Marxism which encourage the hope that ethical conclusions can emerge from scientific propositions still have a large following in Europe and America. C. P. Snow, for instance, throws his whole support on the side of the "scientific revolution" which he hopes will eventually achieve in the social field what it previously did in the realm of nature: to understand the world and to control it. "Applied science has made it possible to remove unnecessary suffering from a billion human lives. . . . It does not require additional scientific discoveries. It depends on the spread of the scientific revolution all over the world. There is no other way. It certainly will happen. . . . When it is achieved, our consciences will be a little cleaner." The solutions for our social ills seem to come from "the knowledge of some potentialities which is theirs [the scientists'] alone."

A similar view is held by many philosophers of the Vienna school, though its basic tenets are starkly opposed to any such inferences. Neopositivism, as "scientific philosophy" or as "philosophy of science," teaches that philosophy must confine itself to analyzing terms and methods for the individual sciences. Like existentialism, it denies that science or philosophy can establish "meaning" either in life or in history. Karl Popper has written a book attacking the attempt to derive a philosophy from the study of social facts. When Marcuse and Kolakowski charged that positivism leads to quietism and prevents commitment to great causes, they may have had in mind Ludwig Wittgenstein, but even he merely meant to clear away rubbish in order to make speculation and ethics possible once again; the stricture hardly applies to Bertrand Russell, a man of many causes. Moritz Schlick, the founder of neopositivism, was murdered by the Nazis; Rudolf Carnap and Otto Neurath were militant socialists, Hans Reichenbach a left-wing Communist.

Where, then, is the misunderstanding? As taught by such modern representatives as A. J. Ayer, Hans Albert, and Ernst Topitsch, neopositivism is a technical academic discipline, not unlike mathematics, concerned with the proper procedures in logic and language, a useful but not necessarily exciting occupation. It does not pretend to reveal great truths, but endeavors to demolish small falsehoods. Like previous agnostics and skeptics, it debunks ideologies, conservative and liberal alike, but particularly the radical ones which confront the world with absolute ideas or visions. To ask for "meaning," in an ethical or metaphysical sense, is to pursue poetry; to pursue political vision requires applying available resources to concrete situations. Hence positivists neither ask "last questions" of metaphysics nor expect apocalyptic solutions in politics. Yet, their function is to criticize. Carnap tried to think in terms of a unitary system of science embracing the logical structure of the universe; others have studied language and the logic of social and cultural sciences, and Wittgenstein himself, at the end of his life, recognized that his own philosophy also was a cultural form.

Positivism thus has become a rigorous tool of science which has sharpened the conception of many other philosophies. Under positivist criticism religious thinkers have repudiated the theological claim that revelation has disclosed scientific truths; existentialist philosophers have admitted that their aim is not scientific "accuracy" but only philosophical "precision," and that they are not dealing with "problems" in the sense that their solution must be verifiable but merely "questioning" the foundations of existence.

When philosophy abandoned its claim to be the queen of sciences, psychology and sociology offered to solve its problems. Max Weber's younger brother Alfred said in 1960: "Our historical condition is that of an age in radical change more thorough than mankind has ever experienced. Therefore we must return to a universal sociology." He also wrote a metahistorical work announcing "The Fourth Man"— technological as well as humanist, master as well as collectivist. Even more ambitious was Arnold Toynbee's ten-volume *A Study of History* (1933–60). But history and sociology clearly could not provide the metaphysical or naturalistic transcendence which people crave in embracing a religion or philosophy. On the contrary, the social and cultural sciences after the war used the behaviorist approach. Following the American example, they studied human behavior without reference to conscious thought. Continental psychologists and sociologists rarely went as far as the Anglo-Saxons; but they, too, in their empirical studies fell under the sweep of the positivist spirit.

This development was unavoidable since European psychologists and social scientists had relied all too heavily on the method of the *Geisteswissenschaften*, emphasizing consciousness, ideas, conceptions. Now the reaction set in. For years an ardent debate raged on the methods and logic of the cultural sciences and whether psychology should be counted among them.

Related to this, another controversy developed among historians of science and philosophy. Up until the 1950's, the "history of ideas" was mainly concerned with tracing parentage and describing the dispersion, migration, and transmutation of ideas as they travel from one civilization to another or mature in one century after having germinated in another. But the ideas themselves were considered true or untrue, valid or mistaken irrespective of their cultural context. When Einstein corrected Newton's model with the theory of relativity, everyone was sure that this new enlargement of our understanding would be either verified or disproved by valid, objective methods of experimentation.

Then, in 1962, the American Thomas S. Kuhn published a book that was revolutionary in its title as well as in content and impact. *The Structure of Scientific Revolutions*[1] contended that scientists have for centuries put up with conflicting evidence and have been able to integrate deviations into established normality. Ptolemaic epicycles, in fact, explained the apparent movement of stars and planets much better than Copernicus's assumptions. But it took a basic "revolution" in the attitudes of the scientific community to make scientists resent the subterfuges and to suggest a different, cleaner, simpler model of the world as a whole. The new model had two advantages. It explained phenomena which only recently had attracted notice, and it gave a more satisfactory view of the universe.

The importance of the new approach, however, went far beyond the history of science; it placed science in a historical-sociological context. The history of ideas no longer looked for systems and structures that followed each other as ever-improving approaches to truth and were to be judged each by its inner coherence, rationality, and logical structure. The new history looked for reasons why scientists act like magicians in retaining or rejecting scientific theories. To accept Newton's explanation of phenomena, one did not have to believe in his "corpuscular" view of matter. To rid us of "particles," "corpuscles," "forces," and similar anthropomorphic conceptions, scientists needed a true "change of world view," a veritable "switch of paradigm." They did not just add here a little and there a little to a basically rational world view; they underwent a radical change so deep that they did not understand any more how their forebears could have been satisfied with the previous world view.

This discontinuity of scientific progress was further elaborated by the group of distinguished scholars who held an International Colloquium in the Philosophy of Science at London in 1965, under the chairmanship of Sir Karl Popper. Their discussions, published by Imre Lakatos and Alan Musgrave, show the disarray into which scientific thinking has been thrown by the new approach. Followers of Thomas S. Kuhn continue to hold that the choice of a theory or philosophy does not depend so much on its logic but on its serviceability. Followers of Sir Karl try to save the possibility of a canon of scientific behavior. But the difficulties in spelling out such a canon suggests to some that "science is what scientists are doing." This discussion has been further complicated by two related developments in the fields of sociology and psychology: the searching inquiries of Jürgen Habermas into the relationship between knowledge and interest, revealing science itself as an ideology; and the whimsical questions which Michel Foucault has asked on the structure of human knowledge.

The implications of these insights are far-reaching. They deepen the relativism of our world view; but they also should encourage scientists to search for better models,

---

[1] In his preface, Kuhn acknowledges the work of several European scholars as helpful in formulating his theory: Emile Meyerson, Hélène Metzger, Anneliese Maier, Jean Piaget, Ludwig Fleck—all dating back to the 1930's. He might have mentioned Henri Poincaré, the mathematician of the previous generation.

not to be glued to observable phenomena but to reach out for a new understanding. In the cultural crisis of Western civilization, they lead scientific philosophy out of the positivist-behaviorist asceticism via new perception toward a new praxis.

One attempt to utilize the new conceptions and to transcend them was made in France by Claude Lévi-Strauss. His "structuralism" originally was nothing more than an anthropological observation; but it soon developed into a universal method challenging the sciences of the preceding age. Traditional anthropologists like Lucien Lévy-Bruhl and psychiatrists like Freud had looked down on the thinking of the "primitives" as couched in affects and "participatory perception," unable to tell fantasy from reality, desire from logic, emotion from thought, subject from object. Lévi-Strauss now showed that the thought processes of the so-called primitives are as consistent, as empirical, and as precise as those of our own scientists, but, in addition, are also as speculative and poetic as those of the alchemists and "natural philosophers" who dominated Western thinking not so long ago. Positivists wish to separate the observer from his subject matter, politics from science, wishful thinking from studies. By contrast, a young generation of "engaged" and enraged thinkers hope to restore the unity of will, feeling, and knowledge; they hailed Lévi-Strauss as a godsend. He liberated studies from the yoke of method and permitted the reunion of theoretical knowledge with subjective experience. Explicitly pointing to Rousseau, he put man back into the totality of his social and natural environment. No doubt this approach placed Lévi-Strauss close to the Marxist romanticism of Ernst Bloch; hence, he became eligible, much against his wishes, to be the philosopher of the Left.

Lévi-Strauss, following Marcel Mauss, argues that kinship relations, exchange relations, and linguistic relations are really of the same kind. Customs are a language, exchanges are messages, rituals are a syntax. It is not unfair to suggest that such an approach owes its inspiration to certain techniques and assumptions of modern information theory and programming; myths and ceremonial behavior store the information in a way reminiscent of electronic circuits or a coded tape. Structuralism is the philosophy of a society that relies on the communications industries and on the manipulative skills of a bureaucracy.

Structuralism proved as temporary and ephemeral as existentialism. The imagination therefore fastened on other sciences, this time in a more naturalistic vein.

A new materialism seized the millions in the 1960's. Whether written by scientists like Konrad Lorenz or by popularizers like Robert Ardrey, books such as *On Aggression* or *The Territorial Imperative* seemed to confirm what many people wish to believe: that human nature is dominated by its animal heritage. Desmond Morris had worldwide success with *The Naked Ape*; Anthony Storr followed up with *Human Aggression*. Such dangerous theories, somewhat reminiscent of the neo-Darwinism which became the mold of racist ideologies, seem to reflect the conservative, restorative mood that took hold of nations. Another variant of this nature worship is the psycho-anarchism preached by the ex-Marxists Wilhelm Reich and Herbert Marcuse. Substituting the liberation of Eros for the liberation of the proletariat, these vanquishers of repression in all its forms reversed the path Marx had traveled from Hegel, and on the way they regressed into the young Hegelians' preoccupation with sex, which Proudhon already had denounced as counter-revolutionary.

Salvation, here, is sought in a return to nature. By contrast, all traditional philosophy shares the view that man is not nature but makes himself. This is true in Catholic personalism, existentialist idealism, and Marxist humanism. These three sustain the heritage of European intellectual history; they also embody the future of a democratic, united Europe.

Summarizing Part X, Western European intellectuals responded to the decline of Europe with perceptions of despair and doom. Their anxieties ranged from the threat of atomic annihilation to the danger of overpopulation, from the fear of domination by the superpowers to the loss of influence overseas, from the powerlessness of the individual *vis-à-vis* large organizations and technology to the individual's total surrender to opportunity and hedonism, from the disappearance of traditional values to the lack of new commandments that might help man understand his new environment and live in it. But the cultural reflections were not realistically related to the genuine problems. Rarely has there been as wide a gap between popular culture and high-brow culture. While the common man was trying to swim in the new technocentric stream and to enjoy his lack of responsibility, the intellectuals told him that this was his doom.

PART XI

The Resurrection of Europe
(1958-74)

CHAPTER I

Winds of Change

So far, we have treated Eastern and Western Europe as social and cultural units. For a more detailed account of recent political developments, we shall now consider each country separately while trying not to lose sight of the Continental aspect.

For all the advances of the welfare state, the regimes which governed the Western half of the Continent during the 1950's were restorative rather than innovative, and NATO came to be identified with the preservation of every *status quo*. Fear of uncontrollable change or a deeply felt need for security produced majorities for the repeated re-election of these governments which the more vocal and more dynamic organs of public opinions were beginning to reject. So far the diverse sources of dissent and dissatisfaction, however, could not converge into the river bed of an opposition because they lacked an ideology, an organization, a leader, and meaningful alternatives. Hence, the changes which ultimately became necessary had to wait until the middle 1960's. Let us recapitulate the conditions which led to these changes.

In 1949, the West German *Länder* (states) approved the constitution of the Federal Republic and elected as its first President, Professor Theodor Heuss, a Weimar liberal. Chancellor Konrad Adenauer emerged as an able leader who guided Germany with a firm hand. A wily politician (the "Fox"), a patriarchical figure of great dignity and integrity, a loyal European, and a staunch anti-Communist, Adenauer built a state which of necessity relied more on make-shift approaches than on solid foundations. Even the capital, Bonn, was chosen for Adenauer's convenience rather than as a national center. He was over seventy years old when he became Chancellor; he was disillusioned to the point of cynicism, righteous to the point of willfulness, and dexterous to the point of deviousness. His Christian Democrats (CDU) and their Bavarian allies (Christian Social Union, or CSU) ruled in coalition, first with the reactionary German Party and then with liberal Free Democrats, the latter party itself a strange mixture of southern liberals and northern nationalists. The CSU provided the Minister of Defense, the fat, strident, aggressive Dr. Franz Josef Strauss, a fanatical anti-Communist who fell when his zeal for the defense of freedom got in the way of some of its nicer points. It was a test of Germany's democracy that a muck-raking weekly, *Der Spiegel*, was able singlehandedly to force the resignation of this cabinet minister who had overstepped the limits of legality. Adenauer hoped to see the temporary become permanent and to win acceptance for a conservative new Germany within a strong Atlantic alliance and with a special relationship to the other two Catholic powers—France, Italy, and sometimes Belgium, the Netherlands—within a united Europe.

Across the Alps, Alcide de Gasperi, likewise a strong personality, a conservative and firm believer in NATO, out-maneuvered the Left until shortly before his death in 1954. He led the Christian Democratic Party (Democrazia Cristiana, or DC) toward a modern republicanism and away from clericalism; but since it never polled more than 40 per cent of the vote and was afraid of the socialists, de Gasperi depended on shifting coalitions with right-wing parties which prevented all the reforms Italy needed so badly. His successor, Giuseppe Pella, even formed a coalition with monarchists and Fascists. Political life remained sharply polarized between bourgeois and pro-letarian parties; at one point the workers threatened a political strike. Moderate Christian Democrats like Giovanni Gronchi and Antonio Segni vainly advocated an "opening to the Left" to let workers' representatives share the burden of responsibility. The socialists stood outside the state. But in 1955, Gronchi was elected President with socialist and Communist votes; his lieutenants Segni and Amintore Fanfani repeatedly served as Prime Minister and Foreign Minister, respectively. They succeeded in winning the small party of right-wing socialists under Giuseppe Saragat for a coalition; their remedies for Italy's ills, however, were no better than those of Pella. They hardly touched the big estates of the south. A hundred thousand peasants were given 1.5 million acres but neither tools, cattle, houses, nor capital. Share-croppers, tenant farmers, and farm workers earned $500 to $800 a year per family, $100 per capita. Skilled workers earned $1,000 to $1,500, university professors $3,000. Property taxes were regressive; 80 per cent of all taxes were indirect. A development plan, adopted in 1955, provided a growth rate of 5 per cent yearly, while job oppor-tunities in northern Europe helped relieve the population problem. But Italy never succeeded in creating the 4 million jobs it needed. The industrial proletariat remained disaffected; the Communist vote rose from 20 per cent to 25 per cent. Another 15 per cent, no less disaffected, but unwilling to support Communism, voted for the left-wing Socialists under Nenni (PSI). In 1960, workers clashed in bloody riots with the police in Genoa, Rome, and elsewhere.

After bitter wrangling in both the Christian Democratic Party and the PSI, Segni was elected President in 1962 and called another centrist, Aldo Moro, to form a government, which for the first time included Pietro Nenni, the left-wing socialist, much to the chagrin of orthodox members in both the DC and the PSI. Moro's cabinet was short-lived since neither party felt comfortable in coalition with the other. The majority of the DC and the powerful interests it represents clashed with the socialists over educational and economic policy. Although the DC had accepted the fact of planning and state ownership in a large sector of the Italian economy, it was not willing to venture very far into the uncharted sea of the welfare state. And though it eventually accepted some land reform, to support public building, and to raise the south from its prostration, its ideas on compensation for the former owners are extravagant.

Nevertheless, the momentum of a Leftist orientation could not be stopped. After the vibrant encyclicals of Pope John XXIII, the left wing in the DC grew bolder and proposed its own policy. It elected Saragat President with the help of the Communist votes; it agreed with the socialists on reform measures such as distribution of more land; it created the Southern Fund for development and farm reform; it favored the expansion of state power in industry and finance, and it helped nationalize the electrical industry. Italy is an instance of state capitalism and directed economy with a private-enterprise ideology. The state owns or directs shipping, the merchant marine, the defense industries, the railroads, power generation and distribution, four leading banks, the steel industry, salt and tobacco, and most mining; it is the sole exporter of rice; it regulates the price of wheat; through its insurance funds it builds residential housing; it settles farmers on former domains. Fanfani created the INA (Istituto Nazionale Assicurazione), which between 1949 and 1956 built 160,000 dwelling units. Mattei, the czar of ENI, was a vigorous proponent of public power and social justice.

The left wing of the DC also advocated a more independent Italian attitude in world politics. Fanfani and Mattei as well as Pope John XXIII and Nenni were viewed with suspicion in Washington, especially when Fanfani and Giorgio La Pira, former mayor of Florence, tried to mediate in Vietnam. In 1961, Segni and Fanfani visited Moscow in search of a possible *détente*; in 1965 Saragat visited Poland.

Such attempts to de-escalate the cold war and to create the foundations for a more independent European policy echoed similar attempts by de Gaulle in France and by a strange combination of the extreme Right and the Left in Germany. Industry was looking to the rich markets in the Soviet empire and the Chinese People's Republic; German nationalists were disappointed that the NATO policy had failed to bring back the lost provinces; the Social Democrats felt that they would never get rid of Adenauer as long as Germany's security depended on that American policy which he sponsored. Thus a general movement got under way to withdraw from American tutelage and to declare the cold war obsolete. In contrast to NATO critics of the late 1940's and early 1950's, however, the new opposition was not based on disaffected classes, alienated intellectuals, and frustrated politicians but rested on solid foundations in the established society of the Common Market countries.

The new critics were, first of all, new people. The Germans who had come out of the war had turned their backs on politics and escaped into vigorous activity for private improvement, building, working, and studying. They gladly accepted a leadership that promised to be firm and averse to "experiments." Konrad Adenauer, whose roots reached back into the monarchy, provided the image of restoration: Forget the misery of the Weimar Republic, the lies of the Nazi period, and the calamity of "the collapse" (they never called it defeat), and go back to the good old days.

Should all be forgotten? Adenauer's Germany was frequently criticized for accommodating former Nazis in the judiciary and even in the Chancellor's own office. His second successor, Kurt Georg Kiesinger, had been a minor official in Ribbentrop's Foreign Office; the second President, Heinrich Lübke, was accused of having supplied construction materials for an extermination camp. In a few West German states the

NPD, a militaristic, Nazi-type party, got more than 5 per cent of the vote, the minimum required for parliamentary representation. Add to this the frustration of Adenauer's foreign policy and his increasing intractability as he approached his eighty-seventh birthday, and the general desire for a change will not be mistaken for ingratitude to a man of infinite merits. When he retired, in 1963, Adenauer could say that he had built a state where there had been chaos, that he had restored Germany's good name in the West and Germans' confidence in themselves, guided his nation toward democracy, and achieved what to many Germans had seemed impossible: reconciliation with their archenemy, France. He had re-established contact with Moscow but had placed Germany firmly in the Western community. He was a good European and a source of strength for his partners, though a martinet to his subordinates and a terror to his enemies. His immediate successor, Ludwig Erhard, an economics professor who was credited with Germany's "economic miracle," had the misfortune of starting his administration in the 1963–64 recession; moreover, he disappointed those who had expected a political and spiritual miracle once the old curmudgeon had gone.

Certainly most Germans recognized the Bonn Republic as a necessary, though not ideal, halfway house and the Western alliance as their only guarantee of survival. Yet nobody seemed to like it. The CDU deputy Gustav Heinemann, a Protestant pacifist who opposed German rearmament and NATO, went over to the socialists—to be elected President of the Federal Republic in 1968. The president of the Bundestag, second chairman of the CDU and likewise a leader of the Protestant Church, Hermann Ehlers, accused Adenauer of "treason against German unity" and demonstratively attended an East German church convention presided over by Communist veteran Wilhelm Pieck—no believer he. Thomas Dehler, chairman of the Free Democrats and at the time Adenauer's coalition partner, charged in 1961 that the government had failed to hold the Allies to their promises, and that the Americans were about to make a deal with the Russians, obtaining a guarantee of free access to Berlin by selling Germany's claim to the lost territories beyond the Oder-Neisse line. Only a year later, after Khrushchev's "wall," such a deal looked very attractive; at the time the nationalists, the refugees, and those expelled from the Eastern territories threatened political death to anyone who would recognize the borders created by the war. West German papers referred to the German Democratic Republic only as "the Soviet-occupied zone" and to its government as the "Pankow gang." It is true that the unspeakable Walter Ulbricht used the most odious crimes to support his rule: murder, kidnapping, torture, blackmail, highway robbery. All Western powers were committed to the fiction that Germany had only one government, in Bonn, which threatened to break off relations with any government that would recognize the German Democratic Republic.

To disabuse the Germans of their illusions, Khrushchev put forth his ultimatum in 1959, threatening to hand Ulbricht the keys to Berlin unless the Western Allies got out voluntarily. Rebuffed, he built a wall which effectively separated Germans from Germans. Western Germans could no longer close their eyes to reality. There were two Germanies, and they had been misled. The Allies had either deliberately broken their word or been impotent to liberate the captive half of Germany. Instead of being an instrument, the alliance seemed to be an obstacle to reunification.

There were other reasons, too, why Germans should wish to conduct a policy more independent of Western tutelage. By the mid-1960's, more than two-thirds of the German population had not been of voting age when Hitler came to power; more than one-third had not been born when he perished. Why should they feel guilty for their fathers' misdeeds?—or accept a political servitude that seemed to be an atonement for Hitler's crimes? In the 1950's, Germans spoke much of "overcoming the past" as a task that had to be faced. In the 1960's, the past was being overcome biologically. A new generation refused to be haunted by the ghosts of yesteryear and demanded an exclusively German politics, which neither Adenauer nor his successors were able to give them.

Even the "economic miracle" now appeared as a mere bribe to accept a humiliating condition. The *Wunderkinder*, as a scathing German movie dubbed them, the children of the *Wirtschaftswunder*, had rebuilt everything, except their souls. The Germans longed to be truly independent again. The American alliance, once considered a precondition of safety, now was resented as tutelage.

In 1966, the liberals broke with the coalition and forced the CDU-CSU to collaborate with the SPD. As Chancellor the new coalition chose Kurt Georg Kiesinger, the suave Swabian who had served the Nazis. Vice-Chancellor and Foreign Minister was Willy Brandt, the illegitimate child of a working woman, once a left-wing socialist who had worn an enemy uniform during Hitler's war—for which chauvinists abused him viciously. Finance Minister was Franz Josef Strauss, a German Gaullist. Together, the three seemed to symbolize the "overcoming of the past."

This coalition benefited from a new economic boom, and it took the first steps toward a new "Eastern policy," or *Ostpolitik*. It established relations with Rumania and was on the verge of reconciliation with Czechoslovakia when the Russians— perhaps for that very reason, among others—marched into that unhappy country. Perhaps West Germany could have helped Dubček by resolutely accepting the *status quo*: renouncing the Polish-occupied area, recognizing the East German Government, dropping the property claims that arose out of the 1938 Munich agreements. But the CDU was a prisoner of its chauvinistic following.

In October 1969, the SPD won a landslide victory, and Willy Brandt formed a "Little Coalition" with the small, liberal Free Democratic Party, which had all along advocated a *rapprochement* with the Soviet Union. Brandt finally drew the lesson of Prague and of America's loss of face in Vietnam. He proposed to the Soviets a non-aggression pact and recognition of the borders created by World War II. German industry offered the Russians a $1-billion credit for a pipeline that would pump gas directly from the Caucasus into the German housewife's kitchen. In return, the Soviets had to give ironclad guarantees for the inviolability of Berlin.

The past was buried completely when West Germany renounced the Munich agreement, recognized the German Democratic Republic, and accepted the Polish borders.

On September 18, 1973, both Germanies became members of the United Nations and supported the Soviet drive for a European Security Pact. The general *détente*—with U.S. blessing—should result in withdrawal of troops from both sides of the Elbe River, in greater freedom for the satellite countries, and in eventual corrosion of the iron curtain, perhaps even of NATO and the Warsaw Pact. Brandt has created a new style in world politics. In revaluating the mark, he has acted most responsibly on behalf of international monetary and economic stability. At home, his ardor for reform was curbed by his coalition partner, the party of big business. In the 1972 elections, the voters approved of these policies. But later, inflation caused a serious strike wave and the government experienced difficulties with the Left wings of both its parties.

The 1970's are a period of great expectations for the German workers. Public-opinion polls show two things to be uppermost in their minds: participation and education. The first means that the workers want a share in decision-making, a check on management, some control of their own economic destiny; the second, that they want an opportunity for their children to go to high school (at present only 20 per cent of all German children of high school age do so, and only 10 per cent graduate). Both demands mean that workers wish to break out of the established German class pattern. The present government cannot fulfill either of these desires; it cannot even meet the trade unions on dollar-and-cent issues. The Social Democratic Minister of Economic Affairs, Karl Schiller, preached moderation, and had to resign. The younger generation, especially the students and the Young Socialists, are pressing for fundamental changes in Germany's social structure. Prompted by his own sons, the personable Chancellor saw that Germany, which under Adenauer had prized safety and security above all, was ready for fundamental changes in attitudes, in customs, in law.

These economic and social tensions translated themselves into strains inside the SPD. Brandt lost his dynamism when a series of misfortunes befell him simultaneously: The *Ostpolitik* and prosperity ran out of steam; the oil crisis provoked a squabble in Western unity; and a spy was discovered in the Chancellor's office. In 1974, therefore, Willy Brandt was succeeded by Helmut Schmidt, a right-wing Socialist who belongs to the post-war generation of no-nonsense political managers. He had been Minister of Defense and Minister of Finance previously, and he had the good fortune of coming to power at the same time as the new French President, Giscard d'Estaing, who, though a conservative, is a man of the same stripe and a close friend. The two were able to restore the shattered confidence in EEC, and they see eye to eye on the important questions which will be discussed in the next chapter. Both fit into the technocratic temper of the 1970's.

A word may be necessary on the danger of neo-Nazism, perceived more often outside Germany than inside. In the 1950's, the whole world watched anxiously as a new party with a frankly nationalistic program arose. The National Democratic Party of Germany (NPD) used some of the symbolism and rhetoric of the former NSDAP. It looked up to a Führer and attracted some unreconstructed admirers of Hitler. It got 5–12 per cent of the vote in areas like Franconia, Holstein, and Hesse, where the

Nazis used to draw their largest crowds, but it also attracted refugees, older people of a strongly conservative outlook, and even some young nihilists. In the national elections of 1969, however, it failed, and soon Chancellor Brandt's dynamic policies put the party out of commission. In 1972 it polled 0.6 per cent of the vote.

History does not repeat itself, and the NPD is not even a good scarecrow. What is more serious is the danger of nationalism in the old parties. The Free Democrats split over this issue. Franz Josef Strauss, of the Bavarian CSU, is an ardent proponent of atomic armament, forcible liberation of the lost provinces, and a more independent German policy; he also happens to be a realist and a strong believer in a united Europe. While his free use of patriotic demagoguery is dangerous, he is not himself given to irrational actions. But he has released the furies of chauvinistic mud-slinging. He has attacked as treason Brandt's policy of opening to the East; other Christian Democrats, too, consider *rapprochement* with the East a menace to the nation's future.

Despite these nostalgias and aberrations, Germany has now accepted the *status quo* and seeks good relations with all her neighbors. Having abandoned all hope of a united Reich, the Germans now are resigned to "two states within one nation." The changes World War II has wrought are recognized as permanent even by the most obtuse German nationalists.

By admitting the obvious, however, West Germany has lost an incentive to perpetuate the NATO alliance, which cannot bring the lost provinces back. The U.S. troops in West Germany will more and more appear to be watchmen over German loyalty to the West rather than guardians of German liberty *vis-à-vis* the East. The *Ostpolitik* has freed West Germany from one-sided dependence on NATO, and some Rightist Chancellor might later on be tempted to play a lone game.

The early 1970's were crucial for the future of Europe as a political entity. The Soviet Union played all its cards in the diplomatic game: the SALT talks for the removal of strategic weapons, the disarmament talks, the European Conference for Security and Co-operation, the negotiations on mutual balanced withdrawal of (occupying) forces—all served the purpose of softening the common defenses of the West, loosening their coherence, and isolating each of the European states before the unity of Europe had time to assert itself. It was very fortunate that in this situation U.S. diplomacy has never wavered in its support for the greatest possible unity of Europe.

CHAPTER 2

The End of the Sterling Club

THE phrase "winds of change" was given currency by Prime Minister Macmillan in a speech to the South African parliament in 1960. White Africa was turning its back on the Commonwealth; black Africa threatened to leave it unless England showed more zeal in promoting equality on their continent. But Macmillan's speech was not directed to Africa. His intention was to tell old England that she must realize what era she was living in. The empire was gone; the Tory government was merely able to arrange for a discreet funeral, it could not revive the imperial era. Resolutely, Macmillan applied for admission to the Common Market, a step not popular with the voters of either party but unavoidable in the judgment of common sense.

Harold Macmillan, who became Prime Minister in 1957 after Eden's defeat at Suez, reduced the armed forces to 375,000 men and acquired an atomic defense posture. But ill luck pursued him. First, Kennedy reneged on a contract to equip the Royal Air Force with tactical missiles; then de Gaulle rudely rebuffed his application to the EEC. Although he bore all this gracefully, there was no grandeur in retreat, and eventually a sordid sex story ended his career: Defense Minister Profumo got involved with a call girl named Christine Keeler, and a shady osteopath, her pimp, had gained *entrée* to high society. The scandalous treatment of this incident by the press belongs in a chronicle of manners rather than in a political chapter; society blamed its own turpitude on the hapless Prime Minister who wanted to provide nothing but boredom and was caught providing sensation. He resigned after seven years of quiet success, which had given most Englishmen modern appurtenances— refrigerators, washing machines, and the like, the basis for his slogan, "You never had it so good"—but also debts, a diminishing currency, a vanishing empire, and that unflappable tedium which gave David Frost of TW3 the chance to think that he was the David Low of TV.

In 1964, Labour won the election by a slim margin. Harold Wilson, the new Prime Minister, introduced the theme of his tenure in the famous "technology" speech at the 1963 conference of his party. The speech really was directed against the Left, which demanded socialization while Wilson advocated modernization, social engineering, melioration. His was to be another administration which sought distinction in not being distinguished.

The Labour government found the old coal problem unsolved and decided simply to abolish it. Henceforth, it decreed, England would burn oil, consume the gas recently discovered under the North Sea, and build nuclear reactors. No wonder the coal miners were radicalized. They rebelled to maintain the subsidies that maintain their employment. Wilson proposed an Industrial Relations Bill requiring the unions to wait for twenty-eight days before calling a strike, but had to drop it in the face of strong back-bench opposition. England was plagued by a great number of wildcat and jurisdictional strikes and by low productivity in industry. Several proposals were made to enforce wage and price guidelines and to make extra raises contingent on higher productivity.

As a man of the Left, Wilson had pledged renationalization of the steel industry. He fulfilled this promise, but in no other respect did he seem to have a well thought-out policy. He did maneuver to maintain the economy on an even keel; with U.S. help he overcame the assaults on the pound. He prepared the conversion of British currency to the decimal system; he bravely kept knocking at the Common Market's door, though substantial numbers in his own party were as averse to this surrender as the Colonel Blimps in the Conservative Party. Cautiously but steadily he also dismantled England's positions east of Suez. Finally, in 1970, having weathered all storms and finding the opinion polls favorable for the first time, he called for new elections—and was repudiated by the voters. Had he been too doctrinaire or too opportunistic? Perhaps both. When all the factors are assessed, the defeat of Labour must be attributed as much to its lack of leadership and decisiveness as to the "end of ideology." Wilson's half-hearted policies could inspire no one; he had overcome his economic problems by routine measures that did not change the rules of the game. What was wrong with his party had been expressed accurately and poignantly by Jimmy Porter, the young trumpeter in John Osborne's play Look Back in Anger: There aren't any big, brave causes left. If there were, Wilson did not name them.

Since Labour had stopped being a cause, it was soon reduced to struggling for its bread and butter. Its adversary was Edward Heath, a modernist and a fighter, a no-nonsense man who very much cared for his principles. He had been England's first negotiator with the Common Market; he was an enemy of all types of nationalism; he had put Enoch Powell in his place. He also was out to put Labour down and to solve England's financial crisis the Tory way. He allowed the nation to be without mail for six weeks until the postal union's strike was broken. He shut power down for industry three days a week rather than give in to the miners' demands. He nationalized the defense-oriented plants of Rolls-Royce but let the rest of the bankrupt firm close its doors. He vowed to expose the superannuated industries of England to the fresh winds of competition in the Common Market. He was determined to break feather-bedding and other impediments to productivity. Featherbedding existed in the railways and even in the most modern industry, aviation. For reasons of prestige England and France had jointly started a mammoth project, the supersonic transport, Concorde. Even on the drawing boards it already was outperformed by the Russian and American projects. All three Western governments have poured billions into this adventure.

But England could not regain her former pre-eminence by any demonstration of force. She had to renounce her prestige ventures and her monopoly practices if once again she was to play a role in the modern world. The decision to try to join the Common Market was taken irrevocably, even if that meant abandoning empire ties and the sterling club. Overseas countries already had declared their monetary independence or re-oriented themselves to the dollar. But the Scandinavian countries still depended very much on the British market and followed the pound sterling in their financial policies. So did Portugal. In abandoning its Free Trade Association, England gave up considerable advantages and also the prestige that went with the position of a leader. The pound is no longer an international yardstick, but London was still the center of international banking and insurance, and the trading post for many staple commodities.

With her entry, in 1972, into the Common Market, England gracefully concluded a period of adjustment to her diminished world status. She was followed by Denmark and Ireland, her NATO and EFTA partners. (The Norwegian voters rejected the option, and the governments of both Denmark and England lost the elections in 1973 and 1974.)

In the fall of 1973, all of Europe was precipitated into the greatest financial and political crisis of the post-war period. After the Yom Kippur War, the frustrated Arabs, unable to beat Israel in the field, took their rage out on the entire West (except France) and incidentally discovered that relations between the old colonial powers and the Third World had undergone a fundamental change. Through an oil embargo, they sought to bring pressure on Israel to make political and military concessions. This created serious energy shortages which sent the prices for petroleum products and derivatives soaring. (Fertilizer and food prices also increased drastically, and this severely hurt some of the poorest countries of the Third World.) Then the Organization of Petroleum-Exporting Countries posted new cartel prices which increased the yearly bill to petroleum importers by the staggering amount of $30 billion, promising to exhaust their reserves of gold and liquidity within a few years.

Oil sheiks, whose countries can absorb only a limited amount of industrial import goods, used to invest their royalties on the London Stock Exchange. Now they conceived the plan to exploit, buy out, and rival their former masters and customers, in addition to blackmailing them politically. The Shah of Iran and King Faisal of Saudi Arabia demanded from the Western countries sophisticated modern weapons, atomic reactors, and heavy industrial equipment. The following year, a special General Assembly of the United Nations put the squeeze on the industrialized countries to pay "reparations" for past unrequited imports; at the same time, India detonated an atomic bomb.

At no time since the war did Europe need unity as badly as at this moment when she was held up for ransom. But the governments panicked, sought bilateral deals with the high-handed Arabs, outbid each other for the Third World's favors, and denounced each other for breaking the unity.

EEC was on the verge of falling apart. NATO lost credibility. The Socialist government of the Netherlands used this weakness to fulfill an electoral promise: It cut its military budget over the NATO partners' protest. England, Ireland, and France allowed their currencies to float. Italy imposed new tariffs; her middle-of-the-road Premier, Mariano Rumor, was not capable of either ruling or resigning.

The British miners, taking advantage of the energy crisis, went on strike either to catch up on inflation or to increase their share in the panic benefit. In the process, they brought down the Heath administration. Wilson campaigned demagogically against EEC; finding himself in power against all expectations, he must renegotiate the terms of Britain's membership, and possibly the basic terms of the Common Market. But he cannot turn back the clock, and England's economic situation will remain grave. The government's position is precarious, moreover, because of the trade unions' increasing radicalization.

It was Europe's good fortune to find oil below the North Sea. With vigorous development of nuclear power, she may close the energy gap in the 1980's. But for the moment most countries find it difficult to balance their payments, and citizens may have to tighten their belts.

Economic stagnation, however, or even loss of income may be small discomfort vis-à-vis the revelation that the West is economically vulnerable as a power. It has created a Frankenstein monster which can choke it: The monopoly power of oil has launched the former beggar-kings on a career of imperialism in reverse.

The crisis of Europe's balance of payments can be overcome only if the Continent understands its new position vis-à-vis the big powers and the Third World. In 1900, five European powers between them determined "world politics"; today, Europe is one of five world powers. Then she owned the world's resources; today her own resources are in thrall to others.

Is it History's irony or retributive Justice that the Sheik of Kuwait now buys a controlling interest in Daimler-Benz and the Shah of Iran one in the Krupp works—two symbols of Europe's former domination?

CHAPTER 3

Reaction and Reform in
Outer Europe

THE rapid development of the Common Market left Outer Europe lagging. Greece and Portugal were members of NATO and Spain was associated with it, but all three countries were ostracized as long as they were ruled by military dictatorships. All three were censured either by the United Nations or by the Council of Europe, and they were ruled for long years by backward elites whose prejudices obstruct modernization of their political and economic structure. EEC blackballed association with these regimes.

In all these countries, though, modernizing forces are at work to overcome their backwardness, either by working inside the system or by preparing its overthrow. A country where either method may eventually triumph is Spain. Its regime, founded in blood and dedicated to the denial of the twentieth century, nevertheless has presided over a remarkable economic development. Its national product rose from 657 billion pesetas in 1955 to 1,372 billion in 1968, its capital formation in the same span from 121 billion to 329 billion (all in 1964 prices). Nor was this simply a matter of quantity; the character of the Spanish economy and society has undergone fundamental changes since the time of the Civil War. Traditionalists and Falangists lost standing in the councils of business and government. Modernizing Catholics formed a masonic association, Opus Dei, which placed efficient managers in many strategic positions. Among them were Luis Carrero Blanco, the *caudillo*'s closest adviser since 1941, and Laureano Lopez Rodo, the architect of the country's prosperity in the 1960's. Lopez initiated the necessary steps for Spain's entry into the OECD, the World Bank, and GATT. Borrowing from French experience, he adopted four-year plans, beginning in 1964, to guide investment and foreign trade.

Despite the regime's troglodytic reputation and its official ostracism by many other countries, tourists began to visit Spain in the 1950's. The shrewd *caudillo*, who had stayed neutral during the war despite his indebtedness to Hitler and Mussolini, exacted a high rental from the U.S. Air Force for military bases. He supported Arab demands against the Anglo-Saxon powers and Israel, voted undogmatically with the Soviet and Third World powers in the U.N. Assembly, maintained good relations with Latin America, and defied the American boycott of Castro. But he could not escape the dialectics of success. As the Spanish middle class grew stronger, it asked for more liberties. To divert their attention, Franco began to harass Gibraltar, demanding the return of the rock to Spain.

Inevitably, as people forgot the Civil War and gained confidence in their own resources, the regions and the classes began to stir. Since wages were the lowest in Europe, workers struck in 1951 and again 1956-57. Vizcaya and Catalonia, the two most highly industrialized provinces, asked for greater self-administration. In 1957, Franco found it necessary to reformulate the Basic Administrative Law, the Statute of the Cortes, and the Principles of the National Movement.

In 1962, unrest among the Asturian miners evoked an echo among students and in Catholic lay organizations. Franco abolished the military courts in 1963, relaxed press censorship a little, gave workers the right to strike, allowed Jews and Protestants to worship in specified locations. In 1966, an Organic Law, for the first time since 1936, established some kind of consultation—however indirect—between the government and the governed. The "vertical" (Falange) syndicates were abolished; the provinces were to send delegates to the Cortes. As his successor, Franco designated Juan Carlos, grandson of the last King, whose education he had supervised personally; but he gave him no power.

It is difficult to imagine that this timid young man will ever master the explosive forces waiting for Franco's demise. The aristocracy is bored, the bourgeoisie frustrated; the regions are suffocating; the church, once the strongest pillar of orthodoxy, is deeply divided; the young army officers are angry because they have no arms, no chance of advancement, and no function. The Falange, the former agent of the regime's ideology and public relations, has fallen into such a rot that its younger members are questioning the foundations of the state. The Opus Dei is undermining political freedom, and began to negotiate with the independence movements in Angola, Mozambique, and Guinea-Bissau. A poor politician and at heart a conservative who did not understand the forces he had unleashed, however, he was overthrown by a junta of younger army officers who were in league with left-wing students and with a well-disciplined Communist Party strongly entrenched in the labor unions. They are setting Portugal on a course that is neutralist in foreign affairs and radical at home. This regime resembles the progressive dictatorships of Latin America.

In Portugal, the regime first seemed to survive its founder, Salazar, who suffered a stroke in 1968 after forty-one years of personal rule. But in 1974 General António de Spínola, long a critic of Portugal's colonial wars, overthrew the government, restored political freedom, and took steps to end the fighting in Africa. He opened the door to further developments, perhaps for the entire Iberian Peninsula, the outcome of which cannot be predicted.

Another country that does not move and yet cannot find stability is Greece. After the monarchy was restored, General Alexander Papagos confiscated all estates over fifty acres (or 250 acres of pasture) and distributed the surplus among settlers. He joined NATO; his successor, Constantine Caramanlis, concluded a treaty of association with the Common Market. But he was drawn into the Cyprus conflict and supported the invasion of the island by General Grivas. Political mistakes discredited the government, the army, and the royal family. In 1963, the left-wing deputy Grigorios Lambrakis was assassinated (apparently with the connivance of the police; the charge, repeated in the movie Z, that the CIA was also involved, is unsubstantiated); in the subsequent elections (1964) the center-Left EK (Center Union Party) won a majority. Its leader, George Papandreou, became Prime Minister and began to purge the army of its political (Rightist) officers. He appeared to harbor Gaullist ideas. His son and a group of younger officers also seem to have discussed plans that aroused the suspicion of the Court and its American advisers. Inexperienced, but backed by the powerful shipping interests (Onassis and Niarchos) and the Americans, Constantine II tried to dismiss Papandreou; but when parliament balked and Papandreou threatened to take his case to the people, parliament was paralyzed, and the country was ruled by the Court's appointees. New elections, called for 1967, were forestalled by an army coup; the ensuing terror was so embarrassing that the American advisers prompted the King to stage a counter-coup and appear as the restorer of democracy. He failed, and had to go into exile.

For six years, Greece was governed by a clique of colonels under George Papadopoulos, whose repressive orders hit indiscriminately all strata of society and all parties, but especially those of the center and the liberals who represented the educated, well-to-do society of the previous regime. It is well to remember that those ostracized, the suppressed newspapers, the censored writers and movie producers, the gagged theater and cabaret directors, belonged overwhelmingly to the upper strata, who had not complained about repression when they were in power. Since the dictatorship itself was inarticulate and its policies were unbelievably inept, practically all intellectuals supported its enemies and pleaded with world public opinion for its overthrow.

Ostracized by the European Parliament and unable to solve Greece's economic problems, Papadopoulos cast about for new ideas in 1973 but was overthrown by a group of officers who only intensified the political repression and tried the remedy of all dictators—foreign adventure. They quarreled with Turkey over oil rights in the Aegean and encouraged a coup to unite Cyprus with Greece. Confronted with Turkish resistance and condemned by world opinion, the regime collapsed, and democracy received another chance in the land where it had been born.

The Greeks blamed U.S. policies and NATO ineffectiveness for their misfortune in Cyprus. Caramanlis, returned from his self-imposed exile after eleven years, gave voice to these feelings and received an overwhelming vote of confidence in the November 1974 elections. The revived EK, under its new leader, George Mavros, polled only 20 per cent of the vote; young Andreas Papandreou's Socialist coalition ran a poor third. In December the Greeks, voting in a referendum on the monarchy rejected decisively the return of the king.

CHAPTER 4

De Gaulle's Fifth Republic

THE Constitution of the Fourth Republic merely provided the framework in which the various interests could battle for their piece of the pie. The inspectorate and the political systems met in the practices of influence-peddling, patronage, corruption, and opportunism. Only the declining classes remained unrepresented and fell prey to the exploiters of resentment on the Right and on the Left.

For all the customary chaos and frustration, the underlying structure of French society was healthy enough, and the economy was in the swing of modernization. The political structure alone seemed to be an impediment, in fact seemed to make France ungovernable. She was divided into three parts: the managed sector, which was doing fairly well; the traditional political circus, to which no one paid much attention any longer; the resentful enemies of the republic—militarists, Communists, Poujadists, and the desperado elements of de Gaulle's party.

The conflict could be resolved in either of two ways: by the appearance of a charismatic leader who put his prestige behind the technocratic program, or by a Jacobin movement whose mystique carried the nation into a fundamental change of its sociopolitical structure. Mendès-France was a man with a mystique whose brief tenure in office set dynamic goals for France; but he had no movement behind him. His attempt to achieve basic reforms within the framework of traditional politics failed, and he was defeated at the precise moment when he tried to overcome traditional politics.

De Gaulle was able to succeed where Mendès-France had failed. He was a national monument; he had style; he was opportunistic on matters of detail but never lost sight of the major goal: to persuade his countrymen that they could regain their place as *la grande nation* about which they learned in school; to design a new policy which would restore to France that self-respect which is the basis not only of law and order but also of modernization and development.

That meant, first of all, doing away with the Fourth Republic, the opposite of all he stood for. It meant, secondly, creating a government which would govern by the lights of technocracy and yet be seen by the nation as its representative. Following the mutiny in Algiers, on June 1, 1958, René Coty installed de Gaulle as head of government. The following day the National Assembly granted him special powers for six months and agreed to its own dissolution; this was to be followed by a new constitution. The Constitution of the Fifth Republic, adopted by referendum on September 28, provided for the election of a President by a complicated indirect process; the President in turn was to name the Premier and the ministers, subject to approval by the two-chamber parliament. He was invested with broad powers, while parliament's powers were minimized and overthrowing the government was made difficult. To assure himself of stable majorities and to reduce the opposition, de Gaulle changed the electoral system back from proportional representation to one-man constituencies, Later he also changed the method of electing the President from the indirect to the direct, plebiscitarian mode, and he relied more and more on this latter device—his personal mystique.

Since his own party, the Union pour la Nouvelle République (UNR), did not have a majority in the National Assembly, de Gaulle ruled by repeated referendums, direct appeals from the leader to the people, and the republicans' fear that he might throw their problems back into their laps. After the Algerian problem had been settled in 1962, de Gaulle's popularity began to decline, but Gaullism still dominated the assembly. In the 1965 election, de Gaulle polled only 43.7 per cent of the vote on the first ballot. (His Popular-Front opponent, François Mitterand, got 32.2 per cent; the three Rightist candidates totaled 23 per cent.)

In 1967, de Gaulle's UNR failed to get a majority of the non-Communist seats; the French voters clearly were returning to party politics, a portent of the coming end of the regime in the following year. The ten-year rule of de Gaulle, built on the general's popularity, gave France governmental stability and freed the technical elites to carry out their far-reaching programs. Having cut her losses and liquidated her colonial liabilities, France was able to devote all her energies to restructuring and solidifying her sound economic heritage. The franc was devalued by one-sixth; subsequently, 100 old paper francs were exchanged for one shining new silver franc, restoring the French pensioner's and the foreign trader's confidence in the country's solidity. The blueprints for an expansion plan, prepared under the Fourth Republic, now came to fruition. First priority was given to the public sector: investments in communications, coal, iron, and electronics took precedent over consumer industries. Hydraulic resources were stepped up for electrification: the harnessing of a forty-foot tide at St. Malo is a miracle of modern engineering. An even greater miracle was the financial and economic concentration of the oil business into ERAP (Entreprises de Recherches et d'Activités Pétrolières), which has done for France what Mattei's ENI did for Italy. Through developments in Algeria, Iraq, Libya and elsewhere it challenged the Anglo-American companies which for so long had dominated the oil supply. In the field of nuclear energy, France also became independent.

The assurance of financial stability in France and the prospect of a six-nation market produced a rush of international corporations eager to buy up businesses on the Continent, to found affiliates, and to mobilize capital in France. In *The American Challenge*, Jean-Jacques Servan-Schreiber says that three thousand firms were created and $10 billion were invested in nine years. The French expansion plan might have succeeded less splendidly without this American participation, which de Gaulle duly denounced as undesirable.

De Gaulle's fame in history, however, will not be measured in terms of economic gains; nor were the results unequivocally fortunate. Wages quickly caught up with the devaluation. A miners' strike in 1963 put the balance of wages and prices to a severe test. Finance Minister Valéry Giscard d'Estaing prescribed austerity measures against inflation; wages, prices, credits, and public spending were frozen. Nevertheless, de Gaulle increased the education budget from 6 to 21 billion francs, and the health budget from 1.3 to 3 billion francs. When incomes fell, Giscard d'Estaing was replaced by Michel Debré.

After the Algerian war was over, the army was halved to 330,000 men, but the defense budget was doubled to 25 billion francs ($5 billion), one-quarter of it for nuclear development. De Gaulle was anxious to have an independent *force de frappe*— a deterrent all his own, proclaiming the grandeur of France—and strongly resisted Kennedy's proposal of a multi-national partnership. It was this show of independence in foreign affairs which has earned de Gaulle the admiration of intellectuals in many countries.

Professor Stanley Hoffmann has written a 520-page love letter to de Gaulle, explaining how he did one thing and then the other to keep France in the news as a world power. But all the admiring disciple has proved is that de Gaulle, once a historical hero, used his destructive capacity to convince others that he was still alive. Having come to power through crisis, he kept creating crises to justify his personal style of authority.

When the Cuban missile crisis revealed the United States's nuclear superiority over Soviet Russia, de Gaulle perceived the chance for small powers to operate independently under the umbrella of American ICBM's. He therefore announced that the danger of a Russian invasion across the Elbe River was over, that the cold war had come to an end, and that France no longer had to integrate her forces with the Atlantic Allies. If, instead, de Gaulle now had worked for a United Europe, he might still deserve the reputation of a great statesman. But he conceived of Europe as a replacement for the empire France had lost in Africa and Asia. He intended to be the leader of the Continent; for that purpose he had to keep England away from the Common Market and to lure the Germans away from their American protectors. In a grandiosely played scene, he offered Chancellor Adenauer friendship and reconciliation, the burial of the centuries-old quarrel between the two neighboring countries. In an equally stately press conference, he announced that England was not yet ripe for membership in the Common Market, and he let it be known that she could not become a member as long as she maintained a "special relation" with the United States. Reviving the policy of Briand and Laval, he threw out the slogans "Europe from the Atlantic to the Urals" and "Europe of the fatherlands," indicating that no loss of sovereignty was implied. On the contrary, in an angry show of state sovereignty, he withdrew the French troops from NATO's military command and ordered NATO headquarters as well as the alliance's installations and communications to leave France. (Its headquarters moved to Belgium.)

Simultaneously, de Gaulle stretched his hands out to Russia and to China, and in the place of these archdevils of NATO he designated *les Anglo-Saxons* as targets for European hate. His obsession with this bugaboo became so strong that he threw himself into disastrous adventures. He used the gold reserves of the Banque de France to launch a run on the dollar. He supported the secession of Biafra from strategic Nigeria where British influence was preponderant—a bloody and sinister affair which ended in failure for France and misery for the Africans. But so effective was Gaullist propaganda among liberal intellectuals that even today this civil war of a puppet general is remembered as a war of black liberation.

Much as the Germans wished to be reconciled with France, they had no desire to subordinate their policies to de Gaulle's designs. They politely declined the proposed *tête-à-tête* and began to play their own game of sovereignty. De Gaulle, furious at his failure, boycotted the EEC meetings for eight months—ostensibly over a technicality in the distribution of farm levies, but actually because the Germans favored majority rule in the community and relied on the technocratic judgment of the Permanent Commission, a supranational civil service, whereas de Gaulle wished to retain a French veto over all decisions. He did not rejoin the talks until the "Europeanists" had been purged from the commission and the commission had promised to make no further proposals for a stronger federation.

Through all these maneuvers, de Gaulle seriously weakened NATO and stalled the process of European unity for at least five years without having anything to show for his troubles. Frustrated, he turned his ambitions back to the Third World. He had gained prestige there by ending the Algerian war; he retained great influence in black Africa. Now he suddenly switched sides in the Arab-Israeli conflict. He was merely trying to please the Third World and to get its backing for his designs on Nigerian oil—which led to the disastrous Biafra war. But his meddling again gave the Russians a decisive advantage in the eastern Mediterranean.

Thus in the end de Gaulle gained nothing for France except a bad reputation for unreliability. His pompous oratory could not hide the hollowness of his nineteenth-century philosophy. Like Churchill in peacetime, he was a relic of past glories, and his followers were cheap imitators of a totalitarian cult which the rest of Europe had discarded only recently. He seemed to be extremely bold and clever in keeping France uncommitted between the Soviet Union and the United States. His admirers may have been dazzled, and French vanity may have been flattered by the erratic blows he dealt the hated Anglo-Saxons: vetoing England's admission to the Common Market; mouthing separatist slogans in Quebec; pulling first the French Navy, then the Army out of the NATO command, and then ordering NATO headquarters to leave Paris, signing a trade agreement with Russia in violation of EEC obligations; abetting Arab truculence in the confrontation with Israel and "Zionism"; recognizing the Peking government (Peking allowed him to recognize it only on the humiliating condition that he oust the Kuomintang Embassy from Paris). As a matter of fact, de Gaulle freely gave the Russians what they never could have won by negotiation: the dismantling of NATO, the paralyzing of the Common Market, the prevention of West European political unity. They therefore gladly advised their friends in France to let the wrecker continue, and their fellow-travelers elsewhere to cheer him on. They even saved him, as will be seen presently, in his hour of greatest need, which came because, over his dreams of glory, he neglected the domestic scene.

De Gaulle procured for France the empty satisfaction that as a sovereign nation she could be a nuisance to her allies. But she was not able to hold on to the Sahara oil. The French-speaking Africans are losing interest in her leadership. Nor has she regained in other fields the position she once held as the world's leader in taste, its legislator in art, its guiding light in political philosophy.

CHAPTER 5

May in Paris

As the Dubček reforms were unfolding "socialism with a human face" in the East, a dilettante revolution was closing ranks in the West. Its roots were first in the Algerian war, then in American student unrest.[1]

Like its U.S. counterpart, the German SDS had originally been a youth division of the Social Democratic Party. In the 1960's it became increasingly independent; it was declared incompatible with membership in the SPD and then fell into anarchist and syndicalist ways. A few professors in Berlin, Göttingen, and Frankfurt supported it. Returned from American exile to Frankfurt, Max Horkheimer and Theodor Adorno had revived the Institute for Social Research, the pre-Nazi tower of Marxist philosophy. Herbert Marcuse meanwhile had become an international prophet of the New Left. Marxist studies grew popular; several publishers—Feltrinelli in Milan, *Nouvelle Revue Française* in Paris, Luchterhand and Suhrkamp in Frankfurt—had given their readers latitude to spread Marxist thought throughout Europe.

This intellectual fermentation preceded the crises that soon were to develop at Western universities everywhere. They resulted from the rapid doubling of the student population, which was not matched by any increase in university facilities and teaching personnel, or in academic jobs, for that matter. Moreover, nothing had been changed in the university's authoritarian structure, its rigid examination system, its less than useful curriculum, and the pompousness of the professors. Assistants and lecturers were impatient with their long wait for professorships; the students wanted to have a share in the planning of curriculum and course content.

This was no proletarian revolution. The sons of workers constitute more than 10 per cent of the academic population only in England (25 per cent), Norway (20 per cent), Italy (15 per cent), and Sweden (30 per cent); and all observers feel that most of these would rather find their places in the establishment. Most of the student activists came from affluent families. As professional revolutionaries, they were

---

[1] Karl-Dietrich Wolff, leader of the German SDS, had taken part in a freedom ride to Mississippi; Rudi Dutschke, the charismatic student leader who escaped from East Germany only to become a rebel in the West too, had an American wife. Before a bullet deprived him of his powers of speech, he was the most intellectual among student insurgents and, by German student standards, the most reasoned.

generals without soldiers. Since their protest was cultural rather than social, they lacked contact with real social movements. They were satisfied with "turning the university around." The one political issue agitating them, if any at all, was anti-Americanism, an attitude that had been assumed by such European intellectuals as Sartre, Hans Magnus Enzensberger, Peter Weiss, and Kingsley Martin long before the Vietnam war.

In 1966, a dispute about the invitation of an anti-NATO journalist to the Free University at Berlin led to riots and to the rector's resignation. The socialist City Hall majority supported reforms which practically disestablished the faculty and left all real power to the ultra-Left student clubs. A year later, when the Shah of Iran visited Berlin, the students received him with noisy demonstrations. The police panicked and fatally shot one (allegedly nonparticipating) student. This provoked huge demonstrations; the students had found a moral cause. In 1968, they attacked the anti-Russian newspaper concern of Axel Springer, tried to prevent publication and distribution of its papers, and rioted at the Frankfurt Book Fair. Once more books were being burned in Germany; universities were occupied by hooting crowds and renamed for revolutionary leaders. The senior faculty lost all their authority when frightened city councils of Berlin, Bremen, and Frankfurt handed the university administrations over to assistants and lecturers. Courses were taught by SDS members, and students elected a self-government that promised relief from exams. Aware of West Berlin's precarious situation, the working population has shown no sympathy for a movement which clearly is weakening the moral defenses of the city: in the elections (1970-72) Communists, pacifists, and the "extraparliamentary opposition" combined polled less than 1 per cent of the total vote in the Federal Republic, and less than 4 per cent in West Berlin.

Nevertheless, the left-wing within the Social Democratic Party and the Young Socialists were a source of perpetual embarrassment to Chancellor Willy Brandt. They decried coalition policies. They demanded direct socialist action, a clear break with NATO, and the more or less unconditional reconciliation with the German Democratic Republic. After the success of the *Ostpolitik*, they turned to direct action on the home front.

Looking at other countries, we find a truly international pattern during the late 1960's. In the spring of 1966, Roman students rioted against antiquated instruction and overcrowding; some eighteen months later, the movement seized all of Italy. Its aims grew more radical through the spring of 1968, when it fell in step with the Paris revolt and came out for the overthrow of capitalism. Even in Spain, under the orthodox dictatorship, students in 1965 started to demonstrate; the agitation increased from year to year, especially among Basques and Catalans.

Was it a mere coincidence that 1968 also was the year when Dubček started his humanist socialism? At least one French movie has bracketed the events of Paris and Prague, and many books speak of an international student movement. If any co-ordination existed, it must have been a very loose, informal exchange of communications between people of like mind. For indeed the German, the French, and the Italian student representations were (and are, due to indifference of the majority) in ultra-Left hands, and hence averse to discipline and organization. They had no idea of what kind of a revolution they wanted.

In May 1968, a happening started a French student revolt and the student revolt led to a movement that nearly toppled the regime. At the bleak new University of Nanterre near Paris, the administration prohibited a pornographic lecture. This touched off a riot not only on the campus but in the streets of Paris. Daniel Cohn-Bendit, the son of German Communists, and Alain Krivine, of Russian extraction, were the leaders of small revolutionary groups which stirred the smoldering resentment in the Latin Quarter. Buildings were occupied; barricades were erected against police authority and against "the system"—more symbolically than for any specific purpose. The revolt did not effectively address itself to any demands; it merely turned the lecture halls into so many circuses and immortalized itself in graffiti, a collection of which became a world best seller. Overreaction by the police then made martyrs out of the revelers, and their barricades lent them the posture of heroes. Despite indignant speeches about police brutality, no shot was fired; but the show of violence recalled to every Parisian the heroic pictures of the great revolutions of 1789, 1830, 1848, and 1871. Millions of workers throughout France, remembering the great sit-ins of 1936, suddenly occupied their factories.

The happening had escalated into a movement that looked like a revolution, and whose spearhead the students appeared to be. Cohn-Bendit with his *enragés* knew how to create violence and gain popularity. The movement had passed the stage where the issue was university reform. Fired by the acclaim of their elders among the intelligentsia, the students went for all-out revolution, though they still did not know what sort of government they wanted. They celebrated, held debates, and acted out their exuberance in more happenings. They were acclaimed by leading intellectuals such as Sartre, Simone de Beauvoir, Nathalie Sarraute, Michel Butor. The teachers' union supported their movement. On May 13, 100,000 Parisians demonstrated. The Christian trade unions and the Communist-led CGT, which disapproved of sit-ins, nevertheless were forced to call a strike; 10 million workers all over France went out and presented stiff demands for higher wages. They even formed soviets; they held sessions in permanence. Yet it was all in good fun, reminiscent less of any real revolution than of famous paintings from the heroic past of the working class.

At this moment, anything seemed possible. The Paris students were for all practical purposes in possession of the street, at least on the Left Bank; the workers were in possession of the factories. The government was paralyzed. De Gaulle had mysteriously disappeared; later it became known that he had gone to confer with the commanders of the occupation army in Germany. Did he think he could reconquer France with bayonets? Mendès-France announced that he was prepared to take the reins of government at the head of a rebuilt Popular Front. Mitterand too held himself available—without acting.

Then the unbelievable happened. The Communist-led CGT cautiously repudiated any connection with the student movement and any desire to overthrow the government. The Communist Party, declaring that the situation was "not revolutionary," refused to enter a coalition government. De Gaulle reappeared and spoke briefly on television, asking the support of all good Frenchmen with common sense. It was forthwith reported that when everybody panicked he had said: "Reforms, yes, but no bed-wetting." Millions of shopkeepers and other right-thinking people, parents of the rebellious students, responded enthusiastically and impressively. Faced with their mass demonstrations, the students abandoned the barricades, the workers their occupied factories. The CGT negotiated a massive pay raise; the students obtained promises of "reform" and "participation." In quickly arranged general elections, the government was given an overwhelming vote of confidence. Not just the bourgeoisie but shopkeepers, peasants, and workers were seeking shelter under the dictator's strong arm. Whatever unity between workers and students might have existed for a day vanished rapidly.

The student movement itself fell apart into ultra-radicals, radicals, moderates, liberals, bystanders, fun-lovers, hippies, ultra-Rightists, and so on. But it left in its wake a flood of enthusiastic and analytical literature, a mystique of the revolutionary May, and a dispersion of agitators who inspired students at other European universities. In Rome, 5,000 students demonstrated before the French Embassy; in Belgrade, students demanded liberalization of the Communist Party; in Madrid, they began to defy Franco's police; in Stockholm, they tried to invade the parliament building; even in staid Zurich they went on strike for a few days. The teachings of Marcuse, Guevara, Regis Debray, and Cohn-Bendit have endowed insurrection with a romantic halo, and pyromaniacs dream of "having many Vietnams in Europe and Latin America." Yet, with all their antics, the students have not changed the structure of the society, and the university reform eventually granted by de Gaulle's successor was hardly worth the price paid.

Just the same, the student movement must be understood as a symptom of a crisis which now is the permanent state of European society. A few months after de Gaulle rescued them from the perils of anarchy, the French voters refused to tolerate his caprices any longer and, defeating by referendum his plan for provincial autonomy, simply accepted his threat of resignation. Less than a year later he died, a hero to his followers, a legend to the outside world, a monument to the dissolution of middle-class society in the country where it had first blossomed. The significance of the May days of 1968 lies not in their success or failure but in the conflict they symbolized and in the trend they brought into the open.

A few features of the student movements stand out. The enemy was neither fascism nor Stalinism but the liberal Establishment. It hit hardest those universities whose professors or administrators were sympathetic, least hard those under conservative leadership. The supreme irony, perhaps, was that it repudiated the mentors of the neo-Marxist counter-establishment; men like Marcuse, Adorno and Habermas in Germany, Sartre and Louis Althusser in France were ostracized. These pundits of the older generation failed to give direction to students who had come to them in great bewilderment, seeking answers to their metaphysical, ethical, social, and personal problems. Students who inclined to revolutionary ideologies or to confrontation politics had flocked to the social-science and humanities departments in great numbers. Far more than by the shortage of stipends and facilities, these students were outraged by their teachers' attitudes to their respective subjects. They gave them science instead of wisdom, method instead of faith, stones instead of bread.

If students want participation, it is not in order to administer the budget but because they suspect that the teachers somehow withhold the truth from them. Hence the attempt to have their own "critical university" which, far from creating a critical frame of mind, indoctrinates its students to follow one leader, one method, and one truth. In other words, the student revolution was nothing so much as a reflection of the crisis of the culture, a revolt against the relativism, skepticism, and liberalism of modern education. In their quest for a new faith, the students resembled the Anabaptists rather than the Enlightenment which they like to invoke as their model, with the "Café Voltaire" and the "Republican Club" as their meeting places.

The Enlightenment rejected neither society nor its elders. Twentieth-century students have conducted a fundamentalist campaign against civilization as represented by their parents. They withdrew into a subculture and refused to formulate any program that might have improved, let alone revolutionized, the society in which they live. Their movement was empty of social content. That was the ultimate reason why eventually they had to abandon the occupied buildings (they could do nothing with them) and why they were unable to form a united front with the workers.

The historic hour of May 1968 passed. The revolution was betrayed by the Communists, transmogrified into a happening by the student Left, sold for francs and sous by the trade unions, purloined and converted into counter-revolution by de Gaulle. The year 1968 ended with a net loss to the Left. The students' revolutionary dynamism was grounded. Cohn-Bendit did what every elder statesman of a revolution has done—he wrote a book. The workers' pay raise soon was eaten away by inflation. De Gaulle was succeeded not by a new republic but by Pompidou, the very incarnation of technocentric capitalism. The subsequent elections were a fiasco for the Fédération des Gauches and for the SFIO as well as for the protagonists of the center-Left: François Mitterand, Gaston Defferre, and Alain Poher.

After de Gaulle, the choice was between three alternatives:

(1) to return to the parliamentary regime of the Fourth Republic, a solution advocated by Poher, candidate of the *juste milieu*

(2) to develop the Fifth Republic along de Gaulle's lines but without his idiosyncrasies (Pompidou provided this solution for the time being)

(3) to revive the Popular Front (this solution, first rejected by both Socialists and Communists, was revived successfully for the 1973 elections, but failed to win a majority)

Pompidou won the election as a Gaullist but moved immediately to pacify the "centrists." He appointed critics of the general like Jacques Duhamel and Valéry Giscard d'Estaing, pillars of the Fourth Republic like René Pleven, and Europeans like Foreign Secretary Maurice Schumann to the cabinet. He moved perceptibly closer to the United States and NATO, and he agreed to admit England to the EEC. And finally, when confronted with the American challenge of a new Atlantic Charter, he saw no other means to counter it than by agreeing to the very thing de Gaulle had feared most, the submersion of French sovereignty in the European Community. Assembled at Copenhagen in the fall of 1973, the Nine agreed to speak with one voice.

The death of Pompidou in 1974 brought on a three-cornered election, from which Giscard d'Estaing, the non-Gaullist conservative, emerged as a youthful, energetic President. A technocrat and realist, he strove to bury the conflict with the Anglo-Saxons, but he has not found the courage to confront the Arab blackmail. Nor has he been able to cope with the tensions in French economy. Whether he can be flexible enough to bring social reform in France up to European standards remains to be seen. He faces crucial choices in meeting British demands for farm price revision inside EEC, and strong pressures in his Ministry of Foreign Affairs to continue the Gaullist quest for an independent French role in world politics.

Apart from the French, the Danish, Norwegian, Swedish, and British socialists lost voters in subsequent years. In Germany Willy Brandt's successful *Ostpolitik* was not matched by a similar dynamism at home, so that the youth became disillusioned with the party. In Italy, the coalition between Christian Democrats and Social Democrats, even with the support of the PSI, found its popular basis wilting and its leadership insecure. Christian Democrats began to see the wave of the future and to flirt with the idea of Communist participation in the government. Communists had shown their ability to govern as mayors of important cities such as Bologna and Florence. They represented one-fourth of the electorate; given the lack of unity in the center, their support was being solicited by aspirants to the leadership of the moderate Left. Sooner or later, it was felt, they would become part of the government, and as far as they were concerned, they had long been converted to "revisionism," the gradual rather than the revolutionary road to power. The so-called polarization, therefore, was leading not so much to the radicalization of the Left but to a drift of impatient Leftists toward a more reformist policy.

An almost bizarre incident will illustrate the acceptance of seemingly radical tactics for reform goals. At Besançon the bankruptcy of a watchmaking concern threatened to make several hundred workers unemployed. These occupied the factory, secured raw materials and half-finished goods and began to sell watches for their own benefit. Though the economics of the venture were highly unorthodox, the government was forced to provide the needed credits, and production continues under joint management.

As a hundred and twenty years earlier the revolutions of 1848, though beaten, were nevertheless followed by profound changes in society, so the cunning of history has provided for new styles in social relations, for the recognition of problems previously ignored, for the general advancement of liberal causes and the increase of radical power in the universities and in society. Maybe these occasional shocks are necessary to ignite the engines of history, after which they may again advance slowly—the reformist way. Of this, the northern countries provide edifying examples.

CHAPTER 6

The Northern Countries

THE five northern countries considered themselves, for a hundred years, a political backwater. They did not take part in the wars and did not share the other countries' concern about the balance of power. Denmark and Norway, however, suffered Hitler's invasion in 1940, and Iceland was occupied by the Americans. Sweden managed to stay neutral. But Finland became a bone of contention and was badly mauled. The Soviet Union took a border strip of land and joined it to the Finnish-Karelian Socialist Soviet Republic; heavy reparations steered the Finnish economy toward the Russian market; a "defense treaty" obliges the Finnish government to "consult" with the Kremlin on whatever the latter pleases, including the make-up of the Finnish Government. Until 1966, the Soviet Union vetoed all socialist ministers but worked along with the Agrarian Presidents, J. K. Paasikivi and Urho Kekkonen. In 1966, the Communists joined Kekkonen's government and took co-responsibility for some unpopular measures. This led to a split within the party. The Stalinist minority wished to return into opposition; the opportunistic majority later on criticized the invasion of Czechoslovakia, but, for diplomatic reasons, managed to stay in the good graces of Moscow.

Helsinki was Russia's chosen place for SALT (the negotiations on the limitation of strategic arms) and her channel for diplomatic and propagandistic offensives such as the plan for a European "conference." The Soviet Union also prevented the formation of a Scandinavian Common Market by forbidding Finland to join it. In declining any commitment, Sweden pleaded her traditional neutrality and Russian pressure on Finland.

Norway, Denmark, and Iceland, on the other hand, joined NATO. Despite this discrepancy in their foreign policy, the Scandinavian countries try to strengthen their economic and cultural ties. They deliberate together in the Nordic Council, and their politicians meet in an inter-parliamentary union. They have a common airline, many interstate trade associations, and common trade-union policies. The Nordic Council initiated hundreds of laws which were adopted by the parliaments of the four countries. These laws cover the development of power resources, atomic energy, schools, broadcasting, investment policies, traffic regulations, passports, taxation, and social security; benefits acquired in one country are payable by another. In 1962, the four countries resolved to unify formally their traffic laws, education, and the penal code. The Joint Committee for Economic Co-operation, founded in 1948, has recommended elimination of all customs; the plan was abandoned, however, when the Six set up the Common Market in 1957. In 1960, three Scandinavian countries joined EFTA, the European Free Trade Area comprising England, Portugal, Sweden, Norway, Denmark, Switzerland, and Austria, or the "Outer Seven." In 1961 Finland acceded by a special treaty. EFTA's purpose was gradually to eliminate all tariffs between member countries by 1969. In that year Sweden also switched to right-hand traffic.

But EFTA is now practically dead. When the Common Market was founded, Iceland associated itself with it through a substantial loan. In 1972 Denmark followed England and Ireland into the Common Market, and Austria (circumventing a Soviet veto) acquired associate status with it. Only Sweden and Switzerland feel that their traditional neutrality is incompatible with membership in such a bloc. Greece, Spain, and Portugal were not acceptable under their pre-1974 regimes. Norway's voters rejected EEC in 1972, and Finland does not dare defy the Soviet Union.

Austria's and Finland's neutrality is imposed. Sweden is neutral by passionate conviction and by the profitable experience of two world wars. She has given the United Nations a Secretary-General and a sizable contingent of its police force. While Western in general orientation, she has given asylum to American deserters. Neutrality has been the main platform of her Social Democratic governments for thirty years; when Prime Minister Tage Erlander resigned in 1969 because of old age, his young successor, Olof Palme, to prove his devotion to neutralism, campaigned on a platform of anti-Americanism. Iceland, in contrast to Norway and Denmark, is at best a reluctant member of NATO. She has feuded with England over fishing rights, and the demand for withdrawal of American troops is popular; yet she simply cannot afford to lose her income from the big NATO base in Keflavik.

The Scandinavian countries resemble each other in their social and political structure. They are sparsely populated and have been able to maintain a healthy balance between town and country as well as between the social classes. Four of them have had long years of Social Democratic or center-Left coalition governments which have systematically expanded welfare-state policies. Though three have retained monarchs as ceremonial heads of state, they are considered the oldest democracies in Europe. The Swedish Communists belong to the most revisionist, unrevolutionary wing of the movement. The Danish Communist leader Aksel Larsen was the only instance of an insurgent able to lead a majority out of the Party. All Communist parties in the North are small; the one exception is Finland's. Largely because of the closeness of the Soviet Union, the Communists gained influence first in the cabinet and then among the voters.

Sweden not only has the highest per capita income in Europe ($3,570 a year), but its Social Democratic government has made a deliberate effort to equalize incomes and to provide equal opportunities for everyone. Where once 5 per cent of the population had academic degrees, now one-half of the college-age group actually is working toward one. Sweden also is the one country in the world where women are the social equals of men in every respect. Moreover, the state provides a wide range of social services, including health care, public housing, recreational facilities, and so forth, which add equal benefits to all incomes. On the other side of the ledger, taxation takes one-third of incomes over $10,000 and up to 84 per cent of the highest incomes; consumer taxes go up to 17 per cent. A strong trade-union movement has pushed the wages of the best-paid factory workers up to $6,000, the highest in Europe, and has forced civil servants, professional people, and even army officers to organize. These groups, whose incomes are about $10,000, felt that they were losing status and went on strike in 1971.

Yet between workers there are inequalities: A Volvo worker earns 15 kroner an hour, an unskilled textile worker not more than 8. The Left-socialist government thinks in terms of *jämlikhet* (equality), but favors neither nationalization nor co-determination. It wishes to retain the mixed structure of the Swedish economy, but also to expand social services and public services. The long rule of socialists has made industrial property safer than it is in England; social rank, conventionalities and forms are loyally observed. Sweden is Western and middle class; in 1973 the socialists did not gain a clear majority, but continued to govern. In these countries the trend toward the welfare state will not be reversed by a change of government.

CHAPTER 7

Problems of Nationhood

THE problem that has plagued Europe throughout its existence is nationalism. Europe's history is the story of tribal wars. Nations secure enough to coexist with others have emerged in the nineteenth century, but this very condition of peace also is the cause that undermined it. Nations will fight. The problem is not how to tame them but how to abolish them. They can either be merged into larger units or they can be broken up into smaller entities; the one may indeed be the precondition of the second.

For indeed, no nation is as stable as its leaders imagine. The loss of empire abroad has given encouragement to minorities and tribes within. Nationalities quarrel because one of them feels that the other is trying to be master in the national state. If both were part of a larger unit, they could both have autonomy without foregoing the advantages of large-scale production and planning.

A case in point are the three countries that make up Benelux. They were the first to form an economic union; they then joined the "Six," and Luxembourg City became the seat of ECSC, Brussels the seat of OECD and later also of EEC and NATO. After the loss of the Dutch and Belgian empires, *dirigisme* was the only workable plan. But apart from trouble in the royal houses, communal problems beset both Belgium and the Netherlands. Flemings fight Walloons in Belgium, Catholics fight Protestants in the Netherlands. In 1963 Belgium was divided into two autonomous regions. Brussels, too, was declared a region, but no one liked the settlement. The problem could be solved only by an over-all European government. The Socialists, at first more favorable to the French-speaking, industrial Walloons, therefore are Europeanists. Their outstanding statesman, Paul-Henri Spaak, several times Prime Minister and Foreign Minister, was one of the most ardent spokesmen for a United Western Europe.

In both Belgium and the Netherlands, Socialists often governed in coalition with Catholics. In 1958, the Dutch Catholics switched partners and formed a coalition with Protestants and conservatives. In the 1960's, the stability of Dutch politics was gravely shaken by doubtful conduct in the royal household, by religious dissension, by radical defections from the two major parties, by the appearance of the Provos, by the emergence of the new Farmers' Party, and by widespread criticism of NATO, which both major parties supported. In the 1967 elections, both lost heavily. Catholics and labor usually polled 30 per cent of the vote each; they slipped to 25 per cent each, while the Farmers' Party and various radical groups increased their share.

In Belgium, too, the settlement of the language question had left everybody dissatisfied. The liberals, who made themselves the mouthpiece of the criticism, gained heavily from both Christian Socialists and socialists in the 1967 elections. But perhaps political parties were becoming as obsolete in Belgium as elsewhere. The Catholics used to get better than 40 per cent of the vote; in the 1960's it declined to a mere 30 per cent, with the Flemish and Francophobe nationalists gaining. The socialists also lost votes.

While Paris students were battling the French police, the language war turned hot at the University of Louvain, Belgium, causing the government to fall; the new Premier, Gaston Eyskens, promised to "make Belgium both more regional and more European."

In France, the homes of regional languages are Brittany and Provence; but other areas also try to establish a peculiar identity for themselves, and politicians are forced to pay tribute to such feelings. First Pétain, then de Gaulle, tried to revive the historical regions, and Mendès-France admonished the Left, which is traditionally unitarian, to "get rid of its Jacobin reflexes." Great Britain has seen the revival of Scotch and Welsh nationalism—antiquarian and ephemeral perhaps, but a warning that, in case of a major crisis, the British nation cannot take its unity for granted. In Northern Ireland, the ostensibly religious strife is obviously grounded in the social differential between the dominant Protestants and the proletarian Catholics; but discriminatory practices and oppressive police measures also serve to maintain the last bastion of the British in the place that was their first conquest.

Usually national minorities are poor or backward, or both. In Spain the roles are reversed. The Catalan and Basque bourgeoisie is modern and uses the regionalist movement in order to wrest concessions from the hidebound dictatorship. Basque fanatics throw bombs and, when brought to trial, find sympathy not only among the world's anti-fascists but in the Vatican, in the White House, and in Spain itself. The *caudillo* saw himself compelled to commute death sentences into life imprisonment.

Regional nationalism plagues governments on both sides of the iron curtain. Latvians, Lithuanians, and Jews try to emigrate from the Soviet Union; Ukrainians resist "Russification." Rumania, intensely chauvinistic under her Communist veneer, struggles to loosen the bloc's hold on her political and economic life and to maintain her sovereignty. Inside Yugoslavia, the regions ask for a fairer distribution of power, and the aging Tito gives them a federal constitution.

Italy also contracted a liability when annexing Trieste and Alto Adige (South Tyrol). Her constitution of 1948 provided for twenty quasi-autonomous regions; but only in the 1960's did the Roman bureaucracy begin to decentralize its power. Riots, instigated by Austrian patriots and sustained by Austrian government propaganda, finally led to the recognition of "South Tyrol" as an autonomous region. But Italy demanded, in return, that Austria renounce all claims to the area. In 1969 the Christian Socialist Foreign Minister Kurt Waldheim, who later was made Secretary-General of the

United Nations, concluded an agreement which was hedged with 120 conditions on whose fulfillment ratification was to depend. Only when the Socialists gained power in 1970 did Chancellor Bruno Kreisky ratify the agreement.

Decentralization has been the device the Soviet Union uses to keep its empire from falling apart. The nationalities and minorities within Russia have been given far-reaching cultural autonomy. The various separatist movements in the Baltic states, in the Caucasian republics, the Ukraine, and elsewhere have been successfully defamed as "petty-bourgeois aberrations" or suppressed by ruthless deportations; the satellite countries are held in thraldom by Communist parties giving recognition, in various degrees, to the national aspirations of the peoples under their control while keeping faith with the Soviet leadership. This is true not only of Poland and Hungary, but even of the Husak regime in Czechoslovakia. There, a technically autonomous government of Slovakia helps the Soviet hegemon to prevent any return of the Dubček deviation. The ancient maxim, divide and rule, may be translated into the modern formula of commonwealth federalism: Empires can maintain their domination over nations by fostering local autonomy below the national level.

In the Soviet Union, autonomy has been denied to certain groups whose identity reaches beyond the frontiers—the Jews, the gypsies, the Catholics. Whether ethnic or religious, their cultural center lies outside the Soviet Union and therefore is considered harmful to the interests of the state. The solution now favored is emigration—which leaves those who do not wish to emigrate the one alternative of henceforth becoming loyal Soviet citizens. (The Moslem and pagan peoples in the Soviet Union have full cultural autonomy and have permission to praise the government in any language.)

The question arises whether the decentralizing features of Soviet administration and empire management might ever degenerate into centrifugal movements of the people concerned. Greater freedom for the satellite countries might permit the building of bridges to the West and the emergence of a middle Europe which, under the most favorable conditions, might bring the Soviet Union closer to Europe, too.

Regional, religious, tribal, linguistic or cultural minorities may help to dissolve the national state. Empires no longer give grandeur to national history. Yet the national state remains the greatest obstacle of European unity, of collective security, of technical and economic progress. The most recent developments in the Common Market have shown how hard the notion of sovereignty dies. States are quarreling, less about matters of substance than about precedence and procedures. The organs of Europe are weak, the fatherlands are strong. Each is seeking accommodation with the big powers and advantage in the Third World. And yet every conference proves anew that their interests are tied together indissolubly, that their differences are small in comparison with their communality. Vested interests of nationals, not of nations, stand in the way of greater unity.

The national state is also being eroded by the multi-national corporations and by transnational group interests, on the one hand, and by special interests, on the other hand. In many Western countries, especially in the democracies, the authority of the state is no longer taken for granted. Civil servants, doctors, pilots, farmers, policemen, firemen, and teachers go on strike; under the guise of direct or participatory democracy, sectional and factional activists usurp the functions of government. In Denmark and France, Poujadists mock the parliamentary process. Occasionally, such protest movements lead to the brink of civil war.

An example of mixed national, communal, and social strife may be studied in the six northern counties of Ireland, which were not included when the Republic of Eire became independent in 1922. De Valera, who was Prime Minister of Eire most of the time between 1937 and 1959, had vowed to unify the island. In 1949, he severed all ties with the British Commonwealth of Nations.

Home rule came to Northern Ireland almost inadvertently. Sir Edward Carson, leader of the Ulster Unionists, did not want it; but his successors, Lord Brookeborough and Terence O'Neill, had to make it work. The latter even tried to come to an agreement with Seán Lemass, de Valera's successor in the Republic of Ireland. This plan provoked a viciously bigoted reaction among the Protestants, led by the fanatical minister Paisley. The Catholics, on the other hand, found an articulate leader in the youthful Bernadette Devlin, who was elected to Parliament by the poorest district of Belfast and went on to challenge the establishment not only in Parliament but in the streets. She led the Belfast riots in 1969, served a term in jail, and emerged as the spokesman of Irish socialism in the tradition of James Connolly, the Irish labor leader and 1916 martyr.

During the riots some cabinet ministers of the southern republic sent arms to Northern Ireland. They were ousted from their posts. Under Seán Lemass and his successor, Jack Lynch, the republic has taken a moderate stance; both these men have tried to divert Ireland's political energies into economic channels. During the past fifteen years, the Republic of Ireland has made enormous strides in developing its resources. Helped by favorable trends in tourism and exports, and thanks to considerable foreign investments as well as government aid, capital formation, and consumer expenditures have doubled in real terms since 1955.

Meanwhile, the Stormont in Belfast also rallied around a moderate government. James Chichester-Clark was able to dissolve the B-Special Reserve, a fascist-like Protestant home guard. But he had to resign in the face of increasing terrorism from both sides.

The British Government was as unable to contain the Protestant bigots in Northern Ireland as it was to rule the white supremacists in Rhodesia. It sent troops to separate the warring parties, but soon the IRA, with at least some support from the south, went into action, and the troops found themselves fighting by the side of the Royal Ulster Constabulary. With pressure from the republic mounting, the three-cornered civil war is likely to drag on and eventually to end in a British withdrawal.

It has been said that a nation is a dialect with a navy. In the future, it may be defined as a language with oil wells. Those petroleum finds below the North Sea (p. 427) have given a lift to Scotch separatism and vindicated Norway's decision to stay outside the Common Market.

CHAPTER 8

Europe, America, and the World

IN January 1958, the Six—France, Germany, the Benelux countries, and Italy— began the venture they saw as the nucleus of a united Europe: the European Economic Community (EEC), popularly known as the Common Market. Its headquarters is in Brussels; its organs are a Council of Ministers, a Parliamentary Council, and a permanent Commission. The Commission supervises an Economic and Social Committee (charged with the adjustment of wage, price, and investment policies) and several other institutions such as a European Investment Bank, a Monetary Committee, a European Social Fund, an Overseas Development Fund, and, among others, a Transport Committee, which soon achieved strikingly visible aspects of unity: uniformity of road signs, abolition of visas and customs inspection, development of European train schedules, and so on. While the ECSC has the authority to close unprofitable coal mines, the Commission regulates farm prices, proposes financial and trade policies to the Council of Ministers, establishes common rules for competition, and negotiates with nonmember countries on behalf of the Community.

Such power, vested in nonelected, supranational managers, has caused considerable resentment against the "Eurocrats," but it also has helped more than one national government by sharing the blame for unpopular decisions. Since individual industries and individual countries have accepted various degrees of *dirigisme*, the structure of EEC planning is jerry-built. It deals with national offices in France and the Netherlands, with individual industries in Germany and Italy, with a Benelux structure, an ECSC structure, and a national farm syndicate in France, with labor unions and migrant workers.

In 1961, the six governments signed a declaration pledging themselves to work toward greater political unity. In 1971, they decided to work for a common currency, which undoubtedly will come one day.[1] However, the political structure of the Common Market still is unsatisfactory. Its Parliamentary Council, composed of delegates sent by the national parliaments, is a private organization. The Council of

---

[1] Technically, ECC currencies (D-mark, franc, lira, guilder, crown, pound) may have different exchange rates *vis-à-vis* the dollar. But their fluctuations vis-à-vis each other must be held within narrow limits.

Ministers meets regularly and deals with pending questions of mutual interest in the manner of a conference, not as an organ of the Common Market. However, it now has a permanent committee which tends to acquire the far-reaching powers of the older Commission. Here lies a chance to circumvent French insistence on the unanimity rule.

The first step toward a European economy was a general reduction of tariffs, with special arrangements made in favor of the French farmers, and the total abandonment of all customs barriers between the Six by 1967. The EEC retained a common tariff of 6 per cent for finished goods and 13–17 per cent for equipment. Negotiations for a tariff agreement with the United States, the so-called Kennedy Round, were not concluded until 1969. But in 1973 an American proposal of a new Atlantic Charter gave the West Europeans an opportunity to answer with one voice for the first time: The Danish Foreign Minister made a counter-proposal in the name of all.

Even while still in the process of formation, the Common Market attracted the unaffiliated countries. Turkey and the French-speaking Africans became "associated." The advantages of a large-scale economy clearly showed in expanding trade, rising living standards, and growth rates consistently better than those of non-affiliated countries. Notably, most of the Outer Seven countries of EFTA have done less well; each had to weigh the question of whether to switch at this late date. Having lost the initial advantage, they now pay a high price for entering with uncertain hopes.

Just the same, the attraction of the Common Market was irresistible. After England, Ireland, and Denmark joined, the 250 million people of the EEC have become an economic power comparable to the United States or the Soviet Union; together, the Nine have a gross product of $600 billion. They are the world's biggest importer and exporter, potentially once again its provider of capital, and likely to attract more countries into their orbit.

A book which appeared in 1969 predicted a world in which only four major powers would count: the United States, the Soviet Union, the more or less united states of Western Europe, and the new Japanese empire. Can we be so sure that Europe's political future is unity? A customs union and a common currency, a joint SST project and a joint atomic installation, uniform road signs and 900 regional associations, from stamp collectors to labor unions, do not yet constitute a federal state. Europe has no integrated army, no parliament elected by all its people, no government whose writ extends beyond national borders. But it now settles its problems through forty-two regional organizations on the governmental level, and EEC as such has a number of treaties with outside nations. The bilateral dealings of the Common Market states with each other constitute only a quarter of their total agreements, whereas three-quarters go through international organizations.

Many Europeans feel that no further steps toward integration are needed or desirable and that a new "model" of a confederation is emerging. The idea of federalism, they say, has been introduced from outside to suit the American conception of partnership within a Western defense community. But Europe is about to loosen the ties of that defense community. It strives to devise an independent policy which might continue to count on American co-operation but should no longer be dictated to by the President of the United States. To develop such a policy, each of the European nations may have to change its thinking. England may have to relinquish the "special relationship" to the United States it once enjoyed; France may have to move her army back into the NATO (or WEU) fold; Germany may have to stop dreaming of unification. Add to these disadvantages the centrifugal blandishments. Should European nations give up the ties—emotional, political, cultural, economic—which they had severally with their former dependencies and with other nations in the Third World?[2] Separately, many feel, they can be stronger than if united. It also stands to reason that a loose association can attract and influence other states where a close federation would appear to be exclusionary. Finally, neither France nor other nations have given up hope that they may regain their former influence in Eastern Europe if they avoid tying themselves down in EEC and NATO.

Such flexibility is deceptive when individual European governments deal with one of the superpowers. Some European leaders may have been tempted, through personal vanity or national ambition, to seek special arrangements with Moscow and Peking. They have been disappointed. China's market is very limited, and Soviet diplomacy has encouraged delusions of "independence" in European leaders merely to weaken the Western defenses. After each such escapade, Moscow's imperialist policies—the Korean invasion, the suppression of the Hungarian revolution, the Cuban missile crisis, the repeated Berlin ultimatums, the invasion of Czechoslovakia, the instigation of Arab fanaticism—have rudely reminded West Europeans that their safety continues to be in unity among themselves and alliance with other Western nations. All of Europe may be "Finlandized" if several of its nations abandon the safety of community. The whole continent may be "Balkanized"—split into quarreling nationalities.

It is tempting to speak of a Hegelian "cunning of history." European unity has been promoted less by any European enthusiasm for unity than by the combined, though quite different, pressures brought by Russia and America. It was fear of Soviet expansionism that called both the economic and the military instruments of a European community into being; it was American initiative that jolted Europe into action. The European Defense Community foundered, as later proposals were to be scuttled, on the rocks of small-state nationalism. Each of the European countries would rather be protected by a special U.S. guarantee than merge its cherished sovereignty with others, which were merely its equals. Nor would they gladly accept the role of being a shield for American strategy, which, so it seemed to some, was being assigned to a United Europe in the councils of Washington.

De Gaulle and Franz Josef Strauss, then Germany's Minister of Defense, would have preferred it the other way: that NATO's nuclear deterrent should be a shield for their independent policies. German nationalists, French neutralists, British imperialists, and pacifists of all these countries were joined in protest against a

---

[2] In the meantime, the Francophone Africans answered that question by deserting France.

European unity which seemed to them restrictive. It excluded the East Europeans and limited West Europeans to the defense of the *status quo*. Moreover, it subordinated the European forces to the "Grand Design" of American strategy.

President Kennedy indeed had such a design: the vision of a United Europe joined in partnership with the United States for common purposes of defense and development. He might honestly have believed that he was offering the Europeans nothing less than equality—provided that they were united and agreed with the U.S. strategy of flexible response.[3] But, in enacting this design, he was less than convincing. Instead of taking council with the British Prime Minister, he treated him like a junior partner. He abandoned the joint project of the Skybolt missile on which England's nuclear striking power depended. Instead of inviting the Europeans to take their seats in strategy councils, he offered them participation in a multinational nuclear navy (MLF) which did not have even symbolic value, except perhaps for the Germans, and left the U.S. commanders substantially in charge. The project had to be abandoned because of the Europeans' indignant protests; but with it was buried the second attempt at an integrated European defense. The idea now was tainted with the dual stigma of cold-war ideology and of American paternity. European unity itself had become suspect as a mere instrument of American policy. For all its efforts, American diplomacy has never been able to allay the fears and resentments born of European inferiority and insecurity feelings.

These erroneous perceptions also have distorted issues and confused party labels. Some politicians who are in fact nationalists have been able to pose as "Europeanists," though their true aim was national grandeur. Vice versa, the cause of European unity was wedded to the Atlantic alliance, while alternative policy proposals were all too easily confused with attitudes that were either pro-American or pro-Russian.

Fifty years ago, the movement toward European unity was associated with pacifist sentiments and internationalist slogans. It was a movement of youth, of the laboring classes, and of the Leftist parties. Today, when there is a real chance that European unity may reach fruition, there is no popular movement to speak of, and the main forces pushing for unity are administrative, economic, and governmental, or even military. The young people, who ought to be in the vanguard, take for granted the

---

[3] I have neither the space nor the competence to deal with strategic concepts. But a layman can readily understand the intimate connection of "massive instant retaliation" with NATO and European unity. This strategy obliges the United States to immediate action against the Soviet center in case of aggression against one member of the alliance. "Flexible response," by contrast, leaves the United States free to negotiate with the U.S.S.R. even while part of Western Europe is being occupied or may already be a theater of conventional war. If "instant retaliation" is no longer a realistic possibility, as de Gaulle charged, the incentive for European governments to seek safety in individual arrangements with the Soviet Union becomes strong indeed. From the U.S. viewpoint, de Gaulle's argument was not quite candid, since it was precisely the certainty of the atomic umbrella that enabled him to play a lone role safely. Egon Bahr, the architect of West Germany's Eastern policy, has said that Germany may pursue independent goals, above all reunification, "because in case of a Russian invasion the Americans have no choice anyway but to help us." To make doubly sure, the Europeans therefore would like to prolong indefinitely the presence of American troops on European soil—as hostages so to speak. The European Security Conference must seek diplomatic means to get out of this dilemma.

new spaciousness and other amenities, the fruits of a political labor they abhor; instead of a militant internationalism, they display either a lazy, vague, and mindless neutralism or a wild, terroristic anti-Americanism which they mistake for internationalism. The radical Left, traditionally pacifist and socialist, has not set itself the goal of a united socialist Europe. Instead, it defends either obsolete empire interests or illusory nationalist aims and, besides, voices resentments against multinational corporations and American domination.

Europe has yet to find her place on the world stage and in history. Right now she is reacting against her recent dependence. Having been rescued by the United States in two world wars and in the cold war, she finds the ever-present liberator more ominous than the banished aggressor. European pamphleteers complain that American companies have bought up firms or established subsidiaries in Europe; European intellectuals complain that American novels, American plays, and American textbooks dominate their intellectual life. The sciences succumb to American behaviorism; American taste and American fashion are denationalizing Europe's old and beloved culture or, worse, American vulgarity is debasing all cultural values. Coca-Cola has conquered Europe while Americans now claim wine connoisseurship; Hilton is defacing every mountainside; rock 'n' roll is displacing the hearty folk songs. Artists and scientists whose education and training has cost millions are lured by the high stipends or modern laboratories of American research institutes. Ironically, even the anti-American protest draws its arguments and images from exclusively American sources—from Henry Miller to C. Wright Mills and the Living Theater.

European culture was in danger. As early as 1930, Franz Werfel, author of *The Song of Bernadette* and *Jakobowsky*, wrote an essay warning that Europe was being ground to death between "the deadly molars of America and Russia." Twenty-five years later, the physicist Max Born said: "Marxism derives its fanaticism from the belief in historical necessity, which is an outflow of celestial mechanics. But physics abandoned these conceptions thirty years ago. . . . American thought, for its part, is based on a superficial pragmatism which confuses utility with truth. I cannot adhere to it. . . . Europe [!] is not bound to any of these absurd doctrines."

Culturally, Europeans have looked down on America as a mere outlying province of Europe. They were unaware of history's ironic twist. To compete with the old powers in world politics, America had discarded her own culture and adopted, developed, exaggerated, and perhaps bowdlerized precisely that European middle-class culture which European snobs always found so laughable and contemptible. America's industrial, gadget-oriented, science-faddist culture was really Europe's own invention, and it showed Europe her caricature as well as her future. Too long had the European middle class concealed its cultural void under the trimmings of the past, of court culture, hierarchy, and paternalism, of the niceties and amenities of a formalistic civilization—what the Germans call *Bildung* and the French *culture*. That frail superstructure of ideologies and arts now had to be defended against "American mass culture."

In the first decade after World War II, the American temper fitted European necessities. Students were eager to succeed, realistic, and almost cynical. They needed no high-flown ideals or visionary politics to see the role they wanted to fill as leaders, managers, celebrants of the new technocratic faith. They seized upon the ideas they mistook to be American—to be cool, to analyze problems, to find solutions by compromise, trusting that science or technology must provide a solution for every problem. No doubt America oversold these attitudes, and even then some Europeans suspected that all was not well in the best of all democracies. They turned to Faulkner and Hemingway, Tennessee Williams and Thornton Wilder, and they sensed that there was more to America than the worship of efficiency. They understood and imitated Norman Mailer, Charles Ives, and Jackson Pollock. European highbrow culture received lasting directions from its American counterpart, and part of that influence was the critique of the official image which American policy-makers were presenting to Europe.

Similar observations might be true of the light muses who inspired consumer culture in the West. America's popular music flowed east as far as Moscow. Joan Baez, Judy Collins, and Bob Dylan as well as the British groups are well known beyond the area of the English tongue. But the tribute Robert Zimmerman paid Dylan Thomas by calling himself Bob Dylan testifies to the unity of the Atlantic culture. America often returns to Europe in modified version what it received, and Europe develops American initiatives. Young people in Europe communicate in the language of jazz and rock, and they use English as an international medium even in Eastern Europe.

Yet, what most fascinated the Europeans who visited the United States in the years of mutual respect and collaboration was neither its particular brand of representative government nor its art, whether light or serious, but its technology and its determination to organize human happiness with efficiency methods. Much later, full of admiration and envy, two Frenchmen told their compatriots that the "American challenge"[4] was not based on any magic or trickery but on techniques which the Europeans could learn and use for their own benefit; and, finally, that the progress of the American working class had not been achieved through ideology ("neither Marx nor Christ"),[5] but through judicious application of management techniques.

The domination of man by his product, the subjugation of the producer by the process of industrial production, were first denounced by Marx as the fruit of modern European capitalism. Jacques Ellul, one of France's finest social critics and a conservative, has acutely recognized the source of the resentment: "After consumer goods came an invasion of productive techniques. Technical invasion is a question not only of colonialism but also ... of simple technical subordination. All political and economic explanations are superficial. ... There are two great technical powers. ... Every other country must subordinate itself."[6]

Massive technology brought the threat of domination. In this respect the United States is potentially more dangerous to smaller countries than the Soviet Union,

---

[4] Title of the book by Jean-Jacques Servan-Schreiber.
[5] Title of a book by Jean-François Revel.
[6] *The Technical Society*, p. 119.

which may have a head start in rocketry and atomic artillery but still has to come to Western Europe for technical know-how and management tools. These cultural and sociological resentments may be only half-conscious; but they provide strong counter-currents to the policies which have dominated Europe between 1946 and 1963, the cold-war period, and which still prevail.

European statesmen must try to define policies that would allow Europe to play a more independent role without, of course, losing the American counterpoise to Soviet encroachments. Such new policies depend on a correct perception of the strategic constellation. The cold war was identical with the polarization of political forces throughout the world—West on the one side, East on the other. Instead of a see-saw, we now have a five-cornered figure with five triangles in it.[7] In the United States–Europe–U.S.S.R. triangle, Europe will try to be the mediator.

It is standard diplomatic practice to seek such a mediating position. De Gaulle tried it and failed. Macmillan, too, strove to mitigate and mediate Soviet-American rivalry; he was humbled. Germany was baited, by the hope of unification, to disengage herself from NATO. But what neither of these small powers can safely attempt, Europe as a whole may well do successfully. For that purpose she must be united and she must catch up with Russian and American technical capacity—a goal Europe can envisage confidently.

As the American sponsors of European unity have perceived, the United States has nothing to fear and much to gain from such a development. The United States did not expect, back in 1945, to maintain indefinitely an occupation army in Europe. It can disengage its troops from this theater of operations only if and when Europe organizes her collective defenses with her own resources. Only a strong Europe can hope to negotiate a satisfactory *détente* with the Soviet Union and her satellites. The new German *Ostpolitik* cannot in itself, without strong American backstopping, improve security in Central Europe; it may even carry the risk that at some future time a weak German government may succumb to Soviet blandishments and abandon its partners for the ephemeral and delusive prospect of another Rapallo honeymoon. A united Europe can be a partner of both the United States and the Soviet Union, provided its members are first of all partners of each other. European unity then may become a center of gravity also for the neutral states which at present are outside the Common Market.

To summarize, the changes expected in the new century have not materialized in the shape their advocates had hoped for. Other changes have come without prompting and prediction. Many European visions of the future have been fulfilled elsewhere—in the United States and in the Soviet Union. Some European inventions have turned against Europe. She is no longer the leading continent; her relations to other continents are overshadowed by new rivalries. On the whole, the dreams of 1900 have not been fulfilled but have been passed by.

---

[7] China between the United States and the Soviet Union; Europe between the United States and the Soviet Union; the United States between Japan and Russia; the Soviet Union between China and Japan; the Soviet Union between Europe and China.

Europe remains an idea. Despite the partition all Europeans still think of their continent as the Occident, a distinct culture whose unity has triumphed over a thousand years of divisions. It is less Roman, less Christian, still less Greek and Judaic than before. Instead it has grown more socialist, more permanently and profoundly democratic and conscious of a European meaning. As long as she strives, she is still Europe—still Faustian, still Promethean, still seeking obstacles and overcoming them.

For all that, the notion of Europe itself is in constant flux. Old cultural values have lost their significance; new ones have emerged. Europe is a living organism that is still developing, transforming herself while retaining an identity *vis-à-vis* other civilizations. She is now experimenting with new forms of economic and political co-operation. Her social system is evolving toward more equality, broader participation. Her cultural development is on the verge of a new explosion. Her youth is eager to redefine its heritage and to discover its own mission. It does not seem to have, at this moment, a new leader, a new party, a new voice or philosophy for that new appointment with destiny. Europe's recent experience with demonic leaders and satanic ideologies has sobered her. Other continents are fighting crusades now; Europe must build for herself.

Although this book goes to press at a moment of doubt and crisis, I still believe that the integrating tendencies are dormant only temporarily and that the various nationalistic, divisive forces are out of step historically. Like other movements, the search for European unity has had its periods of advance and of checks. What makes the present contretemps so dangerous, however, is the simultaneous threat of an economic setback, or at the very least of stagnation in many areas, which suggests beggar-my-neighbor tactics to the several governments while there is, at this time, neither an ideology nor a leader to rekindle the fire. The idealistic youth of Europe is more interested in the revolutions of other continents than in its own.

One of the graffiti that the Paris students, in May 1968, painted on the School of Architecture walls said: "Culture is dead, now let us start creating." The European idea is not dead, but it needs new directions.

A Bibliographical Note

THE following selections for reference and further reading are limited to books available in English. The listings are not necessarily sources of my information or reflections of my own views. Most of the actors in European history have written memoirs of their parts in the story; I have used these titles extensively but am not enumerating them because they can easily be located in public libraries. The same is true of biographies, diaries, and letters.

Governments and international authorities are now publishing important sources of statistical information and of historical documents. Neither are listed here; the hurried student will find current documents in *Keesing's Contemporary Archives* or in the *Survey* and *Documents* series published annually by the Royal Institute for International Affairs, London.

GENERAL HISTORIES AND SURVEYS

The work that has been a model for the present effort is Carlton Hayes's *A Political and Cultural History of Modern Europe*, 10th edn. (New York: Macmillan, 1951), the second volume of which covers the period of 1830–1939; no other history I know of has so well integrated the social, political, and cultural trends in many countries. However, it must now be supplemented with such excellent contemporary books as H. Stuart Hughes, *Contemporary Europe*, 3rd edn. (Englewood Cliffs, N.J.: Prentice-Hall, 1971), and George Lichtheim, *Europe in the Twentieth Century* (New York: Praeger, 1972). Hayes is a Catholic and conservative, Hughes a liberal, and Lichtheim a Marxist. The first two are professional historians with experience in diplomacy; the third wrote in the great tradition of philosophical journalism.

There have also been some notable attempts to interpret recent socio-economic events in the grand manner of Spengler. Foremost among these are: Raymond Aron, *The Century of Total War* (Boston, Mass.: Beacon Press, 1955); Jacques Ellul, *The Technological Society* (New York: Vintage, 1967); Ralf Dahrendorf, *Conflict After Class* (London: University of Essex, 1967); and Andrew Shonfield, *Modern Capitalism* (New York: Oxford University Press, 1965). Aron is a liberal ex-Marxist; Ellul's view is as jaundiced as the more superficial one of Marcuse but, unlike it, conservative;

the other two are deeply involved in the making of the society they describe. So are their American counterparts: John Kenneth Galbraith, author of witty and superficial books, whose viewpoint changes as fast as the linotypists can type; Daniel Bell, whose *Coming of Post-Industrial Society* (New York: Basic Books, 1973) falls short of his ambition to write *Das Kapital* for the managers of the future.

For the period ending with World War II, Fritz Sternberg has given a Marxist interpretation in *Capitalism and Socialism on Trial* (New York: Knopf, 1951); for the post-war period, a similar effort was made by Michael Barrett Brown in *After Imperialism* (London: Heinemann, 1963). Among other interpretative works are Joseph A. Schumpeter, *Capitalism, Socialism, and Democracy*, 3rd edn. (New York: Harper and Row, 1950); Roland N. Stromberg, *An Intellectual History of Modern Europe* (New York: Appleton, 1966) (with a good bibliography); Willson H. Coates and Hayden V. White, *The Ordeal of Liberal Humanism*, vol. II (New York: McGraw-Hill, 1970); James Findley (ed.), *Contemporary Civilization*, vol. IV (Glenview, Ill.: Scott, Foresman, 1967); Kenneth E. Boulding, *The Meaning of the Twentieth Century* (New York; Harper and Row, 1964); Geoffrey Barraclough, *An Introduction to Contemporary History* (Baltimore, Md.: Penguin, 1967); Raymond Williams, *Culture and Society 1780–1950* (New York: Harper and Row, 1958) and *The Long Revolution* (New York: Harper and Row, 1966).

Of special interest here are works speculating on the destiny of Europe: Oscar Halecki, *The Millennium of Europe* (Notre Dame, Ind.: University of Notre Dame Press, 1963); Denis de Rougemont, *The Idea of Europe* (New York: Macmillan, 1966); and Robert H. Beck *et al.*, *The Changing Structure of Europe* (Minneapolis: University of Minnesota Press, 1970), which has a useful bibliography.

As for the quality of life, one is likely to get either glowing reportage on high-society life or gloomy lament on misery, alienation, and the loss of values; or else a nostalgic legend is cultivated to exalt an irretrievable past to the detriment of an accursed present. Although hardly any book is entirely free from any of these faults, we can name at least some that contain antidotes: Peter Gay, *Weimar Culture* (New York: Harper and Row, 1968); Barbara Tuchman, *The Proud Tower* (New York: Macmillan, 1965); and James Lever, *Manners and Morals in the Age of Optimism* (New York: Harper, 1966). The classic work of social history still is Robert Graves and Alan Hodge, *The Long Week-End: England, 1918–1939* (New York: Norton, 1940). Much less satisfactory, despite excellent German models, is Otto Friedrich, *Before the Deluge: Berlin in the 1920's* (New York: Harper and Row, 1972). Still more journalistic are Anthony Sampson, *Anatomy of Europe* (New York: Harper and Row, 1969) and *The New Anatomy of Britain* (New York: Stein and Day, 1972); and John Gunther, *Inside Europe* (New York: Harper, 1940).

ECONOMIC AND SOCIAL HISTORY

Handy reference works are: W. A. Lewis, *Economic Survey 1919–39* (London: Allen and Unwin, 1949); M. M. Postan, *An Economic History of Europe, 1945–64*

(London: Methuen, 1967); Charles Kindleberger, *Europe's Postwar Growth* (Cambridge, Mass.: Harvard University Press, 1967); and Eugene Kulischer, *Europe on the Move: Population, 1917–47* (New York: Columbia University Press, 1948).

More detailed, covering specific countries or periods: Charles Kindleberger, *Economic Growth in France and England, 1851–1950* (Cambridge, Mass.: Harvard University Press, 1964); John Clapham, *The Economic Development of France and Germany, 1814–1914*, 4th edn. (New York: University of Cambridge Press, 1935); Gustav Stolper, *The German Economy, 1870–1940* (New York: Reynal and Hitchcock, 1940); Shepard Clough, *The Economic History of Modern Italy* (New York: Columbia University Press, 1964); Pauline Gregg, *A Social and Economic History of Britain, 1760–1960* (London: Harrap, 1962); Sidney Pollard, *The Development of the British Economy, 1914–50* (London: Arnold, 1962); Keith Hutchison, *The Decline and Fall of British Capitalism* (New York: Scribner, 1950); John Strachey, *The End of Empire* (New York: Praeger, 1964); Roger Clements, *Managers* (London: Allen and Unwin, 1958) (a study of their careers in industry); A. J. Younger, *Britain's Economic Growth, 1920–66* (London: Allen and Unwin, 1968); Eli Heckscher, *Economic History of Sweden* (Cambridge, Mass.: Harvard University Press, 1954); Lionel Robbins, *The Great Depression* (London: Macmillan, 1936); and George Hildebrand, *Growth and Structure in the Economy of Modern Italy* (Cambridge, Mass.: Harvard University Press, 1965).

HISTORY OF IDEAS

No intellectual history of the twentieth century equals the sweep and depth brought to the background of our period by Crane Brinton in *The Shaping of the Modern Mind* (New York: New American Library, 1954) or by John Herman Randall, Jr., in *The Making of the Modern Mind* (Boston: Houghton Miflin, 1940). More like textbooks are George L. Mosse, *The Culture of Western Europe* (New York: Rand McNally, 1961), and Norman Cantor (ed.), *The History of Popular Culture* (New York: Collier, 1958). For detailed information, however, the student might prefer, and will find in most public libraries, specialized surveys such as: John Passmore, *A Hundred Years of Philosophy* (Baltimore, Md.: Penguin, 1968); J. D. Bernal, *Science in History*, 4 vols. (Cambridge, Mass.: MIT Press); Melvin Kranzberg and Carroll Pursell (eds.), *Technology in Western Civilization*, vol. II (New York: Oxford University Press, 1967); Peter Yates, *Twentieth Century Music* (New York: Funk and Wagnalls, 1967); Wilfrid Mellers, *Romanticism and the Twentieth Century* (vol. IV of *Man and His Music*) (New York: Schocken, 1969); and Ben Seligman, *Main Currents in Modern Economics* (New York: Free Press, 1963).

On literature: Boris Ford (ed.), *The Modern Age* (*The Pelican Guide to English Literature*, vol. VII) (Baltimore, Md.: Penguin, 1961); Paul West, *The Modern Novel* (New York: Humanities Press, 1969); Henri Peyre, *French Novelists of Today* (New York: Oxford University Press, 1967); William York Tyndall, *Forces in British Literature, 1885–1946* (New York: Knopf, 1957); Henry C. Hatfield, *Modern German*

Literature (1966); and Edward J. Brown, *Russian Literature Since the Revolution* (London: Collier, 1963).

On *beaux-arts*: Andrew Carduff Ritchie, *Sculpture of the Twentieth Century* (New York: Museum of Modern Art, 1952); Herbert Read, *A Concise History of Modern Painting* (New York: Praeger, 1969) and *A Concise History of Modern Sculpture* (New York: Praeger, 1964); and Werner Haftmann, *Painting in the Twentieth Century*, 2 vols. (New York: Praeger, 1965).

I consider failures two pseudo-Marxist attempts to interpret the development of art on the basis of social developments: Arnold Hauser, *A Social History of Art*, vol. IV (New York: Knopf, 1962), and Donald Egbert, *Social Radicalism and the Arts* (New York: Knopf, 1972).

Quite a few books deal with the intellectual's position in the modern world. The most important are: Thomas Molnar, *The Decline of the Intellectual* (New York: World, 1965); Lewis Coser, *Men of Ideas* (New York: Free Press, 1965); C. P. Snow, *Science and Government* (Cambridge, Mass.: Harvard University Press, 1961), *The Two Cultures* (New York: Cambridge University Press, 1969), and *Corridors of Power* (New York: Scribner's Sons, 1964); Irving Howe, *Politics and the Novel* (New York: World, 1957); Daniel Bell, *The End of Ideology* (Free Press of Glencoe, Ill., 1960); and G. S. Fraser, *The Modern Writer and His World* (New York: Praeger, 1965).

On the literary movements of the post-war period: Robert Brustein, *The Theater of Revolt* (Boston, Mass.: Little, Brown, 1964); Martin Esslin, *The Theater of Absurd* (New York: Doubleday, 1969), and *Brecht*, rev. edn. (New York: Doubleday, 1971); and Richard Ellmann, *Yeats: The Man and the Mask* (New York: Dutton, 1958), and *James Joyce* (New York: Oxford University Press, 1966).

Manifestos of modern art: André Breton, *Manifestoes of Surrealism* (Ann Arbor: University of Michigan Press, 1972); Edmund Wilson, *Axel's Castle* (New York: Scribner's Sons, 1931); Stephen Spender, *The Struggle of the Modern* (Berkeley: University of California Press, 1965); Victor Brombert, *The Intellectual Hero in the French Novel* (Chicago: University of Chicago, 1960); and John Harrison, *The Reactionaries* (New York: Schocken, 1967).

On post-war intellectual trends: Kenneth Allsop, *The Angry Decade* (New York: Fernhill House, 1969); and Jean Améry, *Preface to the Future* (New York: Ungai).

On movies and TV: Paul Rotha, *The Film Till Now* (New York: Twayne, 1960); Penelope Houston, *The Contemporary Cinema* (Baltimore, Md.: Penguin, 1963); Wilson P. Dizard, *Television: A World View* (Syracuse, N.Y.: Syracuse University Press, 1966); Burton Paulu, *Radio and Television Broadcasting on the European Continent* (Minneapolis: University of Minnesota Press, 1967); Siegfried Kracauer, *From Caligari to Hitler* (Princeton, N.J.: Princeton University Press, 1947), a classic.

Modern philosophy: Hans Reichenbach, *The Rise of Scientific Philosophy* (Berkeley: University of California Press, 1951); G. J. Warnock, *English Philosophy Since 1900* (New York: Oxford University Press, 1969); Alfred North Whitehead, *Science and Philosophy* (New York: Philosophical Library, 1948), and *Adventures of Ideas* (New York: Free Press, 1967); Quentin Laner (ed.), *Phenomenology and the Crisis of*

Philosophy (New York: Harper and Row, 1965); Edmund Husserl, *Philosophy and the Crisis of European Man* (New York: Harper and Row, 1965); Karl Jaspers, *Man in the Modern Age*, 2d ed. (New York: Humanities Press, 1966); Ernst Cassirer, *The Problem of Knowledge* (New Haven, Conn.: Yale University Press, 1950); Joseph Kockelmans (ed.), *Contemporary European Ethics* (New York: Anchor, 1972), and *Phenomenology* (New York: Doubleday, 1967); Richard and Fernande de George, *The Structuralists from Marx to Lévi-Strauss* (New York: Doubleday, 1972); and William Barrett, *Irrational Man: The Existentialists* (New York: Doubleday, 1958). A critical history of positivism: Leszek Kolakowski, *The Alienation of Reason* (New York: Doubleday, 1968).

The new sciences: Ernest Jones, *The Life and Work of Sigmund Freud*, 3 vols. (New York: Basic Books, 1953, 1955, 1957); Max Planck, *The Universe in the Light of Modern Physics* (New York: Norton, 1931); Werner Heisenberg, *The Physicist's Conception of Nature* (Westport, Conn.: Greenwood Press, 1958), and *Physics and Beyond* (New York: Harper and Row, 1971), a beautiful autobiography as history of ideas; Albert Einstein, *Relativity: A Popular Exposition* (New York: Crown, 1961); Wolfgang Köhler, *The Task of Gestalt Psychology* (Princeton, N.J.: Princeton University Press, 1969); Robert Thomson, *The Pelican History of Psychology* (Baltimore, Md.: Penguin, 1968); Paul A. Robinson, *The Freudian Left* (New York: Harper and Row, 1969); Adolph Portmann, *New Paths in Biology* (New York: Harper and Row, 1966); Philippe Le Corbeiller (ed.), *The Languages of Science* (New York: Fawcett World Library, 1963); and Claude Lévi-Strauss, *Structural Anthropology* (New York: Basic Books, 1963).

Theology: Andrew L. Drummond, *German Protestantism Since Luther* (Naperville, Ill.: Allenson, 1951); S. Paul Shilling, *Contemporary Continental Theologians* (Nashville, Tenn.: Abingdon Press, 1966); Will Herberg (ed.), *Four Existentialist Theologians* (New York: Doubleday, 1958).

POLITICAL IDEAS AND MOVEMENTS

Political parties and systems: William G. Andrews (ed.), *European Politics* (New York: Van Nostrand Reinhold, 1969); Gwendolen Carter and John H. Herz, *Government and Politics in the Twentieth Century* (New York: Praeger, 1973); Randolph L. Braham (ed.), *Documents of Major European Governments* (New York: Knopf, 1969); Sigmund Neumann (ed.), *Modern Political Parties* (Chicago: University of Chicago, 1959). And, of course, Robert Michels's classic *Political Parties* (Gloucester, Mass.: Peter Smith, 1960); and José Ortega y Gasset's *Revolt of the Masses* (New York: Norton, 1957). These should be read together with other harbingers of intellectual orientation: H. Stuart Hughes, *Consciousness and Society: The Reorientation of European Social Thought, 1890–1930* (New York: Knopf, 1958); Irving Louis Horowitz, *Radicalism and the Revolt Against Reason* (Carbondale: University of Illinois, 1968); Georges Sorel, *Reflections on Violence* (New York: Macmillan, 1961); Henri Bergson, *Creative Evolution* (New York: Modern Library, 1944); Max Weber,

Selected Writings (eds. C. W. Mills and Hans Gerth) (New York: Grosset and Dunlap, 1946); Raymond Aron, *German Sociology* (Free Press of Glencoe, Ill.: 1957); Franz Borkenau, *Pareto* (London: Chapman and Hill, 1936); Hans Rogger and Eugen Weber (eds.), *The European Right* (Berkeley: University of California Press, 1966); René Remond, *The Right Wing in France*, rev. edn. (Philadelphia: University of Pennsylvania Press, 1969).

Church and politics: Mario Einaudi and François Goguel, *Christian Democracy in France and Italy* (Hamden, Conn.: Shoe String Press, 1969); M. P. Fogarty, *Christian Democracy in Western Europe, 1820–1953* (Notre Dame, Ind.: University of Notre Dame Press, 1957); L. C. Webb, *Church and State in Italy, 1947–57* (New York: Cambridge University Press, 1958); Richard A. Webster, *The Cross and the Fasces: Christian Democracy and Fascism* (Stanford, Calif.: Stanford University Press, 1960); Rolf Hochhuth, *The Deputy* (New York: Grove Press, 1964); and Joseph Moody (ed.), *Church and Society* (New York: Arts, 1953).

THE LABOR MOVEMENT

Julius Braunthal, *History of the International*, 2 vols. (New York: Praeger, 1967); James Joll, *The Second International, 1889–1914* (New York: Harper and Row, 1964); Richard H. S. Crossman (ed.), *The New Fabian Essays* (Mystic, Conn.: Verry, 1970); A. M. McBriar, *Fabian Socialism and English Politics, 1884–1914* (New York: Cambridge University Press, 1962); Anne Freemantle, *This Little Band of Prophets* (New York: Mentor Press, 1951); Hugh Clegg, *History of the British Trade Union Movement Since 1889* (New York: Oxford University Press, 1964); Val Lorwin, *The French Labor Movement* (Cambridge, Mass.: Harvard University Press, 1954); Henry Ehrmann, *French Labor from Popular Front to Liberation* (New York: Russell and Russell, 1971); George Lichtheim, *Marxism in Modern France* (New York: Columbia University Press, 1966); Joseph Buttinger, *In the Twilight of Socialism* (on Austria) (New York: Praeger, 1953).

G. D. H. Cole's massive histories of socialism (9 vols.) and of the English working-class movement (3 vols.) may by now be dated.

Carl Landauer's two-volume *History of Socialism* (Berkeley: University of California Press, 1960) evades many important issues. The most radical analysis has been applied to German Social Democracy before 1914; of this vast literature I cite the two most interesting works: Carl Schorske, *German Social Democracy, 1905–1917* (New York: Wiley, 1955), and Guenther Roth, *The Social Democrats in Imperial Germany* (Totowa, N.J.: Bedminster Press, 1963).

Another movement that has often attracted loving curiosity was French syndicalism: Louis Levine, *Syndicalism in France* (New York: AMS Press, 1970); see Sorel and Horowitz above, Broué-Timime below.

On the Communist International, we need an up-to-date, definitive work, though the following older works are quite good: Franz Borkenau, *World Communism: A History of the Communist International* (Ann Arbor: University of Michigan Press,

1962) and *European Communism* (same publisher, 1962); Milorad Drachkovitch, *The Revolutionary Internationals, 1864–1943* (Stanford, Calif.: Stanford University Press, 1966), and *Marxism in the Modern World* (Stanford, Calif.: Stanford University Press, 1965); Milorad Drachkovitch and Branko Lazitch (eds.), *Comintern: Historical Highlights* (New York: Praeger, 1966); House Un-American Activities Committee, 84th Congress, *The Communist Conspiracy*, 4 vols. (No. 835–838 of the Union Calendar, Government Printing Office, 1956); Hugh Seton-Watson, *From Lenin to Khrushchev* (New York: Praeger, 1960); Adam Ulam, *The Bolsheviks* (New York: Macmillan, 1955); Robert V. Daniels (ed.), *A Documentary History of Communism*, 2 vols. (New York: Vintage, 1960); Bertram Wolfe, *Three Who Made a Revolution*, 4th edn. (New York: Dial, 1964), and *Marxism* (New York: Dial, 1965); William Griffith (ed.), *Communism in Europe*, 2 vols. (Cambridge, Mass.: MIT Press); David Cattell, *Communism and the Spanish Civil War* (New York: Russell and Russell, 1965); George Kousoulas, *Revolution and Defeat: The Story of the Greek Communist Party* (New York: Oxford University Press, 1965); Ruth Fischer, *Stalin and German Communism* (New York: Oxford University Press, 1953); Helmut Gruber, *International Communism in the Era of Lenin* (New York: Doubleday, 1972); Jane Degras (ed.), *The Communist International* (New York: Oxford University Press, 1956); Leonard Schapiro, *The Communist Party of the Soviet Union*, rev. edn. (New York: Random House, 1971); Edmund Wilson, *To the Finland Station* (New York: Doubleday, 1953).

On the disintegration of Communism: Leopold Labedz (ed.), *Revisionism* (New York: Praeger, 1962), and *Polycentrism* (New York: Praeger, 1962); Richard Lowenthal, *World Communism: The Disintegration of a Secular Faith* (New York: Oxford University Press, 1966); Chalmers Johnson (ed.), *Change in Communist Systems* (Stanford, Calif.: Stanford University Press, 1970); Dan N. Jacob (ed.), *The New Communisms* (New York: Harper and Row, 1969); Giuseppe Fiori, *Antonio Gramsci: Life of a Revolutionary* (New York: Dutton, 1971); William Shawcross, *Dubcek* (New York: Simon and Schuster, 1971); Z. A. B. Zeman, *The Prague Spring* (New York: Hill and Wang, 1969); Ivan Svitak, *The Czechoslovak Experiment, 1968–1969* (New York: Columbia University Press, 1971); *U.N. Report on the Hungarian Revolution* (Eleventh General Assembly Session, 1957); and Melvin J. Lasky (ed.), *The Hungarian Revolution* (New York: Praeger, 1957).

On the impact of the Russian Revolution in Western Europe: Raymond Aron, *The Opium of the Intellectuals* (New York: Norton, 1962); David Caute, *Communism and the French Intellectuals* (New York: Macmillan, 1964); Gajo Petrovic, *Marx in the Mid-Twentieth Century* (New York: Doubleday, 1967); Richard Crossman (ed.), *The God That Failed* (New York: Bantam Books, 1950); and Czeslaw Milosz, *The Captive Mind* (New York: Random House, 1953).

On the New Left: Tariq Ali (ed.), *The New Revolutionaries* (New York: Morrow, 1969); Alexander Cockburn and Robin Blackburn, *Student Power* (Baltimore, Md.: Penguin, 1969); and Daniel Cohn-Bendit, *Obsolete Communism* (New York: McGraw-Hill, 1969).

On totalitarianism—antecedents and origins: Boyd Shafer, *Nationalism: Myth and Reality* (New York: Harcourt Brace Jovanovich, 1955); Elie Kedurie, *Nationalism* (New York: Praeger, 1961); Ernst Nolte, *The Three Faces of Fascism* (New York: New American Library, 1969); Franz L. Carsten, *The Rise of Fascism* (London: Batsford, 1967), and *The Reichswehr in Politics* (London: Oxford University Press, 1965); Fritz Stern, *The Politics of Cultural Despair* (Berkeley: University of California Press, 1961); Walter Laqueur, *Young Germany* (London: Routledge, 1962); Hannah Arendt, *The Origins of Totalitarianism*, rev. edn. (New York: Harcourt, Brace, Jovanovich, 1966); Carl Friedrich and Zbigniew K. Brzezinski, *Totalitarian Dictatorship and Autocracy* (New York: Praeger, 1961). See also Germany and Italy below.

POLITICAL HISTORY BY COUNTRIES

While this work deliberately minimizes state boundaries, it obviously had to be based on national histories; students looking for further information will undoubtedly have to go back to some of the following books:

For Austria, the successor states, the Balkans, and Eastern Europe: Hugh Seton-Watson, *The Southern Slav Question and the Hapsburg Monarchy* (New York: Fertig, 1969); Charles Gulick, *Austria from Hapsburg to Hitler*, 2 vols. (Berkeley: University of California Press, 1948); Victor Mamatey and Radomir Luza (eds.), *A History of Czechoslovakia, 1918-48* (Princeton, N.J.: Princeton University Press, 1972); Tad Szulc, *Czechoslovakia Since World War II* (New York: Viking Press, 1971); Paul Lendvai, *Eagles in Cobwebs: Nationalism and Communism in the Balkans* (New York: Doubleday, 1969); Robert Lee Wolff, *The Balkans in Our Time* (New York: Norton, 1967); Charles Jelavich and Barbara Jelavich (eds.), *The Balkans in Transition* (Berkeley: University of California Press, 1963); Stephen Fischer-Galati (ed.), *Eastern Europe in the Sixties* (New York: Praeger, 1963); J. F. Brown, *The New Eastern Europe* (New York: Praeger, 1966); and Hugh Seton-Watson, *Eastern Europe Between the Wars* (New York: Harper and Row, 1962).

For France: Henry Ehrmann, *France* (Boston: Little, Brown, 1971); Herbert Luethy, *France Against Herself* (New York: Meridian, 1955); Stanley Hoffmann et al., *In Search of France* (Cambridge, Mass.: Harvard University Press, 1963); Alexander Werth, *France, 1940-1955* (Boston, Mass.: Beacon Press, 1966); David Thomson, *Democracy in France Since 1870*, 4th edn. (New York: Oxford University Press, 1964); Robert Aron and G. Elgey, *The Vichy Regime, 1940-1944* (Chester Springs, Pa.: Dufour Editions, 1966); and Philipp Williams, *Crisis and Compromise: Politics in the Fourth Republic* (London: Longman's, 1964).

For Germany: Friedrich Meinecke, *The German Catastrophe* (Boston, Mass.: Beacon Press, 1963); Arthur Rosenberg, *The Birth of the German Republic, 1871-1918* (New York: Russell and Russell, 1962); Werner F. Bruck, *Social and Economic History of Germany from William the Second to Hitler, 1888-1938* (New York: Russell and Russell, 1962); Alexander Gerschenkron, *Bread and Democracy in Germany* (New York: Fertig, 1943); Erich Eyck, *A History of the Weimar Republic*, 2 vols. (Cambridge,

Mass.: Harvard University Press, 1963) (very unsatisfactory); Klaus Epstein, *Matthias Erzberger and the Dilemma of German Democracy* (New York: Fertig, 1971); Peter Gay, *Weimar Culture* (New York: Harper and Row, 1970); Dietrich Bracher, *The German Dictatorship* (New York: Praeger, 1970); William Shirer, *The Rise and Fall of the Third Reich* (New York: Simon and Schuster, 1960) (largely superseded); Franz Neumann, *Behemoth*, 2d ed. (New York: Octagon Books, 1963) (a masterly study); Claude Guillebaud, *The Social Policy of Nazi Germany* (New York: Fertig, 1971); Helmut Krausnick et al., *Anatomy of the SS State* (New York: Walker, 1965); John Wheeler-Bennett, *The Nemesis of Power: The German Army in Politics* (New York: St. Martin's Press, 1954); Arnold Toynbee and Veronica Toynbee (eds.), *Hitler's Europe: Survey of International Affairs 1939-46* (New York: Oxford University Press, 1965); and Richard Grunberger, *The Twelve-Year Reich* (New York: Ballantine, 1971).

Post-war Germany: Edgar Alexander, *Adenauer and the New Germany* (New York: Farrar, Strauss, 1957); Ardan Crowley, *Spoils of War: The Rise of West Germany* (New York: Bobbs Merrill, 1973); Peter Merkl, *The Origin of the West German Republic* (New York: Oxford University Press, 1963); and Ralf Dahrendorf, *Society and Democracy in Germany* (New York: Doubleday, 1967) (excellent).

On East Germany: Carola Stern, *Ulbricht* (New York: Praeger, 1971); and Peter Lust, *Two Germanies* (Montreal: Harvest House, 1966).

Greece: Bickham Sweet-Escott, *Greece 1939-45* (New York: Oxford University Press, 1954); Irwin T. Sanders, *Rainbow in the Rock: The Rural People of Greece* (Cambridge, Mass.: Harvard University Press, 1962).

Great Britain: Arthur Marwick, *Britain in the Century of Total War* (Boston, Mass.: Little, Brown, 1968) (with an exhaustive bibliography); Eric Hobsbawm, *Industry and Empire* (New York: Pantheon Books, 1968) (superbly written); David Thomson, *England in the Twentieth Century* (Baltimore, Md.: Penguin, 1963); (concise) A. J. P. Taylor, *English History, 1914-45* (New York: Oxford University Press, 1965); and Samuel Beer, *British Politics in the Collectivist Age* (New York: Vintage, 1965) (excellent).

Italy: Denis Mack Smith, *Italy: A Modern History* (Ann Arbor: University of Michigan Press, 1959); Elizabeth Wiskemann, *Fascism in Italy: Its Development and Influence* (New York: St. Martin's Press, 1969); Shepard Clough, *The Economic History of Modern Italy* (New York: Columbia University Press, 1964); E. C. Banfield and L. F. Banfield, *The Moral Basis of a Backward Society* (Free Press of Glencoe, Ill., 1958); Muriel Grindrod, *Italy* (New York: Praeger, 1968); Norman Kogan, *A Political History of Postwar Italy* (New York: Praeger, 1966); and Giuseppe Mammarella, *Italy After Fascism* (Notre Dame, Ind.: University of Notre Dame Press, 1966).

On Italian Fascism: Gaetano Salvemini, *Under the Axe af Fascism* (London: Gollancz, 1936); Ivone Kirkpatrick, *Mussolini; A Study in Power* (New York: Hawthorn Books, 1964); and Carl T. Schmidt, *The Corporate State in Action* (New York: Oxford University Press, 1939).

Poland: Hans Roos, *History of Modern Poland* (New York: Barnes and Noble, 1966); Thad P. Alton, *The Polish Postwar Economy* (New York: Columbia University Press, 1955); and Nicholas Bethel, *Gomulka: His Poland and His Communism* (London: Longman's, 1969).

Portugal: Hugh Kay, *Salazar and Modern Portugal* (New York: Hawthorn Books, 1970).

Rumania: Stephen Fischer-Galati, *New Rumania* (Cambridge, Mass.: MIT Press, 1967); and David Floyd, *Rumania: Russia's Dissident Ally* (New York: Praeger, 1965).

Sweden: Wilfrid Fleisher, *Sweden: The Welfare State* (New York: Day, 1959).

Spain: Salvador de Madariaga, *Spain* (New York: Praeger, 1958); Raymond Carr *Spain, 1808–1939* (New York: Oxford University Press, 1966); and Gerald Brenan, *The Spanish Labyrinth* (New York: Cambridge University Press, 1950) (a good background of the Civil War).

There are four excellent books on the Civil War: Franz Borkenau, *The Spanish Cockpit* (London: Faber, 1937); Pierre Broué and Emile Témime, *Revolution and the Civil War in Spain* (Cambridge, Mass.: MIT Press, 1972) (the German translation is infinitely better annotated); Gabriel Jackson, *Spanish Republic and Civil War* (Princeton, N.J.: Princeton University Press, 1965); and David Cattell, *Communism and the Spanish Civil War* (Berkeley: University of California Press, 1955).

For the Franco regime: Stanley Payne, *Franco's Spain* (New York: Crowell, 1967), and *A History of the Falange* (Stanford, Calif.: Stanford University Press, 1961).

Yugoslavia: Jozo Tomasevich, *Peasants, Politics, and Economic Change* (Stanford, Calif.: Stanford University Press, 1955); Milovan Djilas, *Land Without Justice* (New York: Harcourt, Brace, Jovanovich, 1972); Fitzroy Maclean, *Yugoslavia* (New York: Viking Press, 1969); John C. Campbell, *Tito's Separate Road* (New York: Harper and Row, 1967); and Wayne S. Vucinich, *Contemporary Yugoslavia* (Berkeley, Calif.: University of California Press, 1969).

Soviet Union: it is indispensable to begin with background histories such as R. D. Charques, *A Short History of Russia* (New York: Dutton, 1956); Michael T. Florinsky, *The End of the Russian Empire* (New York: Collier, 1961); Paul Milyukov, *Russia and Its Crisis* (New York: Collier, 1962); Hugh Seton-Watson, *The Decline of Imperial Russia* (New York; Praeger, 1952); Hans Kohn (ed.), *The Mind of Modern Russia* (New York: Harper and Row, 1955); and Nicolas Berdyaev, *The Russian Idea* (New York: Macmillan, 1962). Georg von Rauch, *A History of Soviet Russia*, 6th ed. (New York: Praeger, 1972), includes events up to the end of 1971. Donald W. Treadgold, *Twentieth Century Russia* (Chicago: Rand McNally, 1959) has an excellent bibliography. Important books on the antecedents of Communism have already been named under that heading. There are good biographies of Lenin (for instance: Louis Fischer, *Life of Lenin* [New York: Harper and Row, 1964], and David Shub, *Lenin* [Baltimore, Md.: Penguin, 1967]); of Stalin (Adam Ulam, *Stalin* [New York: Viking Press, 1973], Isaac Deutscher, *Stalin*, 2d ed. [New York: Oxford University Press, 1967], and Robert Tucker, *Stalin as Revolutionary* [New York: Norton, 1973]); and of Trotsky (Isaac Deutscher, 3 vols., *Prophet Armed* [1954], *Prophet Unarmed* [1959], and *Prophet Outcast* [1963] [New York: Oxford University Press]). To these should be added Stephen Cohen's biography of Bukharin (*Bukharin and the Bolshevik Revolution* [New York: Knopf, 1973]). The standard work on the revolution, not easily surpassed, is Edward Hallett Carr, *The Bolshevik Revolution*, 3 vols. (Baltimore, Md.: Penguin, 1966), with its sequel, *History of Soviet Russia, 1923–1926*, 5 vols. (New York: Macmillan, 1954–65). Leon Trotsky's own version is lively and rich: *The History of the Russian Revolution* (Ann Arbor: University of Michigan Press, 1957).

The Stalinist system may be studied in the following works: Merle Fainsod, *How Russia Is Ruled*, rev. ed. (Cambridge, Mass.: Harvard University Press, 1963); Raymond Bauer and Alex Inkeles, *How the Soviet System Works* (Cambridge, Mass.: Harvard University Press, 1956); Abdurakhman Avtorkhanov, *The Communist Party Apparatus* (Chicago, Ill.: Regnery, 1966); Barrington Moore, *Soviet Politics—The Dilemma of Power* (Cambridge, Mass.: Harvard University Press, 1950), and *Terror and Progress USSR* (Cambridge, Mass.: Harvard University Press, 1956); Robert Conquest, *The Great Terror*, rev. ed. (New York: Macmillan, 1973), and *The Soviet Police System* (New York: Praeger, 1968); Andrei Vyshinsky, *The Law of the Soviet State* (New York: Macmillan); and Nathan Leites and Elsa Bernant, *Ritual of Liquidation* (on the great trials) (Free Press of Glencoe, Ill., 1954).

On the in-fighting after Stalin's death: Robert Conquest, *Power and Policy in the USSR* (San Francisco: Gannon, 1970); Michel Tatu, *Power in the Kremlin* (New York: Viking Press, 1969); and Wolfgang Leonhard, *The Kremlin Since Stalin* (New York: Praeger, 1962).

On the domestic opposition: Robert V. Daniels, *The Conscience of the Revolution* (Cambridge, Mass.: Harvard University Press, 1960); and Roy Medvedev, *Let History Judge* (New York: Knopf, 1972).

Aspects of Soviet life: An Observer (George Feifer), *Message from Moscow* (New York: Knopf, 1969); Pierre Sorlin, *The Soviet People and Their Society* (New York: Praeger, 1969); Alex Inkeles and Raymond Bauer, *The Soviet Citizen* (New York: Atheneum, 1968); and W. W. Rostow and Edward J. Rozak, *The Dynamics of Soviet Society*, rev. ed. (New York: Norton, 1967).

On Soviet economy: Oskar Lange and Fred M. Taylor, *On the Economic Theory of Socialism* (New York: McGraw-Hill, 1964); J. P. Nettl, *The Soviet Achievement* (New York: Harcourt, Brace, Jovanovich, 1968) (a fiftieth-anniversary eulogy); Alec Nove, *The Soviet Economy* (New York: Praeger, 1969) (more critical, good bibliography); Roy D. Laird and Ed Crowley, *Soviet Agriculture* (New York: Random House, 1966); David Granick, *The Red Executive* (New York: Doubleday, 1961); Abraham Katz, *The Politics of Economic Reform in the Soviet Union* (New York: Praeger, 1972).

DIPLOMATIC HISTORY AND WORLD POLITICS

On social imperialism, see the classic works by Sidney and Beatrice Webb, *Industrial*

Democracy (Clifton, N.J.: Kelley, 1897), and John Hobson, *Imperialism* (Ann Arbor: University of Michigan Press, 1965); A. P. Thornton, *The Imperial Idea and Its Enemies* (New York: Doubleday, 1968); E. J. Hobsbawm, *Industry and Empire* (Baltimore, Md.: Penguin, 1968); A. M. McBriar, *Fabian Socialism and English Politics, 1884–1918* (New York: Cambridge University Press, 1962); Bernard Semmel, *Imperialism and Social Reform* (London: Allen and Unwin, 1960). Persuasive but journalistic is Lenin's *Imperialism: The Highest Stage of Capitalism* (New York: International Publishers, 1917). Different interpretations of imperialism (notably by Joseph Schumpeter, William L. Langer, and Hannah Arendt) are in Harrison M. Wright (ed.), *The New Imperialism* (Indianapolis, Ind.: Heath, 1961).

The diplomatic aspects of imperialism are discussed in A. J. P. Taylor, *The Struggle for Mastery in Europe, 1848–1918* (New York: Oxford University Press, 1954); Hugh Seton-Watson, *The Russian Empire* (New York: Oxford University Press, 1967); Fritz Fischer, *Germany's Aims in World War I* (New York: Norton, 1967); William L. Langer, *The Diplomacy of Imperialism* (New York: Knopf, 1935); L. C. Seaman, *From Vienna to Versailles* (Gloucester, Mass.: Smith, 1963), and *Post-Victorian Britain* (New York: Barnes and Noble, 1966); Luigi Albertini, *The Origins of the War of 1914*, 3 vols. (New York, Oxford University Press, 1952–57); and Alfred Vagts, *A History of Militarism* (Cleveland: Meridian Books, 1959).

War of 1914: Cyril Falls, *The Great War* (New York: Putnam, 1959); Winston Churchill, *The World Crisis, 1911–18*, 3 vols. (New York: Macmillan, 1923–27); and Barbara Tuchman, *The Guns of August* (New York: Dell, 1963).

On the road to World War II: Louis Namier, *Europe in Decay: A Study in Disintegration, 1936–40* (New York: Macmillan, 1963); Hajo Holborn, *The Political Collapse of Europe* (New York: Knopf, 1951); Martin Gilbert and Richard Gott, *The Appeasers* (Boston: Houghton Mifflin, 1963); H.M. Stationery Office (London), *Documents Concerning German Polish Relations and the Outbreak of Hostilities Between Great Britain and Germany* (1939), and *British Foreign Policy in the Second World War* (1970); Winston Churchill, *The Second World War*, 6 vols. (New York: Houghton Mifflin, 1948–53); U.S. Department of State, *Nazi-Soviet Relations* (Washington: U.S. Government Printing Office, 1948); Charles de Gaulle, *The Army of the Future* (Philadelphia: Lippincott, 1940); Basil H. Liddell Hart, *History of the Second World War* (London: Cassell, 1970); Edward Hallett Carr, *International Relations Between the Two World Wars, 1919–39* (New York: Macmillan, 1959), and *The Twenty Years' Crisis, 1919–39* (New York: Macmillan, 1939).

On Soviet foreign relations: Zbigniew Brzezinski, *The Soviet Bloc*, rev. ed. (Cambridge, Mass.: Harvard University Press, 1967); Anatole Shub, *An Empire Loses Hope* (New York: Norton, 1970); Edward Crankshaw, *The New Cold War* (Freeport, N.Y.: Books for Libraries, 1963); and Adam Ulam, *Titoism and the Cominform* (Cambridge, Mass.: Harvard University Press, 1952). Ulam's *Expansion and Coexistence*, 2d ed. (New York: Praeger, 1974) has superseded all previous books on the subject, but should be supplemented by the following two collections: Alvin Z. Rubinstein (ed.), *The Foreign Policy of the Soviet Union*, 2d ed. (New

York: Random House, 1966), and Alexander Dallin (ed.), *Soviet Conduct in World Affairs* (New York: Columbia University Press, 1960). W. I. Potemkin, *History of Diplomacy* (Moscow: Foreign Languages Publishing House, 1939); and U.S.S.R. Ministry of Defense, *History of the Great Patriotic War* (Moscow: Foreign Languages Publishing House, 1961).

On the cold war: Hugh Seton-Watson, *Neither War nor Peace*, rev. ed. (New York: Praeger, 1962); Herbert Feis, *Churchill-Roosevelt-Stalin* (Princeton, N.J.: Princeton University Press, 1957), *Between War and Peace* (Princeton, N.J.: Princeton University Press, 1960), *The Atomic Bomb and the End of World War II*, rev. ed. (Princeton, N.J.: Princeton University Press, 1966), and *From Trust to Terror, 1945–50* (New York: Norton, 1970); André Fontaine, *History of the Cold War*, 2 vols. (New York: Pantheon, 1968); Louis J. Halle, *The Cold War as History* (New York: Harper and Row, 1967) (outstanding!).

NATO: Carl H. Amme, *NATO Without France* (Stanford, Calif.: Hoover Institution Press, 1967).

THE OUTLOOK

The welfare state: Colin Clark, *Conditions of Economic Progress*, 3rd ed. (New York: St. Martin's Press, 1957); William H. Beveridge, *Full Employment in a Free Society* (New York: Norton, 1945); Ferdynand Zweig, *The Worker in an Affluent Society* (Free Press of Glencoe, Ill., 1962); Walter Galenson, *Trade Union Democracy in Western Europe* (Berkeley: University of California Press, 1961); Marquis Childs, *Sweden: The Middle Way* (Baltimore, Md.: Penguin, 1947); Albert H. Rosenthal, *The Social Programs of Sweden* (Minneapolis: University of Minnesota Press, 1967); and Ralf Dahrendorf, *Class and Class Conflict in Industrial Society* (Stanford, Calif.: Stanford University Press, 1959).

The classic study by P. Lewis and A. Maud of *The British Middle Classes* (1949) has now been supplemented by F. Parkin's *Middle-Class Radicalism* (Portland, Ore.: International Scholarly Book Service, 1968). Great attention has been paid to the double phenomenon of the so-called new middle class and the affluent worker. These questions are dealt with in John H. Goldthorpe *et al.*, *The Affluent Worker* (New York: Cambridge University Press, 1968); Robert McKenzie and Allan Silver, *Angels in Marble: Working Class Conservativism* (Chicago: University of Chicago Press, 1968); and David Lockwood, *The Blackcoated Worker* (New York: Oxford University Press, 1958), as well as his article, "The New Working Class," in *European Journal of Sociology*, 1960.

Basic works are also: D. V. Glass (ed.), *Social Mobility in Britain* (London: Routledge and Kegan Paul, 1954); Richard M. Titmuss, *Income Distribution and Social Change* (Toronto: University of Toronto Press, 1962); D. Wedderburn, "Poverty in Britain Today," in *Sociology Review*, no. 3 (1962); and Eric Hobsbawm, *Labouring Men* (New York: Basic Books, 1965).

On post-war Europe: Walter Laqueur, *Europe Since Hitler* (London: Weidenfeld,

1970); Stephen R. Graubard (ed.), *A New Europe* (New York: Houghton Mifflin, 1966). For class, use: Miriam Camps, *European Unification in the Sixties* (New York: McGraw-Hill, 1966); Walter Hallstein, *United Europe, Challenge and Opportunity* (Cambridge, Mass.: Harvard University Press, 1962); P. E. P., *European Unity: A Survey of European Institutions* (London: Allen and Unwin, 1968); Ghita Ionescu (ed.), *The New Politics of European Integration* (New York: St. Martin's Press, 1972); and Hugh Thomas, *Europe: The Radical Change* (New York: Harper and Row, 1973).

Index of Names

Adenauer, Konrad, 269, 270, 291, 309, 338, 401, 417–20, 433
Adorno, Theodor W., 377, 386, 387, 409, 436, 439
Agnelli, Giovanni, 131, 358
Apollinaire, Guillaume, 63, 65–66, 188, 387
Aragon, Louis, 188, 195, 197
Asquith, Herbert, 40, 50, 52, 140
Attlee, Clement, 143, 267, 274, 281, 291, 343
Auden, W. H., 186, 187, 190, 195, 197
Ayer, Alfred Jules, 205, 410

Baldwin, Stanley, 123–24, 129, 142, 167, 239
Balfour, Arthur, 96
Barbusse, Henri, 94, 126, 188
Barth, Karl, 207–8, 400f., 404
Bauer, Otto, 42, 129, 151
Bebel, August, 35, 36, 42, 44
Beck, Ludwig, 248, 262
Beckett, Samuel, 389, 397–98, 409
Beckmann, Max, 67, 189
Benda, Julien, 214–15, 290
Benedict XV, 96
Beneš, Eduard, 96, 139, 145, 246, 268
Benjamin, Walter, 197, 383
Benn, Gottfried, 67, 68, 147, 195, 211, 215, 226
Bennett, Arnold, 60, 70, 94
Berg, Alban, 66, 69, 83, 190
Bergson, Henri, 32, 65, 70, 71, 74–75, 79, 194, 205, 206, 406
Beria, Lavrenti, 284, 302, 303n
Bernanos, Georges, 207, 373, 404
Bernstein, Eduard, 43–45, 95
Beuve-Méry, Hubert, 290, 365, 403
Beveridge, William, 277, 337
Bevin, Ernest, 274, 291
Bidault, Georges, 260, 296
Bloch, Ernst, 67, 317, 327, 404, 405, 413
Blum, Léon, 129, 143, 236, 239, 248, 253
Böll, Heinrich, 260, 374, 386n, 404, 409
Bonhoeffer, Dietrich, 226, 270, 405
Born, Max, 202, 203, 454
Brandt, Willy, 362, 374, 420–23, 437, 441
Branting, Hjalmar, 45, 139, 144
Braque, Georges, 65, 68, 189
Brecht, Bertolt, 147, 178, 185, 186, 190, 195, 197, 199, 270, 290, 315–16, 374, 397
Breton, André, 59, 187, 188, 195
Brezhnev, Leonid, 308, 321, 322, 325, 326, 332

Briand, Aristide, 14, 44, 92, 123, 124, 126, 129, 143
Broch, Hermann, 67, 192, 373
Bukharin, Nikolai, 104, 159, 160
Butor, Michel, 186n, 389, 438

Caillaux, Joseph, 14, 53
Calvo Sotelo, José, 155, 237, 238
Camus, Albert, 194, 206, 260, 271, 374, 376, 377, 378, 388, 408, 409
Caramanlis, Constantine, 429–30
Carnap, Rudolf, 205, 410, 411
Carson, Edward, 50, 449
Casement, Roger, 96, 112
Céline, Louis Ferdinand, 193, 195, 212, 253, 378
Chagall, Marc, 66, 189
Chamberlain, Joseph, 19, 27
Chamberlain, Neville, 167, 239–40, 247–50, 252
Chaplin, Charlie, 63, 175, 354
Chesterton, G. K., 13, 32, 33, 186, 389
Chirico, Giorgio di, 67, 175, 189
Churchill, Winston, 13, 142, 252, 253, 254, 256, 257, 259, 261, 267, 274, 286, 294, 408
Citrine, Walter, 129, 142
Claudel, Paul, 32, 70, 207
Clemenceau, Georges, 14, 53, 92, 94
Cocteau, Jean, 70, 190
Codreanu, Corneliu, 215, 230
Cole, G. D. H., 43, 143, 185–86
Colette, 39, 63, 70, 345
Conrad, Joseph, 26, 28, 59, 70
Corradini, Enrico, 29, 219
Costa, Joaquín, 11, 155
Cripps, Stafford, 126, 129, 143, 293
Croce, Benedetto, 152, 223
Curie, Marie, 39, 78
Curzon, George, 103n, 249

Daladier, Édouard, 140, 235–36, 239, 248
Daniel, Yuli, 321, 332
d'Annunzio, Gabriele, 58, 110, 193, 215
de Forest, Lee, 173, 202
de Gasperi, Alcide, 261, 291, 418
de Gaulle, Charles, 251, 252, 257, 260, 267, 268, 289, 295–97, 320, 322, 339, 365, 401, 403, 419, 424, 431–35, 438, 439, 440, 447, 452, 453n, 456
de la Rocque, François, 215, 232, 233, 236

473

de Man, Hendrik, 129, 135, 232, 236
de Montherlant, Henry, 126, 195, 253
de Valera, Eamon, 112, 114, 231, 449
de Vries, Hugo, 75, 352
Debré, Michel, 296, 326, 433
Debussy, Claude, 59, 68, 69, 189
Degrelle, Léon, 215, 231–32
Delauney, Robert, 65, 188
Derain, André, 65, 189
Deterding, Henry, 223, 247
Devlin, Bernadette, 345, 449
Dimitroff, Georgi, 224, 235, 272, 273, 286, 287
Djilas, Milovan, 254, 255, 288, 359
Döblin, Alfred, 70, 94, 195, 207
Dollfuss, Engelbert, 151, 154–55, 227, 229
Doriot, Jacques, 218, 220, 232, 253
Dostoevsky, Fyodor, 29, 106, 185, 218
Douhet, Giulio, 89, 251
Doyle, Arthur Conan, 184, 206, 380–81
Dubček, Alexander, 325–27, 421, 436, 437, 448
Duchamp, Marcel, 65, 175
Duhamel, Georges, 70, 192
Durkheim, Émile, 80, 204
Dutschke, Rudi, 333, 436n

Ebert, Friedrich, 45, 97, 98, 129, 147, 273
Eden, Anthony, 239, 274, 291, 294, 424
Ehrenburg, Ilya, 104, 201, 302, 332
Einstein, Albert, 77–78, 203, 204, 411
Eisner, Kurt, 45, 107, 146
Eliot, T. S., 28, 59, 70, 178, 190, 195, 197, 207, 290, 376, 398, 408
Ellis, Havelock, 73, 179
Ellul, Jacques, 359, 455
Éluard, Paul, 188, 195, 197
Enzensberger, Hans Magnus, 374, 390, 437
Erhard, Ludwig, 338, 420

Fadeyev, Alexander, 200, 376
Fall, Leo, 6, 189–90
Fallada, Hans, 139, 222
Fanfani, Amintore, 363, 403, 418, 419
Foerster, Friedrich Wilhelm, 14, 126
Ford, Ford Madox, 94n, 192
Forster, E. M., 60, 70, 106, 113
France, Anatole, 13, 70, 138
Franco, Francisco, 221, 231, 233, 237–40, 246–47, 253, 428–29, 447
Freud, Sigmund, 39, 70, 73–74, 80, 187, 204, 206, 214, 351, 408, 409, 413
Frisch, Max, 375, 386, 389, 398, 408
Fromm, Erich, 222, 364, 409
Fuller, Frederick Charles, 89, 212–13

Galen, Clemens von, 226, 400
Galsworthy, John, 60, 70, 94, 192
Garaudy, Roger, 326, 327, 404
García Lorca, Federico, 195, 238, 240
Gauguin, Paul, 26, 65, 67
Gentile, Giovanni, 154, 222–23
George, Stefan, 28, 218, 227
Gide, André, 57, 59, 70, 71, 73, 178, 179, 192, 193, 195, 253, 373, 374, 408
Giolitti, Giovanni, 11, 93, 111
Giono, Jean, 193, 211–12, 232

Giscard d'Estaing, Valéry, 345, 346, 422, 433, 441
Gladkov, Fyodor, 70, 104, 200
Goebbels, Josef, 221, 223, 225n, 258
Gömbös, Gyula, 156, 215, 230
Gomulka, Wladyslaw, 187, 303, 311, 313, 314, 316, 325, 328, 403
Göring, Hermann, 89, 221, 225, 226, 228
Gorky, Maxim, 36, 70, 200, 201
Grass, Günter, 374, 408
Graves, Robert, 94, 177, 215
Greene, Graham, 207, 404
Grey, Edward, 52, 53, 87
Grimm, Hans, 29, 195
Gronchi, Giovanni, 363, 418
Gropius, Walter, 106, 187, 391–92
Grüber, Heinrich, 226, 270
Guesde, Jules, 42, 44, 45, 91

Habermas, Jürgen, 359, 412, 439
Hallstein, Walter, 279, 280, 358
Hamsun, Knut, 28, 70, 193, 211
Hašek, Jaroslav, 50, 190
Hauptmann, Gerhart, 14, 36, 60–61, 70, 193
Heidegger, Martin, 134, 195, 205–6, 208, 213–14, 408
Henderson, Arthur, 96, 129, 143
Herriot, Édouard, 116–17, 123, 126, 140, 143
Hervé, Gustave, 45, 110, 218
Hesse, Hermann, 14, 28, 59, 70, 94, 106, 192, 194, 408
Hilferding, Rudolf, 19, 42, 129, 131, 135, 227, 359
Himmler, Heinrich, 223, 225, 232, 255–56
Hindemith, Paul, 190, 388, 408
Hindenburg, Paul von, 87, 98, 148–50, 226
Hitler, Adolf, 117, 142, 143, 148–49, 151, 167, 180, 186, 217–23, 224–28, 245–58, 260, 421
Hofmannsthal, Hugo von, 28, 32, 59, 83, 213, 219, 387
Horthy, Miklos, 108, 156, 230
Hugenberg, Alfred, 29, 129, 131, 148, 149, 224
Husak, Gustav, 326, 328, 448
Husserl, Edmund, 205, 206, 213, 214
Huxley, Aldous, 94, 175, 178, 192, 197, 211, 359, 406
Huxley, Julian, 352, 406

Innitzer, Theodor, 226, 400

Jaspers, Karl, 204–6, 213, 214, 270
Jaurès, Jean, 14, 36, 42, 44, 45
John XXIII, 363, 401–3, 419
Johnson, Uwe, 317, 374, 389
Jouhaux, Léon, 41, 129
Joyce, James, 33, 70, 71, 75, 191, 193, 197, 211, 408
Jung, Carl, 33, 74, 195, 204, 206, 211
Jünger, Ernst, 89, 91, 126, 195, 215, 216n, 219, 226, 270

Kafka, Franz, 128, 193, 206, 207, 208, 270, 290, 387, 398
Kamenev, Leo, 99, 158
Kardelj, Edward, 254, 287
Kautsky, Karl, 19, 42, 45, 95
Key, Ellen, 38, 39, 345

Keynes, John Maynard, 60, 116, 140, 277, 295, 337–38, 340, 358
Khrushchev, Nikita, 242–43, 294, 297, 302, 304–11, 313, 314, 315, 319–22, 328, 332, 420
Kipling, Rudyard, 21, 26, 28, 59
Kirchner, Ernst Ludwig, 67, 189
Klee, Paul, 66, 175, 189
Koestler, Arthur, 194, 242n, 373–74, 376
Kokoschka, Oskar, 66–68, 189
Kolakowski, Leszek, 317, 327, 404, 409, 410
Kraus, Karl, 40, 386

Lagerlöf, Selma, 70, 345
Largo Caballero, Francisco, 155, 237–39
Laval, Pierre, 129, 235, 245–46, 252–53, 267
Lawrence, D. H., 58, 70, 71, 73–75, 94, 193, 194, 197, 211, 377, 379, 388
Le Bon, Gustave, 29, 81, 217
Le Carré, John, 185, 389
Le Corbusier, 187, 392
Léger, Fernand, 65, 183, 390
Lehár, Franz, 6, 189–90
Lenin, Vladimir, 25, 42, 43, 45, 46, 47, 79, 87, 95, 96, 99–105, 111, 112, 116, 158, 307, 309n, 318
Leo XIII, 32, 402
Levi, Carlo, 194–95, 373
Lévy-Bruhl, Lucien, 74, 413
Liebermann, Max, 67, 189
Litvinov, Maxim, 124, 242, 243, 246, 249
Lloyd George, David, 3, 11, 12, 13, 92, 104, 106, 140
Ludendorff, Erich, 87, 88, 89, 97, 99, 117, 146, 219
Lukács, George, 214, 313, 389, 409
Luxemburg, Rosa, 39, 41, 42, 45, 46, 107, 108, 346

MacDonald, J. Ramsay, 43, 45, 123, 124, 129, 142, 143
Macmillan, M. Harold, 294, 297, 424, 453, 456
Mahler, Gustav, 59, 68, 76, 189
Malenkov, Georgy, 286, 302–4
Malraux, André, 174, 193, 194, 260, 373, 374, 377, 387
Mann, Heinrich, 14, 39, 70, 94, 292
Mann, Thomas, 28, 29, 57, 59, 70, 71f., 76, 140, 147, 192, 226–27, 270, 292, 373, 387n, 408
Mannheim, Karl, 204, 214, 359
Mansfield, Katharine, 60, 213
Marcuse, Herbert, 176, 290, 333, 359, 366, 377, 409, 410, 413, 436, 439
Marinetti, Filippo, 59, 60, 63, 89, 174, 195, 215
Maritain, Jacques, 32–33, 207, 400, 403
Martin, Kingsley, 290, 365, 437
Martin du Gard, Roger, 70, 94n, 192, 253
Masaryk, Jan, 268, 283, 325
Masaryk, Thomas, 139, 145, 268, 324
Mattei, Enrico, 357, 419, 432
Mauriac, François, 33, 65, 70, 192, 207, 208, 400, 404, 408
Maurras, Charles, 28, 219–20, 233, 253
Mayakovsky, Vladimir, 188, 199, 200, 201
Meinecke, Friedrich, 147, 270
Mendès-France, Pierre, 260, 289, 295, 431, 438, 447

Merleau-Ponty, Maurice, 290, 376
Mikhailovitch, Draja, 254–55, 261, 273
Milhaud, Darius, 68, 190, 388
Mindszenty, Joseph, 282, 312, 313
Molotov, Vyacheslav, 249, 253, 273, 274, 286
Mond, Alfred, 27, 131, 142
Mondrian, Piet, 67, 187, 189
Monnet, Jean, 260, 277, 279, 295, 355, 357, 358
Montessori, Maria, 38, 39, 133, 345
Moore, George Edward, 60, 80, 205
Musil, Robert, 67, 192, 193, 375
Mussolini, Benito, 30, 45, 60, 93, 108, 110–11, 124, 125, 140, 151–54, 157, 194, 217–18, 221, 224, 227–31, 239, 240, 245–48, 257

Nagy, Ferencz, 282, 303, 312, 313
Naumann, Friedrich, 13, 31, 140
Nenni, Pietro, 261, 291, 363, 403, 418–19
Neurath, Otto, 205, 410
Nicolson, Harold, 60, 220
Niemöller, Martin, 226, 401
Nietzsche, Friedrich, 5, 28, 30, 39, 59, 73, 74, 80, 82, 194, 206, 213–15, 367, 407
Nolde, Emil, 66–67, 189, 226, 373n
Norman, Montagu, 168, 247

Ortega y Gasset, José, 11, 134–35, 155, 383
Orwell, George, 194, 197, 264, 333, 359, 373, 383
Osborne, John, 377, 378, 425

Papen, Franz von, 150, 225
Pareto, Vilfredo, 30, 80–82
Pashich, Nikola, 51, 157
Pasternak, Boris, 199, 201, 331–32, 408
Paul VI, 402, 403
Péguy, Charles, 33, 45, 53, 59, 215, 401, 403
Pétain, Philippe, 88, 252–53, 267, 447
Picasso, Pablo, 60, 65, 66, 68, 175, 188, 239n, 289
Pilsudski, Josef, 103, 110, 115, 125, 154, 156, 233, 245
Pirandello, Luigi, 190, 191, 388–89, 397
Pius IX, 32
Pius X, 11, 32
Pius XI, 139f., 154, 155, 226, 245, 400
Pius XII, 226, 254, 400, 401
Poincaré, Henri, 78, 79, 412n
Poincaré, Raymond, 53, 116, 143
Pompidou, Georges, 129, 296, 440
Popper, Karl, 205, 334, 410, 412
Poujade, Pierre, 295, 344, 431, 449
Poulenc, Francis, 68, 190
Pound, Ezra, 28, 58, 70, 195, 197, 387
Prieto y Tuero, Indalecio, 129, 236
Primo de Rivera, Miguel, 154–55, 215, 230
Proust, Marcel, 71, 75, 191, 193, 389, 391
Puccini, Giacomo, 68, 111, 190

Radich, Steven, 109, 137, 157
Rapacki, Adam, 291, 315
Rathenau, Walther, 15, 16, 19, 91, 106, 107, 129, 131, 146, 217
Ravel, Maurice, 59, 76, 189
Reichenbach, Hans, 205, 410
Rilke, Rainer Maria, 28, 32, 39, 82–83, 215, 387
Robbe-Grillet, Alain, 186n, 386, 389

Rolland, Romain, 13, 70, 94, 126, 192
Romains, Jules, 70, 94n, 191, 192
Roosevelt, Franklin D., 166, 256, 259
Russell, Bertrand, 13, 43, 45, 60, 79, 126, 133, 205, 408, 410
Rutherford, Ernest, 78, 203

Saint-Exupéry, Antoine de, 174, 194, 377
Saint-John Perse (Alexis Saint-Léger), 70, 197, 409
Salazar, Antonio, 154–56, 233, 428
Sarraute, Nathalie, 345, 386, 389, 438
Sartre, Jean-Paul, 194, 206, 213, 260, 271, 286, 290, 327, 374, 376–79, 387, 409, 437, 438, 439
Sassoon, Siegfried, 88, 94, 215
Schacht, Hjalmar, 166, 225–26, 228n, 229, 230
Scheler, Max, 71, 204, 205, 213, 214
Schleicher, Kurt von, 107, 150, 225
Schönberg, Arnold, 59, 66, 69, 388
Schuman, Robert, 260, 278, 291, 295, 339
Schuschnigg, Kurt von, 151, 155, 247
Shaw, George Bernard, 43, 57, 58, 70, 75, 94, 191, 194
Sholokhov, Mikhail, 200, 330–31, 408
Silone, Ignazio, 154, 194–95, 373, 374
Sitwell family, 60, 94
Slansky, Rudolf, 287, 324
Smetona, Antanas, 154, 233
Snow, C. P., 359, 407, 410
Solzhenitsyn, Alexander, 306, 321, 332, 408
Sorel, Georges, 30, 41, 74, 82, 195, 217
Soutine, Chaim, 66, 67, 189
Spaak, Paul-Henri, 279, 280, 446
Spann, Othmar, 154–55, 219
Spender, Stephen, 195, 197, 374
Spengler, Oswald, 82, 91, 175, 187, 204, 212, 217, 226
Springer, Axel, 384, 437
Stalin, Joseph, 99, 123, 148, 158–62, 235, 239, 241–45, 249, 253, 255, 256, 273, 274, 284, 286, 287, 301–2, 304, 306, 309, 321, 331, 376
Stauning, Thorvald, 45, 139, 144
Stojanovic, Svetozar, 316, 409
Strachey, John, 113, 129, 220
Strauss, Richard, 57, 64, 68–69, 76, 190
Stravinsky, Igor, 59, 67, 68, 76, 189, 190, 388
Stresemann, Gustav, 116, 117, 118, 123, 129, 140, 147
Strindberg, August, 40, 70, 190

Thyssen, Fritz, 223, 227, 356, 358
Tito, Josip B., 254f., 257, 261, 273, 283, 286–90, 309, 310, 312–13, 315, 316, 329
Togliatti, Palmiro, 261, 316, 327, 375
Toscanini, Arturo, 111, 152, 190
Toynbee, Arnold, 204, 212, 411
Trotsky, Leon, 46, 47, 99–105, 116, 158, 199, 200, 243
Tsankov, Alexander, 109, 154

Ulbricht, Walter, 273, 292, 318, 324, 325, 420
Undset, Sigrid, 70, 206–7

Valéry, Paul, 59, 76, 212
Valois, Georges, 45, 218, 220
van Gogh, Vincent, 65, 66, 189
Varga, Eugene, 243, 277
Vercors, Jean B., 194, 374

Wallace, Edgar, 63, 184
Waugh, Evelyn, 178, 206, 404
Webb, Sidney and Beatrice, 35, 39, 43, 44, 60, 113, 142, 185–86, 362
Weber, Alfred, 18, 411
Weber, Max, 8, 31, 59, 80, 82, 147, 204–5, 214, 217, 359, 411
Webern, Anton von, 66, 388
Wedekind, Frank, 38, 40, 60, 70
Weil, Simone, 211, 405
Weiss, Peter, 390, 397, 398, 437
Wells, H. G., 43, 58, 60, 70, 73, 94
Werfel, Franz, 94, 185, 374, 454
Wilson, Harold, 362, 424–27
Wittgenstein, Ludwig, 205, 410, 411
Woolf, Virginia and Leonard, 60, 70, 191
Wyszynski, Stefan, 314, 316, 403

Yeats, William Butler, 28, 33, 57–58, 70, 94n, 190, 195, 211, 215
Yesenin, Sergei, 201, 332
Yevtushenko, Yevgeny, 306, 331, 332

Zaharoff, Basil, 130, 247
Zhdanov, Andrei, 275–76, 284, 286–87, 330
Zhivkov, Todor, 317, 325
Zhukov, Georgi, 302, 304, 307
Zinoviev, Grigori, 105, 142, 158, 159
Zoshchenko, Mikhail, 104, 199–200
Zuckmayer, Carl, 10, 270
Zweig, Stefan, 57, 94, 126

Index of Subjects

Absurd, cult of, 396, 397, 398, 408
Aeronautics and aviation, 89, 174, 306, 339, 425
Agrarian reform, 47, 99, 106, 108–9. 128, 136–37, 145, 156, 237, 272, 282–83, 305, 418; in Bulgaria, 109; in Hungary, 136, 282; in Rumania, 136; Russian Socialist Revolutionaries and, 45, 46, 99, 101; in Yugoslavia, 157
Anarchists, 41, 102, 107, 237–39
Angry young men, 366–67, 377–78, 425
Anthropology, 28, 74, 204–5, 352, 413
Anti-Americanism, 289–92, 297, 298, 363, 365, 384–85, 397, 419, 421, 430, 433–34, 437, 444, 454
Anti-Semitism, 27, 29, 31–33, 110, 129, 137, 141, 146, 148–49, 198, 212, 217–23, 230, 233, 243, 253, 254, 260, 284, 326–29, 448
Antirationalism, 28–30, 71, 74–76, 81–82, 188, 195, 205, 212f., 222, 413
Appliances, 7, 133–34, 164, 174, 290, 342, 355
Architecture, 4, 6, 66, 187, 218, 391–92
Art Nouveau, 4, 6, 38, 65
Atlantic Charter, 256, 259, 441, 451
Automation, 135, 164, 175, 350, 354–55
Automobile, 5, 6, 62, 134, 173, 174, 306, 339, 342, 356–57, 363
Avant-garde, 58–61, 64–69, 72, 176, 187–99, 341, 368, 379, 386–92, 394–96, 408, 455

Bankers and banking, 130–32, 165–66, 168, 223, 228, 236, 247, 339, 343, 358
Bauhaus, 66, 106, 187
Beatles, 368, 384, 406
Biology and genetics, 75–77, 331, 351, 352
Birth control, 7, 39, 40, 134, 147, 179, 345, 353, 382, 402
Bolsheviks, 45, 96, 99–105, 241–42
Brezhnev Doctrine, 283, 326, 328

Cabaret, 60, 63, 178, 198, 368, 383–84
Carta del Lavoro, 151, 153, 155, 219, 228
Cartels, 18, 23, 25, 165, 339, 343, 357–58
Catholics, 10, 31–33, 138, 139, 206, 237, 262, 270, 291, 345–46, 363, 400–404, 428, 429, 446–47, 449. *See also* Christian parties; Popes
Chemistry, 16, 131, 173–74, 339, 356
Chetniks, 254, 255, 261

Christian parties: Austria, 27, 32, 139, 150; France, 268, 401; Germany, 31, 97, 107, 139, 147–48, 338, 362, 417, 420–23; Italy, 261, 363, 401, 418, 441
Churches: Anglican, 11, 31, 207; Roman Catholic, 11, 31, 139, 153–54, 206–7, 226, 237–38, 270, 314, 316–17, 345–46, 363, 400–404, 428, 429; Witness-bearing, 226, 400, 401
Civil Service, 4, 7, 8, 129–32, 142, 146, 343, 358, 445
Coexistence, 158, 276, 309–10, 315, 316, 322
Cold war, 273, 274, 276, 281, 284, 289, 291–92, 298, 320, 376, 401, 402, 419, 433, 456
Collaborators (in France with Nazis), 231–32, 252–53, 267, 394
Colonialism, 8–9, 25, 29–30, 113–14, 278, 280, 290, 293–94, 296–97, 310, 365, 426, 429, 432, 434, 452, 454, 455
Comecon, 283, 311, 315, 317, 318
Comité des Forges, 23, 141
Common Market, xi, 278–80, 296, 297, 344, 356, 419, 422, 424–29, 433–34, 441, 444, 446, 448–53, 456
Commonwealth, 113–14, 293, 296–97, 424
Communists and communism, 93, 99–109, 117, 141–42, 148–50, 158–62, 224–25, 235–40, 253, 260–62, 268, 272–73, 282–87, 295, 301, 311–19, 326–28, 333, 369, 375, 403–4, 418–19, 429, 431, 437–41, 443–44; International and, 105, 108, 159, 235, 275, 287
Composers, 57, 59, 64, 66–69, 76, 83, 175, 189–90, 386, 388, 390–91, 408
Computers, 330, 349–50, 354–55
Conferences and treaties: Algeciras, 22; Anti-Comintern, 246, 254; Bandung, 310n; Belgrade, 288, 310n; Brest-Litovsk, 101; Geneva, 294; Hague, 22, 89; Locarno, 124, 245; Moscow, 249 (Hitler-Stalin Pact, *1939*), 249 (Security Conference, *1954*), 281 (Nuclear Test-Ban Treaty, *1963*), 349; Munich, 248, 421; Paris (Versailles Treaty, *1919*), 114 (Kellogg-Briand Pact, *1928*), 124 (summit, *1960*), 320; Potsdam, 259, 273–74, 309; Rapallo, 118, 242; Stresa, 245; Westminster Statute, 114; Yalta, 259, 262, 272
Conservative Party, 11, 142–43, 167, 246, 294, 297, 339, 341–42, 424–27
Convergence, 319, 334

Corporations, 16–18, 23, 130–31, 140, 143, 145, 228, 339, 356–57, 427; multinational, 348, 432, 448
Crime, 184, 185, 198, 367. *See also* Vice
Cubism, 59, 65, 71, 199

Dadaism, 66, 188, 391
Dance, 6, 68, 199, 322, 391
Decadence, 57–58, 188, 197, 199, 376, 379
Détente, 322, 419, 422, 456
Disarmament, 22, 245, 291, 322, 349, 423
Divorce, 39, 179, 243, 346, 382
Dopolavoro, 153, 177, 228
Drugs, 178, 198, 367, 382, 384, 406

Education, 8, 10, 31, 35, 39, 106, 132–33, 147, 237, 306, 318, 340, 343, 357, 363–64, 366, 369, 383, 403, 422, 436, 440, 444–45, 454
Electromechanics, 16, 173
Elites, 80, 129, 134, 359. *See also* Avant-garde; Ruling class
Empire, 8, 13, 113, 166, 292, 393–98, 424
Entente Cordiale, 22, 30, 543
Establishment, 71, 343, 358, 367–68, 378, 381, 439
Eugenics, 76, 223, 352
Eurocrats, 343, 358, 450
Europe, xi, 125–26, 263–64, 276–81, 298, 342, 414, 423, 426–28, 433–34, 441, 446, 448, 451–57
European Coal and Steel Community (ECSC), 279, 339, 358, 446, 450
European Defense Community (EDC), 279, 289, 452
European Economic Community (EEC). See Common Market
European Free Trade Association (EFTA), 280, 297, 426, 444, 451
European Recovery Program (ERP), 275
European Security Conference, 422, 423, 453n
Existentialism, 58, 191, 193–94, 205, 206, 213–14, 270, 271, 366, 376, 379, 397–98, 405, 409, 410, 413–14
Expressionism, 59, 67, 188, 190, 199, 284, 390

Fabian Society, 31, 33, 35, 43, 340
Falange, 230–31, 428, 429
Fascism, 89, 93, 110, 126, 152–54, 228–29, 233–34
Fascist groups, 26, 109, 143, 147, 150, 151, 154–57, 215–16, 219–22, 229–33, 253, 449
Fashion, 6, 38–39, 133, 177–78, 367, 381–82
Food, 6, 88, 91, 102, 103, 160, 306, 344
Freemasons, 27, 31, 32, 140, 141, 221
Futurism, 59, 60, 61, 76, 188, 195, 199

General strike, 142. *See also* Sorel, Georges, *in Index of Names*
Genocide, 223, 254, 255, 258, 260, 262, 352

Health services, 12, 306, 339–40, 352–53, 445
Heroes, 59, 186, 194, 331, 367, 378, 380–82, 397
Housing, 174, 306, 340–41, 418, 445

Imperialism, 9, 10, 13, 19, 21–27, 30, 57, 284, 293–98
Industrialists in politics, 129, 142, 223, 239, 357

Inflation, 116, 129, 338, 340, 342
Intelligentsia, 12, 43, 57–58, 60, 141, 147, 201, 214–16, 270, 271, 284–85, 288, 290, 305, 314, 324, 327, 332, 343, 359, 363, 373–79, 407–14. *See also* Avant-garde
Intercontinental missile, 295, 307, 320, 330, 433
Iron curtain, 274, 275, 298, 310, 314

Jazz, 176, 284, 332, 381, 455

Kulaks, 47, 104, 159, 160–61

Labor movement, 36, 41–45, 91, 94–105, 107–10, 126, 129, 132, 135, 138–50, 161–62, 218, 220, 238–39, 343, 362–63, 425, 427, 429, 438, 441, 444
Labor unions, 12, 36, 41–46, 92, 106, 141–42, 150, 155, 220, 224, 238, 262, 295, 342–43, 438–40, 445, 450
Labour Party, 11, 12, 31, 43, 52, 91, 96, 142–43, 167, 235, 267, 281, 291, 297, 339–40, 342, 362, 424–27
League of Nations, 113–16, 118, 124–26, 229, 239, 240, 242, 245, 246, 247
Liberal parties: England, 11–13, 52, 140, 142; France, 10, 140; Germany, 10, 147, 338, 421–423; Russia, 47; Spain, 11
Liberalism, 8, 10–15, 111, 140, 147, 166, 292
Little Entente, 115, 145, 245

Market socialism, 318, 319, 324, 328
Marshall Plan, 275, 277–78, 283, 289
Marxism, 42–45, 91, 99, 359, 404, 409–10, 414, 436
Mass culture, 62–64, 134–35, 178, 180–86, 367–68, 380–85, 393, 396, 407–8, 454
Massive instant retaliation, 453n
Mensheviks, 45, 46, 47, 96, 101, 103
Meritocracy, 128, 133, 348, 359, 369
Metals, 17, 161, 173, 306, 355
Middle classes, 4–8, 15, 17, 18, 26, 38, 39, 57, 63–64, 70, 106, 129, 130, 131, 138, 174, 189, 218, 439, 445, 454
Migrant workers, 338, 342, 346, 450
Militarism, 13–14, 25, 28–29, 83, 89, 194, 215–16, 296
Military strategy, 51–52, 87–89, 124, 251–52, 254–57, 263–64, 303, 309
Movies, 47, 62–63, 88, 95, 129, 133, 174–76, 180–85, 191, 197, 199, 201, 252, 253, 267, 268, 269, 294, 331–33, 354, 374–76, 379, 380, 382, 383, 388, 391, 393–96, 421, 437
Mystics, 29, 33, 74, 211–13, 405, 406

National minorities, 49, 92, 96–98, 100, 102, 106, 114–15, 125, 144–45, 157, 237, 247, 282, 446, 447, 448
Nationalism, 11, 13–14, 27, 30, 45, 52–53, 60, 76, 91–92, 96, 112, 126–27, 161, 200, 217–33, 241, 256, 284, 298, 423, 434, 446–49, 453
Navies, 13, 14, 22, 24, 88, 245, 253, 453
Nazis, 89, 148–49, 214, 216–17, 222–28, 245–46, 419; opposition to, 225
Neo-Nazism and neo-Fascists, 418, 420, 422–23
Neocolonialism, 296, 434

Neutralism, 290–91, 313, 320–21, 401, 429, 434, 444, 454
New Economic Policy (NEP), 103–4, 158–59, 318, 328
Nobel laureates, 331, 332, 408–9
North Atlantic Treaty Organization (NATO), 275–76, 278–81, 289, 291, 295, 297, 298, 309, 310, 320, 322, 365, 417, 419, 422, 423, 426–30, 433–34, 437, 441, 443, 444, 446, 452, 453n, 456
Nuclear bomb, 276, 289, 290, 297, 306, 309–10, 314, 320–21, 349, 426, 433
Nuclear energy and science, 78, 202–3, 279, 349, 425, 432
Nuremberg: laws, 223, 227, 269; trials, 269

OECD (Organization for Economic Cooperation and Development), 358, 428, 446
Oil, 27, 155, 235, 237, 246, 357, 426, 427, 430, 432, 449
Opposition in U.S.S.R., 104, 242, 284, 321–22, 332–33
Ostpolitik, 421–23, 437, 441, 456

Pacifism, 14, 33, 94, 126, 453–54
Painters, 58, 60, 65–68, 175, 187–90, 386, 390–91, 408
Pan-Germanism, 21, 23, 27, 28, 53
Pan-Slavism, 21, 22, 27, 29, 51–53, 218
Parliamentarism, 11–12, 43–44, 92, 97–98, 107, 128, 138–49, 156–57, 222, 236, 361, 365, 418, 429–30, 449
Participation, 93, 142, 146, 287, 326, 342, 422, 439, 440, 445
Parties. See Christian parties; Conservative Party; Labour Party; Liberal parties; *as well as specific movements*
Peasants, 39, 47, 100–104, 108–9, 130, 135–37, 139, 143, 153, 154, 159–60, 164, 165, 236, 262, 282, 288, 305–6, 314, 317, 319, 324, 340–41, 343–44, 356, 418, 439, 443, 446–47
Philosophy, 65, 71, 74–75, 77–80, 204–8, 212–16, 408–14
Physicists, 77–79, 202–5
Planning: Nazi, 167, 227–28; Soviet, 160–61, 306, 318, 319; in West, 167, 236, 277, 295, 337–42, 355–60, 419, 446, 450
Police: French, 438; German, 148, 225; Hungarian, 312; Italian, 152; Nazi, 225; Russian, 47, 101, 105, 241, 302; Spanish, 237–38; Yugoslav, 229, 288
Pop art and music, 367–68, 379, 381
Popes, 11, 32, 96, 139–40, 154, 155, 226, 245, 254, 363, 400–403, 419
Popular Front, 167, 168, 232, 235–40, 245–46, 273, 440
Populations, classes, and shifts, 17–18, 20, 91, 106, 128–36, 337, 340–46, 359, 364–69, 380–85, 436–37, 445
Pornography, 63, 379, 382, 395, 404
Positivism, 12, 79, 82, 205, 410–13
Press, 5, 29, 30, 168, 225, 345, 384, 417
Protestants, 31, 207–8, 226, 262, 270, 291, 401, 404–6, 446
Provos, 367, 446

Psychology, 29, 71, 73–75, 77, 81, 133, 191–93, 204, 211, 212, 409, 411–12

Radio and television, 15, 62, 134, 173, 178, 181, 202, 306, 339, 342, 355, 363–64, 367–68, 383–84, 424
Railways, 15, 21, 91, 155, 167, 339, 425
Reformism, 43–44, 95, 144, 441. *See also* Socialists and socialism
Refugees, 267, 269, 318, 340
Reichstag fire, 224
Relativity, 69, 78, 204, 351, 411
Reparations, 116, 117, 146, 164, 263
Resistance, anti-Nazi, 147, 226–27, 248, 260–62, 374, 394, 400, 401
Revisionism: against treaties, 107, 117–18, 228, 240, 245, 247; within communism, 287, 304, 315–19, 321, 324–39, 359, 409
Revisionist historians, 273n
Rock, 367–68, 381, 384, 391, 454, 455
Ruling class, 106, 129, 288, 343, 346–47, 351, 357–60, 369

Samizdat, 322, 332
Sculptors, 389, 390
Servants, 7, 134, 345
Settlements, 174, 340–41
Sex, 7, 37, 38, 58, 60, 70–71, 73–75, 94, 133, 178–79, 194, 345, 379, 381–82, 384, 395, 402, 414
Socialist Realism, 186, 200, 317, 331–33
Socialists and socialism, 14, 36, 41–47, 93, 104–8, 117, 132, 135, 139, 148–50, 235–39, 261, 262, 268, 272–73, 282, 291, 333, 339–44, 361–64, 378, 418–21, 429, 436–37, 441, 443–47, 454. *See also* Fabian Society; Labor movement; Labor unions; Labour Party; Reformism
Sociology, 29, 80, 82, 193, 204, 205, 350, 408, 411–13
Soviets (councils, shop stewards), 47, 95, 97, 100–101, 146, 254, 287, 312, 327, 438
Space, 306, 320
Sports, 176–77; auto races, 174; bicycling, 6, 35
Stakhanovism, 161
Students, 365, 366, 369, 390, 403, 422, 429, 436–40, 447, 455, 457
Surrealism, 67, 187–88

Technocracy, 128–29, 318, 327, 349–50, 359–60, 369, 431, 440
Technology, 5, 133–34, 173–76, 202–3, 349–60, 391–92, 455–56
Television. See Radio and television
Third World, 219, 287, 310n, 314, 427, 429, 434, 448, 452
Thrillers, 63, 184–86, 380–81, 389, 396
Treaties. See Conferences and treaties
Trotskyists, 239

Unemployment, 36, 135, 149, 164, 165, 167, 168, 337–38, 342
United Nations, 269, 273, 274, 282, 296, 314, 317, 320, 422, 426, 428, 444, 447–48

Vice, 36, 37, 40, 178, 179, 198, 406

Warsaw Pact, 281, 295, 311, 313, 317, 321, 323, 325, 326, 422

Weapons, 89, 251, 264, 295; industry, 17, 23, 91, 130-31, 140, 145, 356-58, 427

Welfare state, 12-13, 32, 43, 135, 139-40, 144, 147, 163, 236, 268, 306, 337-48, 353, 361, 444-45

Western European Union (WEU), 279, 281, 452

White-collar workers, 132, 343, 355, 366

Women, 7, 12, 38-40, 76, 92, 106, 131, 133-34, 174, 177, 178-80, 306, 345, 382, 444-45

Working classes, 4-6, 17, 19-20, 35-37, 39-45, 129, 131-32, 135, 141, 143, 146-48, 153, 161, 163-64, 168, 220-21, 231, 236-39, 284, 287, 342-43, 355, 425, 427, 429, 433, 438-40, 444, 445

Index of Countries, Cities, and Nationalities

African countries, 11, 13, 21, 22, 24, 44, 49, 155, 294–96, 403, 429, 431–34
Albania and Albanians, 49, 261, 329
Austria, 49, 97, 114–15, 150–51, 154–55, 247, 268, 279–80, 309, 444, 447f.

Baltic countries, 49, 102, 109, 115, 233, 249, 253, 259, 272, 282
Belgium, 231–32, 296, 446–47
Berlin, 198, 259, 275, 318, 320–21, 341, 369, 392, 420, 437
Bulgaria, 109, 230, 254, 272, 282, 317

Croats, 49, 98, 115, 137, 156–57, 229, 247, 254, 329
Cyprus, 298, 430
Czechoslovakia and Czechs, 49–50, 96, 102, 108–9, 115, 144–45, 248, 268, 273, 275, 283, 303, 324, 325, 421

Danzig, 115, 248

East Germany, 272–74, 281, 282, 303, 315–18, 327. *See also* Germany
Ethiopia, 21, 125, 215, 229, 245–46

Finland, 144, 251, 279, 280, 282, 309, 443, 444; and Finlandization, 452
France, 10, 14, 143–44, 219–20, 232–33, 235–36, 260, 267–68, 293–96, 339, 431–42

Germany, 97–98, 107–8, 116–17, 146–50, 217, 218, 224–28, 259, 262, 268–70. *See also* East Germany; West Germany
Great Britain. See United Kingdom
Greece, 125, 230, 261, 298, 429–30

Hungary and Magyars, 50, 108, 109, 156, 230, 282, 303, 312–14, 327

Ireland (Eire) and Irish, 11, 31, 49, 50, 96, 112, 114, 231, 449
Italy, 11, 110–11, 152–54, 217–19, 228–29, 261, 268, 279, 375–76, 418–19, 427, 437, 441

Macedonia, 109, 157, 329

Northern Ireland, 50, 112, 447, 449

Poland, 103, 109, 115, 156, 233, 261–62, 273, 282, 303, 311–14, 316–17, 327–28
Portugal, 11, 155–56, 233, 429

Rumania, 109, 230, 272, 303, 317, 327
Russia and U.S.S.R., 46–48, 95–97, 99–105, 158–62, 199–201, 241–44, 282–85, 301–34

Scandinavian countries, 49, 144, 251, 280, 340, 443–45
Serbia. See Yugoslavia and Serbia
Slovaks, 115, 144, 248, 324, 329, 448
Soviet Union. See Russia and U.S.S.R.
Spain, 11, 155, 230–31, 236–40, 339, 428–29; minorities in, 49, 437, 447
Sudeten, 145, 247, 248

Turkey, 21, 49, 111–12, 125, 430, 451

U.S.S.R. See Russia and U.S.S.R.
United Kingdom, 11–13, 50, 112, 142–43, 267, 280, 296–97, 339–40, 377–78, 424–27; minorities in, 49, 167, 447–49

Vienna, 150, 205, 410

West Germany, 274, 279, 291, 309, 338, 374–75, 417–23, 437. *See also* Germany

Yugoslavia and Serbia, 49, 51–52, 113, 115, 156–57, 229, 254–55, 261, 273, 283, 286–88, 316, 329

481

The Fall and Rise of
Europe